HISTORICAL COLLECTIONS
of the *Georgia Chapters*
Daughters of the
American Revolution
Volume III

RECORDS
of
Elbert County, Georgia

Compiled by
Grace Gillam Davidson

CLEARFIELD

Originally published
Atlanta, Georgia
1930

Reprinted with permission of the
Georgia State DAR

Reprinted for Clearfield Company by
Genealogical Publishing Company
Baltimore, Maryland
1995, 2014

ISBN 978-0-8063-4568-0

Table of Contents

	Pages
Wills, Books "A" and "B", 1791-1803	2- 11
Wills, Book 1803-1806	11- 14
Wills, Book 1805	14- 16
Wills, Book "L-F", 1804-1809	16- 18
Wills, Book 1809-1812	18- 21
Wills, Book "K", 1812-1816	21- 26
Wills, Book "L", 1816-1821	26- 34
Wills, Book "M", 1821-1825	34- 40
Wills, Book "N", old no. 1825-1829	40- 45
Wills, Book "N", 1828-1831	45- 47
Wills, Record Book, 1830-1835	47- 53
Index to Will Book, 1829-1860	54- 55

Returns of Administrators and Guardians:

Books "A" and "B", 1791-1803	56- 63
Book 1803-1806	63- 65
Book "L-F", 1804-1809	65- 70
Book 1809-1812	70- 79
Book "K", 1812-1816	79- 88
Book "L", 1816-1821	88- 99
Book "M", 1821-1825	99-107
Book "N", old no. 1825-1829	107-114
Book "N", 1828-1831	114-124
Record Book, 1830-1838	124-132

Minutes of Inferior Court 1791-1830	133-150
Deed Books "A", "B", "C", "D", 1789-1797	151-213
Land Court Records 1791-1822	214-236
Land Lotteries, 1806, 1821, 1827 and 1832	237-265
Tombstone Records	266-270
Marriages 1806-1834	271-304

PREFACE

The Lucy Cook Peel Memorial Committee
GEORGIA DAUGHTERS OF THE AMERICAN REVOLUTION

Present Volume III of the Historical Collections of the Georgia Chapters.

This committee was founded by the Georgia State Conference in 1923, in appreciation of the loyal work given to the D. A. R. by Mrs. William Lawson Peel, Ex Vice President General of the National Society, Honorary State Regent of Georgia, Founder and Regent of the Joseph Habersham Chapter, and First National Chairman of the Committee of Real Daughters in the National Society.

The records of Elbert County, Georgia were abstracted and compiled under the auspices of the Lucy Cook Peel Memorial Committee by Mrs. Grace Gillam Davidson (Mrs. John Lee), State Historian of Georgia D. A. R. 1926-1928.

The Stephen Heard Chapter of Elberton in Elbert County contributed many valuable records to this committee.

Elbert County, Georgia, was created by Legislative Act, Dec. 10, 1790, from Wilkes County and named for Major-General Samuel Elbert. Georgia honored her brave Elbert with the rank of Major-General in the State Militia, while at the same time he was advanced to the rank of Brigadier General in the Continental Army, and upon returning home he was soon made Governor of the State, in which capacity he signed the bill chartering the University of Georgia.

There are few counties in Georgia richer than Elbert in historic names and historic places. First upon the list belongs the world-renowned heroine of the Revolution—**Nancy Hart**. She lived on War Woman's Creek, a little stream some few miles above the ford on Broad river, and here she captured the Tories at the point of her musket. Five acres of land in this immediate vicinity have been purchased jointly by the Stephen Heard Chapter, D. A. R. of Elberton, Ga., and by the Nancy Hart Chapter D. A. R. of Milledgeville, Ga., and the site of the home is marked.

Captain James Jack, an officer of distinction in the Continental army came to Elbert County from Mecklenburg County, North Carolina.

Near Heardmont, in the eastern part of the county, stood the old home of **Stephen Heard**, one of the most noted of Georgia's early patriots and pioneers, and a Governor of the State. Ten acres of land near Heardmont, including the graveyard where Governor Stephen Heard lies buried, have been acquired by the Stephen Heard Chapter for memorial purposes.

Fort James was situated on a point of land between the Broad and the Savannah rivers, and was built to defend the old Colonial settlement at Dartmouth. On the ruins of Dartmouth was built the town of **Petersburg** which was at one time one of the foremost commercial centers of Georgia; a tobacco market in the early days, but now abandoned and one of the lost towns of Georgia.

In the two volumes of Georgia Landmarks, Memorials and Legends, by Lucian L. Knight, former State Historian of Georgia, can be found a most interesting account of Elbert County.

Most of the early settlers of Elbert County were North Carolinians, but along the Broad river in the lower part of the county, there were a number of settlers from Virginia, who came to Georgia with Governor George Matthews in 1784.

The Lucy Cook Peel Memorial Committee desires to make grateful acknowledgement to the Chapters and members who have given encouragement and substantial help in this undertaking, and whose generous co-operation has made possible Volume III of the Historical Collections of Georgia Chapters, Daughters of the American Revolution.

MRS. W. F. DYKES, State Chairman.
MRS. JOHN L. DAVIDSON, Co-Chairman.
MISS HELEN PRESCOTT
MRS. HOWARD H. McCALL
MRS. J. C. GENTRY
MRS. H. Y. TILLMAN
MRS. BLANCHE LA FAR
MRS. MELL KNOX
MRS. DI INGRAM
MRS. B. A. TYLER
MISS VIRGINIA HARDIN
MRS. JULIAN McCURRY
MRS. J. J. HARRIS
MRS. JULIUS TALMADGE
MRS. J. RUCKER

Elbert County Georgia Records
WILLS

Book 1791-1803 "A" & "B"
Book 1803-1806
Book 1805
Book "L-F" 1804-09
Book 1809-1812
Book "K" 1812-1816
Book "L" 1816-1821
Book "M"
Book "N" Old No. 1825-29
Book "N" 1828-31
Book 1830-31
Book 1830-35

GEORGIA D. A. R.

Elbert County, Georgia
Book 1791-1803

This book consists of Books "A", "B" and "C" of mixed records, recently re-bound under the above title.

Wills in Books "A" and "B" abstracted 1925 by members of the Stephen Heard Chapter, D. A. R., under the direction of Mrs. Olin Smith. Miss Edna Rogers, Regent.

BOOK "A"

BIBB, WILLIAM—Page 94—To wife Sally S. Bibb and the children that I have by her, or may have, all property after debts are paid, wife sole Excx. Signed Sept. 9, 1795. Rec. Mar. 30, 1796. Love Statham, Test.

CLEVELAND, JACOB—Page 2—To dearly beloved wife (not named) home, land, furniture etc. To daughter Elizabeth a slave, if she dies without heirs to go to his two youngest sons Reuben and Daniel. To son Jere a bond on John Stogdon besides an equal part of the estate. Wife, Webb Kidd and Jeremiah Cleveland, Excrs. Signed April 4, 1790. Probated May 7, 1791. Reuben & John White, Test.

EASTER, JAMES—Page 13—To wife Sarah all the land whereon they now live, and four slaves, Frank, Jacob, Sam and Hannah, and lends to her four other slaves, Hall, Lucy, Tom and Betty till son Champion comes of age. To daughter Mary Ann horse, saddle and bridle and no more of my estate. To daughters Elizabeth and Dolly five shillings and no more. To son Wm. Thompson Easter the land whereon he now lives and a slave Simon. To son Booker Burton Easter, 250 acres on Long creek, Wilkes Co., and a slave Chas. To daughter Patty Aycock and William Aycock the land on which they live. To daughter Tabby Napier and Thos. Napier a tract adj. Wm. Aycock agreeable to the division made between him and said Aycock. To daughter Lotty a slave, Silvia, household goods etc. To sons Lewis and Champion all the land on which I now live, except what is lent to my wife, when Champion comes of age. To Lewis a slave Caleb, to Champion a slave, Hall, a feather bed, horse and saddle a piece etc. To daughter Sophia a slave, Fanny, feather bed etc. To daughter Tere slave Dilsey, horse and saddle, household good etc. To daus. Lotty, Sophia and Tere my land in Franklin Co., on old Toms creek when they come of age or marry. To dau. Marjary five shillings and no more. Wife Sarah and Wm. Thompson Easter, nephew Richard Easter, friends Wm. Thompson, Sr., Robt. Thompson, Sr., and Benjamin Taliaferro, Excrs. Signed May 19, 1791. Probated

Feb. 11, 1792. Phillip Wray, Wells Thompson, Stephen Ellington, Test. William Booker, Sr., Stephen Ellington, Apprs.

GATEWOOD, RICHARD—Page __—In the name of God, Amen; I intend with God's leave to go to Georgia. It may please God I never return. If not it's my desire that after all my debts and funeral accounts is paid all the rest of my estate I lend to my wife enduring her widowhood all but as much as those children not married to have equal to those that is married, and at her death or widowhood to be equally divided. If any of the children dies without heirs at their death their parts to be equally divided with the rest of their brothers and sisters to them and their heirs forever. Given under my hand this tenth day of December one thousand seven hundred and eighty nine. Signed Dec. 10, 1789. Peter Cashwell, John Ham, Joseph Higginbotham, Test.
Recorded above will the fourth day of November, 1794, and granted letters of administration with the will annexed to Betty Gatewood and John Gatewood. Wm. Higginbotham, Reg. Pro.

GILES, JOHN—Page 50—To wife, not named, plantation and house wherein I now live for life, to dau., who married Jeremiah Wells (not named), and grandson Jonathan Gray to share equally with the rest of the children, not named. Signed Apr. 12, 1794. Probated July 28, 1794. Andrew Elliott, John McNeel, Benjamin Ragland, Samuel M. Thompson, Test.

GRIMES, WILLIAM—Page 57—To daughter Carter slaves Betty, Jane, Harry and Jensy, feather bed, furniture etc., for life to be divided among her children at her death. When son William comes of age, daughter Betsy to have an equal share at the division upon deducting the value of a slave, Big Jancy, which she has already received. To son William 400 acres on Brushy creek conveyed from James McCommon to me. To son Thomas M. the land whereon I now live, both above tracts to be enjoyed by my wife as long as she lives.
Wife Mildred, friends Thos. B. Scott and Wm. Harvie, Excrs.
Signed Dec. 29, 1794. Recorded Jan. 8, 1795.
Thomas B. Scott, Rm. Lindsay, Test.

HIGGINBOTHAM, BENJAMIN—Page 8—of Wilkes Co., To wife Elizabeth all estate real and personal for life. To dau. Anne Higginbotham slaves Lucy and Humphrey. To son Caleb a slave Jack. To son William a slave Lewis. To son Benjamin a slave Charity. To son Joseph a slave Phillis, if he dies without heirs to go to his brothers and sisters. Land to sons Joseph and Francis. To son Francis a slave Rachel. Wife Elizabeth, sons William, Benjamin, Joseph and Francis, Excrs. Signed Feb. 9, 1790 Probated July 25, 1791. Wm. McCutchen, Thomas Willy, James Morrison, Test.

HODGE, WILLIAM—Page 53—To sons John Alexander and Francis L15, eighteen months after my decease, John to have what plank he wants for his own use and my large Bible. To sons William and Elliott the home place to be equally divided between them, they to purchase 200 acres of land for son James when he comes of age. James to be taught to read, write and cipher as far as five common rules. To dau. Mary L20 in four years. To dau. Elizabeth $10.00, the first money got from Penna. To dau. Nancy horse, saddle etc., including what she already has. To dau. Cynthia the same and her board as long as she is single. William Appleby and son John Excrs.

Signed Sept. 20, 1794. Probated Oct. 3, 1794. John Calvert, James McCurdy, Test.

HUMAN, BAZZLE—Page 66—400 acres at the mouth of Holly creek with the mill etc to be sold to pay debts, the remainder to be divided among my dear children, Peggy Wells, Anny, Rutha and Susanna Human and my dear wife Isabel Human. Remaining 400 acres of land to be divided between wife Isabel and my son Alex., for life at her death to son Bazzle. Son Alex. sole Excr. Signed Jan. 10, 1795 Rec. Mar. 12, 1795. Edward Goode, Nathaniel Smith, Test. Thos. Cook, Wm. Aycock, Isaac Coker, and Burton Green, Apprs.

HEAD, JAMES—Page 79—To wife Elizabeth Janet, land on Vans creek to be divided between son Benjamin, Simon and James. To dau. Sarah Fortson a slave Liscy, feather bed, furniture, horse, saddle and bridle now in her possession. Property to be divided beginning with dau. Martha Head and going down to James Head. Land on Kettle creek, Wilkes Co., to be sold to pay debts. Wife Elizabeth Janet Head, Sarah Riddle and Thomas White, Excrs. Signed Oct. 23, 1795. Rec. Jan. 7, 1796

MEREDITH, JAMES—Page 5—To wife Sarah for life, one-fifth part of his estate. Residue at her death to four youngest children Patty, Nancy, Molly and Sally, minors. To dau. Rebeckah the account due him from her dec'd husband Jasper Smith, and a slave Sarah which I lent to her while in N. C., provided she returns a slave Lucy and her children which were also lent to her in N. C. Wife Sally and friend William Moore of Rocky creek, Wilkes Co., Excrs. Signed Jan. 13, 1791.

Probated May 19, 1791. Ja. Williams (Jaret), Drury Ledbetter, John Henley, Test.

PEARPOINT, LARKIN—Page 47—All property to loving dau. Charity, to lie in the hands of my Excrs., James Coil of Elbert Co. and Clement Wilkins of Franklin Co., till she becomes of age. Signed Feb. 28, 1794. Probated Apr. 7, 1794. Robert Megredy, Silas Megredy, Test.

SMITH, JASPER—Page 4—To wife Rebeckah a slave Lucy for life to be divided at her death equally among the children she had by me and her son Thomas, the land to be divided at the wife's death. Everything kept together to raise and educate the children and that there be enough raised annually to keep my son Jasper as long as he lives. Daus. Betty and Sally and son Mark, and to my wife's son Thomas L15 as they come of age or marry. Wife Rebecca, friend James Marks and Thos. B. Scott,

Excrs. Signed Dec. 1, 1790. Probated May 19, 1791. Isaac Tuttle, Jesse Brownen, Test.

STOKES, WILLIAM—Page 90—To wife Sarah all real and personal estate for life or widowhood, at the expiration of either to dau. Elizabeth Pryor three slaves and 20 shillings to buy a ring. To dau. Sarah Grimes a slave Lett and 20 shillings to buy a ring. To dau. Peggy Strong two slaves Antony and Margaret and 20 shillings to buy a ring. Having given dau. Jane Stokes slaves Edy and Nelson now give her 20 shillings as above. To dau. Martha Stokes, 200 acres on Broad river whereon I now live, slaves Dave and Lucy, furniture etc. To son Wm. Munfort Stokes 600 acres of Beaverdam creek, Oglethorpe Co., joining Norris and others, and 300 acres on Oconee river, Franklin Co., slaves Chas. and Amey and all my printed books. To grandson Thos. Burdell a slave Jack when he is 21, if he dies without heirs to go to his brother Robt. Burdell, if Robert dies under 21, slave to go to Elizabeth Grimes, dau. of my dau. Sarah Grimes. Son Wm. Munfort Stokes and son-in-law Wm. Strong and Wm. Stokes, Excrs. Signed Oct. 16, 1794. Rec. Mar. 1, 1796. Johnston Clark, Jon. MacMillian, Sarah Clark, James Elliott, Test.

THOMPSON, JOHN FARLEY—Page 31—A slave and riding horse to be sold on twelve months credit for crop of tobacco at Petersburg and bought by one of the following seven children and equally divided among them, viz: John, Isham, Peter, Sally, Mary, Milly and Tabby. To son William 100 acres where he now lives, slaves etc. To son Robert 300 acres where he now lives and a slave. To dau. Milly Ragland a slave Silas now in her possession. To son Farley land on Bertram's creek, slaves, furniture etc. To son Lewis Bevel Thompson land on Bertram's creek where John Norris now lives, not given to sons Farley and William. Sons Farley and Lewis Bevel app. Excrs. Signed Sept. 3, 1792. Rec. Feb. 5, 1793. Robt. Thompson, Sr., William Thompson, Sr., Stephen Ellington, Test.

WILLIAMS, JOSEPH—Page 23—To son John all the negroes I let him have many years ago. To son Matthew Jouett Williams, all the slaves I let him have many years ago, and all household furniture etc. at my death. To grandson Joseph, son of Matthew Jouett Williams a slave in trust of his father till Feb. 1797. Two sons Excrs. Signed Sept. 13, 1792. Probated Oct. 15, 1792. Wm. Hatcher, Wm. Lankester, Jenny Freeman, Test.

WALKER, JEREMIAH—Page 25—To wife Milly several slaves, bed, furniture, saddle, trunk etc and her dower of one third of the plantation. To dau. Polly Coleman a slave for life, to be divided at her death between her three daus. Elizabeth, Narcissa and Melanda. To son Henry Graves Walker 400 acres of land part of 700 acres bought from Robt. Chambers and a lot in the town of Petersburg, slave etc. To son Memorable 300 acres known by the name of Cabbin Land, slaves, furniture etc. To son Jeremiah 150 acres on south side of Savannah river, part of the Chambers tract and 100 acres off the upper part of the Island, slaves

etc. To son James Sanders Walker 100 acres adj. son Jeremiahs land and the rest of the Island, slaves etc. To son John Williams Walker 250 acres on the river below the above tracts, slaves etc., when he comes of age. To dau. Elizabeth Marshall what she has already received. To all the children a share of his books. Beloved brother Sanders Walker, trusty friend James Tate, Excrs.
Signed Sept. 14, 1792. Probated Oct. 17, 1792.
Wm. Tate, Richard Harvy, John Avren (?), Jesse Jones, Test.

BOOK "B"

ANDREWS, NATHANIEL—Page 60—Land on which he lives and a tract in Franklin Co. to be sold to pay debts. To wife Polly the bed and horse which I received by her, all cattle and household furniture. To brother Robins Andrews horse, slaves, wearing apparel etc.
Bro. Robins Andrews and friend John Andrews, Excrs. Signed April 25, 1799. Rec. Sept. 12, 1799. Henry Brown, Elizabeth Andrew, Test.

BLAKE, WILLIAM—Page 30—To loving wife Lucy life estate in the land where I now live, all cattle, horses, furniture etc., at her decease to go to youngest son Joseph. To dau. Happy Blake a slave Ben. To my children Lucy Adkins, John Blake, Rhoda Rogers, Sarah Hall and Alcy Cook five shillings each. To daus. Patsy, Nancy and Olive Blake at the death of their mother, slaves Hercules, Jude, Meriah and Linder and half of Sue and her increase till the year 1811. Wife Lucy and friend Thos. Jones, son of John Jones, Excrs. Signed Oct. 8, 1796. Rec. Apr. 1, 1798. James Bell, Wm. Mobley, Sally Hudleston, Test.

CUNNINGHAM, WILLIAM—Page 70—200 acres of land in Oglethorpe Co, and $100.00 Francis Howard owes be used to pay debts. To sons Alex., Thomas and William the 450 acres in Elbert Co. whereon I now live at my wife Sarah's death. To son David 4 shillings, bed and furniture. To dau. Patsy horse and saddle, to dau. Polly horse and saddle, furniture. Residue to wife Sarah to give the children as they come of age or marry. Wife Sarah and William Grimes, Excrs. Signed Mar. 18, 1799. Rec. Sept. 12, 1799. Joseph Albert, Anne Grimes, Test.

COOK, BENJAMIN—Page 78—To beloved son-in-law Henry Harden a slave Becky which he has in his possession. To dau. Polly slaves Winny and Burgess, horse, furniture etc. To dau. Rebeckey slaves Silvy and Agnes, horse, furniture etc. To son William a slave Moses, bed and furniture and 287½ acres in Franklin Co. on Grove river, adj. Thomas Gregg and Joel Doss. The residue to wife Effie or Eppy for life, to be divided among all my children at her death. Wife Eppy and son William, Excrs. Signed April 4, 1798. Probated Aug. 10, 1800. Elizabeth Burch, M. Woods, Robert Cosby, Test.

COSBY, CHARLES—Page 90—To wife Elizabeth during life or widowhood land on which I now live and 13 slaves. To grandaughter Lucy Cosby

Harvy a slave Hannibal. To grandaughter Elizabeth Sydnor Harvy a slave Charity. To grandaughter Matilda Hull Andrew a slave Antony in possession of her father, should she die before majority or marriage, to go to my grandaughter Lucy Garland Andrew, the latter to have $20.00 also. To grandaughter Elizabeth Sydnor Cosby, dau. of my son Fortunatus, $20.00. To son Robert Cosby, 260 acres adj. where I now live known as Isham's place. To dau. Patsy Ragland a slave Lucy now in her possession. To dau. Barbara Miner Cosby, slaves, furniture etc. To grandaughter Lucy Hawkins Cosby, dau. of James, a slave Melinda. To sons Richmond, James, David and Chas. Scott the land on which I now live, slaves, stock etc. If dau. Barbara dies without issue her part to be divided among sons named above, and my dau. Mary Overton Andrew. To son David my gun known as Old Coal. To son Scott my gun known as Danell More. Sons Richmond, Robert, James and Scott, Excrs. Signed Mar. 10, 1800. Rec. Aug. 2, 1802. Obediah Jones, Samuel McGehee, Robert L. Tait, Test.

CLARK, CHRISTOPHER—Page 99—That 2000 acres in Kentucky on the Green river and 250 acres on Wahachee creek in Elbert Co., be sold, after the debts are paid the residue be divided into twelve equal parts, viz: Micajah Clark, Christopher Clark, David Clark, Joshua Clark, Mourning Clark Key, children of dec'd. dau. Judith Wyche, Rachel Daly, Agatha Wyche, Molly Oliver, Molly White, Susannah Oliver and Lucy Oliver. To beloved wife (not named) 200 acres on which I now live, all appurtenances and seventeen slaves. To son Joshua all land on Broad river including the home place at his mother's death. Sons Micajah, Christopher, David and Joshua, Excrs. Signed Sept. 12, 1800. Rec. Mar. 17, 1803. Jesse White, Elizabeth White, John White, Test.

DAVIS, BENJAMIN—Page 23—To dau. Ann Mourning Davis a bed and a black horse Jack. To dau. Mary Davis $30.00, to dau. Elizabeth Davis feather bed, butter pot etc. To son Benjamin the land I live on etc., if he dies to return to his sister Elizabeth. John Jones, Sr., John Davis, Excrs. Signed Sept. 2, 1796. Rec. July 24, 1797. Gibson Jarrell, Simeon Jarrell, Elijah Jarrell, Test.

GUTHREE, ROBERT—Page 72—"Sorely afflicted," to wife Betty all estate real and personal for life, and to dispose of as she pleases at her death, she being sole Excx. To every one of my children, William, Thomas, Leroy, Molly, Betsy and John, and Nelly Reaves $1.00 each. Signed Apr. 12, 1797. Rec. Sept. 12, 1799. J. McGowan, Daniel Maddox, Betsy Maddox, Test.

HANSARD, WILLIAM—Page 32—All estate real and personal to wife Jennett until the youngest child comes of age, then 100 acres laid out for her for life, at her death to go to my said youngest child, Thomas Scott. The balance of the land to be equally divided between my other four sons, William, Gessey, Brown and John. To grandaughter, Chaney Hansard a cow and calf. Friends Richardson Hunt, Samuel Higginbotham

and Francis Satterwhite, Excrs. Signed May 10, 1796. Rec. Apr. 1, 1798. Francis S. Meredith, Benjamin Fannin, Test.
(Pencil note over son Wm. Hansard "Born 1768".)

HUBBARD, JOHN—Page 73—To daughter Mary Puryear, a slave Rachel. To son Joseph 200 acres in Franklin Co. on Nail's creek. To dau. Rhoda Burton a slave Fanny, To son Benj. a slave Boson. To dau. Susannah Nunnele a slave Beck. To son John a slave Amia. To loving son Richard 500 acres on Nail's creek, Franklin Co. Four sons Joseph, Benjamin, John and Richard, Excrs. Signed Mar. 1, 1794. Rec. Feb. 15, 1800. James Bell, Thomas Cook, Wm. S. Burch, Test.

HOWARD, NEMEAH—Page 34—To sons Nemiah and Mark plantation where I now live and all adjoining lands except 1½ acres at the mouth of Lightwood Log creek which I gave my friend Elijah Owens to include said Ownes dwelling, warehouse and ferry landing. Also excepting 100 acres given to son Benj. and a tract in Pendleton Co. S. C., which was bought from Thomas Shockley, Sr., whereon James Shockley now lives. To son James Howard a slave Bob. To son Joseph a slave Bess when he is 21. These five slaves, Frank, Len, Sarah, Fan and Hercalaus to be divided between my following children; John Howard, Sarah Putnam, Archer Howard, Hester Torrence, Benjamin Howard, Nancy Owens and Mary Woodward. All property to be in possession of wife Ede as long as she lives. Son-in-law Elisha Owens, son Benjamin Howard, Excrs. Signed Mar. 17, 1796. Ralph Owens, Moses Haynes, Test. Codicil Jan. 4, 1798, confirming gifts to sons Benjamin and Joseph. Rec. Apr. 1, 1798. Isaac Barnett, Thomas Gray, Test.

HUDSON, CUTBERD—Page 80—To beloved wife Elizabeth choice of estate and slaves Stephny, Lucy, and Betty, everything necessary for her support. To son Joacim a slave Solomon. To son Christopher a slave Mary and 287½ acres in Franklin Co., on Little's creek. To son Joshua a slave Harry, To son Gilliom 300 acres in Franklin Co. on Grove river and a slave Elbert. To son Thomas 200 acres of the land on which I now live, all of it at his mother's death or marriage and a slave Olive. To grandson Cuthbert Hudson son of Christopher 50 acres adj. the tract I now live on. To dau. Anphelady Westbrook a slave Pegg. To dau. Elizabeth Northington a slave Amey. To daughter Mary Burton a slave Milly. To dau. Susannah Hudson a slave Nell. To dau. Bethsheba Hudson a slave Nancy, bed and furniture to both. Sons Joacim and Christopher, Excrs. Signed Sept. 30, 1799, Rec. Apr. 20, 1801. John P. Harper, Nathaniel Hudson, Test.

HODGE, JOHN—Page 85—To wife Catrina and my seven children all that I possess. Two oldest sons William and John Hazleton or Hambleton to be put to trades at 17. Friends Wm. Appleby and Alex. Hodge, Excrs. Signed Aug. 20, 1795. Rec. Aug. 3, 1801. John McCurdy, David McCurdy, Test.

HARPER, JOHN P.—Page 86—To wife Sarah 215 acres where we now live and adj. tract of 200 acres and ten slaves, Pete, Bob, Joe, Pompy, Abraham, Sarah, Grace, Amy, Teller and Jenny, stock furniture etc. To son-in-law Middleton Woods 200 acres and slaves Peter, gabe, Edmond, Cate, Jude, and Winny. To nephew William Wilkins, Sr. a lot in Elberton adj. James Kidd and a slave Stephen, horse, rifle gun, all my wearing apparel when he arrives at mature age. Wife Sarah and Middleton Woods, Excrs. Signed June 9, 1801. Rec. Aug. 3, 1801. Wells Thompson, Gilbert Barden, Test.

HARPER, SALLY—Page 92—To nephew Wm. W. Lenore $500.00. To neice Prudence Richardson dau. of Walker Richardson $400.00 to be given her on maturity or marriage. All slaves to be set free, her executors to petition the Legislature. The land including the dwelling, all stock etc. be sold and after payment of all debts the money be equally divided between my son-in-law Middleton Woods and Sophia Walthall, relict of Wm. Walthall of Chesterfield Co. Va. Middleton Woods, Nathaniel Hudson, Richard Hubbard, Excrs. Signed May 15, 1802. Rec. Aug. 2, 1802. J. G. Bardin, Robt. Sanford, Tabby Thompson, Test.

JORDEN, ABSOLOM—Page 39—To wife Mary for life, slaves Chas. and Hanner and 100 acres on the river, at her death to son George Walton Jorden. To sons George Walton Jorden and Joshua Jorden the land whereon I now live, to be divided with the above land to make them equal. Wife Mary and Thomas and Joshua Jorden, Excrs. Signed Oct. 8, 1792. Rec. July 25, 1798. Jeremiah Terrell, Marget Jorden, Sarah Jorden, Test.

JONES, LEWIS—Page 36— To wife Fanny all estate for widowhood, the land to go to son Lewis at her death. To son Cyrus and dau. Polly Jinks $1.00 each, rest of estate to be equally divided amongst the rest of my children. Signed Feb. 17, 1801. Rec. Aug. 3, 1801. Jesse Jones, Thomas Jones, Test.

JOHNSON, JOHN—Page 96—To wife Catharine and son Angus and my three daus. Mary, Elizabeth and Nancy, all movable property to be kept together for their support and then be divided among my above mentioned children. To son Angus the land whereon I live, at the death of my wife, if he is of age. To my four sons Donald, John, Malcom and Neil a slave Susy. Be it remembered that I have already given to my two sons Alex. and Peter all they are to receive. Two brothers in law, Angus and Archibald Johnson, Excrs. Signed Mar. 13, 1802. Rec. Aug. 5, 1802. N. Morrison, Oliver Rock, Test.

MACKIE, THOMAS—Page 19—To wife Rosannah one third of the plantation on which I live for life, the other two thirds to sons John and William during her life, at her death all to fall to son John. To wife Rosannah a slave Hager, at her death to dau. Martha Fleming. To sons Samuel and William slaves Cat, Isaac, Joan and Jan. To daus. Rachel

Strickland, Mary Hemphill and Rosannah Temple $5.00 each. My clothes to Thos. Becxcy. John and Samuel Mackie, Excrs. Signed July 23, 1796. Rec. April 2, 1797. Samuel Hopkins, Elijah Hopkins, Test.

PARNELL, JOHN—Page 93—To daus. Mary Mosely, Martha Philips and Sarah Hill and to sons John and Jesse $5.00 besides the portion given them. To sons Samuel and Daniel $15.00 besides what they have received. To son James half the tract whereon I live, the other half to son Cyrus, the branch to be the dividing line. To dau. Elizabeth Parnell feather bed, dutch oven, cow etc. $10.00. To wife Sarah a horse and household furniture. Wife Sarah and Benj. Mosely, Excrs. Signed July 14, 1797. Rec. Aug. 4, 1802. Lewis & Henry Mosely, Daniel Parnell, Test.

SMITH, NATHANIEL—Page 95—Wife Sarah and son Stephen to share equally a tract of land granted to John Gunnels. At her death or marriage to be sold and equally divided between Alex., Eady, Stephen, Delila Winne, John, William, Sara Margret Smith. To dau. Delilah her bed and furniture. Sons Alex. and Stephen, Excrs. Signed Dec. 15, 1801. Rec. Aug. 4, 1802. Samuel Woods, J. P., Samuel Patten, Test.

TAIT, JAMES—Page 41—To wife Rebecca all estate real and personal for raising and educating the children. To eldest son Charles half the land where I now live, slaves etc. To son Wm. Hudson Tait, slaves James, Lewis, Milly and Randolph. To dau. Nancy Colson, slaves Tom, Webster, Buck, Barbary, Betty, Hager and her child for life at her death to her children. To dau. Barbara Oliver slaves Bob, Winny and her three children. To grandson Hudson Tait Ware, slave Gilbert. To daus. Patsy, Louisa, America and Charity and son James Miner as they come of age or marry, slaves. Calls these his youngest children. Sons Charles and Wm. Hudson Tait, Excrs. Signed Jan. 30, 1798 Nathaniel Allen, Obediah Jones, Test.

Codicil, June 7, 1798. To dau. Barbara Oliver, tract of land on which Wm. Winn now lives adj. Chas. Cosby and Abraham Colson. David Hudson, Robt. Cosby, Robt. L. Tait, Test.

THACKER, WILLIAM—Page 80—Of Granville Co. S. C., To wife Hannah all estate real and personal during her widowhood. To son Voluntine all stock, smiths tools etc. To the rest of my children (not named) one shilling. Son Voluntine and wife Hannah, Excrs. Signed April 3, 1797. Rec. April 20, 1801. Charles Benson, John Leatrem, Test.

THOMPSON, DRURY—Page 83— To son Robert $1.00 and all I have given him. To daus. Nancy Ellington, Elenor Watkins and Jane Watkins $1.00 and what I have already given them. To son Drury land and tenements on which I now live, containing 250 acres, slaves Bevel, Pompey, Larkin and Dolly and one half the stock and household furniture. To son Jesse, a slave Anthony George, commonly called Drummor Vinson and half of all stock. Sons Drury and Jesse, Excrs.

Signed Jan. 23, 1801. Rec. April 20, 1801. H. G. Walker, William Thompson, Sr., George Snellings, Test.

TAIT, ZIMRI—Page 88—To wife Martha all estate to sustain and educate the children. To son Thomas L40 Va. money, feather bed and furniture. To dau. Nancy McGhee a slave worth L40 Va. money to be purchased by executors. All children (not named) to have the same. Bro. James Tait, son Thos. Tait and wife Martha Tait, Excrs. Signed Oct. 2, 1792. Rec. Nov. 27, 1801. A. Colson, Wm. H. Tait, Richard McGhee, Test.

WOLDRIDGE, WILLIAM—Page 37—To wife Sarah, 100 acres where we did live and five slaves, Jack, Rachel, Jenny, Lucy and Isby, all stock, furniture etc for life. To son Richard slaves Cate, Caesar and Pheby now in his possession. To son William, slaves Frank, Sam and Nelly. To son Thomas, slaves Chas., Abel and Nancy. To son Gibson, slaves James, Cain and Suckey. To son Edward, slaves Winny and Sarah, wagon, etc. To dau. Sally Hidspeth, slaves Ceasar, Joan and Nancy for life, at her death to her children. To dau. Patty Davis, slaves Isaac and Peg for life at her death to her children. Mentions debts owing him by Philip Ryons and Blassingame Harvey. Sons Thomas and Gibson and wife Sarah, Excrs. Signed Dec. 6, 1797. Rec. July 25, 1798. Richard Hubbard, Nathaniel Hudson, Walker Richardson, Test.

WALTHALL, GARARD, JR.—Page 89—after debts are paid residue to Thomas B. Creagh and Edward Walthall, Thomas B. to be Excr.
Signed Nov. 7, 1801. Rec. Mar. 23, 1802.
George Cook, Edward G. Winn, Test.

WILSON, JOHN—Page 98—To sons Joseph, William and Benjamin, five shillings each. The rest of the property of every kind to be divided between my five daughters at the death of my wife Mary, to be kept together during her life for support etc of her and my smallest daughters. Wife Mary and Barnabas Pace, Excrs. Signed Sept. 23, 1802. Rec. Mar. 17, 1803. John Cosby, Mary Pace, Test.
No Wills in Book "O."

ELBERT COUNTY, GEORGIA

WILL BOOK 1803-1806

BARNETT, NELSON—Page 57—To honored father and mother(not named) the land whereon they live, to be divided at their death between my brother Peter Barnett and my sisters Elizabeth Speres and Ann Crawford. To friend Joel Crawford my rifle gun. Brother William Barnett, Excr. Signed Dec. 3, 1801. Reg. Aug. 5, 1803. Thos. M. Gilmore, William Barnett, Thomas M. Barnett, Test.

COLLEY, ZACHARIAH—Page 51—To my first wife's children $2.00 apiece. To beloved wife Sarah control of all estate for life or widowhood, to be divided equally among the children of "I, Zachariah Colley and

Sarah Colley my wife" after Sarah is given one third. A negro woman in Va. to be considered part of his estate. Signed Mar. 8, 1804. Reg. Feb. 10, 1805. James Walker, Mary Ward Colley, Zacharias Colley, Test. Page 53—July 4, 1804—Inventory by Samuel Patten, George and David Eberhart shows a bond for £70 Va. currency with interest from Oct. 1, 1799.

COOK, BENJAMIN—Page 63—To grandsons Beverly Crenshaw Cook and George Hiram Cook, a slave Pat after the death of their grandmother. To wife Mary remainder of estate to be at her disposal among her children at her death, she to be sole Excx. Signed Mar. 24, 1805. Reg. April 23, 1805. John Brewer, James F. Nunnellee, Thomas Owens, Test.

FORD, JOHN—Page 19—To wife Mary a slave Ally and 175 acres where I now live, for life or widowhood, then to son Jesse. To son John, a slave Dennis. To dau. Elizabeth bed and furniture. To dau. Dorcas, bed and furniture. Wife Mary, Daniel Ford, Thomas Cook and Henry Gaines, Excrs. Signed Oct. 21, 1803. Reg. June 22, 1804. John Craft, Ephraim Moss, Test.

GATEWOOD, LARKIN—Page 56—To wife Catharine all estate, to be divided at her death between my three daughters, Amy Upshaw, Mary Higginbotham and Dolly Higginbotham. To dau.-in-law Betsy Gatewood cow and calf. My three sons-in-law John Upshaw, Benjamin and Francis Higginbotham, Excrs. Signed Oct. 1, 1802. Reg. April 22, 1805. R. Hunt, Wm. Phelps, Anderson England, Test.

HERNDON, BENJAMIN—Page 65—"Very sick", to wife Susannah all property for life or widowhood, to be divided when the youngest child comes of age, amongst all my children (not named) Wife Susannah and brother Edward Herndon, Excrs. Signed Sept. 18, 1804. Probated April 23, 1805. Wm. Kidd, Test.

KIDD, WEBB—Page 57—To wife Elizabeth land whereon he lives, then to be given to youngest son, Webb at 18 years, and slave Dick. To dau. Nancy Harper furniture etc, now in "their possession. To dau. Polly Jennings land, etc, now in her possession. To dau. Lucy Greenwood land now in her possession. To son William Kidd land, etc, now in his possession. To dau. Rhody Cleveland land, etc. now in her possession. To son Martain, land in Franklin Co. To son John land in Franklin Co., adj. Martain's land. The rest of estate to be equally divided amongst all legatees except son Webb, Lucy Greenwood and Nancy Harper, Nancy's part to go to her dau., Polly and their son Webb. Lucy's part to her son William and dau. Polly Greenwood. Sons Martain, William and John, Excrs. Signed Aug. 16, 1803. Reg. Apr. 22, 1805. John White, Thomas White, Benjamin Herndon, Test.

NORRIS, JAMES—Page 17—To wife Sarah all estate for life or widowhood. To my children Royal Young Norris, Sarah Howard, James Norris, Jr. and Anna Nelms, twenty five cents each. The remainder to be divided among my five last children, Elizabeth, Evins, Samuel, Anny, and Diana.

Wife Sarah and Henry Gatewood Excrs. Signed Oct. 3, 1801. Reg. June 12, 1804. Wm. Howard, Jonl. Thacker, Christian Rice, Wm. Dudley, Frances Gilly, Nathaniel Mennefee, John Staples, Test.

PHARR, FRANCIS—Page 58—"All I possess to my nephew Francis Pharr son of Jonathan." Signed April 4, 1803. Reg. Aug. 5, 1803. William Holt, Test.

PARHAM, JOHN—Page 59—All estate to wife Mary for life, at her death to my several children, viz; Elizabeth Bennett, Cannon Parham, John Parham, Isom Parham, Holebery or Hollyberry Hicks, Mildred Parham, Dickson Parham, Frances Parham, and Lucy Parham. My estate consists of a small tract of land on Dove's creek on which I live, and six negroes, Len, Anthony, Jane, James and Delila, small stock of horses etc. Sons John and Isom and friend William Davis, Excrs. Signed Aug. 2, 1804. Reg. April 22, 1805. David Hicks, Edmond Shackleford, Thomas Parham, Test.

RAGLAND, JOHN R.—Page 52—To wife Franky for life or widowhood, 117 acres near Petersburg known as Giles old Survey, a house in Petersburg known as Lot No. 20, six slaves, bed and furniture. Motherinlaw Patsy Sharp to remain in possession of my 150 acres of land called Stephen's Ford, and seven slaves for life, to go to my wife and children at her death. If John Sharp husband of my motherinlaw should survive her he to have $100.00 a year for life. To dau. Patsy land known as Stephens Ford at the death of her grandmother Patsy Sharp, Lot No. 68 in Petersburg, six slaves, feather bed etc. To son Benj. 500 acres on south side of Broad river in Lincoln Co., and house and Lot No. 28 in Petersburg at the death of his mother, six slaves, feather bed etc., To dau. Pamela, the Giles Survey at the death of her mother, two lots in Petersburg Nos. 59 and 31 and seven slaves, feather bed etc., both daus. under age. Wife Franky and Chas. Tait Atty. Excrs. Signed May 30, 1805. Reg. July 22, 1803. Ro. Thompson, R. Easter, Samuel Watkins, Test.

STRICKLAND, JACOB—Page 15—To wife Elizabeth all property for life or widowhood, to be divided between all my lawful heirs at her death, not named. Signed Jan. 11, 1804. Reg. June 12, 1804. Wm. Sanders and Isaac Strickland, Excrs. Jacob McKleroy, H. Strickland, Test.

TOWNS, ELISHA—Page 52—To wife Ankey or Aukey, all estate for life or widowhood, to be divided between my three daughters, Nancy, Caty and Betsy Towns. My living brothers Drury Towns and Andrew Bell, Excrs. Signed Mar. 21, 1803. Reg. Nov. 10, 1805. James Watkins, Martin Dye, Daniel Tucker, Test.

WALKER, MEMORABLE—Page 56—To wife Sally B., half of all possessions forever. To brother John W. Walker the other half. Wife Sally B., and brothers Henry G. and John W., Excrs. Signed April 26, 1803. Reg. Aug. 5, 1803. Leroy Pope, William W. Bibb, Shaler Hillyre, Test.

WALTHALL, GARRED—Page 61—To son Edward Walthall, two slaves. To dau. Rebecca Creagh four slaves. To grandson Singleton Walthall, seventeen slaves and about 80 acres on which I now live, at majority, the income of which is to be a support for son Wm. Walthall, he dying without heirs to go to Sally Bass and her children, now living in Halifax Co. Va. Friends William Allen and James Banks, Excrs. Signed Nov. 20, 1801. Reg. April 23, 1805. William Tate, John Tate, William Tate, Jr., Test.

WHITE, NICHOLAS—Page 64—Being aged, after the death of me and my wife (not named) cattle, furniture etc. to go to grandaughter Barbary Fowler, if she dies without heirs to grandson John Nix. To daughters Palatere and Barbary five shillings, rest of the estate to be divided between my son Solomon and daus. Mary, Rebecca and Sucka. Son Solomon and Caleb Campbell, Excrs. Signed April 27, 1801. Probated April 23, 1805.

James Norris, James Norris, Jr., Jederson Canterbury, Test.

ELBERT COUNTY, GEORGIA

WILL BOOK—1805

ALEXANDER, WILLIAM—Page 94—Being sick, To wife Nancy all property till the youngest child is 16, then to be divided among all the children. To grandson Edmond Alexander, $80.00 which I have paid to his father, wife Nancy to keep the portions that may fall to her children by me, as I have given $80.00 to four of my children, James, Elijah, John and George Alexander. Joseph Chrystlar, Peter Alexander and wife Nancy, Excrs. Signed Mar. 12, 1805. Reg. June 12, 1806. Lewis Gaar, John McMullin, William Brown, Test.

BRADLY, WILLIAM—Page 118—To wife Elizabeth land on which I live, stock, furniture etc., to be divided at her death between Elizabeth Upshaw, Martha Oglesby, Lucy Christian, and Drury Bradley. To son-in-law Thomas Johnson and wife Mary several slaves until George Stovall (son to said Mary Johnson) comes of age, if he dies without issue, at their death to be put in the hands of Thomas Oglesby, James Christian and John Staples to be equally divided amongst all Mary Johnson's children, the above men to be Excrs. of the will also. Signed Jan. 12, 1799. John Staples, Lewis Phipps, Richard Upshaw, Test. Codicil, Jan. 21, 1799—To grandaughter, Nancy Greenwood, a slave, Susannah. To grandaughter Martha Greenwood, a slave James. If she dies without issue to fall to her mother, Elizabeth Upshaw. Reg. Sept. 26, 1805. John Staples, Test.

HOLLYDAY, TABITHA—Page 56—"Being infirm", to grandson John Gatewood $43.00. To dau. Mary Rowsey $17.00. To negroes Faraoh and Sarah their freedom. The residue to daughters, Betty Gatewood and Mary Rowsey. John Ham and Absolom Stinchcomb, Excrs. Signed

Oct. 2, 1802. Reg. June 4, 1806. Peter Webster, Anna Phelps, Sally Gatewood, Test.

NUNNELLE, WILLIAM—Page 112—To son Walter three slaves. To son James four slaves. To dau. Elizabeth Middleton and her heirs, a slave Molley. To dau. Nancy Burton and her children a slave Levina. To dau. Priscilla Hatcher bed and furniture. To grandson Wm. Nunnelle a slave Hale, slave Peyton to be set free. Residue divided among all children. Sons Walter and James F., Excrs. Signed Nov. 23, 1804. Reg. June 21, 1806. Richard Hubbard, William Oliver, Test.

PARKS, CHARLES—Page 18—To wife Mary lands and stock, furniture etc., for life, at her death the land to go to son Marshall Parks, balance to be divided among my sons here named, John, Charles, Abraham, and Theopeles Parks and my dau. Mary Bobo, and Mary Salmons, dau. of my wife and Benj. and Hannah Bobo, whom I constitute my heirs. This will deposited with my son John to see that it is complied with. Signed Nov. 2, 1805. Reg. May 15, 1806. James Highsmith, Silas Dobbs, Test.

SAXON, HUGH—Page 177—of Elbert Co., in low state of health, all property to be sold at public sale, the proceeds to be divided between my wife Mary and Lewis W. Saxon, dau. Jensy Saxon, sons Drury T. and John M. Saxon. Capt. Robert Thompson my first creditor, first Excr. Lewis W. Saxon, second Excr. wife Mary third Excr. Will made at Col. James Littals in Franklin Co. Signed Feb. 17, 1805. Reg. Sept. 13, 1805. Asa Allen, James Little, Test.

SHAPPARD, JOHN—Page 30—of Franklin Co., to sons Samuel, George Dillard, Peter and Robert Shappard and daughters Anna Ware Coleman, Anna Dillard Nelms, Betsy Ridgdell and Clary Burden, $1.06½ each. To wife Anna all estate for life, to go to George Dillard Shappard, Peter, and Robert Shappard, Clary Burden and their heirs. Signed June 8, 1805. Reg. May 9, 1806. Joakin Hudson, Elen Westbrook, Test.

TURMAN, GEORGE, Sr.—Page 88—"Afflicted in body", all estate to wife Elizabeth for life, at her death the plantation where I live to son Jacob. To my daughter Sarah Lancaster and my son Thomas, a horse each. To Garrett, John, Robert and Isaac (sons?) $1.00 each. To Rebecca Claton and Nancy Turman, $1.00 each. Slave David to be set free. Residue to be divided between Elizabeth Lancaster, Milly Rogers, Zilly Roberts and Elizabeth Higginbotham, relationship not given. Wife Elizabeth, William Hatcher and Thomas Burton, Excrs. Signed July 1, 1805. Reg. June 7, 1806. Richerson Booker, John Turman, Thomas Pace, Test.

WOLDBRIDGE, SARAH—Page 49—To grandson Thomas W. Davis, a colt Jolly etc. The rest of the estate to be sold and divided into five equal parts, one to each of my beloved children, Thomas, Gibson, and Edward Wooldridge and Sally Hudspeth. The fifth part to be divided between my grandchildren, Thomas W., Absolom, William and Sarah F. Davis, minors lawful heirs of Joseph T. Davis. Sons Thomas and Gibson and friend Richard Hubbard, Excrs. Signed Feb. 24, 1804. Reg. May 27, 1806. N. Hudson, J. P., B. Jeter, J. P., Test.

ELBERT COUNTY, GEORGIA
WILL BOOK "L-F"—1804-09

BURGESS, THOMAS—Page 64—Wife Nancy and William Davis, Excrs., if property is well managed etc. to remain in her hands till son Thomas is 18 years old, when an equal division is to take place between my several children, towit, Sanders, James, Betsy, Bethany and Thomas. Signed April 5, 1806. Probated July term, 1808. Philip Wilhite, Reuben Eastin, Test.

CARTER, LEWIS—Page 99—To beloved wife Nelly a sorrel mare in fee simple. To son James tract of land on which I now live. To dau. Polly two colts etc. Brotherinlaw Arthur Jones and friend William Easter, Excrs. Signed Aug. 29, 1803. Above Excrs. refused to serve. William Rose as Admr. with will annexed qualified Sept. 5, 1808.

DAVIS, ABSOLOM, Sr.—Page 30—To sons Frederick, Lewis, Augustine, Richard, Gideon, Chislen, Joseph T., and Wiley Davis, daughters Lucy Howard, Nancy Cunningham and Chirial Wooldridge, $1.00 each. To son Absolom, Jr., residue including slaves, land etc., except featherbed etc., to grandaughter Nancy Davis. Son Absolom sole Excr. Signed Jan. 12, 1807. Probated July 24, 1807. Lucy B. Wooldridge, Martha Henderson, Absolom Davis, Jr., Test.

FAULKNER, JAMES—Page 152—To wife Patsy and sons John and James H. Faulkner all property when the sons come of age. Signed Jan. 11, 1808. Probated May Term 1809. George Oglesby, Francis Cook, Jr., James Cook, Peter Faulkner, Test.

GATEWOOD, BETTY—Page 39—To son John $50.00, to Dau. Sally Gatewood a slave Flora, to grandau. Nancy Ham, bed etc., to grandson Ezekiel Ham $10.00, to grandchildren Richard, Nancy, Henry, Betsy and Chas. C. Gatewood, $10.00 each. Residue to be divided among all other children (not named) Son John Gatewood and John Ham, Excrs. Signed July 1, 1807. Rec. Sept. 24, 1807. John Upshaw, Jr., Beverly Greenwood, James Greenwood, Test.

Inventory shows she lived in the home of John Ham—Page 186—Receipts, Sally Gatewood, John Ham, Betty Gatewood, John Gatewood and of Wm. Phelps who receipts for bed etc., left to Nancy Ham. Feb. 5, 1808.

GARRETT, JOHN—Page 42—To wife Catharine all estate for life, at her death to be divided among my children, Ann Ellington, Catharine Ellington, Maria, Martha, Julian and Margaret, except Ann Ellington who has already received property at her marriage. Friend Benj. Taliaferro and brotherinlaw William Micou of Augusta, Excrs. Signed July 23, 1807. Rec. Jan. 9, 1808. Dabney Berry, Thompson Dye, Lewis B. Taliaferro, Phebe F. Walthall, Test.

JONES, THOMAS—Page 187—"of Elbert Co. and waters of Warhacee creek". To wife Jane, plantation, stock, slaves Bess, Nama and Reuben, for life. To dau. Charlot Jones, slaves, bed etc. To dau. Hulday Jones slaves, bed etc., both minors. James Bell, Richard Hubbard, Excrs. Signed............1809. Probated May Term 1809. Wiley W. Jones, Solomon Jones, John Hathcock, Test.

LONG, JOSEPH—Page 135—of Franklin Co., wife Sarah, horse, saddle and bridle, bed and furniture. The residue to the heirs of my brother Samuel Long. Wife Sarah and friend James Long, Excrs. Signed Sept. 11, 1808. Probated Nov. Term 1808. William Cleghorn, Charles Wheeler, Test.

NAPIER, RENE—Page 14—To wife Dorothy, horse, bed and ett, and $80.00 and possession of the and garden for life if she chooses, the slaves to be hired out and plantation rented. To Polly Shorter, slaves Simon and Easter, and if she dies without heirs to go to Theo., and Cloe Napier and Sally Duncan. James Morrison, McCarty Oliver and Matthew Duncan, Excrs. Signed Feb. 2, 1807. No record of probate. E. Brewer, E. Lyon, Peter Oliver, Test.—Page 178—Receipt of Edward Lyon to James Morrison, Excr., for horse, furniture and other property left Dorothy Napier, wife of said Rene Napier, dec'd. Jan. 11, 1808.

PATTERSON, JOHN, Sr.—Page 65—To wife Margaret land, furniture, stock and two slaves Brown and Saro for life, at her death slave Brown to go to son Wm. B. Patterson, and land to son James Patterson. Land which I drew and now in Baldwin Co., the half of which is the house and spring, to son Robert Patterson, the rest to be sold. To son Samuel Patterson a slave Dave. To dau. Elizabeth Pickens and to son John $5.00, they having received property, the residue to be given to sons Thomas, Joseph, George and Alex. Sons James and Samuel, Excrs. Signed Mar. 19, 1808. Probated July 4, 1808. Wm. F. Underwood, Micajah Terrell, Robt. McCreight, Test.

TURMAN, THOMAS—Page 43—To dau. Catharine 3 slaves, Bob, Lett and Jane. To son George a slave Lewis. To son James a slave Peter. To son John 202½ acres in last purchase. To three grandchildren Prudence, Robert and Abner Turman, $50.00 each. The rent of the plantation, stock, furniture etc., to be equally divided between my son John Turman, Catharine Turman, Joseph Randolph, James Reed and Joseph Chandler. William Goode and Richard Easter, Excrs. No dates. William Hudson, Robert Goode, Test.

THOMPSON, ALEX—Page 136—To sons William and John land whereon I live with grist and saw mills, stills and cotton machines. To dau. Ruth Thompson, alias Strickland $5.00. Slaves to be divided among my sons James, Alex., Robert, William and John and daughters Sarah

GEORGIA D. A. R.

and Esther. Sons James and Alex., Excrs. Signed Dec. 15, 1804. Probated Nov. Term 1808. Samuel James, James McCurdy, Jones (?) McMullen, Test.

WHITMAN, WILLIAM—Page 108—Four minor children now living with him namely, William, Polly, Sally and John Whitman, have $90.00, bed furniture etc, at majority or marriage. Wife Elizabeth to have land etc, for life. She and James Bell, Excrs. Signed Dec. 21, 1807. Probated Sept. 5, 1808. John L. Gordon, William Behannon, Zachariah Clark, Test.

WOODS, MIDDLETON—Page 14—To sister Sally Woods, $100.00. To Nephew William Woods, son of Hugh $5,000.00. To Christopher C. Bowen, a horse. Speaks of a dissolution of partnership with nephew William Woods, all goods etc. to be sold and divided between his brothers and sisters. Excrs. to make titles to Dr. John H. Brewer to the house and lot where he resides. Josiah and William Woods, Excrs. Signed Mar. 12, 1807. Probated May 4, 1807. James Alston, Ro. Middleton, S. Brewer, Test.

ELBERT COUNTY, GEORGIA
WILL BOOK 1809-1812

ALSTON, WILLIAM—Page 37—To son Solomon 2,000 acres on Obyon river which said land he has previously sold. To son James a slave Grace. To daus. Nancy Tait and Elizabeth Thompson slaves. To dau. Sarah Chambers both the tracts of land Thos. Chambers bought of Nathaniel Alston and Thos. B. Creagh. To dau. Christeen L. Alston, slaves. The rest of the slaves, twenty in number, to wife Charity Alston, dau. Mary Alston and sons William H., and Philip H. Alston as they come of age. To two last named sons the land on which he now lives. To sons James, Wm. H., and Philip H., 2,000 acres on Lace or Luce Hatchy river, adj. Gen'l. James Robertson. Wife Charity and son James, Excrs. Signed Dec. 8, 1809. Probated Jan. Term 1810. James Banks, Reuben Tucker, Gabriel Tucker, Test.

ARNOLD, WILLIAM—Page 349—To first wife's children, James, Lucy, Susanna, Jenney and Polly, $1.00 each, having already received their portions. Present wife Nancy and her three children, William, John and Lemuel to have all estate till William comes of age, then to be divided. Wife Nancy and Absolom Davis, Excrs. Signed June 4, 1812. Probated July Term 1812. Sally Childres, Patsy Owens, Barnett Jeter, Test.

BELL, JAMES—Page 34—To eldest son Joseph, $1.00 and what he has already received. To son James, 150 acres on the opposite side of the creek from my dwelling house, adj. William B., and Terrell Key, horse, saddle etc. To son William, 150 acres adj. son James land, horse etc. To son Thomas, 300 acres adj. Posey, horse etc. The remainder of the land including the house where I live to wife Olive until youngest son

David comes of age, when he is to have half, horse, etc. To son Jonathan a slave, horse etc. To dau. Patsy Bell when she comes of age a slave and $200.00. To dau. Nancy Bell notes on Andrew Woodly, Elijah Mosely, Wm. Brown, Wiley Childres and Wm. H. Moon. To three married daus., Polly, Elizabeth and Sarah Moon, $1.00 each and what they have received. Wife Olive to have a number of slaves. Wife and son Joseph, Excrs. Signed Sept. 17, 1807. Peter Wyche, Andrew Woodley, James Glover, Test.

Codicil. Having sold part of the land willed to son Thomas now gives him Lot No. 311, Wilkinson Co. Dau. Nancy having married received most of her legacy. Signed Apr. 2, 1808. Probated Jan. Term 1810. Robins Andrews, Elizabeth Andrews, William Davis, William D. Davis, Reuben Davis, Test.

BURTON, ABRAHAM—Page 84—To son Thomas four slaves. To dau. Dicy Bevill feather bed etc. and three slaves for life to go to her children at her death, and one seal skin trunk. To grandaughter Dicy Tucker, a slave Dilsy. To grandau. Jenny Burton, feather bed etc. To grandson Abraham Burton, a slave Biddy. Son Thomas, Excr. Signed April 10, 1810. Probated Sept. 3, 1810. William Dunlap, Robert Dunlap, Test.

BREWER, SACKVILLE, Page 263—"Weak and afflicted in body," after debts are paid, residue to brother John H. Brewer. My remains to be deposited in a plain pine coffin on Lot No. 7 owned by my brother. John H. Brewer, Excr. Signed Dec. 24, 1811. Probated Jan. 6, 1812. Wm. Woods, Wm. B. Brewer, Test.

BAILEY, EZEKIEL—Page 367—"Low state of health," after debts are paid, all land, stock etc. to wife Rebecca to dispose of as she sees fit. No children mentioned. Signed June 25, 1812. Probated Sept. 17, 1812. Samuel N. Bailey, Fanny Bailey, Test.

COTTLE, DELILA—Page 57—To dau. Lurinna all estate, an inventory of which she gives, including cloth woven and garments made for David Odam, John Hollcom, a slave in possession of Edward Muckleroy of Oglethorpe Co. $100.00 due from John Jones of Montgomery Co., cows lent to Wm., and John Thomasson, Chas. Sorrells, cattle in possession of Samuel Godden of Morgan Co., all to be sold for benefit of said daughter. Signed July 6, 1808. Probated Mar. Term 1810. Nathan Williford, Joel Freeman, William Sorrells, Test.

DEADWYLER, MARTIN—Page 20—To dau. Eve the land whereon I now live for life, after her death to my grandson Martin Deadwyler. Land in Wilkinson Co., to be sold and equally divided among my children (not named) and Nancy Deadwyler, except my son Joseph, grandau. Nancy to have the bed she claims. Son Joseph, Excr. Signed June 1, 1809. Probated Sept. 4, 1809. Joseph Deadwyler, James Murphy, Test.

EBERHART, JACOB—Page 131—To my several children, Christenah McElreath, Jacob Eberhart, David Eberhart, Catherine Patten, George Eberhart, equal portions of my estate. Three sons, Excrs. Signed June 26, 1810. Probated Jan. 4, 1811. James Eberhart, Mary Embry, John Russell, Test.

HIGGINBOTHAM, BENJAMIN—Page 94—To dau. Sarah a slave Daufney, featherbed etc, which she has in her possession. To dau. Anny a slave Milley, featherbed etc. To dau. Elizabeth a slave Letty, featherbed etc., which she has in her possession. To son Benj. Graves, a slave Dainel, cattle, featherbed and horse he is now in possession of. To son Peter a slave Jacob, featherbed, horse etc. To dau. Mary, a slave Rhody, bed, horse etc. To son Larkin a slave Lindsey, horse etc. Residue to be equally divided between the whole of my children. Son Benjamin Graves Higginbotham and John Upshaw, Jr., Excrs. Signed May 20, 1809 Probated Sept. 3, 1810. Jacob Higginbotham, Sr., John Upshaw, Leroy Upshaw, Francis Satterwhite, Test.

LINDSAY, REUBEN—Page 67—To wife Nancy Cannon Lindsay all land, money etc, to her sole use and benefit. Wife, Archelus Jarrett, and Richardson Hunt, Excrs. Signed April 2, 1809. Probated May 7, 1810. S. W. Harris, Bartlet Ham, Benj. Cook, Test.

MOON, WILLIAM—Page 132—To wife Sarah for life or widowhood, the land whereon I now live, slaves Edmond, Jean and Betty, crops, horses etc. Should she marry a childs part or third for life. Son Jacob's orphans to have his part of my estate less $50.00. Sons Robert and William H., to have their part of my estate less $50.00 each. To dau. Martha Blake and her children, a childs part. Son Jesse's orphans to have a childs part. Sons Boller, Pleasant, Archelaus and John, daus. Sally Green Power and Susannah Power to have their equal portion.
Wife Sarah and sons Robert and William H., Excrs.
Signed May 7, 1810. Probated Jan. 7, 1811.
James Wood, James Power, Test.

PATTEN, SAMUEL—Page 80—All property to remain in the hands of wife Catharine for the support of the family during widowhood, then an equal division among all the children except dau. Polly is to have a slave Bet, and dau. Margaret is to have a colt above their shares. Wife Catharine, George Eberhart and William Patten, Excrs. Signed May 12, 1810. Probated July Term 1810. Jonathan Cooper, David Eberhart, Jacob Eberhart, Test.

PENN, WILSON—Page 252—Landed estate and stock to be disposed of at the discretion of executors and more land bought whenever my dear wife may wish, to be kept together for her support and that of the children till they marry or become of age, then to be divided. Dear wife Francis, friends Col. Benjamin Taliaferro, Dr. John T. Gilmer and Thomson Watkins, Excrs. Signed May 19, 1811. Probated Nov. 4, 1819. Caleb Higginbotham, William Brown, Chas. Williford, Test.

THORNTON, REUBEN—Page 130—Lot No. 265, 2nd. Dist. of Wayne Co. Ga. to be sold for paying debts the residue to be kept by my wife Elizabeth for the support of herself and her children. Also the 200 acres on which I live, two slaves Patty and Harry, stock etc., to be possessed by her for widowhood or life then to be divided between her and my beloved children, Priscilla, Thomas, William, Elizabeth, Sally, Reuben and Anne Thornton. True friends Daniel Thornton and Beverly Allen, Excrs. Signed May 1, 1810. Probated Jan. 7, 1811. Simeon Henderson, James Teasley, Drusilla Teasley, Test.

ELBERT COUNTY, GEORGIA

WILL BOOK "K" 1812-16

ALSTON, JAMES—Page 190—To son Nathaniel, slaves Lemas and Nell. To dau. Charity Banks, slaves Tony, Beck and Nell; To dau. Sarah Groves, slaves Ned and Sib; To son John slaves Peter, Easter, Mary and Justine, some time since in their possession. To the first heir of my son John, male or female a slave Alfred; to dau. Hannah Banks, slaves Lemon, Dinah and Ephraim; To grandson James Alston Banks, son of my dau. Charity, a slave Neptine, now in possession of his father; To grandson James Alston Groves, son of my dau. Sarah, a slave Lender, some time since in possession of his father; to grandson William Jefferson Alston, son of Nathaniel, a slave Clarissa in possession of his father; To granddaughter Elmira Banks dau. of Hannah, a slave Beck; To wife Gilley and daus. Martha and Elizabeth Alston, twenty one slaves; To wife Gilley life estate in slaves and the land whereon I live, to go to said daus. Martha and Elizabeth. Wife Gilley and sons Nathaniel and John, Excrs. Signed Oct. 18, 1814. Probated May 1, 1815. James Alston, Jr, Samuel G. Clowd, Wm. H. Alston, Test.

BOND, NATHAN, Sr.—Page 187—To wife Elizabeth, land, stock, furniture etc. for life, to be divided at her death among my children (not named) Son Richard, Admr. Signed Feb. 26, 1815 Probated May 1, 1815. Thomas Davis, Thos. S. Hansard, Test.

BREWER, JOHN H.—Page 50—All debts to be paid, especially $400.00 to the Excr. of Middleton Woods, dec'd., for the lot whereon I now live, part of Lot No. 8. Shop, furniture, medicine, medical books etc to be sold; To my affectionate and beloved wife Fanny C. M. Brewer residue for her use and disposal. Worthy friend Abner McGehee, Excr. Signed June 8, 1813 Probated Sept. 6, 1813. John C. Easter, James Hamilton, Jesse Whipple, Test.

BURTON, ROBERT—Page 85—To wife Tabitha all estate real and personal for life, plantation where I live, and 50 acres of woodland on the Hogpen branch, at her death to be divided between Booker Hudson, Harriet Burton and Eliza Burton. Booker to return a slave to the estate. Wife Tabitha, Booker Hudson and Thomas Burton, Excrs. Signed

Dec. 11, 1813. Probated May 2, 1814. W. Hudson, Daniel Coursey, Ann Burton, Test.

CRAWFORD, JOHN—Page 186—To wife Henrietta all property for raising and schooling my children, except what I am to receive from my mother Lucy Crawford's estate at her death, which is to be divided among "my children" towit, Burton, Earls, Leroy and Wm. Haley. John Craft, Excr. Signed Nov. 12, 1814. Probated May 1, 1815. J. Johnston, Moses Haynes, Sr., Test.

COOK, FRANCIS—Page 11—To wife Betty 200 acres to be divided off the upper end to include the dwelling adj. John Willis, Josiah Cook and Walker Richardson, furniture, stock etc, and $500.00 in fee simple. To grandsons James and Charles Ragans, sons of dau. Nancy Ragans, dec'd. 500 acres in Franklin Co., on Hunters creek which is half a tract granted Thomas Gregg and Wm. Moss. Residue to be divided between the children of my dec'd, son Dudley, the children of my dec'd, dau. Nancy Rogers and my sons Thomas, John, Josiah, Joshua, Benjamin and Elisha Cook and daus. Sarah Long and Elizabeth Mosely. Sons Thomas and Joshua, wife Betty and friend Richardson Hunt, Excrs. Signed Aug. 11, 1804. Probated Mar. 1, 1813. Francis Cook, Jr., William Lane, Jr., W. Woods, Test.

DAVIS, ABSOLOM—Page 261—Wife Nancy all estate for life or widowhood. A slave Sylva to be the property of his wife, at death or marriage to go to son Terry, if he dies to son Thos. F., if he dies to son Absolom T. To dau. Patsy Westley Davis a fourth of a share above her equal portion. Those children having already received property to return it to the estate, viz, Henrietta Tate, Sally Tatum and Terry Davis. Wife Nancy, son Terry and William Holt, Excrs. Signed Mar. 15, 1814. Probated Jan. 6, 1816. John Dailey, John Wilson, Test.

EASTER, RICHARD—Page 101—To wife Mary "horse and chair", and a home such as she desires. To son John C., a slave Abram; To the heirs that are or may be to dau. Elizabeth L. Chisholm, slaves Mary and Zadoc, bed, furniture etc, already delivered to them. To son Richard J., a slave Simeon. To son William F., a slave Henry and beds and furniture to both. John C. Easter, sole Excr. Signed Mar. 23, 1814. Probated July 4, 1814. Wiley Thompson, Britton Capel, Test.

FREEMAN, JAMES—Page 83—of Franklin Co., To John Simmons 350 acres of land on which he now lives. To Holeman Simmons 260 acres on Freeman's creek. To William and James Wheeler, 250 acres on north fork of Broad river. To James Pressel, 250 acres remainder of said tract. To Wiot Cleveland 120 acres on Freeman's creek. To James Simmons 200 acres in Elbert Co., at the mouth of Coldwater creek. Slaves to be sold and money divided amongst my four sisters, Temperance Cleveland, Mary Wheeler, Susannah Pressel and Ann Simmons, also 450 acres in Abbeville Co. S. C. John Simmons and Robt. Barnwell, Excrs.

Signed Oct. 21, 1810. Probated May 2, 1814. E. L. Thomas, Joseph Dobbins, Berry Page, Test.

GAINES, HIEROM—Page 188—To wife Anne Thompson Gaines, slaves Joe and Rachel, the latter in possession of James Adams for life, to be divided at her death between my children. To son James H., land on the Big branch adj. Sally Turner, horse, shot gun etc. To son Wm. Shanklin the balance of the land including my plantation, after the death of my wife, furniture etc, and a slave Billie in possession of James Adams. To dau. Margaret C. Gaines a slave Polly, bed and furniture. To dau. Jeney a slave Edy, furniture etc. To Robert Burk, Sr., a slave, Jack. Confirms a slave each to William Adams, Isham Teasley, Samuel Adams and Ivey Seal. To John Adams a slave Chas., now in possession of James Adams. Certain slaves in possession of father-inlaw James Adams to be divided at his death between William, Samuel and John Adams, Isham Teasley and Ivey Seal. Robt. Burk, Sr., John Johnston and James Gaines, Excrs. Signed Mar. 15, 1815. Probated May 1, 1815. Moses Fleming, R. Banks, James Hamelton, Test.

GLENN, SIMEON—Page 125—To wife Elizabeth the land wheron I now live for life, to go to son James at her death. Son Simeon to continue to hold the tract whereon he lives. Dau. Martha T. Glenn to have horse, saddle, bed furniture etc. at majority or marriage. To grandson Simeon G. Rogers a colt. To grandau. Susannah M. Gray $1.00. Property already given off to sons Clement, William, Joseph, Simeon, Jr., and James Glenn to be accounted for in the final division. James and William Glenn, Excrs. Signed Oct. 8, 1814. Probated Nov. 7, 1814. Hezekiah Gray, Joshua Clark, Reuben Goolsby, Test.

GOSS, ELIZABETH—Page 195—"Being porely of body". To son Charles Goss' four children, Martha Matilda, Mary Sopha, John Colbert and Chas., Lot No. 125 in Wilkinson Co., drawn by Isham Goss. To son Chas., $1.00. To son Jesse a slave Priscilla. To son Horasha J. Goss two slaves Charles and Robin. To dau. Elizabeth Andrews, personalty. To dau. Mary Bragg $1.00. Residue to my children as follows, Benjamin, John, Isham, Micha H. Goss and Anna Webb, John W. Bragg and Isham G. Rogers. To Reuben Brown $1.00. Sons Isham and Horasha J. Goss, Excrs. Signed May 15, 1815. Probated July 3, 1815. George Wyche, Edmond Lowry, Sarah Dillard, Test.

HAMILTON, JAMES—Page 289—Wife Nancy to have a slave Gilbert or Jerry whichever falls to me when the division takes place, the land I live on, stock etc, to bring up and educate my children Jane Ann and Bedford, both minors. A slave Peggy to be kept by his mother as long as she lives. Drugs, books and surgical instruments to be sold. Wife and Bedford Harper, Excrs. Signed April 30, 1816. Probated May 6, 1816. George Wyche, Chiles T. Key, Agatha Wyche, Test.

JONES, THOMAS—Page 214—To wife Jane all land etc. for life or widowhood. To dau. Charlot Jones, slaves etc. To dau. Huldy Jones, bed slaves etc., both daus. minors. Huldy to be educated. Friends James Bell and Richard Hubbard, Excrs. Signed Feb. 18, 1809. Probated May Term 1809. John Hathcock, Wiley W. Jones, Solomon Jones, Test.

RICH, JOHN—Page 124—To wife Mary slaves, land all real and personal estate for life or widowhood. To sons William, James, John, Jesse, Richmond, slaves, money, bed etc. To daus. Mary, Sarah, Elizabeth, Pamelia and Sophia, all minors apparently. Wife Mary and son William, Excrs. Signed Oct. 7, 1814. Probated Nov. 7, 1814. James Morrison, Elisha Brewer, John Snellings, Test.

ROEBUCK, ROBERT, Sr.—Page 232—To dau. Betsy Goss, confirms a slave Barbara received since her marriage. Confirms a slave to dau. Sally Ward received since her marriage, on her husband Richard Ward making titles to the land on which I now live. To dau. Anna Stowers a slave received since her marriage. To dau. Fanny Roebuck a slave, feather bed etc at her marriage. To dau. Harriott Roebuck a slave, bed etc. All property to be held together for the support of two youngest daughters, Fanny and Harriott. Then son William to take it into his possession for the use of my dau. Polly and her child, the remainder to be sold and divided between sons William, George, and Robt. Roebuck, Jr., upon their paying to John Carson $150.00. Sons William, George and Robt. Jr., and Robt. Barker, Excrs. Signed Aug. 30, 1815. Probated Nov. 6, 1815. James Holly, Haley Butler, Jno. Cunningham, Test.

ROSE, THOMAS—Page 303—To wife Sally certain slaves, bed etc. one slave Judy to go to dau. Elizabeth Ansley or Ausley, the rest to be divided among the children by my present wife. To son William, slaves, bed etc, which he has received. To dau. Sarah Barron slaves Lizzie and Fanny. To son Grantham plantation on the west side of the creek, slaves etc, and requests Grantham to assist his son Benjamin when in need. To son Amos the other half of the land on which I now live, my wife to have it for life. To dau. Winny Rose a slave Rhody which she has already received. To two grandchildren James and Lizzie Carrell $25.00 each. All residue to wife Sally Rose for life, to be divided between all children at her death. Son Grantham and wife Sally, Excrs. Signed Nov. 16, 1813. Probated Sept. Term 1816. John Anderson, Smith Cook, John Cook, Test.

ROWSEY, JOHN, Sr.—Page 211—After debts are paid, all property to be put in the hands of beloved wife Mary for life, at her death to be equally divided among my following beloved children, Edmond, Stephen, James and Foster Rowsey, daus. Elizabeth Bond, Cleracy Bond and Polly Bond, and children of my dec'd dau. Tabitha Phipps. To son John Rowsey $1.00 he having already received his portion. John Upshaw, Jr., and Thomas Oliver, Excrs. No date of signature. Probated Sept. 14, 1815. Archer Burden, Penelope Elder, Sarah Powell, Test.

SKINNER, ARCHER—Page 55—All property to be divided between my wife Clary and "all my children", except son James is to have the house and lot now occupied by Dr. James Hamilton. Wm. Woods, and sons Morris and Geo. Martin Skinner, Excrs. Signed Nov. 30, 1813. Probated Jan. 4, 1814. William Holt, Wm. Nunnelee, Frederic Harmon, Test. Codicil—Dec. 2, 1813. James Wood, David Clark, Wm. Holt, Test.

STOKES, THOMAS—Page 41—of Petersburg, Elbert Co. Ga.—To eldest brother Armstead Stokes, $1,500.00. To second brother William Stokes, Jr., $2,000.00, house where I now live, furniture etc. To sister Jane Ware and to brothers Young, Archibald and Richard H. Stokes, $1,500.00 each. Slaves Ben and Sarah to be set free. Archibald and Wm. Stokes, Jr., Excrs. Signed May 6, 1806. Shaler Hillyer, Jos. P. Watkins, Test. When probated July 5, 1813, Shaler Hillyer declared that a bequest of $1,000.00 to John Mallory with horse, saddle and bridle had been stricken out as appears by an entry made in the hand writing of the testator. Archibald Stokes qualified as Excr.

TAIT, WILLIAM—Page 84—To wife Elishaba several slaves, household furniture etc., for widowhood. To son John 100 acres including the plantation whereon he now lives. To son William 100 acres adj. the land he bought of R. L. Tait. To son James 100 acres including the place where he formerly lived. To sons David, Daniel and Enos the other 400 acres of my land to be equally divided, Enos to have the part whereon the dwelling house now stands. To daus. Lucy and Betsy, slave and beds etc. each. To dau. Susanna the legacy I have given her. 490 acres in Wayne Co., to be sold for distribution among all the children. David Hudson and sons John and William, Excrs. Signed Mar. 30, 1814. Probated May 2, 1814. Samuel Watkins, James Watkins, Zimri Tait, Test.

THOMPSON, WILLIAM—Page 54—To sons William, Wells and Asa, slaves To beloved wife Sarah $100.00 a year during her life to be paid by above sons. To grandsons William N. and Richard Richardson slaves Daniel and Tempy and all landed estate. Signed Aug. 3, 1811. Probated Nov. 2, 1813. Robt. P. Haynes, Duke W. Hullum, Thomas Scott, Test.

TERRELL, JEREMIAH—Page 290—To wife Louisa my plantation and mansion house where I now live for life or widowhood, at her death to go to youngest son John. To eldest son William all the land I possess on the south side of Pickens creek. To grandson John Jordan, eldest son of James Jordan, the east end of the tract on which I live adj. Wm. Prewitt, 133 acres according to a deed of gift. To grandson Burden Rice Taylor land adj. that bequeathed to son John, 100 acres sold to Wm. Craft with the consent of my dau. Polly Terrell, she to have the proceeds, etc. To grandaughter Patsy Taylor, bed and furniture. To the heirs of my daus. Rachel and Louisa $5.00. To daus. Rosanna and Susanna $5.00. Sons William and John, Excrs. Mar. 20, 1811. May 6, 1816. William Underwood, Henry Mann, Farley Thompson, Test.

WALTHALL, SUSANNA—Page 213—To grandson Singleton Walthall eighteen slaves and a tract of land in Prince George Co., Va., known as Hopewell on Hopewell creek. To niece Susanna Clark one of the above named slaves Lotty. To nephew James Williams a slave Meranda out of the above mentioned negroes when Singleton Walthall comes of age. If Singleton should die before majority or marriage, all slaves to go to my friend William Allen. Worthy friends William and Beverly Allen, Excrs. Signed Feb. 2, 1805. Probated Sept. 4, 1815. Richard Hubbard, Robt. Hines, Joseph Cook, Test.

ELBERT COUNTY, GEORGIA
WILL BOOK "L" 1816-1821

ADAMS, WILLIAM—Page 128—To wife Nancy 150 acres on north fork of Broad river on which I now live adj. Chas. W. Christian, household goods etc. for life, dau. Anne or Nancy to enjoy it as long as she is single, Anne to have it at wife's death. To son William $1.00. To son John $1.00 and a large Bible. To dau. Rebecca Hendrick 100 acres in Madison Co., on Broad river, divided so as to join Alex. Human, Joseph Bradbury, Robert Woods and James Walker, for life, at her death to her son Pattern Hendrick. James Wood, Excr. Signed Oct. 13, 1817 Probated Mar. 2, 1818. Thos. Staples, Mathew Quinn, C. W. Christian, Test.

BELL, JOSEPH—Page 155—To wife Elizabeth the plantation whereon I now live, furniture, two horses, slaves Jack and Hall. To son Thomas $1.00 in addition to what he has already received. To dau. Anna Bullard, and dau. Mary Bell, $1.00 each in addition to what they have already received. To dau. Rebecca Gunter, $255.00, and to stay on the place where she now lives till my son Joseph is 21. To son Joseph 230 acres adj. James Gunter and James Nash, horse, bed etc. To dau. Elizabeth Bell $330.00, bed, furniture etc. To dau. Eleanor Bell, $330.00, bed, furniture etc. Joseph Bell, Esqr. and son Thomas Bell, Excrs. Signed Feb. 19. 1818. Probated May 4, 1818. James Nash, Nicholas Goode, Benj. Hudson, Test.

BOOTH, GEORGE—Page 181—To wife Nancy stock, plantation, house etc. as long as she keeps it together and uses care, at her death to be sold and divided between my children, towit, Sudith, Sally, Henry, Mary Ann, Nathaniel, Robert and Nancy. Wife Nancy, Reuben Christian and David S. Booth, Admrs. Signed Feb. 23, 1818. Probated July 6, 1818. Nancy Hicks, Drury Ridgeway, Dixon Parham, Test.

BLACKWELL, JOSEPH—Page 284—"To loving wife", plantation where I live, and all personal estate including slaves Sturde, Gemboy, Patt, Charity, Lucy and Lem. All other property to be divided among my six children, viz, Dunston, Banks, Ralph, Joseph, Park and Betsy Chandler Williamson, the third part of her part to be equally divided between Sally Chandler Williamson and Betsy Blackwell Williamson, her daughters. Wife Sally, Ralph Banks and Dunston Williamson, Excrs. Signed Nov. 10, 1804 Probated Sept. Term 1806. Joseph Rucker, James Boatright, Test. Again Mar. 2, 1819, proven by oath of James Boatright.

BREWER, JOHN—Page 231—Children, Sally Childers, James, Susannah Mullins, Martha H. Royal, John Wesley and Leroy have received their portions. To son Wm. Fletcher the mare he got from David Butler, saddle and bridle. Land adj. John Carter to be sold to pay debts. Residue to wife Betsy to be inherited at her death by my youngest son Hundley. Friends James Gunter and Patrick Jack, Excrs. Signed Nov. 20, 1818. Probated Jan. 5, 1819. McKinney Irons, Cynthia Irons, Test.

BANKS, WILLIAM—Page 412—After debts are paid, all estate real and personal to wife Anny to dispose of as she thinks best between my eight children, James Banks, John Henderson Banks, William Randall Banks, Polly Henderson Banks, Betsy Banks, Sally Chandler Banks, Anny Banks and Nancy Banks, and any children my present wife Anny may have. Wife Anny, and two bros. Ralph and James Banks, Excrs. Signed June 22, 1807. Probated Jan. 1, 1821. Excrs. named qualifying. Hierom Gaines, Jr., William Crump, Chas. Crump, Test.

CLARK, CHRISTOPHER, Sr.—Page 331—To my children, Samuel, Margaret, Wm. Davis, Christopher Hull, Thos. Jefferson, Geo. Washington and Mary Clark equal portions of all estate as they come of age or marry. Shelton White, McCarty Oliver, David Hudson, Sr., Excrs. Signed May 14, 1819. Probated Nov. Term 1819. Joshua Clark, David Clark, Milly Satterwhite, Test.

COLBERT, RICHARD—Page 398—To wife Rhoda all property real and personal including a large number of slaves and seven bales of cotton, at her death to be disposed of as follows: To John Colbert son of Nicholas Colbert $200.00; To Isham Morgan, Jr., $200.00; To William Reach $200.00. Residue to be divided equally between Elizabeth Nix's children, Karenhappeck Stone, Patsy Childers, Sally Childers, Gilly Cook, Lucy Colbert, Thomas J. Colbert, and Malinda Colbert, (relationship not given) Friends Beverly and Singleton W. Allen, Excrs. Signed Feb. 5, 1820. Probated May 1, 1820. Tryon Harris, John Dennard, Phebe Dennard, Test.

CRUMP. CHARLES—Page 413—To wife Aggy, slaves Pat and Adams, To son Pleasant D., slaves Jerry and Lewis. To son Lemuel, slaves Isaac and Seburn. The balance of estate to be equally divided among these three, Lemuel's part to be in their possession till he calls for it, he being absent at this time. Friends William Bailey and Thos. A. Banks, Excrs. Signed Oct. 26, 1820. Probated Jan. 1, 1821. R. Banks, John Craft, Joshua Hunt, Test.

CARROL, MARY—Page 430—To dau. Molly Hudson most of personal estate. To son John Cason a bond for $60.00 given by John Hysmith for the hire of a slave Jesse. To grandaughter Betsy Cason a knotted counterpane. Thos. A. Banks, and Wm. White, Excrs. Signed Mar. 5, 1821. Probated July 2, 1821. Henry Bowren, Howard B. Shackleford, Hudson A. Thornton, Test.

FAULKNER, JOHN, Sr.—Page 112—To wife Sarah all estate including a legacy in Va., of several hundred dollars. Sons William, John and Peter, Excrs. Signed July 9, 1806. Probated Dec. 1, 1817. William Davis, Drury Bradley, Nancy Davis, Test.

HUNT, RICHARDSON—Page 130—To wife Nancy M. Hunt, the whole of estate not otherwise disposed of in this will, for life including the mansion house where I live and the spring, and a number of slaves. To son James 250 acres on Savannah river, including the mouth of Cedar creek whereon said James now lives and a number of slaves already in his possession. To dau. Sally Harris 300 acre tract on north fork of Beaverdam creek already conveyed to her by deed of gift, and a large number of slaves. To son Elijah the other third of my thousand acre tract and slaves and household furniture equal to that received by his brother and sister. To bro. Wm. H. Hunt of Halifax Co. Va., 500 acres on Beaverdam Creek, Elbert Co. "I now will and desire my dear children, after what you owe to God in all things to preside to remain always united with each other". Two sons James and Elijah Hunt, Excrs. Signed April 13, 1816. Probated Mar. 2, 1818. Wm. Woods, Edward Sims, James Banks, Test.

HARPER, EDMOND—Page 245—To wife Ann one-eighth part of estate. To daus. Elizabeth Darden, Mary Jones, Lucy Howard, Ann Rucker and Drucilla Harper, $1.00 each. To son Bedford and dau. Elender Harper, Lot No. 58, 9th. Dist., and Lot No. 206, 26th. Dist, Wilkinson Co. Residue to these two children and friend Beverly Allen. Son Bedford and Beverly Allen, Excrs. Signed Aug. 27, 1810. Probated Mar. 1, 1819. John Alston, Dudley Sale, Adam Gaar, Test.

HARBIN, WILLIAM, Sr.—Page 370—"Feeling declining mortality fast giving way". To wife Sally all estate real and personal for widowhood. To children Anna Skels (Scales?), Thomas and John Harbin, Rebecca Brown, Peggy White, Sally and Joanna Brown, $1.00 each. To children Betsy, William, Nancy and Susannah Harbin, feather bed and furniture each. Son Thomas and wife Sally, Excrs. Signed Oct. 16, 1818. Probated May 1, 1820. Leonard Rice, John Duncan, Robert Kennedy, Test.

HAM, JOHN—Page 447—"Infirm in body". To following children, Stephen, James, Gideon, William, John, Clary, Sophia, Sucky, Betsey, Nancy, Samuel, and Willis R., certain sums of money to make them equal with the amount already given dau. Lucinda, the proceeds of crops to pay these legacies. Samuel, Willis R. and Nancy to be educated out of the estate. The entire estate to remain in the hands of my wife Betsy for widowhood. Wife, son William and son-in-law James Upshaw, Excrs. Signed April 21, 1821. Probated Sept. 3, 1821. William King, Levi Stinchcomb, George Upshaw, Test.

JOHNSTON, JOHN—Page 109—Money borrowed of Benjamin Thornton and Ralph Banks to be returned with interest. To son William a slave Samson. To son Thomas a slave Willis. To dau. Elizabeth B. Johnston, slave Clary, bed and furniture to all, to be received when they arrive at majority or marry. To dau. Frances G. Hayley, wife of James Hayley, slave Abbaline. To dau. Sally Gaines, wife of Leavenston P. Gaines, a sum of money. To wife Mary Johnston, money, "it being about one-third of her first husband's estate which I received by her". Sons William and Thomas to have a years schooling. To Jeremiah Warren "his account against me for his fathers estate, as admr. and gdn. in right of my wife", and bed furniture. Sons William and Thomas to have land adj. Ralph Banks and land purchased of Mark and Thomas Thornton and Hieram Gaines and a gun apiece. Friends Robert Burk, Sr., William Bailey, Larkin Johnston and William Banks, Excrs. Signed Nov. 10, 1817. David A. Reese, Samuel N. Bailey, Littleton Johnson, Test. Codicil in regard to cotton crop Signed Nov. 10, 1817. Both probated Dec. 1, 1817. James Rucker, Jeremiah S. Warren, Test.

KERLIN, WILLIAM—Page 157—All estate to be kept together for the mutual benefit of wife and children (not named) till the oldest is of age, then to be divided. James N. Brown, Archelaus Jarrett, Joseph Brawner, Test. Nicholas Meriwether Marks came before the court May 4, 1818, and swore he wrote the above will at the request of the testator in his last illness, Mar. 1, last. James N. Brown and James Brawner qualified as Excrs.

MANN, JAMES, SR.—Page 17—To wife Judith full possession of all estate including slaves Daniel, Dosha and Silva. At death or marriage of wife Judith an equal division amongst my sons viz: John, Joel, Jesse, James, Jr., Jeremiah, Asa and Henry Mann and daus. Martha Shackleford and Elizabeth Roebuck. Wife Judith and son John, Excrs. Signed June 24, 1814. Probated Nov. 4, 1816. John Carroll, James Shackleford, Test.

McDOUGAL, NEAL—Page 310—To Neal McDougal Gordon, son of John Gordon, $300.00; to Neal McDougal McCurry, son of Angus McCurry, Jr., $200.00, to be delivered when they reach majority. To Margaret McDonald, wife of John, $300.00; to Mary and Nancy McDonald daus. of John $100.00 each; To Flora McCurry, wife of Angus, Sr., $100.00. To Katharine Ferguson, wife of Norman, $40.00, all to be delivered when collected. Residue to be divided between Angus McCurry, Sr., John McDonald and John Gordon. John Gordon, Sole Excr. Signed May 17, 1819. Probated Sept. 6, 1819. John Dobbs, Benjamin Head, Test.

McMULLIN, JOHN—Page 123—"Very weak of body", To Elizabeth McMullin, alias Elizabeth Stowers, whom I deem my loving wife, 100 acres including the house and plantation on which I live all personal estate for life or widowhood, including slaves Cato, Sarah, and Milly. To sons James, the eldest, Patrick second, John, third and to my daus. Mary now Mary Powell, and Katharine, now Katharine Shifflet, $1.00, with what they have already received. To my first son by Elizabeth McMullin (alias Eliz. Stowers), Nail, land on which he now resides. To second son, Jeremiah, as above, third son Lewis, as above, fourth son Thomas, as above, land on which they now reside. To fifth son Fielding as above, 300 acres within two years. To sixth son Sinclair as above, 100 acres part of the home tract adj. Benj. Nail and John Dobbs. To seventh son Daniel as above, the land bequeathed to my wife Elizabeth Mc- Mullin, alias Stowers, at her death or marriage. To dau. Nancy, now Nancy Mills a slave Dicy. To dau. Eliza a slave, Edmond. To dau. Levinia, a slave Milly. Son Nail and son-in-law James Mills, Excrs. Signed Dec. 6, 1817. Probated Jan. 6, 1818. Benj. Neal, David Dobbs, John Dobbs, Test.

MOON, PLEASANT—Page 134—All property together with my legacy from my fathers estate and my wife Sarah's legacy from her fathers estate to wife Sarah for life or widowhood, for the use of herself and my five children, viz; William H., James B., Pleasant, John P., and dau. Gabrilla Moon. Wife Sarah and her brother James Bell, Excrs. Signed Jan. 25, 1818. Probated Mar, 2. 1818. Gabriel Booth, James Bell, Test.

MEANS, WILLIAM—Page 329—Three eldest daus. Patsy Gandy, Jamima Wansley and Peggy Daniel having received bed, furniture etc., all daus. now at home, viz; Sally, Betsy, Nancy, Fanny, Patsy Morgan and Rossy Colbert Means to have the same at marriage or majority. Wife Elizabeth to have all other property for life or widowhood for support of herself and the younger children, then the land whereon I live to son John Seal Means. Sons Jacob and Samuel, $50.00 each. If anything should fall to me from estate of Jacob Prewitt, my wife's father, to be equally divided between wife and son Jacob. Wife Elizabeth and Jacob Means, Excrs. Signed Aug. 21, 1819. Probated Nov. 1, 1819. Wylie Ferrell, Tavnah Head, Abner Ward, John Hulmn, Test.

McCUNE, JOHN M.—Page 328—Estate to be divided into two equal parts, one to brother James A. McCune, the other to sister Margaret Ferrell. Brother James A., and friend John Ferrell, Excrs. Signed Sept. 6, 1819. Probated Nov. 1, 1819. James Hunt, Elisha Vick, Test.

MORGAN, ISHAM—Page 458—"Old and infirm". To dau. Sarah Morgan, feather bed, cow, horse etc. To dau. Elizabeth Ridgway, feather bed, cow, horse and slaves Meriah, Sampson and Alabama. To wife Elizabeth land on which I now live and slaves Sam, Jinney, Joe and Charity for life, to be divided at her death amongst all my children except Silus, he to have $120.00 besides. To my six sons, Stephen, Silus, John, Thomas, Isham and Wm. C. Morgan, eight slaves, Cit, Samson, Emericas,

Milly, Jane, Jefferson, Elick and Elbert also my quarter section and a half of land in Dallas Co. Ala., adj. Ridgway. Wife Elizabeth and Stephen and Isham Morgan, Excrs. Signed Aug. 10, 1821. Probated Jan. 8, 1822. James F. Nunnelee, Blackman Burton, Test.

OLIVER, JOHN—PAGE 41—"Of the town of Petersburg", in precarious health. To wife Susannah the land called Sharps Place on Broad river, thirteen slaves, horses and carriage, and a house and half acre lot in Petersburg now rented to Chas. Hudson, and stock in the Bank of Augusta. To dau. Prudence T. Watkins, wife of Robert H. Watkins, nineteen slaves. To dau. Polly X. Bibb, wife of John D. Bibb seventeen slaves. To son John Oliver, the rest of the land I own in Ga., including two lots I own in Petersburg and the small tract called the Ferry landing on the Carolina side of the Savannah river, the houses and ferry boats, and thirty four slaves and stock in the Bank of Ga., at marriage or majority. To my good friend and former son-in-law Daniel Bird, the picture and frame over my chimney piece (The Redeemer). Wife, sons-in-law Robt. H. Watkins, and John D. Bibb, and brother James Oliver, Excrs. Signed Dec. 10, 1816. Probated Jan. 6, 1817. Samuel Watkins, John Watkins, Wm. N. Richardson, Test.

PATTERSON, JOHN—Page 126—To sons William and Jesse and daughters Betsy Smith and Aggie Allen, $1.00 each. To grandson James Allen, $50.00, feather bed etc. to be in trust of his father Joseph Allen for life. To son Nimrod the land whereon I now live, including that bought of Richardson Hunt on north fork of Beaverdam creek, and all personal estate, for the support of my beloved wife Rebecca for life or widowhood. Trusty friends and relatives Nimrod and John Patterson, Excrs. Signed April 16, 1814. Probated Mar. 2, 1818. Wm. Bevers, John S. Kennedy, John S. Heard, Test.

PROTHRO, EVAN—Page 456—To second oldest son James, a bond on Wm. Zimmerman. To third oldest son William a bond on Wm. Zimmerman. To the surviving heirs of my dau. Caty Hughes (?) dec'd. money due from the estate of James Hues, dec'd. To four grandchildren, surviving heirs of my dau. Rachel Myers, dec'd. towit, Patsy, Donel, Eurazemes and William Myers, money due from Daniel Myers. To eldest son, Nathaniel Prothro, slaves, household goods, cattle etc. Son Nathaniel Prothro and Evan Prothro, Sr., Excrs. Signed Dec. 25, 1817. Probated Jan. 8, 1822. David Dobbs, John Dobbs, Moses Haynes, Sr., Test.

RICHARDSON, JAMES R.—Page 135—To my dear friend Rebecca Colson, $250.00, eighty five of which is in Gold Eagles; to my next good friend Miss Lucy Beck $50.00; to my next good friend Reuben C. Beck my new blue coat and masonic breastpin; to my next good friend Wm. A. Beck, my gold sleeve and collar buttons; to my next good friend James Colson my waterloo coat etc. Friend John Beck, Excr. Signed Feb. 10, 1818. Probated Mar. 2, 1818. Larkin Clark, N. Randolph, A. Colson, Test.

GEORGIA D. A. R.

SNELLINGS, GEORGE—Page 220—To sons John and Samuel and daughter Hannah equal portions with the other children after deducting what they have already received. Other children, Elizabeth, Rebecca R., Mary W., and Martha. To wife Rebecca plantation, slaves, etc., for life. Wife and John and Samuel Snellings Excrs. Signed Oct. 4, 1818. Probated Nov. 2, 1818. James Morrison, Joseph Dunlap, Chas. Gunter, Test.

SHACKLEFORD, HENRY—Page 229—To son Henry 109 acres on Vanns creek, adj. Edmond Harper and John Cason, The land I live on to be sold and divided amongst my four daughters Nancy, Betsy, Jenney and Fanny. To son Edmond half of the stock. Grandson Edmond Alexander to have $100.00. Debts to be paid out of a bond on Benjamin Kee. Sons Henry and Edmond and Wm. Brown, Excrs. Signed April 5, 1808 Probated Jan. 5, 1819. Joseph Chipman, John M. White, Peter Alexander, Test.

SATTERWHITE, FRANCIS—Page 244—To sons Francis, John and Reubin, 600 acres according to the plat and grant. To son James 200 acres on Beaverdam creek adj. Thos. Oliver. To son Chas., 200 acres where I now live in which my wife to have a life interest. To said sons and daus. Anna Satterwhite feather bed, furniture etc. To dau. Elizabeth, 100 cents. To wife Elizabeth all slaves etc, for life, at her death to above named children and the children of dau. Elizabeth. Sons Francis, John and Reuben, Excrs. Signed May 5, 1803. Probated Mar. 1, 1819. Peter Stubbs, John Stubbs, Benjamin Higginbotham, Test.

SHACKLEFORD, EDMOND, Sr.—Page 459—All property to wife Judith for life to be divided at her death between all my children "that is to say", sons Philip, Edmond, John, Reuben and Jefferson and my dau. Nancy wife of Drury Oglesby, Elizabeth wife of John Seal, Judith wife of Mordecai Alexander, and Polly or Sally Shackleford. Son Jefferson to be educated out of estate. One eighth of an acre on the land where I live, including a grave yard to remain unmolested. Wife Judith, sons Philip, Edmond and John, Excrs. Signed May 1, 1821. Probated Jan. 8, 1822. Joseph Chimpan, Job Weston, Jeptha V. Harris, Test.

TUCKER, DANIEL—Page 153—To wife Frances all property for life, and daus. Frances and Susannah, and sons Reuben and Shem to live with her till they marry. At her death to sons Ethil, Gabriel, Robert and Eppes, $1.00. To son Daniel my gray mare. After the death of my wife Frances, all residue to daughters Frances and Susannah and sons Reuben and Shem. Sons Reuben and Shem, Excrs. Signed April 4, 1818. Probated May 4, 1818. Beverly Allen, Wm. Stone, Dabney D. Wilkinson, Test.

TOWNS, DRURY—Page 200—To wife Patsy all estate for life, to be divided as the children (not named) come of age.
Signed Nov. 17, 1807. Probated Sept. 1, 1818.
Duke W. Hullum, Abraham Bell, Thomas Bell, Test.

UPSHAW, JOHN, Jr.—Page 198—To wife Rebeckah all estate for the support and education of my two children, Middleton Cook and Elizabeth Burch, till son becomes of age or widow marries, when it shall be equally divided between the three. If wife should have children by a second marriage, her share to go to them. If all children should die without heirs, the property to be divided between my wife and the heirs of my sister Catharine Smith. Signed Jan. 18, 1815. Probated Sept. 1, 1818. William Woods, Bailey M. Woods, Samuel Paxton, Test.

WRIGHT, GABRIEL—Page 179—To wife Mary all estate for life or widowhood, until eldest son Elisha is 21 when he shall have part of the home farm. To second son Henry the remainder of the land at majority. Should both sons die before majority, the land to be divided between the daus. Elizabeth V., and Estley H. Wright. Elisha Vick, Sole Excr. Signed Dec. 22, 1817. Probated July 6, 1818. Wm. H. Underwood, John Dunn, Elijah Vick, Test.

WHITE, REUBEN—Page 352—To wife Elizabeth all estate for life or widowhood. Confirms property already given daughter Sarah Moore and son-in-law Elijah Moore, to be accounted for in a general division with rest of children (not named). Wife Elizabeth, friend James Clark and William White, Excrs.
Signed Jan. 30, 1820. Probated Mar. 6, 1820.
Robert Roebuck, Jeremiah Lewis, Asa Mann, Test.

WEBB, WILLIAM C. Jr.—Page 400—"Very sick", after debts are paid all estate to wife Susannah and son Andrew Jackson Webb.
Wife Susannah and bro. John C. Webb, Excrs.
Signed Sept. 18, 1820. Probated Nov. 6, 1820.
Robert B. Christian, Mial Smith, Test.

WILLIAMS, MATTHEW JOUETT, Sr.—Page 232—To son Thomas Walker Williams half the tract of land purchased of Col. Z. Lamar, desk, sideboard and folding table. The other half of said tract to son Matthew Jouett Williams. To dau. Barbara Williams slaves Caleb, Charlotte, Selina and Burrell, money, gig bought of Mr. Rembert, choice of horses, high bedstead in her room, dining table etc. To daughters Mary Ann Black and Rebecca Anthony and granddaughter Henrietta Jouett Williams $300.00 apiece. To dau. Elizabeth Richardson the interest on money derived from the sale of certain slaves if she stands in need of it" and I expect she will", and my big Bible. To granddaughter Martha Bailey Williams a large Bible. To grandaus. Barbara Floyd, Barbara Cook Harrison, Barbara Williams and Barbara Anthony, $25.00 apiece. To grandsons Matthew W. Black, Matthew R. T. Harrison and Matthew J. W. Anthony my gun, saddle and briddle. If several old slaves become helpless to be treated well. The slaves and household furniture I bought at Sheriffs sale of the estate of Clement K. Harrison, dec'd, the slave Sally to be for the use of my dau. Elizabeth Richardson, at her death to be divided between Clement T. Harrison's children and his grandson E. A. Simmons. Certain slaves in trust of executors to be divided among grandchildren, Henrietta Harrison, Polly B. Simmons, Matt R. T. Harrison, Barbary Harrison, and great grandaughter Elizabeth A. Simmons. After all above legacies are paid property to be divided into six lots, son Thomas W. to have first choice, son Matthew J., second choice, dau. Rebecca Anthony third choice, dau. Barbary William fourth choice. To dau. Mary Ann Black the other half the interest to be used for dau. Elizabeth Richardson, at her death to be divided equally between my grandchildren, Rebecca Richardson, John Walker Richardson, and Robt. Williams Richardson as they come of age or marry.

Sons Matthew J. and Thomas W., Excrs. Signed May 26, 1818 Probated Jan. 25, 1819. Simeon Oliver, Milly Oliver, Frances Wyche, Test.

ELBERT COUNTY, GEORGIA

BOOK "M".

ALSTON, CHARITY—Page 155—To grandson Edward M. Chambers, son of dau. Sarah, wife of Thomas Chambers, $5.00. To grandaughter Charity Ann Tait, dau. of my dau. Ann, wife of William H. Tait, $500.00 to be put at interest till she is 18 or marries, if she died previous, to go to her bro. Chas. Tait. To grandau. Charity A. Clark, dau. of my dau. Mary or Polly, and James Clark, a slave Grace. To sons James, William H., and Philip H. Alston, and dau. Christian Alston slaves Sampson, Ellen, Patsy and Emanuel, and all property of every description. Three said sons Excrs. Signed April 20, 1823. Probated May 5, 1823. R. Banks, Test.

BANKS, JAMES A.—Page 39—Wife Milly T., to purchase a home as soon as possible, and a division of estate to be made at any time she demands it. Son Wm. C. Banks, a minor, and a possible child expected to share equally. Wife Milly T., and friends Willis Banks and Simeon Oliver, Excrs. Signed Feb. 30, 1822. Probated May 6, 1822. Richard Banks, John Alston, Barnard C. Heard, Test.

BURTON, HENRY—Page 79—To dau. Elizabeth Evans, 500 acres of land whereon she now lives adj. Thomas Burton and Dr. William N. Richardson. To son Blackman Burton, 150 acres remainder of above tract. To Daniel Coursey a slave Joe, and to Robt. Dixon a slave Tamer, they to pay to Elizabeth Evans $50.00 each. To Matilda Evans, our bay mare. A tract of land in Dooly Co., all stock etc., to be divided between Abraham, Germain Burton and John L., Roann B., Elenner Ann, Lemuel and Charlotte Dixon, and William Burton. Blackman Burton sole Excr. Signed Aug. 7, 1822. Probated Sept. 2, 1822. Thomas Burton, Leroy Burton, Drury T. Saxon, Test.

BURCH, WILLIAM S.—Page 203—To wife Elizabeth all property for life or widowhood. Upon her marriage, one third to be in the hands of the executors for her support, to be divided at her death into four equal parts, one share to be equally divided among the children of Sarah Hardin, wife of Henry Hardin, one to be divided between the children of Polly Wilbourn, wife of Thomas Wilbourn, one share to be divided between the children of Rebecca and John Upshaw, Jr., these three being sisters of my wife Elizabeth, one share to be divided between Mary Ann and Wm. T. O. Cook, hires of William Cook, dec'd, brother of my wife Elizabeth. "My sister" Betty Cook to have one third of entire estate for her support at her death to be divided betwixt my brothers and sisters towit, Thomas, Benjamin, Moza, John and Cheadle Burch, Polly Johnston, Jinney Divine, Hannah C. Purkins and Sarah Kiser. Wife Elizabeth and friends John Upshaw, Jr., and Wm. Woods, Excrs. Signed May 15, 1817. Probated Jan. 17, 1822. Job Weston, Bailey M. Woods, Wm. Woods, Test.

BULLARD, THOMAS, Sr.—Page 157—To wife Ann for life 16d acres of land, beds, furniture etc, and slaves George and Lucy. To Elixabeth Dye, 100 acres adj. the land whereon I now live. Executor to sell certain slaves, horses etc, and divide proceeds between Allen Bullard, Sarah Murphy, Temperance Woodly, Elizabeth Dye, Delilah Cooks children, Nancy Butler's children and Tapley Bullard's children, Ann widow of Tapley not to return money given Tapley in his life time. Having given Willy and Allen Cook $25.00 each it is to be deducted from what is left to Delilah Cook. Signed April 12, 1823. Probated May 5, 1823. David Hudson, Sr., David Hudson, Jr., James O. Clark, Test.

BANKS, RALPH, Sr.—Page 206—To sons Henry and Lemuel all the land on Savannah river bought of Jos. W. Bibb, all the slaves on the Beaverdam plantation. To son Marion all the land on Little Coldwater creek and 150 acres adj., slaves etc. To wife Rachel all the land on Big Coldwater creek whereon I now live, slaves etc. To son Ralph two adj. tracts of land on Leatherwood creek, Franklin Co. Confirms land etc, given other children (not named). After given his wife Rachel $1500.00, residue to be divided amongst my ten sons and three daus. (not named) Sons Thomas A., and John Banks, Excrs. Signed Oct. 24, 1823. Probated Dec. 3, 1823. William Adams, William Bailey, Richard C. Adams, Test.

BRADLEY, ROBERT C—Page 236—To wife Anna all household goods and a slave Matilda for life to be divided at her death between all my children, Lucy Bradley and Jeptha M. Bradley. Joseph Deadwyler, Sr., Excr. Signed July 13, 1818. Probated Jan. 12, 1824. Robert R. Christian, Joseph Deadwyler, Jr., Test.

BOND, ELIZABETH—Page 236—To sons Joseph and Nathan and the heirs of my dau. Mary Hilly $1.00 each. To son Richard C., a lot of land in Houston Co., drawn in my own name, furniture etc. William Bond and Gaines Thompson, Excrs. Signed Sept. 10, 1823. Probated Jan. 12, 1824. Stephen White, James Christian, Test.

BRANTLEY, JOSEPH M.—Page 293—non-cupative, Frances McGuire, Elizabeth and Frances Dooly swear before Henry White and Joseph Blackwell that they were present at the dwelling house of William Dooly about Jan. 15, during the last illness of said Joseph Brantley and heard him say that his wife Nancy J. Brantley should have his horse and wagon, his slave Naomi, and all the property that was coming to him from his fathers and his grandfathers estates in N. C. Probated July 2, 1824.

BARNETT, NATHANIEL—Page 368—Confirms gift of slaves in 1812 to sons David, William and Joel and dau. Ann Crawford, To children of dau. Elizabeth Spears $800.00, to children of my son———Barnett, $600.00. Sons William and Joel, Excrs.
No date of signature. Probated May 3, 1824.
George Wyche, Agatha Wyche, Joshua O. Wyche, Test.

CARREL or CARROLL, JOHN—Page 38—To wife Mary all estate for life, at her death 125 acres on north side of Coldwater creek and my large Bible to go to John Cason and Molly Hudson, relationship not given.
To Molly Hudson, wife of Nathaniel Hudson the land whereon I now live. Wife Mary and Nathaniel Hudson and John Cason, Excrs. Signed Dec. 24, 1812. Probated July 2, 1821. William Gaar, George Gaar, James E. White, Test.

COOK, JOSHUA—Page 77—To eldest son John, to dau. Elizabeth Patterson and to son Richard, $1.00 each in addition to what they have already received. To dau. Mary, horse, saddle, furniture etc, upon marriage or majority. To youngest son Elijah Mosely Cook, horse, saddle, furniture etc, when of age, he to be educated out of the estate. To wife Sarah all estate real and personal, at her death the land whereon I live to go to son Elijah Mosely Cook. Oldest son John and wife Sarah, Excrs. Signed July 17, 1822. Probated Sept. 2, 1822. James Bell, Smith Cook, Jesse M. Cook, Test.

FLEMING, HENRY—Pages 295—Wife Margaret to have all estate for life, all lands to be divided at her death between two sons Henry and Robert. Henry to have a chest of carpenters tools when he is twenty. Having given dau. Rosanna Fleming a colt, daughter Margaret Fleming to have one. Wife Margaret sole Excx. Signed Aug. 10, 1823. Probated July 5, 1824. William Gray, Delany Chisenhall, William Cunningham, Test.

FORTSON, THOMAS—Page 269—Heirs of son Benjamin Fortson, dec'd, and sons William, Jesse and Richard, and daus. Elizabeth Gibbs and Milly Willis, equal shares, dau. Milly Willis to have also 70 acres of land adj. Durrat Stodgill, to her children at her death. To slave Chaney, nurse in his last illness $50.00. Son Richard, Excr. Signed Jan. 24, 1824. Probated Mar. 1, 1824. Ro. M. Carter, Benajah Houston, John J. Carter, Test.

GRAY, JOSEPH, Sr.—Page 93—To wife Susannah all estate for life, at her death bed and furniture to beloved neice Judy Parrott. To daus. Jane and Sarah Gray a slave and horse each. To dau. Polly Morrison, $350.00. Residue to be divided between my sons Joseph, John, Elijah, William and James Gray and daus. Jane and Sarah Gray. Wife Susannah and Joseph and William Gray, Excrs. Signed Jan. 1, 1819. Probated Oct. 21, 1822. Beverly Allen, David Wade, William S. Parrott, Test.

GAINES, LIVINGSTON P.—Page 337—To wife Sally all estate for life, "to be divided equally amongst my children" at her death. In twelve months the mill and the land adjoining to be sold. Wife Sally and Wm. Johnston, Excrs. Signed Oct. 12, 1824. Probated Nov. 1, 1824. Wm. Crawford, Ralph Gaines, Test.

HIGHSMITH, JAMES—Page 335—To wife Milly, slave Lucy, a horse, furniture etc. To my children, Susannah Bobo, Lucretia Skelton, John Highsmith, Sarah Bobo, Winny Griffin and Nancy Highsmith, four slaves Tom, Malinda, Hizy and Peggy etc. Nancy Highsmith to have bed etc, besides. Son Thomas Highsmith all land on south side of Coldwater creek "whereon I live", a slave Siah etc. Son John and son-in-law Benjamin Bobo, Excrs. Signed Dec. 25, 1819. Probated Mar. 10, 1824. Tavener Rucker, William Rucker, Jesse Wallis, Test.

LEWIS, SARAH—Page 293—To grandson Jeptha Lewis, Lot No. 87, 5th, Dist. Dooly Co. "drawn in my name in the late Land Lottery"., bed and furniture. The value of a slave Debby to be divided among the following children viz: Caty Trimble, Martha More, Sarah Davis, Mary More, John Lewis, Ester Mann, Thomas Lewis, Ellender Lewis, Nancy Jurdin, Philip Lewis heirs, and heirs of Jamima Moore. Son John and son-in-law James Mann, Excrs. Signed Nov. 7, 1823. Probated July 2, 1824. Wm. White, John Cleveland, Reuben Cleveland, Test.

McDONALD, JOHN—Page 207—All estate to wife Margaret for widowhood except that as the children become of age they receive $100.00 or its value in property, viz; Daniel, Angus, John Lauchlin, Roderick, Flora and Margaret McDonald. Residue to be divided at wife's death between the above named children and son Hugh and dau. Nancy McDonald. Margaret, Hugh and Daniel McDonald, Excrs. Signed Aug. 12, 1822. Probated Nov. 3, 1823. Roler (?) Brown, Polly Brown, John Gordon, Test.

OLIVER, JAMES—Page 332—A note due Robt. McGrath & Co., to be paid. Residue divided between all brothers and sisters (not named) My dearly beloved brother Richard Oliver of Mecklenburg Co. Va. and trusty friend Richard Easter of Petersburg, Ga. Excrs. Signed Feb. 15, 1800. Probated Oct. 21, 1824. M. Walker, Robt. McGrath, Jonathan Gray, Test. Proved by the oath of Jeremiah Walker of Lincoln Co. Ga., that he knew all the witnesses that they resided in Petersburg, Ga. at the time and that the signature M. Walker is in the handwriting of Memorable

Walker dec'd. Also by Augustine Edwards for all the signatures, that Memorable is reported dead, that Robt. McGrath is also, or removed to parts unknown. Henry White and Beverly Allen, J. Ps. of Elbert Co.

PROTHRO, NATHANIEL—Page 196—To wife Zilpha all lands, houses, horses, cattle etc. and eleven slaves for life or widowhood. To sons Joshua, William, Nathaniel a slave, horse, saddle and bridle each at majority or marriage. To daus. Mary, Lydia, Elizabeth, Massee and Harriott Prothro a slave, bed etc. at majority or marriage. To grandau. Nancy Gardner $300.00 at majority or marriage. As to my four children, sons Evan, and Solomon and daus. Rachel Corbett and Mehetebal Jones, they have received their protions. Wife Zilpha and John Dobbs, Excrs. Signed Feb. 26, 1823. Probated Sept. 1, 1823. Jesse Dobbs, Thomas Scales, Test.

RICHARDSON, WALKER—Page 80—To dau. Katharine Thornton, and to the children of my dec'd dau. Polly Allen $500.00 each. To wife Prudence one third of all estate for life, at her death to be equally divided between my four children, William N., and Richard Richardson, Martha Head and Prudence Upshaw, to account for former gifts. To son-in-law Leroy Upshaw, husband of my dau. Prudence a slave Wyatt, in consideration of his services in attending to my affairs. Friends Richard Fortson and John S. Higginbotham, Excrs. Signed Mar. 13, 1819. Probated Sept. 2, 1822. Ro. M. Carter, Samuel Turman, Wiley Thompson, Test.

STAPLES, DAVID—Page 94—To wife Fanny a slave Charity, household goods etc. to dispose of at her pleasure. The residue to be distributed amongst my children towit; John Staples, Christian J. Phelps, Elizabeth D. Stovall, Prudence Smith, Barbara Denny, Patsy Staples, Lucy Brown, Melita Denny, the legitimate off spring of my dau. Tabitha Moon, (at majority). To dau. Tabitha Moon $2.00, to Thos Staples, Anna Moon, slaves Gabriel, Hannah, Bridget, Phillis, Jack, Lucinda, Silvey, Benj. and Welborn to be divided amongst above named children. Wife Fanny and son John Staples, Excrs. Signed April 30, 1821. Probated Nov. 19, 1822. C. W. Christian, Wm. Branan, Edmond Smithwick, Test.

STATHAM, JOHN—Page 209—To sons James, John, Charles, and Robert, $1.00 each. Residue to be divided between my sons William, Nathaniel, Jesse and Pleasant Statham and dau. Nancy Barnett. Friends John Brown and James Christian, Excrs. Signed June 27, 1823. Probated Nov. 3, 1823. Chas. Andrew, John Statham, Test.

SELF, SAMUEL E.—Page 491—To dau. Sarah and son Samuel Self, feather bed, stock etc. To daus. Nancy and Mary and son Sinclair $5.00 each "as a balance of their parts". Residue to wife Franky for life or widowhood to be finally divided between my three youngest children. Wife Franky and son Sinclair, Excrs. Signed April 22, 1825. Probated July 4, 1825. Amos Richardson, Joel Scales, Test.

TATE, DAVID—Page 156—To wife Frances 177 acres in Elbert Co. adj. Enos Tate, and Lot No. 194, 12th, Dist. Henry Co., and four slaves. No children mentioned. Wife Frances and brother Enos, Excrs. Signed Mar. 15, 1823. Probated May 5, 1823. Wm. N. Richardson, Zimri W. Tate, Augustine Edwards, Test. (Lived at Petersburg)

TATE, WILLIAM—Page 294—To bro. James four slaves. To brother Enos three slaves, bed, etc. To sister Lucy Andrews (wife of Benjamin), 113½ acres of land on which I now live, and balance of household goods. Brothers James and Enos, Excrs. Signed May 13, 1824. Probated July 5, 1824. William Gibbs, Fortson Gibbs, Hudson A. Thornton, Test.

TEASLEY, WILLIAM—Page 296—To wife Sarah all the lands that adjoin the tract on which I live, in all 750 acres, slaves, household goods etc. to be equally divided at her death between my daus. Anna and Amelia. To John Horton, in right of his wife Winny part of above tract and a lot of land in Wilkinson Co. To Thomas Horton in right of his wife Elizabeth a lot of land in Houston Co. To heirs of Levi Teasley, dec'd, land in the 6th Dist., Baldwin now Jones Co., drawn by Julian Nail. To Thomas Jefferson Teasley $300.00. Thomas Horton and William Lunsford, Excrs. Signed June 16, 1824. Probated July 3, 1824. James O. Landers, Wm. Landers, Lauchlin McCurry, Test.

TYNER, RICHARD, Sr.—Page 339—To dau. Abigail Cridendon $1.00. To son Richard, Jr., the land on which I live. To grandau. Nancy Tyner, a colt. Residue to be divided between my children, Samuel Tyner or his heirs, Harris Tyner, Mary Ryley, Tamer Hunt, Joshua Tyner, Frances McGuire, Noah Tyner, or his heirs, Elizabeth Boatright, Agnes Crump, Martha Bird, Richard Tyner and the children of Charity Bird. Friends Wm. Bailey, Isham Teasley and Thos. A. Banks, Excrs. Signed Sept. 13, 1824. Probated Nov. 10, 1824. Lauchlin McCurry, James Adams, Nancy Tyner, Test.

UNDERWOOD, JOSEPH, Sr.—Page 95—To wife Winnifred home place, a slave to go to dau. Elizabeth Norwood at her death. To eldest son William H., the land on which he lives. The rest to be divided between sons Reuben and Joseph at the death of my wife. To daus. Sally Johnston, Anna Patterson and Polly Haley, $1.00 each in addition to what they have already received. Land in Irwin Co. to be divided among all children except Anna Patterson. Signed Nov. 25, 1821. Probated Oct. 30, 1822. Permelia Norwood, Wm. R. Powell, Chas. Wheeler, Test.

WEST, ANDREW, JR.—Page 57—To wife Elizabeth W., a slave Willis for life, to go to an expected child if it lives, if not to go to my brothers and sisters (not named). Lot No. 183, 12th Dist. Monroe Co., 202½ acres to be disposed of as above slave. To wife Elizabeth, horse, gig etc. All law books to be disposed of to pay debts, any overplus to go to father Andrew West, Sr. and my monogram silver watch. To brother Henry West horse and saddle. Andrew West, Sr., James Olive and Gen. Jeptha

Harris, Exrs. Signed June 5, 1822. Probated July 1, 1822. Joseph Glenn, Archelaus Jarratt, Elijah Pressley, Henry P. Brawner, Test.

WEBB, WILLIAM—Page 125—Slave Abraham and his wife Milly to occupy the part of my plantation on which the Kerlins now live, for life, Pope Webb and Wm. Moore to be their guardians. I give to my sister Lucy Barnett's children, Mary Bellemy's children, Sucky Barnett's children, Sally Colley's children, my brothers John and Austin, Claiborn Webb's children, Pleasant Webb and Patsy Hainey, each one-ninth part of my estate. William Moore, Excr. Signed Oct. 12, 1822. Probated Jan. 6, 1823. Milton P. Webb, Claiborne Webb, David Kerlin, Test.

WATKINS, JAMES, Sr.—Page 334—To daus. Polly Thompson, Sarah Harris, Martha Talliaferro, Jane Tate and Susanna Richardson slaves, having given dau. Sophia Shorter nine slaves. To son Robert H., a slave either Phil or Shock and 12000 weight of cotton delivered to him in Petersburg. To son James, Jr., all cattle, horses, household goods gins etc., all the land on this side of the river where I live, an island opposite the mouth of Beaverdam creek containing 330 acres, another in the Savannah river opposite my mills called Hanna's Island with the saw and grist mills, and land in Abbeville Co. S. C., on the Savannah river and a number of slaves. Sons Robert H. and James, 1 .crs. Signed Jan. 4, 1820. Probated Nov. 1, 1824. Enos Tate, Zimri Tate, Z. T. Watkins, Lewis R. Beaman, John A. Herring, Test.

YOUNG, ELIZABETH—Page 237—All estate to Oliver Threlkeld of Elbert Co., he to be sole Excr. Signed Aug. 23, 1823. Probated Jan. 12, 1824. George Cook, Delila Threlkeld, Test.

ELBERT COUNTY, GEORGIA

BOOK "N"—OLD NO.

1825—1829

ALLEN, WILLIAM—Page—70—To son Beverly 40 acres adj. the land whereon he now lives, and one improved half acre lot in Petersburg, No. 30 Broad St., and four slaves. To son Singleton W., three slaves. To son Thomas 150 acres on which he now lives and four slaves. To son-in-law Zachariah Smith 150 acres adj. Beverly and Thomas Allen. To daughter Elizabeth Thournton 300 acres in Franklin Co., and three slaves. To dau. Drucilla Teasley, 202½ acres in Pulaski Co. orig. grant to Daniel Thornton and three slaves. To daughter Ann Hammond 202½ acres in Pulaski Co., orig. grant to William Allen, and three slaves. To grandsons William A. Lindsey and Singleton W. Smith, and granddaughter Nelly W. Smith a slave each. To granddaughter Almira A. C. Allen a slave at majority or marriage. To Lucy Hines, a horse, saddle and bridle at the death of my wife, or Lucy's majority or marriage, and maintenance till she marries, if she remains with my wife. To beloved wife Sarah, the land, plantation, slaves etc., for life to be divided at her death between my three sons, the slaves between my three daughters, household and kitchen furniture to be divided into seven equal parts, of which Zachariah Smith and his four children are to have one. Sons Beverly and Singleton W., Excrs. Signed Sept. 20, 1825. Probated May 1, 1826. James Banks, Sr., James B. Henderson, Thomas Keys, Test.

BURTON, THOMAS—Page 327—To wife Nancy the land whereon I now live with its appurtenances, a number of slaves, all tools, stock etc. To James M. Tate and Blackman Burton in trust for the heirs of my son Leroy Burton (towit) his wife Harriett, and their three children, Gustus, Robert and Thomas, that part of a tract of land on which he now lives, purchased of Booker Hudson adj. Dr. Richardson, and several slaves, cattle etc, all to be vested in the heirs at the death of Leroy. To son Nicholas residue of tract on which I now live, slaves etc. To dau. Malinda Childers 202½ acres in Laurens, formerly Wilkinson Co., drawn by me in a former Land Lottery, several slaves etc. To dau. Siphia M. Burton, Lot No. 217, 4th Dist., Troup Co., drawn by me in the late Land Lottery, and yet to be taken out of the office, several slaves etc. To James M. Tate and Blackman Burton in trust for grandaughter Martha Ann Childers, 300 acres on Broad river whereon George Rogers now lives, at majority or marriage. To John Childers bed, furniture and horse confirmed. Wife Nancy, James M. Tate and Blackman Burton, Excrs. Signed Oct. 31, 1827. Probated July 7, 1828. Caroline M. Rogers, James F. Nunnelle, Abraham Burton, Test.

CARTER, ELIZABETH—Page 131—The $200.00 willed to me by my brother James Stubbs to be paid to my grandson Chas. Nepolian Bonaparte Carter and all other property. If he dies without heirs to go to my dau-in-law Lucy Carter for life at her death to be put in the hands of my two nephews, Thos. B. Stubbs of Baldwin Co., and Thomas Stubbs of Jones Co., for them to divide equally with all their brothers and sisters living. Friends Richard Fortson, Barnard C. Heard and Leroy Upshaw, Excrs.
Signed July 17, 1824. Probated Dec. 15, 1826.
Benjn. Fannin, Benjamin Fannin, Benjamin Smith, J. P., Test.

GAINES, FRANCIS, SR.—Page 10—To wife Judy all property for life, to be divided at her death among my children, towit; R. T. Gaines, Polly Henderson, Richard S. Gaines, William Crawford, Sally McMullin. "During her life and at her death for the real use of her heirs, that is is to say her children, and Judy Barnett Gaines, Mary Elizabeth Gaines, children of Levingston P. Gaines, dec'd, and Francis Gaines, Jr., Francis to have the shot gun and my draws in the ensuing Land Lottery. R. T. Gaines, Wm. Crawford and Richard S. Gaines, Excrs.
Signed Oct. 12, 1825. Probated Nov. 1, 1825.
Richard Harper, James B. Alexander, John Cunningham, Test.

GIBBS, WILLIAM—Page 451—To dau. Milly Gibbs and son Francis Gibbs a slave each at majority or marriage. Residue to wife Elizabeth for life or widowhood, then to be divided, one share to the children of Ric

Richardson, by present wife Nancy, formerly Nancy Gibbs, one share to the children of Thos. F. Gibbs, one share to Fortson Gibbs, one to the children of Isaac N. Bolton by his present wife Rachel, formerly Rachel Gibbs, one share to Milly Gibbs, one to Francis Gibbs. Sons Thomas F. and Fortson Gibbs, Excrs. Signed July 27, 1828. Probated Mar. 2, 1829. Benajah Houston, Jesse M. Davis, R. L. Critinton, Test.

HANSARD, JANE—Page—132—All estate to remain in the hands of my son John Hansard, who is Excr., with William Patterson.
 Signed Jan. 25, 1803. Probated Dec. 15, 1826.
 John Fannen, Benj. Fannen, Test.

JONES, WILEY W.—Page 190—To wife Charlota seven slaves and Lot No. 239, 3rd, Dist. Henry Co., the land to be sold if she likes. At her death or marriage all property to be divided equally among my five children, Emily, Huldah, Thomas W., Jane and Amanda Jones. No executors named. Signed Jan. 14, 1826. Probated May 7, 1827. John Gray, Jesse Ozley, Jordan Jones, Test.

JETER, BARNETT—Page—119—To brother Dudley Jeter the land whereon he now lives, stock etc. Thomas W. Davis to take under his care my three old slaves, Lewis, Cippio and Isabel, to feed them well clothe them warmly and work them moderately, for which a sum of money is provided. Residue to be sold and divided into four equal parts, one to the lawful heirs of my brother Dudley Jeter, one to my brother Robt. Jeter, one to the children that my sister Caty, now Caty Lowrey had by her former husband, towit, Anderson Jeter, James, Josiah and William Bishop Hicks, and Polly and Patsy Allen, and one to the heirs of Wm. Statham, dec'd, and the lawful heirs of Ransom Davis. Thos. W. Davis, James Arnold and Chas. Statham, son of William Statham, Excrs. Signed Aug. 31, 1823. Probated Nov. 6, 1826.
 Affidavit of Thos. F. Davis, that the above will was found in a small tin trunk in one of the chists of said dec'd, that the name signed is in the handwriting of said dec'd, that the day he died, Thos. F. Davis said he heard him say he had made a will he was satisfied with etc.

JARRATT, ARCHELUS—Page 236—Confirms to sons James D., and Thos. K., twelve slaves, and $800.00 each, already given them. Gives to daus. Martha B., and Eliza D. Jarratt twenty-four slaves and $2,000.00, four beds etc. Sons James D. and Thos. K., Excrs. Signed April 16, 1825. Henry H. Stephens, James King, Willy Thompson, Test.
 Codicil, in which he gives more slaves etc., and new pleasure carriage and two bay horses to his two daughters for their attention during his affliction. Signed May 31, 1827. Probated Sept. 15, 1827. John Barnes, Gardner Ballard, Wiley Thompson, Test.

JONES, STANDLEY—Page 331—To beloved wife Frances a part of the land on which I now live including the home, barns, gin etc, for life. To daus. Ann and Martha $50.00 each. To dau. Sarah and youngest son James, $100.00 each. Residue to be sold and equally divided between my wife and ten children (viz) Garland, Marshall, Elijah, William, John, Thomas, Ann, Martha, Sarah, and James. Wife Frances and bro. William Jones, Excrs. Signed May 12, 1828. Probated July 7, 1828. Samuel McGehee, Mayfield Bell, Thomas Akin, Test.

OLIVER, CALEB—Page 79—To wife Nancy all estate for life or widowhood, at the termination of either to be equally divided among "all my children" (not named). Wife Nancy, Excx. Signed April 15, 1823. Probated May 13, 1826. Henry Shackleford, Stephen A. Mann, Middleton Thornton, Test.

PENN, JOHN—Page 329—To wife Mary, 475 acres of land, including the plantation and mansion house whereon I now live, and all other property except bed etc to daus. now living with me. To dau. Winny Penn, which has left me, bed etc provided she is living. At the death of my wife all to be sold and an equal division among the whole of my children (towit) Elizabeth Penn, Martha Huff, John, Mary, Sarah, Fanny and Sinda Penn. 100 acres in Elbert Co., and 490 acres in Wayne Co. known as Lot 190, 2nd. Dist, to be sold to be loaned out. Also one third of a tract of land on which Sarah Lowremore, wid. lives.
Signed Mar. 24, 1828. Probated July 7, 1828.
Gabriel Booth, Burley Andrew, C. W. Christian, Robt. Booth, Test.

TAYLOR, WINNEY—Page 29—To heirs of son John Taylor, dec'd, fifty cents with what I have already given them. To Rebecca Taylor widow of John, fifty cents. Residue to sons, Nathan and Wm. A. Taylor. Daniel Butler, trusty friend, Excr. Signed Nov. 7, 1825. Probated Nov. 16, 1825. John Nunnelee, Nathan Butler, McKinney Irons, Test.

TERRELL, JOSEPH—Page 117—Confirms gifts of slaves, household goods and cattle to sons Wm. Cook Terrell, Jos. Reed Terrell, James T. Terrell and John W. Terrell, and to daus. Sarah Capell, and Betsy Ham. To dau. Margaret Terrell, slaves, bed, horse etc. To grandson Jabez Britton Capell slave etc at majority, the increase to be given to grandaughter Louisa Capell. Britton Capell and James T. Terrell, Excrs. Signed Apr. 17, 1826. Probated Nov. 6, 1826. James F. Nunnelee, James M. Tate, James Tate, Test.

TATE, ZIMRI—Page 120—To wife Patsy Tate for life, all estate including the land east of Coodie's creek adj. Permelia Tate. All to be divided at her death equally among all my children (not named). John A. Heard, William Rich, and Hugh McGehee, Excrs. Signed May 24, 1823. Probated Nov. 6, 1826. Lewis W. Saxon, Blackman Burton, Augustine Edwards, Test.

TUCKER, GODFREY—Page 165—To dau. Lucy Wall, a slave Martin for life at her death to my grandson Jesse C. Wall. To dau. Lucy Wall all household effects and his interest in two draws in the contemplated Land Lottery. To three sons, Jesse, Robert and Bartlett Tucker $1.00 each.

Son-in-law Wiley Wall and friend Jos. Blackwell, Excrs. Signed Feb. 7, 1827. Probated Mar. 5, 1827. Thos. Allen, Dunston Blackwell, Joseph Davis, Test.

VAWTER, JOHANNAH—Page 78—After debts are paid residue to be divided between two sons, William and Richard Vawter, who are appointed Excrs. Signed July 14, 1805. Probated May 13, 1826. John Harris, Wm. Ward, James Brown, Test.

VAWTER, WILLIAM—Page 332—To brother Lindsey a slave Winney. To brother Russell a slave Jenny. Horse, cattle and household goods to be sold to pay debts. Residue to be equally divided amongst my three brothers, Richard, Lindsey and Russell, who are Excrs. Signed June 11, 1828. Probated July 7, 1828. Micajah Carter, Simeon G. Glenn, J. W. Barrett, Test.

WARD, RICHARD—Page 76—All estate to wife Sarah, till eldest child comes of age, when he shall draw his part, and so on for all the children, not named. Wife Sarah, Wm. Ward and Wm. Roebuck, Excrs. Signed June 25, 1825. Probated May 13, 1826. Abner Ward, Robt. Roebuck, Joseph Terry, John Harris, Test.

WARD, WALTER H.—Page 135—To wife Jane all the property which her father willed her at his death, in fee simple. Plantation upon which we reside, slaves Bob and Amy, horses, cattle, furniture etc for life, at her death to be divided between my two minor children, William B. and Mary Ann Ward. To son John B., 87 acres of land in Laurens Dist., S. C., on Dunkins creek. To Walter H. Jr., son of John B., $150.00 at majority. If he dies previous to go to my three children, Finley, William and Ann Ward. To son Thos. F. Ward, 150 acres in Abbeville, S. C., on Wards Road, at the death of Elizabeth Bailey who holds a dower on said land. To son Wm. R. Ward, $500.00. To dau. Mary Ann Ward, a slave Rachel and $500.00. Thos. F., William R., and Mary Ann minors. Friend John Gray, Excr. Signed Dec. 20, 1826. Probated Jan. 27, 1827. Simeon Henderson, Robt. H. Green, Washington Morrison, Test.

WEBB, MILTON P.—Page 118—To wife Letitia a slave Chania above her proportionate share with my two children Claborn and Alison Mildred Webb, both minors. Wife Letitia, Martin Dedwyler and Abner Webb, Excrs. Signed Sept. 8, 1826. Probated Nov. 6, 1826.

Oath of William Mannen that he and James D. Jarratt wrote this will in the presence of the testator and Miles Smith, which was approved by the testator.

WILKINS, JOHN, Sr.—Page 417—To wife Nancy all estate real and personal for life. At her death son Clement to have the tract of land on which I now live, containing 300 acres on Falling creek, adj. George Wyche and John Butler. Balance of estate to be equally divided between all my children, (towit) Thomas Wilkins, Elizabeth Sutton, Polly Sneed, John Wilkin's heirs, Sally Cox, Rebecca Dye, and Clement Wilkins. Son Clement and friend Isaac Christian, Excrs. Signed Oct. 10, 1828. Probated Jan. 7, 1829. Robt. B. Christian, Thos. Fortson, John Christian, Test.

ELBERT COUNTY, GEORGIA

WILL BOOK "N"

1828-31

BELL, JOSEPH, Sr.—Page 126—To wife Mary plantation, slaves etc, for life or widowhood. If she marries to have one-eighth of said property. Son James to have cow etc, in addition to what I have given him. The rest of my children, Wm. Greene, Thomas, Olive, Elizabeth, Emily and Joseph, the youngest to have $200.00, bed, furniture etc. when they are 21 and to share equally in Lot No. 28, 16th. Dist. of Carroll Co. drawn by Wm. H. Moony, Elbert Co. Wife Mary Excx. Signed June 30, 1829. Probated Jan 5, 1830. James Davis, Samuel Lesuer, William D. Tinsley, Peter P. Butler, Test.

BUTLER, JOHN—Page 146—To sons as they come of age, horse, saddle etc. To daus. as they marry household goods of equal value. To wife Martha all estate for rearing the children, she to be sole Excx. Signed Jan. 11, 1830. Probated Jan. 30, 1830. Horatio C. Bowen, John Snelling, James Bell, Test.

CRAWFORD, WILLIAM—Page 324—To wife Lucy all estate except a bed which I gave my dau. Milly. Several slaves to be sold and divided between my five children, towit; Oliver, James L. Richmond G, Milly L. Crawford and Virginia S. Hunt. Also Lot No. 200, 4th, Dist. Lee Co., and Lot No. 54, 17th, Dist. Lee Co., and Lot No. 202, 8th Dist. Dooly Co. Son Richmond and dau. Milly to have $50.00 more than the rest. Friends Benj. Brown, Barden Rucker and Peter Alexander, Excrs. Signed Jan. 19, 1831. Probated Mar. 7, 1831. John M. Raiford, Anderson Craft, George Hunt, Test.

DEADWYLER, JOSEPH—Page 327—To wife Alice plantation, mill, slaves, except one for life. At her death every thing to be sold and divided equally between my sons, Martin, Asa and John, and daus. Ann Goss, Elizabeth Ford, Letty Webb, Nancy Webb, Polly Black and Arrenna Deadwyler, sons to receive the plantation on which I live and a lot of land in Lee Co. Slave Harriett, bed etc to dau. Arrenna. To grandaughter Margaret Ann Deadwyler, dau. of Joseph, $20.00. Having given son Joseph, Jr. land etc, no further legacy. Sons Martin, Asa and John, Excrs. Signed Nov. 15, 1828. Probated Nov. 10, 1830. William Oglesby, Henry P. Brawner, Simeon Almond, Test.

GUNTER, JESSE—Page 101—To wife Susan all estate for life or widowhood, each child to draw their part as they become of age (not named) Samuel Snellings, Excr. Signed Oct. 12, 1829. Probated Nov. 2, 1829. Jos. Bell, Jr., John Butler, Patsy Butler, Test.

HAYNES, MOSES, Sr.—Page 12—To wife Sarah all property for life, at her death to be sold and divided into eight equal parts, one each to go to sons Stephen, William, Moses and Thomas, dau. Elizabeth Keeling's part to go to her four youngest children towit; L. Matteson, Polly, Susannah and Marcy, after deducting what their father Leonard Keeling owes me; dau Jane, dau. Nancy, dau. Sarah Carden after deducting what Chas. owes me, balance to go to Moses Carden and Jane Glenn. To Leonard Keeling and Chas. Carden $2.00 each. Wife Sarah and son Thomas, Excrs. Signed Dec. 18, 1828. Probated May 4, 1829. John Bagwell, Chas. W. Haynes, James Haynes, Test.

HERRING, WILLIAM ASHUR—Page 123—All medicines, instruments etc, in his shop to be sold at once. After debts are paid all property in fee simple to wife Mary Susan, including paintings, plate, jewels, library etc, and all interest in a tract of land in Spartanburg Dist., S. C., claimed jointly by Z. F. Westmoreland and myself under a verbal gift from my father whom he asks to make clear titles to his wife. No children mentioned, but all given to her that it may descend to her children by me. Shelton White and wife Mary Susan, Excrs. Signed May 17, 1829. Probated Jan. 5, 1830. John Herring, Shelton White, Test.

HALEY, WILLIAM—Page 267—To wife Mary all estate for widowhood to give to the children as they come of age any amount she pleases. To John Haley and Jesse Cash a slave Jo. in trust for my son Thomas. To sons John and Thomas and son-in-law Jesse Cash my river plantation of 450 acres, the part of Thomas to be in trust of John Haley. To Jesse Cash in trust for my dau. Ritter Adams and her children 100 acres off the tract whereon I now live, now rented to James S. Daniel. At the death of my wife the property to be divided into lots and be drawn for and equally divided between James B. Adams, Jesse Cash trustee for Ritter Adams and her children, the children of Henry Mann by my dau. Sally, dec'd, the children of Easton Fortson by my dau. Tabby, Benajah Teasley in right of his wife Lucy, John Teasley in right of his wife Betsy, the children of Thomas Lane, dec'd, towit; John Lane, Eliza Fortson, one share, James Haley, Jesse Cash, John and Thos. Haley and Jesse Cash as trustee for Reuben Haley. Son John, Jesse Cash and Job Teasley, Excrs. Signed Oct. 2, 1830. Probated Dec. 6, 1830. Benajah Houston, James W. Harris, Wm. Crawford, Francis Gaines, Test.

INSHEEP, GEORGE—Page 39—To nephew Geo. I or J. Barr all estate real and personal. July 14, 1829.
Non-cupative—Proved by Cyrus Stewart, John Herring, Robert M. Carter, Voluntine Smith, Thomas Smith, Sr.

LANE, THOMAS—Page 112—To son John A. Lane and dau. Eliza Fortson and her children, Thomas, William and Elizabeth Fortson, half the estate equally to son John A., and the children of Eliza Fortson at majority. If Wm. Fortson, husband of Eliza dies or is divorced Eliza to have one fourth of the estate immediately, she now living away from him. Son John A., sole Excr. Signed Aug. 18, 1826. Probated Nov. 2, 1829. George Cook, William M. Bowen, Beverly C. Cook, Test.

RUCKER, JAMES—Page 38—Nieces Amanda B., and Milly Rucker sole heirs. Thos. A. Banks, Excr. Signed June 28, 1828. Probated Sept. 7, 1829. James F. White, Wesley S. Bailey, Test.

TAYLOR, ELIZABETH—Page 326—To sons John and James and dau. Phillisha Taylor, all estate for their support till majority. Then John to have the land on which I now live and a slave Bob to be equally divided amongst the three. Son John, Excr. Signed June __, 1830. Probated Mar. 7, 1831 John Craft, Edmond Shackleford, Test.

WHITE, WILLIAM—Page 37—To wife Mary a comfortable support for life. Son Jesse to contribute half from what is called the Dobbs tract on which said Jesse lives; son John to contribute the other half from the tract on which I now live, each to fall heir to said tracts at her death. Jesse to allow Lydia White to live in his house, she to have bed etc. At the death of my wife Mary, all personal estate to be sold and equally divided between the heirs of James E. White, David White, Sarah Williams children and dau. Lydia White. Jesse White and John Gordon, Excrs. Signed June 28, 1829. Probated Sept. 7, 1829. John McCurry, Angus McCurry, Reuben L. Tiler, Test.

WHEELER, THOMAS—Page 100—To wife Sarah land and all appurtenances for life, to dau. Sarah Wheeler and her children at wife's death, the personal estate to be sold and divided "among all my children not named) Wife Sarah and Jeremiah S. Warren, Excrs. Signed Sept. 21, 1829. Probated Nov. 2, 1829. F. Cunningham, John Thomason, Ezekiah Bailey, Test.

ELBERT COUNTY, GEORGIA

RECORD BOOK 1830-35

Wills, Administrations, guardians bonds and Marriages

AKIN, THOMAS—Page 133—35—All property to be divided amongst my nine children, viz; Sarah M. Akin, one-ninth, no deductions. After deducting advancements to son Wm. E. Akin, balance of his share to be in trust of Asa V. Mann for his wife and his children till the youngest is 21. The same conditions apply to the share of son Johnson Aken, James Banks, Jr. trustee; to share of dau. Sophia Jones wife of D. H. Jones, to dau. Mary wife of S. H. Tucker, to dau. Jane, wife of R. C. Tucker. To son Warren and daus. Elizabeth and Martha C. Akin their shares in fee simple, no deductions. Beverly Allen, Excr. Signed Jan. or Feb. 1832.

Oath of John M. Radford and Washington Morrison that some time in Jan. or Feb. Thomas Akin sent for Major Beverly Allen to write his will, and gave him special instruction, that they heard what he said, and the will corresponds. May 7, 1832.

ALLEN, JOSEPH—Page 247—To children Joseph J., William, James, John and Rhoda Allen, Elizabeth Head, Piety Reed, Nancy Couch, Sarah Kelly and Polly Blare, $1.00 each. To wife Agnes all estate real and personal, at her death the land to be divided among four sons, Joseph Jr., William, James and John, son James to have $50.00 as it was willed to him by his grandfather Patterson. Friends Williamson Clark, and William Bowers, Excrs. Signed Oct. 29, 1830. Probated May 6, 1833. Henry Duncan, Nancy Hendry, Test.

BRAY, JOHN—Page 32—Son David Bray and dau. Sarah Dean to have $1.00. To dau. Anna Coker $25.00. Wife Patience the land whereon I live for life or widowhood to be sold with other property and divided between my daus. Avy, Nancy, Delinda, Rhoda, Patience, Zoe and Elizabeth Bray. John Sartain and Larkin Coker, Excrs. Signed Dec. 3, 1830 Probated Sept. 5, 1831. John W. Attaway, William C. Cheek, Test.

BROWN, EDWARD—Page 350—To wife Lucy, slaves, bed, horse etc, and the plantation known as the Lowery plantation. Residue to be divided among all my children, viz, Reuben Brown, William Mills, William B. Campbell. I also give to Amos Rows' children an equal part with the other legatees, Milton B., Eliza, Washington, Thomas, Francis, Grantham and Lucy Ann Rows. The part coming to Mrs. Sarah Booth to be equally divided amongst her children, John Westly, Jones R., Catharine and Lucy Ann Alman. To dau. Sarah Booth, $5.00. Only son Reuben Brown of Monroe Co. and Wm. Mills joint Excrs. Signed Jan. 20, 1834. Probated Feb. 10, 1834. James Brawner, Ransom Worrill, Willis Threlkeld, Test.

BLACKWELL, BANKS—PAGE 502—To wife Elizabeth and Lucinda M. Clark all land north of Beaverdam creek, and about 20 acres south of said creek near where Joseph Blackwell formerly lived, and a large number of slaves. To Thomas B. Clark two slaves. Wife Elizabeth and William Jones, Esqr., Excrs.
Signed Mar. 1, 1835. Probated Mar. 16, 1835.
Fleming A. Alexander, William Hall, Isaac M. Tate, Test.

CRAWFORD, LUCY—Page 13—wid. of Oliver Crawford. To children of my son, Wm. Crawford, dec'd, viz; Oliver, James, Richmond, Milly, Nancy B., Lucy A., William, Benjamin and Matilda Crawford and another expected child by his widow Lucy Crawford, and Virginia Hunt, several slaves. To the children of my son John Crawford viz; Burton E., Leroy R., and William H. Crawford several slaves at majority. Balance of slaves and land on which I live, 239 acres on Coldwater creek adj. James Riley and others be sold and equally divided half to children of son William Crawford, and half to children of John Crawford. Signed Mar. 2, 1831. Probated May 2, 1831.
Thomas Johnston, James B. Alexander, John J. Groves, Test.

CANNING, JOHN—Page 143—Benajah Houston to take charge of money and property and to give to Peter Griffith $20.00, my drafts shop furniture and patterns including shears and goose. Balance of estate to be sold and controlled by Benajah Houston for my son Wm. Emit Canning. Should I draw land in the approaching lottery, it to be sold and the proceeds sent to my mother if she be living, if not to son William. James Brawner and Peter Griffith depose that they took this will as expressed by said Canning the day he died. July 2, 1832.

CARTER, JOHN W.—Page 501—$2,500.00 to be put at interest for benefit of my woman Becky, half brother William Woody to have charge of it, and set her free. Residue to half brothers William and Pleasant Woody both of Va., if they are living. Half brother William Woody and friends James Lofton and Robert Hester, Excrs. Signed Jan. 27, 1835. Probated Mar. 14, 1835. Isaac N. Davis, H. H. Cosby, Zachariah Smith, Test.

DICKERSON, ZACHARIAH—Page 12—To wife Nancy all estate for life, at her death to be divided among my six children, viz; David, John, Robert, Polly, Dolly and Rhody. Wife Nancy and Wm. White, Excrs. Signed Nov. 9, 1826. Probated May 6, 1831. Joseph Blackwell, Thomas S. White, Winston Oliver, Test.

HORTON, JAMES—Page 342—To wife Rebecca all property, to be kept together for her support and the support and education of my nine children (not named) some of them minors.
Signed May 16, 1832. Probated Jan. 22, 1834.
Benajah Houston, Job. Weston Robert Hesters, Test.

HENDERSON, SIMEON—Page 22—To wife Nancy all personal property for life, at her death "to my heirs general", except the portion of my dau. Patsy Dickerson and her children to be in trust of my executors. 964 acres on Vanns creek on which I live to belong to wife Nancy for life or widowhood then to go to my three sons, James M., William J., and Thomas B. Henderson. To dau. Amelia Henderson two slaves etc., To dau. Sarah E. Henderson and dau. Syntha Henderson two slaves etc. Residue to my nine children above named and Polly Brown, Anna Gaines and Elizabeth James. James Banks, Jr. and William Bailey, Excrs.
Signed Feb. 17, 1830. Probated July 4, 1831.
John J. Groves, Thomas A. Banks, Joseph Rucker, Test.

HUNT, JAMES—Page 163—To wife Jemima the land on which I live, cattle, horses, slaves etc, for life. Having given a slave to his children, namely, Jesse M. Redwine in right of his wife Elizabeth, Nicholas M. Adams in right of his wife Drusilla, dau. Mary Hunt, sons William, Sion, Henry, James Jr., Moses; Willis, Hullum and Richard Carter Hunt, he leaves it to the discretion of his wife to make further gifts. Sons Sion and Willis, Excrs. Signed Feb. 8, 1832. Probated Sept. 5, 1832 John A. Teasley, Thomas J. Teasler, Benajah Teasley, Test.

HALL, ELIZABETH—Page 169—All property coming to me from the estate of my former husband James Arnold, dec'd, and all I may be possessed of, to two youngest children, Susanna T., and James William Arnold. Singleton W. Allen, Excr. Signed Feb. 24, 1832. Probated Sept. 3, 1832. Henry Hall, Joshua Teasley, Wm. Teasley, Test.

JONES, ARTHUR—Page 480—To wife Mary certain personal estate in fee simple, and the plantation whereon I live for life or widowhood. To sons Hiram and Edmund the land whereon they live and a slave each. To son Arthur, Jr., land purchased of Edward Clark, and a slave. To son Nathan land purchased of Jesse Ozley and a slave. To dau. Patsy wife of Lewis J. Jones and dau. Rhody, wife of Davis Jones, to dau. Lucy wife of David B. Hudson a slave each in trust of Thos. J. Heard. To daus. Cynthia, Harriett and Malinda Jones, slaves, bed and furniture etc. To grandson Thomas Nash son of Henry C. Nash and Polly Nash, now dec'd, a slave and land in Wayne Co., when drawn and a 40 acre gold lot drawn in the late purchase etc., sold to pay debts. Son Hiram Jones and Thomas J. Heard, Excrs. Signed Oct. 9, 1834. Probated Jan. 5, 1835. Joseph W. Davis, Wiley Wall, Dunston Blackwell, Test.

LOWRIMORE, SARAH—Page 248—Widow, all property to two daughters Anne and Sally. Signed June 27, 1814. A. Stinchcomb, William King, Anne King, Test.

Codicil—Apr. 10, 1832—All the land and gold mines drawn by me in the present contemplated land and gold mine lottery to go to daus. Anne and Sally. Probated May 6, 1833. Johnson Hicks, Joseph Sewell, Thomas Pledger, Sr., Test.

LUNSFORD, WILLIAM, Sr.—Page 316—To wife Rachel M., all estate for life, to be divided at her death amongst my children, viz; Rolle, Polly Roberts, James, Katy, William, George, Peggy, Addie and Patsy Lunsford. Sons James and William, Excrs. If any dissatisfaction arises to be settled by William Burden, Abram Brown and Hugh A. Wiley. Signed Feb. 11, 1833. Probated Sept. 2, 1853. Hugh A. Wiley, Wesley Pledger, John A. Teasley, J. P., Test.

McGEE, ANSEL—Page 478—To wife (not named) home place, stock etc, for life, and a note on Josiah Roberts of Hall Co., in fee simple. 159 acres on Coldwater creek to be divided between sons John and Allen. To sons Jonathan and Jesse 40 acres in 2nd. Sec., 2nd. Dist., which they will have to take out the grant. Lot No. 371, 5th. Dist. Appling Co. to five daus., Sarah, Nancy, Mary H., Jane B. and Rachel. Nancy, Jane and Rachel still at home. Sons John and Allen, Excrs. Signed Dec. 18, 1834. Probated Jan. 5, 1835. James Carpenter, Harris Tyner, John H. Johnson, Test.

PACE, BARNABAS—Page 32—To wife Mary all estate for life or widowhood. To grandson Barnabas Pace a sum of money at her death or marriage. Residue to be divided into nine equal parts, one each to sons Thomas,

Bazil, Noel, Dredzil and Paris Pace, and son-in-law John Cary who married my dau. Elizabeth, "to son-in-law who married my dau. Nancy, two shares, Burket Wilborn," and grandson Barnabas Pace. Son Dredzil, son-in-law Burket Wilborn and grandson Barnabas Pace, Excrs. Signed Mar. 24, 1827. Probated Sept. 6, 1831. C. W. Christian, William Moss, J. P., Test.

PLEDGER, SIMEON L.—Page 422—Wife (not named) and my heirs to have use of land drawn by me in Lee Co., some money and draws in the Gold Lottery. To son William, tools, rifle gun etc. Wesley Pledger and my father Thomas Pledger, Excrs.
Signed Dec. 31, 1832. Probated July 22, 1834.
Archibald Burden, John Driver, Simeon Driver, Test.

RUCKER, WILLIAM—Page 477—All property real and personal to my children and grandchildren viz; Bardin, Tavener and William Rucker, Frances Ruckner now by marriage Frances Jones and her heirs and my two grandchildren Wm. Rucker Childs and Susannah Saripta Childs, children of John and Elizabeth Childs and the heirs of Lemuel Rucker, friend David Dobbs to take charge of said property. Sons Bardin and Tavener, Excrs.
Signed Aug. 5, 1833. Probated Jan. 5, 1835.
John Harris, Reuben Thornton, John Highsmith, Test.

RUCKER, WILLIS—Page 479—To two daus. Mary and Margaret Rucker, slaves, bed furniture etc., latter in possession of Jacob M. Cleveland. Residue to sons Jeremiah and Peter Rucker. Friend Peter Alexander, Excr. Signed July 29, 1834.
Codicil—If two daus. die before majority their property to be divided between my remaining children; Permelia Cleveland, Jeremiah and Peter Rucker. Probated Jan. 5, 1835. Dillard Thornton, Wm. A. Beck, Test.

STINCHCOMB, ABSOLOM—Page 328—To wife Mary slaves, cattle etc. and half the household furniture for life. To my grandchildren, children of Levi Stinchcomb all the land on south east side of Doves creek for a home till the youngest is 21. To dau. Lucy M. Hall all my land on Deep creek, slave etc. To son Philip, slave and half a lot drawn in my name in the late lottery, No. 101, 6th, Dist., 2nd. Sec., and $50.00. To dau. Polly C. Sewell, all the land whereon I live etc. To dau. Caty Andrew large iron pot and kittle. To son Nathaniel the other half of land given to son Philip, $150.00 etc. To son Levi all my clothes. Philip Stinchcomb and Joseph Sewell, Excrs. Signed May 20, 1833. Probated Nov. 4, 1833. William Bond, Henry W. Bond, Gaines Thompson, Test.

SIMMONS, JOHN SR.—Page 483—To eldest son Holman F., a slave. To Jane Ann Simmons, dau. of said Holman F., a slave. To second son James B., a slave. To only dau. Susannah Richardson a horse. To Safrony Antionette Richardson, eldest dau. of said Susannah, and to

Livona Josephine Richardson, dau. of said Susannah, a slave each. To Moses W. Simmons, slaves and a tract of land in Franklin Co., on Greggs creek whereon said Moses lives. To youngest son John, slaves. To wife Ann land on Coldwater creek adj. Bedford Harper, and a tract in Franklin, Jackson and Hall counties known as Hickory Level, slaves, household goods etc. To Thos. J. Alexander, horse, bridle and saddle provided he is in employ of my family to the age of twenty. Sons Holman F., and Moses W., Excrs.
Signed Jan. 6, 1830. Probated Jan. 20, 1835.
Henry M. Skaggs, John Beck, John White, Test.

TATE, ENOS—Page 161—To wife Elizabeth all estate real and personal for life, to be disposed of at her death as follows: To my nephew Enos Tate, Jr., certain slaves. To my wife's niece Nancy wife of Enos C. Tate certain slaves. To my nieces Lewcy Andrews and Elizabeth Upshaw $500.00 each. To Agnes Ann Harris, dau. of Rachel Harris, dec'd, and to the children of Wm. A. Nelson dec'd, $500.00 each. To Luther Henry Martin son of Jane Johnston, certain slaves and the tract of land whereon I live. To Enos, son of James Tate, Esqr., a slave now in said James possession. Residue to grand nieces and nephews, Elizabeth, Jane, Milton, and Madison Tate, children of Susan Tate, dec'd, and the children of Philip Johnson and James Arnold, dec'd, and the children of Elizabeth Fortson. Enos Tate, Jr., son of Zimri, James M. and Asbury Tate, Excrs. Signed June 12, 1830. Probated Sept. 3, 1832. Simeon Henderson, H. D. Tucker, Jordan Jones, Test.
Codicil—The $500 to Elizabeth Upshaw to be vested in her children. If Luther Henry Martin dies without heirs, his part to go to his mother Jane Johnston. Henry Bourne, Madison Baker, Geo. Key, Test.

TEASLEY, ISHAM, Sr.—Page 474—To wife Jane all estate for life with the following exceptions: To son Isham, Jr., $100.00. To sons Ausborn G. and Alfred H. certain slaves and $150.00 each when they come of age. Sons Benager and John A. Teasley to share equally in the final division. Signed May 20, 1834. Probated Oct. 27, 1834. Thomas Johnston, Joel Hutchinson, William Johnston, Test.

UPSHAW, GEORGE—Page 124—Whole estate to be divided equally between my three children; John A., Louisa E., and George L. Upshaw. Brother James Upshaw sole Excr. Signed July 17, 1831. Probated May 7, 1832. Richard L. Aycock, John Hall, Isaac M. Tate, Joel Hardman, Test.

UPSHAW, JOHN—Page 472—To son James 196 acres on which said James now lives, a slave and my joiners tools. To son George the land whereon I am now living, blacksmiths tools etc. Residue to be divided among my children and two grandchildren namely Ann Stubbs, Catharine Smith, Leroy, James and George Upshaw and Middleton C. Upshaw. Grandson Middleton C., and Joel Hardman, in right of his wife to have a share jointly. Son James, sole Excr. Signed Feb. 26, 1831.
Codicil—A slave extra to daus. Ann Stubbs and Catharine Smith, sons Leroy and James.

Signed May 11, 1834. Probated Oct. 27, 1834.
Haley Butler, William Bond, Test.

WILKINS, NANCY—Page 412—To son Clement all estate in testimony of my gratitude for his tender care in my declining years, he to be sole Excr. Signed Jan. 23, 1830. Probated July 7, 1834. Thomas F. Willis, Rhoda Rowsey, George Wyche, J. P., Test.

WHITE, JOHN M.—Page 216—Mentions slaves, land etc, already given to dau. Milly Morris, dau. Mary M. Jones, dau. Nancy Mann, son Eppy, son-in-law Asa Mann "his full share", son John M. White, dau. Lucy K. Thornton. Legacies to grandchildren to be received at the final division: Sarah, James F., John M., Elizabeth E., Sabrina L. A., Andrew J., and Reuben H. White, legal heirs of my son Reuben White. Elizabeth Thornton, Elizabeth Warren, Memorable, John Mark, and Eppy Thornton and Sarah Evingson, legal heirs of Thomas Thornton, dec'd, their property to be in possession of Lucy Thornton for their mutual benefit till of age; Polly, Reuben, Jeremiah, Asa, Eliza and Martha E. White, surviving children of my dau. Patsy White, dec'd; Milly Johnson, Eppy Roebuck, Sarah O. Goss, and William Roebuck surviving children of my dec'd, dau. Frances Roebuck; Francis, Milly, Richard, Asa and Charles Rice, legal heirs of Richard Rice, by my dec'd, dau. Eliza Rice. To wife Milly land on which I live, and land in Lee Co., all slaves etc, not heretofore disposed of. Wife Milly and son Eppy, Excrs.
Signed Sept. 21, 1832. Probated Mar 4, 1833.
William Bowers, Edy Bowers, Test.

WANSLOW, JOHN, Sr.—Page 482—All property to be sold and equally divided amongst my children viz: Nancy Young, Eliz. Elliott, Sally Beck, Milly Jenkins, Patsy Davis, Nathan, John, Reuben, Thomas, and Larkin Wanslow, certain amounts already given them to be taken out of their shares. Grandaughter Elizabeth Jenkins to have a bed etc. Son Thomas, William White and William A. Beck, Excrs. Signed Jan. 11, 1835. Probated Jan. Term 1835. Asa Mann, Johnson Maley, Test.

INDEX TO WILL BOOK 1829-1860.

Adams, Thomas
Alexander, William G.
Allen, Beverly
Adams, Nicholas
Allen, Singleton
Adams, William
Alexander, Peter
Alexander, William
Alexander, John B.
Alexander, George
Banks, Thomas A.
Banks, James, Sr.
Banks, James, Jr.
Brawner, Jos., Sr.
Brown, James N.
Bowers, William
Booth, Gabriel
Brown, Benjamin
Bond, Nathan
Brawner, Henry
Blackwell, Joseph
Benton, Nicholas
Burton, Thomas
Blackwell, Ralph
Brown, Elbert
Burch, Elizabeth
Brawner, Jemima W.
Burden, Clareyca
Browner, Dr. James
Bond, Daniel
Colbert, Thomas
Cook, Beverly O.
Cook, George
Carter, James
Cook, Smith
Carleton, Stephen
Cason, Edwards
Clark, Larkin
Clark, James
Clark, David
Cash, Moses
Carpenter, James
Dillard, James
Davis, John
Dickey, Tolley

Denny, Robert
Deadwyler, Susan A.
Deadwyler, Lucinda
Dye, Jane
Eaves, Rhody
Eavenson, Mary
Edwards, Felix
Faulkner, William
Fortson, Easton
Fleming, Sarah
Gapping, John B.
Ginn, Isaac
Goss, Horatio J.
Gaines, William
Gaar, William
Hunt, Elijah
Hunt, Moses
Hunt, Nancy M.
Hansard, John
Haynes, Letty
Higginbotham, Sarah
Hughes, Alexander
Hulme, John
Hopper, Rolly
Hall, Simeon
Jones, Solomon
Johnson, James J.
Jones, Emily
Kelley, Barney
Key, William Bibb
Lunsford, William
Maxwell, Thomas, Sr.
McCurry, Angus, Sr.
Mantz, William
Middleton, Betsey
Merit, John
Middleton, James
McElroy, Henry
Moss, William
Moore, Calvin J.
Newborn, Archibald
Nunnelee, James
Nelms, Jordan
Nelms, Alice
Oglesby, Zachariah

Oliver, James
Ozley, Larkin
Oglesby, William
Ozley, Jesse
Parham, Isham
Pledger, Thomas
Powell, William R.
Parks, Abraham
Patterson, James
Pulliam, William
Patterson, William
Ridgway, James
Rice, Leonard
Rich, William
Rich, Sarah
Rice, Ann
Rich, James
Rich, William, Jr.
Rowzie, Winslow
Roebuck, William
Rucker, Barden
Stinchcomb, Mary
Smith, John
Smith, Drury
Skelton, John
Skelton, John, Jr.
Staples, Fanney
Smith, Margarett
Stiefel, James
Smith, George O.
Shiflet, Picket
Seals, George
Teasley, Benager
Tate, Permelia
Tyner, Harris
Tate, Enos
Thornton, Daniel
Tate, Mary J.
Thornton, Daniel, Sr.
Teasley, James, Sr.
Terrell, William
Thornton, Reuben
Thornton, Benjamin, Sr.
Thornton, Elizabeth

Terry, Joseph
Upshaw, Leroy
Vernon, Robert
Vasser, Jane
Vawter, Richard

Wyche, George
Watkins, John
Walton, Nancy
White, Henry
Wilhite, Philemon R.

Wanslow, Thomas
Worrill, Eleanor
Wilkins, Clement
Wilhite, Calvin F.

GEORGIA D. A. R.

Returns of Administrators & Guardians

BOOK CALLED BOOK 1791-1803 MIXED RECORDS, CONSISTING OF BOOK "A", "B", & "C", BOUND TOGETHER

BOOK "A"

ADAMS, DAVID—Applied for letters of administration on estate of James Adams, dec'd. Jan. 29, 1791. Granted Mar. 2, 1791. James Tuttle, Sr. Thos. Burk, and John Wever, Sr., appraisers.

ADAMS, DAVID—dec'd. James Adams and Archer Burton appointed Admrs., Mar. 8, 1794. Inventory shows slaves Frank and her three children, Peter, George and Silvey, and another slave called Hanner, and a French musket.

AKEN, JOSEPH—dec'd. Sally and Thomas Aken apply for letters of administration Apr. 5, 1796. Granted May 6, 1796. Inventory shows slaves Liddy, Winny, Rose, Jack, Abram, Nan, and Olive, and a note on Chas. Irby of Va. James Tait, George Darden and Cornelius Sale, appraisers.

BRAZDAL, JOHN—dec'd. John Gill applied for letters of administration May 26, 1794. Caveat filed June 2, 1794, Mary Brazdal vs. John Gill.

BREWER, ELISHA—dec'd. John and Elisha Brewer appointed Admrs. Nov. 9, 1793. Inventory shows slaves Sam, Judith, Linda, Ezekiel, and Jeffrey. James Tait, Mat. J. Williams and Zimri Tate, appraisers.

CROCKET, SAMUEL—dec'd. Robert Crocket appointed Admr. May 20, 1793. Inventory shows 287½ acres land in Franklin Co. William Banks, William McKenzie, Solomon McAlpin, appraisers.

CRENSHAW, MAYBOURN—dec'd. Thomas Napier, caveat, Oct. 6, 1794, against Henry Pope obtaining letters of administration. Thos. Cook, William Aycock, Isaac Coker, Burton Green, appraisers.

COOKE, JAMES—dec'd. James Watson Cooke applied for letters of administration Aug. 14, 1792. Granted Oct. 1, 1792. John Sigmon, John Keys, Reuben Cooke, appraisers.

CRENSHAW, MAYBOURN—dec'd. Henry Rose applied for letters of administration Oct. 1, 1792.

DUDLEY, JOHN—dec'd. James Dudley appointed Admr. Dec. 26, 1792. Thos. Haney, Samuel Spears, Manuel McConnell, appraisers.

DIXON, WILLIAM—dec'd. Mary Dixon applied for letters of administration April 19, 1796.

EASTON, CHARLES—dec'd. Wm. Davis applied for letters of administration., Dec. 11, 1792. Granted Jan. 8, 1793. Inventory shows 200 acres land in Va. Richard Coulter, Hezekiah Gray and Absolom Baker, appraisers.

EASTON, JOHN—dec'd. Sally and Reuben Easton apply for letters of administration, Dec. 11, 1792. Granted Jan. 8, 1793. Richard Coulter, Hezekiah Gray and Absolom Baker, appraisers.

EASTER, JAMES—dec'd. William Thompson applied for letters of administration April 19, 1796.

FERRELL, JOHN—Applied for letters of administration on estate of Lewis Davis, dec'd. Granted Feb. 22, 1791. John Pollard, Absolom Davis and Stephen Westbrook, appraisers.

FULGHAM, STEPHEN—Applied for letters of administration on estate of Matthew Fulgham, dec'd. July 27, 1791. Granted Sept. 24, 1791. Estate consisted of horse, bridle, saddle and wearing apparel. John Smith, Peter Sheppard, appraisers.

FERRELL, JOHN—dec'd. Martin Ferrell appointed Admr. June 17, 1793. Outhberd Hudson, John Pollard, and William Davis, appraisers.

GAAR, MICHAEL—dec'd. Amount of estate with that from Va. Travelling expenses to Va. L3. Paid James Brown his part in full and also Abraham Gaar's part. Paid Nicodemus Colbert his part in full. Paid William Kidd for Nancy and Fanny Gaar's schooling, Dec. 28, 1795. A settlement made by Joseph Rucker and Lewis Gaar Dec. 3, 1795, shows by Benjamin Gaar, Excr, of estate of Adam Gaar, Sr. dec'd., negroes hired Jan. 3, 1794, as the property of Sally, Joel, William, Nancy, Frances and George Gaar.

GILES, JOHN—dec'd. William J. Hobby applied for letters of administration, April 19, 1796.

HAINES, STEPHEN, Sr.—dec'd. Moses Haines applies for letters of administration Nov. 23, 1795.

HENDERSON, JOSEPH—dec'd. John Henderson applies for letters of administration May 20, 1791. Granted June 30, 1791.

HAMBLETON, FRANCIS—dec'd. James Cosby applied for letters of administration April 26, 1792.

KINKADE, HUGH—dec'd. Matthew Collers applied for letters of administration Dec. 15, 1791. Granted Jan. 17, 1792. Christopher Clarke, Wm. Walton and Wm. Blake, appraisers.

GEORGIA D. A. R.

MORRIS, JAMES—dec'd. Sally and Isaac Morris applied for letters of administration July 22, 1795. Inventory shows land on which Sherod Morris lives. John Staples, Joseph King and Andrew Johnson, appraisers.

McCURDY, DAVID—dec'd. John McCurdy applied for letters of administration Oct. 23, 1795.

McCLARY, ROBERT—dec'd. Thomas and James Cameron apply for letters of administration Nov. 29, 1791. Granted Jan. 22, 1792. John Hawthorne and John Cameron, appraisers.

MILLER, JOHN—dec'd. Joseph Calvert applied for letters of administration April 20, 1792. Granted May 23, 1792. John Furgus, Arthur Crawford and William Appleby, appraisers.

MONACK, JOHN—dec'd. Mary Monack applied for letters of administration April 19, 1796. Granted May 27, 1796. Inventory shows 250 acres land on Coldwater creek adj. Richard Tiner, 190 acres adj. William Taylor. Mark Thornton, Job Teasley and Richard Tiner, appraisers.

ROGERS, JOHN—dec'd. Nancy Rogers applied for letters of administration July 28, 1795. Inventory shows set of surveyors instruments and note on William Moss for N. C. currency. John Mackey, Jonathan Lear and John H. Johnston, appraisers.

SUTTON, ALSAY, and James McClusky applied for letters of administration on estate of William Sutton, dec'd. June 18, 1791. Granted July 22, 1791.

STROUD, ISHAM—dec'd. William Moss appointed Admr. Oct. 29, 1792. Garrard Walthall and William Alston, appraisers.

SHERMAN or SHEERMAN, ANN—dec'd. Benjamin Head applied for letters of administration Mar. 17, 1795.

STODGILL, JOEL—dec'd. Martitia Stodgill and Caleb Oliver apply for letters of administration, Sept. 14, 1795. Inventory shows slaves Pegg, Mark, Kemp and Sener. Francis Satterwhite, Peter Stubbs, James Carter and Benjamin Fortson, appraisers.

SAIL, ANTHONY—dec'd. Cornelius Sail applied for letters of administration, April 5, 1796. Granted May 6, 1796.

THOMPSON, OLIVER—dec'd. Samuel Watkins, Robert Thompson and Jesse Thompson appointed Admrs. Feb. 22, 1792. Inventory shows a negro in Va. William Thompson, Sr., William Chisholm and Robert Easter, appraisers.

THOMAS, JOEL—dec'd. William Thomas and John Newman appointed Admrs. Sept. 2, 1793. Inventory shows 100 acres land on Savannah river, 200 acres in Franklin Co., on a branch of Hudson's river. Moses Haynes, John Ross, Thos. Scales, appraisers.

THOMPSON, ISHAM—dec'd. John Thompson applied for letters of administration Mar. 26, 1796. Caveat April 3, 1796, by Elizabeth W. Thompson. Judge Taliaferro ordered letters granted Elizabeth. Inventory shows slaves James, Granville, Bob, Pompy, Sall and her four children, Gilbert, Hagar, Hampton and Jack. Rachel and her four children, Fanny Tamer, Moll and Caleb. William H. Tait, William Oliver and Francis Moore, appraisers.

VODAN, BRADOCK—dec'd. Thomas Burton applies for letters of administration Oct. 4, 1791. Granted Jan. 5, 1792. William Hatcher, Evan Ragland, appraisers.

WILLIAMS, PHILIP—dec'd. Rachel Williams applies for letters of administration July 4, 1796.

BOOK "B"

ADAMS, DAVID—Page 10—dec'd. Returns for 1796, receipt of Booker B. Easter and wife Moneyca being late the widow of David Adams, dec'd., for her part in full of said estate.

AKEN, JOSEPH—Page 11—dec'd. Returns shows Thomas, William and Sally Aken, purchasers. Thomas Aken, Admr.

CHAVES, PHILIP—Page 6—Inventory Sept. 20, 1796. Thomas Tate, Martain Sims and Job Hammond, appraisers.

Page 15—Returns Jan. 23, 1797, sales to Harry, Gilbert and Charlotte Chaves, Robert Martain and Martain Sims.

DIXON, WILLIAM—Page 5—Inventory Nov. 19, 1796, shows rifle gun and one note on Francis Gitley for L6 given to Mary Dixon, dated Jan. 2, 1796.

GAAR, MICHAEL—Page 16—dec'd. Returns Jan. 7, 1797, heirs shown, Fanny, Nancy, Joel, William, Sally and George Gaar.

GARNER, STEPHEN—Page 43—dec'd. Inventory, Anthony Oliver, William Easton and Capt. Robert Cowden, appraisers.

GRIFFETH, JOHN—Page 55—dec'd. Inventory April 17, 1799, shows 200 acres land on north fork of Oconee river. Samuel Nelson, John McEny and Robert Cowden, appraisers.

HAYNES, STEPHEN—Page 24—dec'd. Account of sale Jan. 11, 1796. Moses Haynes, Admr. Moses Haynes, Sr., Moses Haynes, Jr., and Stephen Haynes, purchasers.

HUDSON, DAVID—Page 17—dec'd. Nathaniel and Nancy Hudson applied for letters of administration Jan. 11, 1797. Inventory shows 300 acres land including the home place, 180 acres adjoining and 250 acres in Franklin Co., rights to be made by Cudt. Hudson. Slaves Abram and

Jess. James Bell, John P. Harper, William Hightower and David Clark, appraisers.

McCURDY, D.—Page 21—dec'd. Settlement, divided among legatees, John McCurdy, John Calvert, William Appleby, David McCurdy, William Hodge, James McCurdy.

ROGERS, JOHN—Page 1-3 Est. Account of sale Dec. 11, 1795. Purchasers James, Thomas, Nancy, Benjamin and Mary Rogers. James Rogers, Admr.

STOKES, WILLIAM—Page 45—dec'd. Inventory Feb. 14, 1797, shows slaves Tom, Lamender, Davie, Coleman, Lucy, Doll, Jenny, Will, Amy, Robin, Edmond, Jack, Ben and Sally. 600, acres on Beaverdam creek, 300 acres on Oconee river. William Cade, David Ewing, Jas. Leeper, Test.

THOMPSON, ISHAM—Page 9—dec'd. Returns for 1796, shows paid Samuel Watkins for Mrs. Betsy Thompson's gown pattern, paid John R. Ragland for one gallon of rum for the harvest, paid Job Hammond for hauling tobacco to Petersburg, paid accounts of Robert Lewis and Wiley Thompson. George Cook, Admr.

WILLIAMS, PHILIP—Page 21—dec'd. Rachel Williams applied for letters of administration, granted June 21, 1797.

BOOK "C"

ADAMS, SALLY—Page 12—Receipt to Archibald Burton and James Adams, Admrs. estate of David Adams, dec'd. April 3, 1799. Also receipts to Solomon Bridges and Nancy Adams. Alex. Adams, Test.

AKEN, JOSEPH—Page 109—dec'd. Returns 1796-1801. Thomas Aken, Admr. Paid Elizabeth and Sally Aken and George Alexander same amounts 1797, 98, 99. Paid T. Aken for clothing, paid Middleton Woods for T. Aken, paid Fleming Aken and Mary Barden.

BREWER, EDMOND—Page 16—dec'd. Inventory 1793 shows slaves Judith, Linda, Ezekiel and Jeffrey, note on Edmond Taylor, bond on Thomas Napier for bounty land, one obligation to Zachariah Cox respecting land.

Page 17—Copy of sale, Mar. 25, 1794, Elisha Towns, John Brewer, Elisha Brewer, Horatio G. Brewer, William B. Brewer and Sarah Brewer, purchasers.

Page 18-19—Settlement Mar. 24, 1800. John and Elisha Brewer, Admrs. Paid Sarah Brewer, widow of dec'd. Wm. B. Brewer, Sarah More for Elisha Brewer and James Brewer, Sr.

Page 73—Memorandum of the full amount of property now in the hands of the legatees, namely, Robt. Gaines, Reuben Curtis, Thomas Brown, John Brewer, Wm. B. Brewer, Elisha Brewer, Robt. L. Tate,

Horatio G. Brewer. Received cash of estate of Drury Cade, dec'd. by Elisha Brewer. Recorded May 11, 1801.

BURTON, THOMAS, Sr.—Page 70—dec'd. Inventory Aug. 19, 1800, shows slaves Shadrach, Romey, Tab, Diner, Pheby, Reuben, Parthenia, Hiram and 80 acres of land. Evan Ragland, William Hatcher, and William Goode, appraisers.

COOK, BENJAMIN—Page 76—dec'd. Inventory Aug. 30, 1800, shows slaves James, Phillip, Cate, and Betty, 3 Vols. Dodridge Family Exposition, 1 Historical Collections, 2 Vols. Translations of New Testament, Watts Love of God and sundry other authors, 1 pair tooth drawers. Thomas Cosby, James Cosby and M. Woods, appraisers.

CONYERS, JOHN—Page 69—dec'd. Inventory May 3, 1801, perishable property sold by William Conyers, notes on Samuel Young in S. C., Benjamin Allen, Archer Burton etc., 5 doctors books, saddle and saddle bags, 1 brace of pistols, gold weights.
Page 71—Sale Sept. 20, 1800 shows Mrs. Conyers bought six dozen vials.
Page 101—Feb. 27, 1802. Statement by Admr. William Jamison.

CUNNINGHAM, WILLIAM—Page 73—Est. to William Graham paid funeral expenses, cash to David and Martha Cunningham, May 11, 1801.

DAVIS, GIDEON—Page 83—dec'd. Inventory Aug. 10, 1801 shows slaves Will and Ceasor, account on Absolom Davis for L5, N. C. money. Jacob Higginbotham, Robert Pulliam, Roland Brown, appraisers.

FINCHER, MOSES—Page 61—dec'd. Inventory July 28, 1800, shows one tomahawk, one pair compasses. William Arnold, Jere. Walker, J. M. Johnston, appraisers.
Page 62—Sale Aug. 30, 1800, sold to Mary Fincher, horse, bed, furniture, chest, cotton wheel and cards.

GAAR, MICHAEL—Page 24-28—dec'd. Returns 1798-1800 shows Adam Gaar guardian for minors, Nancy, Joel, Fanny, William and George Garr paid for clothes and paid Thomas Perry for schooling for all of them.

GARNER, STEPHEN—Page 22—dec'd. Returns 1799 signed by Daniel Orr, William Hendon and Mary Garner.
Page 72—Returns for 1800 shows Daniel Orr, Admr. in behalf of the whole, paid for schooling the orphans.
Page 100—Returns for 1801, shows plantation leased for five years for benefit of the orphans, and pay to Admr. for three days business in Lexington. "Daniel Orr, Admr. in behalf of the whole".

GILES, JOHN—Page 85—dec'd. Returns for 1800-1801, shows travelling expenses to secure the right of land etc. John Russell, Admr.

GRIFFITH, JOHN—Page 21—dec'd. Returns for 1800. Robt. and Martha Griffith, Admrs.
Page 56—Returns for 1800, Robt. Griffith, Admr.

Page 104—Returns for 1801 shows Robert and Patsy Griffith, Admrs. Corn used for support of the family.

GRIMES, WILLIAM—Page 89—dec'd. Returns for 1795 shows paid Abraham Hill for board for William Grimes, Jr. and for schooling. John Wilhight, Excr.

Page 90—Returns for 1798, shows a slave Amy bought by John Wilhight, slave Phillis bought by Robert Moon, a gun by Thomas B. Scott. John Wilhight, Excr.

HAYNES, STEPHEN—Page 29—dec'd. Moses Haynes, Admr. and guardian for the heirs, namely, James, Sarah, William, Robert, Mary and Walter, nothing expended except nine months schooling for William.

HOLLIDAY, ROBERT—Page 133—dec'd. Inventory Jan. 11, 1803, shows slaves Frank, Pompey, Frazer, Anneyer, Dyne, and a negro man run away in Va., account on John Holliday for L260 Va. money, account on Jeremiah Holliday for L175 Va. money. Signed Richard Tyner, James Ryley, James Jones.

HUDSON, DAVID—Page 32-39—dec'd. Returns for 1797-1801. Paid for recording deed in Franklin Co., paid Mrs. Nancy Hudson $100.00 in 1798, paid expenses of Anne Hudson's tobacco 1799, paid Nancy Hudson part of dower 1798. Nathaniel Hudson, Sr. Admr.

Page 58—Jan. 9, 1800, Receipt of Nancy Hudson for $60.00 "for support of my children".

LOVINGOOD, HARMAN—Page 63-65—dec'd. Inventory July 22, 1800, shows tanners tools, 100 acres of land in Franklin Co. Va., 500 acres in Lincoln Co. Ky., on Richland Creek. 219 acres in Elbert Co. on Cedar creek. Due from Samuel Lovingood by note and Ann Lovingood for cash received since death of Harman. Robt. Selpedy, Patrick Mitchell, Gideon Holmes, appraisers. Moses Haynes, Admr. Ann Lovingood, Admx.

Page 101—Returns for 1802 shows Moses Haynes, Admr.

SCALES, THOMAS—Page 40—dec'd. Bill of sale, Aug. 9, 1797, principal purchasers, Ann Scales, Sr., and Jr., Elizabeth Scales, Moses Haynes, Sr., Moses Haynes, Jr. Stephen, Thomas and Wm. Haynes. Cash found in possession of the widow Ann Scales. Debts against the following men, "who have absconded the state"; Moses Hopper, James Rice, Nathan Pitchford, Joshua Early, William Castle, Peter Scrine, William Biggs, Isaac Land, David Cealor, Zachariah Halcom, Benjamin Slayton, James Roberts, Sr. William Smith, Robert Ellicott, Joseph Woods, William Mitchell, James Shields of S. C., John Russell, Samuel Dewhit, who died insolvent, Joseph Howell, George Lumpkin, Joseph Roberts, Sr., John Moody, John High, John Fleming, Matthew Pedegrew, William Woodson, William Barnett. Signed Moses Haynes, Admr. Ann Thompson, Admx. July 12, 1800.

Page 97-99—Returns for the orphans 1801, Thomas Scales, board, clothing and schooling, same for Benjamin, board only for Elijah and Nathaniel. Ages of the four within heirs of Thos. Scales, dec'd.,

Thomas 13 years 4th, of May last, Benjamin 10 years first of June next, Elijah 7 years 25th, of May next, Nathaniel 3 years 18th, of Dec. last. Recorded Mar. 23, 1802.
Page 121—Receipts, Ann Scales, Admx. Dec. 23, 1799, signed Ann Thompson July 17, 1801.

SHARP, WILLIAM—Page 87—Inventory Aug. 6, 1801, shows a slave Viner, and 170 acres land. Watt Nunnelee, R. Middleton and Samuel McGehee, appraisers.

SMITH, GIDEON—Page 131—dec'd. Inventory, Henry Smith of Franklin Co., Admr. James Brock, John Burrough, Andrew McEver, appraisers. Shows only clothes, horse, saddle and bridle.

SUTTEN, WILLIAM—Page 30-31—dec'd. Amount of sale by Excr. James Sutten, Nov. 2, 1799, slaves Lewis, Lidey and Jack, returns 1792-99.
Page 55—Returns 1800, board and keep for Sally, Joel and George Sutten for one year, expense to Oglethorpe Co. James Sutten, Admr.

THOMPSON, WILEY—Page 30—Receipt of his guardian Middleton Woods for money from George Woods, Admr., of Isham Thompson, dec'd. Feb. 19, 1800.

UPSHAW, ADKINS—Page 60—dec'd. Returns for 1800 by James Patten, Admr, shows funeral expenses, following T. Loveletty to Carolina etc.

VINEYARD, ISHMAEL—Page 13—dec'd. Inventory Sept. 10, 1799. William Fuges, Edward Ware, Allen Leeper, Appraisers.

WILHOIT, ADAM—Page 116—dec'd. Receipt of Adam Gaar that he has received his fathers part of the estate of Adam Wilhoit, dec'd. Signed Michael Wilhoit, George Wilhoit. James Brown and Abraham Gaar, Test. "Each legatee to Adam Gaar for riding to Madison Court House Va., and selling above estate". Dec. 8, 1801. (See Gaar for other legatees.)

WOOD, JOHN—Page 110-116—dec'd. Inventory Nov. 9, 1801, Levin Wales, Samuel Pullen and Geo. Eberhart, appraisers. Purchasers, Susannah Wood, widow of dec'd., Bennett Wood, Sr., James Wood, Penuel Wood, Agrippe Wood.

ADMINISTRATORS & GUARDIANS PAPERS
WILL BOOK 1803-06

BROWN, ROBERT—Page 4—dec'd. Estate appraised Sept. 13, 1802, by Barnabas Pace, James Shields and Absolom Stinchcomb. Caty and Absolom Brown, Admrs.
Page 20-28—Sale April 4, 1803. Purchasers, Caty, Abraham, Polly, Peggy, Betsy and Peter Brown.

GEORGIA D. A. R.

BURTON, THOMAS, Sr.—Page 58—dec'd. Sale Feb. 27, 1802. Purchasers Robert, Thomas, Jr., and Thomas H. Burton.

CHRISTLER, HENRY—Page 29—dec'd. Returns 1801-03. Paid Benjamin Head and Mrs. Bibb for expenses while sick at his house and Dr. Holt for services. Joseph Christler, Admr.

CROCKETT, SAMUEL—Page 74—dec'd. Robert Crockett, Admr. Returns April 18, 1803. Travelling expenses to York Co. S. C. and Franklin Co., Ga.

ELLINGTON, STEPHEN—Page 51—dec'd. Inventory May 9, 1803. Wiley Thompson, Admr.

EASTER, WILLIAM—Page 11—Guardian of Champion Easter. Returns 1803, shows schooling and clothes.

EWING, JAMES—Page 140—dec'd. Returns of William A. D. Ewing, guardian of Charles a school boy, and James Ewing's part in full of said estate Feb. 22, 1804.

GRIMES, WILLIAM—Page 2—dec'd. Receipts in full from the heirs from our fathers estate viz; John Wilhite, John Wilhite, guardian; William Grimes, William Grimes guardian for Thos. Grimes, William and Elizabeth Carter, Robert Moon. April 26, 1802.

GARNER, STEPHEN—Page 73—dec'd. Returns for 1803, shows loss by the death of an insolvent debtor, Moses White, dec'd. July 16, 1803. Daniel Orr, Admr.

GRIMES, PATSY—Page 18—Return of guardian, John Wilhite, paid board etc, 1802.

HIGGINBOTHAM, COL. SAMUEL—Page 89—dec'd. Inventory Aug. 10, 1803 John S. Higginbotham, Admr.

Page 100—Returns for 1803 shows expenses to Augusta on business, expense of going for Parson Cummings, and paying for funeral sermon. Cotton sold by A. Higginbotham and money used for estate. Aron Higginbotham says "money paid by father".

HIGGINBOTHAM, JOHN S.—Page 105—Guardian of Clary, Polly D., and Frances Morrison. Returns for 1798-1803, shows board and clothes.

LAWSON, HENRY—Page 110—dec'd. Inventory and sale May 17, 1804, shows Jonas Lawson, Robert Lawson and Jonas Lawson, Jr., purchasers.

LOVINGOOD, HARMON—Page 136—dec'd. Shows paid William McCune for a judgement obtained by Samuel McCune in Va. Feb. 20, 1804. Moses Haynes, Sr., Admr.

MORRISON, FRANCIS—Page 70—dec'd. His heirs, the heirs of Aron Higginbotham, dec'd, of Amherst Co., Va., division according to his will, viz, Peter and Frances Morrison, John Satterwhite, Ezra Morrison, Washington Morrison, Clary Morrison, and Polly D. Morrison. Feb. 24, 1803.

John S. Higginbotham, guardian. Peter Wyche, James Bell, Thomas Penn, Test.

MORRISON, JOSEPH H.—Page 71—dec'd. John S. Higginbotham, guardian of minors, Clary G., Polly D., Frances, (probably grandchildren of Francis Morrison, dec'd.) Certain fees to be paid by them annually to Clary Higginbotham widow of Aron Higginbotham, dec'd. One slave sold by Joseph H. Morrison in his life time to _____ Barnett, in Amherst Co. Va., suit brought to recover. Expense for bringing their negroes from Virginia mentioned. Reg. Aug. 29, 1803.

McGUIRE, ALLEGANY—Page 134—Account to estate of Robert Holliday, for moving said Holliday and family from Va., to Ga., and boarding said Robert for three years and six months. Reg. May 28, 1804.

RIDGWAY, THOMAS—Page 72—dec'd. Middleton Woods, Admr. Returns 1802.

SHARP, WILLIAM—Page 31-32—dec'd. Sale registered Apr. 7, 1803. Lucrecy Sharp main purchaser.

SUTTEN, WILLIAM—Page 38—dec'd. James Sutten, Admr. Returns 1801-02 expense of law suit in Oglethorpe Co., to boarding and schooling two boys Joel and Geo. Sutten, to boarding Sally Sutten.

WHITE, MOSES—Page 61—dec'd. Pleasant White, Admr. Returns for 1803 show expense to obtain letters of administration.
Page 85—Inventory April 8, 1803. Harry Muckleroy, Enoch Pearson, and Tyree Landers, appraisers.

WOODS, JOHN—Page 112—dec'd. Inventory and debts 1801-1803.

ADMINISTRATORS & GUARDIANS PAPERS
BOOK "L-F" 1804-09

ANDREW, THOMAS—Page 171—Minor, returns of guardian Archelaus Jarratt for 1806, shows paid John Andrew for board etc.

AYCOCK, WILLIAM—Page 57—dec'd. Returns 1807. Thos. Wooldridge, Admr.

BARNES, CORDAL—Page 70—dec'd. Henry Kinnebrew's oath that he left no will, applies for letters of administration.
Page 159—Sale, Priscilla Barnes bought all household effects, Sept. 3, 1808. Dec. 1808 she signs receipt for money for support of family, and Barbara West and Asa Crab sign "in full of all demands."

BOOTHE, JOHN—Page 52—dec'd. Inventory and sale Feb. 24, 1808

BRAZIL, JOHN—Page 141—dec'd. James Glover, Admr., ordered to make clear titles to Benjamin Hubbard. Mar. Term 1808.

GEORGIA D. A. R.

BREWER, JAMES—Page 15—dec'd. Edmond Brewer, Admr. Returns 1806.

BURTON, GERMAN—Page 51—dec'd. Blackman Burton, Admr. Returns 1807

CARTER, THOMAS—Page 101—dec'd. Inventory Oct. 7, 1807.
Page 112—Sale, Dec. 21, 1807, purchasers, Charles, Thomas S., James Carter. Charles and Thomas S. Carter, Admrs.

CHILDS, NATHAN—Page 8—dec'd. Littleton Johnson, Admr. Returns 1806.
Page 93—Settlement May 11, 1807, signed by John Childs, Thomas Head, Nathan Childs, Jane Childs for herself and as guardian of Ann Wilson Childs, Littleton Johnson for James Satterwhite of Granville Co. S. C.
Page 153—James Banks, Thomas Colbert and James Alston released from security for Jane Winn, alias Childs, guardian of Ann Wilson Childs, her present husband John Winn giving security. No date but about 1808.

CLARK, FRANCIS—Page 54—dec'd. Returns 1807. Zacha. Smith, Admr.
Page 156—Returns 1809 shows paid Lewis Clark and Z. Smith, Excrs, for expense. Receipt of Tolliver Hall for his wife Sally's part of the estate. Receipt of Lewis Clark for value received. Test, Edward Clark. Receipt of J. V. Harris, Atty. for having Z. Smith appointed guardian of orphans.

CREWS, THOMAS—Page 110—Praying that William Thompson and Richard Easter, Excrs. and Robert Moore in right of his wife Sarah Moore (formerly Sarah Easter) Excx, of last will of James Easter, dec'd. make titles to 100 acres in Franklin Co., on Toms creek, said Crews holding a bond for same made by the testator Jan. 19, 1791. Sept. Term 1808.

ELLINGTON, STEPHEN, Sr.—Page 194—dec'd. Sale of part of estate, Dec. 12 and 13, 1804. Purchasers of the name, Garland and Rice Ellington. Sworn to by Samuel Watkins.
Page 197—Expense of making clothes for Stephen and Garland Ellington, July 26, 1800. Paid Peter Anderson overseer for 1801.
Page 199—Returns for 1802 show paid for slippers for Jane, spelling book for Robert and cloth for mothers coffin, to which Rice Ellington testifies.
Page 199-206—For different years, 1798 Hat and violin strings bought for son Rice. Receipts from legatees, John Langdon, Jr., Garland Ellington, Wiley Thompson, Rice Ellington, Stephen Ellington, Jr. Tuition paid Wm. Rowe 1805 for Jane Ellington, daughter of Stephen Ellington, Sr. dec'd. Paid Benj. Thurston for tuition for Robert Ellington. Samuel Watkins, Admr.

EVANS, STEPHEN—Page 67—dec'd. Sale May 3, 1808. Matthew J. Williams, Admr.

GARVIN, DANIEL—Page 15—dec'd. Returns for 1806 made by William Dunlap. Expenses of James Hannah to and from Abbeville.

Page 182-185—Returns for 1804 shows expenses to Abbeville Court, Jackson and Lincoln counties and receipt of A. Milligan, Tax Collector to Archabald McMullen for Jane Garvin, Admx. of Daniel Garvin, dec'd. William Dunlap, Admr. Returns for 1808 shows Jane Dunlap, Admx. Returns for 1807 shows schooling paid for Nancy and Robert Garvin.

GATEWOOD, RICHARD—Page 49-50—dec'd. Returns 1794-1808, shows one trip to Va., to settle business, for 1807 shows receipts from Sally Gatewood, Flemming Greenwood and Robt. Laurimore, legatees.

Page 155—Returns for 1808, shows paid Robt. Lowrimore and James Floyd, legatees. John Gatewood, Admr.

GREGG, THOMAS—Page 46—dec'd. Returns 1807 no data.
Page 139—Returns for 1808 shows Howard Cash, Sr. Admr.

HATCHER, WILLIAM—Page 32—Petition for titles to land, given by Robert Turman "in his lifetime Sept. 30, 1802", and on which said Hatcher now lives. July 6, 1807.

HAYNIE, BRIDGER—Page 11—dec'd. Returns 1807 shows paid Thomas Going, William Haynie, Richard Saunders, Jonas Broach "as per receipt", and received of Chas. Haynie on note. Bridgar Haynie, Admr.

HAYNIE, RICHARD—Page 35—dec'd. Inventory May 10, 1807. No data.

GREGG, THOMAS—Page 54—dec'd. Howard Cash and Johannah Gregg, Admrs. Benjamin Head and Wm. Ward pray to be relieved of their security. Feb. 29, 1808.

HIGGINBOTHAM, SAMUEL—Page 91-93—dec'd. Returns 1806, Claibourne Sandridge, Geo. Turman and John S. Higginbotham, Admrs., fees for legal services etc.

Page 156—Returns for 1808. John S. Higginbotham, Admr., signs for amount of property of Claibourne Sandradge and George Turman "rendered in."

HOLIDAY, TABITHA, Mrs.—Page 36-37—Returns for 1807 shows paid John Gatewood and John Rowsey their legacies, John Ham and Absolom Stinchcomb, Excrs.

HOUSE, BRINKLEY—Page 28—dec'd. John Millican, Admr. July Term 1806, paid for letters of administration.

Page 71—Returns for 1808 show plantation rented and property sold.

HUDSON, DAVID—Page 10—dec'd. Returns for 1806, shows receipt of Nancy Hudson for part of her dower and for support of child. Nathaniel Hudson, Admr.

Page 179—Returns for 1808, receipt of Edward Carrell for distributive share of my wife in said estate.

GEORGIA D. A. R.

JONES, JESSE—Page 31—dec'd. Inventory Nov. 6, 1806. John Allgood, James Butler and James Childers, appraisers. Thomas Jones and Arthur Jones, Excrs.

JONES, JAMES—Page 48—dec'd. Returns for 1807, shows paid legatees James Jones, Richard Hubbard, Shadrick Floyd, Nancy, Polly, John, Stanby, and George Jones and Thomas and William Jones, minors, by Admr. (not named)

JONES, NATHAN—Page 153—dec'd. Receipts of legatees, Allen Jones, John Hatchcook, Denton Hatchcock, James Childers, Arthur Jones, Darvin Harris and Thomas and John Jones, Excrs. of Jesse Jones, dec'd. Jan. 28, 1808.

KIDD, WEBB—Page 4-7—dec'd. Inventory and division of estate Dec. 18, 1806. Distributees, Martin Kidd, dec'd., John W. Kidd, William Jennings, John Cleveland, Tarlton Hall, Berry Ryan, Francis Kidd, and the heirs of Charter Harper and John Greenwood.

McCUNE, WILLIAM—Page 7—dec'd. Return against the minors, James and Peggy McCune, Thomas B. McCune, guardian 1805-1807.
Page 86—Receipts of various persons 1807-08, Moses Haynes, Thomas and James McCune, Admrs, shows writ of partition to secure dower for the widow.

MITCHELL, PATRICK—Page 143-44—dec'd. Inventory, Ambrose Dollar, Cornelius Dunahoo, and Edward Harper, appraisers, Jan. 14, 1808 Isaac Mitchell, Admr.

NAPIER, RENE—Page 178—dec'd. Receipts of legatees to John Morrison, Excr. for horse, saddle, household goods ect, left to Dorothy Napier, wife of dec'd. signed Edward Lyon. Jan. 11, 1808.

NORRIS, JAMES—Page 34—dec'd. Returns 1804. Paid Robert Y. Norris, in full of demands, paid Sarah Norris for support of herself and children, paid Betsy Norris her legacy, paid James Norris his legacy, paid Nathaniel Booth in full of all demands. William Dudley, Excr.

RAGLAND, JOHN R.—Page 74—dec'd. Returns show paid for lace 1807 for Miss Patsy at Athens, for medical attendance and medicine 1805, signed George Cleghorn. Receipt of Jay Garvis to Mrs. Franky Ragland for legacy of Sally Ragland, daughter of John R., now his wife., Dated at Petersburg, Dec. 15, 1804. Receipt of William Rowe for schooling Jan. 4, 1808. William Oliver, acting Excr. in place of Mrs. Frances Ragland.

ROGERS, WILLIAM—Page 83-85—dec'd. Inventory and returns 1807-1808. Mary Rogers, Admx.

SALE, CORNELIUS—Page 138—dec'd. Inventory Sept. 2, 1808, William Thompson, John Paxton and Enos Tait, Jr., appraisers. Dudley and Joseph Sale, Admrs.

SCALES, THOMAS—Page 12—dec'd. Returns May 15, 1807, Moses Haynes, Sr. Admr., and guardian of Nathan Scales orphan of said Thomas Scales.

SCOTT, JAMES—Page 44—dec'd. Inventory Jan. 11, 1808, James Ware, Edward Ware and Elisha Johnston, appraisers.

STOVALL, GEORGE—Page 30—Debtor to James Christian guardian for 1806.

STRICKLAND, JACOB—Page 59—dec'd. Returns Mar. 1808 by Elizabeth Strickland, Excx.
Page 175—Returns for 1809 shows 1 History for Hardy, to Samuel Willeford for schooling.

TAIT, JAMES—Page 146-150—dec'd. Returns 1806-08. Receipts of John H. Walton for cotton, it being pay for a family of negroes, Nancy and her three children, of William Tait for acting as overseer after he had absconded, of John Wilson for part of his wife's claim to the proceeds of land in Franklin Co., of Robert Burton for corn furnished the estate. Distributees in division of slaves, James M. Tait, Patsy B. Wilson., Excrs. of James Tait as Trustees, C. Tait. Heirs of B. Oliver, Charity Tait, William H. Tait. Charles Tait, Excr.

TURMAN, GEORGE—Page 1—dec'd. Inventory, James Hatcher, Henry G. Walker and Thomas Turman, appraisers Oct. 3, 1806.

TURMAN, CATY—Page 47—Admx. of Robert Turman, dec'd., ordered to make titles to land to William Hatcher, signed by said Robert 1802. Feb. 17, 1808.

VINEYARD, ISHMAEL & JANE—Page 8-9-10—dec'd. John McCurdy and Samuel Groves, Admrs. Division of estate, Robert Kennedy and Joseph Neal, arbitrators. Legatees, John Vineyard, legatee and representative of Geo. Vineyard, James Vineyard, Ephraim Beasley, legatee and representative of David Vineyard, Joseph Vineyard, John McCurdy representative of William Stephens and Matthew Blackwell, legatees. All receipts signed Feb. 27, 1807.

WALKER, HENRY G.—Page 33—Petition for titles to land on which Richard Easter now lives, bond given by James Tait 1795, assigned by Thomas Tait to James Coleman, by him to Richard Easter, by Easter to Walker. July Term 1807.

WALTHALL, GERRARD, Sr.—Page 16—dec'd. Returns for 1805 by William Allen, Admr.
Page 35—Gerrard Walthall, Jr., debtor to the Excr. Aug. 1, 1807.
Page 56—Gerrard Walthall, Jr., debtor to the Excr. Mar. 7, 1808 Thomas B. Creagh, Admr.
Page 78-82—Gerrard Walthall, Sr. dec'd. William Allen, Admr. Returns 1807-08. Thomas B. Creagh vs. Gerrard Walthall, Sr. dec'd.

1808. To boarding, clothing and tuition for two minors, William and Singleton Walthall.

WILLIAMS, JOSEPH—Page 16—dec'd. Inventory Apr. 4, 1807.
Page 68—Account of hire of slaves Apr. 10, 1807 by Matt. J. Williams, Admr.

WILSON, JOHN—Page 43—dec'd. Debtor to Whited Hendricks, tenant Jan. 2, 1808.
Page 151—Return of Barnabas Pace, Excr. for 1808, paid Benj. Wilson by order of referees certain debts.

WOODS, ANDREW—Page 70—dec'd. Robert and Ann Woods, and James Ewing, Admrs, ordered to make titles to land to Joel Miller, signed by said Andrew Woods 1804.

WOODS, JOHN—Page 60—dec'd. James Wood, Admr. Returns 1807, shows boarding and clothing two children, heirs of the estate.

WHITE, ASA—Page 98—Legatee of Daniel White, dec'd. Jesse Fortson guardian, to boarding and schooling nine months. July Term, 1808.

ADMINISTRATORS & GUARDIANS BONDS
WILL BOOK 1809-12

ALEXANDER, GEORGE—Page 21—dec'd. Application of Mary and William Alexander for letters of administration.
John Hulme, Taliaferro Gaines, Sec. Sept. 4, 1809.
Page 23—Note to William Pickings, signed by Nancy Alexander, Excx. Peter Alexander, Excr. Henry Harper, Oct. 31, 1806
Page 47—Sale of estate, Jan. Term 1810. Purchasers of the name, Mary, Polly, Lucy, Mourning and William Alexander.
Page 65—Second appraisement and allotment, property given by said George in his life time to three of his children, (to wit) Elizabeth Hulme, Sally Gains and William Alexander, Mary, Jr., and Mourning Alexander, Robert T. Gains signs "for said Sally".

ALEXANDER, EZZA—Page 26—Receipt for her part of the estate of William Alexander, dec'd. Aug. 29, 1809.

ALEXANDER, PETER—Page 24—Excr. for Nancy Alexander and the estate of William Alexander. Mar. 24, 1809.

ALEXANDER, WILLIAM—Page 97—dec'd. Returns of Nancy and Peter Alexander, Excrs. 1810. Receipt of Nathaniel Allen, guardian of James Head, for a settlement of bond given Wm. Alexander, dec'd to the legatees of James Head, dec'd. May 30, 1810.
Receipt of William Page for his part of Wm. Alexander's estate, "willed to me before the divison", Sept. 26, 1810.

Page 165—Nancy Alexander, Excx, receipt for cost of schooling 1811.
Receipt of Barden Rucker to Peter and Nancy Alexander for his share of estate of Wm. Alexander, dec'd. Jan. 9, 1811.
Receipt of Standley Jones for his share of said estate.
Page 269—Sale of Wm. Alexander, dec'd, Dec. 19, 1811. Peter and Nancy Alexander, Excrs. Nancy, Peter, George and John Alexander purchasers.

ALEXANDER, GEORGE—Page 149—Returns of William and Mary Alexander, Admrs. for 1810.
Page 260—Receipts of legatees, R. Talliaferro Gains, William Alexander, John F. Cook and John Hulme, Feb. 25, 1811

ANDREW, THOMAS—Page 99—Returns of guardian Archelaus Jarratt for 1809

AKIN, SAMUEL—Page 275—Bound to James E. White as apprentice to learn blacksmiths trade, Jan. 6, 1812.

ALLEN, ASA—Page 179—Guardian of Mary D., and Virginia Hudson, orphans of David Hudson, dec'd. Edward Carrell's receipt for pay for their maintenance for 1810.

ADAMS, HENRY—Page 325—Appointed guardian of Peter, Patsy, Edward and James Bevill, orphans of John Bevill, dec'd. Jan. 6, 1812. Enos Tate, Jr., Security.

BROWN, CATHARINE—Page 14—Guardian of John Brown. Estate of Robert Brown debtor to said Catharine, 1804, 1805, 1808.

BROWN, ROBERT—Page 16—dec'd. Returns for 1808, proved by oath of Abraham Brown.
Page 242—Returns for 1810, Abraham Brown, Admr. Receipts of Silas White for his part of my wife's fathers estate, and of Peggy Brown for her part of her fathers estate.

BELL, OLIVE & JOSEPH—Page 53—Protest to the court that James Bell in his life was Excr of estate of Lewis Jones, dec'd., Thomas Jones, dec'd, and William Whitman, dec'd, and they are unwilling to become responsible for said estates, ask to be releived. Granted 1810.

BREWER, EDMOND—Page 69—dec'd. Robert L. Tait, bond as Admr, George Anderson, William Tate, Sr., and William Tate, Jr., Security. May 7, 1810.
Page 179—Sale Aug. 13, 1810. Robt. L. Tait, 1 Dragoon Sword, William Good, 1 Dragoon Sword. Robt. L. Tait, Digest of Laws of Ga. Robt. L. Tait, Admr.

BREWER, JAMES—Page 143—dec'd. Jacob Turman appointed Admr. George Turman, Security Jan. 7, 1811

BURTON, ABRAHAM—Page 231—dec'd. John Burton's application as Admr. July 1, 1811. Thomas Burton, James Morrison and Richard Hubbard, Security.

GEORGIA D. A. R.

BURTON, THOMAS—Page 234—dec'd. John and Thomas Burton, bond as Admr. Mar. 13, 1811.

BURTON, THOMAS—Page 248—Appointed guardian of Elizabeth Neal Burton, orphan of Thomas Burton, dec'd. Sept. 2, 1811. Abraham and John Burton, Security.

BOOTH, JOHN—Page 237—dec'd. D. S. Booth, Admr. Returns for 1811

BLACKWELL, JOSEPH—Page 281—dec'd. Dunston Blackwell, Admr. Receipts of R. Blackwell, Betsy C. Williamson, Banks Blackwell, Joseph Blackwell, and Parke Blackwell, legatees. Receipts dated 1809, 1810. Returns made 1812.

BOOTH, DAVID S.—Page 331—Appointed guardian of Pridence W., Thomas W., and Martha Booth, orphans of John Booth, dec'd, May 4, 1812. Thomas S. Carter and William H. Moon, Security.

CHILDS, NATHAN—Page 3—dec'd. Receipts of John, Nathan, and Jane Childs, James Satterwhite in right of his wife, Franky formerly Frankey Childs, John Wynn, guardian of Ann Wilson Childs, legatees. Littleton Johnson, Admr. 1808-1809.

CHILDS, RICHARD—Page 183—John Childs bond as Admr. Mat. J. Williams and James Morrison, Security.

COSBY, RICHMOND T.—Page 19—dec'd. James Alston, Admr. Returns for 1808.

CREWS, THOMAS—Page 44—Rule absolute, praying that Richard Easter and William Thompson, Excrs. and Robert Moore in right of his wife Sarah Moore, formerly Sarah Easter, Excx., of will of James Easter, dec'd., to make titles to 100 acres of land in Franklin Co. a bond for which was made 1792 by the testator. July term 1809.

CARTER, THOMAS,—Page 54—dec'd. Returns of Thomas S., and Charles Carter, Admrs. for 1809, shows expense of getting out a grant for land in Jones Co.

CARTER, JAMES—Page 219—Guardian of Thomas Paine Carter. Returns for 1811 shows schooling etc.

CARTER, THOMAS S.—Page 326—Appointed guardian of Blake, Alcy, John and Thomas Hall, orphans of William Hall. May 4, 1812. David S. Booth and Joseph Griffin, Security.

CLARK, ZACHARIAH—Page 64—Guardian of Davis Jones, minor of Nathan Jones, dec'd. Returns for 1807 show paid Charles Gunter for schooling.

CLARK, FRANCIS—Page 68—dec'd. Returns of Zachariah Smith, Admr. for 1810.

CLARK, ZACHARIAH—Page 164—dec'd. Temporary bond of Abigail P. Clark and James Morrison, Admrs. Mar. 4, 1811.

Page 175—David Hudson and Matthew Williams, Sr., Security.
Page 223—Inventory Mar. 9, 1811. E. Brewer, Peter Oliver and David Hudson, appraisers, 41 acres land on Wahachee creek listed.
Page 276—Return of sale Apr. 26, 1811. Matthew J. Williams, Sr. Matthew J. Williams, Jr., McCarty Oliver, Betsy Carter and others purchasers, and sundry articles bought at the Planters Store for the widow Abigail P. Clark, for the use of the family. James Morrison and Abigail P. Clark, Admrs.

CROOK, ROBERT—Page 114—dec'd. Bond as Admr. of William Chisholm, Sr. Caleb Tate, Security Dec. 10, 1810

CARRELL, EDWARD—Page 174—Bond as guardian of Virginia Hudson, orphan of David Hudson. Mar. 4, 1811.
Page 347—He receives her distributive share of David Hudson's personal estate, July 6, 1812.

DAVIS, ABSOLOM—Page 30—Guardian of Sally Davis, Returns for 1809

DOBBS, JOSIAH—Page 76—dec'd. Bond of Luzany and John Dobbs, Admrs. July 2, 1810. Moses Haynes, Sr., and John Cunningham, Security.
Page 189—Appraised July 24, 1810 by John Vawter, Isaac J. Barrott and Amos Richardson. 400 acres land on Little Cedar creek Elbert Co. Lot No. 106, 12th, Dist. Wilkinson Co. 202½ acres, Lot No. 159, 19th, dist., half of Lot No. 20 Dist. 49, listed.
Page 191—Sale Mar. 4, 1810. Luzanna, John and David Dobbs, purchasers.

DUNLAP, WILLIAM—Page 236—Applies for letters of administration on estate of Daniel Garvin, July 1, 1811

DUNLAP, WILLIAM—Page 249—Appointed guardian of Robert M., John E., and William D. Garvin, orphans of Daniel Garvin, dec'd. Abraham Burton and Arthur Jones, Security Sept. 2, 1811

FORTSON, JESSE—Page 183—Guardian of Asa White. Returns for 1809-1810 shows schooling paid.

GRIMES, WILLIAM—Page 4—Returns for 1808-1809 as guardian of Thomas M. Grimes.

GLIN, SIMEON—Page 8—Guardian of Simeon G., and Susannah M. Rogers, returns for 1809 shows paid for schooling.
Page 243—Returns for 1811, shows board and schooling.

GREGG, THOMAS—Page 45—dec'd. Howard Cash, Admr. Returns for 1808 shows paid William Woods for issuing a land warrant in the name of the heirs.

GAAR, WILLIAM—Page 359—Bond as guardian of Amelia Bailey, illegitimate child of Elizabeth Bailey. John Daniel and Geo. Gaar Security. Sept. 7, 1812.

GEORGIA D. A. R.

HENDRICKS, ABIJAH—Page 39—dec'd. estate appraised June 1, 1809 by Barnabas Pace, John Certain, John Turner and John Bray. Purchasers at sale, Elias Hendricks, John Bray, Wm. Hendricks, Camnel Hendricks and Anna Hendricks. Elias and Anna Hendricks, Admrs.

HAM, BARTLETT—Page 82—Proven account, Robert G. Turman, debtor, schooling and board for 1810. A. Jarrett, Esqr., protests because the orphan was bound to said Ham.

HUDSON, DAVID—Page 86—dec'd. Returns of estate for 1809 shows paid Asa Allen guardian of Mary D., and Virginia Hudson. Nathaniel Hudson, Admr.

Page 282—Returns for 1811 shows receipt of Edward Carrell for his part of the personal estate of David Hudson in right of his wife, late Nancy Hudson, and Asa Allen's receipt as guardian of Mary D., and Virginia Hudson for their shares

HIGGINBOTHAM, FRANCIS—Page 115—Appointed guardian of Mary Higginbothan orphan of Benjamin Higginbotham. Charles Carter and John Ham, Security. Jan. 7, 1811.

HIGGINBOTHAN, JOHN S.—Page 116—Appointed guardian of Peter and Larkin Higginbothan, orphans of Benjamin Higginbothan. John Ham and Francis Higginbotham, Security Jan. 7, 1811.

HATCHER, WILLIAM—Page 231—Admrs, bond on estate of Robert Turman, dec'd. Caleb Tait, Security. June 10, 1811

HATCHER, WILLIAM—Page 321—Petition for titles to land adj. James and Thomas Coleman, Julius Howard and Abraham and Nancy Colson, bond for which was given by Jeremiah Walker, dec'd, 1787. Recorded May 15, 1812.

HEAD, WILLIAM—Page 365—Makes oath that William Hall died with will, and asking for letters of administration. Sept. 7, 1812

Page 366—Granted letters, Tavneah Head and John Daniel, Sec.

JONES, JESSE—Page 58—dec'd. Inventory and sale May and June 1809 shows Arthur Jones, surviving Excr.

JARRETT, ARCHELAUS—Page 99—Guardian of Thomas Andrew, returns for 1809 show paid John Andrew for board and clothing.

JONES, JAMES—Page 138—Est. Returns of George and Standley Jones, Admrs. division of estate between Thomas, William, Standley and Nancy Jones, Gilliam Hudson, Richard Hubbard, Shadrick Floyd. Jan. Term 1811.

JONES, ARTHUR—Page 230—Appointed guardian of Davis Jones, orphan of Nathan Jones, William Dunlap, Security. June 1, 1811.

KIDD, WEBB—Page 12—Returns of estate by William, Martin and John W. Kidd, Excrs. for 1808 shows board and schooling for Webb and Frances Kidd.

KENNEDY, CAMPBELL—Page 235—dec'd. Temporary letters administration to Robert Kennedy, June 19, 1811. Caleb Tate, Security.

KING, ELISHA—Page 259—dec'd. William King and James Mills, temp. letters administration, Jan. 7, 1812. Thomas Carter and Martin White, Security.
 Page 319—Permanent bond to the above with Thomas Carter and James Hamilton, Security. Mar. 2, 1812.
 Page 361—Returns for 1812 shows "travelling expenses to the purchase and return"., and paid William King for nursing the dec'd.

LINDSAY, REUBEN—Page 160—Dr. Marshall Durrett's oath as Admr. in right of his wife Nancy, formerly Nancy Lindsay. Mar. 4, 1811.
 Page 161—Benjamin Cooks receipt as pay for clerk in the store Dec. 7, 1810.

LONG, JOSEPH—Page 87—Returns of estate for 1810, shows settlement between Charles Wheeler and the estate "being in a co-partnership in merchandizing". James Long acting Excr.

McELROY, HENRY—Page 32—dec'd. Estate appraised Aug. 15, 1809 by Chas. Wheeler, Geo. Eberhart and Samuel Patten.
 Pellatia and James McElroy, Admrs.

MEREDITH, JAMES—Page 51—dec'd. Returns of Isaac Suttles, Excr. for 1810 show receipts of Zachariah and Nancy Faulkner, Henry and Sally Clift, Buckner and Polly Eaves, legatees. Jabez Butler, John Suttle, James and Patsy Faulkner, Test.

McCURRY, LAUCHLIN—Page 112—dec'd. Lauchlin Johnston and John McDonald apply for letter of administration, Jan. 7; 1811. Angus and John McCurry and Joshua Carpenter, Security.
 Page 113—Angus McCurry applies for letters Aug. 3, 1810, John McDonald, Security.
 Page 114—Granted Lauchlin Johnson and John McDonald, Jan. 7, 1811
 Page 208—Inventory Feb. 15, 1811. Angus Johnson, Roderick McDonald and Moses Haynes, Sr., appraisers. Shows 153 acres land adj. Donald McDonald, 300 acres adj. Joshua Carpenter on Coldwater creek, 100 creek adj. Powell Shiflet on Coldwater creek, 169 acres on both sides of Cedar creek, 287½ acres on north fork of Broad river. Purchasers of the name at sale, Nancy McCurry bought household goods, John and Angus McCurry.

MOON, WILLIAM—Page 167—dec'd. Inventory Feb. 25, 1811, shows 200 acres on south side of Broad river, 80 acres on north side of Broad river and slaves Gabe, Little Gabe, Edmon, Jenny, Lucy, Abby, Ben, Betty and Rafe. James Woods, Robert Woods, Benjamin Witcher, David Staples, appraisers.
 Page 336-39—Receipts of legatees, A. Moon, B. Moon, William Power, Martha and John Blake, David Power, in returns for 1811.

GEORGIA D. A. R.

MOON, SALLY—Page 324—Bound to Sarah Moon, to be taught housewifery, Archilus and Robert Moon, Security. May 4, 1812.

MOON, JESSE—Page 324—Bound to Archilaus Moon May 4, 1812, to be taught the art of farming. William H. Moon, Security.

MOON, STEPHEN—Page 326—Bound to William H. Moon to be taught the art of farming, May 4, 1812. Archilaus Moon, Security.

NAPIER, THOMAS—Page 52—Guardian of James, Richard, Milton, Jewdo (Juda) and Tabitha Aycock, minor heirs of William Aycock, dec'd. Returns for 1810 show Thomas Wooldridge, Admr., giving his receipt for board for children and expense for draw in Land Lottery, and Jacob Lindsays receipt for his legacy.

NAPIER, THOMAS—Page 142—Guardian of James, Terrell, Richard and Milton Aycock orphans of William Aycock, dec'd. Returns for 1809 shows travelling expenses from Putnam to Elbert and back.

NORRIS, JAMES—Page 60—dec'd. William Dudley Admr. Returns for 1810 shows receipt of Sarah Norris for $210.00 for support of herself and children.

NAISH, JEREMIAH—Page 176—Bound to Daniel Tucker to learn the art of farming. Robt. Tucker, Daniel Hudson, Sec. Mar. 4, 1811.

OLIVER, THOMAS—Page 247—and Chas Tait appointed guardians of Maria, Matilda and Mary Ann Oliver, orphans of Wm. Oliver. George Cook, Security. Sept. 2, 1811.

PAXTON, SAMUEL—Page 9—dec'd. Inventory Aug. 22, 1809. Richardson Hunt, Benjamin Higginbotham and Thomas Smith, appraisers.

PATTEN, SAMUEL—Page 108—dec'd. Inventory Aug. 15, 1810. Jonathan Cooper, Archelaus Moon and Chas. Wheeler, appraisers. Shows slaves Harry, Charles, Israel, Frank, Betty, Silvy and child.
Page 177—Returns for 1811 shows paid Benjamin Witcher, schoolmaster and Dr. George Phillips for services.

ROGERS, WILLIAM—Page 197—Est. Returns for 1811. Mary Rogers, Admx, oath signed Mary Bragg.
Page 241—Returns for 1811, signed Mrs. Mary Bragg, Admx.

RUCKER, AZMON—Page 267—Nancy Rucker bond as Admx. John Rucker and John Jones, Jr. Security Jan. 6,.1812.

ROBBINS, PLENNY—Page 323—dec'd. Temp. Admrs., bond to William O. Robbins. Shelton White, Security Mar. 17, 1812.
Page 328—Granted May 4, 1812, Isabella Robins and Shelton White, Security.
Page 369-72—Inventory May 4, 1812 shows Mrs. Isabella Robbins chief purchaser.

ROWSEY, JOHN, Sr.—Page 351—Bond as guardian of Tabitha Lawlis, orphan of John Lawlis. James Rowsey, Geo. Booth, Security. July 6, 1812.

ROWSEY, JAMES—Page 352—Appointed guardian of Betsy Lawlis, orphan of John Lawlis. John Rowsey and William McCoy, Security July 6, 1812.

SIMS, EDWARD—Page 249—Bond to apprentice James Murray to learn the hatters trade. David S. Booth, Security. Sept. 2, 1811

STOVALL, GEORGE—Page 306—Appointed guardian of William, Lindsay, Eouincy, James and Marshall Johnston, orphans of Mary Johnston. George and William Oglesby, Security. Jan. 6, 1812.

TAIT, ROBERT L.—Page 68—Oath that Edmond Brewer died without a will, and he will administer his goods etc. May 7, 1810

THOMPSON, ALEXANDER—Page 173—Est. Returns 1808, James and Alex. Thompson, Excrs. Receipt of legatees, William Langford, Sary Robinson, (Serah Robinson in one place)

THOMPSON, DRURY, Jr.—Page 139—Appraisement of estate Mar. 11, 1809. Samuel Watkins, Willis Thompson, Asa Thompson and Wm. Brewer, appraisers.

TURMAN, MATILDA—Page 182—Bound to Martin Turman to learn housewifery. James Morrison, Security. Mar. 4, 1811

TURMAN, MARTIN—Page 222—Returns as guardian of Prudence Turman for 1811

TURNER, MARTIN—Page 225—dec'd. late of Greene Co. Returns of Sally Turner guardian of Thomas and Elizabeth Martin Turner, orphans of said dec'd., shows boarding and clothing and schooling for both, and Sally receiving her part of estate. July 1, 1811.

WOODS, ANDREW—Page 6—dec'd. Returns by Robert Wood, James Ewing and Ann Woods, Admrs., for 1808 shows titles to 125 acres land on both sides of Fork creek to Joel Miller.

WALTHALL, GARRARD, Sr.—Page 10—dec'd. William Allen, Excr. Returns for 1809, shows clothing and tuition for two minors, William and Singleton Walthall.

Page 148—Returns for 1810 shows board and tuition for two minors, Tom and Singleton Walthall.

WILLIAMS, JOSEPH—Page 310—dec'd. George Wynne, Admr., in right of his wife, returns 1809.

WHITE, DANIEL—Page 15—dec'd. Returns of Wm. Davis, Excr. for 1809, shows paid Martin White, guardian of John White, minor.
Page 222. Returns for 1810 shows paid P. Christian guardian of Eppy White, minor.

WOODS, MIDDLETON—Page 70-75—dec'd. Returns of William Woods, Admr., receipts 1809-1810 from Robert Woods, Sr., Ann Woods, Robert Woods, Jr., Christopher Bowen, Jehu Hale, Joseph Hale, guardian of John Woods, William A. Burwell, guardian of Bailey Woods one of the orphans of Hugh Woods, Joel Shrewsbury, guardian of Josiah W., and Robert N. Dickerson, John Clay, Josiah Woods, Francis Hill, Samuel Hairston, gourdian for heirs of John Woods, dec'd., William Woods, all "on account of their legacy".

Page 198-207—Receipts of legatees, Hugh Martin of Elbert Co., in right of his wife. Francis Hill of Franklin Co. Va., in right of his wife. Robert Woods, Sr., of Franklin Co. Va. Joseph Hale, guardian of John Woods, one of the orphans of Hugh Woods, dec'd., of Franklin Co. Va. Jehu Hale of Franklin Co. Va., in right of his wife Polly Woods now Polly Hale. Robert Woods, Jr., of Franklin Co. Va., J. Woods atty. in fact for William A. Burwell, guardian of Bailey M. Woods, one of the orphans of Hugh Woods, late of Franklin Co., Va., dec'd. J. Woods atty in fact for Joel Shrewsbury, guardian of Josiah W. and Robt. N. Dickenson, two of the orphans of John Dickenson, late of Franklin Co. Va. J. Woods, atty in fact for John Clay, in right of his wife Eliz. one of the heirs of John Dickenson. J. Woods of Elbert Co., one of the legatees. Joab Early, atty in fact for Samuel Hairston, guardian of the heirs of John Woods, late of Franklin Co., Va. Joab Early, atty in fact for Francis Hill.

Page 340-46—Returns for 1811 shows William Woods, surviving, copartner of the firm of M. & W. Woods. Robert Woods, Sr. signs for himself and as atty in fact for Joel Shrewsbury, guardian of Josiah W. and Robt. N. Dickenson, for John Clay in right of his wife, for Wm. A. Burwell, guardian of Bailey Woods, all signed by him in Elbert Co., and receipt of Wm. A. Burwell in Elbert Co. Joseph Hale signs in Elbert Co., as guardian of John Woods one of the minors of Hugh Woods, dec'd., and as atty in fact for Jehu Hale, in right of his wife, Dec. 18, 1811. Josiah W. Dickenson signs for his legacy in Elbert Co. Mar. 28, 1812 showing he was of age, also as atty in fact for Joel Shrewsbury guardian of Robt. N. Dickenson, for John Clay in right of his wife, Dec. 28, 1812.

WOOLRIDGE, WILLIAM—Page 171—Return of Gibson Wooldridge, Excr. for 1811, shows notes etc returned to me by Absolom Davis, guardian of the heirs of Joseph T. Davis. Receipt of Barnett Jeter, guard. of Thomas W. Davis, his distributive share of said estate, Feb. 24, 1810.

Page 314—Returns for 1811 shows receipts of Thos. Wooldridge to Alex. Noble for slippers etc, for Sarah Davis, and Absolom Davis, guardian for the heirs of Joseph T. Davis.

WHITE, SHELTON—Page 328—Pleasant Gray bound to him to learn farming. Wm. O. Robbins, Security, May 4, 1812.

WHITMAN, WILLIAM—Page 316—dec'd. Returns for 1812 by Elizabeth Whitman, Admr. and Excr. also.

WILKINS, JOHN—Page 43—dec'd. Inventory July 1, 1809. Geo. Wych, E. Buckles and Js. Butler, appraisers. Thos. Wilkins, Admr.

WOODS, JOHN—Page 62—dec'd. James Wood, Admr. Returns Mar. Term 1808, shows paid Archelaus Moon for boarding and clothing for Elizabeth and Sarah Wood, orphans of said dec'd. James Wood, guardian. Paid Johathan Cooper and Alex. McMorris tuition. Paid the widow her dower, besides her third in 105 acres on Fork creek.

Page 311-313—Returns for 1811, made Mar. 2, 1812 show paid Archelaus Moon for clothes and board of Elizabeth and Sarah Wood, paid Archelaus Moon the full part of the widows dower of the sale of 105 acres of land Nov. 4, 1811. Signed James Wood, Admr, and guardian.

RETURNS OF ADMINISTRATORS & GUARDIANS

WILL BOOK "K" 1812-16

ALEXANDER, WILLIAM—Page 20-22—Est. Returns for 1812, shows receipts of Standley Jones, John, George and Nancy Alexander, William Page, Willis Rucker, Barden Rucker, and Reuben Cleveland, legatees.

Page 92—Returns for 1813 shows receipt of James Alexander, legatee.

Page 204—Returns up to Sept. 1815. Receipt of Edmund Alexander in full of all claims. Peter Alexander a legatee also.

ALEXANDER, GEORGE—Page 46—Returns of William Alexander, Admr, for 1812, 1813, shows paid Lucy Alexander.

Page 103—Returns for 1813-14, shows Mourning Alexander's receipt in full of her part. Wm. and Mary Alexander, Admrs.

Page 197—Returns for 1815, William Alexander, Admr, shows receipt of William Glenn "in consequence of my part of the est.

ARNOLD, WILLIAM—Page 46—dec'd. Returns for 1813 shows "Mayfield Bell, Excr. in right of his wife Nancy Bell, formerly Nancy Arnold, Excr. of will of William Arnold, dec'd." He pays to Richard Fortson, James Arnold, James Jones, and Philip Johnson, $1.00 each "a legacy left to each in the will."

ALLEN, ASA—Page 52—Guardian of Mary D. and Virginia Hudson, shows paid Edward Carrell for their maintenance for 1810. Apr. 8, 1811. Asa turns over legacy of Virginia to Carrell "now guardian."

ADAMS, HENRY—Page 91—Guardian of Edward, Patsy, and James Bevill, receipt for money signed 1813.

BAILEY, EZEKIAH—Page 6—dec'd. Bond as Admx. of Rebecca Bailey, Samuel N. Bailey and Joshua Clark, Security Nov. 2, 1812.

BURTON, THOMAS—Page 86—dec'd. Division of salves to legatees May 2, 1814. John, Mary, Thomas Burton, Robt. Tucker, Elizabeth Burton, Richard Clark, heirs of A. Burton, dec'd., Richard Burton, John Westbrook, Thomas Hudson. John and Thos. Burton Admrs.

BURTON, ABRAHAM, Jr.—Pgae 47—Inventory Mar. 9, 1813 by Gilliam Hudson and Arthur Jones. John Burton, Admr.

BURTON, THOMAS—Page 102—Guardian of Richard Burton, minor, return for 1813, received of the estate a certain slave.

BURTON, BARSHEBA, Mrs.—Page 139—Guardian of Elizabeth and Rhody Burton, minor heirs of Abraham Burton, Jr. dec'd. Returns for 1814 shows expense of board and clothes and tuition.

BURTON, ABRAHAM, Jr.—Page 159—dec'd. John and Bethsheba Burton, Admrs. Returns for 1814, shows bill for making coffin.

BARRON, WILLIAM—Page 59—dec'd. David Barron, Admr. Returns for 1812 shows paid for letters of administration.
Page 193—Returns made July 1815 shows, By Richard Easter Dep. Paymaster, part of the wages of the dec'd, as a soldier of the U. S., $33.00.

BARNES, CORDAL—Page 174—dec'd. Returns for 1815, show receipt of Priscilla Barnes "in part of my distributive share". Henry Kinnebrew, Admr.

BROWN, ROBERT—Page 68-69—dec'd. Returns of Abraham Brown, Admr. for 1812-13, shows receipts of John Barger for the full sum acoming to my wife Peggy of her fathers estate; of Silas White for his wife Elizabeth's part and of Joel Maxwell for his and his wife's part of her fathers estate.
Returns of Abraham Brown, guardian of Sally and Ann Brown, orphans of Robert Brown, dec'd, shows receipt May 9, 1812 from William Rice in full "for my wife Sally's part of her fathers estate."
Page 128—Returns of Abraham Brown, guardian of Robt. and Ann Brown, minors returns for 1814 shows received of Admr, of Robt. Brown, dec'd. the distributive share of said minors.
Ann Brown's receipt in full for her share "of my fathers est. May 20, 1814."
Page 269—Shows returns for Robert 1814.
Page 127—Returns for 1810 shows Catharine Brown former guardian of Robert Brown, minor, now Catharine Stubblefield.

BOOTH, JOHN—Page 92—dec'd. David S. Booth, Admr. Returns for 1811 shows receipt of Tarlton Shoemaker for "my wife Bellender Ann Shoemaker's part as a legal legatee", daughter of said dec'd." Final receipt Oct. 1812.

BOOTH, GEORGE—Page 133—Guardian of William Booth, minor. Returns 1813-14 shows spelling book and history bought and tuition paid Murrell Pledger.

BOOTH, GABRIEL—Page 272—Guardian of Joel Booth. Returns for 1815 shows tuition paid Murrell Pledger.

BOOTH, NATHANIEL—Page 93-94—dec'd. Inventory Mar. 20, 1813. Austin Webb, Isham Parham, and Sherod Morris, appraisers. David S. Booth, Admr.

Page 95—Sale Apr. 2, 1813 shows Elizabeth Booth, wid., George, Nathaniel, Jr., Robert, D. S., Elizabeth J., and Gabriel Booth purchasers.
Page 276-278—Returns for 1816 shows receipts of Eliz. Booth, wid., and as guardian of Sarah Booth, minor; Robert Booth, George Booth and as guardian of Wm. Booth, Gabriel Booth and as guardian of Joel Booth, John Booth, Nathaniel Booth, Nancy Booth, John Hanna for his wife Elizabeth's part, Joel Faulkner for his wife Polly's part, Thomas Moore for his wife Judith's part, Joseph Murphy of Giles Co. Tenn. for his wife Fanny's part.

BURDEN, EDMOND—Page 122—dec'd. Inventory Dec. 25, 1811. Thomas Penn, Robert Kennedy, Thomas Horton, Abraham Brown, and John Colat, appraisers.

Page 205—Returns for 1815 shows paid for recording inventory and an agreement between Archibald Newbourn, Admr, and Hannah Burden.

Page 210—Returns for 1815 shows account of sales, "Mrs. Sally Bearden debtor to A. Newborn, Admr, of E. Burden, dec'd. for furniture etc bought.

BROWN, JACOB—Page 177—dec'd. James N. Brown, Admr. Returns for 1815, shows receipt of Mary S. Brown in part of her legacy. also Benjamin Brown, Henry Brawner, William Kerlin, Ephraim Godan (Gordan?) Henry P. Brawner, Leucy Brown, John Brawner, James Brown, legatees.

BROWN, EDWARD—Page 260—Guardian of Emily Schofield and Benjamin Ford "on account of his wife formerly Eliza Schofield, orphan of Robert Schofield, dec'd., returns for 1815 shows paid for one shawl for E. Ford and paid Benjamin Ford. Affidavit signed by Edward Brown Jan. Term 1816 as guardian of Benjamin Ford and Emily Schofield".

BELL, JAMES—Page 314—dec'd. Returns of Joseph Bell, Ecxr. for 1816 shows receipt of Harmon Lovingood for $200.00 "which he left his daughter Patsy Bell, which is now Patsy Lovingood.

CARTER, JAMES—Page 54—Guardian of Thomas P. Carter, Returns for 1813 shows board and tuition paid Beckmam Dye.

Page 118—Returns for 1813 and 1814 shows hire of a negro Squire, board and tuition.

Page 223—Returns for 1815 shows man's saddle bought for ward.

CARTER, THOMAS—Page 104—dec'd. Returns of Admrs. Thomas S., and Chas. Carter for 1812 shows "Interest on James and Thos. S. Carter's notes given for his purchase of the real estate, interest on George Carter's note, and receipt of Geo. Cook, atty at law for caveat of heirs of Thomas Carter vs James Carter.

CHILDS, NATHAN—Page 89—dec'd. Returns for Littleton Johnson, Admr. shows paid expense of a re-survey of 275 acres land in Wilkes Co., 1812 by consent of legatees.

CHRISTIAN, PRESSLEY—Page 173—Guardian of Eppy White. Returns 1807-1812, shows tuition paid James Upshaw 1809.

CLARK, ZACHARIAH—Page 19—dec'd. James Morrison, Admr. shows receipt of Planters Mercantile Co. of Petersburg by Amos Baker, Clerk, receipt to Admr. for salt for Mrs. Abigail P. Clark, the widow Jan. 1, 1812.
Page 58—Returns for 1812 shows Mrs. Abigail P. Clark rented the plantation and slaves, and a receipt of John Burton, clerk at Planters Mercantile Co.
Page 167—Returns for 1814 shows receipt of Chas. Gunter to James Morrison, Admr., Zachariah Clark, guardian of Davis Jones for tuition.

COOK, JOSEPH—Page 193—dec'd. Inventory Jan. 30, 1816. Nathaniel Hudson, Samuel McGehee and Jesse O. Tait, appraisers. Shows French and Latin grammar, dictionaries, book-keepers assistant, Greek testament, brace of pistols, saddle bags etc. and various notes.

CRAWFORD, JOHN—Page 312—dec'd. Returns of John Craft, Excr., for 1816, shows wages of said Crawford while in the service of the U. S. as per discharge, $19.37¼.

CUNNINGHAM, WILLIAM, Jr.—Page 118—dec'd. Inventory Aug. 3, 1814 shows only horse, saddle and bridle appraised at $40.00 by Thomas Tate, Henry Adams and Enos Tate, Jr.

DEADWILER, MARTIN—Page 34—dec'd. Joseph Deadwiler, Excr. Returns for 1811 shows receipts of Jeremiah Shewmaker and wife Nancy, Isaac Mobley and wife Frances, Abel Howell and wife Anna, Barrett Ford and wife Barbary "in full of our part of said estate."

DYE, BECKHAM—Page 180—dec'd. Durrett Stodgill, Admr. Returns for 1814 show paid for temporary letters of administration.

ELLIOTT, JAMES—Page 224—dec'd. William Dunlap, Admr. To cash in hand $50.00. Draft on United States $87.10.
Fort Hawkins, Ga.
I do certify on honor that James Elliott, a dec'd, Serjeant of my company, dec'd on the 20th. of Sept. 1814 at Camp Huger, Ga., was enlisted by myself for the period of five years from the 18th, of July 1812 to the 17th, of July 1817, has received all pay, Bounty, clothing and subsistence he was entitled to, and is entitled to such bounty of land as the law allows. Signed Duplicates. William Chisholm, Capt. 7th, Infantry.
Returns for 1815, show paid for pork etc, for the widow and orphans.
Page 235—Inventory and sale Oct. 15, 1815, shows household goods only, bought in principally by Sharlot Elliott.

FANNIN, WILLIAM—Page 119—dec'd. Inventory Aug. 13, 1814. Ephraim Moss, Adam Gaar, and Joseph Henderson, Appraisers. shows only sorrel mare, saddle and blanket, cow and calf, note on John H. Fannin.

FAULKNER, JAMES—Page 116—dec'd. John Faulkner, Excr. Returns for 1814 shows expense of board and clothes kept in hands of Excr., for John and James Faulkner minor heirs from Aug. 1809 to Aug. 1813.

FORD, JOHN—Page 235—dec'd. Inventory Sept. 1, 1815. Adam Gaar, Jeremiah Thornton and Edward Herndon, Appraisers. Shows money due estate by Abraham Moss awarded by arbitration.

FORTSON, JESSE—Page 66—Guardian of Asa White, receipt of said Asa in full for his distributive share of the estate of his father, Daniel White, dec'd. Feb. 3, 1814.

FREEMAN, JAMES—Page 228-231—John Simmons, Excr. Returns show receipt of Wiat Cleveland in full as legatee, July 2, 1814. Mary Wheeler and Ignatius Percel, also.

GLENN, SIMEON—Page 172—dec'd. Receipt of James Gray, guardian of Simeon Rogers to James and William Glenn, Excrs, of Simeon Glenn, formerly guardian of Simeon Rogers for all said minors distributive share. Dec. 28, 1814.
Page 299—Returns of Excrs. for 1815 show receipt of Dr. John Nickols for services in last illness of said dec'd.

GRAY, JAMES—Page 166—Return as guardian of Simeon Rogers for 1814, show paid for letters of guardianship.

GREGG, THOMAS—Page 13—dec'd. Howard Cash, Admr. Returns show receipt Jan. 6, 1812 for recording.

GREGG, POLLY, KEZIAH & ANN—Page 61—Orphans of Thomas Gregg, dec'd. Howard Cash, guardian, returns for 1812.
Page 260—Returns for 1815 the same.

GRIFFITH, JOHN—Page 271—dec'd. Robert Griffith, Admr. Returns show recept of William L. Griffith in full for his share Feb. 6, 1816.

GRAY, JAMES and Simeon Rogers—Page 131-132—Division of slaves belonging to them, James Gray in right of his wife Susannah, formerly Susannah Rogers, agreeable to an order of court May Term 1814. Receipt of James Gray to Simeon Glenn, guardian of Simeon and Susannah Rogers for his part of slaves in full May 12, 1814.

HALL, WILLIAM—Page 39—dec'd. William Head, Admr. Inventory Jan. 1, 1813. Edward Brown, John Rowsey and William Suttle, Appraisers.

HAYNES, MOSES—Page 272—Guardian for minors of Thomas Scales, dec'd. Returns for 1815 shows merchandise bought for Benjamin, Elijah and Nathaniel Scales, minors.

HEARD, STEPHEN—Page 305—dec'd. Inventory July 13, 1816. John A. Heard, Admr. Barnet Jeter, Richard Colbert, Joseph Christler, and James Clark, Appraisers.

HENDRICKS, ABIJAH—Page 9—dec'd. Elijah Hendricks, Admr. Returns for 1812 show receipt of Enoch, James and Cammel Hendrick in full of all demands.

HENDRICKS, NELSON—Page 10—Bound to Elijah Hendricks Sept. 7, 1812 to learn the art of farming. Jacob Coker, Security.

HIGGINBOTHAM, JOHN S.—Page 39—Guardian for Larkin Higginbotham. Returns for 1812 shows note on Benj. G. Higginbotham, Francis Satterwhite and B. C. Higginbotham, Security.

HIGGINS, RICHARD—Page 284—dec'd. Inventory Apr. 23, 1816. William Burden, James Horton and Jesse Ginn, Appraisers, a few household goods.

JARRATT, ARCHELUS—Page 22—Guardian of Thomas Andrew. Shows paid John Andrew board 1812, also John's receipt for slaves and 300 acres land on Newport river, Liberty Co., in full of all legacies of said Thomas Andrew.

JONES, ARTHUR—Page 36—Guardian of Davis Jones, and Excr of Nathan Jones, dec'd., receives from Zachariah Clark legacy of Davis Jones Sept. 7, 1808. Returns 1813.

JONES, JAMES—Page 72—dec'd. Standley and George Jones, Admrs., pay to William Jones, minor son of said dec'd, his full legacy, Feb. 19, 1814.

JOHNSTON, PHILIP—Page 121—dec'd. Inventory Aug. 6, 1814. Barnett Jeter, Larkin Johnston and Standley Jones, Appraisers.

Page 264—Sale Sept. 3, 1814, Susannah Johnston bought most of the household goods.

KIDD, WEBB—Page 160—dec'd. William, Martin and John W. Kidd, Excrs. Returns for 1814 shows sale of 205 acres land on Vanns creek, and 202½ acres in Wilkinson Co. Receipts of Wm. Greenwood and Polly R. Harper for part of their legacies, Feb. 6, 1814.

Page 244—Receipts of Webb Kidd, Polly R. Harper and William W. Harper for part of their legacies, Jan. 2, 1816.

KING, ELISHA—Page 33—dec'd. Sale May 8, 1812, William King and James Mills, Admrs.

McCUNE, WILLIAM—Page 292—dec'd. Returns of Thomas B. McCune, Admr. for 1805, shows paid board and clothing for Wm. S. McCune, minor of said dec'd., tuition to Wiley Ferrel. Expense of Admr. riding to Ky. to bring two horses belonging to the estate.

McELROY, HENRY—Page 192—dec'd. Returns of Pellatia McElroy, Excx, and James McElroy, Excr., pay to John McElroy, son and heir his legacy Oct. 7, 1814.

Page 299—Returns for 1815-16 shows receipts from Littleberry Broach of Madison Co., in right of his wife Sarah, formerly Sarah McElroy; from Edward McElroy for legacy left to Polly McElroy wife of said Edward. James and Pelatia McElroy, Excrs.

MIDDLETON, ROBERT—Page 274—dec'd. Inventory by William Woods and Caleb Tate under temporary letters of administration, Jan. 9, 1816.

Receipt of Joseph Blackwell for Betcy C. Middleton for notes and money found in the secretary.

MOON, ARCHELAUS—Page 103—Guardian of Elizabeth and Sarah Wood, orphans of John Wood. Returns 1814 shows paid board, clothes and tuition, and receipt for their legacy to James Wood, former Admr. and gdn.
Page 296—Returns for 1816 the same.

MOON, WILLIAM—Page 66—dec'd. Returns of William H. Moon one of the Excrs. shows receipt of William Moon for part of his legacy, July 18, 1812. Page 313—Returns Nov. Term 1816, show receipt of B. Moon, Nov. 15, 1814, Jacob Moon, Bird Moon, John Moon, Nov. 9, 1814 one share. John Moon, William Power, A. Moon, David Power, William Moon, Bird Moon, Nov. 9, 1814. Martha and John Blake received of Sarah Moon. All legatees.

NAPIER, RENE—Page 19—dec'd. Returns of James Morrison, Excr. for 1813 shows receipt of Edward Lyon for Mrs. Napier's yearly legacy.

NELLEMS, WILLIAM—Page 274—dec'd. Inventory Feb. 7, 1816. R. Banks, James Rowsey and John Ashley, Appraisers.
Page 295—Sale June 1, 1816, Polly and Nathaniel Nelms principal purchasers. Thomas Hansard and Nathaniel Nelms, Admrs.

PATTERSON, JOHN—Page 227—dec'd. Returns of William Patterson, Admr. for 1815 shows, Sept. 22, 1815 To cash received of Lieut. Easter paymaster 8th Infantry U. S. Balance of his pay as a private Capt. Jones Company $63.25.

PHIPPS, LEWIS—Page 59—Guardian of John and James Faulkner, minors of James Faulkner, dec'd. Returns 1814 show rent of plantation and hire of negro girl.

POWELL, HONORIA—Page 185—dec'd. Inventory Apr. 13, 1814 shows only 50 acres of land on Cedar creek. Wm. R. Powel, Admr.

RAGLAND, EVAN—Page 81—dec'd. Inventory Feb. 11, 1814. Isham Morgan Thos. Burton and E. Brewer, Appraisers.
Page 150—Sale and returns for 1814, Thompson Ragland, Admr., shows Hudson Ragland purchaser and expense of clothes for James and Evan Ragland, minors of the dec'd.
Page 240—Shows tuition for James Ragland, minor for 1814.

RICH, JOHN—Page 147—dec'd. Inventory Nov. 29, 1814. Geo. Snellings, James Morrison and Arthur Jones, Appraisers.
Page 178—Returns for 1814, William Rich, Excr.
Page 221—Returns for 1814 shows paid for probate of will, William Rich, Excr. Mary Rich, Excx.

RUCKER, AZMON—Page 26—dec'd. Inventory Jan. 10, 1812. Joel Doss, Larkin Clark and John Mann, Appraisers.

Page 40—Sale, James and John Rucker, Jr., purchasers.
Page 56—Returns 1811-1813 shows James Hamilton, Admr.

SALE, CORNELIUS—Page 226—dec'd. Joseph Sale, Admr. Returns for 1815. No data.

SMITH, JOHN—Page 279—dec'd. Returns of Robert Kennedy, Admr. for 1815.

STOKES, THOMAS—Page 181—Archebald Stokes, Excr. Returns for 1815.

STOVALL, GEORGE—Page 36—Guardian of William, Lindsay, Yancy, James and Martha Johnston, minors of Thomas Johnston. Returns for 1812.
Page 113—Same as above except they are called minors of Mary Johnston, dec'd. Returns 1813.

STUBBLEFIELD, CATHARINE—Page 67—Guardian of John Brown. Returns for 1813 shows his receipt in full for his part of his fathers estate.
Page 129—Ditto, guardian of Robert Brown, minor. Returns 1810-1812. No data.

TAIT, JAMES—Page 4—Est. Chas. Tait, Excr. Returns for 1811 show receipt of John Wilson for his part of land sold in Franklin Co., in right of his wife.

TAIT, WILLIAM—Page 175—Est. William Tait, Excr. Returns shows receipts of John and James Tait and Lucy Tait for their legacies.

THORNTON, REUBEN—Page 47—dec'd. Beverly Allen, Excr. Returns for 1813.

THOMPSON, ISHAM—Page 315—dec'd. Receipts of G. Walthall, Jr., guardian of Isham Thompson, June 18, 1799; of Tryon Harris, guardian of Sally Thompson, Dec. 29, 1798 and 1802; of M. Woods as guardian of Wiley Thompson, Aug. 9, 1799; of Wiley Thompson, Jan. 14, 1803; of Lewis Mosely, guardian of Patsy Thompson, minor Oct. 1, 1799; of John Alexander for his wife's part Tabitha, daughter of said dec'd. Dec. 10, 1806; of Tyron Harris for his wife's part, Sept. 26, 1808; of Jency E. Thompson, heir of said father, Sept. 19, 1815. George Cook and Elizabeth Cook, Admrs.

TURMAN, ROBERT—Page 8—dec'd. William Hatcher, appointed Admr. Caleb Tait, Security Oct. 23, 1812.

TURNER, SALLY—Page 114—Guardian of Thomas and Elizabeth M. Turner, orphans of Martin Turner, dec'd. Returns show clothes and board for 1813-14, tuition paid to James J. Banks and James Adams.

TYLER, HENRY—Page 76—dec'd. Inventory May 11, 1813. William White Duncan McMartin and Samuel Crow, Appraisers.
Page 179—Returns for 1813 show Moses Haynes, Admr. For 1814 shows Moses Haynes and Reuben L. Tyler, Admrs. Mar. 8 1815 shows Anne Tyler Admx, with the above.

WALTHALL, GARRARD, Sr.—Page 17—dec'd. Returns for 1813 shows Mayfield Bell to hire of a slave and board and clothes for two minors William and Singleton Walthall. Thomas B. Creagh in right of his wife, and Edward Walthall vs. William Allen, Admr.

Page 105—Returns for 1813 show board and clothes for William Walthall and receipt of Singleton Walthall for eight slaves "in full of all demands against William Allen, Admr. or gdn. for me.

WALTHALL, SUSANNA—Page 254—dec'd. Returns of Beverly Allen, Excr, shows receipt of Singleton Walthall for twenty three slaves "in full of my legacy."

Page 264—Dec. 29, 1815 Inventory of above slaves.

WHITE, DANIEL—Page 90—dec'd. Returns of William Davis, Excr. for 1812, shows receipt "in full of a settlement from Stephen Morgan, Martin White, guardian of John White, minor, Isaac Christian, Jesse Fortson, guardian of Asa White, P. Christian.

WEBB, CLAIBORN—Page 74—dec'd. Inventory Dec. 1, 1813, shows "tract of land home house," mill tract, tract in Wilkinson Co., several slaves, household goods, etc. Hezekiah Gray, James N. Brown and James Oliver, Appraisers.

Page 165—Returns for 1813-15, show Margaret and John C. Webb, Admrs, Margaret having rented the home plantation and mill, and the slaves Nancy, Silvy, Sally, Sam, Stephen and Frank, and John C. Webb rented the mill tract. Also a receipt from J. V. Harris for getting Mrs. Webb appointed guardian of the orphans.

Page 236-38—Division of slaves of est. Hezekiah Gray, Nicholas M. Marks and Archelus Jarrett, Commissioners.

To Margaret Webb, Nancy and Milly, To Bridger Webb, Stephen, To William Webb, Maria, To Milton Pope Webb, Silva and Jack, To Abner Webb, Sam, To Martha Webb, Granville and Hamilton, To Evelina Webb, Frank, To Elijah Webb, Sally, To Joseph Glenn, Malinda. Nov. 27, 1815

Page 259—Returns of Margaret Webb, guardian of minors, William, Milton P., Claiborn, Abner, Evelina, Martha, and Elijah Webb, returns for 1815.

WILKINS, JOHN—Page 5—dec'd. Thomas Wilkins, Admr., Shows receipt of Francis Wilkins for his part of said estate "it being one-fourth" Sept. 7, 1812.

WILLIAMS, JOSEPH—Page 253—dec'd. "Matthew J. Williams, Admr, for the estate of his son Joseph Williams". Waddy Tate signs a receipt at Petersburg, Apr. 12, 1811. Tate was a physician. Affidavit of Admr, signed Jan. 23, 1816.

WOODS, MIDDLETON—Page 35—Est. William Woods, Excr. receipt of Hugh Martin of Oglethorpe Co. in right of his wife, Aug. 28, 1812.

Page 87—Returns for 1813 show receipts as follows: Jehu Hale in right of his wife, Elbert Co. Feb. 19, 1813; Robert Woods, Jr. in right of his wife; Robert T. Woods, atty in fact for Josiah W., and Robert N.

Dickenson, and for John Clay in right of his wife, and for Samuel Hairston, guardian of heirs of John Woods, dec'd, dated Augusta, Ga. Sept. 3, 1813; Hugh Martin in right of his wife, Elbert Co. Ga. Nov. 15, 1813.
  Page 184—Returns show receipt of Robert Woods, Sr. legatee, Elbert Co., Aug. 12, 1814.
  Page 280—Returns show receipts of Francis Hill in right of his wife, J. Woods, Robert T. Woods atty for Samuel Hairston, guardian, John Woods, and Bailey M. Woods, legatees all signed in 1815.

WOODS, ANDREW—Page 296—Est. Robert and Ann Woods and James Ewing, Admrs. Returns for 1814-15. No data.

WOODS, WILLIAM—Page 282—Guardian of James O., and Evan Ragland, minors of Evan Ragland, dec'd. Returns for 1815 show board, clothes and tuition paid David Holt for both.

WYNN, JOHN—Page 57—Guardian of Ann W. Childs. Returns for 1813, shows three years tuition, board and clothes, to George Wynne and Edward Watkins for six months.

RETURNS OF ADMINISTRATORS AND GUARDIANS
WILL BOOK "L"

ALEXANDER, GEORGE—Page 185—Estate. William Alexander, Admr. Receipts Feb. 3, 1818 of James B. Alexander and William Glenn, Aug. 16, 1817 for part of their legacies.

BARNES, CORDIAL—Page 6—Estate. Returns for 1816 show receipts of Priscilla Barnes for herself and as guardian of Henry and John Barnes, minors and Henry P. Brawner in right of his wife. Henry Kinnebrew, Admr.
  Page 69—Returns for 1816 show tuition paid for John and Henry.
  Page 160—Returns for 1818 show paid Dennis Tippin and Mede LeSeure tuition for both boys.
  Page 284—Returns for 1819 show paid William Therlkill tuition for John Barnes.
  Page 374—Returns for 1819 show tuition and board for both.

BELL, JAMES—Page 136—Estate. Returns for 1818 show receipts of William and James Bell, and Harmon Lovingood for his wife Martha Bell's share.
  Page 390—Receipt of Thomas Bell, Jr. for his legacy 1819.

BELL, JOSEPH—Page 383—Est. Returns for 1819 show receipt of Burrell Dye for bed etc. left daughter Elizabeth Bell, now Elizabeth Dye, and tuition paid McCarty Oliver.
  Page 436—Returns for 1821, show receipt of John Gunter "which was left his daughter Rebecca Gunter".

BOOTH, GEORGE—Page 15—Guardian of William Booth, minor. Returns for 1815 show tuition paid Fedrick Hicks.

BOOTH, GABRIEL—Page 68—Guardian of Joel Booth, orphan of Nathaniel Booth. Returns for 1817 tax paid.

BRADLEY, WILLIAM—Page 161—Est. Returns for 1817 show articles bought for widow Elizabeth and receipt of Thomas Johnston for his legacy.
Page 178—Shows trips to Putnam and Jackson counties on business for the estate.
Page 227—Cash received of Sheriff of Putnam Co., above the settlement of a suit of Wm. Upshaw vs. Excrs of estate.
Page 260—Returns of Thomas Oglesby one of the Excrs, up to Mar. 1819 shows he retained $100.00 for the support of Eliz. Bradley for the last ten years "who is the widow and relict of said dec'd."

BREWER, Dr. JOHN H.—Page 139—Est. Receipt of Archelaus Jarratt in right of his wife Frances C. M. Jarrett, lately Frances C. M. Brewer, widow of said dec'd, all the property that was devised to his wife. Abner McGehee, Excr. Nov. 17, 1815.

BROWN, EDWARD—Page 19—Guardian of Benjamin Ford and Emily Schofield, returns for 1816 show goods bought.
Page 115—Returns for 1817 shows they held their own plantation and no rent received, called orphans of Robert Schofield, dec'd.
Page 241—Returns for 1818 show paid for cow for the use of Emily Schofield and Eliza Ford.
Page 356—Returns for 1820 says "Return of Edward Brown late guardian for two of minor heirs of Robert Schofield, dec'd, viz; Eliza and Emily, daughters of said Robert". Receipts of Eliza Ford, formerly Eliza Schofield for rent for herself and for her sister Emila Cook, formerly Emila Schofield, and from from Fenton Cook for his wife Emily Cook, their legacies in full,. Legatees of Robt. Schofield, dec'd.

BROWN, ABRAHAM—Page 149—Guardian of Robert Brown, minor of Robt. Brown, dec'd. Returns for 1817 shows bought a saddle for ward.
Page 383—Final returns May 1820 shows receipt of Robt. Brown in full of his legacy.

BURDEN, EDMOND—Page 201—dec'd. Returns for 1818 show receipt of Henry Burden in full of his legacy. Archibald Mewbourn, Admr. Mewbourn as guardian of John Nelson Burden says a certain sum of money being John's distributive share.

BURTON, ABRAHAM, Sr.—Page 5—Est. Returns for 1815 show receipts of Thos. Beville, William Beville, Nancy Beville, Peter Beville, Hudson Prince and Henry Adams for himself and as guardian for minors of the estate. John Burton, Admr.
Page 34—Returns of John and Thomas Burton, Admrs. de bonis non for 1816, shows receipts of John Beville for part of his legacy.

Page 122—Returns for 1817 show receipts in full, as legatees, of Samuel Snelling, Richard Burton, and in part from Robert Tucker and Thomas Hudson by Robt. Tucker. Also Abraham and Nicholas Goode, legatees in full and of Mary Burton for $40.00

Page 314—Returns for 1818 show receipt of Ba Burton in full as legatee.

BURTON, ABRAHAM, Jr.—Page 33—John Burton, Admr. Bathshaba Burton, Admx. Returns for 1816 shows receipt of latter for a sum of money.

Page 311—Returns for 1819 show receipts of Bathsheba Burton for herself as heir and guardian of said estate.

Page 418—Returns for 1819 show receipts as above, and to George W. Heard for medical services.

BURTON, BETHSHEBA—Page 100—Guardian of Elizabeth Hudson Burton and Rhoda H. Burton, minors of Abraham Burton, dec'd. Returns for 1816 her receipts for board and clothes, and Richard Burton's receipt for tuition.

Page 316—Returns 1818, show receipt of William Dunlap for tuition for both minors.

BURTON, GERMAN—Page 402—dec'd. Return of sale of real estate sold to Thomas Walker, Feb. 1, 1820, 202½ acres. Blackman Burton, Admr.

BURTON, THOMAS—Page 31—Est. Returns for 1817 shows the sale of the old plantation to John Burton, the Warhatchee tract to Richard Burton, and receipt of Archer Burton for a bond, called Thos. W. Burton in one place. John and Thos. Burton, Admrs.

Page 315—Returns of John Burton, Admr., shows receipt of Bethsheba Burton as heir and guardian. Mary Burton, Richard Burton, Samuel Snellings, Thomas Hudson, distributees. John and Thomas Burton, Admrs.

Page 56—Receipt in full of Richard Burton to Thomas Burton, "as guardian for me". Mar. 3, 1817.

BOND, NATHAN—Page 325—Est. Receipt of Elizabeth Bond sole legatee to Richard Bond, Excr. July 8, 1817.

BLACKWELL, DUNSTON—Page 354—Guardian of Nancy P., and James L. Middleton. Returns 1820 shows paid Dr. David A. Reese, Dr. J. O. Boucher and Dr. H. Bourne.

BOOTH, JOHN—Page 441—Est. David S. Booth, Admr. Returns for 1822 show receipts of Prudence Booth for her share, received when due, receipt Feb. 17, 1819; of John Booth, signed Dec. 27, 1808; of John Webb as a legatee in right of his wife Barbara, Feb. 10, 1810; of Burrell Webb "in full of all demands", Jan. 4, 1811; of T. W. Booth, by his brother John Booth, Fayetteville, Tenn. Jan. 23, 1819; of Johnston Hicks in full of his wife Patsy's share.

BELL, JOSEPH—Page 383—Est. Returns for 1819, shows receipt of Burrel Dye for his wife Elizabeth Bell, now Elizabeth Dye for her part of her fathers estate.

CARTER, THOMAS—Page 330—Est. Thomas S. Carter, Admr. Returns for 1819 show receipt of J. V. Harris for defending case of Thomas Woods, guardian of John W. Carter vs Admrs. of Thomas Carter, dec'd. Feb. 5, 1819.

CLARK, CHRISTOPHER, Sr.—Page 373—Est. Returns of David Hudson, Sr. for 1819 shows receipt of James Herring, dated Petersburg for Willis Rucker's part of the cotton crop as overseer, and of Woodley & Bell, and Stokes & Sayre, "store keepers".

Page 437—Returns made July 1820, shows receipts of McCarty Oliver for tuition and board at Salem for Margaret Clark, minor; W. C. Davis for tuition and board for Margaret at Salem, and for books and tuition at a Latin School for William Clark; of Zachariah Rhodes for nine months schooling of three minors; of Thomas Childers and Thomas C. Elliott as overseers; of Jones & Juskup for harness; of James Dollar and Thomas W. Williams, blacksmiths work; of Miller & Hanks for making a coat for William Clark, dated at Petersburg Feb. 10, 1821; of Lucy Hudson for making three pairs of shoes; of Wm. Jamison for nineteen months schooling; of Rebecca Clark for three shares of the cotton crop of 1820.

CLARK, ZACHARIAH—Page 55—Est. Returns of Major James Morrison, Admr. Returns for 1816 shows receipts of William Baird for hats; of Bird Saffold for medical services; of Argal Norman and Archd. Stokes for shoes; of William Chisholm for silk for Susanna Clark, minor; of William Colbert for a slave Dolly "my part of the personal property of said estate in my wife's right", and receipt for board for Susannah and Zachariah Clark, minors; of Arthur Jones guardian of Davis Jones for part of the interest of the bond of Zachariah Clark, dec'd., guardian for Davis Jones, minor of Nathan Jones, dec'd.

Page 119—Returns for 1817, shows receipt of William Colbert for board for Susannah A., and Zachariah H. Clark, "minors of said dec'd.

Page 271—Returns for 1818, shows receipt of Alphus Baker for tuition, and William Colbert for board and clothes for above minors.

Page 355—Returns for 1819 shows board for both to William Colbert and spelling books bought for both of Shaler Hillyer.

CARTER, JAMES—Page 159—Guardian of Thomas Paine Carter. Returns show receipt in full of Thomas P. Carter, Oct. 7, 1817

COLBERT, RICHARD—Page 422—dec'd. Inventory Jan. 6, 1821. Barnett Jeter, Joseph L. Chrystler, and Benajah Bibb, Appraisers.

COOK, JOSEPH—Page 106—Est. Thomas Jones, Admr. Paid for letters of administration etc. Nov. 6, 1815.

COOK, WILLIAM T.—Page 170—dec'd. Inventory Jan. 17, 1818 Absolom Stinchcomb, James Christian and David S. Booth, Appraisers. Thomas Cook and Thomas Oliver, Admrs. Frances Cook, Admx.

CRUMP, CHARLES—Page 424—dec'd. Inventory July 20, 1821.

GEORGIA D. A. R.

CUNNINGHAM, JOHN—Page 102—Est. Returns of Gaines Thompson, Admr. Nov. Term 1817 no data.

DAVIS, ABSOLOM—Page 70—dec'd. Returns 1816-17. no data.

DEADWYLER, MARTIN—Page 114—Guardian of Nancy F. and Elizabeth P. Wilhite. Returns for 1817, shows ten months board for both, ferriage paid John Edwards.
Page 302—Returns for 1818 says "orphans of Philip Wilhite, dec'd". Shows receipts of Griffin & Montague for merchandise, morocco slippers, spider net, bonnets, shawls etc. Both debtors to guardian for bed and furniture, and Nancy F., for saddle.
Page 414—Returns for 1820 shows receipt of John B. Wilhite for distributive share of Elizabeth P. Wilhite and of Joseph Y. Wilhite for Nancy F. Wilhites share.

DOBBS, JOSIAH—Page 8—Est. John Dobbs, Admr. Returns for 1810-12-15. no data.
Page 264—Returns for 1818 shows settlement of lawsuit of John Beck & Co., for Robert S. Sayer, and Hugh McDonald vs. Luzanny Dobbs, Admx., and John Dobbs, Admr.

DOLLAR, HENRY—Page 430—dec'd. Inventory Mar. 14, 1821. Horatio J. Goss, John Skelton and Benjamin Bobo, Appraisers.

DUNLAP, WILLIAM—Page 18—Guardian of Hulday Jones. Returns for 1816 shows receipt of Joshua Merrell & Co., and of Jane Jones for board and clothes for Hulday.

DUSKIN, HANNAH—Page 309—dec'd. Inventory May 10, 1819. Jacob Higginbotham, Sr., Nathan Bond and John Maxwell, Appraisers. Shows only clothes and side saddle.

FAULKNER, JAMES—Page 98—Est. John Faulkner, Excr. of will. Returns for 1817 shows received of Forster Rowsey for articles bought at sale, and Benjamin Andrew for rent of land, both by the hands of George Oglesby. Isaac Suttles vs. John Faulkner, Excr., Lewis Phipps, Patsy Phipps, John Faulkner, James Faulkner. In equity for a specific performance. Judgement in Jasper Superior Court in favor of defendant, Isaac Suttles.

FAULKNER, JOHN—Page 189—dec'd. William Faulkner, Excr., shows paid James Huff for going to Wilkes Co., to get the Rev. William Davis to attend court and prove the will.
Page 326—Receipt of Sally Faulkner for all property belonging to the estate, agreeable to the will of dec'd. July 7, 1818.

FORD, JESSE—Page 9—dec'd. John Ford, Admr. Returns for 1816. "Aug. 2, 1816 Received of Major Joshua Clark, paymaster to Col. David S. Booth's Reg. of Ga. Militia the wages of said dec'd, as a soldier, $33.00". Receipts of Jesse Patterson and John Bramblett, in full of their part of said estate Aug. 24, 1816, $75.00 each.

GAINES, HIEROM—Page 28—Est. Returns for 1816 shows receipt of Ivy Seals, Samuel Adams, William Adams, and Isham Teasley for their part of two slaves, Ben and Nance. Receipt in full of Thomas Johnston and wife Margaret C. Johnston, formerly Margaret C. Gaines, daughter of said dec'd, their part in full. Receipt of James Adams, parent and natural guardian of John Adams, a minor for a slave Chas. left said minor in said will.

GAY, ANN—Page 429—dec'd. Inventory Mar. 10, 1821, household goods and several notes.

GLENN, SIMEON—Page 380—Est. Returns of James Glenn, one of the Excrs. shows receipt for two slaves Sam and Sally, $100.00 cash in place of a horse, bed etc, signed Chas. L. Smith in right of my wife formerly Martha T. Glenn, now Martha T. Smith. May 22, 1820.

GREGG, POLLY, Keziah and Anne—Page 234—Orphans of Thomas Gregg. Returns for 1815, Howard Cash, Sr., guardian and admr. shows receipt of Beck & Bowman for dry goods.
Page 375—Shows returns for 1820 no data.

GRIFFITH, JOHN—Page 79—Est. Returns for 1816 show receipts of John Griffith in full of his part.

HEARD, BARNARD C.—Page 86—Guardian of brother Thomas J. Heard, orphan of Stephen Heard, dec'd. Receipts for Latin grammar and of Beverly Martin for board for 1816.
Page 186—Returns for 1817 shows receipt of Barnard C. Heard guardian of Thos. J. Heard for property received of John A. Heard, Admr. of Stephen Heard, dec'd. viz; land and slaves Harry, Bill and Oliver; of William White for three months board; of David McDowel for tuition; of William Pringle for making a coat.
Page 332—Returns for 1819, receipt of William White for ten months board, and Jesse Whipple for dry goods.
Page 408—Returns for 1820 shows receipts of Tate & Verdell and Zachariah Bowman by John Beck for dry goods, J. & W. Clark and Miller & Hawk for goods. Receipt of Josiah Newton, Steward of Franklin College and of Moses Waddle for Asbury Hall, Treas. Board of Trustees, Ga. University for two quarters tuition, room rent and use of library.

HEARD, ELIZABETH—Page 187—Guardian of Sarah H. Heard one of the orphans of Stephen Heard. Returns for 1817-18 shows receipts of Beat. Thompson for first quarters board Powelton Acamedy, of A. Dugger for tuition, J or I Ingraham for tuition and music.
Page 406—Returns for 1819, no data.

HANSARD, SUSANNAH—Page 295—dec'd. Sale Mar. 7, 1818, Thomas S. Hansard, Admr. John, William and Thos. S. Hansard, purchasers.

HENDRICK, ELIJAH—Page 48-97—Admr. of Abijah Hendrick. for 1817. No data.

HIGGINBOTHAM, BENJAMIN—Page 105—Est. Returns of Thomas S. Carter, Admr. with the will annexed for 1817 shows receipts of, Benjamin, Peter, Larkin and William Higginbotham, and James Rowsey for their distributive shares.

HUDSON, DAVID, Jr.—Page 308—Guardian of Malinda and Mary Ann Oliver, orphans of William Oliver, dec'd, Returns for 1819.
Page 394—Returns for 1820, no data.

HUDSON, NATHANIEL—Page 226—dec'd. Inventory Jan. 18, 1821

JACK, PATRICK—Page 420—dec'd. Inventory Feb. 3, 1821. W. H. Jack, James Morrison and William Allgood, Appraisers. Harriett and James Jack, purchasers.

JOHNSTON, JOHN—Page 359—Returns for 1819 shows receipts of Jeremiah Warren for his share, and L. P. Gaines in right of his wife.
Page 446—Returns for 1820 shows Mary Johnston and William Johnston's receipts in full as legatees, Tavner Rucker's receipt for tuition.
Page 225—Returns for 1818 shows receipt of Jermiah Warren in full of his part of Jeremiah Warren's est. "The said John Johnston was Excr. in right of his wife".

JOHNSTON, MARY—Page 188—Orphans of, Geo Stovall, guardian Returns for 1817, no data.

JOHNSTON, PHILIP—Page 190—Est. Richard Fortson, Admr. Returns for 1817, no data.

JONES, ARTHUR—Page 57—Guardian of Davis Jones, minor of Nathan Jones, dec'd. Returns for 1816 shows receipt of Daniel Thornton and John Cook for board for minor.
Page 149—Returns for 1817 shows receipt of A. E. Callahan for tuition.

JONES, JESSE—Page 53—Est. Arthur Jones, Excr. Returns for 1817 shows goods bought of Joshua Merrell.
Pages—148, 256, 419—Show returns for 1817 and 1819, supplies bought for widow and orphans.

KIDD, WEBB—Page 36—Est. William, Martin and John Kidd, Excrs. Returns for 1816 shows receipts of Molly Jennings for William Jennings, Tarleton Hall, Abner Ward, Wm. W. Harper and Berry Ryan and John Cleveland for part of their legacies.
Page 126—Returns for 1818 shows paid John J. Mann in part of his legacy.

KERLIN, WILLIAM—Page 344—Est. James N. Brown, Excr. Returns for 1819 shows receipts of William H. Threckeld for tuition for James Kerlin and Jacob Kerlin, minors. Receipt of Peter Kerlin and of Joseph Y. Wilhite in favor of Mildred Kerlin.
Page 448—Returns for 1820-21 shows receipt of Chas. Presly in right of his wife Mildred, formerly the wife of said dec'd, and as guardian

of Jacob, James, Lucy and Elizabeth Kerlin, minors of said dec'd, a sum subject to an equal distribution.

LEUSEUR, JOHN C.—Page 424—dec'd. Inventory Mar. 7, 1821, slaves Sarah and Matilda, horse and watch listed. Drewry M. Leuseur, Admr.

LYON, EDWARD—Page 348—dec'd. Inventory Dec. 28, 1819, shows slaves Jack, Tempy, Maria, Mary, Franky, "swoards" and household goods.
Page 439—Returns for 1819, Elizabeth Lyon, Admx., shows board, clothes and tuition for Henry, Nathan and Nancy Lyon, receipt of Woodley & Bell, per Joseph Bell.

LYON, JOHN—Page 274—dec'd. Inventory Feb. 3, 1819

McCURRY, LAUGHLIN—Page 371—Est. Returns of John McDonald, Admr. for 1800 shows paid Nancy McCurry for the support of the family.

McGOWEN, ELIJAH—Page 343—dec'd. Inventory Oct. 29, 1819, shows slaves Peggy, Matilda Leah, Joe, Billy and Lewis and one lot of shaving instruments.
Page 401—Returns for 1819 shows John McGowen, Sr., Admr.

MANN, JAMES—Page 107—dec'd. Inventory Nov. 22, 1816.
Page 298—Returns for 1819 shows receipts of Geo. Roebuck, Henry Shackleford, Jeremiah, James, Asa and Henry Mann, for their full legacies, except what is reserved for the support of the widow Judith Mann.

McMARTIN, DUNCAN—Page 258—dec'd. Inventory Jan. 8, 1819.

MEWBOURN, ARCHABALD—Page 201—Guardian of John Nelson Burden. Returns for 1818 shows holds in his hands a certain sum "being his distributive share of his father Edmond Burden's estate.

MIDDLETON, ROBERT—Page 58—Sale of property May 8, 1816, "an inventory having been made".
Pages 73-79—Returns of Betsy C. Middleton, Admx., for 1816 shows paid John K. Charlton for advertising, W. Morrison for a coffin for dec'd., Eliz. Bailey for weaving a counterpane and Joseph and Dunston Blackwell for accounts for Sally C. and Betsy B. Williamson.
Pages 194-197—Returns for 1817 shows cases William Woods vs. Betsy C. Middleton, Nancy P. and James L. Middleton by their gdn. Dunston Blackwell and John Middleton vs. Betsy C., and Betsy C. vs. Samuel Middleton.
Page 286—Returns for 1818 shows suits of Sally C. Williamson, and Betsy B. Williamson an infant, by their next friend Joseph Blackwell, vs. Dunston Blackwell, Excr. of Joseph Blackwell and Betsy C. Middleton, Admx. of Robt. Middleton, dec'd.
Page 409—Returns for 1820 shows paid Adam Gaar for resurveying 740 acres on south side of Beaverdam creek adj. William Allen and Barnard Heard.
Page 467—Returns for 1821 shows paid James Morrison for taking out a grant.

MOON, ARCHELAUS—Page 99—Guardian of Elizabeth and Sarah Wood, orphans of John Wood for 1817 shows Elizabeth's receipt in full for her part of her fathers estate.

NAPIER, RENE—Page 121—Est. Returns of James Morrison for 1818, shows paid part of yearly legacy of Dorothy Napier, widow of dec'd. Signed by Edward Lyon.
Page 472—Returns for 1821 shows receipt of Mary C. D. Nappier for her yearly legacy.

NELMS, WILLIAM—Page 11—dec'd. Returns of Thomas S. Hansard and Nathaniel Nelms for 1816 shows travelling expenses to Milledgeville for a duplicate grant to land granted William Teasley or Feasley, receipt of E. B. Jenkins, Surveyor General.

OLIVER, JOHN—Page 64—dec'd. Inventory Mar. 1817, shows an estensive library, including Wesley Sermons.
Page 142—Returns for 1818 shows receipt of John D. Bibb for seventeen slaves left in the will, one of which he declines to take as he is too old to travel.
Page 282—Returns for 1819, shows receipt from John Burton of Augusta for storage of cotton; of Richardson and Hunt, and Benton Walton of Petersburg, James Herring & Co., and Stokes & Sayre. Also a receipt from Dr. Wm. N. Richardson for $4,121 for produce from the estate; and a transfer of twenty five shares in the Augusta Bank, bequeathed to Susan Oliver according to the will.

PHIPPS, LEWIS—Page 118—Guardian of James and John Faulkner, orphans of James Faulkner. Returns 1817 shows paid Dennis Tippin for tuition and board.

RAGLAND, EVAN—Page 22—Est. Thompson Ragland, Admr. Returns for 1815—show receipt for goods bought of John M. Castins, Petersburg

RAGLAND, THOMPSON—Page 151—dec'd. Inventory Mar. 11, 1818.
Page 269—Returns of James Morrison, Admr. for 1819 shows sale.

RICH, JOHN—Page 12—Est. Returns for 1816 shows receipts of James Rich and Isham Morgan for their legacies. William Rich, Excr.

RICHARDS, REUBEN—Page 428—dec'd. Inventory Feb. 5, 1821.

ROSE, THOMAS—Page 435—Est. Returns for 1821 shows receipt of David A. Reese for "his mothers medical account for 1817, and of James Carrell and Lizzie More for the legacy left them by their grandfather which they transfer to their uncle Drury Rose for money loaned them when in distress.

ROWSEY, JOHN—Page 266—Est. Thomas Oliver, surviving Excr. Returns for 1818, shows receipts of William Bond in right of his wife, Edmond Rowsey as a legatee, and for the maintenance of Mary Rowsey, Stephen Rowsey, James Rowsey for himself and as gdn. of Tabitha and Elizabeth Lawlis, minors of John Lawlis, dec'd. of Lewis Phipps gdn. of Richard and John R. Phipps "my sons by Tabitha Rowsey", of B. G. Higginbotham in right of his wife, of Foster Rowsey.

Page 401—Returns for 1820, shows receipts of Esom, Gabriel, and William Bond in right of their wives.

ROYAL, JAMES—Page 241—dec'd. Inventory, Nov. 10, 1818. Solomon Jones and Abraham Royal, Admrs.

Page 411—Returns Nov. 1819, shows receipts of William Royal; of Benjamin Brown guardian of Averilla Royal; of Henry Hall in right of his wife Leverta Hall formerly Leverta Royal; of Elijah Sneed, legatees.

Page 461—Returns for 1821 shows receipts of Benjamin Brown for Averilla Smith, formerly Averilla Royal; of Elizabeth Royal, of Henry Hall in right of his wife Lavita Hall, formerly Lavita Royal, of Elijah Sneed in right of his wife Sarah, formerly Sarah Royal, legatees and of James Beck by Wm. Beck in full of account at Ruckersville.

Page 444—Returns of Benjamin Brown, guardian for 1821 shows receipt of Averilla and Wills Smith for their distributive share.

SATTERWHITE, FRANCIS—Page 278—dec'd. Inventory Mar. 6, 1819. B. Fortson, Thomas S. Carter and Geo. G. Higginbotham, Appraisers

SHACKLEFORD, HENRY, Sr.—Page 312—Est. Edmond Shackleford, Excr. Returns Sept. 1819 shows receipts of Edmond Alexander, William Brown, Nancy Alexander, Joel Mann, Samuel N. Bailey, legatees.

SNELLINGS, GEORGE—Page 464—Est. Returns Nov. 30, 1821, shows receipt of Richard Burton, in part of his legacy. Samuel and Rebecca Snellings, Excrs.

STANDEFORD, BAILEY—Page 147—dec'd. Abner McGehee, Admr. Shows "Sept. 14, 1815, Cash received of the United States for the services of the dec'd, as a soldier, $74.62½" and a judgement in favor of Jack & McGehee vs. Bailey Standiford and Charles Gordon, April 8, 1809.

TATE, WILLIAM—Page 254—Est. William Tate, Excr. Returns for 1817-18, show receipts of Lucy and Betty Tate for bed and Furniture.

TATE, THOMAS—Page 391—dec'd. Inventory July 17, 1820, Caleb Tate, Samuel Watkins, Thomas Barton and William Rich, Appraisers.

TAIT, JOHN—Page 452—dec'd. Inventory Aug. 20, 1820. Enos Tait, William Allen and Thomas Akin, Appraisers.

TINER, SAMUEL—Page 450—dec'd. Inventory Sept. 28, 1821, shows Lot No. 9, 5th, Dist. Early Co. and book accounts. John Scales, Admr.

THOMPSON, WILLIAM—Page 136—Est. Asa Thompson, Excr. Returns for 1818, shows receipt of Wells Thompson "for which I will credit Asa Thompson, Admr.", and of John C. Rodgers as Agent for Sarah Thompson, wife of Wm. Thompson, dec'd. for her annual legacy of $200.00

Page 145—Returns for 1818, says Asa Thompson, Admr. de bonis non.

GEORGIA D. A. R.

THORNTON, REUBEN—Page 162—Est. Beverly Allen, Excr. of last will. Returns for 1818 shows receipt, Nov. 30, 1816 of Robert Burk, Jr. for horse, bridle, bed and furniture, "on account of my wife Priscilla's legacy", of Elizabeth Thornton "in full of principal and interest collected from the debts of said estate".

THORNTON, THOMAS—Page 451—dec'd. Inventory Sept. 6, 1821.

UPSHAW, JOHN—Page 264—Est. Returns for 1817-18 shows a receipt of Thomas Oliver, surviving Excr. of John Upshaw, dec'd, to Rebecca Upshaw and A. Stinchcomb, Excrs. of John Upshaw for funds belonging to the estate of John Rowsey, dec'd.

VAWTER, JOHN—Page 152—dec'd. Inventory Jan. 12, 1818. Several slaves and household goods.

Page 246—Sale May 30, 1818, Joanna and James Vawter, purchasers. Reuben Brown, Admr.

Page 443—Returns for 1821, shows several slaves set free by Richard Vawter, their guardian, and receipt of Cooper Bennet for part of his legacy.

Page 335—Returns for 1819 of Joannah Vawter, guardian of Lindsay and Russell Vawter, minors of John Vawter.

VINES, ISAIAH—Page 368—dec'd. Sale of estate Feb. 15, 1820, Sarah Vines chief purchaser.

Page 410—Returns for 1820 by Joseph Attaway, Admr.

WOODS, MIDDLETON—Page 83—Est. Returns for 1816, show receipts of Robert Woods, Sr., for Robert, Jr., J. Woods and Thomas McHenry in right of my wife Nancy formerly Nancy Martin, all signed in Elbert Co. Returns for 1818, show receipts from J. Wood, Bailey M. Woods and Thomas McHenry.

WOODS, WILLIAM—Page 84—Guardian of James O., and Evan Ragland, minors of Evan Ragland. Returns for 1817 shows tuition paid Philip Stinchcomb. Returns for 1817 show paid board to William White and John Carroll.

Page 305—Returns for 1818 show paid David McDowell and Zachariah Davis, tuition, and Beverly Martin and Wm. Woods, guardian for board.

WOODS, WILLIAM—Page 113—Temp. Admr. of Evan Ragland, receives from Mrs. Tabitha Clark, Aug. 15, 1817, certain notes which were given to Thompson Ragland as Admr. of Evan Ragland, dec'd.

WATKINS, ROBERT H.—Page 385—Guardian of John Oliver, minor of Maj. John Oliver, for 1820, shows receipts of John D. Beeman for tuition at Mt. Zion Academy, of B. Reid for board and tuition, dated Petersburg, of O. Dumere for his miniature and medallion, dated at Petersburg.

WALLIS, MICHAEL J.—Page 460—dec'd. Inventory Nov. 10, 1821, Jeptha V. Harris, Admr.

WEBB, MARGARET—Page 101—Guardian of William, Milton Pope, Claboan, Abner, Evelina, Martha and Elijah Webb, minors of Clabon Webb, dec'd returns for 1815-16 show maintenance for William, tuition for the rest.
Margaret and John C. Webb, Admrs.
Page 280—Returns for 1816 show maintenance, clothes and tuition for all.
Page 376—Returns for 1819 expenses for all above except Wm.
Page 377—Returns for 1820 show Bridger Webb's receipt for his part of slaves of Claborn Webb, dec'd.

WEBB, CLABORN—Page 470—Est. John C. Webb, Admr. Returns for 1821 shows receipt of Mial Smith, husband of Evelina Webb. Receipt of Milton P. Webb for his share.

WHITE, REUBEN—Page 379—dec'd. Inventory May 2, 1820.

WHITE, DAVID—Page 455—dec'd. Inventory Oct. 15, 1821

WHITMAN, WILLIAM—Page 215—Elizabeth Whitman, Excx. Returns for 1818 show receipts of William Whitman, legatee, Joseph Dunlap, legatee for money given them in the will, both signed 1813.

WILLIAMS, JOSEPH—Page 281—Est. Returns of George Wynne, Admr. in right of his wife and guardian of Henrietta J. Williams a minor. Returns show receipt Apr. 16, 1819 of John Wilkinson for slaves for my wife Henrietta J. Wilkinson.

WILLIAMS, MATTHEW J.—Page 394—Est. Mat. J. Williams one of the Excrs, shows expenses of Mat. J., to N. C. for horse and effects of said dec'd. and by Thomas W. Williams expense to and from N. C. to bring the remains of the dec'd., by his special request, and paid for coffin and winding sheet in N. C. for 1820.

RETURNS OF ADMINISTRATORS AND GUARDIANS

WILL BOOK "M"

ALLEN, BEVERLY—Page 342—Guardian of James B., Sarah W., and Mary A. Henderson, orphans of John Henderson, dec'd. Returns for 1823 shows expense of bringing slaves from Putnam to Elbert Co., of medical services of E. N. Calhoun, Henry Bourn and tuition paid John Cunningham for James B. and Sarah D. Raymond for Sarah W.

BANKS, JAMES & JAMES J.—Page 350—Guardians of Henry and Lemuel Banks, orphans of Ralph Banks. Returns for 1823, no data.
Page 358—Returns of Thomas A. Banks gdn. of Marion Banks minor of Ralph Banks, dec'd. Returns for 1823 shows paid for articles bought at Rachel Banks sale by Willis Banks.

BARNES, PRISCILLA—Page 141—Guardian of John and Henry Barnes, minors of Cordial Barnes, dec'd. Returns for 1822 show board and clothing for both, and Henry's receipt in full for his legacy.
Page 364—Returns for 1823 shows John's receipt in full.

BELL, JOSEPH—Page 98—Returns of estate for 1821 shows receipt of Joseph, Jr. for a horse and saddle left him by his father.

BOOTH, GABRIEL—Page 44— Guardian of Joel Booth, returns for 1822 show receipt in full for his property.

BLACKWELL, DUNSTON—Page 11—Guardian of Nancy P., and James L. Middleton, monors of Robert Middleton, dec'd. Returns for 1821 show his receipt for $5598.00 amount of a judgement against Betsy Middleton, Admx., in favor of said minors, slaves and land excepted.
Page 109—Returns for 1821, show paid Samuel C. Dailey for medical services, Eli Lofton and John Hubbard tuition for both.
Page 246—Returns for 1822 show paid Dr. R. Banks for medical services, and Miss Sarah D. Raymond tuition.
Page 345—Returns for 1823 show same as above.

BRADLEY, ROBERT C.—Page 480—Est. Returns of Joseph Deadwiler, Excr. for 1825 show receipt of Ann and Horatio J. Goss for slave Matilda "according to the will."

BROWN, BENJAMIN—Page 136—Guardian of Averilla Smith, formerly Averilla Royal. Returns for 1822 show her receipt for part of legacy.

BUFFINGTON, JOSEPH—Page 267—dec'd. Inventory Dec. 24, 1823 Ann Buffington, Admx.

BURCH, WILLIAM S.—Page 226—Est. Returns of Mrs. Elizabeth Burch, Admx. for 1822 show receipt of George Alexander for holding an inquest over the body of the dec'd. Jan. 12, 1822.

BURTON, BATHSHEBA—Page 145—Guardian of Elizabeth H. Burton. Returns for 1821-22 show receipt of Gyllum Hudson for tuition.

BURTON, TABITHA—Page 287—dec'd. Inventory May 27, 1824 Leroy Burton, Admr.
Page 483—Sale April 24, 1824. Leroy, Thomas and Blackman Burton purchasers.

BURTON, RICHARD—Page 22—dec'd. Inventory Jan. 11, 1822 William C. Davis and Mary Burton, Admrs.
Page 281—Returns for 1823 shows receipt of Mary Burton, gdn. for money for support of the minors.

CARTER, THOMAS P.—Page 121—Inventory Nov. 5, 1822.
Page 241—Returns for 1823 Ransom Worrell and Benjamin Cook, Admrs.

CASH, HOWARD—Page 170—Guardian of Polly, Keziah and Anna Gregg minors of Thomas Gregg, dec'd. Returns made Mar. 1823 shows receipt of Henry M. Skaggs for Polly Gregg's legacy, now Polly Skaggs, and of David B. Brown for legacy of Keziah Gregg now Keziah Brown, and of Thomas Turner for the legacy of Anna Gregg now Anna Turner.

CHRISTLER, JOSEPH—Page 322—dec'd. Inventory May 8, 1824.

CLARK, CHRISTOPHER—Page 63—Est. David Hudson, Sr. one of the Excrs. Returns for 1821-22 shows receipts of Samuel Clark, John Seale, Rebecca Clark for one-ninth of the cotton crop for 1821, and of David Clark for his legacy, and of James O. Clark for his legacy of one-seventh of the estate in slaves and land. Receipt of Wm. Jameson for tuition for the minors.
Page 191—Returns for 1823 shows James O. Clark rented land of Geo. W., and Christopher Clark, minors., and receipt of Rebecca Clark for pay for board of minors. Receipts to David Hudson, Sr. gdn. of Thomas J., Christopher, Mary, George and Wm. D. Clark.
Page 316—Returns for 1824 shows paid Rebecca Clark for boarding orphans. James McMullen and Wm. D. Clark for tuition, Dr. Samuel Oliver for servises.

COLBERT, RICHARD—Page 67—Est. Beverly Allen, Excr. Returns for 1821 shows receipt of Rhoda Colbert for slave etc., willed her by the dec'd and her permission to divide her life estate. Receipts of John A. Heard, John Childers, John Cook, Holman Childers and Wm. Stone for their wive's legacies, and of Thos. Colbert gdn. of Eliz. Nix's children and Malinda Colbert and Thos. J. Colbert for his legacy.

CLARK, ZACHARIAH—Page 42—Est. Returns of James Morrison, Admr. for 1821 shows receipt of David Hudson, Sr. for boarding Susannah A. and Zachariah H. Clark, also Wm. Colberts receipt for part of 1821, of Shelton White for 1822. Receipt of Davis Jones, minor of Nathan Jones dec'd. for bed furniture etc. willed to him by said Nathan. James Morrison "originally gdn. of said Davis Jones."
Page 278—Returns for 1823 shows receipt of Arthur Jones, gdn. of Davis Jones to James Morrison for a legacy to Davis Jones from Nathaniel Jones, dec'd., and receipt of William Colbert for Susannah A. Clarks board.
Page 443—Returns for 1824 shows paid William Nowlan for board for both.

COOK, BANJAMIN—Page 51—Guardian of Louisey and Eliza C., and Frances Hudson, minor heirs of Nathaniel Hudson, dec'd. shows his receipts for their legacies, 1822.
Page 177—Returns for 1823 shows paid Sarah D. Raymond for tuition for Eliza C., and Louisa.
Page 340—Returns for 1823 show paid Molley Hudson for board. W. D. Tinsley for medical services.

COOK, WILLIAM T.—Page 59—Est. Thomas Cook, Admr. shows receipts from Frances Cook 1818-19-20 for part of her dower.

Page 466—Seperate returns of Thomas Oliver, one of the Admrs. recounting his expenditures for Wm. T. Cook and his family in his life time and since his decease, paying notes and accounts.

CRAWFORD, WILLIAM—Page 275—Guardian of minors of John Crawford dec'd. Returns for 1823 show receipts of Wm. M. Prater and Elijah Dobbs for tuition.

CRUMP, CHARLES—Page 20—Est. Returns for 1821, William Bailey, Thomas A. Banks and Pleasant D. Crump, Admrs., shows receipt of Richard L. Crump in full of all demands against the estate, and Henry Bourne for medical services.

DOLLAR, HENRY—Page 29—Est. Sale June 16, 1821. "Widow Mary Dollar" bought bed etc.

EDWARDS, JAMES—Page 390—dec'd. Inventory Dec. 24, 1824.
Page 449—Sale certified by Sarah B. Edwards, Admx. Feb. 23, 1825 shows fine library.

FLEMING, MOSES—Page 475—A lunatic. Inventory Mar. 10, 1825.

FORTSON, BENJAMIN—Page 235—dec'd. Inventory Nov. 1, 1823. Elizabeth Fortson, Admx., and Eastin Fortson, Admr.
Page 461—Sale Nov. 16, 1824 Accounts of Elizabeth, John, Thomas, Jesse, Tavner W., and Eastin Fortson.

GAAR, ADAM—Page 36—dec'd. Inventory Jan. 19, 1822.
Page 161—Returns of Allen Daniel, Admr., and Nancy Gaar, Admx., Dec. 1822.

GAY, ANN—Page 168—dec'd. Returns of sale of June 23, 1821 by Silvana Ginn, Admx.

GOODE, NICHOLAS—Page 212—Guardian for Eleanor and Milly L. Bell, minors of Joseph Bell, dec'd. Returns for 1822, no data.

HALEY, JAMES—Page 133—Guardian of Burton E., Leroy K., and William H. Crawford, minors of John Crawford dec'd. Returns for 1819 show paid fee for the "draws" of said orphans, and tuition to Tavenah Rucker.

HAM, JOHN—Page 23—Est. Returns of James Upshaw, Excr. for 1822 shows receipts of James, Stephen and Gideon Ham for their part of the cotton crop, and receipts of Drs. John Nickols, P. A. Tabor, Geo. W. Heard and Samuel G. Cloud.
Page 164—Returns for 1822 show receipts of William, Gideon and John Ham for part of legacies.
Page 251—Returns for 1823 sho receipt of Sophia Ham for part of her legacy.
Page 284—Returns for 1823 shows receipt of Elbert Andrews for singing school, and D. E. McLauchlin for "subscription of three scholars."

HAMMOND, JOB, Sr.—Page 173—dec'd. Inventory June 19, 1823. Lucy Hammond, Admx.
　　Page 285—Returns for 1823, shows A. Hammond for Lucy Hammond, Admx.
　　Page 381—Returns for 1824, shows receipt of Archd. Stokes of Petersburg for account paid and receipt of George Cook, Atty. at Law by the hands of Alfred and William Hammond. A case of Lucy Hammond vs. Job Hammond, Jr., caveat.

HAWK, THOMAS—Page 267—dec'd. Inventory Jan. 4, 1824. John and H. M. Watkins and Benj. Baird, apprs. shows only wearing clothes.

HEARD, BARNARD C.—Page 115-375—Guardian of John Hudson, minor of Nathaniel Hudson, dec'd. Returns for 1821-22.
　　Page 374—Returns as guardian for Thos. J. Heard, orphan of Stephen Heard for 1824 shows receipt of Thos. J., in full of his legacy.

HEARD, ELIZABETH—Page 137—Guardian of Sarah H. Heard orphan of Stephen Heard. Returns 1819-22. Receipt of Simeon Henderson Jan. 1, 1821 for a sum of money "to make me equal with Sarah H. Heard in a division of the estate."

HIGGINBOTHAM, JOHN S.—Page 238—Guardian of Peter and Larkin Higginbotham, minors of Benjamin Higginbotham, dec'd. Receipt of Larkin Higginbotham in full of his legacy "from my father Benjamin Higginbotham's estate", July 10, 1816 and receipt of Peter for his legacy in full Oct. 24, 1818, "which I receipted for some years back, which receipt was accidentally burned."

HIGGINBOTHAM, SAMUEL—Page 240—Est. John S. Higginbotham, Admr. Returns for 1823 shows receipts of Geo. Turman for his wife's distributive share, also receipts from Stephen Chatman and William Fortson for their wive's shares, and of Geo. C. Blackley and A. Higginbotham legatees, all of which receipts were "burned some years back", present ones signed 1818-19.

JACK, PATRICK—Page 89—Est. Harriett and James Jack, Admrs. Returns for 1822, no data.
　　Page 142—Returns for 1821-22 shows paid William Jack one of the legatees for board and tuition at Athens.
　　Page 143—Shows James Morrison, William H. Jack and James Bell appointed commissioners to distribute the slaves of the estate into nine equal shares, but they are not assigned to the heirs.

JAMESON, WILLIAM—Page 331—dec'd. Inventory Sept. 22, 1824.
　　Page 455—Returns for 1824 of estate of John Johnston, Larkin Johnston and William Bailey, Excrs, shows receipt of Elizabeth B. Johnston, Thomas Johnston, James Haley, Sarah Gaines, William Johnston, for their part of the last payment on the mills.

JONES, ARTHUR—Page 169—Guardian of Davis Jones, receipt of Davis in full of his legacy by the will of his father Nathan Jones, dec'd, Aug. 29, 1821.

JONES, JESSE—Page 170—Est. Arthur Jones, Excr. Returns show receipt of John Halk for Pyety Halk formerly Pyety Jones, "one of the heirs of said dec'd., Dec. 27, 1822.

KERLIN, WILLIAM—Page 301—Est, Returns for 1824 shows receipt of Charles Presley to Joseph Brawner, Excr., for all property belonging to all the children of said dec'd, towit: James, Jacob, Lucy, and Elizabeth Kerlin. Charles Presley now their guardian he having married the widow. Jan. 12, 1824.

LESUER, JOHN C.—Page 145—Est. Sale 1823 shows Samuel Lesuer, Sr. bought slave, Drury M. Lesuer bought silver watch.

LYON, EDWARD—Page 329—Est. Returns for 1823 show board and clothes for Henry, Nancy, Nathaniel and Mary Caroline Lyon, minors. Elizabeth Lyon, Admx.

McELROY, HENRY—Page 232—Est. James McElroy, Excr. Returns for 1823 in Madison Co., shows receipt of William Hartsfield for the legacy of Peletiah McElroy, daughter of said dec'd, now the wife of said William Hartsfield. Receipt of Henry McElroy and Charles McElroy sons of Henry McElroy, dec'd, late of Elbert Co., now Madison Co. All signed Nov. 1, 1823. Frances P. Eberhart, Test to all.

McMARTIN, DUNCAN—Page 104—Est. Return for 1822, Angus McCurry, Admr.

MARTIN, LEWIS—Page 177—dec'd. Inventory Mar. 8, 1823.
Page 183—Returns for 1823 show Presley G. Christian, Admr.

MIDDLETON, ROBERT—Page 13—Est. Return of the division Jan. 3, 1821 shows lots assigned Betsy C. Middleton, Caleb Tate, William Woods, John Middleton, Nancy Middleton and James L. Middleton.

MORGAN, ISHAM, Sr.—Page 34—dec'd. Inventory Feb. 23, 1822.

MOSLEY, WILLIAM—Page 288—dec'd. Inventory Apr. 27, 1824 shows one counter pane and a gold stock buckle entire estate.

PATTERSON, ELZY—Page 320—dec'd. Inventory May 19, 1824.

POSEY, THOMAS—Page 128—Inventory Nov. 7, 1822.
Page 504—Returns for 1823 show Drury Ridgway, Admr., and only creditor.

RAGLAND, EVAN—Page 35—dec'd. Inventory of slaves Feb. 2, 1822.

RAGLAND, THOMPSON—Page 52—Est. Returns for 1822 show Tabitha Clark vs James Morrison, Admr.

RICH, JOHN—Page 272—Est. Returns of William Rich, Excr., for Jan. 1823 shows receipt of Jesse Rich for his legacy in full.

HISTORICAL COLLECTIONS 105

RICHARDSON, WALKER—Page 302—Est. Returns for July 1824 shows Richard Fortson and John S. Higginbotham, Excrs.
Page 487—Returns of Richard Fortson for 1824 shows receipts of Richard Richardson, Wm. N. Richardson in full "except my portion willed to my mother, wife of said dec'd, now the wife of Benjamin Brown." Receipts of Leroy Upshaw and James Head for their wives legacies and of Henry L. Harris for his wife's legacy "left her by her grandfather."

RICHARDS, REUBEN—Page 70—Est. Nathan Bond, Admr. Returns for 1821 shows, "ten days travelling to Pulaski to collect money from M. McLeod, three days travelling to Jackson after a horse, twenty six days travelling to and from Tenn. to collect money due the estate".
Page 493—Returns for 1825 shows Rachel Richards, Admx.

SKINNER, MORRIS—Page 199—dec'd. Inventory Sept. 12, 1823, Valentine Smith, Admr.
Page 311—Returns for 1824 shows receipt of Sally Skinner to buy bacon.

SNELLINGS, GEORGE—Page 97—Est. Returns of Rebeccah and Samuel Snellings, Excrs., for 1821 shows receipt of John Taylor for his daughter Rebeccah's part when she married.

STAPLES, DAVID—Page 377—Est. Returns of Fanny Staples, Excx. for 1824 shows receipts of John, Thomas, and Patsy Staples, Thomas Phelps, John Stovall, Edward A. Denna, Robt. Denna, Jesse Brown, Jacob Moon, and Thomas Staples for William Smith, each for $391.00 their distributive shares, and Tabitha Moon for $2.00 as per will.

TATE, JOHN—Page 308—Est. Returns of Sarah Tate, Admx. for 1823 shows board and clothes for Sarah Ann, John D., William J., and Joseph P. Tate, minors of said dec'd, and receipt of Chas. Hunter for tuition.

TATE, THOMAS—Page 45—Return of Zimri Tate one of the Adnrs. for 1822, shows paid Dr. E. Hunt and Permelia Tate, Admx.
Page 84—Division of estate shows Permelia Tate(widow), Anderson Riddle, Catharine, Thomas J., Beatrice A., and John W. Tate, and Martha Klugh, distributees. Eleven lots were taken, only these received theirs.

TEASLEY, LEVI—Page 54—dec'd. Inventory April 13, 1822.
Page 223—Returns for 1823 shows William Teasley, Admr.

TAYLOR, JOHN—Page 118—dec'd. Inventory Oct. 15, 1822.

THORNTON, THOMAS—Page 253—Est. Returns of Lucy K. Thornton, Admx. of sale Jan. 10, 1822.

THRELKELD, JOHN—Page 33—dec'd. Inventory Jan. 14, 1822 William H. Threlkeld, Admr.

GEORGIA D. A. R.

THRELKELD, THOMAS—Page 55—dec'd. Inventory Mar. 16, 1822.
Page 86—Returns of sale Apr. 25, 1823 shows Willis and Delilah Threlkeld, Admrs., they and Oliver Threlkeld principal purchasers.

TURNER, SARAH—Page 133—Guardian of Thomas and Elizabeth Turner who has since married Ralph Gaines. Receipts of Ralph Gaines and Thomas Turner in full, "of Sarah Turner widow of Martin Turner late of Green Co., dec'd. Jan. 4, 1823.

VAWTER, JOHN—Page 30—Est. Returns of Reuben Brown, Admr. for 1821 show receipts of Joanna, Richard, William, Elizabeth, Nancy and James Vawter, and of Joannah as gdn. of Lindsey and Russel Vawter, minors, and Cooper Bennett, distributees.
Page 298—Returns for 1824 shows receipts of Joanna for herself and as gdn. Nancy, Richard and William Vawter, R. D. Crump in right of his wife Elizabeth, formerly Elizabeth Vawter, and Cooper and Frances Bennet jointly.

WARD, WILLIAM H.—Page 518—dec'd. Inventory June 16, 1825.

WALLIS, MICHAEL J.—Page 88—dec'd. Sale Jan. 9, 1822.

WATKINS, ROBERT H.—Page 239—Guardian of John Oliver. Returns for 1823 shows John's receipt in full to Watkins as Excr. of John Oliver, dec'd., for his distributive share.

WEBB, MARGARET—Page 87—Guardian of Claborn, Abner, Martha, and Elijah W., minors of Claiborn Webb, dec'd. Returns for 1820 show maintenance for all above.
Page 365—Returns for 1824 show maintenance for above minors and Bridger Webb, adult 1813. Wm. C. Webb minor 1819, Milton P. Webb minor 1821, Miles Smith husband of Evelina Webb, 1821, all charged with bed furniture and household goods.

WILHITE, MESHAC T.—Page 188—Guardian of Geriah G., and Philip A. Wilhite. Returns for 1821 shows clothes and board.
Page 489—Returns for 1825 shows receipt of Martin Deadwyler for part of the distributive share of Philip A. Wilhite, minor of Philip Wilhite, Dec'd., and receipt of Robt. C. Oglesby for distributive share of Geriah G. Wilhite, now Geriah G. Oglesby's share.

WILLIAMS, MATTHEW J.—Page 99—Est. Returns for 1822 by Thomas W. Williams one of the Excrs, shows receipt of Micajah Anthony for his wife Rebecca, his dau. Barbara and his son Matthew J. W. Anthony; of Barbara Williams; of John Wilkinson for his wife, at the time Henrietta J. Williams; of Lemuel Black for his wife Mary Ann.
Page 254—Retruns for 1823, shows receipt of Thos. W. Williams for property left in trust for Rebeccah and Robt. Richardson, children of William Richardson, and his receipt as gdn. of Barbara C. Harrison and Matthew R. T. Harrison; receipt of Micajah Anthony for remainder of his legacy.

HISTORICAL COLLECTIONS   107

WOODS, WILLIAM—Page 181—Guardian of John W. Carter, returns for 1821 shows case John W. Carter, by his guardian vs Thos. S. Carter, Admr. of Thos. Carter, dec'd. Full settlement as John W. is now of age.

WILLIS, JOHN—Page 129—dec'd. Inventory Dec. 1, 1822.
    Page 228—Sale Mar. 7, 1823 shows Richard Fortson one of the Admrs. Later returns show Milly Willis, Admx., and indicate John Willis had the contract to build the Elberton Academy.

WOODS, WILLIAM—Page 392—Sale beginning Feb. 26, 1824, Jeptha V. Harris, Admr.

WYNN, GEORGE—Page 19—Excr. of John Wynn, dec'd., who was guardian of Ann W. Childs. Returns for 1822 show paid for merchandise.

RETURNS OF ADMINISTRATORS AND GUARDIANS
WILL BOOK "N" OLD NO.

ALSTON, CHARITY—Estate—Page 300—Returns of William H. Alston, Excr. Mar. 1828, shows receipts of Christian L. Alston, William A. Tate, gdn. of Charity Ann Tate, and Philip H. Alston in full of their legacies.

ALLEN, BEVERLY—Page 23—Guardian of orphans of John Henderson, dec'd. Returns for 1824 shows paid E. N. Calhoun for medical services, paid for coat for James B., and tuition etc for Mary A. Henderson.
    Page 113—Returns for 1825 shows William Whitfield Admr. "in right of his wife". Paid Wm. Whitfield for board and clothing for Sarah W. and Beverly A. Henderson, board, clothing and tuition for Mary A., John A., and Joseph W. Henderson. Also receipt in full of John Sharman for his wife Sarah W. Sharman, formerly Sarah W. Henderson, share of personal estate.
    Page 231—Returns for 1826, show board and tuition for all except Sarah W. Henderson.

BANKS, JAMES J.—Page 37—Guardian of Henry and Lemuel Banks, minors of Ralph Banks, Dec'd. Returns for 1824 shows paid John S. Willson tuition and Asa Thompson board for both.
    Page 315—Returns shows receipt of Lemuel Banks all the property and money that has come into his guardians hands Dec. 27, 1827.

BANKS, JAMES A.—Page 261—Division of estate between Milly T. Banks, wid. and Wm. C. Banks minor orphan of said dec'd. Dec. 29, 1826. Simeon Oliver, one of the excrs.

BARNETT, NATHANIEL—Page 150—Est. Returns for 1826 shows Daniel McDowell, Admr. de bonis non.

BRADLEY, ROBERT C.—Page 148—Est. Return of Joseph Deadwyler, Sr., Dec. 25, 1826 shows receipt of Daniel C., and Lucy C. Thornton for a slave Piety in full of a legacy designated in will of dec'd to Lucy C. Bradley.

BELL, THOMAS, Jr.—Page 276—Guardian in right of his wife Mary Bell, formerly Mary Dye of George W., Susan A., and Martin B. Dye, minor heirs of Brown Dye, dec'd. Returns for 1827.

BLACKWELL, DUNSTON—Page 25—Guardian of Nancy P., and James L. Middleton, minors of Robert Middleton, dec'd. Returns for 1825 shows paid E. G. Harris tuition for both and R. Banks for medical services.
Page 133—Returns for 1826 shows paid J. F. Wallis for board and tuition, and Dr. John Geridine for services for Nancy P. Paid E. G. Harris tuition and R. Banks medical service for James L.
Page 249—Returns for 1827 show paid bills same as above.

BREWER, HORATIO G.—Page 234—Inventory June 1, 1827.
Page 346—Returns of Susannah Brewer, Admx. July Term 1828. No data.

BURTON, RICHARD—Page 36—Est. William C. Davis, Admr. Returns for 1825 shows receipt of Nancy Burton for cash for support of the minors.
Page 191—Returns for 1826 shows the same.
Page 303—Returns for 1827 shows paid William D. Tinsley for medical services, and receipt of R. D. Hudson for cash for support of the minor orphans, George Thomas and Richard Abram Burton, calling himself admr. and guardian in right of his wife Mary formerly Mary Burton.
Page 405—Final settlement Sept. 3, 1828, showing receipt of Richard D. Hudson, admr. in right of his wife, widow of said dec'd., and gdn. of said minors.

BURTON, TABITHA—Page 109—dec'd. est., Leroy Burton, Admr. Returns for 1826 shows paid Amos Baker for coffin.

CHRISTLER, JOSEPH—Page 110—Est. Singleton W. Allen, Admr. Returns of sale Dec. 4, 1824. Julius Christler one of the purchasers.

CLEVELAND, JOHN—Page 389—dec'd. Inventory Sept. 12, 1828.

COOK, BENJAMIN—Page 40—Guardian of Louisa and Eliza C. Hudson, orphans of Nathaniel Hudson, dec'd. Returns for 1825 shows paid William White tuition, and M. M. A. Elsworth tuition by William White.

COOK, BEVERLY C.—Page 364—Guardian of James, Zimri and Horatio Tate, minor orphans of Zimri Tate, dec'd. Returns for May 1828 shows spelling books and clothes bought for all.

COOK, JOSHUA—Page 35—Estate. Returns of John Cook, Excr. for 1826 shows receipt of Mary Cook for horse etc, part of her legacy.

COOK, JOSHUA—Page 390—dec'd. Inventory Sept. 19, 1828. William A. Herring, Admr., shows only a sow and pigs and one note of hand.

DAVIS, THOMAS—Page 325—dec'd. Inventory May 7, 1828. Benajah Houston and William White Admrs.
Page 336—Returns of notes belonging to the estate in possession of Geo. Carter, temp. admr. May 1828.

DEADWYLER, MARTIN—Page 166—Guardian of Philip A. Wilhite. Returns show board and clothes for 1824 and schooling 1825-26.

DUNLAP, WILLIAM—Page 170—Guardian of William D. Garvin, minor of Daniel Garvin, dec'd. Returns for 1827 shows affidavit of John E. Garvin that said minor had received his part of estate before the death of said dec'd.

DYE, BROWN—Page 14—Sale of estate Apr. 1, 1825. Polly Dye, Admx. Polly, Burwell, David, William and Jane Dye purchasers.
Page 48—Division of slaves, Mar. 19, 1825, signed by William, David, Elizabeth, and Burwell Dye. By Polly Dye for herself and as gdn. of minor heirs of Brown Dye. By Jane Dye as gdn. of heirs of Thompson Dye, dec'd.
Page 63—Returns of Polly Dye, Admx. Mar. 6, 1826, shows paid Amos Baker for coffin.
Page 155—Returns Jan. 1827, shows Thomas Bell, Jr. Admr. in right of his wife Polly Bell, formerly Polly Dye shows paid for building a vault over said dec'd. Built by Edward H. Ball.

DYE, JANE—Page 73—Guardian of Francis, Elizabeth, Sarah, George J. Thompson B., and Mary Dye, orphans of Thompson Dye, dec'd. Returns Mar. 7, 1826 shows board, clothes and tuition for all.

DYE, JOHN A.—Page 81—dec'd. Polly Dye, Admx. inventory Nov. 12, 1825.
Page 57—Returns for 1825 shows her account for board and clothes and paid for burial expenses.
Page 156—Returns of Thomas Bell, Jr., in right of his wife Polly shows paid for building vault over said dec'd.

DYE, THOMPSON—Page 173—dec'd, estate, Jane Dye, Admx. Returns Mar. 1827 shows hire of slaves.
Page 429—Returns for 1828 shows hire of slaves.

EDWARDS, JAMES—Page 100—dec'd. estate, Sarah B. Edwards, Admx. Returns for board and clothes for my five children for 1825 and receipt of Wm. D. Tinsley for medical services.
Page 238—Returns of Sarah B. Edwards, admx. for 1826 show paid Alvin Dean and Dr. Amstead for medical services, A. Donovan tuition, and Wm. D. Tinsley for board and clothes "for my four orphans".
Page 391—Returns Nov. 1828 shows Wm. D., and Sarah B. Tinsley, formerly Sarah B. Edwards, Admrs., show sale of land and premises on which said dec'd lived, house and lot in Elberton.

ELLIOTT, JAMES—Page 170—Estate. Returns of William Dunlap, Admr. Mar. 1827 shows paid Robert Hines for cash for the use of the widow,

Jan. 12, 1819, and of Sharlott Elliott in part of estate of said dec'd. Aug. 29, 1823.

FLEMING, SARAH—Page 54—Guardian of Moses Fleming, lunatic, Returns for 1828 (not data).

FORTSON, BENJAMIN—Page 52—Estate, Easton Fortson, Admr. Mar. 6, 1826 (no data).

Page 355—Returns for 1827 shows receipts to Easton Fortson one of the admrs. of Edward B. Tait and of Thos. Fortson, of John Fortson agent for Jonathan Harris for his distributive share, of John and James Fortson for their distributive shares, of Eliz. Fortson for her share and as gdn. of Eliz. E., Richard, Benjamin G., and Amanda M. Fortson.

FORTSON, JESSE—Page 362—dec'd. Inventory July 17, 1828.

GARVIN, DANIEL—Page 168—dec'd, estate. William Dunlap, Admr. Returns Mar. 1827 shows receipts of Edward Smith 1811, 1812, 1814, and 1827 "in right of my wife"., receipt of 1827 dated Tuscaloosa; of Robert M. Garvin, 1816, 1821, in full, of John E. Garvin 1821, in full as "legatees."

GLENN, SIMEON, Jr.—Page 31—Inventory Nov. 18, 1825. James Glenn, Admr.

Page 141—Sale Dec. 20, 1825. Mitchell Glenn, purchaser.

Page 279—Returns for 1826 show receipt of Radford Glenn "as per note and account" and Mitchell W. Glenn "within account".

Page 426—Returns for 1828 shows case Isaac W. Johnson, Admr. of William Glenn, dec'd, vs. James Glenn, Admr. Simeon Glenn, dec'd.

GOODE, NICHOLAS—Page 32—Guardian of Milly L. Bell. Returns for 1825 paid for her draw in the Lottery and receipt of William W. Downer, "in right of my wife Elenor Downer, formerly Elenor Bell."

GAINES, SALLY—Page 455—Guardian of Judith B. and Mary Elizabeth Gaines, minors of Levingston P. Gaines, dec'd. Returns Mar. 1829 shows a note on William Crawford for $555.00, their proportionate share of the estate of Francis Gaines, dec'd.

HAM, JOHN—Page 67—Estate, James Upshaw one of the Excrs. Returns shows receipt in full of Sophia Ham for her legacy Dec. 28, 1825.

Page 126—Returns Nov. 6, 1826 show "Received of Jesse Beck and Chas. Monday excrs, of Stephen Ham, late of Va., dec'd, $950.00. Receipts of Wm. Ham for himself and as gdn. of Samuel and Betsy Ham, minors and legatees, of James Upshaw, of Sophia Ham, of Sucky Ham, of Stephen Ham, of William Glenn, of Gideon Ham, all legatees of Stephen Ham of Amherst Co. Va.

Page 205—Returns show receipt of William Glenn in full of his legacy due by the last will of John Ham, dec'd., and of Betsy Ham for cash, April 1827.

Page 313—Returns show receipt of Betsy Ham for cash, of Sucky and Samuel Ham in full of their legacies and of John W. Black in full in right of his wife by the last will etc. All signed Mar. and April 1828.

HAM, STEPHEN—Page 306—Guardian of Willis R., and Nancy Ham, shows paid for bed for each in 1828.

HALL, SEALS—Page 209—dec'd. Inventory Apr. 20, 1827. Wagon, harness, saddle, slave, entire estate.
Page 299—Sale, Oct. 2, 1827. John and Simeon Hall purchasers. John, Admr.

HAMMOND, JOB, Sr.—Page 43—dec'd. estate Lucy Hammond, Admx. Sale Feb. 1, 1825, 286 acres on Savannah river to A. Hammond, and 490 acres in Irwin Co. Lot No. 405, 6th. Dist.

HARPER, EDMOND—Page 88-91—Est. Returns of Bedford Harper, Excr., show receipts of Beverly Allen, of Ransom Worrill, of Eliz. Dardin, of Nancy Jones, of Drusilla Harper, of Lucy Howard, of John Dickey, all "in full of legacies and demands against said estate". Signed 1824-25.

HEARD, BARNARD C.—Page 233—Inventory June 20, 1827.
Thomas J. Heard, Admr.

HENDERSON, JOHN—Page 104—Est. Slaves ordered to be divided so as to give John A. Sherman who intermarried with Sarah W. Henderson, one of the heirs, his share.

HINTON, PETER—Page 376—dec'd. Inventory Aug. 2, 1828 James L. Hinton, Admr.

HULME, WILLIAM—Page 440—dec'd. Inventory Nov. 13, 1828.

JACK, HARRIET—Page 58—Guardian of Patrick C., Spencer A., Abner McG., Archabald E., Margaret E., and Harriet K. Jack, minors of Patrick Jack, dec'd. Returns for 1824 show board, clothing and tuition for all except Archibald E., only board and clothes.

McCURRY, LAUCHLIN—Page 74—dec'd. Inventory April 26, 1826.
Page 194—Returns of Benjamin Penn Admr. for 1826 show receipts of Wm. Horton, gdn., of Wm. and Thos. Teasley, minors of Levi Teasley, dec'd., for their property and of William Lunsford gdn. of Thos. J. Teasley, minor of Ann Teasley for their property, for whom Lauchlin McCurry, dec'd, had been guardian in his life time.
Page 307—Returns for 1828 show receipts in full from these guardians.

MEWBORN, ARCHEBALD—Page 376—Guardian of John N. Burden, a minor, shows tax paid 1821-27, and paid for plat and grant.

MORRISON, JAMES—Page 157—dec'd. Inventory Feb. 5, 1827.
Page 384—Returns for 1828 shows Thomas Morrison one of the Admrs.

OLIVER, JOHN—Page 56—Est. Robert H. Watkins, Excr. Returns for 1823 show receipt of John Oliver in full, dated Lawrence Co. Ala., to Robert Watkins, Petersburg, Ga.

GEORGIA D. A. R.

PATTERSON, ELIZA—Page 61—Est. Returns of William Patterson, Admr., Mar. 1826, no data.

RAGLAND, THOMPSON—Page 378—Est. Thomas Morrison one of the Admrs. of James Morrison, dec'd, makes returns of returns made by James Morrison dec'd, in 1825 not recorded. Shows receipt of Dr. Geo. W. Heard for services. Division of slaves into five parts, P. Ray, by J. N. Pulliam, atty in fact, E. Ragland, Admx, of est. of Hudson Ragland, dec'd, Tabitha Clark, En. Ragland receive their lots, that of James O. Ragland levied on by William Woods and sold. All signed Dec. 31, 1825.

RICH, JOHN—Page 26—Est. William Rich, Excr. Receipt of Elijah Berry, gdn. of Sophia Rich, for her share and of Jesse Rich for part of James Rich's share. Mar. 28, 1825.

RICH, WILLIAM—Page 403—Guardian of Jacob M. Tate for 1828 shows paid for a gray horse.

RICHARDSON, WALKER—Page 92—Est. Returns of Richard Fortson, Excr. shows receipt of Thomas Allen, gdn. of Permelia, Caroline, Martha, and Richardson Allen for their legacy.

ROAN, JOHN—Page 209—dec'd. Inventory Mar. 23, 1827.
Page 333—Returns of William Rich, Admr., of sale May 13, 1828. Frances Roan, purchaser.

RUCKER, JAMES—Page 73—dec'd. Inventory May 2, 1826.
Page 427—Returns for 1828 show Tavner and Wm. Rucker, Admrs.

SHACKLEFORD, EDMOND—Page 12—Est. Philip Shackleford, Excr. Returns for 1824 shows paid Jesse Hayes for a gig for his mother, and paid C. W. Rawson for medical services to Judith Shackleford.
Page 130—Returns for 1825 shows receipt of James Kenny for board of T. J. Shackleford at school, July 1825, and receipt of Thos. J. for what was due him from said est. Mar. 14, 1826 paid for a horse for Judith Shackleford.
Page 278—Returns for 1826 show receipts of E., R. E., Thos. J., and Sally W. Shackleford and Mordecai Alexander for cash, and articles bought by Philip for Judith Shackleford.

SHACKLEFORD, HENRY, Sr.—Page 268—dec'd. Inventory Nov. 8, 1827.
Page 335—Sale Jan. 3, 1828, William White Admr. Martha, Henry and Asa C. Shackleford, purchasers.

SNELLINGS, GEORGE—Page 286—Est. James Snellings, Excr. Returns for 1827 shows receipt of John H. Hudson, in right of his wife Martha, formerly Martha Snellings. Receipt of Daniel Butler in full of Rebecca Snellings, dec'd. account with me, May 12, 1827; of Patrick Butler for helping to make a coffin.
Page 316—Returns for 1828 shows receipts of John H. Hudson in right of his wife, Martha, John Snellings, Rebecca Taylor, formerly

Rebecca Snellings, R. D. Hudson in right of his wife Mary, formerly Mary Snellings, Peter P. Butler in right of his wife Hannah, formerly Hannah Snellings, Eliz. Snellings, all in full of their legacies.

TATE, BEATRICE J. A.—Page 246—dec'd. Inventory Nov. 5, 1827. Five slaves listed.

TATE, JAMES M. & JOHN W.—Page 189—dec'd. Inventory Apr. 27, 1827. Only slaves listed.

TATE, THOMAS—Page 174—Est. Zimri Tate, Admr. Returns Mar. 1827 for 1820-27.

Page 246—Returns for 1827 show affidavit of Permelia Tate that a certain note was given the est. of Thomas Tate, dec'd, as a balance of purchase money of three negroes bought in Va.

TATE, WILLIAM—Page 308—dec'd. Sale Oct. 15, 1824.

TEASLEY, WILLIAM—Page 5—Est. Thomas Horton and Wm. Lunsford, Excrs. Returns for 1824 show receipts of Lauchlin McCurry gdn. of heirs of Levi Teasley, dec'd, of John Horton in right of his wife Winny, of Wesler Christler in right of his wife Anna, of Thomas Horton in right of his wife Eliz., of Wm. Lunsford in right of his wife Amelia. All signed April 4, 1825.

Page 101—Returns Sept. 1826 show receipts of Jeremiah Horton, atty, for Thos. Horton in right of his wife Winny, of Wesler Christler in right of his wife Anna, by Reuben Thornton, Atty, of Wm. Horton as gdn. of Wm. and Thos. Teasley, minors of Levi Teasley, dec'd, of Wm. Lunsford in right of his wife Amelia.

TURMAN, GEORGE—Page 44—dec'd. Inventory Nov. 16, 1825.

Page 105—Sale. Jan. 6, 1826. Mrs. Violetty Turman principal purchaser. Samuel Turman, Admr.

Page 216—Returns for 1826 show receipts of Seaborn J. and Violetty Turman for their distributive shares, and of Samuel Turman as gdn. of Mariah and Thos. J. Turman, minors.

TYNOR, RICHARD—Page 33—Est. Returns for 1824 show receipts of Robt Crump, Nancy Tyner, Harris Tyner, Thompson McGuire and Moses Hunt in right of his wife Tamer in part of their legacies.

Page 152—Returns for 1825 show receipts of Wm. Boatright in right of his wife Eliz., of John Bird in right of his wife Martha B., and of Elijah Bird gdn. of Sarah, Martha, Nancy and Mary Bird orphans of Billings B. Bird and Charity Bird. Also receipts of David Dobbs, atty. for Richard Tyner for fees for acting as atty., and expenses in establishing the claim and collecting money which was approriated to said Tyner for a Revolutionary claim for property lost in the war between the U. S. and Great Brittian. William Bailey and Isham Teasley, Excrs.

UNDERWOOD, WINNEY—Page 406—Est. Returns Nov. 1825 shows sale of Lot 41, 6th, Dist., Troup Co., to James Culberson, cash paid for plat and grant. Reuben Underwood, Admr.

VAWTER, JOHN—Page 288—Est. Reuben Brown, Admr. Returns for 1827 show receipt of William Crump in full of distributive share.

WEBB, CLABORN, Jr.—Page 67—dec'd. Inventory Jan. 28, 1826.
Page 242—Returns of Martin Deadwyler, Admr. de bonis non for property received from former admr., Milton P. Webb. Receipt of Sheriff of Newton Co. for crying a tract of land in that county, property of said dec'd.

WEBB, BURRELL—Page 173—Guardian of Prudence U. Booth. Her receipt for $750.00 in full of her distributive share of est. of John Booth. David S. Booth, Admr. Mar. 5, 1817.

WEBB, MARGARET—Page 139—Guardian of minors of Claborn Webb, dec'd. Returns for 1824 shows paid board, clothing and tuition for Martha P. and Elijah W. Webb. Abner Webb charged with bed and furniture. Receipt in full of Claborn Webb, Jr., Sept. 5, 1824, of Abner Webb for a slave Sam, of Joseph Deadwyler, Jr. Mar. 22, 1826 in full of his share of slaves, Granville and Hampton. May 20, 1826.
Page 454—Returns as gdn. of Elijah W. Webb shows board, clothes and tuition for 1827-28, and her receipt for his distributive share of William Webb, Sr's, estate.

WEBB, WILLIAM—Page 289—Est. William Moore, Excr. Returns show John Webb of Putnam Co., sells his share of said estate to William Moore of Elbert Co. Receipt of Pleasant Webb "in full of all claims on my brothers estate". Claborn Webb, Jr. purchases share of Abner Webb, Oct. 15, 1823. Claborn having already purchased the shares of Joseph Glenn, Mial Smith and Bridger Webb, sells them to William Moore Sept. 9, 1823. Receipt of John Webb for his share May 11, 1823 (probably the same who sold to Wm. Moore) Receipts of Mose Bailey, Milton Pope Webb, Austin Webb, David Barnett, Benj. J. Barnett, Bridger Hainey in right of his wife Patsy, Edward Colly, Zacharias Colley, Wm. Cockran, Leonard Barnett, John Bellamy and John C. Webb, legatees.

WILLIAMS, MATTHEW J.—Page 269—dec'd. Inventory Jan. 3, 1828.
Page 441—Returns show Frances E. Williams, Admr. 1827. Thomas Hearn, Admr. in right of his wife 1828.

WOODS, MIDDLETON—Page 376—Est. Christopher Bowen, Admr. de bonis non Sept. 1828.

RETURNS OF ADMINISTRATORS AND GUARDIANS
WILL BOOK "N" 1828-31

ALEXANDER, PETER—Page 96—Guardian of Eliza Banks. Returns 1828-29 No data.
Page 208—Returns 1829 as guardian for Eliza, minor of William Banks shows interest received on Ann Banks note.

Page 207—Returns 1829 as guardian of Mary, orphan of William Banks, cash received from Ann Banks.

Page 349—Returns for 1830, shows notes on John H., and Ann Banks for hire of slaves.

Page 206—Return as guardian of William Jones, minor of Standly Jones, dec'd. for 1829 shows tuition paid James Loftin.

Page 350—Returns for 1830 show cash received from William Jones, Excr., of Standly Jones, as gdn. of James Jones, minor of Standly.

ALLEN, BEVERLY—Page 60—Guardian of the orphans of John Henderson, dec'd. Returns for 1827 show receipt of James B. Henderson in full of his legacy in slaves and cash, and his part of a tract of land in Monroe Co., drawn by the said orphans. Cash paid Henry Bourne for medical services; paid for clothing for Mary A. Henderson for 1827-28; paid Josias R. Banks tuition for John J. Henderson for 1827; paid William Whitfield for board and tuition for Joseph W. and Beverly A. Henderson for 1827, tuition to Reuben C. Beck. Receipt of John A. Sharman for his wife's part of a lot of land drawn by said orphans, Feb. 10, 1827.

Page 259—Returns for 1829-30, shows receipt of John M. Raiford for medical services, goods brought in Petersburg for Mary A., and Wm. Whitfield for board and tuition of Joseph W. and Beverly A. Henderson.

BANKS, JAMES A.—Page 93—Est. Returns for 1828 by Simeon Oliver, Admr. No data.

BANKS, WILLIAM—Page 106—Est. Returns of James Banks, Jr., one of the Admrs. for 1828 shows interest received on notes of Ann Banks and Willis Alexander, James Banks, Jr. Receipts of Willis Alexander, Thos. W. Davis, and William W. Bowen "in part of my legacy". Receipt of Peter Alexander as guardian of Eliza and Martha Banks and also as legatees. Receipt of Thos. W. Davis as gdn. of Thomas Banks. Receipt of Thomas D. Wooldridge; of James Banks, Jr; of John H. and William R. Banks all for part of their legacy.

BLACKWELL, DUNSTON—Page 113—Guardian of James L. Middleton, minor of Robert Middleton, dec'd. Paid James Loftin tuition and board for 1828.

Page 273—Returns for 1829 shows bought saddle and bridle for ward.

BRADLEY, ROBERT C.—Page 11—Est. Joseph Deadwyler, Excr. Returns for 1828-29 shows paid Horatio J. Goss for board and tuition for Jeptha M. Bradley, minor of said dec'd.

BERRY, ELIJAH—Page 147—Guardian of Sophia Rich. Returns for 1825 shows his receipt to William Rich, Excr. of John Rich dec'd. for Sophia's part of estate, and cash received of Richmond Rich, Admr. of Mary Rich, dec'd, for Sophia's part of Mary's estate, also paid for Sophia's part of expense of grant of land.

Page 184—Returns for 1829 shows paid Jamerson 1823, William Whitman 1824, William Davis 1825 for tuition; paid Watkins and Speed for her board Nov. 1822 to Jan. 1830, except ten months she was absent; receipt from James Nix "who intermarried with said Sophia."

BELL, THOMAS—Page 237—Admr. John A. Dye, dec'd. Returns for 1830 show David Dyes relinquishment and receipt Nov. 12, 1828. Receipts in full of Burrell, Jane, Elizabeth and Wm. Dye, and Vinson Hubbard. Also Thomas Bell's return as guardian for Geo. W., Martin B., and Susan F. A. Dye, shows David Bells receipt for tuition for M. B., and Susan A., and paid for board of all three.

BRANTLEY, JOSEPH M—Page 275—Est. William Dooley, Admr. Returns made 1830 shows paid for coffin, and paid Dr. R. Banks in 1824.

Page 303—Returns for 1830 shows receipt of Moses Hutcherson for a slave Naomi "being the whole of the property in the hands of the Admr. coming to my wife Nancy J. Hutcherson, formerly Nancy J. Brantley. Dec. 25, 1830.

BREWER, HORATIO J.—Page 196—Est. Returns of Mrs. Susanna J. Brewer Admx. shows pd. Wm. N. Richardson for Medical services for 1827 and Wm. Whitman tuition for minors 1828.

BREWER, JOHN—Page 217—dec'd. Inventory Aug. 11, 1830 shows only a slave Charity and her child Henry. Wm. F. Brewer, Admr.

BUTLER, JOHN—Page 289—Est. Returns of Martha Butler for 1830 shows paid for goods for the family.

CARTER, ELIZABETH—Page 23—Est. Richard Fortson, Excr. Returns for 1829 shows hire of slaves and rent of plantation.

Page 228—Returns for 1829 shows books bought for Chas. N. B. Carter.

CARTER, JOHN W.—Page 134—Guardian of William C. Woody. Returns for 1829, no data.

CLARK, CHRISTOPHER—Page 1—Est. David Hudson one of the Excrs. Returns for 1828 shows paid S. C. Oliver "medical account". Receipt of Christopher H. Clark in full of his proportionate share of Geo. W. W. Clark's est. Also Christopher H's receipt for his part of slaves etc. of his grandfathers and fathers estate. Receipt of Wm. D. Clark, gdn. of Thos. J. Clark for his part of Christopher Clark's est. and of his brother George W. Clarks est. Also Wm. D's receipt as gdn. of Mary Clark for her distributive share of her father Christopher and her brother Geo. W. Clark's estates.

Page 302—Returns of Wm. D. Clark gdn. for 1830 shows receipt of Thos. J. Clark in full of his legacy from his fathers est. and his brother Geo. W. Clark's est. Oct. 23, 1830. Receipt of Thos. Burgs (?) (Burgess?) in right of his wife Mary formerly Mary Clark in full of her legacy from her father's est. and her brother Geo. W. Clark's est.

CLARK, JAMES—Page 62—Est. Beverly Allen, Admr. Mary Clark, Admx. Returns for 1828-29 shows travelling expenses to Lincolnton to secure a tract of land sold by Hezekiah Dodge to James Clark, and travelling to S. C.

CLEVELAND, JOHN—Page 109—dec'd. Sale Dec. 16, 1828, Jacob M. Cleveland, Admr. Rhoda, Sarah W., James M., Jacob M., and Reuben Cleveland purchasers.

COOK, BEVERLY C.—Page 105—Guardian of James, Zimri, and Horatio Tate, minors of Zimri Tate, dec'd. Hire of slaves, and board for minors May 1828 to May 1829.

DAVIS, THOMAS—Page 5—Est. Sale of balance of property (except land and slaves) Dec. 12, 1828. Benajah Houston, Admr.
 Page 7—Returns for Mar. 1829 shows receipt of George Carter for his services as a temporary admr.
 Page 193—Division of slaves, Dec. 28, 1829. Legatees: Mrs. Susannah Wyche, Alfred Wyche signing as her Atty., and for Mary Johnson also. Thomas Williamson, signing as Atty., for Wm. Rosser, Thomas Davis, William Davis, Nancy Emory, Mary Fielding and John Davis. Cullen C. Knight signs as Atty. for Edward Davis; Wm. White's receipt for the distributive share of Jeptha Rosser "as a legatee."
 Page 292—Returns of Wm. White one of the Admrs. for 1830 shows paid Dr. D. W. Hammond for services.
 Page 301—Returns for 1831 shows receipt of Thos. Williamson, agent for residue of shares of Thomas, William, and John Davis and Mrs. Nancy Emory and Mrs. Mary Fielding and William Rosser. Receipt of Joseph Henry Lumpkin, Atty. for Mrs. Wyche, Mrs. Johnson and Mrs. Bass.

DAVIS, THOMAS F.—Page 309—Guardian for Thomas F. Rone. Returns for 1830 shows paid William Whitman tuition.

DEADWYLER, JOSEPH, Jr.—Page 35—Inventory July 14, 1829.
 Page 216—Sale Dec. 22, 1829 Alex. P. Houston, one of the Admrs. Rent of plantation and slaves.

DEADWYLER, MARTIN—Page 54—Guardian for Philip A. Wilhite. Returns for 1829 shows receipt of Philip A. Wilhite in full of his distributive share of the estate of Philip Wilhite, dec'd.

DEADWYLER, MARTIN—Page 350—Guardian of Jackson Oliver declares nothing has ever come into his hands as such. Jackson Oliver states the same and says he is twenty one years old. Feb. 28, 1831.

DYE, BROWN—Page 237—Est. Thomas Bell, Admr. Rent of land mentioned. Receipts of David Dye, Burrell, Jane, Elizabeth and William Dye and Vinson Hubbard in full, heirs of said est.

EDWARDS, JAMES—Page 13—Est. Returns of William D. Tinsley, Admr. in right of his wife Sarah B. Tinsley, formerly Sarah B. Edwards, Admx. Returns for 1828-29 show paid R. L. Crittenton for schooling Emaline Edwards in music, board of Emaline, board and clothes for Gilbert, Laura, and Sarah and tuition to Albert M. Spaulding for Gilbert and Laura; paid medical services rendered by Dr. Wm. D. Tinsley.
 Page 213—Returns for 1830 shows paid board for Felix G., Laura G., and Sarah M. Edwards and tuition to McCarty Oliver.

GEORGIA D. A. R.

Page 299—Division of est. into five equal parts, taken by Felix G., Laura G., and Sarah M. Edwards, Emily E. Patterson, formerly Emily E. Edwards and Sarah B. Tinsley, formerly Sarah B. Edwards. Recorded Dec. 6, 1830.

Page 318—Returns for 1830 shows paid tuition to R. W. Christian for Felix, Laura and Sarah.

FLEMING, SARAH Mrs.—Page 69—Returns of Moses Fleming, a lunatic No data.

FORTSON, JESSE—Page 20—dec'd. Sale April 7, 1829. Richard Fortson, Admr.

Page 269—Returns for 1830 show receipts of Isaac Almond for himself as legatee, and as gdn. for Jane M., Thomas, and Harriett Fortson, minors of said Jesse; of Simeon Almond legatee; of William F. Brewer, legatee.

FORTSON, RICHARD—Page 277—Guardian for Jesse M. Fortson, minor of Jesse Fortson, dec'd. Returns Nov. 1830 shows receipt of Richard for Jesse M's distributive share, and paid Cyrus Stewart tuition.

GATES, JAMES—Page 24—dec'd. Inventory May 21, 1829, shows one mattock and iron wedge.

GIBBS, WILLIAM—Page 10—dec'd. Inventory Mar. 30, 1829.

Page 102—Returns of Admr. Fortson Gibbs Nov. 1829 shows 23 bales of cotton sold in Augusta.

GOODE, NICHOLS—Page 166—Guardian for Milly L. Bell, now Milly L. Butler show paid Peter P. Butler in right of his wife, her legacy as left by the will of Joseph Bell, dec'd. July 24, 1828.

GROVES, JOHN J.—Page 163—Guardian for Francis F., and Amanda E. Terrell, orphans of William Terrell, dec'd. Returns show paid for passage of Francis F. Terrell from New York, paid board for both from July 1, 1828, paid for schooling of both, paid Francis's expenses to Lexington "to bind her out", paid Mrs. Terrell board for both for 1829, paid expenses of making titles to land sold by the heirs of Joseph Terrell. Received notes of W. Waldough Spearer atty. in fact for John W., and James F. Terrell, Elizabeth A. Ham, and Darby Henley, their proportionate share due the heirs of Wm. C. Terrell from the estate of Jos. Terrell, dec'd. By notes received of Joseph R. Terrell as his proportionate share of the est. of Joseph Terrell, dec'd., due the heirs of William C. Terrell. Also shows receipt of Brittian Terrell for expenses of Francis from New York to Ruckerville and board for both, and tuition paid James Loftin.

GUNTER, JESSE—Page 168—dec'd. Inventory Nov. 10, 1829. Susan Gunter, Excx.

Page 289—Returns for 1830 shows Susan Hubbard, formerly Susan Gunter, Excx.

HAM, JOHN—Page 18—Est. Returns of James Upshaw, one of the Excrs. Returns for 1829 shows Stephen Ham's receipt in full for the legacy of Nancy Ham, of whom Stephen is guardian.

HAYNES, MOSES—Page 209—Est. Returns of sale June 25, 1829 shows 190 acres of land on which L. Keeling lives, and 202½ acres in Coweta Co., Lot No. 169, 4th, Dist.

HEARD, JOHN A.—Page 24—dec'd. Inventory Mar. 4, 1829.

HEARD, BARNARD C.—Page 158—Est. Return of the sale Jan. 15, 1829 Page 187—Returns of Thomas J. Heard, Admr. for 1829 shows receipt of Samuel Edmondson for articles purchased in Augusta for Mrs. Mary Heard, wid. of dec'd; of James Banks, Sr., for tuition of Stephen Thomas Heard, minor of said Barnard C. Heard; of John Hudson what is due him, said Barnard C. Heard having been my guardian, John being a distributee of the estate of Nathaniel Hudson, dec'd.

HEARNE, THOMAS—Page 305—Guardian in right of his wife Frances E. Hearne for Barbara and Frances Williams, minors. Returns for 1829 shows receipt of Thomas Jones one of the Trustees of Elberton Female Academy for tuition for both.

HENDERSON, JOHN—Page 59—Est. Divided so as to give James B. Henderson, one of the heirs his share at the end of the present year. Dec. 27, 1827.

HICKMAN, MARTHA—Page 9—dec'd. Inventory Nov. 21, 1828. Benjamin Neal, Admr.

HUDSON, WILLIAM—Page 290—dec'd. Inventory Jan. 18, 1831 David Hudson, Admr.

HULME, WILLIAM—Page 180—dec'd. Sale Dec. 3, 1828. Purchasers, Margaret Hulme, John R. Hulme, Admr. Receipt of John T. Hulme in full of his distributive share Feb. 26, 1830.

JETER, BARNETT—Page 135—Est. Chas. Statham one of the Excrs. Returns for 1829 shows receipt of Benjamin Allen for part of his legacy of money; of Barnett Statham for part of his legacy in money; of R. Banks for interest on the legacy of Anderson Hicks and William Allen; of James Hicks for his distributive share; of Wm. R. Statham; of Peter Lamar in part of the portion due Wm. Quinn, a legatee; of Dunston Blackwell for legacies of Robert Jeter, Josiah R. Hicks, Bishop Hicks, Barnett Jeter, and Nancy Jeter, "I having an order from said legatees for their part; Robert Jeter and Josiah R. Hicks of N. C., Barnett and Nancy Jeter and Wm. B. Hicks of Decalb Co. Ga.

JONES, STANDLY—Page 70—Est. Sale Nov. 17, 1828. William Jones, Excr. Frances Jones, Excx. Returns show paid M. Chandler for making a coat for Elijah Jones one of the minors.

Page 322—Returns for 1830 shows receipt of Marshall Jones, Elijah Jones, Peter Alexander, guardian of Wm. Jones and James Jones, Frances Jones, legatees.

JONES, THOMAS—Page 127—Guardian of George I. Barr. Returns for 1830 no data.

JONES, WILEY W.—Page 172—Est. Returns of James Bell, Admr. with will annexed Mar. 1830, shows expense of going to Henry Co., and sale of slave Edmund.

JONES, WILLIAM—Page 331—Guardian of Thomas Jones, minor. Returns for 1830 shows paid board.

Page 333—Guardian of Martha Jones. Returns for 1830 show board paid.

Page 334—Guardian of Ann Jones. Returns for 1830 shows receipt for her legacy and tuition paid James Loftin and account of Sophia Eliza Metzler.

Page 337—Guardian of John Jones. Returns for 1830 show paid Samuel Collins for shoemaking and James Loftin tuition. All above are minors of Standley Jones, legacies according to will.

KNOTT, THOMAS—Page 315—Sale of estate Feb. 15, 1831. James Oliver, Admr.

McCURRY, LAUCHLIN—Page 88—dec'd. Benjamin Penn, Admr. Returns Sept. 1829 shows receipt to Sion Hunt, surviving co-partner of dec'd. Receipt of Thos. S. Hickman in right of his wife one of the legatees.

MORRISSON, JAMES—Page 148—Est. Thomas Morrisson one of the Admrs. Returns for 1829, no data.

Page 274—Returns for 1830, no data.

NIX, LUCY—Page 40—Est. James Nix, Admr. Returns for 1829, shows sale of Lot No. 135, 11th. Dist. Henry Co., for which expense of grant had to be paid before sale. Case, George and Joseph Nix, et al by James Nix vs Hardie Blackwell.

OLIVER, SIMEON—Page 95—Guardian for William C. Banks. Returns for 1828 shows hire of several slaves and receipt of Milly T. Meriwether for cash to be applied to clothing etc. of said Wm. C. Banks.

Page 271—Returns for 1829 calls Wm. C. Banks, minor of James A. Banks, dec'd.

PENN, BENJAMIN—Page 91—Guardian of Flora M., Daniel N., Patsy B., and Benjamin C. McCurry, orphans of Lauchlin McCurry, dec'd., Board for all for 1829.

Page 279—Returns for 1830 shqws board and clothing for all.

PROTHRO, NATHANIEL—Page 133—Est. Returns for 1829 of·John Dobbs, Excr., and Zilpha Prothro, Excx., shows receipt of Linsey Neal in full for principal and interest of what was willed to Nancy Gardner, now his wife.

ROAN, JOHN—Page 86—Est. William Rich, Admr. Returns Sept. 1829 no data.
Page 282—Returns for 1830, no data.

RICHARDS, REUBEN—Page 279—Est. Returns of Rachel Richards one of the Admrs. for 1830, shows paid Seaborn Jones for services in her suit vs Murdoch McLeod, expense of board for six orphans for ten years ending Sept. 7, 1830, and receipt of Oliver Threlkeld and Duncan C. McLauchlin for tuition.

ROEBUCK, ROBERT—Page 115—dec'd. Inventory Sept. 29, 1829.
Page 211—Sale Dec. 18, 1829, William White, Admr. Purchasers, Elizabeth L. Roebuck, widow, William and Eppy W. Roebuck.
Page 346—Returns for 1830 show paid James Loftin tuition.

ROYAL, JAMES—Page 335—Est. Solomon Jones one of the Admrs. Returns for 1830 shows receipt of John Royal "one of the heirs of said dec'd, and of Henry Hall in right of his wife Lavita Hall, formerly Lavita Royal.

RUCKER, JOSEPH—Page 17—Guardian of Eliza C. Hudson, minor of Nathaniel Hudson, dec'd. Returns for 1829 shows receipt of guardian to Linsey Oglesby, Sec. for Benjamin Cook former guardian and tuition paid Sarah D. Raymond.

RUCKER, ZACHARIAH—Page 114—dec'd. Inventory Sept. 29, 1829.
Page 215—Sale Dec. 3, 1829. Joseph Rucker, Admr.

SATTERWHITE, FRANCIS—Page 186—dec'd. Inventory Mar. 8, 1830.
Page 338—Returns for March 1831 of James Satterwhite, Admr. with will annexed shows he paid for supplies for the family in 1829 before he became admr., and the hire of a slave payable to Elizabeth Satterwhite "pr. sister".

SHACKLEFORD, HENRY—Page 204—Est. William White, Admr. Returns for 1827, no data.

STUART, CYRUS—Page 167—dec'd. Inventory Jan. 6, 1830.
Page 281—Sale Feb. 23, 1830, Thomas Hearne, Admr., estate consists of books and wearing apparel.

STATHAM, JOHN—Page 272—Est. John Brown one of the Excrs. Returns for 1830 shows lawsuit of Leonard Barnett, Jesse Harris and Memory Statham by their atty. in fact Nathaniel Statham vs. James Christian and John Brown, Excrs. Verdict for plaintiffs.

TATE, BEATRICE J. A.—Page 41—dec'd., est., Zimri W. Tate, Admr., and former guardian. Returns Sept. 1829 shows his commission for handling said dec'd, proportion of perishable property of Thomas Tate, dec'd in 1827. Receipt of B. W. Sayre for making wall around grave of dec'd, Oct. 30, 1828; of Drs. A. D. Statham and Wm. N. Richardson for services, and of Sarah D. Raymond for tuition.

GEORGIA D. A. R.

TATE, ZIMRI W.—Page 43—Admr. and former guardian of James M. Tate. Returns show cash advanced 1825 while at school at Franklin Paid for funeral sermon and burial clothing; paid B. W. Sayre Oct. 30, 1828 for walling grave; Dr. Ajax Armstead and Dr. Henry Bourne for services 1827. Also perishable property of Mrs. Tate 1827.

TATE, ZIMRI W.—Page 45—Admr. John W. Tate. Returns show same as above.

TATE, THOMAS—Page 48—dec'd. est. Zimri W. Tate, Admr. Returns Sept. 1829 shows paid the widow Permelia Tate, she having taken her dower, and B. W. Sayre for walling grave.

TATE, ZIMRI W.—Page 240-249—Admr, of James M., John W., and Beatrice J. A. Tate. Returns Sept. 1830, shows receipts of Permelia Tate of Wilkes Co., one of the legatees; of Augustine D. Statham of Wilkes Co., in right of his wife, Lucy B., formerly Lucy B. Tate; of Paschal D. Klugh of Wilkes Co., in right of his wife Martha M., formerly Martha M. Tate; of Taverner W. Fortson of Elbert Co., in right of his wife Katharine D., formerly Katharine D. Tate, and also in right of his child Laura P. E. Fortson for whom he is guardian, as respects her interest in the estate of Beatrice J. A. Tate; of Thomas J. Tate as a legatee of all three estates; of Sarah Y. Riddle of Wilkes Co., all signed 1829 and 1830. Receipts of all for their legacies from the estate of Thos. Tate, dec'd also due 1822. T. W. Fortson signing as Admr, of Katharine D. Fortson, dec'd. Mar. 19, 1830.

TATE, ZIMRI—Page 78—Est. Returns of William Rich and John A. Heard, Excrs. for 1829 shows paid Dr. Ajax Armstead and Dr. Wm. N. Richardson for services.

Page 91—Distribution of slaves 1828 shows receipts of Isaac M. Tate; of Tavner W. Fortson for the share of Eliz. D. Tate, now Eliz. D. Fortson; of Beverly O. Cook guardian for Horatio, James and Zimri Tate, for their share; of Enos Tate, Sr., and Jr., guardians for William M., Uriah M., Zimri M., and Martha J. Tate, legatees; of William Rich for share of Jacob M. Tate.

Page 260—Returns for Nov. 1830 shows William Rich surviving Excr.

Page 339—Returns Mar. 1831 shows receipt of Martha Tate for ten slaves "willed me by Zimri Tate, dec'd."

TERRELL, TIMOTHY—Page 33—dec'd. Inventory July 4, 1829.

Page 199—Sale Sept. 3, 1829, Sarah Terrell bought most of household goods, Phillip Terrell shot gun etc. John J. Groves and Robert L. Edwards, Admrs.

THRELKELD, MARCUS DELEFAETT—Page 313—dec'd. Sale Nov. 8, 1828 Delila Threlkeld bought horse etc, Oliver Threlkeld bought shot gun, also bought 202½ acres of land in Meriwether Co.

TUCKER, GODFREY—Page 96—dec'd. Inventory of property he did not give away by his will, May 8, 1829. Wiley Wall and Joseph Blackwell, Excrs. Books, trunk, man's saddle etc. listed.

TURMAN, GEORGE—Page 227—Est. Return of Samuel Turman, Admr. Sept. 1830, no data.

UNDERWOOD, WINNEFORD—Page 41—Est. Return Sept. 1829 shows amount retained by Reuben Underwood, Admr., for board and keep of dec'd for four years and eight months.

WARD, WALTER H.—Page 82—Est. Returns of sale of personal property Apr. 8, 1827, John Gray, Excr. Jane Ward bought bed and clothing. James Gray bought 202½ acres land in Henry Co.
Page 103—Returns May 1829 shows four slaves hired by Jane Ward and articles bought for the family. Expense of a business trip to S. C.
Page 232—Returns Sept. 1830, Abner Ward, Admr. Show part of slaves hired to William and Abner Ward, the rest kept by Martha Ward to assist her and the children. Receipt of Harris Walton atty in fact for Martha W. Ward for a part of her distributive share.

WARD, ABNER—Page 314—Guardian for Salley Ward, minor of William H. Ward, dec'd. Returns for 1831 shows receipt of Martha Ward for board for Salley.

WARNER, ELIZABETH—Page 276—Guardian for Nathan R. Warner, minor of Nathan Warner, dec'd. Returns for 1829 show paid William N. Richardson for medicine.

WEBB, CLAIBORN, Jr.—Page 49—dec'd. Martin Deadwyler and Abner Webb, Admrs. de bonis non. Returns July 1829 show receipts of Letty Webb for distributive share of Milton P. Webb, dec'd, signing as guardian, and also signs for Miles Smith's share. Also receipts of Abner Webb for his share; of John C. Webb for himself and for Joseph Glenn; of Bridger Webb for himself and for Joseph Deadwyler, Jr.; of John C. Webb as guardian of Andrew J. Webb; of Margaret Webb for herself and as guardian of Elijah Webb, minor.

WEBB, MILTON POPE—Page 53—Est. Returns July 1829, Martin Deadwyler one of the Admrs. Receipts of Letty Webb for a slave Jack, property of said dec'd.

WEBB, JOHN C.—Page 200—Guardian of Andrew Jackson Webb. Returns Mar. 17, 1830.

WEBB, LETTY—Page 230—Guardian of Alice A. M. and Claborn Webb, clothing and maintenance for both 1827-29.

WHEELER, THOMAS—Page 263—Est. Sale Jan. 1, 1830. Leroy, George, Thomas B., and Sarah Wheeler, purchasers. Jeremiah S. Warren, Excr.

WILKINS, JOHN—Page 149—Division of slaves. He having left his wife Nancy sole heir, she is willing to have a division. The other heirs sign the agreement Dec. 28, 1829 as follows; Clement Wilkins, Thomas Harris, Wilson White, Abner Sutton, Jacob Cox, David Dye, Israel Sneed.

GEORGIA D. A. R.

WILLIAMS, MATTHEW J.—Page 56—Division of est. Legatees, Frances E. Williams, Frances E. Hearne, gdn. of Barbara E. W., and Frances M. A. Williams, Shelton Oliver in right of his wife Martha B., formerly Martha B. William and Frances E. Hearne "as former wife of said dec'd. All signed May 9, 1829.
Page 175—Returns Feb. 1830 made by Thos Hearn, Admr. in right of his wife.

WOODS, WILLIAM—Page 128—Est. Jeptha V. Harris, Admr. Returns Jan. 1830 show receipt of Middleton G. Woods for himself and as guardian of Wm. H. C. Woods.
Page 160—Returns for 1830 says the above are the only legatees of said estate.

RECORD BOOK 1830-38
RETURNS OF ADMINISTRATORS AND GUARDIANS

ALLEN, BEVERLY—Page 43—Guardian, orphans of John Henderson, dec'd. Returns Nov. 1831 shows paid Thomas J. Sheppard in right of his wife Mary A., formerly Mary A. Henderson, slaves and cash from the sale of land in Monroe Co., drawn by said orphans. Paid board and tuition for Joseph W., and Beverly A. Henderson to William Whitfield, receipt signed by Matilda J. Whitfield for William.
Page 180—Returns for 1832 shows paid for coffin for John J. Henderson, and receipt of William A. Beck, Admr. of John J., for John J's share of estate. Paid Wm. Whitfield for board and tuition for Joseph Wm., and Beverly A. Henderson.

ALEXANDER, PETER—Pages 413-414—Guardian of Eliza Banks now Eliza Bryson, shows receipt of James Bryson in full of all demands, and guardian of Martha Banks now Martha Hudson, and receipt of John R. Hudson in full. July Term 1834.

ARNOLD, JAMES—Page 123—dec'd. Inventory Mar. 14, 1832. Beverly Allen Admr.

ALLEN, BEVERLY—Pages 425-428—Guardian of Susan T., and James Wm. Arnold, minors of James Arnold, dec'd. Shows board paid Jordan Jones for 1833.

ALLGOOD, PETER—Page 497—dec'd. Inventory Feb. 7, 1835

BREWER, HORATIO |G.—Page 14—Sale of estate Apr. 25, 1831 Susan Brewer, Admx.

BREWER, JOHN—Page 78—Est. William F. Brewer, Admr., with will annexed. Returns for 1831 shows paid James Brawner for medical services.
Page 355—Returns Jan. 1834 shows receipt of John Royal in right of his wife Martha formerly Martha Brewer for property which came

into the hands of Wm. F. Brewer as Admr. of John from the estate of Elisha Brewer.

BREWER, SUSAN—Page 101—Guardian of minors of Horation G. Brewer, dec'd. Board and clothes for Frances K., Sarah Ann R., Mary A., and Martha G. Brewer for 1831.
Page 386—Paid Moses W. Houston tuition for Frances K. for 1832.

BULLARD, THOMAS B.—Page 137—Guardian of Tapley Bullard, minor of Tapley Bullard, dec'd. Returns Feb. 1831, no data.

BANKS, RALPH—Page 137—Est. Thomas A. Banks one of the Excrs. Returns July 1832 shows receipts in full of Richard, Henry, James J., Lemuel and Ralph Banks, and Moses Butt in right of his wife, daughter of said dec'd.

BELL, MAYFIELD—Page 91—dec'd. Inventory Nov. 14, 1831. William A. Beck, Admr.
Page 302—Sale, Dec. 25, 1832. Azmond B. Bell, purchaser. Returns for 1832 shows paid Daniel Thornton board for Ann Bell, one of the minors, and paid a fine to the Sheriff for Lucious Bell, one of the legatees.

BURTON, RICHARD—Page 184—Est. William C. Davis, Admr. Returns 1830-31 shows sold and rented land in Fayette Co.

BURTON, WILLIAM C.—Page 288—Inventory Feb. 28, 1833.
Page 307—Sale, July 1, 1833. Abraham Burton, Admr. Mrs. Jane Burton, Abraham, German, Blackman, Nicholas and Leroy Burton, purchasers.

BELL, MARY—Page 241—Excx. of Joseph Bell, dec'd. Returns of Joseph Bell as Excr. of James Bell, dec'd, Mar. 1833. Receipts of Harmon Lovingood, James Bell, Thomas Bell, Jr., for himself and as guardian of David Bell, William Bell, Sarah Moon, William H. Moon, Elizabeth Moon, all signed Dec. 11, 1822.

BROWN, BENJAMIN—Page 338—Guardian of Milly L. Crawford, minor of William Crawford, dec'd. Nov. 1833, no data.

CRAWFORD, WILLIAM—Page 252—Est. Returns of Peter Alexander and Barden Rucker, Excrs. May 1833, shows cash received for a lot of land in Lee, now Sumter Co., sold for the benefit of the first set of children. Will says this property was for Oliver, James L., Richmond G., and Milly L. Crawford and Virginia Hunt. Receipts of Oliver Crawford, James L. Crawford, of Smith Cook, guardian of Richmond G. Crawford, of B. Brown, guardian of Milly L. Crawford, of Joel Hunt for his distributive share, and of Lucy Crawford for her share above paying of debts for herself and her children by William Crawford.

COOK, SMITH—Page 354—Guardian of Richmond L. Crawford, Richmond's receipt in full for what was coming to him from his father William Crawford. Sept. 2, 1833.

CHRISTLER, JULIUS—Page 313—dec'd. Inventory July 23, 1833.
Page 380-87—Returns of sale, Elizabeth Christler, purchaser. Gardner McGarity and Bardin Rucker, Admrs.

COLBERT, THOMAS—Page 460—Guardian of Malinda Colbert, James, John, Lucy and Sarah Nix, minor heirs of Richard Colbert, dec'd. Receipts of Walker Horton in right of his wife Malinda, 1826, of John Nix, 1833, of James Nix, 1824, of Lemuel N. Arnold in right of his wife formerly Sarah Nix, 1832, of Lucy Nix to Thomas Colbert guardian of Joseph Nix's children, 1825.

CLEVELAND, JOHN—Page 493—Est. Return of Jacob N. Cleveland, Admr, shows Rhoda Cleveland rented the land, 1829-30-31-32-33 and bought it Nov. 1833.

DEADWYLER, JOSEPH, Sr.—Page 19—dec'd. Inventory Apr. 14, 1831, Martin Deadwyler, Excr.

DAVIS, THOMAS F.—Page 84—Guardian of Thomas F. Roan. Returns show his receipt to William Rich, Admr. of John Roan, for the minors part of the estate. Paid board etc for 1828-31.

DEADWYLER, JOSEPH, Jr.—Page 155—dec'd. Division of property Dec. 21, 1831, between Alex P. Houston, in right of his wife Martha, formerly the widow of said dec'd, and Margaret A. Deadwyler, daughter of said dec'd.

DEADWYLER, MARTIN—Page 160—Guardian of Philip A. Wilhite. Returns Sept. 1832 shows bought saddle and bridle for ward, and expense of going to Jackson Co. on business.

DYE, BROWN—Page 430—dec'd. Returns of Thomas Bell, Jr. in right of his wife Polly Dye, shows receipt of John H. Butler for claims in right of his wife formerly Polly Hubbard, on estates of Brown and John A. Dye, dec'd. Dec. 29, 1830.

DEADWYLER, MARGARET A.—Page 416—A. P. Houston, guardian. Returns for 1833 shows paid board, clothing and tuition.

DYE, JANE—Page 495—Guardian of minors of Thompson Dye, dec'd. Returns show receipts of Richmond Rich in right of his wife Frances W. Rich, formerly Dye, minor heir of Thompson Dye, dec'd, Jan. 6, 1832; of Mary J. Dye for her part of her grandfather Brown Dye, dec'd, estate. Nov. 6, 1833; of Lewis R. Jones, in right of his wife Elizabeth K., formerly Dye, minor heir of Brown Dye, dec'd. Jan. 6, 1832; of Sarah T. Dye for legacy from grandfather Brown Dye, dec'd, Mar. 27, 1832.

FORTSON, THOMAS—Page 176—dec'd. Sept. 12, 1832—
Page 333—Returns of sale, Samuel Kerlin, Admr.
Page 345—Returns 1834 shows Samuel Kerlin, Admr., in right of his wife.

FORTSON, TAVNER W.—Page 423—Return as guardian of Permelia L. E. Fortson, shows received money from estates of Zimri W., and Beatrice J. A. Tate, dec'd.

GROVES, JOHN J.—Page 18—Guardian of Francis F. and Amanda E. Terrell, minors of William O. Terrell, dec'd. Receipt of Brittian Terrell for board and clothes for both for 1830.
Page 197—Returns for 1831 same expenses.
Page 367—Returns for 1832-34, same expenses.

GAULDING, ALEX.—Page 41—dec'd. Inventory Aug. 9, 1831.
Page 168—Sale Dec. 26, 1831. Nancy Gaulding rented plantation, Richard and William Gaulding hired slaves. Nancy, Admx.
Page 369—Division of slaves, Jan. 11, 1834. Distributees, Elizabeth Gaulding, Leslie G. Carter who married Mary Ann Gaulding one of the children of said dec'd., Richard Gaulding, Wm. B. Gaulding, Lucy Gaulding, Nancy Gaulding, widow of said dec'd., Wm. B., signs as guardian of Elizabeth and Lucy Gaulding and renders a statement of what he received from his father in his lifetime.

GUNTER, JESSE—Page 89—dec'd. Est. Vinson Hubbard, Admr., in right of his wife Susan formerly Susan Gunter. Returns for 1831 shows paid for coffin and paid Wm. D. Tinsley for medical services.

HULME, WILLIAM—Page 106—dec'd. Joseph R. Hulme, Admr. Returns for 1831, shows all slaves hired by Margaret Hulme, and receipt of John T. Hulme for part of his legacy.

HULME, MARGARET—Page 238—Guardian of minors of William Hulme, namely, Thomas M., Henry B., Agnes M., Susannah, Wm. A. Hulme. Returns for 1833 shows paid board and tuition.

HAYNES, MOSES, Sr.—Page 366—Est. Returns of Thomas Haynes, Admr. for 1833 shows receipts of Moses Haynes in full of his legacy, of Mary Arnett for her legacy, of John Dobbs in right of his wife Jane Dobbs, dec'd, in full of her legacy, of Sarah Haynes in part of her legacy.

HEARD, BERANRD C.—Page 417—dec'd. Division of slaves so as to give Henry Bourne in right of his wife Mary, formerly Mary Heard, widow of dec'd, his share. Dec. 27, 1833.

HEARNE, THOMAS—Page 452-454—Guardian in right of his wife of Barbara E. and Frances N. A. Williams. Returns 1830-34 shows hire of slaves etc.

JETER, BARNETT—Page 39—dec'd. Returns of Chas. Statham one of the Excrs. for 1831 shows receipts of legatees, Richard W. Statham, Thomas Stribling, Samuel Davis, Peter Lamar, Augustine J. Davis, Wm. R. Statham, Aug. D. Statham, Wm. Jeter, Barnett Jeter for himself and as guardian of Willis B. Hicks, and of Mary E., James, Robert, and Samuel Jeter, minors of Dudley Jeter, and of James Lawlis for the legacy of Catharine Lawlis formerly Catharine Jeter.

GEORGIA D. A. R.

JONES, JESSE—Page 26—Est. Arthur Jones, Excr. Returns for 1831 shows receipts of Edmond Jones in right of his wife Keziah, and Hyram Jones in right of his wife Litha, daughters of dec'd.

JONES, WILEY—Page 36—Est. James Bell, Admr. Returns for 1831, No data.

JONES, STANDLEY—Page 432—Est. William Jones, Excr. Returns for 1834 shows sale of land in Early Co., for which Fleming A. Alexander gives receipt in right of his wife Ann, of John, William, Frances, Elijah, Marshall, and Garland Jones, and of Peter Alexander guardian of James Jones.

JONES, WILLIAM—Page 103-105—Guardian of Sarah Jones. Returns for 1831, show tuition paid and receipt of Fleming A. Alexander in full of the legacy of Ann Alexander formerly Ann Jones, and tuition paid for Martha Jones, and for Thomas Jones all minors of Standley Jones.

JONES, SIMEON—Page 237—dec'd. James Jones, Admr. Returns Mar. 1833 shows expenses paid to Habersham Co., to sell the real estate of said dec'd.

KIRLEN, DAVID—Page 5—Guardian of James Kerlen. Returns for 1830 shows clothes charged to minor, and credit for minors work.

KERLIN, SAMUEL—Page 404—Guardian of Richard E., Benjamin H., Edward K., and Rachel A. Fortson, orphans of Thomas Fortson, dec'd., also Admr. of said dec'd estate, having married the widow. Returns 1834 shows guardian having received the property.

LANE, THOMAS—Page 6—dec'd. Return of John A. Lane, Excr. Returns for 1829 shows paid Job Weston for copying will.

LUNSFORD, JAMES—Page 196—Guardian of John W., and Armstrong Roberts. Returns show tuition paid for John W.

LOWREMORE, ANDREW—Page 359—Guardian of Jacob Kerlin. Returns show receipt of Jacob Jan. 14, 1834, "for all my services rendered my guardian".

MILLER, JEDEDIAH S.—Page 27—dec'd. Inventory, Jan. 30, 1831. Elizabeth O. Miller and James Edwards, Admrs.
Page 140—Returns show receipt for rent for a house and lot in Petersburg, for 1831.

MOSS, BEVERLY—Page 176—dec'd. Inventory Oct. 3, 1832.

MALEY, JOHNSON—Page 449—Guardian of Sidney Maley minor Returns July 1834 shows "received from the estate of John Maley, dec'd of Va. his part", and Sidney's receipt in full.

McMULLAN, LEWIS—Page 464—dec'd. Inventory Aug. 15, 1834. Sinclair McMullan, George McCurdy, Test.

Page 491—Sale Jan. 21, 1835. Elizabeth, Frances, Joice, Thomas, Daniel, and Patrick McMullan, purchasers.

OLIVER, SIMEON—Page 113—Guardian of William C. Banks, minor of James A. Banks, dec'd. Returns 1831.
Page 337—Returns show tuition paid Wm. H. Threlkeld 1831.
Page 450—Returns for 1833 shows paid V. Smith board.

OLIVER, THOMAS—Page 291—Guardian of William T. O. Cook. Shows William's receipt to Thomas Oliver and Frances Housley, formerly Frances Cook, "my guardians" in full of his distributive share of estate of William T. Cook, dec'd.

PENN, BENJAMIN—Page 49—Guardian of heirs of Abijah Hendrick. Returns for 1831 shows receipts of John L. Barnes for his distributive share in full in right of his wife, Polly Seals Hendrick, now Polly Barnes, of Nelson Hendrick in full of his distributive share "of my fathers estate for himself and as atty. in fact for John Mason and Ann his wife, formerly the widow of Abijah Hendrick, she choosing a childs part. All mention land sold in Jones Co. as part of each legacy.

PENN, BENJAMIN—Page 80—Guardian of minor heirs of Lauchlin McCurry, dec'd. Returns 1831 shows receipt of Abner J. Penn for tuition for Daniel N., and Martha B. McCurry for 1831.
Page 340—Returns for 1832 shows board for two minors, and tuition for Daniel N., and Benj. C. McCurry, paid A. J. Penn.
Page 356—Returns for 1833 shows board and tuition for all three.

PROTHRO, ZILPHIA—Page 54—dec'd. Inventory Nov. 26, 1831.
Page 205—Sale Jan. 27, 1832. William and George Prothro purchasers. Jesse Dobbs, Admr.

PATTERSON, WILEY—Page 86—Guardian of Felix G., Lamar G., and Sarah B. Edwards, minors of James Edwards, dec'd. Felix G. received pay for work done for Wm. D. Tinsley, 1831.
Page 275—Returns for 1832, shows paid tuition for all, Robert G. Clowney, teacher.
Page 364—Returns for 1833 shows paid Wm. D. Tinsley board for all three.

PREWIT, WILLIAM—Page 187—dec'd. Inventory Nov. 24, 1832. John Prewit, Admr.
Page 385—Returns for 1833, shows receipts of Willis Prewit in full of his share, and of Zilpha Prewit for cash for use of the family.

PULLIAM, WILLIAM—Page 467—Guardian of Lucious K. M. Bell. Returns for 1834 shows receipt of Dr. Thomas F. Gibbs for "attention on Lucious when stabbed".

RUCKER, JOSEPH—Page 41—Guardian of Eliza C. Hudson, minor. Returns Sept. 1831, no data.
Page 155—Returns Dec. 1831 says minor of Nathaniel Hudson, dec'd.

GEORGIA D. A. R.

RUCKER, ZACHARIAH—Page 70—Est. Joseph Rucker, Admr. No data.

RUCKER, JAMES—Page 107—Est. Willis B. Jones, Admr. Return Mar. 1832. No data.
Page 358—Returns for 1833 shows receipt of W. B. White in right of his wife.

RUCKER, WILLIAM—Page 487—Dec'd. Division of slaves Jan. 5, 1835. Tavener, William and Barden Rucker, William and Susan Childs, Lemuel Rucker's children and Frances Jones, Legatees.

ROAN, JOHN—Page 49—Est. William Rich, Admr. Returns show receipt of Peter Bevell in full of his distributive share, of Thomas F. Davis, guardian of Thos. F. Roan for wards share. Jul. 30, 1831.

ROEBUCK, ROBERT—Page 60—Est. William White, Admr. Sold several tracts of land 1831.

RICH, WILLIAM—Page 235—Guardian of Jacob M. Tate. Returns show Jacob's receipt in full for his distributive share of his father Zimri Tate's estate. Nov. 13, 1832.

SATTERWHITE, FRANCIS—Page 97—Est. James Satterwhite, Admr, with will annexed. Returns show receipts of Anderson and Elizabeth McGuire for pay for taking care of the widow Eliz. Satterwhite 1831.
Page 229—Receipts as above for 1831-32 and paid Benj. Smith Feb. 5, 1833 for draws for Elizabeth, widow in the land and Gold Lotteries.

STUART, CYRUS—Page 119—Est. Thomas Hearn, Admr. Returns 1831 No data.

SMITH, VALENTINE—Page 208—Guardian of Louisa E., Geo. L., John A., Upshaw, minors of George Upshaw, dec'd. Returns 1833.
Page 400—Returns Mar. 1834, shows board and clothes for all, James Loftin tuition, James Brawner medical services.

SHOCKLEY, JAMES A.—Page 344—Guardian of James M. Henderson, minor of Simeon Henderson. Receipt in full of James M. Henderson Jan. 6, 1834.

STONE, WILLIAM—Page 409—Inventory Mar. 5, 1834.
Page 434—Sale. May 15, 1834. Eastin Fortson, Admr.

TAYLOR, ELIZABETH—Page 19—Inventory May 25, 1831.

TURMAN, SAMUEL—Page 33—Guardian of Mariah and Thos. J. Turman. Returns show receipt of Thos. J. for slaves, his part of his father Geo. Turman's estate. July 7, 1828, and of John Hall in right of his wife Mariah formerly Turman, May 1, 1827.

TURMAN, GEORGE—Page 34—dec'd. Samuel Turman and William Pulliam, Admrs. Returns show receipt of John Hall in right of his wife Mariah formerly Turman, as a distributee. Aug. 11, 1831.

TATE, ZIMRI—Page 236—dec'd. Final settlement, William Rich surviving Excr. Legatees, Beverly C. Cook, guardian, Jacob M. Tate, William A. Johnson, T. W. Fortson, Enos Tate, Jr. guardian.

THRELKELD, MARCUS D. F.—Page 146—Est. Oliver Threlkeld, Admr. Returns July 1832 shows paid burial expenses and expenses to Meriwether Co. to sell land, and expense of grant of land. Receipts of Stephen Wilson, Samuel David, Delilah Threlkeld, for their proportionate shares.

TUCKER, STEPHEN H.—Page 165—Guardian of Martha W., and Sarah H. Tucker, minors. Returns Sept. 1832 shows guardians receipt to Thomas J. Heard, Admr. of John A. Heard, dec'd for money.

TERRELL, TIMOTHY—Page 181—dec'd. John J. Groves and Robert L. Edwards, Admrs.

Page 352—Returns show receipt of Sarah Terrell for herself, and as guardian of Mary E., Nancy W., and Sarah Ann Terrell; of Booker S. Terrell for himself and as agent for Joel Terrell; of Philip Pane Terrell as Admr. of Timothy Terrell, Jr., dec'd. a legatee of said estate, and for himself as a legatee, and as guardian of James Terrell minor of Timothy Terrell, dec'd.

TERRELL, SARAH—Page 277—Guardian of Elizabeth Ann, Nancy W., and Sarah Ann Terrell, minors of Timothy Terrell, dec'd.

Page 387—Returns for 1833 show tuition for Nancy and Sarah Ann, and extra clothing for Mary E. Terrell "she being a young lady".

TERRELL, TIMOTHY, Jr.—Page 419—dec'd. Philip P. Terrell, Admr.

TERRELL, PHILIP P.—Page 419—Guardian of James Terrell, minor, shows Philip's receipt for James part of Timothy Terrell, Sr's estate. Dec. 23, 1833.

THORNTON, JOHN—Page 310—dec'd. Inventory July 12, 1833.

Page 361—Returns for 1833 shows Benjamin Thornton, Admr.

TATE, WILLIAM, Sr.—Page 322—dec'd, Returns of David Hudson, one of the Excrs. showing property in hands of Elishaba Tate, widow of dec'd, at her death. Receipts of legatees for their part of the slaves, namely Daniel, James, and John Tate, George Upshaw, B. Andrews, John Watkins, agent for Samuel Watkins.

TATE, ELISHABA—Page 435—dec'd, widow of William Tate, Sr., dec'd. Return of Inventory May 5, 1834.

UPSHAW, GEORGE—Est. James Upshaw, Excr. Returns for 1833 show V. Smith, guardian of minors.

VAWTER, JOHN—Page 361—est. Reuben Brown, Admr. Returns Nov. 1833 Shows receipt of John Ray "as an Atty" in full of my distributive part.

GEORGIA D. A. R.

VICKERY, JAMES—Page 311—dec'd. Inventory July 12, 1833. Mary Vickery, Admx.
    Page 333—Sale Aug. 15, 1833. Mary Vickery principal purchaser, and Aaron Vickery, Jr.

WOODS, WILLIAM—Page 2—Est. Jeptha V. Harris, Admr. Returns show receipt of Middleton G. Woods for himself and as guardian of William H. C. Woods, April 10, 1830.

WARD, WILLIAM H.—Page 56—Est. Abner Ward, Admr. Returns Nov. 1831 Division of slaves between Martha W. Ward, widow of dec'd. and Sarah Ward, minor of said dec'd.
    Page 193—Returns show receipt of Martha Ward, widow in full, except lot No. 141, 8th Dist. Dooly Co. Feb. 7, 1831.

WHITE, WILLIAM—Page 87—Est. Jesse White, Excr. Returns show receipt of Wm. Williams, guardian, "for use of my children" Dec. 15, 1831, and of Lydia White for part of her legacy Dec. 30, 1831.

WHEELER, THOMAS—Page 100—dec'd. Jeremiah S. Warren, Excr. Returns show receipts of George, Thos. B., Leroy, Benjamin Wheeler by his Atty, Colby Wheeler, Job Franklin and Ezekiel Underwood. All signing as legatees, 1829-30.

WEBB, LETTY—Page 167—Guardian of Claborn and Alice Ann Mildred Webb. Returns for 1831 show paid tuition.

WILHIGHT, YOUNG—Page 411—dec'd. Inventory Mar. 6, 1834. Philemon R. Wilhight, Admr.

Minutes of Inferior Court, 1791-1830

SEVERAL BOOKS BOUND TOGETHER

Jan. Term 1830—Page 2—Sarah Terrell, widow of Timothy Terrell appointed guardian of her three young daughters, Mary E., Nancy W., and Sarah Ann Terrell.

Page 2—William W. Downer appointed guardian of William G. Bullard, over 14 years old, minor of Tapley Bullard, dec'd.

Page 3—Peter Alexander appointed guardian of James Jones under 14, minor of Stanley Jones.

John Lewis appointed guardian of his own minor children, Hester, John W., Mary M., and Thos. W. Lewis.

March Term 1830—Page 9—Ordered that Sophronia J., James M., and John A. H. Kennedy, children of William J. O. and Elizabeth Kennedy be bound to John Cason till they are 21.

Page 10—Alex. P. Houston, having married Martha P. Deadwyler, widow of Joseph Deadwyler, Jr., asks that he be appointed Admr. with Mial Smith of said estate. He is also appointed guardian of Margaret Ann Deadwyler, minor of said Joseph, dec'd.

Page 11—Francis Dunn an orphan of Francis Dunn, dec'd. 14 years old bound to Westly Bailey.

May Term 1830—Page 15—Susan Brewer, widow of Horatio G. Brewer appointed guardian of her four young children, Frances K., Mary M., Sarah Ann R., and Martha J. Brewer.

Ann Walker a minor of 11 years, daughter of Sally Walker having been bound to John Bullis now dec'd., she is now bound to Robert Hinton.

July Term 1830—Page 17—Catharine and William Brantly, over 14, orphans of Black Brantly, choose Wm. W. Dooly, guardian.

Sept. Term 1830—Page 19—Return of Thomas Bell, Admr. on estate of John A. Dye, in right of his wife, ordered recorded. Also guardian of George W., Martin B., and Susan A. F. Dye.

Page 20—Letters of administration granted Zeuriah King on estate of Thomas King, dec'd.

Alfred Hammond appointed guardian of Chas. N. P. Carter minor orphan.

Page 21—Brockman A. Bell, 17 years old chooses Isaac N. Davis guardian.

Page 24—Abner Webb, Elisha Ford, Matthew J. Black and Horatio J. Goss legatees enter caveat to will of Joseph Deadwyler, dec'd.

Nov. Term 1830—Page 25—Martha and Sarah Tucker, under 14 years, Stephen H. Tucker appointed guardian.

Page 26—Beverly Allen and Mary Clark, Admrs. of James Clark, dec'd. dismissed, having finished.

Page 28—Jane Dye, guardian of minors of Thompson Dye given leave to sell real estate.

Page 29—Will of Joseph Deadwyler, dec'd. ordered recorded. Martin, Asa and John G. Deadwyler appointed Excrs.

Page 30—Estate of James Edwards, dec'd. be divided into five equal shares.

Page 32—Tapley Bullard, a minor over 14 chooses Thomas B. Bullard guardian.

Page 33—Return of Elizabeth Warner, guardian of Nathan B. Warner, a minor recorded.

Jan. Term 1831—Caveat of David Hudson against John Gunter being appointed Admr. of William Hudson, dec'd., upon which David is appointed.

Page 35—Return of sale of Jesse Gunter, dec'd. made by Susan Gunter now Susan Hubbard be recorded. Felix G. Edwards, minor of James Edwards, dec'd., over 14, chooses Wiley Patterson guardian.

Page 37—Leave to sell a tract of land in Carroll Co. for the benefit of the orphans of Zimri Tate, dec'd. said land having been drawn by them.

Page 38—Wiley Patterson appointed guardian of Laura G., and Sarah M. Edwards, both under 14.

Page 40—Return of William D. Clark guardian of Thomas J., and Mary Clark minors recorded. Return of Andrew Lawremore, guardian of Jacob Kerlin, minor recorded.

March Term 1831—Page 47—Easton Fortson appointed guardian of his own children, Haley, Benjamin, Thomas J., and George G. Fortson all under 14 years, to take care of a legacy left them in the will of William Haley, dec'd.

Page 48—Notice of Isaac N. Davis to be dismissed as guardian of Brockman Bell, minor of Mayfield Bell, dec'd.

Page 49—Richard G. Crawford, minor of William Crawford, dec'd., over 14 chooses Smith Cook guardian.

Page 50—Return of Martin Deadwyler guardian of Jackson Oliver, a minor, recorded.

April Term 1831—Page 51—Return of David Kerlin, guardian of James Kerlin recorded.

May Term 1831—Page 52—Letters of administration granted Eliz. Miller and James Edwards on estate of Jedediah H. Miller, dec'd.

David N. Hudson appointed guardian of Mary, David N., and Elizabeth A. Hudson minors of William Hudson, dec'd., all under 14.

Page 53—Returns of Isaac Almond guardian of Thomas D., Jane M., and Alemede H. Fortson, orphans of Jesse Fortson, dec'd.

Page 53—Returns of John J. Groves guardian of Frances F., and Amanda E. Terrell orphans of William O. Terrell recorded.

Will of Zachariah Dickerson, dec'd. recorded, Wm. White, Excr.
Page 54—Will of Lucy Crawford probated, Peter Alexander and David Dobbs, Excrs.

July Term 1831—Page 58—Nancy Gaulding appointed Admr. of Alex Gaulding, dec'd. Will of Simeon Henderson ordered recorded and James Banks, Jr., and William Bailey appointed Excrs.

Page 60—Six slaves of Joseph Deadwyler ordered divided between A. P. Houston in right of his wife, and Margaret A. Deadwyler daughter of said dec'd.

Sept. Term 1831—Will of John Bray, dec'd., ordered recorded. Larkin Coker named Excr. in said will qualifies.

Page 62—James M. Henderson over 14 chooses James A. Shockley guardian. William Bailey appointed guardian of Amelia and Cinthy Henderson, minors of Simeon Henderson, dec'd. William J. Henderson over 14, chooses Beverly Allen guardian, and he is appointed guardian of Thomas B. Henderson, both minors of Simeon Henderson, dec'd.

Page 63—William Williams appointed guardian of his own children, William, Mary Ann and Harman Williams, and heirs of Sarah Williams wife of William, to take care of a legacy left by the will of William White, dec'd. William A. Beck appointed Admr. of John J. Henderson, dec'd.

Page 66—Will of Barnabas Pace, dec'd. ordered recorded, Dreadzil Pace named Excr.

Nov. Term 1831—Page 68—Jesse Dobbs appointed Admr. of Zilphy Prothro, dec'd.

Page 69—Nancy Bell applies for letters of administration on estate of Mayfield Bell, dec'd., she refusing to give bond and William A. Beck entering caveat he is appointed.

Dec. Term 1831—Page 70-71—It appearing to the Court that by the last will of Lucy Crawford certain slaves are to be divided among Burton E., Leroy R., and Wm. H. Crawford, children of John Crawford, so that they should receive their distributive share upon majority, Burton E., being of age this month, commissioners appointed to divide said slaves.

Jan. Term 1832—Page 72—Will of Dionysius Oliver, dec'd., offered for probate, Caveat entered.

Page 73—Caveat of Thomas Oliver one of the legatees, by his attorney Isaac N. Davis, claims that the testator was unduly influenced, and expresses his intention not to allow it to remain, that Superior Court in 1820 refused to admit it to record. Reuben Goolsby security for Nancy Galding, Admr. of Alex. Galding, dec'd., withdraws as such claiming mismanagement. John Seals application to be appointed Admr. of James Arnold, dec'd. caveated by Beverly Allen and he is appointed.

Page 75—Will of Dionysius Oliver, dec'd. ordered recorded.

Page 76—Margaret C. Hines, illegitimate daughter of Polly Hines, seven years old next March bound to Amos Richardson.

Page 77—Return of David Kerlin, guardian of James Kerlin, minor recorded. Return of Thomas F. Davis, guardian of Thos. F. Roan recorded. David Daniel appointed guardian of Emily Mitchell under 14, reputed daughter of Polly Harper.

Page 78—Return of Vinson Hubbard, Excr. in right of his wife, of Jesse Gunter, recorded.

May Term 1832—Page 84—Will of George Upshaw ordered recorded. James Upshaw qualifies as Excr.

Page 84-85—Zimri W. Tate having been appointed guardian for the minor heirs of Thomas Tate, dec'd. Jan. 8, 1822, namely: Lucy B., James M., John W., Lawrence P., and Beatrice J. A. Tate, that Pemelia Tate, Anderson Riddle and Paschal D. Klugh were security, the latter now reports that said guardian has failed to make returns etc.

Page 85—Letters of administration on estate of Nancy Cardin, dec'd. wife of Robert Cardin, and formerly a daughter of Moses Haynes of this county dec'd. Granted Thomas Haynes.

Page 86—Division of part of property of Lucy Crawford, dec'd. recorded, Peter Alexander and David Dobbs, Excrs.

Page 87—Will of Thomas Akin, dec'd. recorded, Beverly Allen qualifies as Excr. Slaves and real estate of Mayfield Bell ordered sold. William A. Beck, Admr.

July Term 1832—Page 88—Agnius M., and William A. Hulme choose Margaret Hulme guardian they being over 14 years old. She is appointed guardian of Susanna, Thomas M., and Henry B. Hulme minors under 14. Returns of Thomas B. Bullard guardian of Tapley Bullard recorded.

Page 89—Benjamin Brown appointed guardian of Milley L. Crawford orphan of William Crawford, dec'd. Letters of administration de bonis non granted Beverly Allen on estate of Thos. Akin, dec'd.

July Term—Page 89—Valentine Smith appointed guardian of John A., Louisa E., and George L. Upshaw. Jesse Dobbs, Admr. of Zilphy Tate, allowed to sell real estate.

Page 90—Sidney Maley minor of John Maley chooses Johnson Maley guardian. Will of John Canning, dec'd, probated, Benajah Houston qualifies as Excr.

Page 91—Lemuel N. Arnold appointed Admr. with the will annexed of William Arnold, dec'd. Returns of Alex. P. Houston as Admr. in right of his wife of Joseph Deadwyler, recorded.

Sept. Term 1832—Page 93—Will of Enos Tate, dec'd, probated. Zimri A., and Enos Tate, Jr. qualify as Excrs.

Page 94—Samuel Kerlin appointed Admr. of Thomas Fortson, dec'd. John Prewet appointed Adr. of William Prewet, dec'd. Will of Elizabeth Hall probated, Singleton W. Allen qualifies as Excr.

Page 95—Samuel Kerlin appointed guardian of Benjamin H., Richard E., Edwin K., and Rachel A. Fortson, minor heirs of Thomas Fortson dec'd., all under 14.

Page 96—Will of James Hunt probated, Sion and Willis Hunt qualify as Excrs. Lucresy B. Moss appointed Admr. of Beverly Moss, dec'd. Sale of property of Alex. Gaulding by Nancy Gaulding ordered recorded.

Nov. Term 1832—Page 98—Elizabeth Akin, minor of Thomas Akin, dec'd. over 14, chooses Beverly Allen, guardian

Page 99—Lucius J. B. Bell, minor of Mayfield Bell, over 14, chooses William Pulliam, guardian.

Jan. Term 1833—Page 100—Philip P. Terrell appointed Admr. of Timothy Terrell, Jr. dec'd. Abraham Burton appointed Admr. of William O. Burton, dec'd.

Page 101—Returns of James Lunsford guardian of John W., and Armstrong Roberts minors recorded.

Page 103—Elizabeth and Benjamin H. White, over 14, orphans of David White, dec'd, choose William White, guardian. He is appointed guardian of George W. White, under 14.

Page 105—Ann Bell, over 14, minor of Mayfield Bell, dec'd, chooses William D. Thornton guardian. Rhoda Cleveland appointed guardian of Ibrey Cleveland, minor of John Cleveland, dec'd.

March Term 1833—Page 105—Shelton White, Excr. of Thomas Bullard, dec'd, applies for leave to sell land and slaves of said estate. Will of John M. White probated.

Page 108—William Gaulding, minor and orphan, over 14 chooses Joshua O. Wyche, guardian.

MINUTES OF INFERIOR COURT, 1791—1830

Another section of this book

Jan. 4, 1826—Page 1—Abner Ward appointed guardian of Sally Ward, minor of William H. Ward, dec'd.

March Term 1826—Page 5—Return of William Patterson, Admr. of Elza Patterson recorded. Rule nisi granted at July Term last at the instance of James M. Tate and Asa Thompson in right of their wives ordering James Watkins, Jr., Excr. of a paper purporting to be the will of James Watkins, Sr., to show cause why said will should not be annulled.

Page 6—Thomas J., and John A. Heard appointed Attys. to take out bond of Presly and James Christian as Admrs. of John R. Wilhite and of Meshack T. Wilhite as guardian of Philip A., and Geriah G. Wilhite.

Page 9—Nace Roberts, illegitimate child of Patsy Roberts, now about 13, bound to Hosey Hathcock.

July Term 1826—Page 9—Sally Ward App. Admr. Richard Ward, dec'd.

Page 10—Job Weston, Clerk of Court ordered to deliver to Thomas O. Wilhite the bond of Martin Deadwyler as guardian of Nancy F., and

Elizabeth P. Wilhite minor heirs of Philip Wilhite, dec'd. for the purpose of commencing action in favor of John B. Wilhite in right of his wife Elizabeth P., and Joseph Y. Wilhite in right of his wife Nancy F. Richard Fortson and Milly Willis dismissed as Admrs. of John Willis, dec'd. Rebecca Pucket, about 13, and John Pucket about 9, children of James Pucket, unprotected and unsupported by their father, bound to their grandfather John N. Legrand. John Page, minor of William Page "upwards of 14" chooses William Lunsford, guardian.

Sept. Term 1826—Page 13—Application of Daniel McDowell, Admr. de bonis non of Nathaniel Barnett, dec'd. to sell real estate.

Page 14—James Jones appointed guardian of Mary Elizabeth Jones under 14, minor of Simeon Jones.

Nov. Term 1826—Page 17—Violet Turman claims her dower in the estate of her husband George Turman, dec'd.

Page 18—Petition of Milley T. Banks widow of James A. Banks to divide the estate between her and her son Wm. O. Banks. Eliza Hudson, minor of Nathaniel Hudson, dec'd. over 14, chooses Joseph Rucker, Esqr, guardian.

Page 20—Gaines Thompson applies for letters of administration de bonis non on estate of Sarah Thompson. Caveat by James Olive sustained by Court.

Page 22—Jacob M. Tate, one of the heirs of Zimri Tate, dec'd, over 14, chooses William Rich, guardian.

Page 23—Elizabeth D., and Uriah R. Tate, two of the heirs of Zimri, Tate, dec'd. over 14, chooses Enos Tate, guardian. The Court appoints him guardian of Martha J., and Zimri M. Tate, under 14.

Nov. Term 1826—Page 23—Zachariah H. Clark one of the heirs of Zachariah Clark, dec'd. over 14, chooses John A. Heard, guardian.

Jan. Term 1827—Page 25—Mary Clark and Beverly Allen appointed Admrs. of James Clark, dec'd.

Page 28—Petition of Martha Ann Clark, Lucindia Malecia Clark, Mary Anthona Elsworth Clark and Thomas Banks Clark, sisters and brother of John Houston Clark by their next friend Banks Blackwell depose that Joannah Hall widow, late of said county, dec'd. on the 13th, of Aug. 1821 made bond to said John Houston Clark, son of Robert Clark who is Admr. of said Joannah, for a lot of land drawn by her in the then contemplated Land Lottery, that she drew No. 94, 11th, Dist. Monroe Co., and they ask that Robert Clark, Admr. make clear titles to said land.

March Term 1827—Page 31—John Hall appointed Admr. of Seals Hall, dec'd.

Page 32—William D. Clark appointed Admr. of George W. Clark, dec'd. Lafayette Cabbeness about 8 years old, bound to Wm. Runnels.

May Term 1827—Page 36—Richmond Rich appointed Admr. of Mary Rich, dec'd.

Page 37—Henry K., and James Philips, minors of Wm. Philips, dec'd, over 14, choose Thomas Haynes, guardian. James Booker about 7 years old bound to Hardie Blackwell.

Sept. Term 1827—Page 46—Mary Alexander, minor of Isaac Alexander, dec'd. over 14, chooses Elam Alexander, guardian.

Nov. Term 1827—Page 49—John J. Groves appointed guardian of Francis F. and Amanda E. Terrell, minors of William C. Terrell, dec'd. Wesley Ham son of Reuben Ham bound to John Ashworth till he is 21, "which will be thirteen years from this date.
Page 50—Tavner W. Fortson appointed guardian for his infant daughter Permelia E. L. Fortson a legatee of Beatrice J. A. Tate dec'd.
Page 51—James Lunsford appointed guardian of John and Armstrong Roberts, minors of Martha Roberts. William D. Clark, Admr. given permission to sell real estate of George W. Clark, dec'd. Receipt of Simeon Brawner to John C. Webb, Excr. of William C. Webb, dec'd. in full for all claims as a legatee or distributee of said estate and of a slave Moriah, which Simeon's wife Susannah formerly Susannah Webb, widow of said William C. Webb to which while a widow she made a deed of gift to her son Andrew Jackson Webb, of record in Oglethorpe Co. Also to relinquish his guardianship of said Andrew J. Webb.
Page 55—Napoleon Bonaparte Cabbeness, son of Henry Cabbeness bound to Joseph Parker till he is 21 "which will be fourteen years the first day of next Jan.

Nov. Term 1827—Page 56—Martha B. Williams, over 14, chooses Frances E. Williams guardian, and she is appointed guardian of Barbara E., and Frances M. Williams, all orphans of Matthew J. Williams, dec'd.

Jan. Term 1828—Page 58—Thomas F. Davis appointed guardian of Thomas F. Rone, minor of John Rone, dec'd.
Page 59—William White, Admr. of estate of Henry Shackleford petition to sell slave to pay debts, notice having been served on Asa, Henry and Martha Shackleford (wid) and as natural guardian of John, James, Stephen, Madison, and Martha Shackleford, minors.
Page 60—Permission given Richmond Rich, Admr. of Mary Rich, dec'd. to sell Lot No. 214, 5th, Dist. Monroe Co. original survey 202½ acres. Mary Heard, widow of Barnard C. Heard relinquishes her dower, and takes a childs part.

March Term 1828—Page 63—Sterling Carter appointed admr. of William Grimes, dec'd.
Page 65—Valentine Smith appointed guardian of Martha B., Lyon Hunt, Daniel N., Edmond Shackleford, Benjamin C., Gardner McGarity, Flora M., all orphans of Lauchlin McCurry, dec'd.

May Term—1828—Page 66—Beverly C. Cook appointed guardian of James, Zimri, and Heratio Tate, orphans of Zimri Tate, dec'd.
Page 67—Jesse Marion Fortson, minor of Jesse Fortson, dec'd. over 14, chooses Richard Fortson, guardian. Isaac Almond appointed guardian

of Thomas D., Jane M., and Almeda H. Fortson, orphans of Jesse Fortson, dec'd. Benajah Houston and George Carter apply for letters of administration on estate of Thomas Davis, George refusing to serve, William White is appointed.

Page 71—William Lunsford, guardian of Thomas J. Teasley, minor of Ann Teasley, permission to sell land.

July Term 1828—Page 72—Sarah Gaines appointed guardian of Judith B., and Mary E. Gaines, orphans of Levingston P. Gaines, dec'd.

Page 73—William C. Davis, security for Mary Burton, now Mary Hudson wife of Richard D. Hudson, guardian of George and Richard Burton, Heirs of Richard Burton, dec'd. refuses to act as such longer.

Page 75—John A. Heard appointed Admr. of Thomas Graves, dec'd.

Sept. Term 1828—Page 75—Benjamin Nail appointed Admr. of Martha Hickman, dec'd.

Nov. Term 1828—Page 79—Ordered that Job Weston, Clerk deliver to Garnett Andrews or J. V. or S. W. Harris the original will of William Grimes to be used as evidence in court.

Page 80—John Watkins appointed and qualified as Excr. of last will of Robert Watkins late of Abbeville Dist. S. C., dec'd. is appointed Excr. in this state.

Nov. Term 1828—Page 81—Thomas Hearn Admr., in right of his wife Frances E. Hearn, formerly Frances E. Williams, prays that the estate be divided among the legatees (towit) Frances E. Williams now Frances E. Hearn, Martha B. Williams, now Martha B. Oliver, Barbara and Frances Williams all legatees of Matthew J. Williams, dec'd. Return of Reuben Underwood, Admr. of Winnifred Underwood, dec'd, caveat by Samuel Patterson as to that part which we charged for her support.

Page 82—Elijah and John Jones, upwards of 14 years minors of Standley Jones, dec'd. choose William Jones, guardian, and he is appointed guardian of Thomas, Ann, Martha and Sarah Jones, under 14. William Jones, minor of Standley Jones, dec'd. "upwards of 14 years, chooses Peter Alexander guardian.

Page 84—William Rich, Excr. of Zimri Tate, dec'd, notifies the heirs and guardians of the minors (towit) Isaac M. Tate, Tavner W. Fortson, in right of his wife Elizabeth, Enos Tate and Beverly C. Cook guardians that he will call for a division.

Page 85—Margaret and Joseph R. Hulme appointed Admrs. of William Hulme, dec'd.

Jan. Term 1829—Page 86—Stephen W. Jordan, over 14, chooses B. Houston guardian.

Page 87—Mary Clark, aged 14, chooses Wm. D. Clark guardian.

Page 91—Jackson Oliver, over 14, chooses Martin Deadwyler guardian.

March Term 1829—Page 92—Samuel Kaar appointed Admr. of James Gates, dec'd.

Martha Deadwyler widow of Joseph Deadwyler, dec'd. caveat of the will. Verdict in her favor, because he was not of sound mind.
Page 95—William A. Herring appointed guardian of Margaret O. Hines.
Page 96—Hughy S. Hall, minor over 14 chooses John Merrit guardian.

May Term 1829—Page 100—Martha Deadwyler and Mial Smith appointed Admrs. of Joseph Deadwyler, dec'd. Martha P. Deadwyler appointed guardian of Margaret Ann Deadwyler, minor of said dec'd.
Page 101—William W. Dooly appointed guardian of William and Elizabeth Dooly orphans of Allen Dooly, dec'd. Elizabeth having been born since his death.
Page 102—Elizabeth Warner appointed guardian of her son Nathan Rembert Warner, infant son of Nathan Warner, dec'd.
Benajah Houston guardian of Stephen W. Jordan given permission to sell Lot No. 120, 23rd Dist. Muscogee Co.

Sept. Term 1829—Page 103—Richard L. Aycock appointed Admr. of James E. Aycock, dec'd.
Page 106—James Kerlin, over 14, minor of William Kerlin, dec'd. chooses Daniel Kerlin guardian. Andrew Lawremore chosen guardian of Jacob Kerlin, over 14, minor of William Kerlin, dec'd.
Page 108—Middleton G. Woods as an heir, and as guardian of William H. C. Woods, a minor and other distributees asks for a division of estate of William Woods, dec'd.

Sept. Term 1829—Page 110-122—Returns of Jeptha V. Harris, Admr. of William Woods, dec'd. who was Admr. of Middleton Woods, dec'd. show following receipts given Wm. Woods as Excr. of M. Woods: Of Josiah Woods of Franklin Co. Va. for all his share of the estate of his brother, Middleton Woods and his claim to what his father Robert Woods, Sr. had in said estate, which was conveyed to Josiah by deed of gift in Franklin Co. Va. Apr. 25, 1821. Of Francis Hill of Franklin Co. Va. in right of his wife Elizabeth, formerly Elizabeth Woods, July 11, 1815. Of Robert Woods, Jr., John Woods and Jehu Hale in right of his wife Mary formerly Mary Woods all of Franklin Co. Va., which was paid them by Bailey Woods, agent for William Woods, Aug. 12, 1815. Of Robert Woods, Sr. of Franklin Co. Va. paid him by Bailey M. Woods, Agt. Aug. 17, 1815. Of Citizen Stovall Woods for himself and as Atty for Robt. T. Woods and Robt. Hairston in right of his wife Elizabeth, formerly Elizabeth H. Woods, and Samuel Hairston guardian of Samuel H., Peter M., and Geo. Woods minors, all of Franklin Co. Va. and heirs of John Woods late of said county, dec'd. brother of said Middleton Woods, Dec. 3, 1819. Of Reuben Woods of Madison Co. Terr. of Miss., in right of his wife Lucy, formerly Lucy Martin. George Philips, Christopher Bowen Test. Given in Oglethorpe Co. Ga.
Order of James Ormond to William Woods to pay to Christopher Bowen the share of Giles M., and Marion Ormond, heirs of Peggy Ormond formerly Peggy Martin lately dec'd, of whom James Ormond is guardian. Feb. 5, 1820. Of Robert Woods of Franklin Co. Va. brother of said Middleton Woods, by Josiah Woods, Apr. 25, 1821. Order of Dr. George

Phillips of Pleasant Valley Dallas Co. Ala. to pay his share to John K. Binford. May 17, 1823. (The above is a very interesting personal letter to Wm. Woods) Receipt of Robt. N. Dickerson for himself and as Atty in fact for Josiah W. Dickerson and John Clay in right of his wife Elizabeth formerly Elizabeth Dickerson, all of Franklin Co. Va. Jeptha V. Harris, Admr. of William Woods who was Excr. of Middleton Woods presents these papers as having been found among the papers of William Woods, dec'd., but they are rejected.

Page 124—Sept. 8, 1829—Andrews and Chandler, Attys. appointed to prosecute a suit of Entreken Raney and his wife Matilda on the bond of Bridger Haynie, Archibald Prior and Bridger Haynie, dated Oct. 18, 1805, that Bridger Haynie should well and truly administer on the estate of Bridger Haynie, dec'd.

Page 126—Returns of Martin Deadwyler as guardian for the minor heirs of Philip Wilhite, dec'd.

Page 127—Benjamin Nail, Admr. of Martha Hickman given permission to sell a slave. Returns of James Lunsford, guardian of minors of Martha Roberts, recorded.

This book seems to be an index or brief record of names of administrators and executors, with dates of appointment, probably.

Page 1—Jan. 29, 1791—David Adams, Admr. of estate of James Adams, dec'd. James Tuttle, Sr. Security.

Feb. 22, 1791—John Ferrell, Admr. of estate of Lewis Davis, dec'd. William Head, Security.

May 20, 1791—John Henderson, Admr. of Joseph Henderson, dec'd. Richard Rain, Security.

May 9, 1791—Milly Cleveland, Webb Kidd, and Jeremiah Cleveland, Excrs. of estate of Jacob Cleveland, dec'd. Rice Cleveland, Sec.

May 19, 1791—Rebecca Smith, James Marks and Thos. B. Scott, Excrs. of estate of Jasper Smith. Sarah Meredith, Wm. More, Excrs. of estate of James Meredith, dec'd. James Almond, Security

June 16, 1791—Alcy Sutton and James McClusky, Admrs. of estate of William Sutton, dec'd James Almond, Security.

Page 2—July 21, 1791—Elizabeth Williams, Joseph and Francis Higginbotham, Excrs. of estate of Benjamin Higginbotham, dec'd.

Sept. 24, 1791—Stephen Fulghum, Admr. of Matthew Fulghum, dec'd. John Smith, Security.

Jan. 5, 1792—Thomas Burton, Admr. of Braddock Voden, dec'd. Robert Middleton, Security.

Jan. 17, 1792—Matthew Collers, Admr. of Hugh Kincade, dec'd. William Barnett, Security.

Jan. 22, 1792—Thomas and James Cameron, Admrs. of Robert McClary, dec'd.

Page 3—Feb. 24, 1792—Samuel Watkins, Robert and Jesse Thompson, Admrs. of Oliver Thompson, dec'd.

Feb. 24, 1792—Sarah Easter, William Thompson Easter, Richard Easter, William Thompson, Sr., Excrs. of James Easter, dec'd.
May 23, 1792—Joseph Calvert, Admr. of John Millor, dec'd. Thomas Carter, Sr. Security.
Oct. 1, 1792—James Watson Cook, Admr. of James Cook, dec'd. Henry Cook, Security.
Oct. 15, 1792—John and Matthew Jouett Williams, Excrs. of Joseph William, dec'd. Isham Morgan, Security.
Oct. 17, 1792—Sanders Walker and James Tate, Esqr., Excrs. of Jeremiah Walker, dec'd. Robert Martin, Security.

Page 4—Dec. 26, 1792—James Dudley, Admr. of John Dudley, dec'd. Samuel Speers, Security.
Jan. 8, 1793—William Davis, Admr. of Chas. Easton, dec'd. Reuben Easton, Security. Sally Easton and Reuben Easton, Admrs. of John Easton, dec'd.
Jan. 19, 1793—William Moss, Esqr. Admr. of Isham Stroud, dec'd. William Hansard, Security.
Feb. 5, 1793—Farley and Lewis Bevel Thompson, Excrs. of John F. Thompson.
May 20, 1793—Robert Crocket, Admr. of Samuel Crocket, dec'd Samuel Young, Security.

Page 5—June 17, 1793—Marten Ferrell, Admr. of John Ferrell, dec'd. William Head and James Ferrell, Security.
Oct. 3, 1793—William Thomas and John Newman, Admrs. of Joel Thomas, dec'd. John Ross, Security.
Nov. 9, 1793—John and Elisha Brewer, Admrs. of Edmond Brewer, dec'd. Middleton Woods, Security. John Coleman, Security for John Brewer. Matt. J. Williams, Security for E. Brewer.
Mar. 8, 1794—Archer Burton and James Adams, Admrs. of David Adams, dec'd. William Hightower, Security.
July 28, 1794—_____Giles and Wm. J. Hobby, Excrs. of John Giles, dec'd.
Oct. 3, 1794—William Appleby and John Hodge, Excrs. of William Hodge, dec'd.
Nov. 4, 1794—Betty and John Gatewood, Admrs. with will annexed of estate of Richard Gatewood, dec'd. Tabitha Holliday, Security.

Page 6—Jan. 2, 1795—Thos. B. Scott, William Harvey and Mildredge Grimes, Excrs. of William Grimes, dec'd.
Mar. 12, 1795—Alex. Human, Excr. of Bazzle Human, dec'd.
Apr. 15, 1795—Benjamin Head, Admr. of Ann Sherman, dec'd. William Ward, Security.
Apr. 1, 1795—Thomas Napier, Admr. of Maybourn Crenshaw, dec'd. Walker Napier, Security.
Aug. 22, 1795—Sally and Isaac Morris, Admrs. of James Morris, dec'd.
Oct. 14, 1795—Martitia Stodgehill and Caleb Oliver, Admrs. of Joel Stodgehill, dec'd. Thomas Fortson, Security.

GEORGIA D. A. R.

Page 7—Sept. 29, 1795—Nancy and James Roggers, Admrs. of John Roggers, Esqr. dec'd. Thomas Roggers, Security.
Dec. 22, 1795—Elizabeth Janet Head, Sally Riddle and Thos. White, Excrs. of James Head, dec'd. Moses Haynes, Admr. of Stephen Haynes, dec'd. Thomas Scales, Security.
No date—Adam Gaar, Admr. of estate of Michael Gaar, dec'd.
Oct. 23, 1795—James and John McCurdy, Admrs. of David McCurdy, dec'd.
Apr. 7, 1794—John Coil and Clement Wilkins, Excrs. of Larkin Pearpoint.

Page 8—Mar. 1, 1796—William Montford Stokes, William Strong and William Stokes, Excrs. of William Stokes, dec'd.
Mar. 30, 1796—Sally S. Bibb, Excx. of William Bibb, dec'd.
May 6, 1796—Sally and Thomas Aken, Admrs. of Joseph Aken, dec'd. George Darden and Cornelius Sale, Security.
May 6, 1796—Cornelius Sale, Admr. of Anthony Sale, dec'd. George Darden, Security.
May 27, 1796—Mary Monack, Admr. of John Monack, dec'd. Mark Thornton, Security.
Apr. 19, 1796—George Cook and Elizabeth W. Thompson, Admrs. of Isham Thompson, dec'd. James Tait, Security.

Page 9—June 4, 1797—Rachel Williams, Admr. of Philip Williams, dec'd. Thomas Griffeth, Security.
Dec. 16, 1796—Gilbert Chaves, Admr. of Philip Chaves, dec'd. Richard Easter, Security.
Feb. 10, 1797—Nathaniel and Nancy Hudson, Admrs. of David Hudson, dec'd. John P. Harper and Cuthburt Hudson, Security. Also security for Nancy Hudson, Chas. Hudson and Nathaniel Allen.
Sept. 19, 1797—Nancy Gileylen, Admr. of Jacob Gileylen, dec'd. Samuel Shields, Security.
Oct. 4, 1797—Mary Garner, Daniel Orr and William Hendon, Admrs. of Stephen Garner, dec'd. Robt. Cowden, Security.
Dec. 20, 1797—Joseph Higginbotham, Admr. of Robt. C. Burton, dec'd. Robert Pulliam, Security.

Page 10—June 24, 1799—Moses Haynes and Ann Scales, Admrs. of Thomas Scales, dec'd. Hugh McDonald, Security.
April 2, 1797—John and Samuel Mackie, Excrs. of Thomas Mackie, dec'd.
July 27_____John Jones, Sr., and John Davis, Excrs. of Benjamin Davis, dec'd.
April 1, 1798—Lucy Blake and Thomas Jones, Admrs. of estate of William Blake, dec'd. Richardson Hunt, Samuel Higginbotham and Francis Satterwhite, Excrs. of William Hansard, dec'd. Elijah Owens and Benjamin Howard, Excrs. of Nemiah Howard, dec'd.

Page 11—July 25, 1798—Thomas Gibson and Sarah Woldridge, Excrs. of William Woldridge, dec'd. Joshua and Mary Jorden, Excrs. of Absolom

Jorden, dec'd. Chas. Tate and William Hudson Tate, Excrs. of James Tate, dec'd.
Nov. 27, 1798—Patsy and Robert Griffeth, Admrs. of John Griffeth, dec'd. Alex. Elliott, Security.
Sept. 12, 1799—Betty Guttery and James Ryley, Excrs. of Robert Guttery, dec'd. Robins and John Andrews, Excrs. of Nathaniel Andrews, dec'd.

Page 12—Sept. 12, 1799—Sarah Cunningham and William Grimes, Excrs. of William Cunningham, dec'd.
Oct. 19, 1799—Mary Dixson, Admx. of William Dixson, dec'd. James Crow, Security.
July 16, 1800—William Jamerson, Admr. of John Conyers, dec'd. William Hatcher and George Cook, Security.
Feb. 7, 1800—John and Richard Hubbard, Admr. of estate of John Hubbard, dec'd.
July 16, 1800—Frederick Crowder, Admr. of Moses Fincher, dec'd. Moses Haynes, Security. John Russell, Admr. with will annexed of John Giles, dec'd. Chas. Taylor, Security. Thomas and Robt. Burton, Admrs. of Thomas Burton, dec'd. Evan Ragland, Security. Effy Cook, Excx., and William Cook, Excr. of Benjamin Cook, dec'd.

Page 13—July 16, 1800—James Patten, Admr. of Adkins Upshaw. Samuel Patten, Security. Ann Lovingood and Moses Haynes, Admrs. of Harmon Lovingood, dec'd. Frederick Crowder, Security. Zachariah Shammel, Admr. of Robert Tait, dec'd. James Alston, Security. George Thomason, Admr. of Solomon Dunnal, dec'd. William Teasley and Jesse Ginn, Security.
Feb. Term 1801—Moses Haynes, guardian of Thomas, Benjamin, Elijah and Nathaniel Scales, Minors.
Feb. Term 1801—Nathaniel Allen, guardian of James Head, minor. William Pulliam, Security. Middleton Woods, guardian of Flemin Akens, minor. William Moore, guardian of Patsy McAlpin, minor. Solomon McAlpin, Security. Solomon McAlpin guardian of Ann McAlpin. William Moore, Security. Ann Lawson, Admx. of James Lawson, dec'd. David and Henry Lawson Security.
July Term 1801—Joseph and Milly Davis, Admrs. of Gideon Davis, dec'd. John S. Head and W. Blankenship, Security.

Page 14—July Term 1801—Joseph Christly, Admr. of Henry Christly, dec'd. Julias Christly, Security. Robert Kennedy, Admr. of Lauglin Finny, dec'd. Henry Gatewood and James Patten, Security. Lucy Sharp and John S. Head, Admrs. of William Sharp, dec'd. Joseph Davis and W. Blankenship, Security. Hannah and Voluntine Thacker, Excrs. of William Thacker, dec'd. Joacim and Christopher Hudson, Excrs. of Outbird Hudson, dec'd. Drury and Jesse Thompson, Excrs. of Drury Thompson, dec'd. William Appleby and Alex. Hodge, Excrs. of John Hodge, dec'd. James Bell and James Childreys, Excrs. of Lewis Jones, dec'd. Sally Harper and Middleton Woods, Excrs. of

GEORGIA D. A. R.

John P. Harper, dec'd. Lucy Ridgway and Middleton Woods, Admrs. of Thos. Ridgway, dec'd. Thomas Johnson, Security. Alisany McGuire, Admr. of Robert Holliday, dec'd. James H. Kidd and John Nelmns, Security.

Page 15—July Term 1801—James Wood, Admr. of John Wood, dec'd. Robt. Moon, Security. James H. Kidd, Admr. of James Adams, dec'd. George Cook and Allegany McGuire, Security. Henry Smith, Admr. of Gideon Smith, dec'd. Richard Ross and Israel D. Mundy, Security. Henry G. Walker, Admr. with will annexed of Jeremiah Walker, dec'd. Robt. Middleton and Thos. Colbert, Sec. John McCurdy and Samuel Grove, Admrs. of Ishmael Vineyard, dec'd. Joseph Calvert and Robert Kennedy, Security. Caty and Abraham Brown, Admrs. of Robt. Brown, dec'd. Barnabas Pace and James Shields, Security. Robt. Richmond and James O. Cosby, Excrs. of Charles Cosby, dec'd. Middleton Woods, Nathaniel Hudson and Richard Hubbard, Excrs. of Sally Harper. Sarah Parnell and Benjamin Mosely, Excrs. of John Parnell, dec'd. Angus and Archabald Johnson, Excrs. of John Johnson. Stephen Smith, Excr. of Nathaniel Smith, dec'd.

Feb. Term 1803—Micajah, Christopher, David and Joshua Clark, Excrs. of Christopher Clark.

Page 16—Feb. Term 1803—Mary Wilson and Barnabas Pace, Excrs. of John Wilson, dec'd. Jonas Lawson, Admr. of Henry Lawson, dec'd. Henry Nash, Security. Elizabeth Ellinton and Wm. Thompson, Admrs. of Stephen Ellington, dec'd., Wyley Thompson and Walter Nuneler, Security. Thomas Smith, Admr. of Voluntine Smith, dec'd. Thos. S. Carter, Security. Larken Gatewood, Admr. of James Gatewood, dec'd., Benjamin Higginbotham, Security.

July Term 1803—Chas. Tait, Admr. of John Filson, dec'd., R. T. Cosby and Richardson Booker, Security. Geo. Fitch Garald, Admr. of Robt. Harris, dec'd., John Fitchgarrald and John Royal, Security. Pleasant White, Admr. of Moses White, dec'd., Mark Renolds and Andrew Muckleroy Security. Jane and John S. Higginbotham, Admrs. of Samuel Higginbotham, dec'd., Francis Satterwhite and Peter Stubbs, Security. William Hudson, Admr. of Charles Hudson, dec'd., C. Tait and N. Hudson, Security.

Page 17—Frankey Ragland and Chas. Tait, Excrs. of John R. Ragland, dec'd. John Walker, Excr. of Memorable Walker, dec'd. William Barnett, Excr. of will of Nelson Barnett, dec'd. Elizabeth Strickland, Wm. Sanders and Isaac Strickland, Excrs. of Jacob Strickland, dec'd. Jane Garven and Middleton Woods, Admrs. of Daniel Garven, dec'd., Robt. Middleton and J. H. Kidd, Security. William Dudley, Admr. with will annexed of James Norris, dec'd., Samuel Akens, Security. Jacob Odam, Admr. of Levy D. Smith, dec'd., Beckham Dye, Security. Thomas Woldridge, Admr. of William Aycock, dec'd., Thomas Napier, Security. Mary and Daniel Ford, Thomas Cook and Henry Gains, Excrs. of John Ford, dec'd.

Page 18—July Term 1804—Samuel Watkins, Admr. of Stephen Ellington, Sr., dec'd., Joseph Watkins, Security. Maynard and John Colly, Excrs. of Zachariah Colly, dec'd. Drury Towns and Abraham Bell, Excrs. of Elisha Towns, dec'd.

Feb. Term 1805—Caty Gatewood, John Upshaw, Benjamin and Francis Higginbotham, Excrs. of Larkin Gatewood, dec'd. Martain, William and John Kidd, Excrs. of Webb Kidd, dec'd. John Childs and Littleton Johnson, Admrs. of Nathan Childs, dec'd., Nathan Childs and Thomas Wooldridge, Security. John and Isham Parham and William Davis, Excrs. of John Parham, dec'd. William Allen and James Banks, Excrs. of Garred Walthall, dec'd. Mary Cook, Excr. of Benjamin Cook, dec'd. Caleb Campbell and Solomon White, Excrs. of Nicholas White, dec'd. Susannah and Edward Herndon, Excrs. of Benjamin Herndon, dec'd.

Page 19—July Term 1804—George and Standly Jones, Admrs. of James Jones, dec'd., Larkin Clark, Security. Absolom Davis, guardian of Absolom, William, Edward and Sally S. Davis, B. Jeter, Security. Middleton Woods, guardian of Fleming Aken, William Holt, Security.

July Term 1801—Martha Tait, guardian of James Tait. Chas. Tait, Security. William Grimes, guardian of Thomas M. Grimes, Jacob Odam, Security. Middleton Woods, guardian of Tabby Thompson, William Holt, Security. William Hightower, guardian of Thomas, Absolom, William and Sally Davis. Archer Burton, Security.

July Term 1801—John McCurdy guardian of Mary Ann Miller. Samuel Groves, Security. Wiley Thompson, guardian of Isham Thompson. Richmond T. Cosby, Security.

Feb. Term 1803—Leroy Pope guardian of Willis Carter, a mulatto boy. Charles Tait, Security. William Thompson, guardian of Alsomain Thompson. Wiley Thompson, Security.

Page 20—Feb. Term 1803—Larkin Higginbotham, guardian of Lewis Freeland. Hugh McDonald, guardian of William Scales. L. McCurry, Security. Archalas Garrett, guardian of Thomas Andrew. James O. Cosby, Security.

July Term 1803—Wiley Thompson, guardian of Patsy Thompson. Feb. Term 1804—Wm. Easter, guardian of Campain Easter. William Aycock, Security. James Christian, guardian of Geo. Stovall. James Ewing, guardian of Charles and James Ewing. Caty Brown, guardian of John, Sally, Amy and Robert Brown. Luke White and Thos. Horton, Security. Richard Collins, guardian of Wm. Jarvis., Joseph Pulliam, Security. William Thompson, Sr. guardian of Averelle Harper.

Page 21—Feb. Term 1805—Thomas Tait, guardian of James Tait. Abraham Bell, Security. William Allen, guardian of William and Singleton Walthall. James F. Nunnelee, Security. James O. Cosby, guardian of John Anthony Virdal. Robt. Middleton, Sec.

July Term 1805—Archelas Prier, Admr. of Harden Prier, dec'd., Bridger and Chas. Haynie, Security. Ann Underwood, Admx. of Joshua Underwood, dec'd., Wm. Smith and Geo. Wheeler, Security. Jane and

GEORGIA D. A. R.

Thomas McCune and Moses Haynes, Admrs. of William McCune, dec'd., Benjamin Head and Howard Cash, Security. Bridger Haynie, Admr. of Bridger Haynie, dec'd. Archibald Prier and Chas. Hayne, Security. Blackbourn Burton, Admr. of German Burton, dec'd., Patrick Butler and Henry Burton, Security. Jacob Odam, Admr. of Levy Smith, dec'd., Beckham Dye, Security. Joannah Gragg and Howard Cash, Admrs. of Thomas Gragg, dec'd., William Ward and Benjamin Head, Security. Mary Braddy and Thomas Wilkins, Admrs. of James Braddy, dec'd., Benjamin Glover and John Sertain, Security. Thomas McCune, guardian of James, and (?) Alexander McCune, Margaret and Peggy McCune, Moses Haynes, Security. Jane McCune, guardian of Polly Baskens McCune and Washington McCune, Moses Haynes, Security. Ann and Robert Woods, Admrs. of Andrew Woods, dec'd., Francis and Samuel Woods, Security. James Christian, guardian of George Stovall, William Bradley, Security.

Page 22—Feb. Term 1806—John Ham and Absolom Stinchcomb, Excrs. of Tabitha Holliday, dec'd. Wallis and James F. Nunnellee, Excrs. of William W. Nunnelee, dec'd.

Feb. Term 1806—Anna, Peter and Robert Sheppard, Excrs. of John Sheppard, dec'd. John, Charles, Abriam, and Theophilus Park, and Mary Salmons and Mary, Benjamin, and Hannah Bobo, Excrs. of Charles Parks, dec'd. Thomas and Gibson Wooldridge and Richard Hubbard, Excrs. of Sarah Wooldridge, dec'd.

May Term 1806—Joseph Christly, Peter and Nancy Alexander, Excrs. of William Alexander, dec'd.

July Term 1805—Thomas Napier, guardian of Richard, Milton, Tabitha and Terrell Aycock. Leroy Pope, Security. Moses Haynes, guardian of Waller Haynes. William Oliver, Admr. of Daniel Britt. William Holt, Security. John Millican, Admr. of Brinkley House. Lemuel Groves and David Staples, Security. Barnet, Jeter, guardian of Thos. W. Davis. Littleton Johnson, Security. Jane Childs, guardian of Ann W. Childs. Thomas Colbert, James Aulston and James Banks, Security. Sally Turner, Admr. of Thomas and Elizabeth Turner. John Johnson, and Hiram Gaines, Security. Matthew J. Williams, Admr. of Stephen Roan. Jas. F. Nunnelee, Security. Howard Cash, guardian of Polly, Keziah and Ann Graig, minors of Thomas Graig. Moses Haines, Security.

Page 23—May Term 1806—Samuel Paxton, Admr. of Lemuel Paxton, dec'd. Middleton Woods, Security.

Items from this book that do not seem to appear elsewhere. The following seems to be a list of soldiers for Georgia Militia for the War of 1812. No doubt there was an oath of allegiance preceding it, and other names following.

Pages 35-36.   Autograph Signatures.

Archer Burton, Capt.	David Eberhart	James Christian
Francis Higginbotham	William Allen	Zachariah Clark
John Higginbotham	Peter Wyche	Gilbert Barden
John Staples	Moses Fleming	Eli Eavenson
Richard Colbert	Jacob Odom	Edward Ware
John Mackie	William Mackie	Edward Storey
Jacob Kees	William Haley	Thos. Woodward
Robert Moon	James Lawson	John Shields
Elias Alexander	Josiah Dobbs	Ralph Smith
Robert Cowden	James Ware	David Dickson
Joseph Blackwell	David M. Curdy	Benjamin Turman
George Alexander	Charter Harper	Jno. Montgomery
Samuel McGehee	John Oliver	William Brown
Shaler Hillyer	Robt. L. Tait	James Morrison
William Rowe, Capt.	Wm. Watkins, Lt.	Dionysius Oliver, Ensign
James Baker, Lt.	Jas. W. Muse, Lt.	Azmon Rucker, Major.

Winslow Rowzie, Lieut.
William Chisolm, Lt. Col.
William Patterson, Troop Horse
Thompson Ragland, Capt.
Eliam Evans, Ensign
Thomas Oliver, Maj. 3rd. June 1809
Charles Carter, Capt. 3rd. June 1809
John Higginbotham, Capt. 3rd. June 1809
Welcome Whipple, Lieut. 6th. May 1809
William Fortson, Capt. 3rd July 1809
John Dudley, Capt. 17th, July 1809
James Oliver, Capt. 17th. July 1809
George Eberhart, Capt. 17th, July 1809
John Brown, Lieut. 17th. July 1809
Drury Lesuer, Lieut. 17th. July 1809
William O. Robins, Ensign 17th. July 1809
Payton Bibb, Capt. 3rd. June 1809
Jas. Clark, Lieut. 3rd. June 1809
Shadrick Dean, Ensign
Jesse Edwards, Ensign 24th. Feb. 1810
Joshua Clark, Capt. 13th. Nov. 1809
James Rhodes, Lieut. 6th. April 1811.
Robert Orr, Ensign 6th, April 1811
Gaines Thompson, Lieut. 22nd. Feb. 1812
Peyton Bibb, Lieut. Col. 21st. July 1812
Benjamin G. Higginbotham, Lieut. 1st. Aug. 1812
Benjamin Penn, Ensign 1st. Aug. 1812.

Court of Ordinary 1805.

Page 40—On motion of William Allen that William Walthall a deaf and dumb man and Singleton Walthall a minor orphan, need attention, William is appointed guardian.

Page 52—Feb. Term 1806—James Glover appointed guardian of Eli and Sally Brady, minors of James Brady, dec'd.

Page 54—May Term 1806—Sally Turner, relict of Martin Turner of Greene Co. dec'd. appointed guardian of her two minor children, Thomas and Elizabeth M. Turner.

Page 57—Nov. Term 1806—Nathan Bond, Jr. appointed guardian of Nancy Aken, minor. Return of William Grimes as guardian of Thomas M. Grimes.

Page 58—Returns of Thomas Wilkins, Admr. of James Braddy, dec'd. Return of James Head, Admr. of William Sharp, dec'd.

Page 59—Jan. Term 1809—Absolom Davis appointed guardian of Absolom, William and Sarah Davis in lieu of William Hightower. Jesse Fortson appointed guardian of Mildred and Asa White. Presley Christian appointed guardian of Epaphodetus White, and Martin White appointed guardian of John White, all orphans of Daniel White, dec'd. Returns of Lewis W. Saxon, Excr. of Hugh Saxon. Blackbourn Burton appointed guardian of William, Elizabeth, Abraham and German Burton, orphans of German Burton, dec'd.

Page 60—James Wood appointed guardian of Elizabeth and Sarah Wood, orphans of John Wood, dec'd.

Page 61—March Term 1807—Polly J., and Matthew J. Williams appointed Admrs. of Joseph Williams, dec'd.

Page 62—May Term 1807—Jemmima Haynie appointed Admx. on estate of Richard Haynie, dec'd.

Elbert County, Georgia Records

DEED BOOKS "A", "B", "C" & "D"

DEED BOOK "A".

ALMAND, JAMES—Folio 102—To Isaac Suttles, receipt for slaves, York, Sarah, Bobb and Edd. Aug. 11, 1792. John Almand, James Heatley, Test.

ADAMS, DAVID, planter—Folio 124—To James Tuttle, 36 acres on N. Fk. of Broad river. Jan. 13, 1793. John Furgus, J. P.

ALFORD, JAMES of Greene Co.—Folio 143—To Wm. Cunningham of Wilkes Co., 108 acres on S. Fk. of Broad river in Wilkes Co. Aug. 27, 1791. Michael Rogers, J. P., John Thompson, Test.

BRADFORD, WILLIAM of Va.—Folio 21—To John Depriest of Ga. 200 acres on N. Fk. of Doves Cr., granted July 20, 1786. Dec. 5, 1789. Thomas B. Scott, J. P., Test.

BROWN, FRANCIS of Elbert Co.—Folio 36—Power of Atty. to son George Brown of Va., to recover from Wm. Spier as Excr. of Benj. Spier of Hanover Co. Va., all he is due from said estate. Oct. 3, 1791. R. Hunt, J. P., Wm. Barnett, J. P.

BARNETT, MIAL, planter and wife Polley—Folio 40—To Isaac David both residentures of Wilkes Co., 200 acres on S. Broad river, original grant to said Barnett 1788. Nov. 10, 1789. Thomas B. Scott, J. P., Test.

BONDS, ELIZABETH—Folio 46—To Nathan Bonds, Jr., both of Wilkes Co., cattle, household goods, etc., "as well in behalf of Nathan Bonds, Sr. as for myself. Mar. 15, 1790. Richardson Hunt, Thos. Hillery, Test.

BROWN, THOMAS of Elbert Co.—Folio 46—To Edward Baldwin of Wilkes Co., 200 acres on Fork Cr. Elbert Co., adj. Sailors, Powers, McCarty and Alford. Nov. 24, 1791. Evan Ragland, J. P.

BAKER, JOHN—Folio 74—To Wm. Barnett, James Tait, Evan Ragland and Richardson Hunt, Esqrs., 50 acres comprehending the court house, and jail for the county, part of 950 acres granted said John Baker 1792. June 5, 1792. M. Woods, J. P., Test.

BURK, THOMAS, Sr.—Folio 101—Power of Atty. to John Staples to settle all his affairs in the counties of Caroline, Hanover etc. Va. Oct. 1, 1792. R. Hunt, J. P., Frans. Satterwhite, Test.

GEORGIA D. A. R.

BARNETT, BENJ. JOHNSON and his sister Patsy Barnett—Folio 104—To Claborn Webb, 100 acres on Broad river adj. Thos Webb, orig grant to the heirs of Wm. Barnett 1784. Feb. 8, 1792. Thos B. Scott, J. P., Bridgor Haynie, Test.

BAKER, ABSOLOM and wife Mary—Folio 106—To Issac Suttle, land granted said Baker 1788, adj. McCleskey and Webb. June 9, 1792. James McCleskey, J. P., Test.

BROWN, WILLIAM and wife Sarah—Folio 115—To Isaac Coker, 160 acres on south side of Beaver Dam Creek. June 12, 1792. Francis Cook, Test.

BARNETT, NATHAN and wife Lucy—Folio 115—To Wm. Hatcher, 350 acres, orig. grant to said Barnett 1787. Jan. 17, 1791. Thos. B. Scott, J. P., Test.

BARNETT, NATHAN and wife Lucy—Folio 135—To Edmond Shackleford 400 acres, orig. grant to said Barnett 1785. Jan. 24, 1791. Jo. Barnett, John Crossley, Chas. Coulter, Test.

BOSLER, HENRY, of Richmond Co., Folio 125—To John Hutchins Johnson of Elbert Co., 600 acres in Franklin Co. on Curries Cr. Nov. 10, 1792. John Depriest, John Rogers, Jas. Tait, J. P., Test.

BELL, JOSEPH and wife Elizabeth—Folio 128—To David Martin 300 acres on both sides of Falling Cr., orig. grant to George Martin 1786. Dec. 29, 1792. James Bell, J. P., Archer Skinner, Test.

BUTLER, JAMES and wife Salley—Folio 130—To Patrick Butler 200 acres orig. grant 1790 to said James. Feb. 7, 1793. James Bell, J. P., Jesse Jones, Test.

BURTON, JACOB and wife Nancy—Folio 131—To James Brown, all his plantation and all the said grant to Mary Edes and conveyed to said Burton, except 10 acres Abel Pennington sold to Jones Brock, or Broak. Mar. 14, 1791. Thos. B. Scott, J. P., Test.

BOND, NATHAN—Folio 146—Deed of gift for life of a slave Rachel to his mother Elizabeth Bond. Oct. 1, 1792. R. Hunt, M. Woods, Test.

CRISWELL, DAVID of Wilkes Co.—Folio 6—To Thos. Brown of Elbert Co., land in Elbert Co., adj. Powers and Alford, orig. grant to John Watson, for whom David Criswell is attorney. Feb. 1, 1791. George Walton, W. Williamson, Test.

CUNNINGHAM, JOHN and wife Ann—Folio 13—To Geo. Rucker 400 acres in Wilkes Co., granted said John 1784. Jan. 1, 1790. Hugh McDonald, Robt. Jackson, Test.

CARR, GEORGE and wife Judith—Folio 28—To Reuben White, all of Wilkes Co., 200 acres on Van's Cr. Wilkes Co., July 19, 1789. J. Gresham, J. P., John White, Test.

COOK, FRANCIS and wife Sarah—Folio 33—200 acres on Beaverdam.

COWDON, ROBERT—Folio 33—To David Vineyard, 200 acres adj. Richard Call and Isham Vineyard. Aug. 13, 1791. Thomas B. Scott, J. P.

CHAMBERS, ROBERT, and wife Lettice—Folio 42—To John Scales, 200 acres on Cedar Creek, orig. grant 1784 to Wm. Lovell. Jan. 22, 1791. J. Walker, J. P., Richard Floyd, Milly Walker, Test.

CHAMBERS, ROBERT and wife Lettice—Folio 92—To Jeremiah Walker 150 acres the upper part of an island in the Savannah river formerly known as Collin's Island, divided by a line across the island from the land of Culbird Hudson. Mar. 22, 1791. Stephen Heard, James Hanna, Edoshus Cook, Test.

COULTER, RICHARD and wife Rebecca—Folio 43—To Thomas Scott, all of Wilkes Co., 200 acres on Doves Creek, part of orig. grant 1787 to said Coulter. July 28, 1789. John Fergus, J. P., Test.

CLARK, CHRISTOPHER—Folio 54—To Wm. B. Key, 350 acres on the dry fork of Falling Creek "for good will and affection". Feb. 14, 1792. David Clark, Chas. Goss, Judith Clark, Test.

CLOUD, JEREMIAH and wife Sarah—Folio 69—To Ezekiel Cloud, all of Wilkes Co., 200 acres on S. Fk. of Broad river. Dec. 2, 1788. David Harr, Andrew Evins, Test.

CLOUD, EZEKIEL—Folio 70—To George Elliott, all of Wilkes Co., above land. April 13, 1789. Richard Harvie, Alex. Thompson, Test.

CARTER, THOMAS, Sr.—Folio 74—To James Carter, 200 acres on Beaverdam Creek, comprehending a plantation now occupied by Peter Stubbs, part of a grant of 1000 acres 1785 to said Thomas Carter. June 4, 1792. Thos. L. Carter, Test.

CARTER, THOMAS—Folio 78—Marriage contract, to Elizabeth Stubbs, life estate in 100 acres of land adj. James Carter, Samuel Higginbotham and Wm. Hansard, Thomas reserving for the life time of Peter Stubbs and his wife Mary, that part of the land on which they live. After the death of Elizabeth Stubbs her son Harrison Yerby Stubbs to have the land in fee simple. To Elizabeth during her widowhood, slaves, cattle etc, to be divided amongst said Carters children by said Elizabeth, if any. If none, to said Carters three youngest children by his first wife. June 1792.

CARTER, THOMAS—Folio 89—To Thomas Fortson, 330 acres on Beaverdam Creek, part of a grant of 1100 acres to said Carter 1785. May 31, 1792. Francis Satterwhite, James Head, John Maxwell, Benson Henry, Test.

CARTER, THOMAS—Folio 105—To Jonathan Webster, a slave Emelia and her infant. Oct. 29, 1792. Geo. Crutchfield, M. Woods, Test.

COOK, JAMES—Folio 93—To William McCune, 100 acres part of a larger grant, 1787 for Wilkes Co., to Isaac Jones. July 18, 1792.

GEORGIA D. A. R.

COOK, JAMES and wife Deborah—Folio 99—To David Brown and James Camron, 275 acres, it being the other half of the land Robt. Martin sold to Benj. Cook, orig. grant 1787 to Thos. Brown. Dec. 6, 1791. Peter Miller, Elisha Goin (?) Test.

CARRELL, PETER and wife Mary—Folio 109—To Thos. Pinnel, 200 acres on Falling Creek, orig. grant 1787 to John Mobley, conveyed by him to said Peter. Dec. 19, 1791. Francis Cook, J. P., Test.

COULTER, FRANCIS and wife Sarah—Folio 117—To Francis Alice and her son Chas. Alice, 130 acres on Doves Creek. Oct. 26, 1792. Signed Seara Coulter. W. Higginbotham, J. P.

COLSON, ABRAHAM—Folio 120—To James Tait, six slaves. Dec. 3, 1792. Wm. H. Tait, John Owens, Test.

COSBY, SYDNOR and wife Cynthia—Folio 123—To John Jack all of Wilkes Co., 200 acres on N. Fk. of Broad river, Wilkes Co. granted 1787. Feb. 9, 1790. Benj. King, Wm. Barnett, Evans Long, Test.

CARGYLE, JOHN, planter of Wilkes Co., Folio 127—To James Scott of Elbert Co., 300 acres on Bluestone creek, Broad river, orig. grant 1787 to said Cargyle. May 9, 1791. John Cleghorn, James Cleghorn, Test.

CLARK, JOHN, High Sheriff of Wilkes Co.—Folio 129—To John Heard, Jr. of Wilkes Co., 300 acres in Elbert Co. formerly a part of Wilkes Co., on Beaverdam creek, the property of Bernard Heard, dec'd. Feb. 26, 1791. John King, J. P., W. Pope, Test.

COLLINS, ZACHARIAH—Folio 134—To John Statham, 250 acres on Dove's and Falling creeks. Feb. 15, 1792.

COLEMAN, JOHN and wife Polly—Folio 137—To Wm. Goode, 470 acres on Broad river, orig. grant 1787 to said Coleman. Nov. 9, 1792. James F. Nunnelee, M. Walker, Test.

COLBERT, SUSANNA—Folio 141—To Jacob Gilleylen, 100 acres granted 1786 to said Susanna in originally Wilkes Co., now Elbert. May 15, 1792. Isaac Suttle, Martha Turman, Test.

COLSON, ABRAHAM—Folio 148—To James Coleman, 99½ acres on Savannah river. May 8, 1793. Wm. J. Hobby, Jacob Bugg, Test.

CROSBY, JOHN—Folio 152—To Lindsey Shewmaker, 200 acres on Doves creek. Apr. 20, 1791. Nyal Barnett, D. Wyter, Test.

COSBY, ROBERT, Esqr. T. C.—Folio 151—To John McDonald, 150 acres on Fork creek adj. said John, the property of Major Evens. April 2, 1790. Francis Cook, Test.

DANIEL, WILLIAM and wife Amy—Folio 16—To Wm. Head, all of Wilkes Co., 400 acres on Cold Water Creek, Wilkes Co., part of 800 acres granted Nicholas Long. Signed Nancy Daniel. May 19, 1789. Reuben Allen, J. P. Test.

HISTORICAL COLLECTIONS 155

DEPRIEST, JOHN—Folio 20—To Absolom Stenchcomb, 200 acres on N. Fk. of Doves creek. July 4, 1791.

DOOLY, GEORGE—Folio 25—To Collin Reed, Lot No. 40 in town of Petersburg, half acre, agreeable to the plan first laid down. Nov. 19, 1790. Thomas Russell, J. P. Test.

DANIEL, WILLIAM and wife Nancy—Folio 31—To Nathan Childs 550 acres on Beaverdam creek adj. lands of Wiley Davis, Walker Richardson, Robt. Middleton, Thos. Burton, Walter Nunnelee, Womack Blankenship and James Madkin. Jan. 14, 1791. John Patterson, Wm. Arnold, Test.

DAVIS, LEWIS and wife Sarah—Folio 31—To Stephen Westbrook all of Wilkes Co., 100 acres on Beaverdam creek, granted 1786 to said Davis. Nov. 10, 1789. J. Gresham, J. P. John Terrell, Test.

DANIEL, WILLIAM and wife Nancy—Folio 38—To William Arnold, 200 acres on Beaverdam creek, orig. grant 1784 to said Daniel. Oct. 15, 1791.

DANIEL, WILLIAM and wife Nancy—Folio 39—To Thomas Head, land on both sides of Beaverdam creek. Oct. 13, 1791. Wiley Davis, Robt. Middleton, James Tait, Test.

DANIEL, WILLIAM—Folio 68—To Samuel Blackburn, a slave, Charles. April 20, 1792. John Matthews, M. Wood, Test.

DANIEL, WILLIAM and wife Nancy—Folio 106—To James Matkin, 200 acres on Beaverdam creek. Oct. 16, 1792. Allen Daniel, Daniel Matkin, Test.

DAVIS, WM. HACKNEY and wife Suckey—Folio 42—To daughter Rody one gray mare etc. Nov. 10, 1791. Wiley Davis, Test.

DAVIS, BENJAMIN—Folio 68—To Wm. Pulliam, both of Wilkes Co., 10 acres including a grist mill on Beaverdam creek, known as Pulliam's Mill, part of orig. grant of 200 acres 1786 to said Davis. Jan. 17, 1789. Benj. Sanders, Test.

DAVIS, JOHN and wife Ann—Folio 112—To Chas. Kennedy, all of Wilkes Co., 100 acres orig. grant to Wm. Strong, 1786, on Fork creek. June 12, 1790.

DOUGHTY, JOSEPH—Folio 72—To Samuel Sewell, 130 acres on Falling creek. Sept. 28, 1791. Wm. Barnett, Test.

DUNCAN, HENRY and wife Joanna—Folio 95—To John White, 200 acres on Broad river. Oct. 22, 1791. Thos. Perry, John Morris, John Depriest, Andw. McEver, Test.

DARDEN, JOHN—Folio 144—To Arthur Bridge Dickson, 800 acres on Mill Shoal creek. April 4, 1793.

GEORGIA D. A. R.

DUNCAN, MARK and wife Mary—Folio 146—To David Eberhart, 125 acres on both sides of Fork creek. Feb. 19, 1793. Jacob Aberhart, Geo. Aberhart, Test.

DOSS, JOHN and wife Jean of Richmond Co. Folio 14—To William Alexander of Wilkes Co. orig. grant to Doss. Sept. 14, 1789. Wm. Dean, John Cunningham, J. P., Test.

EDWARDS, WILLIAM of Richmond Co. Folio 23—To Barnabas Pace of Wilkes Co., 200 acres on Big Shoal creek. Jan. 14, 1790. John Gorham, Susanna Fannin, Test.

EDWARDS, WILLIAM and wife Susannah—Folio 73—To Bazzle Human, all of an orig. survey to said Edwards dated Nov. 1784 on N. Fk. of Broad river. Dec. 24, 1791.

EASTER, JAMES of Wilkes Co.—Folio 79—To Wm. Aycock, bill of sale two slaves, Crias and Chito. Mar. 6, 1789. Peter Thompson, Wm. Easter, Ricd. Aycock, Test.

EASTER, JAMES, and wife Sarah—Folio 79—To William Aycock both of Wilkes Co., 200 acres on Beaver and Falling creeks. ----------6, 1789.

EASTER, SARAH—Folio 104—Widow of James Easter, dec'd. about to intermarry with a certain Edmund Brewer, desirous to do justice to the children of said dec'd., delivers all slaves, furniture etc., she is entitled to under the will of James Easter, dec'd. to Samuel Watkins, Robt. Thompson and Richard Easter to be held by them for the use of said Sarah during her life, after which the above men shall pay to Lotty, Sophy and Tere Easter, children of said James Easter, dec'd, L30 each upon majority or marriage and transfer by proper title all the remaining property by virtue of said will of James Easter, dec'd, to Patty Easter, now Patsy Aycock, William Thompson Easter, Booker B. Easter, Tabby Champion Easter, Sophia Easter and Tere Easter children of James Easter, dec'd. May 23, 1792. Ben Taliaferro, Jeremiah Walker, Wm. Thompson, Sr. Farley Thompson, William Scott, Test.

EVENS, GEORGE—Folio 113— To Richard Gatewood, 100 acres on Deep creek. Feb. 23, 1793. Robert Loveman, Test.

ELLIOTT, JAMES—Folio 47—To Cuthberd Hudson, both of Wilkes Co., 200 acres on Savannah river, Wilkes Co., adj. land of said Hudson on which he now lives. July 8, 1786. J. Gorham, Test.

ELLIOTT, WILLIAM and wife Sarah—Folio 78—To Jonathan Arnold, 100 acres on Cedar creek. July 2, 1790. John Clarkson, Test.

FARROW, PERIN—Folio 11—To John, Willie, Needham, Sally, Micajah and Britton Farrow, slaves, horses, cattle, household goods and land. Apr. 25, 1791. J. Gorham, J. P. Jenny Gorham, Test.

FREEMAN, JAMES—Folio 45—To James Hanna, 200 acres on Cedar Creek. Jan. 3, 1792. Chas. Hutchings, Moses Haynes, Jno. Cunningham, Test.

GRAY, JAMES and wife Mary—Folio 7—To Thos. Lovelady, all of Wilkes Co., 380 acres. Oct. 18, 1790. Wm. Leach, Robt. Ross, Test.

GREGG, THOMAS—Folio 8—To Richard Colbert, both of Wilkes Co., 100 acres part of a grant of 300 acres on Dry Fork of Vanns creek. May 10, 1789. John Colbert, Thos. Colbert, Test.

GREGG THOMAS—Folio 49—To Esaias Harbour, both of Wilkes Co. 100 acres on Cedar creek. Sept. 10, 1789. William Dean, John Cunningham, Test.

GREGG, THOMAS—Folio 57—To William Cothers, 300 acres on Cold Water creek, orig. grant 1784 to said Gregg. Mar. 30, 1792.

GLOVER, WILLIAM and wife Anna—Folio 9—To James Shepherd, all of Wilkes Co., 240 acres on Falling creek, orig. grant 1786 to said Glover. Aug. 19, 1790.

GLOVER, JOHN—Folio 27—To his grandson John Brown, son of Meroday Brown, 200 acres on Falling Creek, part of orig. grant 1786 to said Glover, this land to be in trust of Meroday Brown, or Mary Brown, his wife as long as they live. July 21, 1791. Evan Ragland, J. P.

GUNNOLDS, JOSEPH and wife Marget of Franklin Co. Folio 88—To James Crow of Elbert Co., a survey of land in Elbert Co., on Broad river and Fork creek adj. Wm. Edwards, Christ, Sayler, David Aberhart and Nathaniel Smith. Mar. 20. 1792. Alex. Hodge, James Nailer, Test.

GRAVES, HUMPHREY—Folio 98—of Richmond Co. Ga., to Joseph Fuqua, Jr. of Charlotte Co. Va., 550 acres in Wilkes Co., now Elbert Co., conveyed to Humphrey Graves by Thos. Graves, to said Thomas by Joshua Bradley, and wife. Dec. 16, 1791. Dr. Hunter, J. P., Thomas Carter, Test.

GUTTERY, ROBERT and wife Betsy—Folio 103—To Austin Webb, 100 acres on Broad river agreeable to a grant signed 1785. Aug. 11, 1792.

GUNNELS, WILLIAM—Folio 113—late a soldier in the 1st. Va. Regt. of Light Dragoons, commanded by Col. White, Power of Atty. to Francis Baldwin of Wilkes Co. Ga., to ask for etc., any pay or bounty of land for said service from the United States or the State of Va. Jan. 17, 1793. Sworn to before Francis Cook, J. P. of Elbert Co., even date.

GILLEYLEN, JACOB and wife Agness—Folio 119—To Wm. Hailey, 100 acres, orig. grant to Susanna Colbert from Edward Telfair, sold by her to said Gilleylen. Jan. 6, 1793.

GOSS, BENJAMIN and wife Elizabeth—Folio 155—To Claban Webb, 100 acres adj. Benj. Merrett and Thos. Harbour. Dec. 17, 1792.

HILL, JOHN and wife Ann—Folio 14—To Absolom Trantham, all of Wilkes Co. Land on Beaverdam and Vanns creeks. Aug. 26, 1790. John McKenzie, J. Cunningham, J. P., Test.

GEORGIA D. A. R.

HILL, MOSES—Folio 65—To Christ. Harmar, 200 acres in Elbert formerly Wilkes Co., Sept. 14, 1791. Robt. H. Taylor, Test.

HUMAN, ALEX.—Folio 18—To William Grimes, 136 acres on north side of Broad river, orig. grant 1787 to said Human. Mar. 8, 1791. Edward Goode, Robt. Moon, Test.

HAWSEY, JOHN and wife Sarah—Folio 26—To Wm. Arnold all of Wilkes Co., 10 acres on Vanns creek. May 31, 1790. J. Gorham, J. P., Reuben Allen, J. P., Test.

HUTCHINGS, CHAS.—Folio 34—To Thos. Scales, 200 acres on south side of Savannah river, orig. grant to Samuel Hunter adj. James Freeman and Richard Jones, also slaves, cattle, houses etc. Sept. 9, 1791. Moses Haynes, Samuel Hunter, Test.

HEAD, WILLIAM and wife Peggey—Folio 48—of Wilkes Co. Ga., To Noah Harbour of Halifax Co. Va., 400 acres on Coldwater creek, Wilkes Co., part of orig. grant of 800 acres to Nicholas Long. Aug. 14, 1790.

HARBOUR, NOAH—Folio 48—of Halifax Co. Va., To Esaias Harbour of Elbert Co. Ga., the above tract for L30. June 6, 1791. John Boyd, Talmon Harbour, Test. Wm. McCune, J. P.

HARBOUR, ESAIAS and wife Catharine—Folio 121—To Wm. McKenzie, 400 acres on Coldwater creek, adj. Solomon McAlpin. Feb. 8, 1792. Donald McDonald, John King, Test.

HARBOUR, ESAIAS—Folio 136—To son Talmon Harbour, 500 acres in Franklin Co., on Nails creek adj. Stephen Westbrook, two slaves, George and Hannah, cattle, horses and all goods and chattels in my house in said county. Deed of gift. Jan. 7, 1793. Robt. Skelton, John Skelton, Test.

HEAD, BENJAMIN—Folio 137—To Thompson McGuire, a slave boy Jack, Mar. 25, 1793. John Beck, Test.

HUDSON, CUTBIRD and wife Elizabeth—Folio 52—To William Guy, 200 acres on Savannah river below the land and plantation of said Hudson, orig. grant 1785 to James Elliott, Apr. 12, 1790. Wm. Hudson, Nathaniel Hudson, James Tait, J. P., Test.

HUDSON, CUTBERD and wife Elizabeth—Folio 91—To Jere. Walker, land on Savannah river, orig. grant 1784 to said Hudson. Dec. 22, 1791. Christopher Hudson, Test.

HIGGINBOTHAM, JOSEPH and wife Frances—Folio 53—To Thomas Penn 200 acres on Beaverdam creek, orig. grant 1787 to said Higginbotham adj. Francis Higginbotham and Carters land. May 14, 1791. Larkin Gatewood, R. Hunt, J. P., Test.

HARRIS, JOHN and wife Mary—Folio 58—of Pendleton Co. S. C. To Jeams Sutton of Wilkes or Elbert Co. Ga., 200 acres on Purkins fork of Davis creek. Nov. 4, 1791. William Ashley, Reuben Sutton, Test.

HENDRICK, HILLERY and wife Elizabeth—Folio 53—To Wm. Bibb Key, 150 acres, the lower part of a tract on which said Hendrick now lives, orig. grant 1788 to said Hendrick, on Falling creek. Feb. 12, 1791. James Bell, William Brown, Test.

HUBBARD, JOHN and wife Sally—Folio 88—To Benjamin Glover, 200 acres adj. Frederick Brasel. July 26, 1792. James Bell, J. P., Augustine Bryan, Test.

HUBBARD, JOHN and wife Sally—Folio 97—To Josiah Certain, 200 acres, other half of above tract. July 26, 1792. James Bell, J. P., Augustine Bryan, Test.

HUBBARD, BENJAMIN and wife Caty or Catron—Folio 103—of Wilkes Co. To Thomas Burton of Elbert Co., 200 acres on Warhatche creek. Oct. 8, 1792. Richard Hubbard, James Bell, J. P., Test.

HOWELL, JOHN—Folio 96—of the town of Augusta, To James McDonald of Elbert Co., a negro boy York. April 5, 1792. Abraham Jones, J. P., Hugh McDonald, Test.

HUNT, RICHARDSON—Folio 97—To John Greenwood, 45½ acres adj. said parties, part of orig. grant 1787 to said Hunt. Aug. 19, 1791. William Barnett, J. P., James Tait, J. P., Test.

HIGHTOWER, JOHN and wife Sarah—Folio 111—To Dionysius Oliver, Sr. part of a 550 acre tract on north side of Broad river, orig. grant 1786 to said Hightower. Dec. 7, 1792. Wm. Oliver, Test.

HIGHTOWER, JOHN and wife Sarah—Folio 153—To Robt. Huddleston, the rest of above tract. Dec. 6, 1792. Thomas Oliver, Test.

HATCHER, ROBERT—Folio 118—of Columbia Co. To William Hatcher of Elbert Co., three slaves, Sall and her two children Luce and Ben. Jan. 14, 1793. Mat J. Williams, Milley Walker, Test.

HERRINGTON, JOHN—Folio 108—of Franklin Co., To Valentine Smith of Elbert Co., 250 acres orig. grant 1789 to said Herrington. Oct. 9, 1792.

HALEY, WILLIAM and wife Mary—Folio 122—To Zimry Tait, 100 acres with appurtenances adj. said Tait and Turman W. Colbert. May 10, 1791. Robert Middleton, J. P.

HOWARD, JULIUS and wife Susannah—Folio 139—of Wilkes Co., To William Alston of Elbert Co., 800 acres on Savannah river, included a mill. May 22, 1792. Leroy Pope, Test.

JONES, JOHN—Folio 37—of Elbert Co. Power of Atty. to friend Thomas Bell of Chaham Co., N. C. to appear in court of said county and make a lawful deed of conveyance to John Lambeth, Sr. for 100 acres part of the tract on which I formerly lived on Buffalo branch and for the remaining part to the heirs of Robert Ryland, dec'd. Nov. 2, 1791.

GEORGIA D. A. R.

JONES, ISAAC and wife Elizabeth—Folio 51—To James Cook, 100 acres on Cedar creek, half of a tract that did belong to said Jones. Nov. 30, 1791.

JOHNSON, ANDREW and wife Nancy—Folio 62—To Leonard Rice, 200 acres on Doves creek orig. grant 1788 to said Johnson. Jan. 6, 1790. John Staples, Robert Burke, Test.

JONES, JOHN and wife Elizabeth—Folio 71—To Henry Mosely, all of Wilkes Co., 32 acres adj. both. Sept. 13, 1791. Francis Cook, J. P. Test.

JOHNSTON, GEORGE—Folio 94—To Richard Woods both of Wilkes Co., 200 acres on Broad river, orig. grant to Alex Reeves. adj. John Barnett. Oct. 13, 1790. Robt. Magary, Major Pulling, James Aycock, Test.

JOHNSON, JOHN H. and wife Sarah—Folio 133—To John McDonald, 300 acres on south fork of Broad river in Elbert and Wilkes counties. May 11, 1791. Andw. Hemphill, Test.

KERSEY, STEPHEN—Folio 20—To Richardson Hunt both of Wilkes Co. 200 acres on Doves creek adj. said Hunt. April 20, 1790. John Jourdan, Test.

KENNEDY, ROBERT and wife Elizabeth—Folio 59—To John Patterson 138 acres on Savannah river orig. grant to said Kennedy. May 19, 1791. Wm. Higginbotham, J. P., James Ware, Larkin Gatewood, Test.

LITTLE, JAMES, Sr. and wife Isabell—Folio 25—To William Daniel 214 acres on Savannah river including a small island. Feb. 17, 1791. James F. Nunnelee, Allen Daniel, Reuben Allen, Test.

LUMPKIN, GEORGE—Folio 12—of Wilkes Co., To Thomas Shockley of Albeville Co., S. C. one quarter of an acre in Wilkes Co. on Savannah river whereon Shockley's Ferry is situated. May 2, 1790. James Giles, William Elliott, Test.

LUMPKIN, GEORGE, and wife Ann of Wilkes Co. Folio 81—To Elijah Owens of Elbert Co., 100 acres between Powderbag and Lightwood Log creeks, adj. James Greenstreet, John Tweedle and Nehemiah Howard, including the school house, part of a grant of 400 acres to said Lumpkin. June 22, 1792. James Greenstreet, Sarah Haynes, Moses Haynes, Test.

LEGETT, JOHN—Folio 71—of Wilkes Co., To Nathan Acheson of Elbert Co., 200 acres on Fork creek, Elbert Co., adj. Robt. Cowdon and John Talbot. Sept. 10, 1791. Jacob Odom, Jacob Eaverhurt, Test.

LAMAR, BASIL and wife Mary—Folio 101—of Wilkes Co., To Robert Mosely of Elbert Co., 200 acres in Wilkes, now Elbert Co., on Falling creek, orig. grant 1786 to said Lamar. Jan. 1, 1791. Z. Lamar, Henry Ware, J. P., Test.

LOVELL, JOHN—Folio 128—of Granville Co. S. C., To Patrick Mitchell of Wilkes Co., Ga., 140 acres part of a grant of 400 acres to said Lovell. Aug. 18, 1789. Jacob Hill, Gideon Holmes, Test.

LOVELADY, THOMAS and wife Jane—Folio 138—To Alex. Stinchcomb, 200 acres on Doves creek part of a survey of 800 acres to James Gray 1790, adj. Edmond Johnson, Wm. Bradford and Basil Brawner. Dec. 26, 1792.

LOVILL, JOHN—Folio 148—of Granville Co. S. C., To Moses Hill of Wilkes Co. Ga., 100 acres on Cedar creek, part of orig. grant of 400 acres to said Lovill. Aug. 18, 1789. Jacob Hill, Patrick Mitchell, Gideon Holmes, Test.

McDONALD, HUGH—Folio 10—of Elbert Co., To David Criswell, Esqr., of Wilkes Co., for 20 shillings 350 acres on Scull Shoals a branch of Broad river, Elbert Co. Mar. 2, 1791. Robert Christmas, J. P., William Sansom, Test.

McDONALD, HUGH and wife Helen—Folio 61—To James High Smith, all of Wilkes Co., 100 acres on Cedar creek. Mar. 23, 1790. Thomas Berrien Creagh, Moses Rush, Test.

McDONALD, HUGH and wife Helen—Folio 15—of Wilkes Co., To William Little, gunsmith of Wilkes Co., 250 acres on Falling creek bounded on all sides by said McDonald's land. Dec. 14, 1789. Isaac Little, Richard Richardson, Test.

McDONALD, HUGH—Folio 96—To William Elliot, a slave Muncratt. Aug. 18, 1792. John King, Test.

McDONALD, HUGH and wife Helen—Folio 102—To James Hunt, 300 acres on Coldwater creek, Elbert Co. Dec. 29, 1791. Samuel Baker, Murdock Martin, Test.

McCLESKEY, DAVID and wife Mary—Folio 22—To William Daniel all of Wilkes Co., 350 acres on Broad river at the mouth of Bluestone creek. Oct. 26, 1789. John Fergus, J. P., Test.

McCLESKEY, DAVID and wife Mary—Folio 55—of Elbert Co., To Thos. Hemphill of Burke Co. N. C., 300 acres orig. grant 1788 to said McCleskey, in Elbert Co. on Bluestone creek. June 1, 1791. Samuel Mackie, Thomas Mackie, Jno. Crosby, Test.

McCONNELL, JAMES—Folio 66—of Abbeville Co., S. C., To John McConnell of Wilkes Co. Ga., 200 acres on Broad river, Wilkes Co., orig. grant 1785 to said James. Sept. 21, 1787. John Johnson, Joseph Carey (?), Test.

McKEEN, WILLIAM—Folio 85—of S. C., To Henery Shackleford of Elbert Co, 300 acres on Vanns creek, orig. grant to said McKeen. Jan. 16, 1792. Edmond Shackleford, Edward McGarry, Test.

McDONALD, JAMES & HUGH—Folio 140—To John Smith, a slave York. Mar. 30, 1793. John Neal, Test.

McDONALD, PATRICK and wife Elizabeth—Folio 83—of Richmond Co., To James Crow of Wilkes Co., 245 acres on Fork creek Wilkes Co., July, 9, 1790. Thos. White, J. P., Samuel Devereux, Test.

MARTIN, ROBERT—Folio 1—To Barkley Martin and Thos. Posey, his security as guardian of Peter, Robert, Archibald, Elizabeth and John Martin as relates to a legacy to them from their grandfather John Martin, mortgage on 200 acres in Abbeville Co. S. C. on Savannah river, and slaves Neptune, Phillis, Harry, Charles, Lett and Jenny. Feb. 1, 1791. George Walker, Test.

MARTIN, ROBERT—Folio 29—To Robert Middleton, a slave Charles about 25 years old. Jan. 12, 1791. Bradock Voden, M. Woods, Test.

MARTIN, ROBERT and wife Eliza—Folio 99—To James Walker, 275 acres on Beaverdam creek it being the other half of the land sold Benj. Cook, orig. grant 1787 to Thomas Carter. Nov. 14, 1791. James Cook, John Allbritton,Test.

MARTIN, GEORGE and wife Elizabeth—Folio 37—To Joseph Bell, all of Wilkes Co., 200 acres, orig. grant to said Martin 1785. Dec. 26, 1789. James Bell, Jesse Jones, Test.

MARTIN, GEORGE and wife Elizabeth—Folio 39—To Joseph Bell, 57 acres in Wilkes Co., orig. grant 1786 to said Martin. Dec. 26, 1789. James Bell, Jesse Jones, Test.

MORSE, SAMUEL—Folio 16—To his son John Julian Morse, land, house, cattle, horses etc. Deed of gift. May 16, 1791. Robert Cosby, John Davis, Test.

MATLOCK, JAMES—Folio 20—of Rutherford Co. N. C., To Samuel Blackburn of Elbert Co., Ga., 350 acres on Cedar creek, part of a grant of 400 acres Apr. 19, 1790 to said Matlock. Apr. 20, 1790. John Jourdan, J. Cunningham, J. P., Test.

MATLOCK, JAMES—Folio 27— of Franklin Co., To Wm. Flanigin of Elbert Co., 100 acres on Little branch, including the plantation where said Flanigin now lives in Elbert Co. Jan. 19, 1790. George Cockburn, John Tweedle, Test.

MIDDLETON, ROBERT—Folio 36—High Sheriff of Elbert Co., To Robt. Corethers, 200 acres on Vanns creek property of John Cunningham. Oct. 3, 1791.

MIDDLETON, ROBERT and wife Elizabeth—Folio 49—To William Woldridge, 100 acres on Beaverdam creek. Aug. 18, 1791.

MIDDLETON, ROBERT—Folio 82—Sheriff, To Allen Daniel, 300 acres on Broad river, sold as property of Wm. Daniel to satisfy judgement of John Dunn. Feb. 17, 1792.

MOSELY, HENRY and wife Mary—Folio 40—To John Jones, all of Wilkes Co., 32 acres adj. Basil Lamar and said Mosely, orig. grant 1787 to Robt. Mosely. Sept. 13, 1791. Francis Cook, J. P.

MOSLEY, ROBERT and wife Sarah—Folio 47—To John Wilkins, all of Wilkes Co., 200 acres adj. Robert and Henry Mosely, orig. grant 1788 to said Robert. Mar. 10, 1790. James Bell, Littleberry H. Talley, Olive Bell, Test.

MEADOWS, ISAAC and wife Mary—Folio 144—To William Moore, 130 acres on Vanns creek. Sept. 20, 1792. Reuben Thornton, Reuben Allen, J. P., Test.

MERRITT, BENJAMIN and wife Mary—Folio 156—To Claban Webb land on Cedar creek. Dec. 16, 1792.

NUNNELEE, JAMES FRANKLIN and wife Keziah—Folio 56—To James Tate 150 acres on Coodye creek adj. James Tate, William and Drewry Thompson and said Nunnelee, orig. grant 1783 to Henry Wideman. Feb. 16, 1792.

NUNNELEE, JAMES FRANKLIN—Folio 121—To Joseph Akin both of Wilkes Co., 200 acres on Cudies creek. May 25, 1789.

NUNNELEE, Wm. WOMACK—Folio 29—To Elizabeth Nunnelee, bill of sale of two slaves, Doll and Lucy. April 7, 1788. Eli West, William Hatcher, Test.

NAIL, JULIAN and wife Mary—Folio 86—To John Patterson, 200 acres on Savannah river, orig. grant to said Nail. July 13, 1792. Rolen Brown, Test.

OLIVER, DIONYSIUS and wife Mary Ann—Folio 1—To Middleton Woods, lot No. 66 on west side of second Street and Lot No. 77 on east side of Second Street in the town of Petersburg in the forks of Savannah and Broad rivers. Aug. 14, 1786. Martha Vann, Jesse Cox, Test.

OLIVER, DIONYSIUS and wife Mary Ann—Folio 30—To James Oliver 200 acres on Broad river adj. John Coleman and John Easter. May 20, 1791. John Oliver, William Oliver, Test.

OLIVER, DIONYSIUS, Sr. and wife Mary Ann—Folio 64—To Peter Oliver 600 acres on Doves creek obtained by a warrant 1783. Oct. 22, 1791. Thomas Oliver, Dionysius Oliver, Jr., Test.

OLIVER, DIONYSIUS—Folio 76—To John Oliver, Lot No. 70 on west side of 2nd. Street in town of Petersburg, containing half acre. May 21, 1792. John Oliver, Jr. Wm. Thompson, Jr., Test.

OLIVER, DIONYSIUS—Folio 77— To John Oliver Lot No. 16 on west side of Front Street in town of Petersburg, also Lot No. 13 on east side of Front Street, also Lot No. 60 on west side of 2nd. Street. May 21, 1792. John Oliver, Sr., Wm. Thompson, Test.

OLIVER, JOHN and wife Frances—Folio 46—To John Peterson Harper, Lot No. 16 on west side of Front Street in the town of Petersburg. Jan. 20, 1792. O. Whyte, Harry Caldwell, J. P., Test.

GEORGIA D. A. R.

PETTIGREW, GEORGE—Folio 18—To James Cook, 150 acres on Savannah river. May 19, 1791.

PACE, BARNABAS and wife Agnes—Folio 43—To David Adams, 100 acres on Wahatchee creek. Jan. 6, 1791. John Thompson, Harry Caldwell, J. P., Test.

PORTER, BENJAMIN—Folio 60—To William Allen, Lot No. 30 in town of Petersburg containing half acre. Feb. 24, 1792. Parent Farer, William Moss, J. P., Test.

POLLARD, JOHN and wife Polly—Folio 67—To William Patterson, two acres on Beaverdam creek, part of a patent to Joseph Pulliam. Dec. 6, 1791. Richard Pollard, Reuben Allen, J. P., Test.

PAYTON, WILLIAM—Folio 96—To George Johnston, both of Wilkes Co., 200 acres adj. John Barnett. Aug. 5, 1790. Hez. Luckie, John Crosby, Test.

PEEK, JOHN C.—Folio 131—To William Dudlee, all that tract of land granted Sept. 18, 1786. Dec. 1, 1792. Thos. Collier, J. P., Test.

RICE, LEONARD and wife Sary or Sarah—Folio 9—To John Staples 50 acres on Doves creek orig. grant 1786 to Wm. Strong. Jan. 6, 1791. Andrew Johnson, Robert Burke, Test.

REED, COLLIN—Folio 25—To John McDowell of Charleston, Lot No. 26 on the west side of Front Street in the town of Petersburg, containing half acre. July 25, 1791. John Buchanan, Evan Ragland, J. P., Test.

READY, JAMES and wife Elizabeth—Folio 50—To Benjamin Brown, all of Wilkes Co., 200 acres on Beaverdam creek. June 12, 1790.

ROSS, JOHN and wife Marget—Folio 61—To Richard Bonds 200 acres on Coldwater creek_____ 1791. Samuel Baker, Joseph Bond, George Wood, Test.

RICHARDSON, WALKER—Folio 63—To Dionysius Oliver, Sr., 334 acres Dec. 28, 1791. Dionysius Oliver, Jr., Thomas Oliver, Test.

RICHARDSON, WALKER—Folio 64—To Dionysius Oliver, Sr., 900 acres Dec. 28, 1791. Dionysius Oliver, Jr., Thomas Oliver, Test.

RICHARDSON, WALKER—Folio 114—late a Lieut. in 1st. Va. Regt., commanded by Col. Chas. Harrison, power of Atty to William Higginbotham of Elbert Co., Ga., to receive all pay due for such service from the State of Va., or the United States. Feb. 1, 1792. James McCleskey, J. P.

ROGERS, JOHN—Folio 125—To Thomas Rogers 170 acres on Scull Shoal Creek. April 18, 1791. James Rogers, Benj. Rogers, Test.

ROGERS, JOHN—Folio 147—To Mary Rogers "in consideration of the many favors he has received of said Mary", 94 acres on Scull Shoal creek, adj.

HISTORICAL COLLECTIONS   165

Jason Wilson and John Rogers. May 5, 1791. Thomas Rogers, Thos. Barren, Unity Rogers, Test.

RUCKER, GEORGE and wife Catharine—Folio 150—To Wm. Alexander, all of Wilkes Co., 122 acres on Savannah river adj. John McGowan. Aug. 13, 1790. Thos. Keyes, Daniel Matkin, Test.

SCOTT, THOMAS and wife Betsy—Folio 12—To Thomas Hilley, all of Wilkes Co., 200 acres on Coldwater creek, granted 1786. July 17, 1790. Thomas Scott, J. P. Test.

SCOTT, THOMAS—Folio 38—To Richard Coulter, Jr., and Major Nelson a horse and saddle to settle a debt. Dec. 1, 1791. Alex. Stephen, Chas. Coulter, Test.

SCOTT, THOMAS and wife Nancy—Folio 44—To James Ryelye, 200 acres on Doves creek part of a grant 1787 to Richard Coulter, Sr., Nov. 4, 1789. John Crosby, Francis Cook, J. P., Test.

SMITH, JOHN and wife Mary—Folio 19—of Franklin Co., To Zachariah Butler of Wilkes Co., 32 acres adj. said Butler, James Butler and Clement Wilkins. Jan. 17, 1791. M. Woods, Nancy Matthews, Test.

SMITH, JOHN and wife Priscilla—Folio 22—of Wilkes Co., To Moses Davis of Amherst Co. Va., 400 acres on Beaverdam creek. July 20, 1790. Wm. Higginbotham, Absolom Stinchcomb, Peter Brown. Test.

SMITH, BENJAMIN and wife Jemima—Folio 24—To Wm. Arnold, all of Wilkes Co., 10 acres on Vanns creek. May 31, 1790.

SHEARMAN, ROBERT—Folio 29—of Wilkes Co., To William Graham of Elbert Co., 200 acres on west side of S. Fk. of Broad river, orig. grant 1785 to said Shearman. Aug. 8, 1791. Henry Mounger, J. P., Test.

SHACKLEFORD, EDMOND—Folio 75—of Elbert Co., To John Douglas of Orange Co. Va., power of Atty to receive from Geo. Terrell of Culpepper Co. Va., a certain large bay horse. June 13, 1792 John Jones, Test.

STREETMAN, GARRETT and wife Mary—Folio 120—To William Halley, both planters, 100 acres on Shoal creek, part of a grant of 200 acres to John McConnell, conveyed by him to James Tuttle, by Tuttle to said Streetman. Oct. 19, 1792. John Fergus, J. P.

SMITH, WILLIAM—Folio 140—To daughter Elizabeth Smith, a mulatto girl called Annaka, now living at my fathers, John Smith, Sr. Sept. 20, 1790. Geo. Cockbun, John Tweedle, John Shields, Test.

STUBBLEFIELD, SETH—Folio 142—To William Cunningham, both of Wilkes Co., 200 acres on south fork of Broad river. Sept. 25, 1788.

SUTTLES, ISAAC—Folio 67—To James Almand, to settle a proven account of estate of James Meredith, dec's., three slaves, Sary, Bob and Ede. Feb. 4, 1792. Thos. Harbin, John Brawner, Test.

GEORGIA D. A. R.

TOLLETT, JOHN and wife Margaret—Folio 4—To Wm. Higginbotham, both of Wilkes Co., 100 acres on Beaverdam creek orig. grant 1785 to Moses Trimble. Dec. 1, 1790. Richardson Hunt, Philip Wingom, Test.

TOLLETT, JOHN and wife Marget—Folio 5—of Wilkes Co., To Jesse Holbrook of Union Co. S. C., 100 acres on Beaverdam creek, orig. grant by Samuel Elbert to said Tollett. Jan. 17, 1790. John Allbritton, Test.

TOLLETT, JOHN and wife Marget—Folio 7—of Wilkes Co., To John Allbritton of Union Co. S. C., 200 acres on Beaverdam creek. Jan. 17, 1790. Thomas Carter, Jesse Holbrook, Test.

TOLLETT, JOHN and wife Marget—Folio 15—To Moses Trimble, all of Wilkes Co., 600 acres on Beaverdam creek, "it being the balance of tract on which Philip Vineyard now lives". orig. grant 1785 to said Tollett. April 5, 1790. Richardson Hunt, Will Higginbotham, Jean Mouson, Test.

TOLLETT, JOHN—Folio 41—To Philip Vineyard, both of Wilkes Co., 300 acres on Beaverdam creek, it being part of orig. grant of 600 acres, 1785 to said Tollett. Dec. 30, 1789. Richardson Hunt, J. P., Wm. Higginbotham, Test.

THOMPSON, ISHAM and wife Sally—Folio 10—To Benjamin Porter Lot No. 30, in town of Petersburg. Mar. 22, 1791. Stephen Ellington, James Tait, J. P., Wm. Hatcher, Test.

THOMPSON, ISHAM and wife Sarah—Folio 17—To Esther Singletary Starnes, all of Wilkes Co., Lot No. 31, in town of Petersburg. Sept. 8, 1790. Thomas Russell, J. P.

THOMPSON, ROBERT and wife Sarah—Folio 57—To Robert Watkins, six lots in the town of Petersburg, Nos. 5, 7, 15, 17 and 33 all on the east side of Front Street and No. 2 on west side of Front Street, and 3 acres of low ground on the Savannah river. Feb. 22, 1792. Drury Thompson, Harry Caldwell, J. P., Test.

THOMPSON, ROBERT and wife Sarah—Folio 59—To James Watkins of Charlotte Co. Va., 206 acres on Bartram's creek, adj. Oliver and Wm. Thompson, James Tait, David Hudson and Evan Ragland, being the tract I last bought of Chas. Hudson. Mar. 22, 1792. John Watkins, Oliver Thompson, Test.

THOMPSON, JOHN FARLEY—Folio 117—To Joseph Terrill, 270 acres on Coody's creek. Sept. 28, 1791. R. Easter, Wm. Christopher, Test.

THOMPSON, WILLIAM and wife Mary—Folio 118—To Nathaniel Allen, 400 acres, on Wahatche creek. Dec. 21, 1792.

TUTTLE, NICHOLAS and wife Betty—Folio 32—To John Rowzy, 200 acres on Beaverdam creek whereon said Rowzy now lives. Aug. 2, 1791. Chas. Ellis, Clabourn Sandidge, Test.

TUTTLE, NICHOLAS—Folio 114—late a soldier in Col. Clark's Regt. of Va., forces raised for the defense of the western territory, power of atty. to Francis Baldwin of Wilkes Co., to demand, and receive pay etc. due me as a soldier aforesaid from the State of Va., or the United States. Jan. 17, 1793. Wm. Higginbotham, J. P.

TUTTLE, JAMES, Sr.—Folio 94—To the Rev. Mr. John White, 200 acres on Doves creek, orig. grant 1784 to Benj. Davis. Dec. 9, 1791. John Depriest, Andw. McEavert, Test.

TUTTLE, JAMES, Sr.—Folio 110—of Elbert Co., To John Barnett of Franklin Co., 200 acres on Big Beaverdam creek, adj. Nicholas Tuttle. Sept. 10, 1791.

TUTTLE, JAMES, Sr.—Folio 126—To James Tuttle, Jr., 250 acres on north fork of Broad river. Sale. Jan. 30, 1793. John Fergus, J. P.

TUTTLE, JAMES, Jr.—Folio 109—of Elbert Co., To John Barnett of Franklin Co., 200 acres on Big Beaverdam creek. Sept. 10, 1791.

TEASLEY, SILAS and wife Fanny—Folio 31—To Oliver Crafford 200 acres on a branch of Coldwater creek. Mar. 26, 1791. R. Banks, J. P.

TRIMBLE, MOSES and wife Katharin—Folio 35—To John Ballenger, 600 acres on Beaverdam creek "being the balance of the tract of land whereon Philip Vineyard now lives", orig. grant 1785 to John Tollett. April 1, 1791. J. Gorham, J. P. Jared Bass, John Trimble, Test.

TRIMBLE, MOSES—Folio 141—To Isaac Meadows 130 acres on south fork of Vanns creek adj. Joseph Moore, Tukedmark Colbert and Thos. Colbert. Feb. 26, 1790. Philip Lewis, Test.

TRENTHAM, ABSOLOM—Folio 44—To Anthony Beverly 150 acres on branches of Beaverdam and Vanns creeks orig. grant 1786 to Ann Trentham, "it being the place whereon the said Beverly now lives", conveyed by John Hill and Ann alias Trantham his wife to said Absolom Trentham, Aug. 26, 1790. Dec. 2, 1791. R. Hunt, J. P., Wm. Shackleford, Test.

TUREMAN, GEORGE and wife Elizabeth—Folio 52—To Martin Tureman 250 acres on Coodye creek. Nov. 3, 1791.

TWEEDLE, JOHN and wife Sarah—Folio 81—To Elijah Owens, 600 acres on Savannah river, it being the plantation whereon said Tweedle now lives, adj. George Lumpkin. June 16, 1792. Nehemiah Howard, Jesse Vinson, Moses Haynes, J. P., Test.

TATE, WILLIAM and wife Elisheba—Folio 90—To Jere. Walker 190 acres on the north side of the road from Petersburg to Tugaloo, part of a 600 acre tract granted 1789 to said Tate. Mar. 28, 1791. Wm. Hatcher, John Sigmon, Test.

GEORGIA D. A. R.

TAIT, JAMES and wife Rebecca—Folio 91—To Jeremiah Walker, 206 acres being an island in the Savannah river, formerly called Collins Island, divided by a line across the island, formerly sold to Robert Chambers. Mar. 22, 1791. William Hatcher, William Tait, Robert Chambers. Test.

TERONDET, DANIEL and wife Salley—Folio 107—of Wilkes Co., To Nathan Bond of Elbert Co., 200 acres on Beaverdam creek, Elbert Co., orig. grant 1786. Oct. 10, 1792. John M. Carter, R. Worsham, J. P., Test.

WIDEMAN, HENRY and wife Mary—Folio 2—of Abbeville Co. S. C. To Edward Walthall of Wilkes Co. Ga., 200 acres on Coodys creek, adj. James Tate, Isham Morgan, Chas, Hudson and Isham Thompson. Dec. 31, 1790. John Turman, Martin Turman, Test.

WATTSON, JOHN—Folio 3—To David Criswell to make a grant etc, to Thomas Brown, which warrant is in the hands of said Criswell. Oct. 4, 1790. Evan Ragland, Test.

WIMBISH, SAMUEL—Folio 56—of Elbert Co., power of Atty to Alex. Gorden of Charlotte Co. Va., to attend to all business in Va. Feb. 16, 1792. John Dailey, John Ells, Test. M. Woods, J. P.

WYCHE, THOMAS—Folio 60—of Burke Co., To Peter Wyche of Elbert Co. a slave Doll. May 20, 1791. C. Clark, D. Clark, Agatha Clark, Test.

WATKINS, WILLIAM and wife Susannah—Folio 78. To John Oliver Lot No. 10 in the town of Petersburg which lies on the west side of Front Street with a store and stable thereon. April 14, 1788.

WALTHALL, EDWARD and wife Nancy—Folio 80—To James Tait 4 acres on Coodys creek. July 20, 1792.

WHITE, JOHN and wife Milley—Folio 87. To Henry Duncan 400 acres on Beaverdam creek, adj. Wm. Pulliam, orig. grant to James Kidd and Milley. Oct. 22, 1791. Thomas Perry, John Morris, John Depriest, Andw. McEver., Test.

WALKER, JAMES and wife Elizabeth—Folio 100. To James Cook 225 acres on Beaverdam creek, it being the upper and other half of a tract Robert Martin sold to Benjamin Cook, part of orig. grant 1787 to Thomas Carter. Nov. 19, 1791. Jona. Rosel, Joshua Sled, Test.

WATTS, EDWARD—Folio 118. To John Buchannan both of Wilkes Co., 200 acres orig. grant 1784 to said Watts which included three islands in the Savannah river which are reserved. Apr. 22, 1790. Jacob Gillylen, Thomas Turner, Test.

WATTS, EDWARD—Folio 122. of Wilkes Co., To Thomas Turner of Abbeville Co. S. C., above islands. Mar. 1, 1788. Jacob Gilleylen, John Buchannon, Test.

WEBB, WILLIAM—Folio 132—To John Bowen, both of Wilkes Co., 300 acres on Falling creek it being the tract said Webb sold to Audley Maxwell of Va. June 20, 1789.

WILKINS, THOMAS and wife Elizabeth—Folio 145—To John Armstrong Baker, 163 acres adj. Absolom Baker, James Shepherd and William Harbin. July 9, 1792.

ELBERT COUNTY GEORGIA

DEED BOOK "B".

ALLEN, BENJAMIN and wife Elizabeth—Folio 3—To John Hubberd Fannin 125 acres on Beaverdam creek, adj. Wm. Hansard, William and Middleton Woods. April 10, 1790. (Signed Betty) James Bell, J. P., Chas. Hudson, Test.

ALLEN, NATHANIEL and wife Pamelia—Folio 3—To Benjamin Fanning, 250 acres on Beaverdam creek adj. James Carter, Robt. Hall, John Walton, Benj. Brown and Wm. H. Tait. April 9, 1793.

ALLEN, BENJAMIN and wife Elizabeth—Folio 4—To Benjamin Fanning, 125 acres on Beaverdam creek, adj. Wm. Hansard and Thos. Adkins. April 10, 1793. (Signed Betty)

ALLEN, BENJAMIN and wife Elizabeth—Folio 42—To Zimri Tate, 200 acres on Codys creek adj. Edward Walthall, Wm. Tait and William Haley. April 9, 1793. (Signed Betty)

ALLEN, BEVERLY—Folio 81—of the State of S. C., but now of the town of Augusta to Reuben Allen, all estate real and personal to secure said Reuben as security for Beverly Allen & Co., for a debt of three thousand pounds to John Wray of Charleston. Feb. 20, 1794. James Richards, Allen Daniel, S. Alston, William Allen, Test.

ALLEN, NATHANIEL and wife Pamelia—Folio 97—of Elbert Co., To Joseph Wilson of Prince Edward Co. Va., 500 acres on Beaverdam creek, adj. Thomas Carter, Daniel Casey, Wm. H. Tait and Zachariah Butler., Mar. 20, 1794.

ALLEN, NATHANIEL and wife Pamelia—Folio 131—To Thomas Akins 360 acres on Beaverdam creek adj. Middleton Woods, Benjamin Allen, Thos. Carter, Hudson Tait, part of 1000 grant to said Nathaniel 1792. April 9, 1793.

ALLEN, NATHANIEL and wife Pamelia—Folio 151—To John Bray 200 acres it being the upper part of orig. grant 1785 to William Thompson on north fork of Wahatchee creek. Jan. 11, 1794. James Bell, J. P., Olive Bell, Test.

ALLEN, NATHANIEL and wife Pamelia—Folio 152—To Nathan Jones 127 acres being the middle part of above tract. Jan. 11, 1794.

ALLEN, NATHANIEL and wife Pamelia—Folio 180—To Jesse Jones 236 acres, lower part of above tract. Aug. 31, 1793.

ALLEN, BEVERLY—Folio 181—of St. Thomas Parish in the State of S. C. and William Allen of Elbert Co., Ga. agreement that William Allen is to divide profits on sale of mdse. expenses equally shared. Feb. 10, 1792. William Moss, Test.

ALLEN, WILLIAM—Folio 189—of Elbert Co. To John Waller of Hancock Co., two slaves David 14 and Isaac 12 years old, horses, cattle, feather beds and furniture (1 pr. fire dogs) Sept. 30, 1794. Thomas Colbert, Jeremiah Walker, Test.

ALLEN, WILLIAM—Folio 189—of Elbert Co., To John Waller of Hancock Co., 800 acres the plantation on which said Allen now lives on Beaverdam creek, adj. John Key, Wm. Arnold and Blankenships land. Sept. 29, 1794. Stephen Heard, Thomas Thornton, Test.

ALLEN, NATHANIEL and wife Pamelia—Folio 191—To William Hudson Tate 200 acres on Beaverdam creek whereon the said Tate now lives orig. grant 1786 to said Allen. Aug. 14, 1793.

AKIN, THOMAS and wife Mary—Folio 4—To Benjamin Fannin, for L5, 100 acres on Beaverdam creek, beginning at Hudson Tate's corner. May 25, 1793. Richard Hansard, Test.

ALFORD, JAMES and wife Luraner—Folio 120—of Green Co., To William Head of Elbert Co., 400 acres orig. grant 1786 to said Alford. Mar. 7, 1794. Abraham Womack, J. P.

ASH, THOMAS LEWIS—Folio 192—of Washington Co., in the Southwestern Territory, power of Atty to John Clarkson of Elbert Co. Ga., to secure a certain bounty of land due me from the State of Ga. for services done to said State as will fully appear by discharge dated the 9th, day of Feb. 1790. Dec. 24, 1794. H. M. Donald, John B. Alexander, Test.

ARMSTRONG, JOHN, Jr.—Folio 194—of Franklin Co. Ga., To Daniel Parker 300 acres on Hannah's creek, Elbert Co., orig. grant 1795 to said Armstrong. Mar. 30, 1795. Jason Wilson, Test.

BAKER, BENJAMIN and wife Comfort—Folio 53—To Edmond Lowry, 87 acres on Falling creek, orig. grant 1786 to said Baker. Mar. 8, 1792.

BAKER, BANJAMIN and wife Comfort—Folio 166—To John Armstrong Baker, 112 acres part of above grant. Mar. 17, 1794. Benjamin Baker, James Baker, Test.

BAKER, JOHN A. and wife Jane—Folio 76—To James Shepherd, 163 acres on west side of Falling creek. Dec. 14, 1793.

BAKER, JESSE and wife Susannah—Folio 152—To William Blake, Jr., 198 acres on Falling creek adj. William Blake, Sr., and Jane Mitchell. Regisered Oct. 20, 1794.

BUGG, JACOB and wife Nancy—Folio 6—and Abraham Colson and wife Nancy, To James Tait, 300 acres on Savannah river adj. William Watkins, Julius Howard and John Coleman. Dec. 17, 1792. H. Graves Walker, Test.

BURKE, ROBERT and wife Sally—Folio 53—To Wm. Howinton, 200 acres on Doves creek. May 25, 1793.

BROWN, BEDFORD—Folio 58—of Wilkes Co., To Newton Foote of Chester Co. S. C., 360 acres on Shoal creek and Broad river, Elbert Co. Oct. 18, 1792. Wm. G. Gilbert, Abm. Tyson, Test.

BROWN, BENJAMIN and wife Nancy—Folio 56—of Elbert Co., To Michael Border of Franklin Co., 200 acres on south fork of Beaverdam creek adj. Peter Brown and John Tollett at time of original survey. Dec. 10, 1792.

BARNETT, WILLIAM, Folio 63—James Tait, Evan Ragland and Richardson Hunt, To William Cook, Lot No. 10 at the Court House, it being part of the 50 acres that was conveyed to us by John Baker, June 5, 1792, it being part of a larger survey of 950 acres. orig. granted 1793 to said Baker. Jan. 29, 1793.

Folio 67—Ditto to Wamack Blankenship, Lot No. 12 at the Court House as above. Jan. 29, 1793.

Folio 82—Ditto to Richard Coulter, Lot No. 32 at the Court House. April 4, 1794.

Folio 103—Ditto to James and Chas. Flood Lot No. 29 at Court House April 1, 1794. S. Blackburn, Samuel King, Test.

Folio 121—Ditto to Eli Eavenson, sadler, Lot No. 19 at the Court House. April 1, 1794. S. Blackburn, Samuel King, Test.

BONDS, ELIZABETH—Folio 66— To son Nathan Bonds, a slave Rachel during the natural life of said Elizabeth. Feb. 27, 1794. M. Woods, Eli Eavenson, Test.

BLANKENSHIP, WAMACK—Folio 67—of Elbert Co. To James Kidd of Richmond Co., Lot No. 12 at Court House, Elbert Co., Feb. 5, 1794.

BOBO, LEWIS—Folio 113—planter To Robert Skelton both of Wilkes Co., 10 acres adj. said Skelton. Aug. 20, 1789. John Tweedle, James Giles, J. P., Test.

BAILEY, HEZEKIAH and wife Rebeckah (?)—Folio 124—To Thomas Patterson, 100 acres part of orig. grant 1786 to Absolom Jackson. July 19, 1794. John Patterson, Test.

BARDEN, GILBERT and wife Charlott—Folio 130—To William Oliver 100 acres on Wahatchee creek including part of Powder branch. Mar. 20, 1792. Edward Clark, Thomas Hancock, Test.

BOYD, JOHN, Sr.—Folio 135—To his dear grandson John Purcell, a negro man Will, now in possession of John McKenzie, Sr. Mar. 28, 1793. James McDonald, John Boyd, Jr., Test.

GEORGIA D. A. R.

BUTLER, ZACHARIAH and wife Mary—Folio 154—To William Brown, all of Elbert Co., 250 acres on Beaverdam creek which said Butler bought of Nathaniel Allen. Dec. 15, 1792. James Bell, J. P.

BROWN, JOHN and wife Amy—Folio 164—To Elizabeth Smith and the heirs of William Smith, 130 acres on Falling creek. Jan. 28, 1792.

BURKE, THOMAS—Folio 169—To William Harrington, 58 acres on Doves creek. Oct. 10, 1794. John Staples, Robt. McDowell, Test.

CARTER, THOMAS, Sr.—Folio 16—To Thomas Penn, 25 acres on Beaverdam creek it being a part of the tract whereon said Carter now lives. July 19, 1793.

CARTER, JAMES and wife Lucy—Folio 34—To Thomas Carter, Sr., 400 acres on Beaverdam creek, orig. grant to said James 1787. June 4, 1792.

CARTER, WILLIAM—Folio 40—To William Gunns, three slaves, Betty, Harry and Jane. Jan. 2, 1793. Jacob Burton, Mary Johns, Joseph Stocks, Test.

CARTERS, THOMAS, Jr. and wife Elizabeth—Folio 44—To Benj. Fortson 100 acres on Beaverdam creek part of a larger survey of 1100 acres 1785 to said Carter. Oct. 7, 1793. R. Hunt, J. P., Wm. Fortson, Test.

CARTER, THOMAS, Sr. and wife Elizabeth—Folio 77—To Joel Stodgill, 250 acres on Beaverdam creek, part of a larger survey of 1100 acres 1785 to said Carter. Dec. 18, 1793. David Cosby, Test.

CLARK, ZACHARIAH—Folio 1—To Benson Henry, land on Coldwater creek a part of a survey to Wm. Taylor adj. an orig. grant to Hambleton Blackwell. May 20, 1793.

CROW, JAMES and wife Hannah—Folio 21—To Wm. Gordon, 245 acres on Fork creek orig. grant to Patrick McDonald. Apr. 25, 1791.

CROW, JAMES and wife Hannah—Folio 175—To Samuel Woods, all the orig. survey to Joseph Gunnels 1784, 150 acres on Broad river and Fork creek Feb. 20, 1794. Wm. Hodge, J. P. Edwd. Goods, Test.

COBBS, JOHN and wife Mary—Folio 23—To William Toms, all of Columbia Co., 250 acres a part of a grant of 1000 acres in 1786 to said Cobbs. Sept. 10, 1793. John de Yampert, J. P. Thomas Dawson, William Buckham, Test.

COSBY, ROBERT, T. C.—Folio 36—To Moses Haynes, the property of Isaac Land, 97½ acres on Savannah river adj. said Haynes and Liab (?) Vinson. Oct. 10, 1793.

CLEMM, ADAM and wife Jemmia—Folio 39—To Wm. Pickings, 250 acres on a branch of Coldwater creek. Oct. 20, 1792. John Walraven, Hugh Hairon (?) Test.

COMMISSIONERS—Folio 63—Wm. Barnett, James Tait, Evan Ragland, and Richardson Hunt, To William Cook, Lot No. 10 at the Court House. Jan. 29, 1793. John Fergus, J. P., John Coleman, Test.

COMMISSIONERS, as above—Folio 67—To Wamack Blankenship Lot No. 12, at the Court House. Jan. 29, 1793.

COMMISSIONERS as above—Folio 82—To Richard Coulter, Lot No. 32 at or near the Court House. April 4, 1794.

COMMISSIONERS as above—Folio 121—To Eli Evanson, sadler, Lot No. 19 "at the Court House April 1, 1794. Samuel Blackburn, Samuel King, Test.

COSBY, ROBERT, T. C.—Folio 44—To Henry Tuggle, 150 acres on Broad river, the property of Hezekiah Dailey. Dec. 2, 1793.

COSBY, ROBERT, T. C.—Folio 94—To Humphrey Graves of Wilkes Co., 550 acres on Savannah river the property of Joseph Fuqua, Jr. April 5, 1794.

COKER, ISAAC and wife Nancy—Folio 58—To William Cook, 160 acres on Beaverdam creek on the south side of Wm. Brown's mill creek. Mar 7, 1793. Francis Cook, J. P., Test.

CRISWELL, DAVID—Folio 70—of Wilkes Co. To Thomas Smyth, Jr., of the town of Augusta, 1000 acres in Elbert formerly Wilkes Co., orig. grant the 14th, of this month "to said Criswell. Nov. 15, 1792. P. Clayton, J. P., B. Jones, Test.

CONWAY, PETER—Folio 80—"of the State of S. C., to Edwin Conway of Newberry Co., S. C., 1000 acres on Coldwater creek, which land was granted said Peter by Horatio Marbury by deed of bargain, Jan. 22, 1788. Ephraim Sanders, Jesse Sanders, Test. June 15, 1792.

COLSON, ABRAHAM and wife Nancy, Jacob Bugg and wife Nancy—Folio 78—all of Wilkes Co; To Drury Bradley of Buckingham Co. Va., 300 acres on both sides of Doves creek. Dec. 25, 1790. John Coleman, Test.

CARGILL, CHARLES and wife Mary—Folio 96—To John Calvart, all of Wilkes Co., 400 acres on Broad river, now Elbert Co. Dec. 20, 1791. John McCurdy, Stephen Groves, Test.

COOK, JOSEPH—Folio 98—To William Rogers, both of Wilkes Co., 1000 acres on Coldwater creek, orig. grant 1786 to said Cook. July 1, 1790.

CLARK, BOLIGN (BOLLING)—and wife Martha—Folio 176—To Benjamin Allen, 270 acres on Waughthatchee creek. Sept. 25, 1792. James Bell, J. P., Henry Mosely, Test.

CALHOUN, JOHN—Folio 109—of 96 District S. C., To Hezekiah Bailey of Elbert Co., 500 acres on Pickens creek half an orig. grant to Absolom Jackson 1786 first conveyed to John Hardin by deed, by him to said

174   GEORGIA D. A. R.

Calhoun. July 9, 1793. Edward McGarry, Joseph Dolings, William McCune, J. P., Test.

COULTER, RICHARD—Folio 118—To Chas. Coulter, 100 acres on Doves creek, orig. grant 1786 to said Richard. April 2, 1792. James McCleskey, J. P., Robert Coulter, Test.

COLSON, ABRAHAM—Folio 182—Power of Atty. to James Coleman to collect his part of the dower of Milly Walker, late widow and relict of Jeremiah Walker, dec'd, as her dower at common law of the estate of my father Jacob Colson whose widow and relict Milly was. Dec. 9, 1792. William Goode, Test.

DANIEL, WILLIAM—Folio 8—To Allen Daniel, a slave Buck about 14. June 28, 1793. J. Davis, Test.

DARDEN, GEORGE and wife Martha—Folio 17—Power of Atty. to John Good, Henry Crittenden and Chas. Harrison of Brunswick Co. Va. to take possession of a slave Moll and her progeny so far as our hereditary right shall extend by virtue of devise of Sampson Lanier to his daughter Elizabeth Burch in his last will bearing date Jan. 8, 1742/3. Aug. 26, 1793. William Goode, J. P. James Ginnings, Test.

DUDLEY, WILLIAM and wife Mary—Folio 33—To Andrew Millican, 300 acres on south side of north fork of Broad river. Feb. 26, 1793.

DEPRIEST, JOHN—Folio 55—To Elizabeth Cunningham, 250 acres on Pendleton's Fork. April 1, 1793. Andrew McEver, Andrew Cunningham, Test.

DANIEL, WILLIAM and wife Nancy—Folio 61—To William Allston, 214 acres on Savannah river including a small island. May 4, 1792. A. Daniel, William Moss, J. P. Test.

DIXON, JOHN LIDDELL—Folio 99—of town of Augusta, To John Swepson of Greene Co., 468 acres on Cedar creek in Wilkes Co. Nov. 2, 1787. T. McCall, John King, J. P., Test.

DECKER, JOHN and wife Edey—Folio 179—To John Algood, 100 acres on Wahachee creek, part of orig. grant 1787 to said Decker. Dec. 24, 1794. James Bell, J. P., Christ. Clark, Jr., Test.

DAVIS, WILEY—Folio 184—of Elbert Co., To Aron Jones of Abbeville Co., S. C., 150 acres on Pickings creek including Mountain Spring. Aug. 23, 1794. John Morris, Test.

DIXON, OUTLERBRIDGE—Folio 193—To James Brock, Peter a slave 11 years old. Mar. 13, 1795. John McConnell, James Brock, Test.

DAUGHERTY, JOHN—Folio 170—of Talbot Co. Md., To David McCleskey, three slaves Doll, Amy, and Jane. Oct. 29, 1791. William Rose, Samuel White, Test.

EDWARDS, WILLIAM and wife Susannah—Folio 25—To William Dudley 33½ acres on north fork of Broad river, being part of orig. survey 1784 to said Edwards. Dec. 24, 1791.

ELLIS, ROBERT—Folio 170—To Charles Isom, 200 acres on Deep creek adj. Peter Brown and Wm. Richardson, Oct. 8, 1794. Stephen Handlin, Abadiah Finney, Test.

EADES, JOHN, Sr.—Folio 187—of Columbia, Co., To Nathaniel Barnett of Columbia Co., land on both sides of Falling creek, Elbert Co. Oct. 6, 1792. Peter Barnett, Test.

FOSTER, SAMUEL—Folio 20—To Nathan Jones, 200 acres on Falling creek. May 10, 1793.

FLANIGIN, WILLIAM—Folio 63—To Jonathan Arnold, both of Franklin Co., 100 acres on Little Beaverdam and Cedar creeks, being part of orig. grant of 440 acres to James Medlock. Oct. 19, 1792.

FERGUS, JOHN—Folio 105—of Elbert Co., To William Butt of Halifax Co. N. C., 100 acres on the branches of Broad river adj. Franklin Co. line and Milly Mann. Feb. 22, 1794.

FREEMAN, JAMES—Folio 144—To Jacob Prewett, 8 acres on Savannah river. Mar. 21, 1792.

FULGHAM, STEPHEN—Folio 158—Excr. of Matthew Fulgham, dec'd. To Robert Ellis, 200 acres on Deep creek. Oct. 3, 1791.

GLOVER, JOHN and wife Ellender—Folio 120—To Robert Huddleston 120 acres on Falling creek part of orig. grant 1786 to said Glover. Oct. 14, 1793.

GLOVER, JOHN and wife Ellender—Folio 186—To Joseph Huddlestone part of a 600 acre grant 1786 to said Glover, one boundary being a line said Glover had marked out to his grandson John Brown. Oct. 14, 1793. James Bell, Joseph Bell, Test.

GATES, JOSIAH—Folio 7—of Newberry Co. S. C. To John Cook of Elbert Co. Ga., 200 acres on Dry fork of Falling creek. orig. grant 1785 to said Gates. Jan. 9, 1793.

GORDON, WILLIAM and wife Catharine—Folio 22—To Chas. Kennedy, 245 acres on Fork creek, orig. grant to Patrick McDonald. July 9, 1792. William Carter, Test.

GORHAM, JOHN and wife Jean—Folio 46—of Franklin Co., To Thomas White of Elbert Co., 450 acres on Vanns creek orig. grant 1785 to Wm. Pulliam. Feb. 18, 1793. Thos. Fortson, Shelton White, Test.

GILLEYLEN, JACOB and wife Agness—Folio 136—To James Allston, 100 acres orig. granted 1786 to Susannah Colbert, sold to said Jacob 1792, except one acre on which is Wm. Hailey's house, which is conveyed to said Hailey by said Allston. Stephen Heard, James Tait, Test. April 29, 1793.

GEORGIA D. A. R.

GAAR, LEWIS and wife Catharine—Folio 148—To Hezekiah Bailey all of Elbert Co., 375 acres in Washington Co., Ky. formerly Jefferson Co. Va., orig. grant 1785, by Patrick Henry Gov. of Va., to said Gaar. June 19, 1794. James Bailey, R. Banks, Test.

HERNDON, JOHN—Folio 16—To John Calhoun, both of 96 Dist. S. C. 1000 acres in Wilkes Co., on Pickings creek, orig. grant 1786 to Absolom Jackson. April 25, 1793. James Spivey, Patrick Forbis, John Calhoun, Test.

HANDLEY, GEORGE—Folio 26—Sheriff of Richmond Co., To Robert Middleton of Washington Co., for 25 shillings, 400 acres on Coldwater creek Wilkes Co., property of Horatio Marbury to satisfy a suit of Richard Wylly and Leonard Cecil Vs Samuel Jack, Robert Middleton and Horatio Marbury. May 25, 1793.

HUDDLESTON, ROBERT—Folio 52—To Joseph Bell, 275 acres on Broad river, bought of John Hightower. Oct. 4, 1793. James Bell, J. P. Jesse Jones, Test.

HUDDLESTON, JOSEPH and wife Sarah—Folio 171—To David Martin 600 acres on Falling creek, orig. grant 1786 to John Glover. Oct. 18, 1794. William Brown, Test. (Signed Salley)

HUDDLESTON, ROBERT and wife Patsey—Folio 172—To David Martin 50 acres on Dry fork of Falling creek. Oct. 18, 1794. Thomas Cook, Test.

HOLBROOK, JESSE and wife Susanna—Folio 60—To Peter Tidwell, 100 acres on Beaverdam creek, orig. grant 1785 to John Tollett. Dec. 27, 1792. B. Pace, J. P., Robt. Ballenger, Rot. Brown, Test.

HARRIS, JOHN and wife Mary—Folio 65—of Pendleton Co. S. C., To John Wilson of Elbert Co., 200 acres on Big Shoal creek alias Beaverdam creek adj. land of said Harris. Aug. 13, 1793. Benjamin Ashworth, John Pickens, Test.

HEAD, BENJAMIN—Folio 75—To Wiley Davis slaves Dave, Rachel, Moll, Emma, Lyd, Ceasar and six negro children, Bob, Esther, Bell, Sarah, Jack and Squire. Jan. 22, 1794. River Jurdon, John Jurdon, Test.

HEAD, JAMES and wife Elizabeth—Folio 172—To Shelton White, 94 acres on Vanns creek, Jan. 20, 1795. Thos. and John White, Test.

HEAD, WILLIAM, Jr. and wife Ritter—Folio 178—To James Pearson 100 acres part of orig. survey to James Alford. Dec. 31, 1794. William Wear, James McCurdy, Test.

HIGGINBOTHAM, WILLIAM and wife Dorothy—Folio 82—To Robt. Pulliam 200 acres, part of a 600 acre grant 1792 to said William. (Signed Dolly Higginbotham). Feb. 15, 1794. John Crowder, Jacob Higginbotham, M. Woods, Test.

HIGGINBOTHAM, WILLIAM—Folio 187—To Thomas Napier two slaves, Jack and Major. Feb. 7, 1795.

HISTORICAL COLLECTIONS 177

HIGGINBOTHAM, WILLIAM—Folio 188—To Robert Middleton, four slaves, Philis, Sarah, and Anthony and a little girl. Feb. 7, 1795.

HARPER, EDMOND and wife Ann—Folio 90—To beloved children, Mary, Elizabeth, Lucy, James, Nancy, Drucilla, Bedford, Ellander and Williamson Harper, all property, real and personal. May 13, 1794. David Cosby, Eli Eavenson, Test.

HILL, MOSES—Folio 106—To John Hill, 10 acres, adj. said John's mill on Cedar creek. Dec. 28, 1791. Archelaus Walker, Test.

HOLMES, RICHARD and wife Mary—Folio 115—To Amos Richardson, all of Wilkes Co., 100 acres on Savannah river. Dec. 12, 1788. John Cane, Gideon Holmes, Test.

HARBOUR, ESAIAS and wife Catherine—Folio 127—To John Skelton, 400 acres on both sides of Cedar Creek, being the place whereon said Harbour lives. Jan. 4, 1793. Talmon Harbour, Test.

HAYNES, MOSES, Esqr.—Folio 133—To Jesse Vinson, planter, 97½ acres on Savannah river formerly belonging to Isaac Land. Feb. 19, 1794.

HUDSON, CHARLES and wife Martha—Folio 137—To David Hudson, 200 acres on Burtram's creek. Feb. 5, 1793. Benjamin Allen, William Hudson, Patrick Butler, Test.

HARPER, JOHN, P. and wife Sarah—Folio 142—To Eli Eavenson, Lot No. 21 "at the Court House"., for Ll, 25, 4d. Sept. 8, 1794. Edward Lyon, Test.

HARMAR, CHRIST., and wife Rebeckah—Folio 145—To Jacob Prewett, 100 acres on Pickens creek. Feb. 9, 1795. Abraham Duke, David Franklin, Test.

HARMAR, CHRIST. and wife Rebeckah—Folio 147—To Thomas King, land as above, being the lower part of one grant 1792 to Moses Hill. Oct. 22, 1794. James Means, Test.

HOBSON, NICHOLAS and wife Sally—Folio 143—of the State of Ga., power of Atty., to our faithful friend William Cowan of Luneburg Co. Va., to to receive a legacy bequeathed to said Sally Hobson by the last will of Trehamer de Graffenreidt of said county of Lunenburg. Jan. 30, 1795. Samuel Strong, Reuben Jourdan, Test.

HUNT, RICHARDSON—Folio 157—To William H. Tait, 373 acres on Beaverdam creek. Feb. 28, 1795. Samuel Higginbotham, J. P. Samuel Higginbotham, Jr., Test.

HUMAN, BAZELL and wife Isabell—Folio 162—To Richard Stickall or Steagall, original grant 1786 to said Human. May 25, 1792. Edward Goode, Alex. Human, Test.

HOWINGTON, WILLIAM—Folio 180—To John Staples, 58 acres on Doves creek. Oct. 18, 1794. Robt. McDowel, Thos. Burk, Test.

JOHNSON, EDMOND—Folio 14—To James Tuttle, Sr., both of Wilkes Co., Land on Doves creek. April 14, 1789. John Crosby, John H. Johnson, Elisha Johnson, Test.

JACKSON, ABSOLOM—Folio 15—of Wilkes Co., To John Herndon of Edgefield Co. S. C., 1000 acres in Wilkes Co., having such form as shown by a grant Feb. 1786. Mar. 7, 1789. Forts Cosby, John Henley, Edward McGarry, Test.

JONES, NATHAN and wife Cartna—Folio 37—To Thos. Wilkins, 45 acres on Falling creek which said Jones bought of said Wilkins, to whom it was granted 1786. Oct. 1, 1792.

JOHNSTON, JOHN H.—Folio 83—To Sarah and William Deskins, land on Scull Shoal creek. July 7, 1793. Garrett Turman, Josiah Hopkins, John Rogers, Test.

JURDIN, RIVER—Folio 85—of Elbert Co., To Francis Smith of Columbia Co., 150 acres on branch of Coldwater creek. Dec. 31, 1793. John Walton, Wm. Mathis, Aber or Over River Jourdin, Test.

JONES, JESSE—Folio 90—To John Cook, land on Falling creek, orig. grant 1787 to said Jones. Feb. 22, 1794. James Bell, J. P. Thomas Oliver, Test.

JONES, ARON and Sarah Jones—Folio 183—of Abbeville Co. S. C. To Thomas B. Creagh of Elbert Co., all the legacy given to us by Isham Stroud dec'd, late of Elbert Co. Aug. 5, 1794. Gerard Walthall, John Morris, Test.

JONES, ARON and Sarah—Folio 185—of Abbeville Co. S. C., To Thomas Creagh of Elbert Co., 150 acres on Pickings creek. Aug. 2, 1794. Gerard Walthall, John Morris, Test.

KING, THOMAS and wife Elizabeth—Folio 146—To Jacob Prewitt, 20 acres a part of a grant 1792 to Moses Hill. Oct. 27, 1794. James Means, Robert Means, Test.

KING, THOMAS and wife Elizabeth—Folio 168—To William Means, 1 acre adj. said Means. Oct. 22, 1794. Robert Means, Test.

KAIN, RICHARD—Folio 97—and Ruth, Rosanna, Christian and John resign all right, title etc., to Chas. Quirys part of William Quirys estate, dec'd., which was left to said Chas., namely the land which Alex. McConnell sold to William Quiry, dec'd. April 1, 1794. William Cain, Barnabas Pace, J. P., Test.

KAIN, RUTH—Folio 78—Rosanna, Christian and John, all of Elbert Co., sell all their rights etc to L80 Penn. currency which was left to us as our share by Wm. Quiry, dec'd., of Elbert Co., Mar. 31, 1794. Chas. Quiry, B. Pain, Test.

LONG, JOSEPH and wife Sarah—Folio 23—To William S. Burch, 200 acres on Falling creek, orig. grant 1785 to Sarah Cook. Sept. 11, 1793. William Brown, Ben Cook, Test.

LAMAR, BASIL and wife Mary—Folio 29—of Wilkes Co., To Christopher Clark of Elbert Co., 200 acres on Falling creek, part of orig. grant 1784 to said Lamar. Feb. 4, 1794. George Holman, Test.

LAMAR, BASIL and wife Mary—Folio 57—of Wilkes Co., To William Walton of Elbert Co., 400 acres on Broad river and Falling creek part of above grant. Nov. 25, 1793. Chas. Simpkins, J. Pannill, J. P. Test.

LEWIS, SARAH—Folio 84—To Philip Lewis, a slave Jane about 14. Mar. 12, 1794. William Joseph, John Moore, Test.

LUCKIE, JOHN and wife Jane—Folio 85—To Wm. A. D. Ewing, 100 acres on south fork of Broad river. Jan. 9, 1792. John McElhanen, Wm. Fos. Luckie, Test.

LUMPKIN, GEORGE—Folio 132—of Wilkes Co., To Jesse Vinson of Elbert Co., several tracts of land on Savannah river orig. grant 1787 to Samuel Foster. June 21, 1792. Elijah Owens, Janes Jones, Test.

LUMPKIN, GEORGE—Folio 148—of Oglethorpe Co., To James Greenstreet of Elbert Co., 76 acres on Lightwood Log creek, orig. grant 1792 to said Lumpkin. Feb. 9, 1795. John Lumpkin, J. P., Test.

LOWRY, WILLIAM—Folio 159—of the State of S. C., to Benjamin Cook of Elbert Co., 125 acres orig. grant 1790 to said Lowry. Feb. 28, 1794.

McELROY, AVINGTON and wife Sarah—Folio 9—To William Brewer, 178 acres part of a grant of 200 acres to said McElroy, adj. James Aycock and Walker Richardson. April 8, 1793. Mat J. Williams, Test.

McELROY, AVINGTON and wife Sarah—Folio 27—To Elisha Brewer and Lemuel Black, 400 acres on south side of Broad river. April 8, 1793. Evan Ragland, Mat J. Williams, Test.

McELROY, EVINGTON—Folio 68—of Pendleton Co. S. C. To George Cook of Elbert Co. Ga., power of Atty. for all business. Feb. 2, 1794. Joseph H. Morrison, James Adams, Test.

McCLUSKEY, DAVID and wife Mary—Folio 13—To James Tuttle, Sr., 117 acres on Falling creek, orig. grant 1788 to said David. Feb. 13, 1792. John Crosby, John H. Johnston, Elisha Johnston, Test.

McCLESKEY, DAVID and wife Mary—Folio 89—To James Allmand, 200 acres on Falling creek, orig. grant 1792 to said David. Nov. 9, 1793.

McDONALD, HUGH and wife Helen—Folio 31—To James Brady of Wilkes Co., 200 acres on Falling creek, Elbert Co., orig. grant 1788 to Allan McDonald. Aug. 1, 1791. Samuel Baker, Geo. Wood, Test.

McDONALD, HUGH and wife Helen—Folio 35—To John Morris, land on Lightwood Log creek, Elbert Co. Feb. 11, 1793. Lewis Stowers, James McDonald, Test.

McDONALD, HUGH and wife Helen—Folio 86—To Isaac Suttle, 157 acres on Falling creek. Sept. 30, 1793.

McNEIL, JOHN—Folio 81—To George Turman, Jr., Lot No. 37 in town of Petersburg on Front Street. April 12, 1794. William J. Hobby, Andrew Elliott, Test.

McDONALD, JAMES and wife Sarah—Folio 107—To Robert Skelton, 200 acres on Cedar creek adj. Lewis Bobo. Aug. 25, 1792. Donald McDonald, John Newman, Test.

McGARRY, EDWARD—Folio 108—To George Rogers and Jennet McGarry 100 acres on Coldwater creek, orig. grant to said Edward 1784. July 10, 1794.

McELROY, AVINGTON and wife Sarah—Folio 196—To Benjamin Cook, 100 acres on Warhatche creek. April 9, 1793. John Conyers, Test.

MOSELY, HENRY and wife Polly—Folio 10—To Henry Hunt, 180 acres adj. George Mosely, Robt. Mosely, Henry Mosely, and Joseph Bell. Jan. 31, 1793. James Bell, Joseph Bell, Test.

MATTHEWS, JOHN—Folio 11—and Christopher Clark, Admrs. of John Bowen, dec'd, To Absolom Baker, 300 acres on Falling creek, a tract Wm. Webb sold Audley Maxwell of Va. April 15, 1793. John Armstrong Baker, John Baker, Test.

MOSELY, ROBERT and wife Sara—Folio 65—To Thomas Bullard, 100 acres being the upper part of a 200 acre tract granted 1785 to Basil Lamar. May 27, 1793. Sterling Hightower, Test.

MIDDLETON, ROBERT—Folio 64—Sheriff,—To William Mecune, 100 acres on Savannah river, property of Isaac Jones, Oct. 4, 1792.

MIDDLETON, ROBERT—Folio 101—Sheriff, To Thomas Rodgers, cattle, sheep, household goods, property of John Rodgers to satisfy a debt to Julius Howard. May 1, 1794. R. Cosby, George Menefee, Test.

MIDDLETON, ROBERT—Folio 68—of Columbia Co., To William Goodwin of Baltimore, Md. Esqr., 400 acres on Coldwater creek, formerly Wilkes Co., adj. Hugh King, orig. grant 1786 to Horatio Marbury. Jan. 2, 1794. Abram Jones, Samuel Jack, Test.

MIDDLETON, ROBERT—Folio 115—Sheriff, To William Patton, 140 acres property of John Watson to satisfy a debt to Samuel Nelson. Feb. 1, 1790.

MIDDLETON, ROBERT—Folio 123—Sheriff, To Thomas Scales, 200 acres property of Samuel Hunter, sold to satisfy a debt to Caleb Phips. Sept. 4, 1792.

MARBURY, HORATIO—Folio 79—of Chatham Co. Ga., To Peter Conway of State of Va., 100 acres in Wilkes Co., granted to said Marbury, with houses etc. Jan. 23, 1788. J. Hall, Thomas Watkins, James McNeil, Test.

MILLICAN, ANDREW—Folio 128—of Elbert Co., To William Cleghorn of Washington Co., cows, horses, sheep etc. Sept. 27, 1794. John Millican, David Adams, Test.

MILLICAN, ANDREW, Folio 129—To John Millican, 300 acres on Broad river, orig. grant to William Dudley and conveyed by him to said Andrew. Sept. 27, 1794.

MIDDLETON, ROBERT—Folio 160,—Sheriff, To Isaac David, 200 acres property of Chas. Kennedy and Thos. B. Scott, to satisfy a debt to Matthias Maher & Co. Jan. 6, 1795.

MEANS, WILLIAM and wife Elizabeth—Folio 166—To Thomas King, land on Pickens creek. Oct. 2, 1794. Robert Means, Test.

NELSON, SAMUEL—Folio 5—To Thomas Harbin, 100 acres on Cedar creek and Broad river. July 10, 1792. Signed Samuel Nelson, Matthew X Nelson. her mark Stephen Stephens, John McAlhenan, Test.

NELSON, SAMUEL and wife Martha—Folio 87—To Wm. A. D. Ewing, 350 acres on south fork of Broad river, 150 acres of which was granted Thos. Patton 1786, 200 acres granted said Nelson. Jan. 9, 1792. John Luckie, Wm. Elliott, Test.

NORRIS, WILLIAM and wife Jane or Geen—Folio 156—of Franklin Co., To William Ward of Elbert Co., 450 acres on Coldwater creek, orig. grant to said Norris. Jan. 20, 1793.

OLIVER, DIONYSIUS, Sr., and wife Mary Ann—Folio 2—To their son John Oliver "for natural love and affection", a tract of land of triangular shape in the confluence of the Broad and Savannah rivers, formerly supposed to contain 300 acres, bounded on one side by the Broad river, on the other by lands of John Oliver, in which tract is located the town of Petersburg containing 80 one-half acre lots, and six of low ground, conveyed to Robt. Thompson and Robt. Watkins, adj. the lot whereon Robt. Watkins now resides. Also one-half acre of low ground conveyed to Wm. Thompson, Sr., which lots, that is to say the town of Petersburg and forty one acres yet to be laid off to Dionysius Oliver Sr., are hereby excepted. May 20, 1793. Wm. Thompson, Sr., Dionysius Oliver, Evan Ragland, J. P., Test.

OLIVER, DIONYSIUS—Folio 54—To John Oliver for L40, Lots 3, 57 and 59, containing half-acre each, No. 3 on east side of Front Street, Nos. 57 and 59 on the east side of 2nd. Street, in the town of Petersburg. Sale. July 7, 1793. Elinr. Oliver, Francis Oliver, Rot. Watkins, J. P., Test.

OLIVER, DIONYSIUS, Sr., and wife Mary Ann—Folio 130—To William Oliver for L150, 275 acres on the north side of Broad river. Signed by both. Mar. 18, 1794. James Bell, J. P.

OLIVER, DIONYSIUS, Jr., and wife Polly—Folio 41—To Peter Oliver, 500 acres on Broad river, adj. Wm. Adams and Dionysius Oliver, Sr. Sale. June 5, 1793. Thomas B. Scott, J. P.

OLIVER, JAMES—Folio 37—To Peter and John Oliver, 200 acres on north side of Broad river, adj. lands of John Coleman and James Easter, when surveyed. Oct. 22, 1793. Thos. B. Scott, J. P.

OLIVER, PETER and wife Elizabeth—Folio 38—To James Oliver, 700 acres on east side of Doves creek, it being a survey obtained in two grants, one in 1783, one in 1790. June 5, 1793. John Post, Thomas B. Scott, J. P., Test.

ORR, DANIEL—Folio 59—To Stephen Garner, 21 acres on south fork of Broad river. Feb. 4, 1794. William Hodge, Test.

PACE, BARNABAS and wife Agnes—Folio 56—To Zachariah Clark, 133 acres on Wahatchee creek. Aug. 23, 1793.

PACE, BARNABAS and wife Agnes—Folio 65—To James Morrison the remainder of above tract, surveyed 1786 for said Pace. Aug. 24, 1793.

PENN, PHILIP—Folio 24—To Absolom Stinchcomb, a slave Charity, about 11 years old "which girl I gave to said Stinchcomb about 7 years ago. Sept. 16, 1793

POWERS, FRANCIS and wife Elizabeth—Folio 51—To Bridger Haynie, 220 acres on Fork creek, surveyed 1785. Nov. 3, 1792. William Hodge, Test.

PINION, THOMAS and wife Ann—Folio 66—To William Black and William Rogers, jointly, 200 acres orig. grant 1787 to John Mobley, this being the north tract of said tract divided by agreement, adj. John Brasel John Gill and John Ferguson. Nov. 17, 1792. James Bell, J. P., Francis Cook, J. P., Test.

PULLIAM, ROBERT and wife Elinor—Folio 105—To William McCutchen, 150 acres on north fork of Beaverdam creek, orig. grant 1791 to said Pulliam. Feb. 22, 1794.

POLLARD, JOHN and wife Mary—Folio 110—To John Childs, 150 acres on Beaverdam creek, orig. grant 1784 to Joseph Pulliam. Jan. 14, 1794. W. Richardson, Stephen Satterwhite, Test.

REYNOLDS, WILLIAM and wife Patty—Folio 41—To John MacNeill, Lot No. 37 on east side of Front Street in town of Petersburg. Mar. 30, 1793—Robt. Watkins, J. P.

RAGLAND, BENJAMIN—Folio 93—of Elbert Co., To John R. Ragland of Wilkes Co., 150 acres on Broad river, adj. John Giles, Sr., orig. grant 1788 to Nancy Stephens. Jan. 31, 1794. James Coleman, William Reynolds, Test.

ROGERS, JOHN, Esqr.—Folio 114—To George Menefee, 200 acres adj. David Robinson, orig. grant to said Rogers. Feb. 13, 1794. John Templeton, Rosannah Templeton, Test.

ROGERS, JOHN and wife Nancy—Folio 122—To James Ware, 350 acres adj. Willson, said Rogers and Thos. Rogers, orig. grant to Wm. Moss. Jan. 3, 1794. John Templeton, Larkin Davis, Sally Davis, Test.

ROGERS, JOHN—Folio 134—To David Robinson, 160 acres adj. Thos. Rogers, part of two tracts orig. grant to said John Rogers and Wm. Moss together. Jan. 27, 1794. Martha Rogers, John H. Johnson, Test.

ROSE, HENRY and wife Jemima—Folio 126—To John Daily, a tract of land on both sides of Little Beaverdam creek, orig.grant 1785 to said Rose. Aug. 16, 1794. Lembird King, Larkin Higgason, Test.

ROSE, HENRY—Folio 167—To the heirs of Maben Granshaw, 100 acres on Beaverdam creek. Jan. 29, 1795.

RUSSELL, THOS. C. }
ROSSITER, NATHANIEL } Folio 197—Whereas a co-partnership between us in Petersburg since Jan. 1791 to this time, which being now dissolved, agreement to bear expenses, pay for goods in New York, and divide final profits. May 1, 1794
"I do assign and make over all right and claim to the within business to Mr. Andrew Elliott for value received.
         Thos. C. Russell. April 22, 1795

SUTTLE, WILLIAM and wife Margret—Folio 18—To John Lowery, 250 acres on Falling creek bounded on all sides by lands of Hugh McDonald. Jan. 13, 1792. James Lowery, Jr., Mashack Lowery, Test.

SANDIDGE, JOHN—of Franklin Co., Folio 28—To Martin Turman of Elbert Co., 90 acres on Coodys creek, Elbert Co. June 21, 1792. Joseph Chandler, Jas. Tait, J. P. Test.

SANDEDGE, CLAIBOURNE—Folio 30—To Christopher Millirons, both of Wilkes Co., 100 acres on Beaverdam creek, part of a tract of orig. grant of 200 acres 1786. Sept. 13, 1788. Richardson Hunt, J. P., Nancy Hunt, Test.

Christopher Millirons relinquishes all claim in said land to John Tollett for L100. Oct. 2, 1788. Registered Oct. 2, 1793.

SKINNER, ARCHER and wife Clary—Folio 50—of Wilkes Co., To Joseph Bell of Elbert Co., 360 acres in Elbert Co., agreeable to the plat of orig. grant 1790 to said Skinner. Dec. 29, 1792 James Bell, J. P., David Martin, Test.

STODGILL, JOEL—Folio 51—To Thomas Carter, Sr., a negro boy Dennis about 15 years old. Dec. 18, 1793. David Cosby, Test.

SMYTH, THOMAS, Jr.—Folio 74—To William Patterson, merchant of the city of Baltimore, Md., 5000 acres in Wilkes Co., now Elbert, orig.grant

1792 to David Criswell. May 10, 1793. George Salmon, Test. Geo. Gould Presbury, J. P. of Baltimore, Md., before whom Thos. Smyth, Jr., appeared.

STEPHENS, NANCY—Folio 92—To Benjamin Ragland, 150 acres on Broad river adj. John Giles, Sr., orig.grant 1788 to said Nancy. June 7, 1791. Thos. C. Russell, M. Walker, Test.

SMITH, JOHN—Folio 95—of Franklin Co., To Nathaniel Hudson of Wilkes Co., 300 acres on Beaverdam creek. Jan. 25, 1788 James Tait, J. P., Test.

STEPHENS, NANCY, Folio 177—To Robert Allen, 200 acres on Wahatchee creek, part of orig.grant 1785 to said Nancy. April 9, 1793.

SMITH, JOHN—Folio 183—of Pendleton Co. S. C., to John Clarkson of Elbert Co. Ga., 150 acres on both sides of Cedar creek, being the land said John Smith sold to Wm. Smith, adj. said William Smith's old line and Randolph Depriest's land. Sept. 23, 1794. Esaias Harbour; Amos Richardson, Test.

SAYLORS, ELIZABETH—Folio 99—To Robert Guttery, 33 acres on Broad river, orig.grant 1785 to said Elizabeth.

STUBBLEFIELD, WILLIAM—Folio 111—of Wilkes Co., To John McConnell of Elbert Co., 200 acres on Broad river, Elbert Co., Dec. 30, 1793. Robert Ellis, Fielding Rucker, Test.

SULFRIDGE or SELFRIDGE, ROBERT and wife Agnes—Folio 112—To Archeles Walker, 100 acres on Cedar creek. April 1, 1793.

STUART, JAMES M.—Folio 125—of Liberty Co., To Marmaduke Ricketson of Richmond Co., 200 acres on Coldwater creek, Wilkes Co., adj. Wm. Teasley, orig.grant to John Appling, by him conveyed to said Stuart. April 4, 1793. Geo. Foster, J. P., Geo. Handley, Test.

SPURLOCK, JOHN—Folio 137—To loving son and daughter Charles and Judy Fain, all of Elbert Co., horses, cattle and household goods. March 31, 1794. John Baker, James Fain, Test.

STEAGALL, RICHARD and wife Elizabeth—Folio 163—To Andrew Walker, 100 acres orig. grant 1786 to Bazell Human. Aug. 1792.

TAIT, JAMES and wife Rebecca—Folio 9—and William Hatcher and wife Priscilla, To Samuel McGahee, 230 acres on Beaverdam creek, adj. Wm. Thompson, Watters Nunnelee and James Tait. July 13, 1793. Wm. H. Tait, Test.

TRIMBLE, MOSES and wife Katharine—Folio 20—To James Head, 150 acres adj. Webb Kidd's land. Sept. 5, 1791. J. Gorham, J. P. Robt. Woodward, John Trimble, Test.

TRIMBLE, MOSES—Folio 195—of Wilkes Co., To Walker Richardson, one mulatto girl Dargus. May 17, 1787. Reuben Allen, J. P. John Cunningham, Test.

TATE, JAMES and wife Rebecca—Folio 95—To Nathaniel Hudson, 100 acres on Beaverdam creek. Sept. 3, 1791 M. Woods, W. Hudson, Test.

TATE, WILLIAM and wife Elisaba—Folio 112—To William Haley, 75 acres on Coodys creek, adj. Zinny Tait. Feb. 21, 1792. Barbara Tate, James Tait, J. P., Test.

THOMPSON, ISHAM and wife Sarah—Folio 47—of Elbert Co., To Roland Taylor of Wilkes Co., land on Coodys creek, orig. grant 1787. Oct. 7, 1791. Samuel Hollinshed, Solo. Potter, Test.

THOMPSON, ROBERT and wife Sarah—Folio 54—of Wilkes Co., To Stephen Ellington of Elbert Co., 300 acres on Bertrams creek, Elbert Co., adj. Wm. Thompson, Sr., Col. Ragland, and James Watkins, Jr. Jan. 16, 1792. Wm. Thompson, Sr., Drury Thompson, Jr., Jesse Thompson, Test.

TOLLETT, JOHN and wife Margrett—Folio 31—To John Nelms all of Wilkes Co., 100 acres on Beaverdam creek, being the upper part of orig. grant to Claibourn Sandidge. May 4, 1790. R. Hunt, Nehemiah Williams, Thomas Davis, Test.

TALBOTT, JOHN and wife Phebe—Folio 84—To Thomas Ewing, 200 acres on Fork creek, orig. grant 1786 to Thomas McCall. Feb. 9, 1792. Thomas Talbot, Matthew Ewing, Matthew Talbott, Test.

THORNHILL, LEONARD and wife Mary—Folio 88—To Aron Vanhook, 287½ acres, to which Leonard and his wife have full right of inheritance in fee simple. June 16, 1792.

TEASLEY, JOHN—Folio 149—To Charter Harper, 190 acres, no adjoiners mentioned. Jan. 19, 1793.

TAYLOR, BENJAMIN and wife Susannah—Folio 155—of Wilkes Co. To Dionysiue Oliver, Sr., of Elbert Co., 200 acres on Wahatchee creek, Elbert Co., adj. land surveyed for Barnabas Pace and Walker Richardson. Jan. 14, 1793. William Oliver, Thomas Hancock, Test.

TUTTLE, JAMES, Jr.—Folio 195—To David Adams, 100 acres on north side of north fork of Broad river, adj. John Johnson, being part of orig. grant of 150 acres to James Tuttle, Sr. April 10, 1794. Thomas Mayes, Test.

WILKINS, JOHN and wife Ann—Folio 7—To Henry Mosely, 200 acres on Falling creek adj. Henry and Robert Mosely and Basil Lamar, orig. grant 1788 to Robert Mosely. Jan. 5, 1793. John Decker, Test.

WHITE, REUBEN—Folio 40—planter, "To loving children (not named) all lands, cattle, household goods etc, an inventory of which he has filed with the Clerk of said Co. Oct. 28, 1793. David Cosby, Test.
Inventory gives 242 acres of land on which said Reuben now lives.

WINGFIELD, JOHN and wife Mary—Folio 42—To James Lowry, 100 acres on Falling creek, orig. grant 1785 to Robert Neal. Nov. 4, 1791.

GEORGIA D. A. R.

WALTON, WILLIAM and wife Mary—Folio 62—of Elbert Co., To Daniel Hervey of Wilkes Co., 440 acres on Broad river and Falling creek, Elbert Co., adj. Lewis Clark and Peter Edwards, orig. grant 1784 to Basil Lamar. Jan. 10, 1793. Christopher Clark, Robert Huddleston, Test.

WILLIAMS, MATTHEW JARRETT—Folio 104—of Elbert Co., Power of Atty. to Matthew Walton of Ky. and Jonathan Patterson of Va., to dispose of a 900 or 1000 acre tract of land on Buck Fork of Salt river in Ky., located by said Matthew Walton, and entered in the names of said Matthew Jarrett Williams and John Williams. July 22, 1794. Thomas Wooten, Test.

WILLMOUTH, WILLIAM—Folio 138—To Minor Marsh, 50 acres on Savannah river, part of orig. grant 1785 of 200 acres to Thos. Wilmouth. July 12, 1794.

WALKER, HENRY G.—Folio 117—To William Tate, 450 acres on Savannah river bounded by said Wm. Tate, Jere. Walker and James S. Walker, heirs of Jere. Walker, dec'd, and Geo. Darden, part of a grant of 700 acres to Robert Chambers. July 11, 1794. David Hudson, George Cook, Test.

WILMOTH, THOMAS—Folio 139—To William Williams, 200 acres on Savannah river adj. Jesse Rowel, Wm. Wilmoth and Marsh's land, orig. grant 1785 to said Thomas Wilmoth. Oct. 25, 1791. Signed; Thomas Wilmoth, Nancy Wilmoth, Ezekiel Wilmoth, William Wilmoth.

WILLIAMS, WILLIAM and wife Nancy—Folio 140—To Minor Marsh above tract. May 26, 1794. (signed Ann)

WOODS, MIDDLETON—Folio 143—To James Christian, 204 acres on Doves creek, Jan. 7, 1795. Wm. Phillips, Wm. Bradley, Test.

WILLIFORD, STEPHEN—Folio 168—To John H. Johnson, 175 acres where said Stephen now lives, with growing crops, hogs etc. June 9, 1794. Wm. Daniel, Allen Daniel, Test.

ELBERT COUNTY GEORGIA

DEED BOOK "C"

ALLSTON, WILLIAM and wife Charity—Folio 18—of Elbert Co., To John Howard of Edgefield Co. S. C., 400 acres part of a tract purchased by said Allston from Julius Howard adj. Martin Sims, Leroy Pope, Daniel Shaw, James Tait and Richard Easter. July 1, 1794.

ALLEN, NATHANIEL—Folio 31—To Francis S. Carter, 419 acres on Carters fork of Beaverdam creek, Oct. 30, 1793. Betsy Allen, Test.

ALEXANDER, ELIZABETH—Folio 41—To Edmond Shackleford, a gray horse and side saddle. Mar. 9, 1795. Henry Shackleford, Jr., Test.

ALLEN, JOSEPH and wife Aggey—Folio48—To Leonard Rice, 50 acres on north fork of Beaverdam creek, it being part of a tract of 200 acres upon which said Allen now lives, orig.grant 1791 to said Allen. Oct. 1, 1793.

ARNOLD, JONATHAN—Folio 53—at present of the town of Augusta,, Ga., To Chas. Snowden of the city of Charleston, S. C., mortgage on 200 acres on north fork of Cedar creek, 100 of which was orig. grant 1786 to Robert Chambers. July 15, 1795. Will Barden, Jr. Test.

ADAMS, JAMES—Folio 55—bond as Admr.of David Adams,dec'd. Archer Burton, Benj. Cook, Wm. Hightower, Sec. Mar. 8, 1794.

BAKER, CHRISTOPHER, Folio 6—of Cobarcus (Carrabus) Co. N. C. To Jesse Baker of Elbert Co. Ga., 200 acres on Falling creek. Aug. 10, 1793. John Baker, Isabella McCleskey, James McCleskey, J. P., Test.

BAKER, ABSOLOM and wife Mary—Folio 39—To John Cook, 200 acres on Falling creek. Sept. 30, 1795. Chas. Cosby, Test.

BAKER, JOHN and wife Susannah—Folio 88—To Samuel Talbot, 100 acres on Falling creek, adj. Benj. and Absolom Baker, part of a 950 acre tract orig. grant 1792 to said John. July 4, 1795. Robt. Cosby, John Depriest, Test.

BAKER, JOHN—Folio 89—of Greenville Co. S. C. To Eli Eavenson of Elbert Co. Ga., 10 acres on Falling creek adj. the town lots. ------------------ 1796. Wm. S. Burch, Test.

BAKER, JOHN—Folio 97—of Greenville Co. S. C., To Middleton Woods of Elbert Co. Ga., 134 acres on Falling creek. Feb. 11, 1796. James Kidd, Wm. Brown, Test.

BAKER, ABSOLOM and wife Mary—Folio 104—and John A. Baker and wife Jennett, To Archibald Jarrett, 370 acres on Falling creek, Jan. 8, 1796. R. Hunt, John Baker, Test.

BURTON, THOMAS, Jr., and wife Ann—Folio 24—To Henry Burton, 200 acres whereon the said Henry Burton now lives, adj. James Easter and said Thos. Jr. April 23, 1795. W. Hatcher, Test.

BRAZEL, FREDERICK and wife Elizabeth—Folio 46—of Washington Co., To Elias Hendricks of Elbert Co., 76 acres on Falling creek. Sept. 22, 1795. John Sertain, Test.

BOBO, MARY, THOMAS HOOKER & MATTHIAS WARD—Folio 48—To Angus Johnson, a slave Grace and her increase. Oct. 27, 1795. Archibald Johnson, Test.

BURTON, THOMAS—Folio 74—To John Hubbard, Lot No. 38 in town of Petersburg. Oct. 8, 1792. Richard Hubbard, Test.

BREWER, ELIJAH—Folio 71—of Elbert Co., To Thos. Black of Oglethorpe Co., a slave Sam and his wife Jude, horses, cattle, feather beds etc. Sept. 7, 1795. John & Wm. Black, Edwd. Herrin, Test.

BREWER, ELISHA & JOHN—Folio 60—Bonds as Admrs., of Edmund Brewer, dec'd. Nov. 9, 1793. Middleton Woods, Sec.

BARNETT, JOHN and wife Caroline—Folio 76—of Franklin Co., To John McCleary of Elbert Co., 500 acres on Fork creek, adj. Thomas Ewing, Richard woods, Harden Evans and Alex Hodge. Jan. 29, 1794. Wm. A. D. Ewing, Test.

BARNETT, WILLIAM, JAMES TAIT, EVAN RAGLAND & RICHARDSON HUNT, Folio 113—To John P. Harper, Lot No. 16 "at the Court House". April 5, 1794.

BLACKWELL, JOSEPH and wife Sally Chandler Blackwell—Folio 84—To Julius Chrysler, 120 acres on both sides of Nelms Big Branch. Nov. 11, 1793. Reuben McClary, Dosster Blackwell, Test.

BROWN, PETER—Folio 113—of Abbeville Co. S. C. To James Miller of Elbert Co., 200 acres in Elbert Co., bounded on all sides by vacant land when surveyed. July 29, 1795.

BROWN, WILLIAM and wife Sarah—Folio 117—To Joseph Bell, 125 acres on Beaverdam creek which said Brown bought of Zachariah Butler, including a new grist mill which Brown built and 40 acres part of a tract of 200 acres which said Brown bought of Francis Cook, which includes the old mill. Dec. 17, 1794. James Bell, J. P., Reuben Cook.

BROWN, PATRICK—Folio 133—of Union Co. S. C., To Thomas B. Scott, 115 acres on Broad river. Mar. 27, 1795. Isaac Popwell, Arch Jarrell, Test.

BROWN, JOHN and wife Amy—Folio 135—To Joseph Downer, 130 acres on Falling creek, orig.grant 1790 to said Brown, adj. lands of William Smith, dec'd. Dec. 22, 1792.

BUTLER, PATRICK and wife Elizabeth—Folio 101—To James Butler, 300 acres adj. Zachariah Butler, Wm. Thompson and vacant land when surveyed 1790. Feb. 7, 1793. James Bell, J. P., Jesse Jones, Test.

BIBB, WILLIAM and wife Salley—Folio 102—To James McGowen, 120 acres on north fork of Beaverdam creek. April 21, 1795. Samuel Bailey, Test.

BIBB, SALLY B.—Folio 119—To her stepmother Sally B. Bibb, for her attention to her from infancy, boarding, clothing etc. deed of gift to her two youngest sons, John Dandridge Bibb, a slave Patrick, to Joseph Wyatt Bibb a slave Pleasant, when said John and Joseph come of age. Jan. 9, 1796. William W. Bibb, Test.

BLAKE, WILLIAM, Sr.—Folio 143—To James Rogers, two slaves Fillis and Isaac. Oct. 4, 1796. Peleg Rogers, William Mobley, Test.

COOK, BENJAMIN and wife Mary—Folio 1—To John M. Whitney, 375 acres on Broad river. April 25, 1795. Cornelius Sale, Test.

COOK, FRANCIS and wife—Folio 39—To Josiah Cook, 200 acres on Beaverdam creek. Aug. 31, 1795. Benjamin Cook, Test.

COOK, WILLIAM—Folio 38—To Tabither Thearmond, bond to properly provide for Fanny, a child of said Tabitha, 4 years and 7 months old. Aug. 5, 1795.

COOK, JOHN and wife Aley—Folio 66—To Patrick Butler, 200 acres on Falling creek. Nov. 14, 1795. William Blake, Test.

COULTER, CHARLES and wife Mary—Folio 43—To Richard Coulter, Jr., 100 acres on Doves creek, orig.grant 1786. Nov. 28, 1794. Richard Coulter, Robert Coulter, Test.

COULTER, RICHARD—Folio 42—To Wm. Phelps 100 acres on Doves creek, being part of a grant to said Coulter, adj. lands of heirs of Richard Gatewood, dec'd. Oct. 9, 1795.

COULTER, RICHARD, SR.—Folio 79—To Richard, Jr., land on Doves creek whereon Richard, Sr., now lives, orig. grant 1784 to Richard, Sr. Dec. 18, 1795. Absolom Stinchcomb, Test.

COULTER, RICHARD and wife Rebekah—Folio 136—To John McEaver, all of Wilkes Co., 200 acres on Doves creek, orig. grant 1786 to said Coulter. July 28, 1789. Francis Coulter, Test.

COULTER, RICHARD, Sr. and wife Rebeccah—Folio 111—To John Gatewood 120 acres being part of two tracts orig. granted said Richard Mar. 15, 1791. John Crosby, Robt. Smith, Henry Gatewood, Test.

COULTER, RICHARD, Sr. and wife Rebecky—Folio 126—To Wm. Crittenton 170 acres on Doves creek it being the land whereon said Richard now lives. July 2, 1796. Absolo. Stinchcomb, Chas. Coulter, John Gatewood, Robt. Smith, Test.

COULTER, RICHARD, Jr. and wife Elizabeth—Folio 127—To Richard Coulter, Sr. 165 acres on Doves creek where Richard, Sr. now lives. April 30, 1796. Absolo. Stinchcomb, John Penn, Test.

COULTER, RICHARD, Jr. and wife Elizabeth—Folio 130—To Wm. Dudley, 25 acres on Doves creek, adj. land on which Richard Coulter, Sr. now lives. April 26, 1796. Sarah Dudley, Louise Crump, Test.

COSBY, ROBERT, T. C.—Folio 44—To Matthias Williamson, 200 acres in Franklin Co., on Broad river, the property of Richard Eubanks. Sept. 12, 1795.

COSBY, ROBERT, T. C.—Folio 47—To Michael Grant, 300 acres on Cedar creek, property of Christopher Mooney, adj. Jonathan Arnold and Amos Richardson. Aug. 5, 1795.

COSBY, ROBERT, Sheriff—Folio 72—To Matthew J. Williams of Elbert Co., and Thos. Black of Oglethorpe Co., planters, property of Lemuel Black and Elisha Brewer to satisfy a debt to George Cook. Jan. 6, 1796.

GEORGIA D. A. R.

COSBY, ROBERT, Sheriff—Folio 73—To Samuel Higginbotham, planter Lot No. 21 in town of Elberton property of James Flood to satisfy a debt to Richard Hubbard. Jan. 12, 1796.

COSBY, ROBERT, T. C.—Folio 75—To William Jones 100 acres on Coldwater creek, property of John Turk. June 2, 1795.

COSBY, ROBERT, Sheriff—Folio 105—To Vilet (Violet) Morrison, goods and chattels of Joseph H. Morrison, including a rifle and musket, cattle, horses, slaves etc. April 13, 1796. Thomas Bibb, Test.

COSBY, JAMES O., T. C.—Folio 134—To William Chisholm, 435 acres on Hannah's creek, Sept. 6, 1796. James Alston, Test.

COLEMAN, JAMES—Folio 41—and Henry G. Ragland, To John R. Ragland Lot No. 20 on west side of Front Street in the town of Petersburg. Sept. 23, 1795. John Oliver, Asa Thompson, Test.

CREAGH, THOMAS BIVE and wife Rebecca—Folio 50—To Thomas Perry 150 acres on Savannah river, part of orig. grant to Margret Steel by George Matthews, Gov. July 11, 1795. Aron Jones, Test.

CROCKET, ROBERT—Folio 56—Bond as Admr. of Samuel Crocket, dec'd. Samuel Young, Sec., James Cosby, Test.

CRESWELL, DAVID—Folio 67—To Abell Howell, both of Wilkes Co., 200 acres on Doves creek, Elbert Co., Nov. 14, 1795. John Depriest, E. Offutt, Test.

COKER, ISAAC—Folio 70—To Mallicha Coker (he), 150 acres on Beaverdam creek, part of orig. survey to Wm. Cochran. Dec. 25, 1795.

COKER, MALICHA—Folio 98—To Spencer Allgood, above tract. April 1, 1796. R. Cosby, Test.

CERTAIN, JOSIAH and wife Elizabeth—Folio 117—To John Certain 100 acres being the plantation whereon said Josiah now lives. May 4, 1794.

DOBBS, JOHN, Sr.—Folio 10—To Jacob Skelton, 75 acres on Cedar creek for L5, orig. grant to Gabriel Smith. Feb. 8, 1794. William Skelton, Moses Haynes, J. P., Test.

DANIEL, WILLIAM—Folio 46—To Elizabeth Daniel, a slave girl Betty, 6 year old. July 26, 1795.

DUDLEY, JAMES—Folio 55—Bond as Admr. of John Dudley, late of said county, dec'd. Dec. 28, 1792. Samuel Spears, Sec.

DAVIS, WILLIAM—Folio 56—Bond as Admr. of Chas. Easten, late of said county, dec'd. Jan. 8, 1793. Reuben Easten, Sec. Carter Miller, Test.

DECKER, JOHN and wife Eady—Folio 90—To Christopher Clark, 200 acres adj. Clement Wilkins, Dec. 24, 1794. Christopher Clark Jr., Test.

DEADWILER, JOSEPH and wife Eales—Folio 91—To Alex. Hodge 200 acres on Fork creek. Mar. 27, 1792. Wm. & Francis Hodge, Test.

DEPRIEST, JOHN and wife Jean—Folio 122—To William Faulkner, 100 acres on Doves creek. April 28, 1796. R. Hunt, J. P. Elizabeth Cunningham, Test.

DEPRIEST, JOHN—Folio 132—To William Faulkner, 100 acres on Pennington's fork of Doves creek, orig. grant 1792 to Ebenezer Smith. June 3, 1796. John Goss, William Faulkner, Test.

EASTEN, SALLY & REUBEN—Folio 55—Bond as Admrs. of John Easten, late of said county, dec'd. Jan. 8, 1793.

FORTSON, THOMAS and wife Rachel—Folio 51—To James Arnold, 80 acres on Carters creek, which said Fortson purchased of Thomas Carter. Oct. 3, 1795. William Fortson, Test.

FERREL, MARTIN—Folio 57—Bond as Admr. on goods and chattels etc. of said dec'd, not named. Jan. 17, 1793. Wm. Head, James Ferrell, Security. John Dingler, Test.

FLINT, WILLIAM—Folio 61—Power of Atty. to friend Jesse White, both of Elbert Co., to collect what is due him from his fathers estate. Sept. 10, 1795. Isaac Popplacell, Test.

Sir: Pay to Mr. Jesse White L10, 8s, 4d. it being my legacy from my father, John Flint, dec'd etc.

Yours, Wm. Flint.

To Capt. Moses Taylor, Excr. for John Flint, dec'd. Northumberland Co., on Great Wecomoco, State of Va.

FERGUS, JOHN—Folio 111—To Armstrong Herd, 300 acres on Scul shole creek, orig. grant to said Fergus. Feb. 17, 1794. James Coffee, John Herd, Test.

GATEWOOD, RICHARD—Folio 4—To Walker Richardson, a slave Hannah. Feb. 5, 1794.

GATEWOOD, BETTY & JOHN—Folio 64—Bond as Admrs. of Richard Gatewood, dec'd. Tabitha Holliday, Sec. Nov. 4, 1794. Gabriel Higginbotham, Test.

GLOVER, JOHN and wife Ellender—Folio 5—To James Certain, part of a 600 acre grant 1786 to said Glover, it being the plantation whereon said Glover now lives, including the mill. Jan. 16, 1794. William Rogers, Test.

GREENWOOD, JOHN, Sr., and wife Anne—Folio 26—of Elbert Co., To Peter Brown of Abbeville Co. S. C., 100 acres on Savannah river, adj. John Greenwood, Jr. and Fleming Greenwood. July 25, 1790.

GEORGE, WILLIAM—Folio 96—of Elbert Co. Power of Atty. to friend James George of Wilkes Co., to attend to all business in S. C. especially to sell

192   GEORGIA D. A. R.

land in S. C., granted to his father David George. April 8, 1795. George Doss, James Cunningham, Test.

GOODWYN, THOMAS—Folio 116—Receipt to John Wilkins for twenty Spanish milled dollars for a negro fellow Tom, with a crooked knee. Dec. 24, 1795.

GUTTERY, ROBERT and wife Betty—Folio 116—of Elbert Co. To Chas. Beddingfield of Wilkes Co., 233 acres on Broad river orig. grant 1785 to said Guttery. May 22, 1794. Archelaus Jarrett, Test.

GREENSTREET, JAMES and wife Jean—Folio 141—To Ralph Owins, 200 acres on Powderbag creek, orig. grant to said Greenstreet from George Matthews, Gov. 1794. (Signed Jane) Not registered. Clement Owins, Elijah Owins, Test.

HUNT, RICHARDSON and wife Nancy Martin to Josias P. Adams (late of Va., but of Augusta, Ga. at the time of making a contract for this land), 1000 acres on Beaverdam creek, then Wilkes, now Elbert Co., originally granted 1787 to said Hunt from Gov. George Matthews, for five likely young negroes. Aug. 11, 1794. Francis S. Carter, Test.

HUNT, RICHARDSON—and wife Nancy Martin—Folio 131—To Nathan Bonds, Jr., 250 acres on Carters creek, orig. grant 1787 to said Hunt. July 30, 1796.

HUNT, FITZ. M.—Folio 107—of Columbia Co., Atty. for Henry Hunt, To James Alston of Elbert Co., 300 acres orig. grant 1785 to said Henry Hunt. Aug. 7, 1793. Nathaniel Alston, Test.

HUNT, FITZ. M.—Folio 109—of Columbia Co. Atty. for Henry Hunt, To George Darden, 450 acres on Beaverdam creek. Aug. 7, 1793.

HATCHER, WILLIAM and wife Pricilla—Folio 20—To William Thompson, Jr., 70 acres on south side of Bertrams creek. Feb. 20, 1793.

HEARD, ARMSTRONG and wife Jenny—Folio 26—To James Coffee, 200 acres part of an orig. grant to John Fergus. Feb. 17, 1794.

HEARD, JOHN, Jr. and wife Elizabeth—Folio 28—of Wilkes Co., To George Darden of Elbert Co., 2 acres on Big Beaverdam creek, including said Darden's distillery. April 27, 1795. Archibald Riddle, Theodrick Stubblefield, Test.

HAWTHORN, ROBERT—Folio 27—To Turner Christian, 400 acres on Deep creek. July 9, 1795. Henry Gatewood, John Carson, Test.

HEAD, WILLIAM, Sr.—Folio 35—Sale of slaves, Bob, Sary, Nan, Lill and Synth, To William Head, Jr. Sept. 14, 1795. John Hanna, Daniel Head, Test.

HEAD, BENJAMIN—Folio 58—Bond as Admr. of estate of Ann Sheeman, dec'd. April 15, 1795. William Ward, Sec.

HEAD, WILLIAM—Folio 137—To Walter Nunnelee, a slave Ciller for six thousand weight of tobacco. Jan. 2, 1792.

HARRIS, SHERWOOD—Folio 68—To Joseph Moses, 110 acres, adj. Shackleford. Dec. 12, 1795. Samuel Morgan, Test.

HUNTER, DAVID—Folio 36—of Oglethorpe Co., To Henary Muckleroy of Elbert Co., a slave Abram, horses, cattle, household goods and growing crops. Sept. 20, 1795. John McElroy, Wm. Muckleroy, Test.

HOWELL, THOMAS and wife Ann—Folio 79—To William Falkner, 100 acres on Doves creek "which I purchased from John Roberts". Aug. 5, 1795. William Davis, John Falkner, Test.

HOWELL, THOMAS—Folio 103—To Abel Howell, 475 acres on Broad river, Franklin Co., adj. Grant Taylor. Aug. 15, 1795.

HALL, WILLIAM—Folio 97—and Josiah and Elijah Aliven, power of Atty to Robt. Cowdon all of Elbert Co., to receive all money real estate etc., to which we are entitled in Cumberland Co. Penna. April 19, 1796. Robert Barnwill, Test.

HARBIN, THOMAS and wife Mary—Folio 120—To Hezekiah Gray, 100 acres at the mouth of Cedar creek, adj. Wm. Barnett and Wm. Brown. Jan. 7, 1794.

HUDSON, CHARLES and wife Martha—Folio 127—and Benjamin Allen and wife Betty, To Zimri Tait, 400 acres on Cudys creek. Mar. 29, 1794. William Hudson, Test.

JENNINGS, ROBERT—Folio 96—of Guliford Co. N. C., To Jean Carson, all claim to 500 acres on Lightwood Log creek, 500 acres on Powderbag creek, 200 acres on Cedar creek, Elbert Co., and all notes, bonds and book accounts due to her, horses and all other property. Nov. 9, 1794.

KEES, JOHN, Sr. and wife Winny—Folio 109—To James Alston, Sr., 76 acres part of orig. grant to said Kees. Aug. 28, 1795.

KIDD, JAMES and wife Elizabeth—Folio 135—To Walker Richardson, 100 acres on Smiths branch adj. Benj. Davis and Wm. Pulliam. Sept. 6, 1796.

LUMPKIN, GEORGE—Folio 4—To William Hay, both of Wilkes Co., for 5s· 7 acres on Savannah river, Elbert Co. May 10, 1792.

LUMPKIN, GEORGE—Folio 7—To William Skelton of Elbert Co. 100 acres on Cedar creek, which said George purchased of John Smith and whereon the said Skelton now lives. May 24, 1792. Thomas Woodward, Archer Smith, Test.

LONG, NICHOLAS and wife Rebeccah—Folio 128—To William Teasley, 300 acres on Coldwater creek, adj. land whereon said Teasley lives. July 18, 1795. G. Hay, Jesse Ginn, Test.

McCLESKEY, JAMES—Folio 25—To James Brock, 200 acres granted 1792 to said McCleskey. July 28, 1795.

McDONALD, HUGH—Folio 82—To Mark Thornton, 800 acres on south fork of Coldwater creek, orig. grant 1788 to said McDonald. Dec. 5, 1792. James, William and Ralph Banks, Test.

MOSS, WILLIAM—Folio 16—Admr. of Isham Stroud, dec'd. To Thomas B. Creagh, 200 acres on Beaverdam creek, orig. grant to the heirs of said Isham Stroud. May 6, 1795.

MIDDLETON, ROBERT—Folio 18—Sheriff, To John Wingfield, planter 200 acres on Falling creek, property of Robert Neal. July 16, 1791.

MIDDLETON, ROBERT—Folio 32—Sheriff, To Richardson Hunt, 1000 acres on Beaverdam creek, property of Josias P. Adams. Sept. 1, 1795.

MIDDLETON, ROBERT—Folio 65—Sheriff, To John Brawner, 730 acres property of Hugh McDonald to satisfy a debt to Thomas C. Russell. Nov. 4, 1795.

MIDDLETON, ROBERT—Folio 142—Sheriff, To George Evans, planter 100 acres, property of John Watson, to satisfy a debt of Samuel Nelson. July 29, 1795.

MARTIN, ROBERT—Folio 23—of Abbeville Co. S. C., To James Harthorn of Elbert Co., 275 acres on Beaverdam creek orig. grant in Wilkes Co. 1787 to Thomas Carter. Aug. 16, 1792.

MARTIN, JAMES—Folio 37—of Elbert Co., To James Thurmand of Wilkes Co., 150 acres on both sides of Wahachee creek. Mar. 24, 1794.

MOORE, JOSEPH—Folio 52—To John Moore, 180 acres on north fork of Vanns creek, part of an orig. grant 1785 to said Joseph Moore. Nov. 3, 1795. William Davis, Test.

MORRIS, SALLEY & ISAAC—Folio 58—Bond as Admr. of James Morris, dec'd. Aug. 22, 1795.

MOSELY, HENRY and wife Polly—Folio 118—To Joseph Bell a certain parcel of land on Falling and Wahatchee creeks, a part of three grants, some of which has already been conveyed to Lewis Mosely, adj. Lewis Mosely, Henry Hunt and Benj. Mosely, part to John Jones, all this land adj. that of Henry Mosely, Sr. the grantor. Nov. 23, 1795. James Bell, J. P., Thos. Bullard, Test.

NELSON, SAMUEL and wife Martha—Folio 9—To James Leper, 269 acres on south fork of Broad river, part of orig. grant 1785 to said Nelson. Aug. 16, 1794.

NAPIER, THOMAS—Folio 59—Bond as Admr. of Maybourn Crenshaw, dec'd. April 1, 1795. Walker Napier, Sec.

OLIVER, DIONYSIUS and wife Mary Ann—Folio 14—To William Hatcher, Lot 29 on east side of Front Street in town of Petersburg. Sept. 29, 1786. John Oliver, Elizabeth Ragland, Test.

OLIVER, DIONYSIUS and wife Mary Ann—Folio 30—To Jaramah (Jeremiah) Walker, Lot 20 on west side of Front Street in Petersburg. April 28, 1786. John Thompson, Isham Thompson, Test.

OLIVER, DIONYSIUS, Sr. and wife Mary Ann—Folio 33—To William Oliver, 200 acres on Wahachee creek. June 21, 1795. P. Hancock, Test.

OLIVER, JOHN—Folio 70—of Elbert Co., To Thomas Hancock of Edgefield Co. S. C., 275 acres on north side of Broad river sold by John Hightower to Dionysius Oliver, Sr. adj. Lewis Clark and Joseph Bell. Jan. 17, 1795. Elinor Oliver, Dionysius Oliver, Jr., Test.

OLIVER, DINOYSIUS, Sr. and wife Mary Ann—Folio 80—To McCarty Oliver, 500 acres on north side of Broad river, part of orig. grant 1784 of a 1000 acres to said Dionysius. Feb. 12, 1796. Peter and William Oliver, Test.

OLIVER, DIONYSIUS, Sr. and wife Mary Ann—Folio 81—To McCarty Oliver, a negro boy Jessa about 9 years old. Feb. 12, 1796.

OLIVER, DIONYSIUS, Sr. and wife Mary Ann—Folio 81—To James Oliver a slave Dick about 18 years old. Feb. 13, 1795.

OLIVER, DIONYSIUS, Sr. and wife Mary Ann—Folio 85—To Fanny Oliver two slaves, Rachel about 6 years old, Moses about three years old. Feb. 12, 1796.

OLIVER, DIONYSIUS, Sr. and wife Mary Ann. Folio 85—To Fanny Oliver 400 acres in Washington Co., adj. John Culpepper, being part of a survey of 900 acres conveyed to said Dionysius by Hugh McCelley (?). Feb. 12, 1796.

OLIVER, DIONYSIUS, Sr. and wife Mary Ann—Folio 85—To Ellinor Oliver two slaves, Poll about 13 years old and Nead about four. Feb. 12, 1796.

OLIVER, DIONYSIUS, Sr. and wife Mary Ann—Folio 86—To Elinor Oliver 338 acres on south fork of Oconee river, Greene Co., orig. grant to Curtis Welborn. Feb. 12, 1796.

OLIVER, DIONYSIUS, Sr.—Folio 90—To Peter Oliver, a slave Hannah about 40 years old, two cows and calves, feather beds, household furniture etc. Feb. 13, 1796.

OLIVER, DIONYSIUS, Sr.—Folio 92—To William Oliver, two slaves, Rose and Dave "both country born", Rose about 19, Dave about 13, cows, furniture etc. Feb. 11, 1796.

OLIVER, DIONYSIUS, Sr. and wife Mary Ann—Folio 93—To Wm. Oliver 281 acres on Wahachee creek. Mar. 5, 1796.

GEORGIA D. A. R.

OLIVER, DIONYSIUS, Sr. and wife Mary Ann—Folio 124—To Evan Ragland "a naked lot" in the town of Petersburg, No. 18 on west side of Front Street. June 21, 1795. P. Hancock, Test.

OLIVER, DIONYSIUS, Sr. and wife Mary Ann—Folio 132—To McCarty Oliver, 15 acres on Broad river adj. McCarty and Joseph Bell. Mar. 24, 1796. Epaphroditus Hightower, Thomas Oliver, Peter Oliver, Test.

OLIVER, WILLIAM and wife Barbara—Folio 139—To Thomas Jones, 281 acres on Wahachee creek, Mar. 21, 1796. Nothias Taylor, James Jones, Test.

POPE, LEROY and wife Judith—Folio 29—To Outbird Hudson, 470 acres on Wahachee creek, it being the whole of the tract said Pope purchased of Benj. Allen. Mar. 2, 1795—James Coleman, Test.

PRUETT, JOHN & SAMUEL—Folio 30—of Abbeville Co., S. C. Oath before A. O. Jones, J. P. of said county that they were in company of Thomas Lovelady in Ga., when he took Robt. Crump on suspicion as he said, for being concerned in taking of John Dickerson's horse, that Crump left them and that said Crump never said he knew where the horse was and several times after he said he had never seen the horse or knew anything about it. May 16, 1795.

PETTIGREW, GEORGE—Folio 78—of Franklin Co., To Edward Ware of Elbert Co., 400 acres on Broad river, Elbert Co., adj. William Hall and James Tuttle, orig. grant to said Pettigrew. April 10, 1794. Thomas Mayes, Test.

POWERS, FRANCIS and wife Elizabeth—Folio 137—To Samuel Long, 220 acres on Fork creek of Broad river. Orig. grant 1786 to said Powers. April 10, 1791. William Hodge, Test.

RILEY, JAMES—Folio 45—To Joseph King, 225 acres on Doves creek orig. grant 1792 to Andrew Johnson. Nov. 6, 1794. William Howington, Ezekiel King, Test.

RILEY, JAMES and wife Ann—Folio 99—To Mitchell Coleman, land on Doves creek as per grant, adj. Drury Bradley. Mar. 15, 1796. Dionysius Oliver, Thomas Oliver, Test.

ROGERS, JOHN and wife Nancy—Folio 100—To John Templeton, a tract of land orig. granted to William Moss and by him conveyed to said Rogers. Jan. 16, 1794. John Machel, Thomas Selman, James Scott, Test.

ROGERS, NANCY—Folio 63—Bond as Admr. of John Rogers, dec'd. Sept. 20, 1795. James & Thomas Rogers, Security.

RICKERSON, MARMADUKE and wife Mary Ann—Folio 83—of Richmond Co., To Caleb Higginbotham of Elbert Co., 200 acres in Elbert Co. formerly Wilkes, adj. Wm. Teasley. Feb. 5, 1795. John Leith, J. P. Receipt given in Columbia Co. Feb. 5, 1795.

RICHARDSON, WALKER and wife Prudence—Folio 94—To Dionysius Oliver, Sr., 281 acres on Wehatchee creek. Mar. 1, 1796.

RAGLAND, JOHN R.—Folio 105—His oath that on Jan. 22, 1791 John Oliver agreed that said Ragland and his family should cross the ferry across Savannah and Broad rivers free during the natural life of said Ragland. Sworn to Jan. 26, 1796 before Evan Ragland. Robert O. Burton, John Sharp, Test.

RAGLAND, EVAN—Folio 125—To James Coleman, "one naked lot", No. 18 on west side of Front Street in the town of Petersburg, the improvements excepted as I never owned any of them. April 5, 1796. Joseph Groves, John Ooleman, Test.

SHACKLEFORD, HENRY—Folio 3—of Elbert Co., To Edmond Shackleford of Orange Co. Va., 123 acres on Doves creek, adj. Edmond Harper, Reuben White and Middleton Woods, whereon said Henry Shackleford now lives. Feb. 21, 1795.

SHACKLEFORD, JOHN, JR.—Folio 15—To Sherwood Harris, 110 acres adj. Middleton Woods, all other sides by Shackleford's land. May 22, 1795.

STONE, URIAH—Folio 8—of Elbert Co., Power of Atty. to Marbil Stone of Franklin Co. Va., to attend to all business, especially to collect for negroes sold, for next ten years. May 14, 1795.

STAPLES, JOHN—Folio 11—To Larkin Gatewood, 53 acres adj. John Upshaw and said Staples and Gatewood's land. Jan. 27, 1795. John Upshaw, James Gatewood, Test.

STAPLES, JOHN—Folio 12—To John Upshaw of Louisa Co. Va., 63 acres adj. John Upshaw and said Staples. Jan. 27, 1795. Larkin Gatewood, James Gatewood, Test.

SOALES, JOHN—Folio 21—To William Skelton, 50 acres on north side of Cedar creek. Mar. 7, 1792. H. McDonald, John Skelton, Test.

SHEARMOND, TABITHA—Folio 38—Binds to William Cook a girl Fanny four years and seven months old till she is 10. Aug. 5, 1795.
(This may be Thearmond)

SHARP, WILLIAM—Folio 51—from Justices of Inferior Court, a boy William Arnold, bound as apprentice till 21 years of age. Sept. 30, 1795.

STODGILL, MARLITIA or MELITIA—Folio 64—and Caleb Oliver, bond as Armrs. of Joel Stodgill, dec'd. Oct. 14, 1795. Thomas Fortson, Security.

STEEL, HENRY—Folio 101—To James Alston, 164 acres adj. Watters Nunnelle and Wm. Moore. May 13, 1794. Henry Collin, Henry Cook, Test.

SEWELL, SAMUEL—Folio 124—of Franklin Co., To Charles Goss of Elbert Co., 135 acres on both sides of Falling creek, orig. grant to Joseph Docth (Dorcth?). July 19, 1796.

STRICKLAND, SOLOMON—Folio 140—To James Rogers, 40 acres on Bluestone creek. Feb. 27, 1795.

SHAW, DANIEL and wife Molly—Folio 141—To Richard Easter, 400 acres on Savannah river, near Spring Meeting House, orig. grant to Julius Howard. Oct. 5, 1795.

THOMPSON, WILLIAM, Sr. and wife Mary—Folio 23—To son William Thompson, Jr., 1300 acres on east side of Bertrams creek adj. James Morrison, Benjamin Cook, Walker Richardson, Elijah and Wm. Brewer, Matt J. Williams, Wm. Hatcher and Stephen Ellington. Deed of gift. Mar. 25, 1793. Samuel Watkins, Isam Watkins, Drury Thompson, Jr., Test.

THOMPSON, WILLIAM, Sr. and wife Mary—Folio 49—To John Seel or Seal, 100 acres on Bertrams creek part of orig. survey to Wm. Thompson, Sr., adj. Drury Thompson. May 2, 1795. Drury Towns, Test.

THOMPSON, WILLIAM, Sr. and wife Mary—Folio 87—To Darvin Harris, 62 acres on dry fork of Wahatchee creek, adj. Nathan Johnson. Jan. 16, 1795. Wells and Asa Thompson, Test.

THOMPSON, FARLEY—Folio 122—To Henry G. Walker, Lot No. 32 on west side of Front Street in town of Petersburg. Nov. 17, 1794. M. Walker, Jn. Coleman, Test.

THOMPSON, JOHN and wife Sarah—Folio 138—To Nathan Butler, 100 acres on Wahatchee creek being cut off from the east end from a 300 acre tract by a line of marked trees, whereon said Nathan Butler now lives, orig. grant to David Adams, dec'd. Dec. 11, 1795.

TUTTLE, JAMES, Sr.—Folio 28—To Joseph Deadwiler, 250 acres on Doves creek, orig. grant to Edmond Johnson, adj. John White and John Williamson. July 28, 1795.

TURMAN, GARRETT and wife Mary—Folio 38—To William Hightower, all of Wilkes Co., 200 acres on Falling creek, Jan. 26, 1788.

TURMAN, GEORGE—Folio 115—son of Thos. Turman, To Martin Turman 200 acres on Beaverdam creek, orig. grant 1784 for Wilkes Co. Dec. 12, 1795. William Calhoun, R. Burton, Test.

THURMAN, JOHN—Folio 42—of Wilkes Co., To James Adams and Archibald Burton of Elbert Co., 150 acres on Wahatchee creek. Mar. 24, 1794. Tobitho Wootten, Thomas Wootten, Test.

THOMAS, WILLIAM—Folio 61—and John Newman, bond as Admrs. of Joel Thomas, dec'd. Oct. 3, 1793—John Ross, Sec.

TOWNLEY, HENRY—Folio 77—of Pendleton Co. S. C., To Nicodemus Colbert of Elbert Co., 170 acres on Vanns creek. Feb. 5, 1795. James Walker, Test.

HISTORICAL COLLECTIONS 199

TOLBERT, SAMUEL—Folio 91—To Jesse Jones, 100 acres on the branches of Falling creek, adj. James Kidd, Valentine Smith and Benjamin Baker. Feb. 13, 1796. Theodocus Cook, Test.

TWEEDLE, JOHN and wife Sarah—Folio 143—To Ralph Owins, 44 acres on Powderbag creek, part of a grant of 248 acres 1793 to said Tweedle. Dec. 8, 1794. Clement Owins, Test.

VINEYARD, DAVID—Folio 39—To Jonathan Vineyard, 200 acres on Vineyards creek, orig, grant 1790 to Robt. Couden. Aug. 29, 1795.

VINEYARD, PHILLIP—Folio 69—To Pearson Duncan, 300 acres on Beaverdam creek, part of a grant of 600 acres 1785 to John Tollett. Sept. 3, 1795. Leroy Pace, Test.

WILKINS, JOHN and wife Ann—Folio 6—To James Certain, 30 acres on both sides of Falling creek, for a mill site, part of a grant of 500 acres to said Wilkins. Jan. 7, 1794. John Wilkins, Jr., Test.

WILKINS, CLEMENT and wife Clary—Folio 130—To John Hubberd, 760 acres on Wahatchee creek. July 9, 1796. J. H. Little, J. P. Joakim Hudson, J. P., Test.

WILLIAMS, NEHEMIAH and wife Peggy—Folio 16—To Thomas Maxwell, 213 acres on Coldwater creek, part of a grant of 400 acres to said Williams 1788 in Wilkes Co. Oct. 3, 1792.

WILLIAMS, MATT. J.—Folio 89—To James Morris, a negro boy, Bartlet, Dec. 24, 1795. Elisha Brewer, Lemuel Black, Test.

WALTON, JOHN JENNINGS and wife Nancy—Folio 34—To Benj. Brown 200 acres "as the same had been actually granted to said Benj. Brown. Dec. 20, 1791. Rowland & Reuben Allen, Test.

WEBB, AUSTIN—Folio 44—To William Whaley, part of orig. grant 1785 to Robt. Guttery on Broad river. Oct. 23, 1795. Absolom Stinchcomb, Robt. McDowell, Test.

WEBB, CLABURN and wife Peggy—Folio 120—To Hezekiah Gray, 100 acres on cedar creek. May 2, 1795.

WEBB, CLABOURN and wife Peggy—Folio 129—To John Webb, 100 acres on Cedar creek adj. Samuel Nelson. May 2, 1795.

WILLEFORD, STEPHEN—Folio 66—Power of Atty. to John Willeford to collect all debts in N. C. Jan. 4, 1796. Thos. Rogers, Test.

WALTHALL, GERRARD, Jr.—Folio 74—planter, To Thomas B. Creagh, three slaves, Jack, Phil and Sarah, now in Chesterfield Co. Va. May 26, 1791. James Highsmith, Test.

WILSON, JOHN & CO.—Folio 87—Receipt to James and Thomas Oliver for pay for tobacco, Augusta, Feb. 8, 1796. John Blair, John Wilson, Jr., Test.

WESTBROOK, JOHN—Folio 98—of Franklin Co., to Walker Richardson of Elbert Co., land on Beaverdam creek, Elbert Co. _____ 1795 John Little, John Ellison, Test.

ELBERT COUNTY GEORGIA

DEED BOOK "D"

ALEXANDER, ADLY—Folio 4—To John Montgomery, Jr., a certain dark bay mare, sale. Aug. 26, 1795. H. McDonald, J. P. J. Alexander, Robt. Black.

AKEN, THOMAS and wife Mary—Folio 8—To Benjamin Fannin, 50 acres on Beaverdam creek. Nov. 14, 1796.

AKEN, THOMAS and wife Mary—Folio 10—To Dozier Thornton, 243 acres on Beaverdam creek. Nov. 14, 1796. Jacob Dyer, Test.

ALSTON, WILLIAM and wife Charity—Folio 21—To James Tait, 227 acres whereon Leroy Pope now lives. April 29, 1793. Stephen Heard, Jacob Gilleylen, Test.

ARNOLD, JAMES and wife Nancy—Folio 36—To Benjamin Fannin, 40 acres on Carters creek. Feb. 14, 1797.

ALEXANDER, WILLIAM and wife Nancy—Folio 59—To John McGowan, land on Coldwater creek adj. said McGowan. May. 3, 1796.

ARNOLD, WILLIAM and wife Susanna—Folio 120—To John Dingler, 100 acres on Beaverdam creek. Dec. 16, 1797.

ALLEN, WILLIAM—Folio 135—of Elbert Co., To John Waller of Hancock Co., Lot No. 30, in Petersburg. Sept. 29, 1794. Stephen Heard, Thomas Thornton, Test.

BAKER, JOHN A. and wife Jeen or Jency—Folio 6—To Thomas Akins, 112 acres on Falling creek. Oct. 27, 1796.

BAKER, JOHN A. and wife Jean—Folio 23—To Edmond Lowry, for L1., 10s., 4 acres on Falling creek. Mar. 4, 1796.

BAKER, JOHN, Sr.—Folio 29—of Greenville Co. S. C., To Wm. Oliver of Elbert Co. Ga., 200 acres on which the said Baker built an overshot mill, adj. the town of Elberton. Dec. 21, 1796.

BAKER, ABSOLOM and wife Mary—Folio 45—To John Mackie, 150 acres on Falling creek. Aug. 22, 1794. James Baker, Test.

BAKER, ABSOLOM and wife Mary—Folio 67—To James Armstrong, 100 acres on Falling creek. Sept. 5, 1795.

BROWN, JAMES and wife Julia—Folio 18—To Jos. Rucker, 200 acres on Vanns creek. Dec. 15, 1794. Adam Gaar, John Smith, Benjamin Head, Test.

BROWN, JINCEY—Folio 52—of Richmond Co., To Jos. Glenn of Elbert Co., the middle lot of orig. survey to Wm. Brown of 400 acres. May 13, 1796. Anthony Hanie, Edwin Glenn, Test.

BROWN, WILLIAM and wife Sarah—Folio 88—To Wm. S. Burch, 45 acres on a branch of Falling creek. Sept. 7, 1797.

BARNETT, JOHN and wife Caroline—Folio 19—To Jason Wilson, all of Wilkes Co., 200 acres on both sides of Doves creek. Dec. 23, 1789.

BELL, JAMES and wife Olive—Folio 24—To George Wyche, 216 acres including the plantation where John Gill formerly lived. Dec. 20, 1796. Peter Wyche, Test.

BELL, JOSEPH and wife Elizabeth—Folio 78—To Henry Mosely, 179 acres on Falling creek, orig. grant 1786 to George Martin. Nov. 23, 1795—James Bell, J. P., David Porterfield, Test.

BURK, THOMAS—Folio 43—To Michael Saylors, 200 acres on Doves creek. Aug. 20, 1795.

BUTLER, ZACHARIAH and wife Mary—Folio 52—To John Rich, 125 acres adj. Benjamin Cook. Nov. 15, 1796. William Oliver, James Kidd, Test.

BUTLER, PATRICK and wife Elizabeth—Folio 33—To Benj. Fanning 200 acres on Falling creek. Jan. 30, 1797.

BUCKHANNON, EBENEZER—Folio 35—of Pendleton Co. S. C., To Jos. James, a certain island in Savannah river, orig. grant 1790 to Thos. Wilmoth. April 16, 1796. Alex. Patterson, Test.

BURTON, BENJAMIN—Folio 60—To John McCombs, tract of land on Broad river "where I now live". Nov. 10, 1796. Edward Ware, Polley Thurmond, Test.

BLAKE, WILLIAM, Sr. and wife Lucy—Folio 97—To Allen Mobley, 125 acres on north side of Falling creek. Mar. 22, 1796. William Mobley, Happy Blake, Test.

BLAKE, WILLIAM, Sr.—Folio 98—of Elbert Co., To the orphans of Wm. Mobley of N. C. dec'd. viz: Allen Mobley, Jos. Huddleston, and Sally his wife, Thos. Jones and Gilly his wife, William and Stephen Mobley, heirs of said Wm. Mobley, dec'd., three slaves "after my death and not before", and half interest in another at the end of 15 years "if my present wife be dec'd"., to satisfy a debt to said heirs. May 5, 1796. James Bell, Arthur Jones, Josiah Allen, Test.

Sept. 6, 1796, Slaves delivered to Jos. Huddleston "in behalf of the whole". Signed Wm. X Blake.

BURTON, ARCHER—Folio 126—and James Adams, Admrs., David Adams, dec'd. To Thomas Napier, 200 acres on Wahatchee creek. Dec. 23, 1797.

BARNETT, WILLIAM—Folio 122—and R. Hunt and Samuel Higginbotham, To Eli Eavenson, Lots No. 17 & 20 "at the Court House for the county". Dec. 19, 1797.

BIBB, SALLY S.—Folio 138—Excx. Wm. Bibb, dec'd, To Richardson Hunt, 500 acres on Beaverdam creek, part of a larger survey granted to said Wm. Bibb. Oct. 8, 1797.

BARNETT, WILLIAM—Folio 71—James Tait, Evan Ragland and Richardson Hunt, To Thomas Carter, Lot No. 2, "at the Court House" part of 50 acres which was conveyed to us by John Baker. Jan. 29, 1793.

COULTER, CHARLES—Folio 40—To Beverly Greenwood, 200 acres on Doves creek, orig. survey 1784 to said Coulter. Feb. 7, 1797. James Christian, Test.

COSBY, ROBERT—Folio 48—Sheriff, To Timothy Saxon, planter, 200 acres, property of John Johnson to satisfy a suit of John Millican. April 4, 1797. John M. Whitney, M. Woods, Test.

COSBY, ROBERT—Folio 53—Sheriff, To Leroy Pope, Lot No. 25 in Petersburg sold as the property of Thos. C. Russell to satisfy a debt to James Perry. Mar. 7, 1797. W. Nunnelee, Test.

COSBY, ROBERT—Folio 59—T. C., To Middleton Woods, 100 acres on Bluestone creek adj. Wm. Kellet, property of Solo. Kellet. Mar. 19, 1796. Wm. Brown, Test.

COSBY, ROBERT—Folio 65—T. C., To Stephen Groves, 300 acres, property of Wm. Kilgore, to satisfy a debt to Aron Vanhook. April 18, 1797. John Brawner, Test.

COSBY, ROBERT—Folio 95—T. C., To the heirs of Benj. Hendricks, dec'd, of Wilkes Co., 54½ acres on north fork of Broad river, adj. John H. Johnson, the property of Patrick McDonald. Aug. 1, 1795.

COSBY, ROBERT—Folio 104—T. C., To Thomas Camron, Sr., 1850 acres on Beaverdam creek adj. John Albritton, property of Robert Hawthorn. June 2, 1795.

CRISWELL, DAVID—Folio 57—of Wilkes Co., To John McCurdy of Elbert Co., 200 acres on Holly creek adj. where William Appleby now lives. Aug. 28, 1794. Stephen Groves, John McCarty, Test.

CRISWELL, DAVID—Folio 69—of Wilkes Co., To Wm. Appleby of Elbert Co., 200 acres on Holly creek. Aug. 28, 1794.

CARTER, THOMAS—Folio 70—To William Guy, 200 acres on Beaverdam creek, part of a larger survey to James Carter. June 24, 1797.

CALDWELL, Harry and wife Catharine—Folio 73—of the State of N. Y. To James Manning of Petersburg, Ga., Lot 14, on west side of Front Street in said town. Jan. 12, 1797.
    O. Whyte, Lit. B. Wilson, Test.

CERTAIN, JOSIAH and wife Elizabeth—Folio 81—To Josiah Certain, Jr. 100 acres on dry fork of Falling creek. May 4, 1794.

CLOUD, EZEKIEL—Folio 86—To Daniel Orr, 105 acres on South river. June 17, 1797. James Walker, Wm. Preston Elliott, Test.

CARGILE, JOHN—Folio 110—of Oglethorpe Co., To James Leeper of Elbert Co., 400 acres on Forge creek, a branch of Broad river. Aug. 1, 1797. Peter Wyche, James Crow, Test.

COLBERT, THOMAS and wife Anne—Folio 117—To Philpot Colbert, 100 acres on Vanns creek. Oct. 8, 1794.

CROCKETT, ROBERT—Folio 127—Admr. Samuel Crockett, dec'd of York Co. S. C., To Stephen Heard, 200 acres of land on Savannah river where said Samuel Crockett resided when he made bond for title. Oct. 17, 1791. Wm. Sharp, Thos. Thornton, Test.

CHAMBERS, ROBERT and wife Lettice—Folio 136—of Greene Co., To Stephen Heard of Elbert Co., 899 acres on both sides of Beaverdam creek adj. Chas. Cosby, Wm. Moss and Wm. Daniel. Aug. 22, 1793. Alex. Reed, Jr., H. McDonald, James Chambers, Test.

COLEMAN, MICHAEL—Folio 140—To John Hawthorn, land on Doves creek, adj. Drury Bradley. Sept. 19, 1796. John Hawthorn, Robert Hawthorn, Test.

COSBY, JAMES O.—Folio 7—T. C., To Wm. Criddenton, land on Doves creek, property of Richard Coulter, Sr., adj. Chas. Coulter, and Richard Coulter, Jr. Nov. 8, 1796.

COLBERT, THOMAS—Folio 11—As guardian of Fanny and Patsy Colbert, John Colbert, Chas. Goss, Nicodemus Colbert & Thomas Colbert guardian of Philpot Colbert of Elbert Co., To William Bibb of Wilkes Co., 150 acres on Vanns creek, orig. grant to Thos. Gregg and formerly conveyed to John Colbert, dec'd. Nov. 16, 1792. H. G. Walker, Wm. Moss, J. P. Test.

Signed; John Colbert, Chas. & Martha Colbert, Nicodemus Colbert Thomas and Fanny Colbert. Thomas Colbert for Philpot Colbert as guardian.

COLBERT, THOMAS and wife Anne—Folio 117—To Philpot Colbert, 100 acres on Vanns creek. Oct. 8, 1794. Nicodemus Colbert, Thomas Wootten, J. P., Test.

COOK, JAMES WATSON—Folio 15—To Sally, Allen and Patsy Cook, 200 acres, 100 being part of Geo. Pettigrew's survey, 100 being part of a survey 1785 to James Cook, Sr. Jan. 4, 1797. John Conyers, James Little, Test.

COOK, JOSIAH and wife Elizabeth—Folio 17—To Benjamin Fannin 70 acres. Dec. 20, 1796. Thomas Cook, Test.

COOK, G. W.—Folio 50—To William Moore, a slave levied on as the property of Wm. Head for a debt to Benj. Cook. Feb. 6, 1797.

CUNNINGHAM, ELIZABETH—Folio 16—of Elbert Co., To Thos. Oglesby of Buckingham Co. Va., 250 acres on Penningtons Fk., otherwise called Doves creek, orig grant 1785 to Joshua Pickins. Dec. 3, 1796. Allen Jones, Test.

COULTER, FRANCIS—Folio 20—To John Greenwood, 200 acres on Doves creek "including the improvements" where I now live. Dec. 15, 1796. Henry Gatewood, Test.

COLEMAN, JAMES—Folio 22—To James Tait, a certain tract of land sold by Abraham Colson to said Coleman, May 8, 1793. Jan. 5, 1794. A. Colson, Wm. J. Hobby, Test.

CONWAY, PHILIP and wife Marget—Folio 25—To Christopher Starr, 250 acres on Broad river adj. James Patten and John Thornhill. July 30, 1792.

COLLINS, ZACHARIAH and wife Sally—Folio 27—To John Gaddis, 100 acres on Doves and Falling creeks. Jan. 17, 1797.

CHISOLM, SARAH—Folio 77—To Margaret Davis a slave Filidy and bed and furniture, no consideration mentioned. Sept. 5, 1796 Wm. C. Davis, Rebecca Davis, Test.

COMMISSIONERS—Folio 71—Wm. Barnett, James Tait, Evan Ragland and Richardson Hunt, To Thomas Carter, Lot No. 2 at the Court House, part of a 50 acre tract conveyed to us by John Baker, June 5, 1792, which is part of a larger survey of 950 acres granted to said Baker, April 9, 1792.

COMMISSIONERS—Folio 122, as above, To Eli Eavenson, Lot No. 18 at the Court House, known as Elberton. Dec. 19, 1797. Also Lots Nos. 17 and 20.

DICKINSON, JOHN—Folio 5—To David Adams, 186 acres on north fork of Broad river. Aug. 29, 1796. Thos. Lovelady, Jos. Dickinson, Test.

DAVIS, ABSOLOM—Folio 7—To Salvannah Randall, daughter of Nany Randall, her freedom. July 2, 1796.

DIXON, OUTERBRIDGE—Folio 33—To Eleven Dixon, slaves etc, bill of sale. Feb. 6, 1797. Leroy Pace, B. Pace, J. P., Test.

DIXON, OUTERBRIDGE—Folio 34—To Joshua McConnell, land on Mill Shoal creek, on which said Dixon now lives which is part of a survey bought of John Dardin. Feb. 6, 1797.

DOSS, JOHN—Folio 58—To Daniel Parker, a slave Jacob 14 years old and lame. April 19, 1797. Edward Grove, John Parker, Test.

DEPRIEST, RANDOLPH and wife Amey—Folio 62—To Mathias Ward, 100 acres on both sides of cedar creek. Jan 15, 1794. Amos Richardson, James Highsmith, Test.

DARDEN, JOHN—Folio 64— of Wilkes Co., To Bazdel Human of Elbert Co., 270 acres on Holly creek waters of Broad river. Jan. 31, 1794. Basiell Human, Ezekiel Wells, Test.

DUGLASS, THOMAS—Folio 118— and Lewis Sale, To Memorable Walker for $1200.00 one house and lot in Petersburg, No. 38 west side of Front Street. Nov. 2, 1797.

EVANS, GEORGE—Folio 1—To_____(Folio lost)

EASTER, RICHARD and wife Mary—Folio 31—To Geo. Whitfield, Jr. Lot No. 32, west side of Front Street in town of Petersburg, Jan. 14, 1797. Jos. Bukley, of Beckley, Test.

EASTER, RICHARD and wife Mary—Folio 31—To Littleberry & Whitfield Wilson, Lot No. 34 on west side of Front Street in town of Petersburg, Jan. 14, 1797.

EASTER, RICHARD and wife Mary—Folio 45—To John Oliver, 300 acres on Savannah river, formerly belonging to Daniel Shaw, including the mill known as Howard's Mill ("he being the original builder"). Aug. 3, 1796. Evan Ragland, Chas. Scott Cosby, Test.

FANNING, BENJAMIN and wife Avery—Folio 9—To Jos. Moss, 100 acres on Beaverdam creek. Nov. 12, 1796.

FANNING, BENJAMIN and wife Avery—Folio 9—To Middleton Fanning, 160 acres on Beaverdam creek, adj. Benj. Brown and Edward Clark. Nov. 14, 1796.

FANNIN, BENJAMIN and wife Aberialer—Folio 87—To Wm. S. Burch, 75 acres adj. said Burch. Sept. 6, 1797.

FOSTER, SAMUEL—Folio 134—of Abbeville, Co. S. C., To Stephen Heard of Elbert Co., 200 acres adj. Thos. Colbert, on Beaverdam creek, orig. grant 1785 to said Foster. Sept. 15, 1794. Samuel Wimbish, William Spear, Jos. Turnbull, Test.

FERGUS, JOHN—Folio 139—of Franklin Co., To Benjamin Burton of Elbert Co., part of a tract of land on Broad river on which said Benjamin now lives, including the Fishery. May 4, 1796. Little B. Battle, William Cain, Test.

GREENWOOD, JOHN, Sr.—Folio 31—To Thomas Oliver, 400 acres on both sides of Beaverdam creek, whereon Geo. Blackwell and Michael Coleman now live. April 8, 1796. Dionysius Oliver, John Hawton, John Greenwood, Test.

GREENWOOD, JOHN and wife Lucy—Folio 61—To Henry Cridington, 200 acres on Doves creek adj. Chas. Ellis, Wm. Criddington, John and Larkin Gatewood. Jan. 4, 1797.

GREENWOOD, JOHN, Jr. and wife Lucy—Folio 88—To Robert Pulliam, 200 acres on south fork of Beaverdam creek. Aug. 30, 1796.

GREENWOOD, JOHN—Folio 121—To James Sartain, 200 acres on Doves creek, orig. grant 1784 to Chas Coulter. Dec. 19, 1797.

GREENWOOD, BEVERLY—Folio 90—To George Greenwood, 200 acres on Doves creek. Mar. 27, 1797. Leroy Upshaw, Henry Criddington, Test.

GREENWOOD, GEORGE—Folio 91—To John Greenwood, 200 acres on Doves creek. July 9, 1797.

GUY, WILLIAM and wife Mary—Folio 14—To William Cunningham, 200 acres on Savannah river, adj. the heirs of Jeremiah Walker. Oct. 3, 1795. Elisha Towns, Abraham Bell, Test.

GOSS, BENJAMIN—Folio 25—farmer of Elbert Co., To John Andrew of Oglethorpe Co., 200 acres on Cedar creek whereon said John Andrew now liveth, adj. Jesse White and Chas. Goss. Dec. 21, 1796.

GOSS, BENJAMIN and wife Elizabeth—Folio 138—To John Andrew, all of Elbert Co., 200 acres on Doves creek as described in above deed, "it being part of a tract of land formerly conveyed verbally by said Benj. Goss, Sr., to Benj. Goss, Jr. Dec. 30, 1797.

GILES, JOHN M.—Folio 43—To John R. Ragland, all he is entitled to in lands, personal estate etc., of his father John Giles, dec'd. Feb. 25, 1797. Hudson Ragland, John Murrah, Test.

GARRETT, JOHN—Folio 56—of Augusta, Ga., Power of Atty., to William Daniel of Elbert Co., to sell land now in his possession. May 7, 1796. John Henderson, Thomas Hanay., Test.

GRAHAM, WILLIAM and wife Nancy—Folio 73—To Richard Sanders, 184 acres on south fork of Broad river. Oct. 19, 1796. Nathaniel Smith, Samuel Woods, J. P., Test.

GLOVER, WILLIAM—Folio 85—To James Jones, 180 acres on Falling creek. Sept. 15, 1796. Elias Hendrick, Test.

GAINES, HIRAM, Sr.—Folio 93—To William Gaines, slaves and a horse. Bill of sale. Sept. 27, 1797.

GLENN, JOSEPH—Folio 105—To Jos. L. Glenn, a slave. Sale Oct. 28, 1796. Chas, Goss, Robt. Huddleston, Test.

GREGG, THOMAS—Folio 105—To Joel Doss, 290 acres according to a grant 1784. Sept. 12, 1797. James Freeman, Robt. Mains, John Carrell, J. P., Test.

GRIFFITH, JOHN and wife Ann—Folio 123—of Oglethorpe Co., To Hardin Evins of Elbert Co., 125 acres on Fork creek, adj. James and Robert Griffith and John McClary. Feb. 25, 1795 James Griffith, Test.

HUDDLESTON, ROBERT and wife Patsy—Folio 7—To David Clark, 70 acres on dry fork of Falling creek. Nov. 9, 1795. Chas. Goss, William Blake, Test.

HEARD, H—Folio 42—T. C., To Ruth and Rosannah Kain, 250 acres on Broad river, adj. B. Pace, sold as property of Wm. Kain. May 4, 1795. Rich'd. Kain, John Coffee, Test.

HEARD, JOHN, Jr. and wife Elizabeth—Folio 49—of Wilkes Co., To George Darden of Elbert Co., 150 acres on south side of Beaverdam creek. Jan. 10, 1796. Buckner Darden, Jesse Heard, Robt. L. Tait, Test.

HEARD, JOHN, JR. and wife Elizabeth—Folio 55—of Wilkes Co., To James Alston, Sr., of Elbert Co., 201 acres, part of orig. grant 1784 to Barnard Heard. Jan. 30, 1797. Ledford Parrott, Nathaniel Alston, John Abenathee, J. P., Test.

HEAD, WILLIAM—Folio 51—To James Lockhart, 468 acres on Codys creek. May 3, 1796. William Moon, William Allen, J. P., Test.

HEAD, WILLIAM—Folio 58—To James Head, 100 acres on Broad river. June 20, 1796.

HAYNIE, ANTHONY—Folio 54—To Edwin Glenn, all the land on the north side of Broad river which was laid off to said Anthony as a legatee of William Brown, 130 acres a part of orig. survey to William Brown, and granted to his heirs. Mar. 9, 1796. Chas. Goss, Claburn Webb, Test.

HENDRICKS, JESSE and wife Frances—Folio 62—To Reuben Cook, 50 acres on Falling creek, being part of 200 acres orig. grant to said Hendricks and whereon he now lives. May 12, 1797. John Cook, Test.

HOWARD, JULIUS and wife Susannah—Folio 72—To Richard Easter, 200 acres, adj. Thos. Burton, Martin Turman, Martin Sims, and Collins orphans. Jan. 10, 1794. Elizabeth Howard, Test.

HATCHER, WILLIAM and wife Priscilla—Folio 100—To Wm. Reynolds, Lot No. 29 on east side of Front Street in Petersburg. Jan. 24, 1797. John Martin, Test.

HODGE, WILLIAM—Folio 111—and Elliott, To Allen Leeper, 172 acres on Fork creek adj. said grantors and John Griffith and John Calvert. Feb. 18, 1797.

HUDSON, NATHANIEL—Folio 141—To John P. Harper, 5 acres on Wahatchee creek. Feb. 10, 1792.

JONES, THOMAS and wife Gilley—Folio 5—To William H. Moon, 281 acres on Wahatchee creek part of a tract said Jones bought of William Oliver. Oct. 6, 1796. John Jones, Test.

JONES, JAMES—Folio 84—To Elias Hendrick, 50 acres on the branches of Falling creek, part of a tract Wm. Glover sold said Jones. Sept. 15, 1796. William Glover, Test.

KIDD, JAMES and wife Elizabeth—Folio 30—To William Oliver, half of a certain lot of land in Elberton, whereon said James Kidd now lives on which there is a large two story house etc. Dec. 21, 1796. J. Moon, Test.

GEORGIA D. A. R.

KIDD, JAMES, and wife Elizabeth—Folio 30—To John M. Whitney, 100 acres near Elbert Court House. Jan. 19, 1797.

KIDD, JAMES H.—Folio 61—To Archer Skinner, Lot No. 12 at the Court House part of 50 acres bought of Womack Blankenship. Mar. 10, 1795-. William Brown, Philip Thurman, Test.

KIDD, WEBB—Folio 96—To William Jennings, 100 acres on Vanns creek. Oct. 5, 1797.

KENNEDY, CHARLES—Folio 92—of Pendleton Co. S. C., To John Wilhite of Elbert Co., 100 acres orig. grant 1786 to William Strong. Sept. 19, 1797. Warren Stow, William Gerdan, Test.

KERR, SAMUEL and wife Charity, alias Charity Bowers when granted.—Folio 103—To John Carson, 100 acres on Coldwater creek, orig. grant 1784 to Charity Bowers. Aug. 12, 1797.

KEYS, JOHN and wife Winny—Folio 133—To Stephen Heard, 300 acres orig. grant 1787 to John Keys. Dec. 8, 1797. Nicodemus Colbert, Test.

LOWERY, JAMES—Folio 3—To Meshach Lowery, 100 acres on Falling creek. May 9, 1796. John Lowery, James Lowery, Jr., Test.

LOWERY, WILLIAM and wife Mary—Folio 21—To Edmond Lowery, 25 acres on Falling creek. Mar. 1, 1794. John Lowery, Meshach Lowery, Test.

LAMAR, BASIL—Folio 119—of Lincoln Co., To John Parnall of Elbert Co., 75 acres on north side of Falling creek. Feb. 24, 1797. Thomas Vining, Robert Ware, William Stokes, J. Ps.

LOVELADY, THOMAS and wife Jane—Folio 126—To William Lunsford, 200 acres on a branch of Deep creek adj. Wm. Johnson. July 16, 1796. James Norris, Roy Norris, Test.

McDOUGALL, ALEX. and wife Elizabeth—Folio 12—of Elbert Co., To Joel Crane of Franklin Co., 200 acres on main Lightwood Log creek, orig. grant to said Alex. from George Matthews. Dec. 9, 1795. Cornelius Cain, William Wilbourn.

McCLESKEY, DAVID and wife Mary—Folio 36—To James McCleskey, all of Wilkes Co., for L20, 300 acres on Falling creek, orig. grant 1788 to said David. Jan. 15, 1790.

McCLESKEY, JAMES and wife Isabella—Folio 37—To Benjamin Goss, 328 acres part of a survey to David McCleskey and part of a survey to said James McCleskey. Feb. 23, 1797. Elizabeth Kidd, Test.

McCARTY, DANIEL—Folio 68—of Wilkes Co., To Robert Cowden of Elbert Co., 50 acres, all the land that is in said Cowden's survey belonging to an old survey of James Gillespy. April 14, 1792.

McDONALD, HUGH and wife Helen—Folio 72—To James McCleskey, 200 acres on falling creek, adj. Francis Webb. May 8, 1797.

McGOWEN, JOHN and wife Hannah—Folio 91—"of the town of Alexandria, Elbert Co., To Lewis Gaar, Lots 5 and 6 in said town. April 5, 1797. Henry Harper, Test.

McGOWEN, JOHN and wife Hannah—Folio 113—of the town of Alexandria, Elbert Co., To Henry Harper, Lots 13 and 14 in said town. April 5, 1797.

McALPIN, ROBERT—Folio 107—of Greene Co., To John Moore of Abbeville S. C., 400 acres on Deep Creek Elbert Co., purchased by said McAlpin at a sale Jan. 3, last, property of Thomas Lovelady. Mar. 27, 1797. J. W. Carter, Wm. Foster, Test.

McKEE, JOHN and wife Mary—Folio 128—of Franklin Co., To Thomas Colbert of Elbert Co., 150 acres on south west side of Falling creek. Mar. 8, 1797. Robt. B. Huddleston, John Dorsey, Test.

MORRIS, JOHN and wife Sarah—Folio 2—To Cornelius Cain, land on Lightwood Log creek. Dates effaced. Abraham P. Casey, Test.

MARBURY, HORATIO—Folio 26—of Columbia Co., To Peter Carnes, Esqr. of Richmond Co., 800 acres on south fork of Coldwater creek, adj. Hugh McDonald and Mark Thornton. Feb. 7, 1791. B. Porter, Elihu Lymon, Test.

MOORE, DAVIS—Folio 118—and John Cowdery of S. C., To Pope & Walker of Petersburg, Ga., twelve slaves. Oct. 25, 1797. William J. Hobby, John Martin, Test.

MATKIN, JAMES—Folio 124—of Pendleton Co. S. C., To William Sharp of Elbert Co., 200 acres on both sides of Beaverdam creek. Feb. 2, 1797. Thomas Head, Test.

MANN, JAMES, Sr. and wife Judah—Folio 129—To James Mann, Jr., 200 acres on south side of Vanns creek. Dec. 30, 1797. Reuben Whyte, Test.

MANN, JAMES, Jr.—Folio 136—To John Whyte, 11 acres part of above tract. Dec. 29, 1797.

NELMES, DAVID and wife Unity—Folio 83—To Thomas Price, 200 acres on north fork of Beaverdam creek. May 10, 1797.

NEAL, JULIAN—Folio 130—To son Benjamin, the tract of land on which I live on Cedar creek. Deed of gift, _____1797 Stephen Haynes, J. Neal, Jr., Moses Haynes, Test.

NEAL, JULIAN—Folio 130—To his daughter Elizabeth Neal, a slave Hannah, bed etc. _____1797 Stephen Haynes, J. Neal, Jr., Moses Haynes, Test.

OFFUTT, WILLIAM JOHNSON—Folio 125—of Columbia Co., To Thomas Keys of Elbert Co., 500 acres surveyed 1785, then in Wilkes now in Elbert. Jan. 4, 1794.

OLIVER, DIONYSIUS and wife Mary Ann—Folio 64—To Peter Oliver, 200 acres on Broad river. Mar. 17, 1796. Sale. McCarty Oliver, James Oliver, Test.

OLIVER, DIONYSIUS, Sr. and wife Mary Ann—Folio 113—To McCarty Oliver, 500 acres on Broad river, part of a 1000 acre grant to said Dionysius, 1784. April 4, 1797. Thomas Oliver, Eleanor Oliver, Test.

OLIVER, DIONYSIUS, Sr., and wife Mary Ann—Folio 114—To McCarty Oliver, a slave boy Jesse about 9 years old. April 4, 1797.

OLIVER, DIONYSIUS, Sr.—Folio 137—To Thomas Hancock of Edgefield S. C., a slave. Mar. 9, 1796. Wm. Oliver, James Oliver, Test.

PERKINS, JOSHUA—Folio 17—of N. C., To John Depriest of Elbert Co. Ga., 50 acres on Pennington Fork, orig. grant April 1785 to said Joshua. Jan. 3, 1792.

POPE, LEROY and wife Judith—Folio 45—To John Oliver, 400 acres on Savannah river, known by the name of Howard's Mill seat. May 3, 1796. Wells Thompson, Test.

POPE, LEROY and wife Judith—Folio 112—To Martin Sims, 100 acres on Savannah river, adj. John Howard. May 16, 1796.

PRICE, Thomas and wife Elizabeth—Folio 83—To Stephen Rowsey, 100 acres on south side of north fork of Beaverdam creek. Aug. 9, 1797.

PEW, ISAAC—Folio 89—To Garrett Turman, a certain roan horse, Bill of sale Sept. 7, 1797. Thomas Turman, Ephriam Beasley, Test.

REED, COLLIN—Folio 100—To Chas. Taylor, Lot No. 40 in town of Petersburg. Jan. 1, 1796. Richard Aycock, Augustine Edwards, Test.

ROYSTON, ROBERT—Folio 10—of Newberry Co. S. C., Marriage settlement with Sally Riddle, widow of Elbert Co. Relinquishes all claim to 16 slaves and all other property. Nov. 18, 1796.

RUSSELL, THOMAS COMMANDER—Folio 47—of Lincoln Co. and wife Mary, To Wells Thompson of Elbert Co., Lot No. 22 in the town of Petersburg, bounded east by Front Street, west by Commons or Broad Street, south by Cross Street and north by Lot No. 24, containing half an acre. Aug. 9, 1796. John Oliver, Wm. Woods, Test.

ROSS, JOHN and wife Margaret—Folio 95—of Elbert Co., To Owen Shannon of Pendleton Co., S. C., 200 acres on Cedar creek, adj. Francis Powell and Evan Ragland. Aug. 20, 1797.

ROSS, ROBERT—Folio 104—To James Brown, both of Wilkes Co., 200 acres on Cedar creek in Wilkes Co. Dec. 30, 1789. John Ross, Wm. Carithers, Test.

REYNOLDS, WILLIAM and wife Martha—Folio 99—To Oliver White, all of the town of Petersburg, Lot No. 28 on north side of Front Street. April 25, 1797 (Signed Pattey)

STARR, CHRISTOPHER and wife Mary—Folio 41—To Thos. Connolly, 250 acres adj. James Patton, John Darden and William Dudley. Mar. 1, 1797. William Brawner, Test.

SHOEMAKER, LINDSAY and wife Elizabeth—Folio 43—To Thos. B. Scott, 200 acres on Doves creek. Nov. 14, 1793. Rn. Lindsay, A. Jarratt. Test.

STEEL, MARGARET—Folio 80—of Abbeville Co. S. C., To Thos. B. Creagh of Elbert Co. Ga., 300 acres orig. grant 1785 to said Margaret. April 15, 1795. James Alston, John Morris, Test.

SCOTT, THOMAS B., and wife Betsey—Folio 56—To Jos. Glenn, 115 acres on Broad river. Aug. 6, 1796. Archilus Jarratt, Claborn Webb, Test.

SCOTT, THOMAS B., and wife Elizabeth—Folio 79—To William Hall, 200 acres on Doves creek. Mar. 17, 1797. John Andrew, Test.

SHAW, ZACHARIAH—Folio 83—of Wake Co. N. C., in consideration of L62 Va. currency, to Moses Fleming of Elbert Co. Ga., a slave Lew. Dec. 13, 1796. Thomas Jones, J. P., Major Pollard, Test.

SAXON, HUGH and wife Mary—Folio 109—of Washington Co., To Christopher Harris of Elbert Co., 200 acres adj. Robert Thompson. Mar. 6, 1795. Thos. Barton, Jr., Wm. Thompson, Test.

TWEEDLE, JOHN and wife—obliterated—Folio 2—To Elijah Owens, date and description obliterated. Ralph Owen, Clement Owen, Test.

TUTTLE, JAMES—Folio 4—To John Dickenson, 156 acres on Broad river adj. William Dudley. Mar. 4, 1795. Holleman Battle, Edward Ware, Test.

TUTTLE, NICHOLAS H., and wife Betty—Folio 116—To John Greenwood 200 acres on both sides of Beaverdam creek, half of a grant of 400 acres, the other half having been deeded to John Rowsey. July 2, 1796. Thomas Oliver, Test.

TUTTLE, JAMES—Folio 132—To Isaac Tuttle, 117 acres on Falling creek, orig. grant to David McCluskey, who sold it to said James. Dec. 28, 1797. Jesse Tuttle, Test.

TAIT, JAMES and wife Rebecca—Folio 23—To Edward Walthall, 400 acres on north side of Coody's creek. July 12, 1797. Evan Ragland, J. P.

TAIT, JAMES and wife Rebecca—Folio 46—To Thomas C. Russell, Lot No. 22 in Petersburg, bounded east by Front St. south by Cross St., west by Common, Broad St., north by Lot No. 25. July 9, 1796. Eanos Tait, Test.

THOMPSON, ISHAM and wife Elizabeth Williams Thompson—Folio 50—To Robert L. Tait, 44 acres on Coody's creek. April 6, 1795. L. B. Thompson, Test.

THOMPSON, FARLEY & LEWIS—Folio 75—Excrs. of John Farler Thompson, dec'd, To Richard Easter, 200 acres on Bertram's creek, adj. Wm. Thompson, Sr., and said Easter. Mar. 30, 1793.

THOMPSON, JOHN and wife Sarah—Folio 74—To Richard Easter, 200 acres on Bertram's creek, adj. Wm. Thompson, Jr. Jan. 19, 1793.

THORNTON, THOMAS and wife Molly—Folio 84—To William Arnold 123 acres on Beaverdam creek. July 10, 1797.

TURMAN, MARTIN and wife Nancy—Folio 82—To George Turman son of Thomas Turman, 232 acres on Coody's creek. Dec. 12, 1795.

THOMPSON, LAMENTATION—Folio 94—To Lewis Gaar, 400 acres on Vanns and Coldwater creeks, adj. Perrin Farrar and Wm. Colson_____ 1797.

THORNTON, MARK and wife Mary—Folio 63—of Elbert Co., To Hiram Gaines, Jr., of Fluvanna Co. Va., land on Coldwater creek, adj. Wm. Gaines, John Teasley and Chas. McDonald. May 7, 1797. William Gaines, Test.

WILLIAMS, THOMAS—Folio 32—To John R. Ragland all his right etc, and his wife's in the estate of John Giles, dec'd. Petersburg, Jan. 3, 1797. Jos. Beckley, Hudson Ragland, Test.

"Received of John R. Ragland seventeen pieces of gold one dollar, being in full of the legacy John Giles, Sr. gave Becky Wells, my wife etc. Jeremiah T. Wells, Petersburg, Nov. 7, 1796. Little B. Wilson, Chas. Harrison, Allen Thompson, Test.

WILMOTH, THOMAS—Folio 34—To Ebenezer Buckhannon, all of Wilkes Co., 200 acres on Savannah river and one island, orig. grant to said Wilmoth 1784, by Stephen Heard. Nov. 16, 1790. Jacob Gilleylen, Test.

WILMOTH, WILLIAM and wife Elizabeth—Folio 68—To William Shives or Sharyar, 100 acres a half of orig. grant to Stephen Wilmoth 1795. June 1, 1797. Randolph Depriest, Test.

WOODS, MIDDLETON—Folio 41—To Luke White, 200 acres, including the plantation whereon said White lives. Jan. 1, 1797.

WALTON, JOHN and wife Nancy—Folio 57—To Edward Clark, 100 acres adj. James Hutson. June 22, 1795. Robt. Mosely, M. Walker, Test.

WHITNEY, JOHN M., and wife Bridget—Folio 66—To Joseph Long, 50 acres. May. 29, 1797.

WILSON, JOS.—Folio 76—of Elbert Co., To Ferdinand Phinizy of Oglethorpe Co., 270 acres on Cedar creek, adj. Harmon Lovingood, Geo. Watts, Archilus Walker and Patrick Mitchell. Aug. 14, 1797. Robert Cosby, Test.

WILSON, JASON—Folio 115—To Isaac Ford, 200 acres on Doves creek, orig. grant 1785 to John Barnett. Dec. 7, 1797. Frances Cook, Test.

WILSON, JOS.—Folio 108—Merchant, To Jonathan Phair, planter, 300 acres on north fork of Coldwater creek. July 9, 1796. Archeleus Walker, Edward Wallace, Test.

WALTHALL, EDWARD and wife Nancy—Folio 77—To Zimri Tait, 106 acres on Coodie's creek. Dec. 27, 1796. Benj. Cook, Test.

WALTHALL, GERRARD, Sr.—Folio 120—To grandson John G. Creagh, a slave Daniel, now in possession of Thos. B. Creagh, Deed of gift. Oct. 22, 1795. Edward Walthall, Aaron James, Test.

WALKER, HENRY G.—Folio 76—To Richard Easter, Lot No. 32 in town of Petersburg, 44 yards on Front Street. Jan. 1, 1795. Winsley Hobby, John R. Ragland, Test.

WOLDRIDGE, WILLIAM, Sr.—Folio 115—of Elbert Co., To William Woldridge, Jr., of Surry Co. N. C., a slave Phebe. Bill of sale. May 22, 1797. Walker Richardson, Thomas Woldridge, Test.

WATKINS, JAMES, JR, and wife Jane—Folio 102—To Wm. Thompson, Sr., 206 acres on Bertram's creek, adj. Stephen Ellington, Wm. Thompson, James Tait, David Hudson and Evan Ragland, for 30,000 weight of tobacco. April 3, 1797. Elizabeth Tait, James Tait, J. P., Test.

WHITE, THOMAS and wife Elizabeth—Folio 108—To Caleb Oliver and wife Nancy, 112 acres on Vann's creek, given, granted etc, the said bequeathed land. April 17, 1797. William Kidd, John White, Henry White, Test.

WHYTE, JOHN—Folio 127—To loving daughter and son-in-law William and Mary Jones, 200 acres on Broad river, orig. grant to Henry Duncan. Deed of gift. Dec. 29, 1797. Reuben Whyte, Test.

WHYTE, JOHN—Folio 132—To loving son Reuben Whyte, 287½ acres in Franklin Co., on Little's creek, orig. grant to Lewis McLean of Wilkes Co., William Jones, Test. Dec. 29, 1797.

WIMBISH, ALEX., and wife Frances Scott Wimbish—Folio 131—of Abbeville Co. S. C., To Jos. Bond., 419 acres on Carters Fork of Beaverdam creek. Dec. 29, 1797. Nathan Bond, Test.

WELLS, DAVID—Folio 102—of Franklin Co., by his Atty, Samuel Sewell, To Andrew Brown of Elbert Co., land on Cedar creek orig. grant 1785 to David Wells. June 17, 1796. Elias Baker, Benj. Baker, Henry Sewell, Test.

YOUNG, LEMUEL—Folio 38—of Richmond Co., To James Ware of Lincoln Co., 200 acres on Beaverdam creek, granted 1784. Jan. 6, 1797. Chas. Tait, A. Colson, Edmond Lyon, Test.

Land Court Records, 1791-1822

EXPLANATORY

There was passed at Savannah on the 7th, of June 1777, "An Act for opening a land office and for the better settling and strengtheining this State".

Headrights and bounty warrants were issued during the Revolution by the Executive Council, and the grants signed by the Governor. Land courts were established later in the counties and the Justices of the Peace were Commissioners to issue warrants. Many of these were no doubt bounty grants which had not been taken up, although no reference is made to this. Others were headrights, a single man being entitled to 100 acres, men of family to the same for themselves, and 50 acres each for wife and children. In some instances a grant of 50 acres was issued as children were born. Many of these warrants were sold by the grantees which explains certain men taking up large tracts.

Feb. 7, 1791—Thomas Cook 200 acres in lieu of an old warrant Wilkes Co. (in name) Peter Wyche.
William Bibb, 1000 acres in lieu of an old warrant for Wilkes Co.
John Baker, 1100 acres in lieu of old warrant, Wilkes Co., one for 950 acres, one for 150 acres, in the name of Wm. Lowry.
Archebald Johnston 1000 acres in lieu of old warrant for Franklin Co., one in the name of James Finley, for 250 acres, one in the name of Anquish Johnston, 100 acres in name of James Shields, 100 acres in name of Donald McDonald, balance in name of Hugh McDonald. Issued to Hugh McDonald.
James Freeman in lieu of an old warrant 100 acres to be in the name of Hugh McDonald.
Francis Filps 200 acres in lieu of old warrant, Wilkes Co., to issue in the name of John Staples.
John Staples self and 4 in family.
Francis Higginbotham, 3 in family.
Jonathan Rossell, self and 2 in family
Bridger Haynie, self and 4 in family
Bridger Haynie, Jr., self and 4 in family
Eli Eavenson, self and 4 in family
George Wood, 1000 acres in lieu of old warrant for Franklin Co., to be issued to John Staples, Alexander and Hugh McDonald.
John Allbritton, self and 6 in family
Reuben Cook, 6 in family
Daniel Moulder, self and 8 in family
Leroy Upshaw, self and 15 in family

John Nelms, self.
William McCune, 400 acres in lieu of old warrant for Wilkes Co.
Richard Saunder, 114 acres of Brigg Haney headright.

April 4, 1791—Present, Richardson Hunt, Ralph Banks, and William Higginbotham, Esqrs.
Edward McGarry, 2 in family, Issued to L. Stowers.
John McGown, 3 in family.
Robert Shepard, old warrant 200 acres.
Thomas Cook, old warrant 240 acres.
Valentine Smith, old warrant 200 acres.
Charles Parks, old warrant 200 acres, 175 issued in name of Howard Cash.
Jesse Hendrick, self. William Howington, self and 3 in family
James Ready, self. Francis Satterwhite, 1 in family.
James Carter, 71 acres issued. Wm. Harbin, own and 71 acres.
James Spurlock, 1 in family. Robt. Marten, old warrant, 550 acres.
William Watkins, self and 9 in family. John Hall, self.
John Ferrill, 1 in family. Robt. Martin, self and 16 in family.
Samuel Hunter, 3 in family. William Elliott, 11 in family.
Nehemiah Williams, old warrant 200 acres.
Nehemiah Williams, old warrant 283 acres.
Middleton Woods, old warrant 315 acres.
Edmond Taylor, warrant of 1000 acres each, old warrant of R. Worsham, William Stubblefield and N. Coats.
Nimrod Long has four warrants in lieu of old warrant of Elijah Clarke, Sydnor Cosby, Benj. Cleveland and Wm. Edwards.

May 2, 1791—Ordered that Stephen Heard have a warrant for 800 acres in lieu of a grant dated 26th, Oct, 1784, by J. Houston for 800 acres including Budd's Island.
John Peterson Harper, self and 16 in family.
William Thompson, Jr. Jacob Hill, family.
Major Evens, self. Jos. Underwood, self and 5 in family
Stephen Haines, self. Jesse Hide, old warrant.
Wm. Thompson, Sr., old warrant. J. Matlock, 200 acres.
Wm. Thompson, Sr., 1500 acres two warrants.
Robert Fleming, self and 3 in family old warrant.
James Patton, 200 acres in lieu of old warrant, Jesse Hide.
Robert Middleton, 200 acres old warrant, B. Voden
James Tait, 445 acres old warrant of Warren Philpot, Robert Middleton.
James Tait, 838 acres, old warrant of his own, John Sandidge and Robert Middleton.

June 6, 1791—Present, Richardson Hunt, Ralph Banks, Wm. Higginbotham, Esqrs.
Robert Pulliam, 4 in family. Robt. Middleton, self and 7
Wm. Hightower, 45 acres. A. Heard, 115 acres
Jesse Ross, 156 acres. Henry G. Walker, self.
Elijah Alcorn, self, issue to William Hall.

GEORGIA D. A. R.

William Hall, 3 in family carried to Jan. 1793.
Peter Brown, 5 in family.   Ben Davis, 2000 acres.
Mordecai Shackleford, old warrant 200 acres.
John Crosby, old warrant 522 acres.
William Fergus, old warrant 400 acres, Jo. Fergus.
Robert and Silas McCredy, old warrant 200 acres, Jo. Rogers.
John Akin, 4 in family, to issue in the name of Jacob Akin.
John Greenwood, Jr., self, to issue to John Sr.
John Greenwood, Sr., old warrant 350 acres, and two to issue in his own name.
Moses Fleming, self and 1 in family.
John Fleming, Sr., 600 acres in lieu of old warrant, Jean Carew, John Sandidge and James Tate.

July 4, 1791—Present, Richardson Hunt, Reuben Allen, Thos. Scott, Esqrs.
John Shackleford in lieu of old warrant.
Right Nicholson, 200 acres.
William Pitchford in lieu of old warrant of 200 acres.
John Gill, in lieu of old warrant.
John Terrell, 1 in family.   James McCleskey, 1 in family.

Sept. 5, 1791—Present, Wm. Barnett, Ralph Banks, Frank Cook, Esqrs.
John Henderson, himself.   Robt. Henderson, himself.
Thos. Gilmer, self and 14.   Thos. Akin, 2 old warrants
Richardson Hunt, 6 old warrants of Wm. Tidwell.
John Collins, self to issue in name of Alex. Steward.
John Turke, 2 in family.   John Bray, self and old warrant.
John Coleman, 1 in family.   Conrod Aderhold, self.
Thomas Hilley, 2 in family.   Nathaniel Allen, old warrant.
David Franklin, 100 acres to be renewed.
John Ryal, 200 acres to be renewed.
Drury Ross, old warrant 200 acres.   Fleming Greenwood, self.
Stephen Westbrook, 114 acres in lieu of old warrant of William Thompson.
A. Stinchcomb, 20 acres on R. Hunt family headrights.
Thomas Lovelady, 200 acres in lieu of old warrant, Jos. Long.
Gilbert Bardin, 250 acres in lieu of old warrant of John P. Harper.

Oct. 3, 1791—Present, Wm. Barnett, Richardson Hunt, Wm. Higginbotham, Esqrs.
Robert McFarlin, self and 2 in family,
Drury Ross, 2 in family.   James Hanna, 1 in family.
John Hodge, 200 acres to be renewed.
John McDowell, 200 acres issued, 100 acres to be renewed.
George Dardin, 225 acres in lieu of old warrant of John McKenzie for 250 acres.
Jesse Brawner, 100 acres in lieu of old warrant of Mary Smith.
Jesse Brawner, 85 acres in lieu of old warrant of Wm. Howington.
Isaiah Hambleton, 1 in family.   Reuben Allen, 5 in family.

Nehemiah Williams, 2 in family.   David Nelson, self and 3.
J. Nail, 150 acres.   G. Davis, 120 acres.
John Robertson, 200 acres in the name of C. Clark, Jr.
James Spurlock, old warrant 50 acres issued to V. Smith.
Jasper Smith, 150 acres in lieu of old warrant of Samuel Hunter.
Daniel Shaw, 305 acres in lieu of old warrant of Thos. Thornton.
Absolom Davis, 100 acres to issue in name of Jos. T. Davis.
Wiley Davis, old warrant, 50 acres to be recorded in name of Absolom Davis, Sr.

Feb. 6, 1792—Land Court held at Court House—Present, R. Hunt, Wm. Higginbotham, Francis Cook, Esqrs.
Wm. Winn, self and 16 in family.   Geo. Wyche, self.
John Thomason, 4 in family.   Peter Wyche, self and 7
William Smith, old warrant rend. Esaias Harbour.
Wm. Lowry, John Baker, Jr., Rachel Baker, all to issue to John Baker, Sr.
Francis Batey, self and 3 in family.
Benjamin Davis, to be charged to Ferrell.
William Hall, 100 acres, 44 to James Glass.
William Harbin, 150 acres own and family.
Thomas Silman, 450 acres old warrant.

Mar. 5, 1792—Land Court held at Court House—Present, R. Hunt, Wm. Higginbotham, M. Woods, Esqrs.
James Reily, self and 7 in family.
Thomas Bryan, self and 4 in family.
James McDonald, 300 acres to be recorded for Woods, 100 acres to James Little, 150 acres to B. Baker.
John Speers, 100 acres in lieu of J. Smith.
David McCleskey, 200 acres in lieu of warrant of Barnes Strickland.
Samuel Higginbotham, 330 acres in lieu of old warrant of Francis Satterwhite.

May 7, 1792—Land Court held at the Court House—Present, R. Hunt, Francis Cook, M. Woods, Esqrs.
Nicholas Sewell, self to issue to William Sewell.
William Brown, old warrant.
William Hightower, 8 in family.
John Palmer, 1 in family   John Pollard, 1 in family.
Heirs of James Colbert, old warrant 400 acres.
Benjamin Baker, 150 acres in lieu of old warrant of James McDonald.
Two old warrants one for 287½ acres in name of James Freeman, 200 acres in name of Joel Thomas to be issued to E. McGarry.
Ledford Parrott, 12 acres in lieu of part of R. Hunt's headright.
John Royal, 200 acres to be renewed in name of E. Clarke.

June 2, 1792—Same Esqrs.
Jacob Myers to have warrant for 100 acres in lieu of one lost.

Christopher Mooney, self and 4 in family.
John Smith, 2 in family.

Aug. 6, 1792—Present—Wm. Higginbotham, Francis Cook, M. Woods, Esqrs.
Absolom Jourdan, 8 in family.   Jeremiah Terrell, 9 in family.
Absolom Stinchcomb, 1 for R. Hunt.
John Lowery, self and 3 in family, 250 acres to issue to J. Fulgum.
Michael Fry, self, 100 acres to issue
James Means, self, 100 acres to issue.
Luke Hambleton, old warrant, 100 acres.
Jeremiah Terrell, 650 acres in lieu of an old warrant.
John McCann, 315 acres old warrant.

Oct. 1, 1792—Present, Thos. B. Scott, Wm. Moss, M. Woods, Esqrs.
James Maxwell, self.
Thomas Maxwell, 2 in family to issue in the name of James.
John Sigmon, 450 acres, old warrant.
John Fergus, old warrant, 500 acres.   John Rogers, 275 acres.
Patrick Murdock, 290 acres to bear date of today when issued.
Robert Martin, old warrant 550 acres to be renewed.
John Prewet, 335 acres, old warrant, 267 to issue to David Nelms.
William Hall, 100 acres old warrant to be renewed in name of James Hanna.   John Baker, Sr., 30 acres on headright of R. Hunt.

Jan. 7, 1793—Present, R. Hunt, Wm. Higginbotham, Francis Cook, Esqrs.
William Bennett, self and 6 in family.
James Butler, 5 in family to issue to C. Wilkins.
Thomas Lovelady, 4 in family to issue to Joseph Long.
Robert Brown, three warrants, 400, 450, 200 acres, three of his family and headright.   Benjamin Cook, 500 acres old warrant.
Moses Davis, self and 4 in family, to issue in name of Robert Brown.
Archibald Burden, 60 acres on Hunt headright.
Benjamin Cook 200 acres in lieu of old warrant, A. Davis.
Robert Martin, 550 acres renewed to Peter Martin.
William Hall, 350 acres.
Benjamin Cook 300 acres in part of an old warrant for 500 acres.

Mar. 4, 1793—Present, Richardson Hunt, Francis Cook, and James McCleskey, Esqrs.
Samuel Morgan, self and 9 in family.
David Porterfield, self.   James Lowry, 200 acres renewed.
John Barnett, 1000 acres, 200 issued.

April 1, 1793—Present, R. Hunt, F. Cook, M. Woods, Esqrs.
Allegany McGuire, 3 in family, to issue to Thompson McGuire.
James Wood, self to issue to S. Epperson.
John Rogers, 275 acres on part of John Fergus.
Jesse Ginn, 283 acres in lieu of N. Williams.
Armstrong Heard, 43½ acres in lieu of Robt. Middleton's headright, "Bob to pay".   John P. Harper, 107 acres.

HISTORICAL COLLECTIONS 219

Moses Fleming, 600 acres old grant of John Fleming and Hugh McDonald.

May 6, 1793—Present, R. Hunt, F. Cook, W. Higginbotham, Esqrs.
Gerrard Walthall, Sr., self, 100 acres to issue, balance issued Thomas B. Creagh.
John Glover, 1 in family, Francis Cook, 2 in family, to John Glover.
Heirs of James Carter on the affidavit of Richardson Hunt, 450 acres.
Nehemiah Williams, 200 acres to be renewed in the name of Thomas Maxwell.

June 3, 1793—Present, R. Hunt, F. Cook, M. Woods, Esqrs.
Joseph Underwood, old warrant 138 acres renewed.
Peter Stubbs, 4 in family.

Aug. 5, 1793—Same Esqrs.
Rice Cleveland, 1 in family. Turner Christian, self.
Thomas Penn, old warrant 498 acres.

Sept. 2, 1793—Present, R. Hunt, Wm. Higginbotham, F. Cook, Esqrs.
Warren Sto, self 100 acres to issue to Joel Miller.
John Clarkson, 100 acres. Joseph Long, 200 acres.
Samuel Epperson, 200 acres.

Oct. 7, 1793—Present, R. Hunt, John Fergus, M. Woods, Esqrs.
Patrick Murdock, 4 in family, old warrant of 200 acres.
Charles Sarr (?) 4 in family.
Alex. Stewart, 200 acres to be renewed to Thos. Lovelady.

Dec. 2, 1793—Present, James McCleskey, Francis Cook, M. Woods, Esqrs.
Thomas Bryant, old warrant.
Jesse Ross, 115 acres on Robert Middleton's headright.
John Shackleford, Sr., 33 acres on Robert Middleton's headright.
James Alston, 24 acres on R. Allen's headright

April 7, 1794—Present, R. Hunt, F. Cook, John Fergus, Esqrs.
John Hawthorn, self and 8 in family to issue to A. Forbes.
A. Forbes, self, all to issue in his own name.
John Fergus, 4 in family, 100 acres to issue to J. Tuttle, Sr.
James Hawthorn, self and 8 in family, to issue to A. Forbes.
Jesse Baker, 8 in family to issue to J. Baker, Sr.
William Harbin, 350 acres in lieu of old warrant and part of his headright. John Dardin, 431 acres, old warrant.

May 5, 1794—Present., James McCleskey, Thos. Cook, M. Woods, Esqrs.
Burwell Morris, self. Flemin Burk, 3 in family.
Allegany McGuire, 240 acres. Thompson McGuire, 250 acres.

June 2, 1794—Present, R. Hunt, Francis Cook, M. Woods, Esqrs.
James Leeper, 2 in family. Fleming Burke, self.
Daniel White, 250 acres. D. Nelms, 250 acres.
John Nelms, 250 acres.

GEORGIA D. A. R.

July 7, 1794—Present, R. Hunt, S. Higginbotham, F. Cook, Esqrs.
John Williams, self, Lee Guthrie, self 100 acres, Robert Guthrie, 2 in family, all to issue to Robt. Guthrie.
John Gill, old warrant 600 acres, 316 issued to J. Bell.
Joseph Davis, 126 acres issued A. Davis, Sr.
Jeremiah Terrell, 650 acres, renewed.
Burrell Morris, 200 acres old warrant 6 and 7 issued to H. Still.

Oct. 6, 1794—Present, R. Hunt, F. Cook, John Fergus, Esqrs.
William Cohorn, 300 acres old warrant renewed.
Peercon Duncan, self, 155 acres issued balance carried to Jan. 1809.
M. Shackleford, renewed.
H. Rose, old warrant, renewed.   D. Porterfield, old warrant
125 acres issued to Jesse Baker.

Nov. 3, 1794—Present, Francis Cook, James McCleskey, S. Higginbotham, Esqrs.
Samuel Kaar, self, 16½ acres.
Thos. B. Creagh, 100 acres part of G. Walthall's headright.
Thos. Gilmer, 900 acres, 300 issued to William Oliver, 600 to B_____

Dec. 1, 1794—Present, R. Hunt, James McCleskey, M. Woods, Esqrs.
John Blake, 3 old warrants, 100 acres renewed.
Heirs of Isham Stroud, 250 acres.
William Moss, headright, proven 1792.
Thomas Carter, 200 acres renewed to R. Hunt.
Thomas Watts, 200 acres old warrant renewed to G. Turman.
John Clarkson, old warrant and part of headright.
W. Richardson, 1330 acres, lost.   James Little, 100 acres, lost.
William Turman, 200 acres renewed to Garrett Turman.
Heirs of James Colbert, 400 acres duplicate.

April 6, 1795—Present, R. Hunt, F. Cook, Thomas Cook, Esqrs.
Samuel Nelson, 2 in family.   S. Nelson, 100 acres.
John Albritton, 200 acres on his own headright.
John Hall, 200 acres old warrant renewed.

July 6, 1795—Present, same Esqrs.
Robert Kennedy, 3 in family and part of a certificate of 62 acres, 200 acres issued to Francis Baty.
John Camron, self and 2 to John Fargus.

Aug. 3, 1795—Present, R. Hunt, S. Higginbotham, Francis Cook, James McCleskey, Esqrs.
Joseph McConnell, self and 6, 400 acres to issue to John Fergus, 100 to John McConnell.   Ab. Trentham, self, 74 acres
William Aycock, self, 50 acres.

Sept. 7, 1795—Present, R. Hunt, F. Cook, M. Woods, Esqrs.
Luke White, self and 7 in family.   David White, self and 9.
John Pollard, old warrant renewed.

Oct. 5, 1795—Present, Wm. Barnett, R. Hunt, M. Woods, Esqrs.
  Jesse Ginn, self and 4 in family. Thos. Maxwell, self and 3.
  John M. Whitney, 5 in family. James Dudley, self.
  William Elliott, old warrant, 550 acres.
  Nicholas Long, 800 acres.

Nov. 2, 1795—Leonard Rice, 5 in family, Wm. Teasley, 4 in family.
  Richard Kain, old warrant renewed.

Jan. 7, 1796—Present, S. Higginbotham, Thos. B. Scott, M. Woods, Esqrs.
  Joshua McConnell, self and 2 in family.
  James Brock, self and 8 in family. James Brown, self.
  Julius Crisler, 1 in family. James Maxwell, 300 acres.

Mar. 7, 1796—Present, R. Hunt, J. McCleskey, M. Woods, Esqrs.
  James Sutten, 2 in family. Joseph Rucker, 1 in family.
  Wm. Oliver, self and 9 in family. W. H. Tuttle, 2 in family.

April 4, 1796—Present, R. Hunt, F. Cook, M. Woods, Esqrs.
  John Rucker, self. John Patterson, 2 in family.
  Rosannh Cain, old warrant renewed 200 acres.
  Ruth Cain, old warrant renewed 200 acres.

July 4, 1796—Present, F. Cook, Wm. Higginbotham, R. Middleton, Esqrs.
  Wm. Whaley, self and 5 in family. James Ware, 20 in family
  Wm. Payton, 2 in family. L. Davis, self and 4 in family.
  James Crow, 1 in family. Samuel Patton, 2 in family.
  Robert Fleming, old warrant 500 acres.

Sept. 5, 1796—Present, R. Hunt, F. Cook, M. Woods, Esqrs.
  William Thompson, Jr., old warrant 350 acres to William, Sr.
  Arthur Forbes, 2 old warrants
  Turner Christian, 12 in family. David Neil, self and 1 in family.
  Frederick Hart, self and 4 in family.
  John Conyers, self and one in family, on the affidavit of John Fergus
    that he lost a warrant of Francis Baty of 250 acres.
  William Dudlie, 7 in family. Jesse Statham, self and 4 in family.

Oct. 3, 1796—Present, Edward Goode, R. Hunt, F. Cook, Esqrs.
  Stephen Groves, self, 2 warrants. Henry Gragg, self.
  Matthew McRight, self. James Banks, self and 10 in family.

Nov. 7, 1796—Present, F. Cook, R. Middleton, M. Woods, Esqrs.
  John Duncan, self. William Fergus, self and 8 in family.
  Jacob Higginbotham, old warrant 400 acres renewed.

Jan. 2, 1797—Present. Wm. Higginbotham, Thos. Cook, Wm. Hightower,
    Esqrs.
  Alegany McGuire, 4 and old warrant on R. Hunt.
  Joshua Underwood, self and 10 in family.
  R. Hunt, 1 in family. Jacob Watkins, self and 4 in family
  Joshua McConnell, self. Garrett Turman, 9 in family.

GEORGIA D. A. R.

Feb. 6, 1797—Present, R. Hunt, Francis Cook, Thos. Cook, Esqrs.
Joel Miller, 3 in family.   Isaac Morris, self.
Julian Nail, old warrant 120 acres.

Mar. 6, 1797—Present, Wm. Barnett, Wm. Higginbotham, M. Woods, Esqrs.
William Hemphill, self, 166 acres.   John Depriest, 1 in family.
Joshua Underwood, 220 acres.

Mar. 3, 1797—Present, R. Hunt, Wm. Higginbotham, Barnabas Pace, Esqrs.
Thos. Maxwell, self and 10 in family.   Quinton Shannon, self and 2.
Edward Ishams, old warrant, 400 acres.

May 1, 1797—Present, J. Cunningham, F. Cook, M. Woods, Esqrs.
Robt. Shepperd, 1 in family.   James Mann, 1 in family.
Archelaus Walker, self   Thos. Lovelady, 4 in family.
John Smith, old warrant 200 acres.

June 5, 1797—Present, J. Cunningham, F. Cook, M. Woods, Esqrs.
Wm. Oliver, 16 acres to issue on his own headright proven Mar. 1796.
John Cunningham, self and 7 in family. William H. Tait, self. Bridger Haynie, Sr., 135 acres proven Feb. 1791. Robt. Guthrie, old warrant 400 acres. John Blake, 100 acres proven Dec. '94. Leroy Pope, old warrant. Hugh McDonald, 1000 acres old warrant.

July 3, 1797—Present, S. Higginbotham, Joseph Rucker, M. Woods, Esqrs.
Thomas C. Russell, 16 in family.

Aug. 7, 1797—Present, R. Hunt, John Cunningham, R. Lindsay, Esqrs.
Thompson McGuire, self. John Taylor, self and 4 in family. John Cunningham, 200 acres renewed. Joshua Underwood, 2 old warrants renewed.

Sept. 4, 1797—Present, James Bell, Wm. Hightower, J. P. Harper, Esqrs.
William Cade, self and 6 in family.   F. Phinizy, 1 in family.
Wm. Fergus, self and 8, renewed from Nov. '96.

Oct. 2, 1797—Present, R. Hunt, S. Higginbotham, Wm. Hightower, Esqrs.
Paschal Borders, self.   John Bonds, self.
Jesse Rowell, 100 acres.   John Beck, one of his family.

Nov. 6, 1797—Present, Wm. Higginbotham, Edwd. Goode, Jonathan Farr, Esqrs.
Stephen Bradberry, self.

Dec. 4, 1797—Present, R. Hunt, S. Higginbotham, Reuben Lindsay, Esqrs.
Samuel Speers, self and 2 in family.   Robt. Corithers, 5 in family.
John Maxwell, self and 1 in family.
A. Stinchcomb, old warrant renewed.

Jan. 1, 1798—Present, R. Hunt, S. Higginbotham, Wm. Hightower, Esqrs.
John Cook, self and 4 in family.   Benj. Baker, 3 in family.
William Harbin, 3 in family. On petition of James Colbert, Jr. warrant issued to heirs of James Colbert, dec'd.

Mar. 5, 1798—Present, Wm. Higginbotham, Nathaniel Hudson, John P. Harper, William Allen, Esqrs.
Bazil Brawner, old warrant, 1 family headright.
Abner Ponder, 4 in family.   Avros (?) Ham, 1 in family.
Turner Christian, old warrant 600 acres.
Moses Haynes, self.   William S. Burch, one in family.
A. Trantham, 100 acres from Aug. '95. Thomas Maxwell, old warrent 350 acres.   Henry Gatewood, self and 5 in family.

April 2, 1798—Present, S. Higginbotham, Wm. Higginbotham, William Allen, Esqrs.
Samuel Clark, self.   Christopher Harris, self and 6 in family.
John Andrew, old warrant 954 acres.
Christopher Clark, Sr., old warrant 400 acres renewed.

June 4, 1798—Present, S. Higginbotham, Moses Haynes, James Ware, Esqrs.
John Scales, self and 11.   Eliab Vinson, self and 6.
Jeremiah Fowler, self and 7.   Thos. Scales, self and 13.
William Shelton, self and 6.   Robt. Smith, self and 5.
William Brawner, not self but 1.   Moses. Haynes, self and 16.
Hezekiah Gray instead of Moses Haynes.
Hugh McDonald, not self but 7.

July 2, 1798—Present, Nathaniel Hudson, Jos. Rucker, John Staples, Esqrs.
Quinton Shannon, 2 in family.   Thos. Williford, self.
William Thompson, Jr., 150 acres old warrant.

Sept. 3, 1798—Present, Ralph Banks, Nathaniel Hudson, John Staples, Esqrs.
John Mason, 2 in family.   Benjamin Burton, self.
Reuben Allen, 130 acres from Jan. '92.

Nov. 5, 1798—Present, Wm. Hightower, John Coleman, Nathaniel Hudson, Esqrs.
Timothy Saxon, self and 6 in family.   Wm. K. Floyd, self.
John Vineyard, self and 2 in family.   Ephrain Beasley, self.
H. G. Walker, 100 acres from '91.   Robert Cosby, self.

Dec. 3, 1798—Present, Wm. Higginbotham, John P. Harper, Hezekiah Gray, Esqrs.
James Sutten, 5 in family.   Robert Cade, 2 in family.
James Hanna, 1 in family.   Henry Harper, self.
Wm. Howington, 180 acres old warrant.
Timothy Saxon, old warrant, 300 acres.
James Sutten, 2 old warrants.
John Rucker, old warrant 75 acres.

Jan. 7, 1799—Present, R. Hunt, A. Stinchcomb, N. Hudson, Esqrs.
Leroy Pace, self and 2 in family.   Samuel Self, self and 2.
Moses Webster, self.   Joshua McConnell, old warrant.
Robert Middleton, 156 acres, family.

Mar. 4, 1799—Present, John P. Harper, John Staples, Jos. Rucker, Esqrs.
Newell McConnell, 2 in family. Sherod Morris, 1 in family.
John McCleary, self and 5 in family. John Decker, 1 in family.
Benj. Higginbotham, 1 in family. Wm. Burden, self and 1 in family.
Thos. Oliver, self and 1 in family. Richard Kain, old warrant renewed.

April 1, 1799—Present, James Banks, James Shields, Moses Haynes, Esqrs.
Wm. Haynes, self, 50 acres. Edward Denny, self and 8 in family.
Elijah Alcorn, 4 and 200 acres part of old warrant.
Oliver Rock, self and 6 in family. John Patterson, 1 in family.
Moses Fleming, 50 acres from 1791.

June 3, 1799—Present, Richardson Hunt, Samuel Higginbotham, Hugh McDonald, Esqrs.
Francis Powell, self and 13 in family. Wm. Adams, self and 8.
John McMullen, self and 12 in family.
David Crawford, self and 4 in family.
James Vineyard, five in family.
Andrew McEaver, self 4 in family.
Pleasant Statham, self and 1 in family.
John Decker, certificate of surveyor on family rights.

July 1, 1799—Present, R. Hunt, James Shields, John P. Harper, A. Stinchcomb, Esqrs.
James Burden, self. William Smithwick, self and 2 in family.
Nathaniel Booth, self and 2 in family.
Samuel Speers, 8 in family. Eli Eavenson, self, brought Feb. 1791.
Edward Denny, 17½ acres on county Surveyors Certf.

Aug. 5, 1799—Present, R. Hunt, S. Higginbotham, Thos. Cook, Esqrs.
Thos. Gregg, 1 in family. Wm. Whaley, cert. for 113 acres.
William Adams, self and 8 from June '99.

Sept. 2, 1799—Present, Thos. Fortson, Thos. Cook, R. Hunt, Esqrs.
Ambrose Ham, to include an old warrant of his own.
John Blake, 1 in family.
Thomas Ridgway, his own and six of his family.

Oct. 7, 1799—Present, Wm. Barnett, Wm. Higginbotham, N. Hudson, Esqrs.
Robert Cowden, 3 in family.

Jan. 6, 1800—Present, S. Higginbotham, Wm. Higginbotham, Thos. Fortson, Esqrs.
Robert Black, self and 6 in family. Andrew Millican, self.
Thos. Price, self and 11 in family. Samuel Eakin, 6 in family.
Samuel Shepperd, self and 3 in family. Wm. Guy, 2 in family.
Samuel Runnolds, self and 6 in family.
Ephraim Moss, self and 7 in family.

Mar. 3, 1800—Present, R. Hunt, S. Higginbotham, Joseph Rucker, Esqrs.
Darvin Harris, self and 6 in family.
John Kennedy, self and 10 in family.

HISTORICAL COLLECTIONS

William Singleton, self and 2 in family.
Henry Gaines, 1 in family.   Ector Thacker, self and 2 in family.
Thomas Silmon, old warrant from 1792.

April 7, 1800—Present, R. Hunt, Wm. Higginbotham, James Banks, Esqrs.
Daniel Tucker, self and 5 in family. Thos. Tait, self and 13.
James Banks, 200 acres brought from Oct. '96.
Joannah Wells, old warrant.

June 2, 1800—Present, Richn. Hunt, Wm. Higginbotham, Thomas Fortson, Esqrs.
Chas. Tait, self and 9 in family.   William Oliver, 3 and old warrant.

Aug. 4, 1800—Present Same Esqrs.
John A. Ragland, self and 16 in family.   Milly Davis, self.
Nathias Taylor, self.

Aug. 8, 1800—Present, R. Hunt, Thos. Fortson, Jno. Carrell, Esqrs.
James Allen, hisself, 200 acres. Benj. Brown, two family, 100 acres.
Edward L. Wailes, self and 9, 650 acres.
Samuel Paxton, self and 2, 300 acres.

Dec. 1, 1800—Present, R. Hunt, R. Banks, Wm. Higginbotham, Esqrs.
Samuel Runnolds, 300 acres.   Eli. Eavenson, old warrant, 200 acres.
Elijah Alcorn, 1 and old warrant 400 acres.
Joshua Gross, self and 7 in family.

Jan. 5, 1801—Present, Wm. Barnett, S. Higginbotham, Wm. Higginbotham, Esqrs.
Isom Morgan, 1 in family.   James Colbert, self.
Daniel Thornton, self and 5 in family.   Thos. Lane, self.
James Riley, brought from Mar. '92, 300 acres.
Hugh McDonald, 2, brought from June '98.
Stephen Heard, 2 carried to Sept. 1808.
Affidavit of Robert Smith that he lost a land warrant for 450 acres.
   Prays that it be renewed, and include an addition to his family.

Feb. 2, 1801—Present, R. Hunt, S. Higginbotham, Thos. Fortson, Esqrs.
Beverly Greenwood, self.   Jesse Mann, 1 in family.
Thomas Johnson, self and 13 in family.

Mar. 2, 1801—Garrett Turman, 6 in family. Fodrick Crowder, self and 8
Samuel Bently, Jr., self and 2.   William Cross, self and 3.
James Rhoads, self and 2.   David Allen, self.
William Holt, self and 8.   Wm. Means, 5 in family.
Thomas Gregg, 1 in family.   William Perkins, self.

April 6, 1801—Present, R. Hunt, S. Higginbotham, Nathaniel Hudson, Esqrs.
William Means 2 and old warrant.   Geo. Darden, Sr., 1.
Nathaniel Hall, self.

June 1, 1801—Present, R. Hunt, Thomas Fortson, Esqrs.
Daniel Parker, 4 in family. Archer Skinner, 7 in family.
Garrett Turman, 6, old warrant 250 acres.

July 6, 1801—Present, R. Hunt, S. Higginbotham, Thos. Fortson, Esqrs.
John Hubbard, 5 in family.

Aug. 3, 1801—Present, John Cunningham, Thomas Fortson, James Alston.
Hezekiah Gray, 1 in family. Noah Cloud, 1 in family.
Samuel Eakin, brought from Jan. 1800.
E. McGarry, old warrant 400 acres.

Oct. 5, 1801—Present, Leroy Pope, James Shields, A. Jarratt, Esqrs.
James Brock, self and 2 in family. William Mason, 3 in family.
Nathan Willeford, 8 in family.

Jan. 14, 1802—Present, Thos. Fortson, A. Jarrett, Wm. Higginbotham, Esqrs.
Thos. Story, self and 1 in family. A. Stinchcomb, 1 in family.
James Griffith, self and 9 in family.
Aron Stinchcomb, self. W. Blankenship, self and 4 in family.

Mar. 1, 1802—Present, Wm. Hightower, Thos. Fortson, James Alston, Esqrs.
Gabriel Tucker, self. Wm. Brown, 9 in family.
Sherod Morris, self. James Sewell, 2 in family.
William Post, 1 in family. James Hannah, old warrant renewed.

May 3, 1802—Present, R. Hunt, S. Higginbotham, James Alston, Esqrs.
David Graham, self and 5. A. Richardson, self and 4.
Thomas Hooker, self and 1.

July 5, 1802—Present, Thomas Fortson, James Alston, James Christian, Esqrs.
George Fits Gerrald, self. Geo. Eberhart, self and 8, 300 acres.
Bridger Haynie, old warrant 75 acres.

Sept. 5, 1803—Present, R. Hunt, R. T. Cosby, James Christian, Esqrs.
Roland Brown, self, 200 acres. Benj. Nail, self 100 acres.

Oct. 3, 1803—Present, Allen Daniel, Elijah Owens, Chas, Sowell, Esqrs.
Wm. McKie, 9 in family. Chas Gunter, self and 2 in family.
A. Stinchcomb, 2 in family. A. Daniel, self and 2 in family.
Elizabeth Riley, self. Barnaby Stricklan, 5 in family.

Jan. 2, 1804—Present, Thos. Cook, Wm. H. Tait, H. Gray, Esqrs.
Robt. Lowrymore, 2 in family. Luke White, 1 in family.
John Norman, self and 9 in family. Lewis Mosely, self and 1.
Jacob Slack, old warrant 600 acres renewed.
Andrew McEaver, old warrant 400 acres renewed.
Edward McGarry, 50 acres old warrant.
Henry Gatewood, 2 old warrants 300 acres.

Feb. 6, 1804—Present, Wm. Hightower, James Alston, R. T. Crosby, Esqrs.
Benj. Higginbotham, 16 in family. Reuben Jones, self and 7.

Thos. Dula (Dooly) self and 11. Thos. James, self and 6.
William Dula, self and 1. Robt. B. Christian, self and 5.
Joshua Carpenter, self and 7.

Mar. 5, 1804—Present, R. Hunt, J. Alston, H. McDonald, Esqrs.
William Bradberry, self and 8. William Gaines, 6, in family.
Stephen Suttles, self and 2.
H. McDonald, certificate from Surveyor.
Hugh McDonald, 450 acres old warrant on J. Terrell's headright transferred back to the original.
John Cunningham, old warrant 200 acres.

July 2, 1804—Present, Wm. Barnett, Reuben Lindsay, R. Hunt, Esqrs.
John Maxwell, 1, also warrant 250 acres. John Coil, 2.
Francis Higginbotham, old warrant.

Aug. 6, 1804—Present, Reuben Lindsay, A. Jarrett, R. Kennedy, Esqrs.
Isaac Coker, self and 4 in family.

Oct. 1, 1804—Present, James Alston, R. Banks, A. Stinchcomb, Esqrs.
Thos. Burton, 4 in family. John Brawner, 4 in family.
Thomas Story old warrant 250 acres.

Dec. 3, 1804—Present, A. Stinchcomb, R. Kennedy, R. Lindsay, Esqrs.
William Stewart, self.

Jan. 7, 1805—Present, John Johnson, N. Hudson, Thomas Cook, Esqrs.
Lewis Phipps, self and 2 in family.
William McCoy, self and 5 in family.
Reuben Christian, self and 4 in family.
Enoch James, Jr., 5 in family.
Allen Daniel's affidavit that he had lost a warrant, ordered to obtain a duplicate.

Feb. 4, 1805—Present, R. Lindsay, R. Hunt, J. S. Higginbotham, Esqrs.
Thos. Haynes, self and 3 in family. James Shields, 5 in family.
Archibald Newman, self and 1 in family.
William Bowers, self and 2 in family.
Luke White, 4 in family, two old warrants.

Apr. 1, 1805—Present, R. Hunt, R. Lindsay, James Christian, Esqrs.
Charles Willeford, self.

July 1, 1805—Present, R. Hunt, Thomas Cook, W. Hightower, Esqrs.
Joseph Blackwell, 1 in family. Robert Jones, self.

Nov. 4, 1805—Present, Thos. Cook, A. Stinchcomb, N. Hudson, Esqrs.
John Carrell, self. Arthur Elliott, 6 in family.
Joseph Neal, self and 1 in family.

Feb. 3, 1806—Present, R. Lindsay, Thos. Cook, Wm. Hightower, Esqrs.
Siah Hendrick, self and 6 in family.

GEORGIA D. A. R.

Aug. 4, 1806—Present, R. Hunt, James Christian, B. Jeter, Esqrs.
Abner Jordon, self.   Benjamin Wilson, self and 4 in family.

Sept. 1, 1806—Present, Allen Daniel, A. Jarrett, Wm. Hightower, Esqrs.
Joseph Nix, self and 3 in family.   Joseph Stephens, Jr., self.
Stephen Suttle, self and 3 in family.

Oct. 6, 1806—Present, Samuel Patton, Ro. Kennedy, Robert B. Christian, Esqrs.
Turner Drake, self and 5 in family.   Samuel Groves, self.
Robert Groves, self.

Nov. 3, 1806—Present, A. Jarratt, W. Nunnelee, Samuel Paxton, Esqrs.
A warrant for 50 acres in favor of Benjamin Davis, dec'd. passed July 5, 1802 in favor of his heirs, having been lost, a duplicate issued.

Dec. 1, 1806—Present, Wm. Hightower, Rn. White, N. Hudson, Esqrs.
Howard Cash, self and 5 in family.
Micajah Anthony, self and 12 in family.
George Stovall, 1 in family.
A. Skinner, 1 in family, lost warrant established.

Jan. 5, 1807—Present, Thos. Cook, N. Hudson, John Carrel, Esqrs.
John Stone, self, 100 acres issues.

Feb. 2, 1807—Present, R. Hunt, R. Lindsay, A. Jarratt, Esqrs.
Burrell Bobo, self and 1 in family.   Wm. Magee, self.
H. G. Walker, 550 acres on old warrant.
James Anglin, self and 3 in family.
Robert Baskin, self and 3 in family.
Zach. Hutchens, self and 3 in family.
Wm. Bowers, 300 acres on old warrant.

May 4, 1807—Present, R. Lindsay, Jas. F. Nunnelee, N. Hudson, Esqrs.
Gabriel Guthrie, self and 2 in family.

June 1, 1807—Present, Thos. Cook, J. P. Christian, Robt. B. Christian, Esqrs.
William Means, 1 of family renewed.   Sherwood Toney, self and 3 in family.   Thos Hopper, self and 2 in family.
James Pace, self and 5 in family.

July 6, 1807—Present, William Allen, B. Jeter, Dad Ewing, Esqrs.
James Dickson, self and 1 in family.
Micajah Anthony, balance of self and 12 of family.
Hugh McDonald, 5 in family.   John McDonald, self and 7 in family.
Anquish McCurry, self and 3 in family.

Sept. 7, 1807—Present, R. Hunt, J. Johnston, Jas. F. Nunnelee, Esqrs.
Robt. Kennedy, 6 in family.   Robt. Skelton, self and 5 in family.   Henry Bramblet, self and 8 in family.

Oct. 5, 1807—Present, A. Stinchcomb, N. Hudson, H. McDonald, Esqrs.
Jeremiah Fields, self and 5 in family.
Robert Middleton, 2 in family.   Robt. Moon, self and 11 in family.

Dec. 7, 1807—Present, R. Hunt, A. Stinchcomb, Ro. Kennedy, Esqrs.
Reuben Little, self and 6 in family. Stephen Carlton, self.

Jan. 4, 1808—Present, H. McDonald, John Carrell, M. Haynes, Esqrs.
Howard Cash, Jr., self. Jesse Cash, self and 2 in family.
Thos. Wheeler, self and 5 in family. Chas. Wheeler, self and 2 in family. Chas. Sorrells, self and 6 in family.
Chas. W. Christian, self and 1 in family.
Howard Cash, Sr., 50 acres, old warrant.
Robert Skelton, surveyors certificate, 350 acres.

Feb. 1, 1808—Present, Thos. Cook, B. Pace, R. Lindsay, Esqrs.
Reuben Ponder, self and 1 in family. James Jordan, self.
Thomas Haynes, 275 acres on old warrant.

Mar. 7, 1808—Present, A. Stinchcomb, Jas. F. Nunnelee, John Carrell, Esqrs.
William Ward, self. Richard Easter, self and 14 in family.
William Chisolm, self. Robert Bramblett, self and 4 in family.
Robert Rice, self. William Woods, self and 12 in family.
Voluntine Warren, 5 in family.

May 2, 1808—Present, R. Hunt, A. Stinchcomb, Wm. Allen, Esqrs.
Leonard Rice, 4 in family, 100 acres. Thos. Harbin, self.
Abraham Brown, self and 2 in family. John Harbin, self.
John Collett, self. Siah Kendrick, 100 acres on old warrant.
Amos Richardson, 100 acres on old warrant.
William Harbin, 150 acres on old warrant.
Joseph Nix, 200 acres, balance on headright Sept. 1806.

June 6, 1808—Present, R. Hunt, James Christian, Thos. Cook, Esqrs.
Thos. Nix, self and 9 in family. John Nix, self.
Michael Blackwell, self and 5 in family. John Brown, self.
William Page, self and 3 in family. Wm. Teasley, 4 in family.
Elias Hendrick, self and 1 in family. Jesse Ponder, self and 5 in family.
Elias Sanders, self and 1 in family.
Jonathan Payne, self and 2 in family.
Archd. Newborn, 100 acres on old warrant.

July 4, 1808—Present, Aln. Daniel, W. Nunnelee, A. Jarratt, Esqrs.
John Gates, self and 3 in family. Benj. Rogers, self and 3 in family.
Gabriel Tucker, 200 acres on old warrant.

April 1, 1808—Present, R. Hunt, H. McDonald, R. Lindsay, Esqrs.
Patrick McMullan, self and 15 in family.
Lewis Stowers, self and 13 in family.
Ambrose Dollar, self and 13 in family.
Rn. Bramblett, 300 acres from Mar. 1808.

Sept. 5, 1808—Present, Robt. Kennedy, Thos. Cook, R. Christian, J. R. Hunt, Esqrs.
Stephen Heard, 100 acres brought from Jan. 1801.
Thomas Cook, 5 in family.

GEORGIA D. A. R.

Oct. 3, 1808—Present, Allen Daniel, Barnett Jeter, Samuel Patton, Esqrs.
Isaac Cook, 200 acres old warrant, 200 acres from Aug. 1804.
Wm. Stephens, self and 2 in family.
Claiborn Reatherford, self and 7 in family.

Nov. 7, 1808—Present, Thos. Cook, A. Jarratt, J. F. Nunnelee, Walter Nunnelee, Esqrs.
Joseph Nix, self and 5 in family.   Robt. Childers, self.
James F. Nunnelee, 16 of his family.

Dec. 5, 1808—Present, R. Hunt, Jas. Christian, A. Stinchcomb, Thos. Cook, Esqrs.
John Franklin, self and 3 in family.
Wm. Redwine, self and 4 in family.
Peter Smith, self and 4 in family.
Hillery Hendrick, 5 in family.   Nimrod Hendrick, self.
Archibald Newbourn 2 in family.   Henry Sanders, 5 in family.

Jan. 2, 1809—Present, A. Jarratt, W. Nunnelee, Wm. Hatcher, Esqrs.
Thomas Burton, 1 old warrant renewed for 200 acres.
William Haley, 7 in family, 238 acres issued to your son R. Mar. 1810.
John Jordon, self and 3 in family.
Abraham Davis, self and 3 in family.
Peerson Duncan, 45 acres from Oct. 1794.

Feb. 6, 1809—Present, R. Hunt, Thos. Cook, Ro. Kennedy, Esqrs.
John Childs, self and 9 in family.   Thomas Maxwell, 2 in family.
William Ballenger, self and 4 in family.

Mar. 6, 1809—Present, Thos. Cook, A. Stinchcomb, John Jones, Esqrs.
John Daniel, 1 in family.   Thomas Cook, 6 in family.
Simeon Henderson, self and 1 in family.
Ordered John Blake have warrant for 46 acres, being a balance on a warrant Sept. 2, 1799.

April 3, 1809—Present, Thos. Cook, A. Stinchcomb, R. B. Christian, Jas. Christian.
Chas. W. Christian have a warrant for 120 acres due him on old warrant. Jan. 4, 1808.

May 1, 1809—Present, R. Hunt, Wm. Barnett, A. Jarratt, Esqrs.
John Childs, 8 in family.   Luke White, 1 in family.
Pleasant Moon, self and 3 in family. Ordered that an old warrant in the name of Thos. Gregg, dec'd. for 50 acres be renewed in the name of his heirs, viz; Joannah Harris, Polly, Keziah and Anna Gregg.

Aug. 7, 1809—Present, R. Hunt, Thos. Cook, John Wilson, Esqrs.
Nathan Thomson given a warrant for 200 acres out of 650 acres, his own and nine of his family headrights proved. Nathan Thompson, 200 acres.

HISTORICAL COLLECTIONS

Sept. 4, 1809—Present, Wm. Allen, Ro. Kennedy, Thos. Cook, Esqrs.
Wm. Hansford, self and 6 in family.
James Vineyard, 2 in family.

Oct. 2, 1809—Present, R. Hunt, Jas. Christian, John McCurdy, Esqrs.
Richard Tyner, 1 in family.   Thos. Burton, 7 in family.
John Collins, self and 3 in family.
Moses Haynes, old warrant for 200 acres renewed.
Wm. Hayley, old warrant for 100 acres renewed.

Dec. 4, 1809—Present, R. Hunt, Wm. Hightower, Thos. Cook, Esqrs.
Banks Blackwell, 1 in family.   Daniel Tucker, 150 acres renewed.

Mar. 5, 1810—Present, Allen Daniel, Thos. Cook, Rm. White, Esqrs.
Mark Thornton, 25 acres.   Reuben Haley, 200 acres.
Joel Freeman, 300 acres.
Issued to Allen Daniel 100 acres and 112½ acres in lieu of old warrants.

Mar. 5, 1810—Present, W. Nunnelee, Wm. Allen, Rn. White, Esqrs.
James Shackleford, self and 2 in family.

July 2, 1810—Present, A. Stinchcomb, Wm. Allen, James Christian, Esqrs.
Robert Rice, 1 in family.   Wm. Griffin, self and 2 in family.
Abraham Parks, self and 3 in family.   Geo. Scales, self.
Robt. Floyd, self and 6 in family.
Amos Richardson, self and 5 in family.

July 2, 1810—Present, A. Stinchcomb, Wm. Hightower, Jas. Christian, Esqrs.
William Allen, self and 14 in family.

Sept. 3, 1810—R. Haley, 100 acres he proved 5 of his family.

Oct. 1, 1810—Issued to J. Cunningham tha balance of his own and family headrights May 1, 1797, on land adj. William Roebuck, and Robt. Burke, specially.   William Alexander, self and 3, 50 acres.
Wm. Christian, self and 5 of his family.
John McCormick, self and 6 of his family.

Dec. 3, 1810—Jesse Moore, self only, 200 acres. Rt. Smith, self only 200 acres.
William Fergus, renews old warrant for 400 acres into two of 200 acres each.

Jan. 7, 1811—Nathaniel Hudson, self and 16 of his family 700 acres.

Feb. 3, 1812—Robert Middleton and 10 of his family all at this date, 500 acres.

Jan. 7, 1811—Thos. Cook allowed to renew two old warrants. To Thos. Cook, 550 acres. R. Blackwell, 50 acres all he proved.

Mar. 4, 1811—Booker B. Easter, self and 7 in family.
Wm. Adams, self, 200 acres.   Wiley Thornton, self 150 acres.
Littleton Johnston, self and 16 in family 1000 acres.

Apr. 10, 1811—Benjamin Higginbotham, 200 acres on his own headright.
W. Y. Thompson, 1000 acres on his own and 16 of his family.

May 6, 1811—Caleb Tait proved his headright for 200 acres.
Thos. L. Tait, 7 acres on application of B. Allen, county surveyor.

Sept. 2, 1811—Wm. Duncan, self and 9 of family 450 acres.
Warrant for 200 acres given Dec. 1810 to Robt. Smith renewed, original having been lost.

Oct. 1, 1811—George Rucker, self and 3 in family, 290 acres in one, 60 acres in one, all he proved.

Oct. 7, 1811—Banks Blackwell, self, 200 acres.

Nov. 4, 1811—Thomas Watson, self and 2, 300 acres. Moses Haynes, Jr. 2 in family, 100 acres. Philip Shackleford, 2 in family, 100 acres. Moses Haynes, Jr., 200 acres on old warrant, renewed.

Feb. 3, 1812—Jas. Carter, 50 acres all he proved.
Nathaniel Hudson, 300 acres.

Jan. 7, 1811—Rt. Smith proved 5 of his family 240 acres.
William Dula, 100 acres part of old warrant.

Mar. 2, 1812—John Wilson, self and 16 of his family, 300 acres.
Edward Sims, self and 12 in family.

May 4, 1812—Littleton Johnson, 387 acres in part of 1000 acre warrant.

July 6, 1812—James Carter, four of his family all he proved.

Sept. 7, 1812—Williamson Clark, 1 of his family 25 acres.
Archd. Newbourn, old warrant renewed.

Dec. 7, 1812—Chas. Berryman, 500 acres for himself and 10 of family. John S. Higginbotham for self and 2 of family. G. Booth, self and 6 of family.

Jan. 4, 1813—Samuel Carr, 3 in family. Moses Duncan, self and 7 in family. James Carter returns 200 acre warrant and proved two more for 300 acres.

Mar. 1, 1813—Harris Tyner, self and 2, 300 acres. Benj. Ashworth, 3 in family, 150 acres. John Ashworth, self and 4, 400 acres.
Robt. Kennedy, 1 of his family, 50 acres.
Thos. Dula, Sr., 50 acres on old warrant.

May 3, 1813—Rn. Jones, 400 acres (balance. G. Booth, 100 acres in part. Tom Merrett, 150 acres. John Carr, 200 acres.

July 5, 1813—Gains Thompson allowed to return an old warrant of his brother W. Thompson for 1000 acres and receive a new one. Jesse Hendrick, 300 acres all he proved. Isaac Hendrick, 200 acres all he proved. Thos. Nix, Jr., 200 acres, all he proved.

Sept. 6, 1813—Robt. Baskins, 100 acres on headrights.

Feb. 7, 1814—Mary Smithwick proved her own headright.

Mar. 7, 1814—Samuel Self, 4 of his family.

April 14, 1814—Thos. B. McCune, proved for self and 12.

May 2, 1814—Alex. McDonald, proved for self and 3 of his family.

June 6, 1814—David Carr his own headright.

July 4, 1814—Chas. Fanning proved his own headright.

Aug. 1, 1814—Peter Alexander proved his headright.
Hillery Hendrick proved self and two of family.
Gaines Thompson, self.

Sept. 5, 1814—Stephen Williamson, self and 1 in family.
Jesse Ford, self. Jesse Ginn to have 78 acres a balance on 200 acre warrant, Oct. 5, 1795, per certificate of Ro. Kennedy, C. S.

Oct. 3, 1814—Lewis Salmons, self and 9 in family.
Hierome Gaines, 7 in family.   Robt. Burk, Jr., self.
Jacob Coker, self and 6 in family. Littleton Johnston, 112 acres a balance of old warrant.

Mar. 6, 1815—John Ashworth, 100 acres balance of warrant Mar. 1, 1815.

June 5, 1815—Reuben Haley, old warrant 200 acres renewed.
George Scales, old warrant, 50 acres renewed.
Howard Cash, Jr., old warrant 200 acres renewed.

Aug. 7, 1815—Mary Simpson, self and 4 of family.
Lewis Stowers, old warrant 850 acres renewed.
Patrick McMullen, old warrant 950 acres renewed.
Ambrose Dollar, old warrant 850 acres renewed.
Hugn McDonald, old warrant 360 acres renewed.

Sept. 4, 1815—James Rowsey, self and 4 in family.

Oct. 2, 1815—John Roberts, self and 7 in family.
John Beard, self and 16 in family.

Nov. 6, 1815—James Hunt, for one of his family. Wm. Rice, headrights.
James Shackleford, old warrant, 50 acres.

Dec. 4, 1815—James Shackleford, 50 acres balance warrant in 1810.

Jan. 1, 1816—Abraham McGehee, self.   George Thompson, headright.
Martin Deadwyler, self and 4 in family.
Alex. Henry, headright.

Feb. 5, 1816—John Webb, self 200 acres. Wm. Faulkner, self and 8 in family. Wm. Brown, headrights. Abner Pealer, self 200 acres. Samuel Self, balance of 191 acres.

GEORGIA D. A. R.

Mar. 4, 1816—William Brown, balance 50 acres. John Sartan, 274 acres balance on his own and 8 of family.
Mathis Huff, headright, 200 acres.   John Carr, 50 acres.
Anderson Shellnut, self and 10 in family, 700 acres.
Wm. Faulkner, 450 acres. Angus Johnson, 50 acres on his headright.

April 1, 1816—John Edwards, self and 5, 200 acres.
Joshua Carpenter, Sur. Gen'l's. duplicate, 525 acres in full.
Howard Cash, old warrant 50 acres renewed.

May 6, 1816—Austin Webb, self and 6 of family 300 acres.
John C. Kennedy, his own, 200 acres. James F. Nunnelee, 100 acres part of his family headrights proved Nov. 7, 1808.

June 3, 1816—Level Page, self and 4 in family.
Samuel Lourimore, self and 6 in family. James Webb, self and 9 in family. Austin Webb, balance in full.

Sept. 2, 1816—Tryon Harris, 200 acres warrant all he proved.
Moses Cash, 50 acres all he proved.

Jan. 6, 1817—Asa Jones, 9 of family headrights.

Mar. 3, 1817—Leroy Oglesby, self and 4 of family 240 acres.
Wiley Childers, his own, 200 acres.

May 5, 1817—Jo. Bragg, 200 acres all he proved.
Edmd. Shackleford, 50 acres proved self and 4 of family.

Aug. 4, 1817—A. Richards, balance 100 acres. C. Berryman, 200 acres.

Aug. 4, 1817—James F. Nunnelee, 103 acres in part.
Daniel Ross, 500 acres self and 6. James Jordan, 100 acres part of 200 acres. William Hall, 100 acres on old warrant. Wm. Faulkner, 7 of family headrights, 200 acres. Henry A. Harper, self and 3 of family.

Sept. 1, 1817—Martin Deadwyler, one of his family 16 acres.
Affidavit of Robt. Kennedy, Dist. Sur., that he had lost a warrant for 300 acres granted James Rowsey Sept. 4, 1815 when Robt. was Co. Sur., a duplicate issued.

Oct. 6, 1817—David Ballenger, self and 4, 121½ acres.

Nov. 3, 1817—James Clark, 200 acres all he proved.
L. P. Gaines, 200 acres all he proved. Shem Tucker, 200 acres all he proved. James Wootan, self and 3 of family, 100 acres.

Jan. 5, 1818—Charles Carden, self and 3 of family.

Feb. 2, 1818—Tyree Landers, self and 3 of family, 350 acres.

April 6, 1818—Jesse Brown, self and 5 of family.

May 4, 1818—Howard Cash, Jr., 200 acres renewed. Thomas Posey, headrights, 200 acres.

June 1, 1818—Martin Deadwyler, one of his family 50 acres.

July 6, 1818—Richard Richardson, 150 acres, headright.

Sept. 7, 1818—William Steedley, 200 acres headright.

Nov. 2, 1818—Amos Rose, own headright, 50 acres. John Childers, own headright, 50 acres. McKinne Irions, own headright, 50 acres. Sally Turner, one of her family headrights, 50 acres. Joseph Downer, one of his family headrights, 50 acres.

Jan. 4, 1819—Sally Turner, two warrants of 10 acres each, her own headrights. William Nolan, two warrants of 10 acres each, his own headrights.

April 5, 1819—Mary Simpson, on her own and part of her family headrights in lieu of an old warrant, 60 acres.
Gaines Thompson, 200 acres in lieu of an old warrant and 50 acres on one of his family headrights.
John Collett, self and 7 of family, 500 acres.

May 3, 1819—Edmond Shackleford had a warrant May 5, 1817 for self and 7 of family. Received 100 acres.

June 1, 1819—John Watkins, self and 15 of his family.
John Beck, self and 13 in family, 250 acres.

July 5, 1819—William Rice, self and 4 of his family.

Aug. 3, 1819—Micajah Anthony, four family headrights, 200 acres.
Burrell Bobo, seven of his family, 150 acres.
Patrick McMullen, in lieu of old warrant.
Ambrose Dollar, in lieu of old warrant.

Sept. 6, 1819—Job Hammond, self and 10 in family. John Penn, self and 9 in family. Simeon Oliver, self and 6 in family.

Nov. 1, 1819—Aron Vickery, self and 10 of his family.

Jan. 3, 1820—Joel Doss, one of his family. Isham Morgan, self for 200 acres. Job Hammond, Sr., 20 acres in compliance with order. George Lunsford, self and 2 of family, 300 acres. Reuben Christian, 200 acres in lieu of old warrant Jan. 7, 1805.

May 1, 1820—Affidavit of John Collat that he had lost a warrant for 550 acres dated Apr. 5, 1819. Ordered renewed.
James Nash, self and 11 of his family.

June 5, 1820—Samuel Adams, self and 9 of his family.

Nov. 6, 1820—Zimri Tait proved 2 of his family. Thos. Scales proved 2 of his family. James Dodds proved 2 of his family. Thomas Haynes proved 2 of his family.

Dec. 4, 1820—Jos. Parker, self and 8 of his family, 600 acres in full.
John Booth, self and 6 of his family, 500 acres in full.

Lewis Salmons, 56 acres balance of old warrant.
Reuben Brown, self and 16 of his family 300 acres in part.
Edward Brown, self and 13 of his family, 300 acres on part.
Rufus Christian, self and 13 of his family, 475 acres in part.

Jan. 8, 1821—Joseph Smith, self and 6 of family, 500 acres in full.
    Thos. S. Hansard, self 200 acres in full. Ralph Blackwell proved one of his family's headrights, 50 acres in full.

April 2, 1821—Benjamin Brown, 12 of his family, 600 acres in full.
    Ephraim Moss, 300 acres, self and part of family, proved Jan. 6, 1800.
    Thos. S. Hansard, 3 of his family, 150 acres in full.
    John Ballenger, Jr., headrights, 200 acres in full.
    Joseph Gray, Jr., headrights, 200 acres in full.

Oct. 1, 1821—James Clark, 8 of his family, 400 acres in full.

Nov. 15, 1821—John White, own headright, 100 acres in part.
    James Pledger, his own and 3 of his family, 350 acres in full.

Jan. 7, 1822—Absolom Stinchcomb proved one of his family, 50 acres in full.

Mar. 4, 1822—John Watkins on family headright, 100 acres.
    William Woods, on family headright, 100 acres.
    Wiley Childers, 300 acres in part of family headrights.

Land Lotteries 1806-1821-1827 and 1832

NAME OF BOOK; LAND GRANTS AND REVOLUTIONARY SOLDIERS CONTAINS LOTTERIES OF 1806, 1821, 1827, 1832. GOLD LOTTERY TAX DIGEST OF 1825 (Not taken)

Lottery of 1806

EXPLANATORY

The lands given out in this lottery were acquired from the Creek Indians, situated in Baldwin and Wilkinson counties.

Those entitled to draw were every free white male twenty one years of age and upwards a citizen of the United States and an inhabitant of this state three years immediately preceding the passage of this act, and who had paid tax, entitled to one draw; every free white male of like description having a wife and legitimate child or children under twenty one years of age, entitled to two draws; all widows with like residence, all free white females, all families of orphans, under twenty one years, whose father is dead, one draw; those having neither father or mother living, two draws, provided the person did not draw a prize in the late land lottery.

No mention is made of Military service in this law and no provision is made for the soldiers of any war.

Capt. Thos. Oliver's District.

Name	Draws	Name	Draws
Allgood, John	2	Christian, Jesse	2
Burden, Archibald	2	Chrittington, Henry	2
Bradley, Drury	2	Chrittington, Pryor	2
Burden, James	2	Chrittington, Henry P.	1
Burgamy, Nathaniel	2	Chrittington, Robert	1
Burden, Hannah, wid.	1	Coker, Abraham	2
Burden, Edmond	1	Coker, Malachi	2
Burden, William	2	Christian, Presley	2
Childers, Thomas	2	Christian, Wm. P.	2
Christian, James	2	Carter, Charles	2
Chrittington, Wm.	2	Carter, Thomas	2

GEORGIA D. A. R.

Name	Draws
Davis, Hickman	2
Davis, Nancy	1
Ellis, Zillar	1
Fowler, Arthur	2
Ferington, Aaron, dec'd Orphans	1
Gatewood, Catharine, wid.	1
Greenwood, Beverly	2
Greenwood, George	2
Hunt, Richardson	2
Hendricks, Elias	2
Hendricks, Abijah	2
Higginbotham, William	2
Hatchcock, Oziah	2
Higginbotham, Benj.	2
Hendricks, Sarah, wid.	1
Hawthorn, Eliz., wid.	1
Higginbotham, Anna	1
Higginbotham, Sarah	1
Higginbotham, Joseph	2
Hawthorn, Joseph	2
Higginbotham, Francis	2
Hatchcock, William	2
Ham, Ambrose	2
Hatchcock, Harbert	1
Harris, Jeptha V.	2
Ham, John	2
Higginbotham, Gabrile	2
Jorden, Redden	2
Jorden, James, Sr.	2
James, Enoch	2
King, William	2
Kannady, William M.	1
Lawremore, Sarah, wid.	1
Lawremore, Nicholas, dec'd. Orphans of	1
Lawremore, Sally	1
Lawremore, Anna	1
Lawless, John, dec'd, Orphans	2
Lawremore, Alex	1
Lawremore, James	1
Lawremore, Samuel	1
McCoy, William	2
Martin, John	1
McCoy, Reuben	2
Oliver, Dyonecious	2
Penn, Eliz. R.	1
Penn, Fanney	1
Penn, Thomas	2
Purkins, William	2
Penn, Benjamin	2
Penn, Philip	2
Pledger, Thomas	2
Penn, Lewcy	1
Pledger, Sally	1
Penn, Salley	1
Purkins, Elizabeth	1
Paten, Mary	1
Paten, Margarette, wid.	1
Penn, William	1
Page, Lèvil	1
Rogers, Elisha	2
Rowsey, John, Sr.	2
Ridgedale, David	2
Rowsey, Edmond	2
Rowsey, Clary	2
Shepard, Robert	2
Shepard, Samuel	2
Shepard, Peter	2
Sumner, Nazareth	2
Shepard, Anna, wid.	1
Satterwhite, Nancy	1
Shepard, Nancy	1
Smith, John, Sr.	2
Staples, John	2
Stephens, John, dec'd, orphs.	1
Upshaw, John, Sr.	2
Upshaw, Ann	1
Upshaw, Sarah	1
Upshaw, Catharine	1
Upshaw, Leroy	1
Upshaw, John, Jr.	2
Varner, James	1
White, Joshua	2

We certify the foregoing statement for Capt. Thos. Oliver's Company in Major Richardson Hunts Battalion to be correct as far as we know or believe. Given under our hands as Commissioners for said Battalion, for the ensuing Land Lottery, this 26, of Aug. 1806

(Signed) William Banks
Chas. Carter

HISTORICAL COLLECTIONS 239

Capt. Dunston Blackwell's District.

Name	Draws
Arnold, James, Jr.	2
Anglin, James	2
Adams, James, Sr.	2
Allen, Thomas	2
Brown, James N.	2
Brown, Benjamin	2
Burks, Robert	2
Beverly, Anthony	2
Bramblett, Henry	2
Bramblett, John	2
Bramblett, Reuben	2
Bailey, Julin	2
Bailey, Samuel	2
Bailey, James	2
Bonds, Nathan, Jr.	2
Bramblett, Margrett	1
Bramblett, Lott	1
Brown, Margrett	1
Bonds, Nathan, Sr.	2
Bowers, William	2
Bailey, Elizabeth	1
Bailey, Hezekiah	2
Blackwell, Banks	1
Blackwell, Dunston	1
Blackwell, Ralph	1
Blackwell, Sally N.	1
Blackwell, Jos., dec'd Orphans of	1
Banks, William	2
Clark, Francis, dec'd Orphans of	1
Carr, Samuel	2
Clark, Williamson	2
Carrel, Jessy	2
Christler, Julius	2
Craft, John	2
Carter, James	2
Clement, Simon	1
Dudley, Nicholas	2
Davis, Meredith	2
Driver, Betsey, wid.	1
Driver, Bird, dec'd, orphs.	1
Davis, Sarah	1
Dutton, James	2
Eavenston, George	2
Eavenston, Susannah	1
Eavenston, Eli	2
Easter, Champion	2
Fanning, Laughlin	2
Faulkenberry, Jacob	2
Ford, Sarah, wid.	1
Ford, John, dec'd, orphs.	1
Fanning, Benjamin	2
Fleming, Moses	2
Fleming, John	1
Fortson, Benjamin	2
Gaar, Lewis	2
Gatewood, Eliz. wid.	1
Golden, Matthew	2
Gaar, Joel	2
Gaar, Adam	2
Gaines, William	2
Gunn, Elisha	2
Ginn, Jesse	2
Gaar, Mikel, Dec'd, orphs.	1
Hulme, William	2
Hall, Robert, Sr.	2
Hall, Robert, Jr.	2
Henderson, Simeon	2
Higginbotham, Jacob, Jr.	2
Hilley, Sarah	1
Hilley, Milley	1
Hansard, Susannah	1
Hansard, Wiliam	2
Hansard, John	2
Henderson, William	2
Henderson, Joseph	2
Hunt, Nathaniel	1
Hansard, Jane wid.	1
Hansard, Wm., dec'd, orphs.	1
Herndon, Edward	2
Higginbotham, John	1
Higginbotham, Jacob, Sr.	2
Hilley, Thomas	2
Higginbotham, James	2
Higginbotham, John S.	2
Henderson, James	2
Hall, William	2
Kettler, John	2
Lions, John	2
Meret, Towan (?)	2

	Draws		Draws
Megarity, Kindred	2	Robertson, William	1
Magee, William	2	Rucker, John Sr.	2
Maxwell, Thomas, Jr.	2	Sandidge, Claiborn	2
Maxwell, Joel	2	Smith, John	2
Moss, Ephraim	2	Smith, Zachariah	2
Morrison, Peter	2	Smith, David	2
Murrah, Tabitha	1	Smith, Jesse	2
Murrah, Nancy, wid.	1	Smith, Jemima, wid.	1
Murrah, John, dec'd. orphs.	1	Smith, Benj., dec'd, orphs.	1
Magee, Lewis	2	Stubbs, Peter	2
Magee, William, Sr.	2	Sullivant, Patsy	1
Maxwell, Thomas, Sr.	2	Thornton, Mark, Sr.	2
Newborn, Archabald	2	Taylor, Benjamin	2
Nix, Joseph, Sr.	2	Thornton, Dozer, Sr.	2
Norris, James	2	Thornton, Jeremiah	2
Nelms, Jurden	2	Teasley, James	2
Nelms, Ann wid.	1	Teasley, Isom	2
Nelms, Wm., dec'd. orphs	1	Tomason, George	2
Nelms, Polley	1	Teasley, William	2
Nelms, Penelepy	1	Underwood, Ann wid.	1
Nix, Lewcy	1	Underwood, Joshua, dec'd orphs. of	1
Nail, Julian, Sr.	2		
Patterson, John, Sr.	2	Underwood, Ezekiel	1
Ponder, Abner	2	White, Henry	2
Ponder, Jesse	2	White, Daniel	2
Powell, Honourrias	1	White, William	1
Ponder, Reuben	1	Witt, Charles	2
Ponder, Betsy	1	Woodall, Joseph	2
Pulliam, Joseph	1	Williamson, Betsy C.	1
Rucker, Azmon	1	White, Thomas	1

We certify the foregoing sheets for Capt. Dunston Blackwell's Dist., in Maj. Richardson Hunt's Battalion to be correct as far as we know or believe. Given under our hand as Commissioners in said Battalion for the ensuring Land Lottery, this 26 day of Aug. 1806

(Signed) William Banks

Chas. Carter

Capt. Geo. Roebuck's District.

Adams, William	2	Breeden, Richard, orph. of	1
Alexander, William	2	Cash, Jesse	2
Allen, Ephraim	2	Cash, Howard, Jr.	1
Boughtright, William, Sr.	2	Cunningham, Franklin	1
Boughtright, William, Jr.	2	Clark, James	1

HISTORICAL COLLECTIONS 241

Name	Draws
Cash, Nancy	1
Cash, Howard, Sr.	2
Cunningham, John, Sr.	2
Crump, Charles	2
Chipman, Joseph	2
Cash, John	2
Cash, James	2
Doss, Joel	2
Dutton, Thomas	2
Franklin, Polley	1
Franklin, David	2
Ferrell, Micajah	2
Franklin, Henry	2
Franklin, Sarah, wid.	1
Franklin, Edmond, orphs of	1
Franklin, Mary, wid.	1
Franklin, Philemon, orph of	1
Franklin, Milly E.	1
Franklin, Samson	1
Ferrell, Wiley	1
Gaines, Francis	2
Gaines, Talefaria	2
Gulley, Richard	2
Gaines, Richard S.	1
Gregg, Joanas, wid.	1
Gregg, Thomas, orphs of	1
Hulme, John	2
Hinton, Peter	2
Hailey, Reuben	1
Head, William	2
Humber, John	1
Hailey, William	2
Johnston, John	2
Jones, James	2
Jurden, John	2
Jinkens, Samuel	2
Jurden, Fountain	2
Jurden, James	2
Jurden, Margaret	1

Name	Draws
King, Thomas	2
Lockhard, James	2
Lively, Charles	2
Lovell, Gabrile	2
McAlpin, Mary, wid.	1
McCune, Thomas	2
McCune, Jean, wid.	1
McCune, Wm. orphs by Jane McCune	1
McCune, Wm. orphs by Mary McCune	2
McGowing, John	2
McGuire, Anderson	2
Meanes, William	2
Meanes, Hugh	2
McGuire, Allegana	2
Patterson, John, Sr.	2
Patterson, Joseph	2
Prewitt, William	2
Patterson, James	2
Patterson, Alex.	2
Pealer, Abner	2
Riley, James	2
Roebuck, Robert, Jr.	1
Shifflet, Pickett	2
Smith, Richard	2
Shackleford, James	2
Turner, Martin, orphs. of	1
Terrell, William	2
Taylor, William	2
Terrell, Jeremiah	2
Terrell, Mary	2
Underwood, William H.	2
Underwood, Joseph	2
Wheeler, Thomas	2
Wheeler, George	2
Wade, Anna, wid.	1
Wade, Joshua, orphs of	1
Warren, Jeremiah, orphs of	1

Capt. Isaac J. Barrett's District.

Name	Draws
Bennett, Moses	2
Bobo, Benjamin	2
Barrett, Isaac J.	2
Braden, William	2

Name	Draws
Bennett, Joel	2
Brown, Daniel	1
Bobo, Lewis, dec'd, orphs	1
Cunningham, John Jr.	2

GEORGIA D. A. R.

Name	Draws
Crow, Samuel	2
Cautih (?), John	2
Cautih, Polley	1
Carter, Thomas Sr.	2
Childrus, Robert	2
Carter, Sarah	1
Carden, Robert	2
Cook, William	2
Dobbs, Josiah	2
Dobbs, Silus	2
Dunnyhoo, Cornelius	2
Dollar, Ambrus	2
Dollar, James	2
Dobbs, John	2
Dobbs, Lewcey, wid.	1
Dobbs, Peter	2
Dobbs, Lot	2
Fitzjarreld, George Sr.	2
Gore, Lydia	1
Haynes, Moses Sr.	2
Haynes, Stephen, orphs of	2
Harper, Edward,	2
Holms, Shadrack	2
Harper, Sarah	1
Holmes, Joshua	2
Holmes, Gideon Sr.	2
Howard, Nehemiah	2
Hooker, Thomas Sr.	2
Haynes, Moses, Jr.	2
Holmes, Gideon, Jr.	2
Howard, Joseph	2
Holmes, Richard	2
Haynes, William	2
Hooker, Thomas, Jr.	2
Holmes, Ezekiel	1
Hooker, William	2
Hatchcock, Wm., orph of	1
Jarrell, Samuel F.	2
Jarrell, Archabald	2
Jarrell, William F.	2
Kidd, Martin	2
Kees, Cornelous	2
Lovengood, Polly	1
Lovengood, Harmon	1
Mitchell, William	2
Mitchell, John	2
Mitchell, Patrick	2
Moor, Nancy	1
Mitchell, Elizabeth	1
Megarity, Abner	2
Moor, John, dec'd, orphs	1
McDonald, John, Sr.	2
McMartin, Dunkin	2
McMullen, John, Sr.	2
McGarrita, Gardner	1
Mitchell, Isaac	1
McMullen, Neal	1
Nail, Benjamin	2
Parks, Mary, wid.	1
Pritchett, George	1
Pritchett, Nicholas	2
Rumsey, Thomas	2
Rumsey, John	2
Rumsey, Fanney	1
Rumsey, Polly	1
Rumsey, William	2
Rumsey, Henry	1
Richardson, Amos	2
Richardson, Ann, Wid.	1
Scales, Thos. dec'd orphs of	1
Sammons, Lewis	2
Skelton, Reecy	2
Smith, Ralph	2
Smith, Patsey, wid.	2
Smith, Archer, dec'd, orphs of	1
Scales, John, Jr.	2
Skelton, Zachariah	2
Thompson, Samuel	1
Tweedle, James	2
Thompson, Solomon	2
Thompson, Nathan	2
Taylor, Elisha	2
Thompson, Jesse	2
Thompson, Andrew	1
Williamson, John	2
Willmath, William	2
Ward, Mathias	2
White, William	2
Woodward, Thos. dec'd, orphs of	1

Capt. William McGuire's District

Name	Draws	Name	Draws
Ashworth, Benjamin	2	James, Angus	2
Adderson, Thomas	2	James, Samuel	2
Ashley, John	2	Johnson, Archabald	2
Ashworth, Joab	1	Johnson, Rachel, wid.	1
Ashworth, John	2	King, Catharine, wid.	1
Bevers, William	2	King, John	2
Bevers, Alsa	1	McMullin, Patrick	2
Braden, Hannah, wid.	1	McCurry, Angus	2
Brown, Polly	1	McDonald, Donald, Sr.	2
Braden, Rachel	1	McDonald, Rodrick	2
Brown, Andrew	2	McDonald, John	2
Brown, James, Sr.	2	Magee, Ansell	2
Brown, Roland	2	McDonald, Ronnald	2
Beedon (?), Ephraim	2	McCurry, John	2
Braden, John	1	McDonald, Donald, Jr.	2
Banks, John	2	McCurry, Flora, wid.	1
Cason, John	2	McCurry, Daniel, orphs of	1
Childs, John	2	Montgomery, Elizabeth, wid.	1
Dodd, William	2	McGuire, William	2
Dooly, William, Sr.	2	Page, William	2
Dooly, William, Jr.	2	Powell, Killis	2
Driver, William	1	Powell, Francis, Sr.	2
Dodd, Elizabeth	1	Powell, Lanston	1
Dooly, Nancy	1	Powell, Francis, Jr.	1
Faguson, Norman	2	Powell, William R.	2
Foster, Worsham	1	Parks, Abraham	2
Gay, Ann, wid.	1	Powell, Lurany	1
Gordon, Gilbert, orph of	1	Rice, Robert	2
Herndon, Israel	2	Roe, Susannah	1
Harper, Rhoderick	2	Skelton, John	2
Harper, Henry	2	Selfridge, Robert	2
Harper, Thomas	2	Stowers, Lewis	2
Hill, Jacob	2	Scales, John, Sr.	2
Highsmith, James	2	Sharyer, William	2
Harcrow, Hugh	2	Sharyer, Joseph	1
Hunt, James	2	Scales, Thomas	1
Hendon, Thomas	2	Scales, George	1
Hutchings, Zachariah	2	Shifflett, Powell	2
Herndon, Geo. dec'd, orphs of	1	Sawyer, Robert	1
James, Enoch, Sr.	2	Selfridge, Nancy	1
Johnson, Malcom	2	Standerfer, Anderson	1
Johnson, Caty, wid.	1	Standeford, Benjamin	2
Johnson, John, dec'd, orphs of.	1	Teasley, Silus	2
James, Thomas	2	Tyner, Richard, Sr.	2
Johnson, Angus	2	Tyner, Richard, Jr.	1

	Draws		Draws
Tyner, Harris	2	Wood, Sarah, wid.	1
White, Jeany	1		

We certify the foregoing statement for Capt. Wm. McGuire Co. Dist. in Major Richardson Hunt's Battalion for the ensuing Land Lottery this 26 day of Aug. 1806.

(Signed) William Banks

Chas. Carter.

LAND LOTTERY OF 1821

Explanatory

The land disposed of by this lottery was obtained by treaty from the Creek and Cherokee Indians, covered by five original counties at the time of survey, Dooly, Houston, Monroe, Henry and Fayette counties, since divided into twenty one counties.

Maj. Chas. W. Christian's Batt. No. 152

Capt. Rufus Christian's Dist. No. 202

	Draws		Draws
Almand, John	2	Moon, Stephen	2
Beard, Robert	2	Moore, William	2
Beard, Samuel	1	Moon, John	2
Bradley, Ann, wid.	1	Nix, Edward	1
Bradley, Robt. C., orphs. of	1	Oglesby, Lindsay	1
Boothe, Nancy, wid.	1	Oliver, James	2
Boothe, Prudence	1	Parham, Southern	1
Boothe, Nathaniel, orphs. of	1	Parham, Sarah, wid.	1
Chambless, James E.	1	Ridgeway, Bazel	1
Christian, Ira	1	Ridgeway, James	2
Chappell, Thomas B.	2	Webb, Margaret, wid.	1
Deadwyler, Joseph	1	Webb, Claibourn's, orphs.	1
David, Jacob W.	2	Webb, Clabourn	1
Deadwyler, Martin	2	Wells, William	2
Edwards, John	2	Wilhite, John R.	1
Falkner, John	2	Webb, Archer	1
Johnson, James	1	White, Sally, wid.	1
Jones, Micajah	2	White, Anderson	2
Kerlin, Elizabeth	1	Wood, Francis	1
Kerlin, Samuel	1	White, Nicholas, orphs. of	1
King, James	2	Woods, Bennett	1
Lesuer, Samuel, Sr.	2	Unis, Samuel	1
Lesuer, Mede	1	Upshaw, William	2

HISTORICAL COLLECTIONS 245

Capt. James Hanna's District

	Draws		Draws
Boothe, Joel	1	Jordan, Rachel, wid.	1
Dudley, John T.	2	Legrand, John N.	1
Dudley, James L.	1	Largent, Jesse, orphs. of	1
Denny, Robert	2	Moon, Sarah, wid.	1
Davis, William	1	McCommack, John	2
Dudley, Jarrott	1	Nelmes, William	2
Dudley, John B.	2	Nelmes, Jonathan	2
Elder, William	1	Nix, Samuel	2
Falk, Thomas	1	Rains, Dabney	2
Hendrick, Whitehead	2	Ruff, Stephen	2
Hanna, James, Jr.	1	Ruff, Allen	1
Hendrick, Brantley	1	Robbards, John	1
Hendrick, James	1	Penn, Philip	2
Hendrick, Milam	1	Quinn, Matthew	2
Hendrick, Eli	1	Seemore, Zachariah	2
Ham, Jinny, wid.	1	Story, Lucy, wid.	1
Ham, Reuben, orphs. of	1	Skinner, Clary, wid.	1
Handley, Drury B. P.	1	Skinner, George M.	2
Handley, Jarrett, Sr. orphs. of	1	Tucker, Robert	1

Capt. John Merritt's District

Baskin, Robert	2	Davis, Thomas L.	1
Bray, David	2	Gates, James	1
Ballenger, John, Jr.	2	Ginn, Jesse	2
Ballard, Jesse	2	Gentry, Wiatt	2
Brown, Abraham	2	Harbin, Sally, wid.	1
Brown, Henry	1	Harbin, William, orphs. of	1
Ballenger, David	2	Hendrick, Jesse	2
Blackwell, Sarah, wid.	1	Head, James B.	2
Bray, John	2	Horton, Elizabeth	1
Burnett, Jeremiah	2	Horton, Walker	1
Brantlet, Henry	2	Hagins, Richard, orphs. of	1
Brantlet, Lott	1	Jordan, Matthew	2
Bates, George	2	Legrand, Jesse	1
Cheek, Burgess	2	Lagrand, William	1
Carr, David	2	Merritt, John	1
Cheek, William	2	Magarity, Kindred	2
Clark, Edward	2	Merritt, Torren	2
Carr, John	2	Nix, Lucy, wid.	1
Coker, John	1	Page, William	2
David, Humphrey	1	Patterson, Rebecca, wid.	1
Duncan, Nathaniel	1	Parker, Benjamin B.	1
Duncan, Henry	1	Rice, Leonard	2

246   GEORGIA D. A. R.

Name	Draws	Name	Draws
Spears, Salian, wid.	1	Wallis, Thomas	2
Spears, Joshua, orphs. of	1	White, Martin	2
Spears, Shadrick	1	Vines, Sarah, wid.	1
Smith, Nathaniel	1	Vines, Isaac, orphs. of	1
Smith, Fulden	1	Vines, John	1
Steel, Robert	1	Vines, Parnal	1
White, Eppy	2	Vines, James	1
Winn, Benjamin	2		

Capt. Benj. Penn's District

Name	Draws	Name	Draws
Andrew, Benjamin, Jr.	2	Mann, William	2
Allgood, John	1	Mann, James W.	1
Bond, William	2	Pledger, Isaac M.	1
Brawner, Joel	2	Penn, William	2
Coleman, Jesse	2	Pucket, James	2
Carter, George	2	Peeler, Benjamin	2
Chambers, John	2	Pledger, Lemuel	2
Chambers, William S.	2	Pruit, William	1
Christian, William P.	2	Pruit, Susannah wid.	1
Christian, Elijah D.	1	Pledger, Joseph P.	1
Crittenten, Elijah	2	Pruitt, David	2
Christian, James G.	1	Pledger, Thomas, Jr.	2
Christian, Elijah W.	1	Peeler, Abner	2
Christian, James, Sr.	2	Richards, Rachel wid.	1
Critendon, Juda wid.	1	Richards, Reuben's orphs.	1
Ford, Joseph	1	Stinchcomb, Levi	2
Fitts, William H.	2	Standerford, Tilman	1
Harmon, John Sr.	2	Shepherd, Samuel	1
Hicks, David	2	Scales, George	2
Hendrick, Abijah's orphs.	1	Stephens, Fereby wid.	1
Hicks, Samuel	1	Shepherd, Nathan	2
Hicks, Frederick	2	Shepherd, Richard H.	1
Jordan, William	2	Stinchcomb, Nathaniel	1
King, John	1	Statham, John	1
King, Ambrose B.	1	Statham, William	1
McCoy, Nancy	1	Thompson, Gaines	2
McCoy, William's orph.	1	Turman, Seaborn	1
Mann, William H.	2	Roberts, Jesse	2

Capt. Leroy Upshaw's District

Name	Draws	Name	Draws
Akins, Absolom's orphs.	1	Burns, William	2
Andrew, Charles	1	Carter, Robert M.	1
Brown, Reuben	2	Cook, Fenton	2
Brown, Edward	2	Cook, William's orphs.	1

	Draws		Draws
Chandler, Washington	1	Mason, Joseph P.	1
Depriest, James A.	2	Oliver, Thomas, Sr.	2
Dailey, Samuel C.	1	Pledger, John S.	torn
David, Isaac	1	Rowsey, Edmond	1
Ellington, Stephen orphs. of	1	Ragland, Evan	1
Fortson, Richard	2	Stodghill, Willis	1
Fortson, William	2	Skinner, Morris	2
Fortson, Thomas, Sr.	2	Skinner, Archer, orphs. of	1
Green, Castoe	1	Smith, Thomas	1
Griffin, Margaret wid.	1	Turman, Samuel	1
Griffin, Joseph, orphs. of	1	Thornton, Thomas A.	2
Gibbs, William	2	Tait, William	2
Hickman, Walker	2	Verdel, John A.	2
Hendrick, William	2	Weston, Job	1
Hall, Thomas	1	Wilhite, Lewis	2
Hall, Samuel	1	Wilhite, Joseph G.	2
Hall, John	1	Wood, James L.	1
Insheep, George	1	Wilhite, John B.	2
King, Jacob W.	2	Winkfield, John Y.	1
King, William, Sr.	2	Williams, John	1
Maxwell, Simeon	2		

GEORGIA, ELBERT COUNTY

We James D. Jarratt and Samuel Bentley appointed by the honorable, the Inferior Court of the state and county aforesaid to take a return of the amount of draws claimed in the Land Lottery contemplated and authorized by an act of the General Assembly of said state passed at an extra session thereof, assented to the 15th, day of May 1821, by persons residing in the 142 Battalion Georgia Militia in said State and county, do hereby certify that the foregoing is a correct list and return of the same.

Given under our hands this 13th, day of July 1821.

(Signed) Samuel Bentley,
James D. Jarratt.

LIST OF THOSE ENTITLED TO DRAWS IN THE LAND LOTTERY FOR 1827

Copied by the Stephen Heard Chapter D. A. R., under the direction of Mrs. Olin Smith. Miss Edna Rogers, Regent.

EXPLANATORY

The land disposed of by this lottery embraced the five original counties of Muscogee, Troup, Coweta, Lee, and Carroll counties. This teritory was ceded by the Indian Springs Treaty February 12, 1825.

GEORGIA D. A. R.

Those eligible for participation were white males over 18, who had been residents of the state three years, Revolutionary soldiers, widows of Revolutionary soldiers, orphans, soldiers of late wars with Great Britain and Indians and others who had not drawn land in previous lotteries.

KEY

h. of f.___Heads of families.
s._____Single
r. s._____Revolutionary soldier.
w. r. s.___Widow of Revolutionary soldier.
wid._____Widow of other persons.
orphs.____Orphans.
h. a._____Women whose husbands have been three years absent.
f. a._____Minors whose fathers have been three years absent from the State.
id._____Idiots.

Major Thomas Allen's Battalion
Capt. Tate's District.

	Draws		Draws
Burton, Thomas r. s.	2	Coleman, James h. of f.	2
Bevvill, Thomas h. of f.	2	Cunningham, Abraham s.	1
Miller, Jedidah S. h. of f.	2	Banks, John s.	1
Watkins, Henry M. s.	1	Speed, Wade s.	1
Tate, Zimry W. s.	1	Tate, Thos. orphs. of	2
Tate, Thos. J. s.	1	Tate, Jesey C. s	1
Hamilton, Elisha s.	1	Saxton, Eliz. M. w. r. s.	1
Evans, Eliz. wid. & w. r. s.	2	Burton, Nelson B. h. of f.	2
Tate, Elizabeth w. r. s.	1	Rich, Richmond s.	1
Evans, Elam s.	1	Rembert, Samuel H. s.	1
Tate, Enos Minor s.	1	Burton, Girman s.	1
Urquhart, John A. s.	1	Burton, Paten S. s.	1
Dickson, Blackman s.	1	Barron, Briton B. s.	1
Tate, Isaac M. s.	1	Roan, John h. of f.	2
Hudson, David B. h. of f.	2	Dickson, Samuel orphs. of	1
Burton, Nicholas s.	1	Hudson, John H. h. of f.	2
Rich, John orphs of	1	Colbert, Susannah w. r. s.	1
Flemming, Margaret wid.	1	Flemming, Margaret w. r. s.	1
Flemming, Henry orphs. of	1	Chisenhall, Dilany h. of f.	2
Cunningham, Minter orphs.of	1	Cunningham, William r. s.	1

Capt. Bell's District

Clark, Samuel s.	1	Clark, Zacheriah, orph. of	1
Naish, Frances, wid.	1	Davis, Wm. C. h. of f.	2
Williams, Matthew J. Orphs. of	1	Edwards, Sarah P. wid.	1
Snellings, Rebecka w. r. s.	1	Edwards, James, orphs. of	2

HISTORICAL COLLECTIONS

	Draws		Draws
Cook, John r. s.	2	Carter, Elizabeth w. r. s.	1
Jones, Jesey orphs of	1	Cannada, Elizabeth orph.	1
Cook, Mary wid. and w. r. s.	2	Cape, Meriam h. of f.	2
Jack, Margaret wid. and w.r.s.	2	Cook, Samuel h. of f.	2
Clark, Rebecka wid. and w.r.s.	2	Hubbard, Vincent h. of f.	2
Turman, Robert G. s.	1	Childers, William s.	1
Cook, Jesse M. s.	1	Bell, Joseph orph. of	1
Cook, Joshua, orphs. of	1	Cook, Smith, Jr. s.	1
Carter, Nathias, orphs. of	1	Allgood, Mary wid.	1
Moon, William H. s.	1	Allgood, Peter orphs of	2
Clark, Christopher H. s.	1	Barr, Robert S. h. of f.	2
Kemp, David V. h. of f.	2	Mobley, William s.	1
Bell, David s.	1	Allgood, John r. s.	1
Martin, Nathaniel s.	1	Bullard, Ann wid. and w.r.s.	2
Martain, Henry s.	1	Burton, Joseph s.	1
Dye, Jane wid.	1	Jones, Jesse s.	1
Dye, Thompson orphs. of	1	Cook, Beverly C. s.	1
Williams, John h. of f.	2	Moon, Elizabeth wid.	1
Key, William B. r. s.	2	Clark, James O. h. of f.	2
Perrian, John s.	1	Cook, Theodosius h. of f.	2
Wodley, Temporine wid.	1	Burton, Richard orphs. of	1
Wodley, John orphs. of	2	Dye, Brown orphs. of	2
Key, Thomas J. s.	1	Mobley, Frances wid.	1
Bell, James h. of f.	2	Hudson, David r. s.	2
Taylor, Nathias, orphs. of	1	Clark, Christopher orphs. of	1
Naish, Frances w. r. s.	1	Taylor, Rebecca wid.	1
Williams, Frances E. wid.	1	Taylor, John C., orphs. of	1
Tinsley, Wm. D. s.	1	Cook, Thomas r. s.	2
Royster, Robert s.	1	Moon, Jesse, orphs. of	1
Anderson, Ann h. a.	1	Snellings, Samuel h. of f.	2
Cook, Daniel s.	1	Burton, Mary wid.	1
Brown, Aaron h. of f.	2	Dye, Mary wid. and w. r. s.	2
Cook, Joshua s.	1	Bell, Elizabeth w. r. s.	1
Brewer, Hundley J. s.	1	Mobley, Isaac orphs. of	2
Rich, John h. of f.	2	Hudson, William h. of f.	2
Maupin, Jesse r. s.	2	Oliver, Berrien h. of f.	2
Turman, Mary wid.	1	Oliver, Peter r. s.	2
Good, John M. s.	1	Cook, Theodosius r. s.	2
Cook, Sarah wid.	1		

Capt. Butler's District

Martin, Rebecca wid.	1	Brawner, Simuel h. of f.	2
Head, William, orphs. of	1	Kerlin, Eliz. wid. and w. r. s.	2
Butler, David C. h. of f.	2	Allman, Usry orphs. of	2
Hardy, Mary orph.	1	Rodgers, John W. h. of f.	2
Rowsey, Forester h. of f.	2	Thrilkill, Wm. H. h. of f.	2

GEORGIA D. A. R.

Name	Draws
White, Thomas J. s.	1
Hall, Seales s.	1
Wyche, William H. s.	1
Wyche, Joshua O. s.	1
Stephens, Henry H. h. of f.	2
Hall, Thomas s.	1
Allgood, William h. of f.	2
Webb, Abner h. of f.	2
Butler, Patrick r. s.	2
Brown, James N. r. s.	2
Hardy, Jetha, minors of f. a.	2
Glenn, Mitchell s.	1
Thrilkill, Willis h. of f.	2
Allmand, Sarah wid.	1
Dennard, John r. s.	2
Dennard, John citizen	2
Thrilkill, John W. s.	1
White, John H. s.	1
Campbell, Daniel, h. of f.	2
Cook, Lewis h. of f.	2
Christian, John M. s.	1
Rodgers, Isham G. h. of f.	2
Wright, Warren s.	1
Wright, Charles h. of f.	2
Algood, Spencer r. s.	2
Brown, Asa A. h. of f.	2
Adams, George s.	1
Bragg, Mary wid.	1
Dennis, Stephen orphs. of	1
Dillard, James cit. & r. s.	3
Taylor, William h. of f.	2
Kerley, Samuel s.	1
Kinnebrew, Edwin s.	1
Christian, Samuel s.	1
Golden, Alexander Sr. h. of f.	2
Golden, Alex. orphs. of	1
Wilkins, John r. s.	2
Bowen, Horatius C. h. of f.	2
Fortson, Thomas h. of f.	2
Dillard, Nehemiah V. s.	1
Dillard, Isaac s.	1
Butler, John h. of f.	2
Snellings, John h. of f.	2
Kerlin, Wm. orphs. of	1
Brawner, Asa. s.	1
Butler, Peter D. s.	1
Brawner, William M. s.	1
Brawner, John W. s.	1
Brawner, Joseph s.	1

Capt. Tucker's District.

Name	Draws
Brewer, Horatio orphs. of	2
Brewer, Susan wid.	1
Hudson, Chas., minors of f. a.	2
Nunnelee, James F. r. s.	2
Tate, Sarah wid.	1
Tate, John, orphs. of	2
Davis, Absolom, orphs. of	1
Edwards, Robert L. h. of f.	2
Jones, Fannie, wid. & w. r. s.	1
Middleton, Robt., orphs. of	1
Terrill, Jowel s.	1
Terrell, Timothy s.	1
Tate, Enos, Sr. r. s.	2
McGehee, Thomas G. s.	1
Tucker, Godfry r. s.	2
Jones, Edmond h. of f.	2
Hudson, Richard D. s.	1
Whitman, William h. of f.	2
Hudson, Lucy h. a.	1
Childs John cit. & r. s.	4
Jones, Samuel s.	1
Brewer, Edmond H. h. of f.	2
Wall, Cade s.	1
Davis, Thomas F. s.	1
Cholston, Charles T. s.	1
Terrell, Joseph r. s.	2
Davis, Nancy w. r. s.	1
Seals, Eliz., wid. & w. r. s.	2
Bray, Banister R. h. of f.	2
Lane, John A. s.	1
Johnson, James s.	1
Foster, William h. of f.	2
Tatum, Jese r. s.	2
Wall, Bud C. s.	1
Childs, Lewis G. s.	1
Hudson, William h. of f.	2

	Draws		Draws
Johnson, John H. s.	1	Statom, John h. of f.	2
Martin, Beverly h. of f.	2	Johnson, Susan wid.	1
Johnson, Philip, orphs. of	2	Owens, James S. s.	1
Owens, Barashaba wid.	1	Arnold, William s.	1
Owens, Barashaba w. r. s.	1	Smith, Wells h. of f.	2
Owens, John, orphs of	1	Collins, Samuel h. of f.	2
Hudson, Eliz. wid. & w. r. s.	2	Rose, Sarah wid.	1

Capt. Allston's District

Chandler, Mordecai s.	1	Banks, Richard s.	1
Oliver, Nancy wid.	1	Cleveland, Jacob M. s.	1
Oliver, Cabeb, orphs of	2	Alston, Gilley w. r. s.	1
Jones, William h. of f.	2	Alexander, Elam s.	1
Statham, Augustus D. s.	1	Cleveland, Early s.	1
Arnold, John s.	1	Akin, Johnson s.	1
Rucker, Zacheriah h. of f.	2	Fortson, Tavner h. of f.	2
Grag, Susannah w. r. s.	2	Banks, Ann wid.	1
Clark, Larkin r. s.	2	Banks, Henry h. of f.	2
Banks, William R. s.	1	Lyon, Thomas s.	1
Rucker, James s.	1	Perryman, Wm. J. h. of f.	2
Rucker, Milly wid.	1	Nix, John s.	1
Rucker, John, orphs of	1	Henderson, James B. s.	1
Gillespie, Geo. J. h. of f.	2	Jones, Marshall s.	1
Howard, Lucy h. a.	1	Allen, Thomas h. of f.	2
Beck, Sary wid. & w. r. s.	2	Naish, Jeremiah h. of f.	2
Lewis, Jeptha s.	1	Harper, Bedford h. of f.	2
Heard, Eliz. wid. & w. r. s.	2	Henderson, John, orphs of	1
Jeter, Barnett, Jr. s.	1	Nellums (Nelms) Wm. s.	1
Keys, John D. s.	1	Ramsey, B. h. of f.	2
White, Rheubin, orphs of	2	Alexander, Willis h. of f.	2
Banks, William, orphs of	2	Arnold, Wm., orphs of	1
Rosser, Jeptha h. of f.	2	White, Mary wid.	1
Bourne, Henry s.	1	White, David, orphs of	2
Clark, William D. s.	1		

GEORGIA, ELBERT COUNTY

This is to certify that we have made a true list of the names for a draw or draws in the approaching land lottery on the above state and county and Major Allen's Battalion,

This 1st. day of October, 1825.

(Signed) William Jones
Banister R. Bray,
Receivers.

GEORGIA D. A. R.

Major David Dobb's Battalion

Capt. Horton's District

Name	Draws	Name	Draws
Mills, Moses r. s.	2	Dodds, William orphs. of	2
Higginbotham, Jacob r. s.	2	Maxwell, Thomas, Sr. r. s.	2
Thornton, Benj. h. of f.	2	Maxwell, John r. s.	2
Molding, Thomas h. of f.	2	Hunt, James r. s.	2
Thornton, Elizabeth wid.	1	Dickerson, John h. of f.	2
Thornton, Reuben, orphs of	1	Lunsford, William h. of f.	2
Bond, Nathan r. s.	2	Mewbourn, Thomas h. of f.	2
Bond, Willis h. of f.	2	Hilley, Thomas, Sr. r. s.	2
Haircrow, Ezekiel s.	1	Hilley, Thomas, Jr. s.	1
Haircrow, Hugh s.	1	Johnson, Angus s.	1
Ginn, Transylvania wid.	1	Teasley, Sarah, wid. & w. r. s.	2
Ginn, Transylvania w. r. s.	1	Burden, Hannah wid.	1
Maxwell, Jesey s.	1	Thornton, Daniel s.	1
Maxwell, Martin s.	1	Sandidge, Clairborne r. s.	2
Maxwell, Thomas s.	1	Teasley, James S. h. of f.	2
Maxwell, Wm. Jr. s.	1	Sandidge, Thomas J. s.	1
Teasley, John s.	1	McCurry, Lauchlin, Jr. s.	1
Teasley, Levy, orphs. of	1	McCurry, Lauchlin, Sr. h. of f.	2
Adams, Nicholas M. s.	1	Pulliam, Robert r. s.	2
Adams, Calvin M. h. of f.	2	Tibis, Thomas h. of f.	2
Adams, William h. of f.	2	Teasley, Isham b. of f.	2
Adams, Lawrence M. s.	1	Thornton, Elsey B. s.	1
Ashworth, Elisha h. of f.	2	Thornton, John h. of f.	2
McCurry, Kathrine wid.	1	Thornton, Thos., orphs of	5
Nelms, Joshua B. h. of f.	2	Murry, Nancy, wid. & w. r. s.	2
Underwood, Ann wid. & w. r. s.	2	Higginbotham, Riley s.	1
Ginn, Thos. h. of f.	2	Adams, Thomas r. s.	2
Ginn, William s.	1	Adams, James, Sr. r. s.	2
Wallis, Rhody wid.	1	Runnals, William s.	1
		Cabennis, Henry r. s.	2

Capt. Carpenter's District

Name	Draws	Name	Draws
Wooldridge, Thos. h. of f.	2	Tinar, Tolison h. of f.	2
Rumsey Richard h. of f.	2	McMullan, Daniel h. of f.	2
Rumsey, Richard r. s.	2	Sittin, William h. of f.	2
Skelton, John s.	1	Teasley, Beverly A. s.	1
Vacray, Jos. h. of f. & r. s.	4	McCurley, Moses h. of f.	2
Coulston, Mariam, wid. & w. r. s.	2	Stowers, Jeremiah s.	1
		Sadler, James R. h. of f.	2
Watson, Thomas h. of f.	2	Wright, Gabriel, orphs of	1
Chrislar, Benj. h. of f.	2	Fain, Charles s.	1
Tinar, William s.	1	Pritchett, Thos. h. of f.	2
Tinar, Cabel s.	1	Dutton, William s.	1

HISTORICAL COLLECTIONS 253

Name	Draws
Hickman, Martha wid.	1
Hickman, Waker, orphs of	1
Scales, William s.	1
Richardson, Amos r. s.	2
Bryan, Sarah wid.	1
Pritchet, Delpha wid.	1
Pritchet, Nicholas, orphs. of	1
Pritchet, Nicholas orph.	1
Brown, Rolen s.	1
Dutton, Thomas h. of f.	2
Carpenter, Joshua S. h. of f.	2
Ashworth, John h. of f.	2
Ray, James H. s.	1
Bobo, Lewis s.	1
Hickman, William s.	1
Stowers, Lewis, Sr. r. s.	2
Skelton, Jabez h. of f.	2
Adams, Robert h. of f.	2
Macgehee, Jonathan s.	1
Macgehee, Jesse s.	1
Macgee, John s.	1
Adams, Solomon s.	1
Dooley, Allen D. h. of f.	2
Johnson, Daniel s.	1
Johnson, John s.	1
Jones, Jos. H. h. of f.	2
Jones, Rebecca wid.	1

Name	Draws
Jones, Simeon, orphs. of	1
Lovingood, Samuel s.	1
Hutarsen, Moses h. of f.	2
Highsmith, John h. of f.	2
Highsmith, Thos. H. h. of f.	2
Harper, William G. s.	1
Ashworth, Noah s.	1
Rucker, William r. s.	2
Teasley, Silas r. s.	2
Shiflet, James s.	1
Shiflet, Picket s.	1
Johnson, Linsey s.	1
Johnson, Neal s.	1
Johnson, Alexander s.	1
Totman, Rebecca wid.	1
Hill, Ealum s.	1
Hickman, Thomas S. s.	1
Thompson, Jesse h. of f.	2
Scales, Joel h. of f.	2
Skelton, Richmond h. of f.	2
Crump, Pleasant D. h. of f.	2
Healing or } Thos. J. s.	1
Keeling	
McGuire, Thomas M. s.	1
Powell, Francis, Sr. h. of f.	2
Highsmith, Milly wid.	1
Highsmith, Milly w. r. s.	1

Capt. Dobb's District

Name	Draws
Self, Frances wid.	1
Self, Samuel L. orphs. of	1
Prothro, James h. of f.	2
Sullivan, Wm. H. h. of f.	2
Bradley, Robt. C. orph. of	1
McCurry, Angus, Sr. r. s.	2
Sanders, Calvin P. h. of f.	2
Sanders, Lewis M. h. of f.	2
Neal, Lindsey s.	1
Vaughters, Linsey s.	1
Vaughters, Russell orph.	1
Boatwright, Daniel h. of f.	2
Prothro, Joshua h. of f.	2
Prothro, Zilpha wid.	1
Prothro, Nathaniel orphs. of	2
Prothro, William s.	1
Enlo, John h. of f. & r. s.	4

Name	Draws
Scales, Thomas h. of f.	2
Rhodes, Hannah wid.	1
Rhodes, John W. { orph. of Moses R. Rhodes	
McCurry, John s.	1
Gill, Elizabeth { orph of Robert Gill	1
White, Tabitha h. a.	1
Minors of John W. White, f. a.	2
McDonald, Margaret wid.	1
McDonald, John orphs. of	1
Fowler, Rachel wid.	1
Fowler, James orph.	1
Salmon, Jeremiah s.	1
Vickery, James h. of f.	2
Ferguson, Daniel s.	1

GEORGIA D. A. R.

	Draws		Draws
McDonald, Angus s.	1	Neal, Chriswell s.	1
Ferguson, John s.	1	McDonald, Donald s.	1
Kelley, Wm. h. of f. & r. s.	4	Keeling, Leonard W. s.	1
Dobbs, Louisania wid.	1	Gardner, Nancy, minor of	
Dobbs, {orph of Silas {Josiah Dobbs	1	Gardner, Elijah f. a.	1
		Sadler, Wm. B. h. of f.	2
Childers, Jesse C. h. of f.	2	Williamson, Walker h. of f.	2
Tiller, Reuben L. h. of f.	2	Fain, John h. of f.	2
Smith, Archibald h. of f.	2	Fain, John H. s.	1
Alexander, Isaac r. s.	2	Dobbs, Josiah s.	1
McGarity, Willson s.	1	Haynes, Moses G. s.	1
White, William, Sr. r. s.	2	Carden, Moses s.	1
White, Jesse h. of f.	2	Haynes, Moses, Jr. h. of f.	2
Couch, Sarah wid.	1	Dean, John h. of f.	2
Coulston, Nancy h. a.	1	Park, Mary w. r. s.	1
Skelton, Martin, h. of f.	2	Fain, Robert s.	1
McMullan, Willis s.	1	Fain, Epperson s.	1

Capt. Dunn's District

Underwood, Joseph h. of f.	2	Hinton, Peter r. s.	2
Hailey, William r. s.	2	Allen, Edmond h. of f.	2
Hailey, Thomas, minor f. a.	1	Chapman, Frederick s.	1
Jourdain, Fountain, h. of f.	2	Crawford, Oliver s.	1
Jourdain, Fountain r. s.	2	Ganes, Henry S. s.	1
Jourdain, John s.	1	Preuit, Joshua s.	1
Ganes (Gaines), Francis r. s.	2	Preuit, John h. of f.	2
Hinton, James S. s.	1	Jourdain, Isaac h. of f.	2
Craft, John, Jr.	1	Skaggs, Tabitha wid. & w. r. s.	2
Roberson, Samuel s.	1	Alexander, Mary wid.	1
Head, Benjamin s.	1	Bell, Rhoda wid.	1
Means, Jacob h. of f.	2	Bell, John orphs. of	1
Means, Elizabeth, wid.	1	Dodds, William s.	1
Means, Wm., orphs. of	2	Jourdain, John, Jr. s.	1
Crawford, Lucy wid.	1	Buffinton, William s.	1
Johnston, Mary wid. & w. r. s.	2	Hinton, Robert s.	1
Taler (Taylor), Wm. Jr. s.	1	Alexander, Geo. C. s.	1
Chapman, David, h. of f.	2	Taylor, Jesse W. h. of f.	2
Hunt, Henry orphs. of	1	Teasley, Benager S. h. of f.	2
Davis, John r. s.	2	Harris, John, Jr. h. of f.	2
Craft, William, Jr. s.	1	Harris, Ezekiel s.	1
Wright, Isaac h. of f.	2	Bowman, Willis W. s.	1
Lockhart, James r. s.	2	Ganes, Sarah wid.	1
Cook, David h. of f.	2	Ganes, Levingston W. orphs. of	1
Preuit, Jacob G. s.	1	Hunt, George h. of f.	2
Dunn, Joseph s.	1	Hunt, Moses r. s.	2
Ham, Reuben orphs. of	2		

HISTORICAL COLLECTIONS 255

	Draws		Draws
Smether, Gabriel h. of f.	2	Tailer, Elizabeth wid.	1
Smether, Gabriel r. s.	2	Tailer, Garrett s.	1
Strickland, Joseph h. of f.	2	Tailer, John s.	1
Terrell, Levisa wid. & w. r. s.	2	Smith, Robert h. of f.	2
King, Zuriah h. of f.	2	Cash, John r. s.	2
Yoes, Katharine wid. & w. r. s.	2	Terrell, Robert W. s.	1
Snoe, Eli h. of f.	2	Faubes, Henry h. of f.	2
Allen, Reuben h. of f.	2	Hunt, John S. h. of f.	2
Underwood, Wyneford wid.	1	Hunt, Joel s.	1
Underwood, Wyneford w. r. s.	1	Terry, Thomas s.	1
McGuire, Anderson r. s.	2	Riley, James r. s.	2
Grissop, James r. s.	2	Harper, John s.	1
Prather, William M. s.	1	Sadler, John F. s.	1
Craft, Washington h. of f.	2	Powell, Wm. R. h. of f.	2
Harris, John, Sr. r. s.	2	Daniel, John, Jr. s.	1
Craft, John, Sr. h. of f.	2	Davis, James s.	1
Craft, Samuel h. of f.	2	Rowzee, John s.	1
Hinton, John L. s.	1	Daniel, John, Sr. r. s.	2
Hinton, Peter, Jr. s.	1	Word, Wm. Sr. h. of f. & r. s.	4
Shiflet, Joseph s.	1	Mabry, Thos. W. h. of f.	2
King, Thos. s. & r. s.	3	Cunningham, John Sr. h.of f.	2
Turner, Thos. h. of f.	2	Buffington, Ann wid.	1
Tailer, John orphs. of	2	Buffington, Joseph, orphs. of	2

Capt. Blackwell's District

Cunningham, Joseph, h. of f.	2	Thornton, Dozier, Sr. r. s.	2
Rucker, John h. of f. & r. s.	3	Word, Sarah wid.	1
Banks, Lemuel s.	1	Word, Richard, orphs of	2
Anderson, Thomas h. of f.	2	Carter, Lucy wid.	1
Brown, Dozier T. h. of f.	2	Carter, Chas. N. B. orph. of	1
Alexander, William h. of f.	2	Carter, Thos. P.	
James, William s.	1	Carter, Robert M. s.	1
Henderson, Richard S. s.	1	Carter, John J. s.	1
Ganes, Wm., h. of f. & r. s.	4	Carter, Elizabeth w. r. s.	1
Wansley, Reubin h. of f.	2	Hansard, Janet w. r. s.	1
Wansley, John s.	1	Rodlander, William B. s.	1
Wansley, John, Sr. r. s.	2	Dickerson, Robert W. s.	1
Davis, Susannah wid.	1	Henderson, Simeon, Jr. s.	1
Nelms, James s.	1	Bailey, Henry s.	1
Thornton, Jonathan h. of f.	2	Adams, Abner s.	1
Royal, Eliz. wid. & w. r. s.	2	Patterson, Wiley s.	1
Williford, Maxfield H. s.	1	Henderson, James h. of f.	2
Harper, William M. s.	1	Hulme, Joseph s.	1
White, Jas. E., minors of f. a.	2	Hulme, John T. s.	1
Herndon, Edward h. of f.	2	Eavenson, Willis s.	1

GEORGIA D. A. R.

	Draws		Draws
Tait, Edmond B. h. of f.	2	Brown, Elbert s.	1
Fortson, Elizabeth wid.	1	Blackwell, Park h. of f.	2
Fortson, Benj. orphs. of	2	Blackwell, Sally Chandler w. r. s.	1
Ford, Mary wid. & w. r. s.	2		
Hall, Katharine wid.	1	Wansley, Larkin s.	1
Hall, Robert orphs. of	2	Ward, William, Jr. orphs. of	1
Eavenson, Eli r. s.	2	Ward, Martha wid.	1
Harris, Rebecca w. r. s.	1	Shackleford, James id.	1
Brown, James s.	1	Faulkner, James M. orph.	1
Brown, Benjamin, r. s.	2	Shackleford, Asa. O. s.	1
Wheeler, Thomas, Sr. r. s.	2	Hudson, Nathaniel, orphs. of	1
Smith, Joseph h. of f.	2	Newberry, Nancy w. r. s.	1
Roebuck, William s.	1	Banks, Marion orph. of Banks, R., dec'd	1
Hudson, Molly wid. & w. r. s.	2		
Rice, Richard h. of f.	2	Banks, Thos. A. h. of f.	2
White, John M. r. s.	2	Alexander, Katharine wid.	1
Landers, Jas. O. h. of f.	2	Alexander, Edward orphs. of	1
Mann, Thomas s.	1	Mann, Judith w. r. s.	1
Shackleford, Henry s.	1	Hinton, Thomas h. of f.	2
Maxwell, Reuben h. of f.	2	Andrew, Joseph s.	1
Craft, Archable s.	1	Morgan, Andrew s.	1

GEORGIA, ELBERT COUNTY

We do hereby certify that the foregoing is a correct list of the persons with the number of annexed to each of their names in Major Dobb's Battalion in said County who have given in their names for a draw or draws in the present and contemplated Land Lottery of this State.

Given in under our hands, this 31, October, 1825.

(Signed) Thomas S. White

John A. Virdel

Receivers of names for draws.

GOLD LOTTERY (1832)

This land was known as the "Cherokee Purchase", and extended from the Chattahoochee river to the state of Alabama on the west, to Tenn. and N. C. on the north. Lots of 40 acres were supposed to contain gold, and were known as "gold lots". Land lots contained 160 acres.

Revolutionary soldiers, widows of Revolutionary soldiers, citizens, citizens widows and orphans were eligible for participation.

HISTORICAL COLLECTIONS 257

KEY

Married men....2 draws.
Single men....1 draw
s. l. w..........Soldier Late War.
s. i. w..........Soldier Indian War 1784–1797.
r. s.............Revolutionary Soldier.
w. r. s.........Widow Revolutionary soldier.
wid............Widow.
orphs.........Orphans.

Maj. James E. Chambers Battalion
Capt. John Cannings District

	Draws		Draws
Heard, George W.	2	Smith, John M.	1
White, Benjamin B.	1	Fortson, Easton	2
Holmes, James	2	Booth, Henry	1
Perryman, Albert G.	1	Allen, Nathaniel R.	1
Rich, James	1	Clark, Thomas J.	1
King, William, Sr.	2	McLester, Horatio	1
Worrill, Edmund F.	1	Housley, William	1
Weston, Job	1	Jones, Thomas	2
Smith, Thomas	1	Stone, William	2
Black, John W.	2	Chisholm, Ann w. r. s.	1
Smith, Francis M.	1	Taylor, William T.	2
Young, Thomas	1	Willis, James M.	1
Lofton, James	2	Johnson, Julius (Jasper Co.)	2
Adams, William H., Jr.	1	Harris, James W.	2
Baker, Madison	1	Speed, Terrell	2
Fortson, Benjamin W.	1	Chisholm: orphs. of Andrew Chisholm given in by their mother Ann Chisholm	1
Darracott, Rebeckah wid.	1	Patrick J.	
Chisholm, Ann wid.	1	Andrew J.	
Bentley, Hiram	2	Sarah Ann	
Barr, George I.	2		
Willis, William	1	Almand: orphs. of Usry Almond	1
Basinger, John N.	1	Mahulda K.	
Campbell, William B. s. l. w.	2	Lucyann F.	
Davis, Isaac N.	2	Willis, Milley wid.	1
Brown, Edward	2	Willis:	
Perryman, Anthony A.	2	Benj. orphs. of John Willis	1
Hendrick, Frances wid.	1	Eliz. C.	
Hester, Robert	1	Louisa, A.	
James, David R.	2	Bowen, Frances D.	1
Fortson, Tavner W.	2	Brawner, Middleton s. l. w.	2
Smith, Voluntine	2	Ragan, John	1

GEORGIA D. A. R.

Name	Draws
Almand, Jones R.	1
Reece, Alford B. of Morgan Co. s. l. w.	1
Carter, John W.	1
King, Francis W.	2
Higginbotham, Jeane wid.	1
Higginbotham, Jeane w. r. s.	1
Oliver, Thomas s. i. w.	1
Anderson, James	2
Burch, Benjamin	2
Griffen, William W.	2
Griffen, Marshall W.	1
Almand, Sarah wid.	1
Griffen, Margaret wid.	1
Willis, Milley w. r. s.	1
Wilhight, Thomas C.	1
Herring, John	1
Aycock, Richard L.	2
Willis, Richard	2
Bond, Martin	1
Seamore, John W.	1
Smith, Zachariah s. l. w.	1
Eades, Sarah D. } orph. of Ramey Eades	1
Aycock, Fielding	2
Satterwhite, Eliz. wid.	1
Satterwhite, Eliz. w. r. s.	1
Smith, Benjamin s. l. w.	1
Burch, Eliz. wid. & w. r. s.	2

Capt. Jos. G. Wilhite's District

Name	Draws
Cabaniss, Henry r. s.	2
Fortson, Thos. D. Jane M. Almedia H. } orphs. given in in by their gdn. Isaac Almand	2
Webb, Letty wid.	1
Almand, John	2
Faulkner, Wm. s. l. w. & s. i. w.	2
Booth, Nancy wid.	1
Parham, George W.	1
Almand, Isaac s. l. w.	1
Webb, Claborn Alcean M. } orphs. given in by their mother Letty Webb, gdn.	1
Webb, Bridger s. l. w.	1
Johnson, Lindsay orph.	1
Parham, Isham, Jr.	2
Parham, John	1
Christian, Drewry	1
Booth, Mary Nancy Geo. J. } orphs. given in by their gdn. Nancy Booth	2
Stinchcomb, Levi s. l. w.	1
Booth, Joseph G.	2
Webb, Elijah W.	2
Ridgway, John T.	1
Oglesby, James	2
Oliver, James s. i. w.	1
Kerlin, Jacob	1
Morris, Sherod s. i. w.	1
Christian, Elijah L. s. l. w.	1
Vaughan, Isaac D.	2
Faulkner, James J.	2
Booth, John s. l. w.	1
Booth, William N.	1
Colvard, John S. s. l. w.	1
Oglesby, Adkin	1
Almand, Simeon	2
Webb, Walton P.	2
Booth, Robt. Sr. s. l. w.	1
Deadwyler, Henry R.	1
Mobley, Martin D. } orph. of Isaac Mobley	1
Wilhight, Philip A.	1
Ridgway, Robert C.	1
Brown, Thomas H.	1
Ridgway, James Sr. s. l. w.	1
Mabry, Thomas W.	1
Deadwyler, Margaret Ann } orph. of Jos. Jr.	1
Mabry, Thomas W., Sr. s. l. w.	1
Arnold, Davis	2
Phelps, James Jr.	1
Stovall, Thomas	1
Webb, Fortunatus	2
Bentley, John E.	1
Deadwyler, Asa	1

Draws

	Draws
Ridgway, Lemuel T.	1
Hammond, Furney	2
Phelps, Thomas s. l. w.	1
Montague, Susan G. wid.	1
Wooton, Hannah wid.	1
Edwards, John s. l. w.	1
Bray, Lewis	2
Page, James B.	1
More, William J.	1
Moore, John N.	2
Wiley, William S.	2
Wilhite, Lewis r. s.	2

	Draws
Banks, { orph. of Jas. A. Banks, given in by Wm. C. Simeon Oliver, gdn.	1
Ridgway, James E.	1
Mobley, Frances wid.	1
Wilhite, Jos. Y. s. l. w.	1
Brag, Maston H.	2
McFerron, William	1
Vasser, William O.	1
Webb, Margaret wid.	1
Houston, Alex. P.	2
Almand, Micajah T.	1
Almand, Ann, wid. of s. i. w.	1

Capt. Jesse Nellum's District 201

Booth, Gabriel s. l. w.	1
Moon, Pleasant	1
Trammell, William s. i. w.	1
Hill, Elum	2
Eagin, John r. s.	2
Fits, Mary Jane / Tandy W. / John T. / Rhoda Ann / Wm. Green / Elizabeth / Keziah D. } orphs. of John Fits given in by their mother Jincy Fits.	1
Dudley, Ignatius s. l. w.	1
Cooper, Thomas	2
Denny, Edward A. s. l. w.	1
Coker, John	1
Blanget, Jeremiah } orph. given in by Robt. Smith	1
Smith, Elijah	2
Raines, John W.	2
Bentley, Jesse	2
Hendrick, Eli	1
Bentley, Samuel s. l. w.	1
Denny George W.	1
Roberts, Jos. Sr. r. s.	2
Seamore, Zachariah, Jr.	2
Oliver, John { orph. given in by his mother Nancy Rumsey.	1

Booth, Victor E.	2
Staples, Frances w. r. s.	1
Hathcock, Oziah r. s.	2
Raines, Josiah F.	2
Penn, Mary wid.	1
Duncan, Nathaniel	2
Legrand, John N. r. s.	2
Wadson, Abner	2
Tucker, John M. s. l. w.	1
Tucker, William	2
Fits, Mary w. r. s.	1
Smith, Micajah M.	1
Duncan, Pearson Jr.	1
Fits, James O.	1
Denney, Robert s. l. w.	1
Payton, George	1
Ginn, Wiley	2
Moon, James B.	1
Gay, James	2
Steedley, James P.	2
Anderson, Henry	2
Smith, Isham	1
Downes, James	2
Hendrick, Whitehead s. l. w.	1
Hendrick, Wesley	1
Denny, David s. l. w.	1
Christian, Washington	1
Raines, Dabney s. l. w.	1
Hendrick, Russell s. l. w.	1

GEORGIA D. A. R.

Draws

Moon, John B., Gabrilla } orphs. of Pleasant Moon, given in by their mother 1

7th. April 1832. This is the only date in this book.

Smith, William W. 2
Christian, Turner 2
Brumfield, Ann C. w. r. s. 1
Penn:
  Frances, Lucinda } orphs. of John Penn 1

Draws

Henry, Sarah Ann, James M. } orphs. of Alex. Henry .. 1
Payton, William 1
Jones, Jemima wid. 1
Pearce, Jacob 2
Payton, John 1
Nelms, William s. l. w. 1
Smith, Asa 1
Page, John S. 1

Capt. Joel Bowers District

Evas, Rhoday r. s. 2
Brown, Middleton, W. 1
Peck, Elizabeth, wid. 1
Peck, Abel, Stephen, Winny { orphs. of Abel Peck, given in by their mother Eliz. Peck 1
Robert, Moses J. 2
Chambers, Edward M. 1
Hall, Hugh S. 1
Smith, Larkin 1
Smith, Drury 2
Lines, Joseph 2
Bray, Patience w. r. s. 1
Bray, Avy, idiot given in by his mother, Patience Bray 1
McGarrity, Sarah { orph of Kindred McGarrity given in by her mother Delilah McGarrity 1
Mason, Elizabeth wid. 1
Mason, Jane Ann, Evelina, Polly, Kitty, Wm. J., Joshua, Lucinda } orphs. of Andy Mason given in by their mother Eliz. Mason .. 2

Maxwell, William T. 2
McGarrity, Kindred 1
Roland, Mastin 2
Brown, William H. 1
Peck, Solomon 2
Robert, Presley B. 2
Karr, Samuel S. s. i. w. 1
Smith, John, Sr. s. i. w. 1
Allen, James 1
Peeler, Cader 2
Smith, John, Jr. 1
Walas, Thomas, Jr. 1
Kelly, Barnabas 2
Clark, Larken 1
Harbin, Sarah w. r. s. 1
Ginn, Sarah w. r. s. 1
McGarrity, Delilah wid. 1
Horton, Elizabeth w. r. s. 1
Duncan, John Jr. 1
Mann, Robert B. 1
Brown, Wiley B. 2
Williford, Reuben S. 2
Redwine, Jacob r. s. 2
Rice, Aaron 2
Smith, Singleton 1
Bray, John 1
Bray, Benjamin 1
Burnett, Pleasant 2
Philips, Wiley 2
Haynes, Thomas s. l. w. 1
Burnet, John 1

	Draws		Draws
Parker, Joseph H.	1	Ballenger, John Jr.	2
Ballenger, John Sr.	2	Brown, John Jr.	2
Haynes, James W.	1	Horton, Joshua P.	1
Haynes, Moses M.	1	McGee, William	1
Eaves, James	1	Steel, Robert	2
Carlton, Isham W.	1	Eaves, Alford	2
Merritt, John	1	Rice, Walton	1
Jordon, Obedience wid.	1	Carlton, Henry S.	1
Jordan,		Winn, Gustavus A.	1
James N. { orphs. of		Carlton, John M.	1
Littlebury { James		Ray, William C.	2
Joshua R. { Jordan		Burden, Wm. s. i. w. and s. l. w.	2
Eliz. C. { given in		Allen, Agnes wid. and w. r. s.	2
Levy H. { by their		Allen,	
James B. H. { mother		John { orph of	
{ Obedience		{ Joseph Allen	1
{ Jordan	1	Bramblet, Levi	1
Davis, Moses	2	Allison, John	2
White, Eppy s. l. w.	1	Bray, David	2
Harden, Mary absent husband	1	Harden, Rhoda (minor) f. a.	1
Brown, James E.	1	Henry, Daniel N.	2
Bowers, Joel	1	Bowers, Edy	1
Gully,		Brown, Andrew s. i. w.	1
Eliz. } Idiots given in		Horton, Jeremiah T.	1
Geo. } by father	1	Horton, James J.	1
Hendry, Charles	2	Hendry, Charles s. i. w.	1
Reed, Sarah w. r. s.	1	Jones, Drewry N.	1
Bramblet, Elizabeth w. r. s.	1	Smith, Wm. W., Sr. s. l. w.	1
Smith, William W., Jr.	1	Kelly, John	1
Ginn, Jesse	2	Wade, John s. l. w.	1
Burnett, Reason	2		

Capt. Rowland Lunsford's District

Brewer, William F.	2	Burton, Thos. J., Jr.	1
Upshaw, James	2	Lowrimore, Samuel s. l. w.	1
Carter, George s. l. w.	1	Young, Reuben	1
Christian, Lindsay	1	Ham, Willis R.	1
Harmon, James M.	1	Dickey, John	2
Carter, Thos. S. s. i. w. and s. l. w.	2	Pledger, Thomas r. s.	2
Hudson,		Richards,	
Mary L. { orphs, given		Piety { orphs. of	
David N. { in by gdn.		Letha { Reuben	
Eliz. Ann { David Hudson	2	Wm. { Richards	
Bond, Henry W.	1	Mary { given in by	
Threlkeld, Marian F.	1	Reuben { mother Rachel	
		{ Richards	2

	Draws		Draws
Hunt, Nancy wid. of s. i. w.	1	Lowreymore, Sarah w. r. s.	1
Threlkeld,		King, William s. l. w.	1
Thomas D. Banebridge — orphs. of Thos. Threlkeld given in by mother Delila Threlkeld	1	Turman, Viletty, wid. s. i. w.	1
		Webb, Urbin A.	2
		Christian, Jesse G.	1
		Pulliam, John	1
		Polestone, Jesse	1
		White, Martin	2
Upshaw,		Head, William O.	1
John A. Louisa Geo. L. — orphs. of Geo. Upshaw given by James Upshaw	2	Pledger, Mary S. — orph. of John S. Pledger, given in by Wesley Pledger	1
Burton, Thomas, Sr. s. l. w.	1	Ham,	
Head, Sarah wid. and w. r. s.	2	Nancy — orph of John Ham	1
Smith, Thomas J.	1		
Christian, George W.	1		
Harmon, John, Sr. r. s.	2	Scales, George	2
Butler, Haley s. l. w.	1	Penn, William	2
Phelps, Johnson	1	Lunsford, Rollin s. l. w.	1
Means, Alex. Sr.	2	Oliver, Jane, wid. and w. r. s.	2
Critenton, Elijah	2	Hardiman, Elizabeth B.	1
Upshaw, Middleton	2	Palmore, Catharine W. absent husband	1
Bond, Ephraoditus	1		
Threlkeld, Tuly	1	Ham, Elizabeth wid.	1
David, Samuel	2	Stinchcomb, Absolom s. i. w.	1
Threlkeld, Dilila wid.	1	Mann, John B.	2
Bailey, Henry	2	Scales, George s. l. w.	1
Pledger, Isaac M.	2	Upshaw, John r. s.	2
Tabor, Benjamin K.	2	Booth, Prudence, wid. and w. r. s.	2
Ham, Theophilus	2		
Sandridge, James M.	2	Hardiman, Joel's, orphs.	1
Cook, William T. O.	2	Shoemaker, John B.	1
Cook, Abraham	2		

GOLD LOTTERY

Names taken from what seems to be a repetition of the foregoing lottery, these names not found in the foregoing. Married men, single men, widows and orphans entitled to draws, no mention of military service. The only date being on the margin in one place only, April 7, 1832.

Chambers Battalion. Capt. John Cannings District.

	Draws		Draws
Turman, Thos. J.	1	Ragan, William	1
Higginbotham, John S.	2	Worrill, Ransom	2
Brawner, James	1	Whitman, William	2
Winkfield, John	2		

Capt. Jos. Y. Wilhites Dist.

	Draws		Draws
Deadwyler, Martin	2	Oglesby, Thomas, Sr.	1
David, Jacob W.	2	Parham, Isham, Sr.	2
Brown, Jesse	2	Booth, Robt., son of Nancy	1
Andrew, Burley	2	Booth, Robt., son of Robt.	1
Culbreth, A.	2	King, James	2
Ridgway, Burrel	2	Hicks, William	2
Phelps, James, Sr.	2	Oliver, Shelton	2
Phelps, Thomas	2	Vaughn, Alex.	2
Wilhite, John B.	2	Johnson, Lindsay	2
Moore, Thomas	2	Oglesby, William	2
Watson, Moses	2	Brawner, James M.	2
Oliver, Simeon	2	Booker, Alex.	2
Webb, John D.	2	Vasser, John	2
Webb, John B.	1	Brown, Lewis	2
Oglesby, Drewry	2	Wilhight, Philemon R.	2
Butler, Peter P. Sr.	2	Wiley, George	2

Capt. Jesse Nellums Dist.

	Draws		Draws
Threlkeld, Oliver	2	Jones, Jemimah wid.	1
Staples, Thomas	2	Nelmes, Jesse	2
Coker, Alsea	2	Northern, John	2
Fork, Henry	2	Dudley, James L.	2
Payton, Moses	2	Ruff, Shadrick	2
Payton, George	1	White, Martin	2
Smith, Robert	2	Eaves, William	2
Pace, Dredzil	2	Hendrick, Milum	1
Denny, George W.	1	Moon, Sarah wid.	1
Birdin, Nelson	1	Lyon, John	1
Roberts, John	2	Smith, William W.	2
Roberts, Joseph Jr.	2	Brumfield, Anny C. wid.	1
Rumsey, Benjamin	2	Henry, Sarah wid.	1
Miles, Thomas	2	Henry:	
Moon, John	2	Sarahann, James M. — orphs. of Alex. Henry, given in by their mother	1
Payton, John	1		
Payton, William	1		
Nelmes, William	2		

GEORGIA D. A. R.

Draws		Draws
Tucker, Robert W.	2	Hendrick, Brantley	1
Page, Wadson D.	2	Hendrick, James	2
Page, Laval	2		

Capt. Joel Bower's Dist.

White, John M.	2	Duncan, Pearson, Sr.	2
Horton, William	2	Brown, William A.	2
Brown, Abraham	2	Carlton, Stephen	2
Rice, Leonard	2	Merrit, John	1
Merritt, Toren	2	Duncan, John, Sr.	1
Nelms, Wiley	2	Ray, William C.	2
Peeler, Cader	2	Kelley, Barney	2
Reed, William P.	2	Holbrook, Fleming	2
Vines, Joseph	2	Cheek, John, Jr.	2
Smith, Nathaniel	2	Bowers, William	2
Parker, William H.	2	Kelly, William	2
Allen, Joseph	2	Horton, James	2
Harbin, John	2	Ginn, Luke W.	2
Smith, Jesse	2	Burnet, Jeremiah	2
Blair, Middleton	2	Rice, Aaron	2
Cocks, George	2	Smith Singleton	1
McGarity, Archabald	2	Hansard, Thomas S.	2
Clark, Williamson	2	Winn, Benjamin	2
Kelly, Barnabas	2	Haynes, William D.	2
Dodds, Thomas	2	Haynes, John M.	1
Clark, James	1	Haynes, Thomas J.	1
Clark, Larken	1	Jordan, Stephen W.	2
Hendrick, Jesse	2	Brown, Andrew	2
McGarrity, John	2	Brown, Adam	2
Duncan, Henry	2	Jones, Elwylie	2
Balenger, William	2	Burden, Hannah wid.	1
Maxwell, William T.	2	Burden, William	2
Rice, William	2	Horton, Thomas	2
Duncan, Moses	2	Parker, Joseph, Sr.	2
Duncan, Aaron	1	Tabor, Brittain C.	2

Capt. Rowland Lunsford's Dist. No. 197

Harmon, John S.	2	Hall, John	2
Christian, George W.	1	Oglesby, Robert C.	2
Bond, William	2	Ford, Elisha	2
Pledger, Simeon L.	2	Upshaw, Haston	2
Tabor, Benjamin K.	2	Sewell, Joseph	2
Rowsey, William	2	Christian, Jesse G.	1
Shoemaker, Talton	2	Christian, Thomas J.	2
Threlkeld, Willis	2	Burton, Thomas, Sr.	2

	Draws		Draws
Nicks, Joseph	2	Andrew, Benjamin	2
Ginn, Jesse	2	Oliver, Jackson	2
Mann, John R.	2	Christian, William P.	2
Scales, George	2	Edwards, Jesse	2
Brewer, Elizabeth wid.	1	Pulliam, Joseph	2
Parrham, Harrison	2	Pledger, Wesley	2
Penn, John	2	Upshaw, Leroy	2
Depriest, James A.	2	Hall, Thomas	1
Dickey, John	2	Rosser, Jeptha	2
Pledger, Thomas, Sr.	2	Chambers, James E.	1
Cook, Abraham	2	Moon, William H.	2
Richards, Rachel, wid.	1	Hicks, Johnson	2
Johnson, Thomas, A.	1	Upshaw, Rebecca wid.	1

GEORGIA D. A. R.

Toombstone Records

INSCRIPTIONS FOUND ON SOME OF OLDEST GRAVES IN ELBERT COUNTY.

COPIED BY STEPHEN HEARD CHAPTER, D. A. R.

Heardmont Cemetery.

Sacred to the memory of COLONEL STEPHEN HEARD

He was a soldier of the American Revolution and fought with the great Washington for the liberties of his country. He died on the 15th, of November 1815 in the 75th, year of his age.

Old Key Cemetery on the Bell Ferry Road about six miles from Elberton on the original Key plantation.

In Memory of WILLIAM BIBB KEY, who was born in Albermarle County, State of Va., Oct. 2, 1759 and died in Elbert Co. Ga., Dec. 7th, 1836. Erected by Nathan & Lucy Mattox 1850.

In Memory of MOANING KEY, wife of Wm. B. Key and daughter of Christopher Clark, who was born in Albermarle County, State of Va., Aug. 12, 1764 and died in Elbert County Ga., Jan. 22, 1840

Erected by Nathan & Lucy Mattox 1850

Old Maxwell Cemetery in Centerville District.

THOMAS MAXWELL	MARY PEMBERTON
Born Sept. 8, 1742	wife of Thomas Maxwell
Died Dec. 12, 1837	Born 1744 Died 1827

Bethelehem Cemetery at Bethelehem Methodist Church

Sacred to the memory of SARAH G. VERDELL. Born Feb. 12, 1795 and departed this life June 27, 1846.

In Memory of JAMES L. MIDDLETON, son of Robert & Betsy C. Middleton. Born July 10, 1814. Died Oct. 20, 1845.

Sacred to the Memory of ELIZABETH C. MIDDLESTON who was born August 11, 1780 and died October 2, 1841.

Sacred to the Memory of CAPT. DUNSTON BLACKWELL who was born April 7, 1775 and died Nov. 5, 1843.

Sacred to the Memory of MARGARET EDWARDS late concort of John F. Edwards, who was born Jan. 22, 1814 and died Mar. 12, 1838.

Sacred to the Memory of REV. THOMAS HEARN, M. D., who departed this life Jan. 25, 1857, aged 71 years and 10 months. He was a minister of the Gospel in the communion of the Methodist Episcopal Church 51 years, and died as he lived a Christian.

R. B. NELMS
Born July 31, 1815
Died Apr. 23, 1833

JAMES F. NUNNALEE
Born Jan. 2, 1760
Died 1838

JANE NASH
wife of James F. Nunnalee
Born Nov. 5, 1788
Died Jan. 1864

Petersburg Cemetery

Lower part of Elbert Co., at the confluence of Broad and Savannah Rivers—commonly called The Point.

In Memory of JANE WATKINS, who died on the 21st of Dec. 1798 aged 70 years.

In Memory of MARY daughter of John Watkins, who died on the 12th, day of May 1818, aged 12 years and 4 months.

In Memory of JOHN WATKINS, born Feb. 12, 1766, died Apr. 6, 1841 Leaving a wife and five children to deplore their irreparable loss.

Sacred to the Memory of LOUISA REMBERT who was born Nov. 16, 1822 and died June 13, 1823

Sacred to the Memory of MARGARET M. REMBERT consort of Andrew Rembert, who was born Dec. 10, 1799 and died May 8, 1823.

Sacred to the Memory of MRS. ELIZABETH S. STOKES, consort of Archibald Stokes and daughter of Samuel and Margaret Sayre, of the State of New York, who was born July 31, 1790 and departed this life Nov. 1, 1819.

Sacred to the Memory of CATHERINE STOKES, consort of Archibald Stokes and daughter of Col. James and Hannah Paton, of Woodbridge, N. J., who was born Oct. 24, 1788 and died Mar. 15, 1814.

Sacred to the Memory of GEORGE PATON of Woodbridge, N. J., who died June 18, 1826, age 86 years

Sacred to the Memory of MARGARET STOKES consort of Archibald Stokes and daughter of Col. James and Hannah Stokes of Woodbridge, N. J., who was born June 1, 1782 and died Aug. 9, 1826.

Sacred to the Memory of WILLIAM POPE, JUNIOR a native of the State of Delaware. Obit 4th, Dec. 1808—Etat 35 years. who in attempting to visit his friends in this state, after an absence of four years on the wilds of Louisanna, was overtaken by sickness on the way, which terminated in death two days after he had reached the home of his brother, Alexander Pope in Petersburg.

Sacred to the Memory of MRS. SARAH W. BIRD who died Dec. 3, 1812 in the 21st, year of her age.

Sacred to the Memory of EDWIN RUTHVEN, son of Drury and Julia A. Cade who was born Dec. 26, 1839 and died Sept. 27, 1841.

Rembert Cemetery

In lower part of Elbert Co., on the Tate land, now owned by Zimri Tate.

Sacred to the Memory of EZRA O. REMBERT who died Sept. 24, 1821 aged 16 years.

Sacred to the Memory of ASBURY W. REMBERT who died Sept. 27, 1821 aged 9 years and 12 days.

Sacred to the Memory of HARRIET R. L. C. REMBERT consort of Andrew Rembert, who was born Sept. 25, 1806 and died July 22, 1827.

Vans Creek Baptist Church at Ruckersville

In Memory of JOSEPH and MARGARET RUCKER. United during their lives and in death they were not divided.

MARGARET RUCKER, born Dec. 1, 1792 died Sept. 5, 1864.

JOSEPH RUCKER born Jan. 5, 1788 died Aug. 27, 1864.

Sacred to the Memory of Wm. S. RUCKER son of Joseph and Margaret Rucker, born June 28, 1820 died Oct. 11, 1850.

Sacred to the Memory of MARTHA S. DURRETT wife of Richard Durrett and daughter of Joseph and Margaret Rucker., born July 15, 1815 died Oct. 11, 1847.

Sacred to the Memory of GEORGE GAAR, who died April 18, 1836 aged 47 years.

Sacred to the Memory of MARY GAAR, wife of George Gaar who died Jan. 26, 1811, aged 52 years.

Sacred to the Memory of MRS. MILDRED WHITE, wife of Wm. B. White who was born Dec. 7, 1814 and died Jan. 26, 1845.

Sacred to the Memory of WILLIAM BOWLING WHITE, husband of Eliza White, who was born on the 13th, day of Dec. 1811 and departed this life on the 16th, day of July 1858.

MRS. JANE CHANDLER, wife of Rev. Asa Chandler, aged 27 years Died Jan. 6, 1836.

Sacred to the Memory of POLLY DICKEY, who died 20th, Feb. 1844 aged 66 years.

Sacred to the Memory of MATTIE O. BARRETT, who was born the 15th, and departed this life July 16, 1857.

THOMAS J. ROUSEE
1829—1854

Ruckersville Methodist Church Cemetery.

Sacred to the Memory of WILLIAM U. BOWEN, who was born Feb. 23, 1788 and departed this life on the morning of Oct. 27, 1851.

Sacred to the Memory of MRS. ANN BOWEN consort of Wm. U. Bowen who was born Dec. 30, 1800 and departed this life July 29, 1843.

Sacred to the Memory of WILLIAM BANKS, born Feb. 2, 1766 and died Dec. 17, 1820. Also ANNE BANKS consort of the above, born Jan. 24, 1771 and died Oct. 11, 1838.

Sacred to the Memory of DR. JOHN BANKS ALEXANDER who was born Oct. 29th, 1826 and died Oct. 16, 1858.

MAJOR ROBERT W. TERRELL, died Apr. 23, 1848 in the 42nd. year of his life.

Sacred to the Memory of JEREMIAH PROCTOR born Nov. 10, 1803 in Fleming County, Kentucky, died Dec. 14, 1834.

Sacred to the Memory of CHARITY ANN, daughter of Gilly Yancy and Bedford Harper, who was born Aug. 13, 1827 and died July 3, 1853.

Sacred to the Memory of GILLY YANCY, consort of Bedford Harper, born Feb. 23, 1801, died June 22, 1852.

Sacred to the Memory of BEDFORD HARPER, born Sept. 1788 died Aug. 25, 1852.

Designed to mark the spot where rests the remains of JOSEPH BLACKWELL, who was born on the 13th, day of Mar. 1756 and departed this life May 6, 1851.

In Memory of CAROLINE RAMSAY, daughter of D. B. & Mary J. Ramsay who died July 6, 1833 aged 7 years.

Sacred to the Memory of MAJOR THOMAS A. BANKS, who died July 23, 1835 aged 45 years.

Two graves, one unmarked, found on what is known as the old Hunter Place, about two miles beyond Bethelehem Church.

The remains of MARTHA M. TERRELL who died Aug. 1, 1820 in the ninth year of her age.

Sacred to the Memory of LUCINDA M. ALEXANDER, born Feb. 26, 1822 died Nov. 5, 1851.

Sacred to the Memory of PETER ALEXANDER, born June 22, 1783 died May 15, 1856.

Sacred to the Memory of ELIZABETH ALEXANDER, born Feb. 6, 1796, died Dec. 11, 1852.

MRS. MILLY ADAMS, consort of R. G. Adams, born Mar. 18, 1799 died Jan. 11, 1853.

MRS. NANCY MURRY, consort of John Murry, born 1756 and died 1850.

In Memory of MRS. LOUISA HAMMOND, consort of Maj. Alfred Hammond, who was born Oct. 28, 1808, was married Jan. 24, 1826 and departed this life May 30, 1833.

In Memory of
MAJOR ALFRED HAMMOND.

The old Wall Cemetery on the Stephen Heard Highway About halfway between Elberton and Rosehill Plantation.

MRS ANN WALL
Born in 1768
departed this life
Mar. 18, 1850

MISS MARTHA HICKS WALL
Born Jan. 5, 1800
departed this life
June 8th, 1838

The Old Turman Cemetery, several miles this side of Balchin's store, in lower Elbert Co.

Sacred to the Memory of FRANCES TURMAN, consort of Thomas J. Turman, who departed this life Apr. 27, 1849. In the 37th, year of her life.

Sacred to the Memory of MRS. JANE TAIT, who departed this life on the 26th, April 1820 in her 77th, year. A. T.

Evidently an old family grave yard on the road between Ruckersville and Pearle Station on S. A. L. Ry.

In Memory of JAMES CLARK, who died in the 47th, year of his age Oct. 26, 1826.

In Memory of WILLIAM A CLARK who died in his 30th, year Nov. 7, 1843.

Marriages

The marriages from the two following books were copied by J. A. LeConte, who made a personal gift of them to Mrs. John L. Davidson.

BOOK "H" re-bound into BOOK "L-F"

Marriages recorded in BOOK "H" re-bound into BOOK "L-F".

Arranged alphabetically as to men's names

Groom	Bride	Date	Page
Ansley, Jesse	Betsy Rose	Sep. 30, 1807	28
Almond, Ezra	Sally Brown	Oct. 22, 1807	28
Burton, Blackman	Jinsy Saxton	Mar. 30, 1806	28
Booth, Gabriel	Betsy Stinchcomb	Jul. 26, 1806	28
Bird, Daniel	Sarah Oliver	Dec. 25, 1806	28
Bullard, Tapley	Anna Bell	Jun. 29, 1807	28
Barnett, William	Sally S. Bibb	Mar. 21, 1807	28
Berry, Robert	Mary Fincher	Dec. 17, 1807	42
Bevill, Thomas	Eliz. Cunningham	Nov. 26, 1807	44
Bragg, William S.	Polly Rogers	Feb. 24, 1808	54
Ballard, Jesse G.	Judah Clark	Sep. 9, 1807	55
Bevers, Ansley	Susanna Dunahoo	Jan. 14, 1808	55
Beavers, Allen	Elizabeth Braden	Jun. 19, 1807	57
Butler, Peter	Hannah Snellings	Jan. 21, 1808	133
Butler, Christopher	Mahala Cole	Jan. 8, 1809	133
Brown, Benjamin	Ann Griffith	Dec. 22, 1808	151
Brown, Hardie	Delilah Lowry	Jan. 5, 1809	151
Cape, Lewis	Elizabeth Ooker	Dec. 18, 1806	28
Coursey, Daniel	Catty Burton	Jan. 26, 1806	28
Christian, Isaac	Milly White	Feb. 12, 1807	28
Christian, Chas. W.	Nancy Ruff	Jun. 6, 1807	39
Childs, Benjamin	Catharine Irons	Oct. 22, 1807	42
Crittenden, Henry P.	Kizzia Fitts	Dec. 10, 1807	42
Cole, Samuel	Charlotte B. Harper	Dec. 12, 1807	45
Clay, Simeon	Mary Lockhart	Feb. 21, 1808	55
Crider, David	Permelia Bond	Oct. 22, 1807	55
Cranshaw, Cornelius	Milly Parham	Dec. 27, 1807	97
Cash, Moses	Nancy Hudson	Sep. 6, 1808	111
Cash, Howard	Susanna Scales	Nov. 21, 1808	151
Crawford, William	Peggy Holbrook	Mar. 9, 1809	151
Crock, Robert	Martha Walker	20, 1809	151
Dunlap, William	Jane Garvin	Jul. 10, 1806	28
Davis, Shadrack	Betsy Stephens	Jul. 20, 1806	28

GEORGIA D. A. R.

Groom	Bride	Date	Page
Davis, Edward	Frances Ragland	Feb. 19, 1807	28
Dean, Frederick	Sally Bray	Jan. 8, 1807	42
Dye, Randolph	Elizabeth Bell	Jan. 9, 1808	44
Denay, David	Polly Ruff	Dec. 2, 1807	55
Davis, William	Sally Dickson	Jun. 15, 1807	55
Dobbs, David	Dosha Walters	Nov. 4, 1807	58
Ellington, Garland	Catherine Garrett	Sep. 25, 1806	28
Evans, Robert	Mahala Granger	Feb. 12, 1807	28
Ewing, William D.	Rebecca Ewing	Oct. 11, 1808	63
Etchison, William	Tabitha Hays	Nov. 15, 1808	151
Ewin, James D.	Mary E. McClary	Nov. 9, 1809	151
Ferrenton, Edward F.	Eliz. Robertson	Feb. 25, 1808	55
Ferrell, John	Peggy McCune	Oct. 1, 1807	55
Falkner, Peter	Nancy Cook	Oct. 31, 1807	55
Ford, John	Jinsey Head	Jan. 21, 1808	133
Gilmer, Francis	Patsey Barnett	Jan. 28, 1808	45
Groves, Samuel	Rachel Forgus	Jul. 14, 1808	63
Harthcock, Debton	Polly Jones	Oct. 26, 1806	28
Hubbard, Richard	Patsey Jones	Jan. 22, 1807	28
Hailey, Reuben	Sally Wood	Aug. 13, 1807	38
Harris, Stephen W.	Sarah H. Watkins	Jan. 19, 1808	44
Hailey, Martin	Betsy Jennings	Mar. 3, 1808	55
Henderson, Joseph	Frances Johnston	Jun. 6, 1808	110
Hall, Taliaferro	Sarah Clark	Jun. 16, 1808	110
Horton, William	Jane Crawford	Oct. 9, 1808	110
Harris, John	Joannah Gragg	Jan. 22, 1809	151
Haley, John	Polly Underwood	Jan. 5, 1809	151
Jones, Asa	Martha Butler	Jun. 10, 1808	63
James, Samuel	Ruth Hendon	Jun. 6, 1806	151
Langdon, John	Jane Ellington	Nov. 11, 1806	28
Love, James K.	Jane Rucker	Apr. 25, 1807	38
Lowrymore, Andrew	Sally Bentley	Oct. 14, 1808	63
Mauchett, Samuel	Mary Eastridge	Mar. 27, 1806	28
McMullin, Neal	Polly Thornton	Aug. 1, 1807	39
Morgan, John	Nancy Towns	Dec. 20, 1807	44
McMartin, Duncan	Catharine McCurry	Apr. 8, 1806	58
Martin, Cluf	Martha Vaughn	Sep. 8, 1808	110
Martin, Ewel	Nancy Vaughn	Sep. 8, 1808	110
Maxwell, Elijah	Betsy Jordan	Oct. 13, 1808	110
Oliver, William	Frances Ragland	Dec. 27, 1807	42
Orr, Barrett or Burrell	Betsy Hendrick	Sep. 24, 1807	55
Osley, Willis	Sally Butler	Jan. 26, 1809	133
Pritchet, George	Eliz. Mitchell	Jul. 26, 1807	55
Power, David	Susanna Moon	Oct. 15, 1807	55

Groom	Bride	Date	Page
Parum or Parham } Dixon	Elizabeth Hicks	Mar. 8, 1807	55
Page, Dempsey	Margaret Ashworth	Mar. 20, 1806	55
Powell, Losten	Sally McKinney	Aug. 28, 1806	58
Ragland, Evan	Sally Evans	May 21, 1806	28
Rucker, Willis	Milly Alexander	Oct. 29, 1807	45
Roberts, William	Polly Lunceford	May 14, 1807	55
Rowsey, Foster	Polly Dennard	Dec. 15, 1808	97
Stinchcomb, Levi	Polly Ridgway	Jul. 25, 1806	28
Saxon, Lewis	Sally Spencer	Jan. 14, 1806	28
Smith, Valentine	Catharine Upshaw	Dec. 23, 1806	38
Sherrod, Benjamin	Eliza H. Watkins	Jan. 1, 1808	44
Smith, Leonard	Charlotte Lain	Dec. 29, 1807	45
Scales, Aaron	Anna Harbin	Nov. 29, 1808	97
Sale, Dudley	Nancy Hatcher	Nov. 1, 1807	42
Stubblefield, William	Caty Brown	Feb. 23, 1809	151
Tait, Enos	Mary J. Tait	Aug. 28, 1806	35
Tait, Caleb	Polly Middleton	Dec. 25, 1806	35
Turman, Jacob	Polly Brewer	Oct. 15, 1807	42
Tate, Waddy	Eliza E. Thompson	Jan. 4, 1808	44
Talliaferro, Benj.	Martha Watkins	Oct. 15, 1807	44
Tatom, Thomas	Sarah Davis	Oct. 6, 1808	110
Thompson, Allen C.	Charlotte Thompson	Mar. 3, 1808	133
Vineyard, George	Patience Bassile	Mar. 9, 1807	28
Vaughn, Alex.	Elizabeth David	Aug. 20, 1807	55
Vawter, Richard	Cynthey McGuire	Nov. 11, 1806	57
Vincent, Pleasant	Susan Edwards	Jan. 14, 1808	63
White, Joseph	Avariller Harper	Aug. 28, 1806	28
Willis, Samuel	Piety Skinner	Jan. 8, 1807	28
Worrell, Richard	Lucy Hammond	May 8, 1806	28
Woodward, Henry	Betsy Figgs	Aug. 24, 1806	28
White, Martin	Patsy White	Feb. 11, 1807	28
Woods, William	Martha N. Middleton	Sep. 16, 1807	38
Webb, Burrell	Sarah Booth	Oct. 18, 1806	39
White, John	Barshaba Gunter	June. --, 1803	42
Ward, Abner	Frances Kidd	Dec. 24, 1807	45
Watkins, William Jr.	Ruth Pope	May 15, 1806	45
Witcher, Benjamin	Frances McLeroy	Sep. 10, 1807	55
Wiley, George	Milly David	Feb. 4, 1808	63
Wynn, George	Polly Ingraham	Dec. 30, 1807	111
Winn, John	Jane Childs	Nov. 10, 1808	133
Wheeler, Benjamin	Patsy Dutton	Sep. 3, 1808	151
Warren, Harrison	Susannah Gaines	Oct. 20, 1808	151
Walker, Robert	Sally Cole	Aug. 8, 1808	151

GEORGIA D. A. R.

MARRIAGES 1809—1812

IN BOOK OF MIXED RECORDS

Groom	Bride	Date	Page
Alston, John	Charity Tait	Oct. 4, 1810	118
Ashworth, Joab	Nancy Teasley	Jun. 4, 1809	251
Bond, Gabriel	Clary Rowsey	Mar. 9, 1809	1
Brown, Dozer	Polly Herndon	Sep. 5, 1809	1
Bradley, Drury	Sally Ridgway	Sep. 9, 1809	2
Brawner, Russell	Sally Tidwell	Aug. 10, 1809	2
Bray, David	Lucy Hall	Apr. 9, 1810	66
Brawner, Bazel	Nancy Campbell	Sep. 27, 1810	78
Banks, James, Jr.	Milly Jones	Sep. 11, 1810	98
Brown, Reuben	Dosha McMullen	Jun. 6, 1810	136
Brewer, William	Anny Bates	Oct. 12, 1810	136
Brown, Jesse	Lucy Staples	Jan. 17, 1811	137
Bradley, Robert C.	Anna Deadwilder	Dec. 11, 1810	196
Baker, George	Polly Brown	Jun. 13, 1811	242
Booth, John	Anna Faulkner	Sep. 3, 1811	251
Bailey, William	Amely Reily	Sep. 9, 1811	251
Barnett, Thomas N.	Margaret Micou	Sep. 23, 1811	251
Burdon, Edward	Sally White	Dec. 22, 1811	307
Bentley, William A.	Charlotte C. Nunnelee	Jan. 23, 1812	315
Bibb, John D.	Mary Oliver	Feb. 6, 1812	335
Blackwell, Joseph	Eliz. McGehee	Mar. 3, 1812	335
Brown, John	Polly Statham	Dec. 12, 1811	339
Colly, Zachariah	Eliz. D. Saunders	Apr. 20, 1809	1
Capel, Brittain	Sarah Terrell	May 25, 1809	1
Cook, Francis, Jr.	Anna Swet	Nov. 12, 1809	2
Cook, Benjamin	Jane England	Apr. 30, 1810	42
Cabaniss, Henry	Nancy Crittenden	Feb. 10, 1810	66
Cheatham, Stephen	Clarysa Higgenbotham	Apr. 5, 1810	66
Clark, Micajah T.	Tabitha Raglin	Jul. 17, 1808	66
Carlton, Stephen	Susanna Childs	May 3, 1810	75
Childress, Robert	Sarah Carter	Aug. 8, 1809	76
Crawford, John	Henrietta Haley	Feb. 25, 1810	76
Cook, James	Rhoda Falkner	Aug. 15, 1807	76
Chisholm, Wm. Jr.	Eliz. L. Easter	May 13, 1810	79
Cook, Benjamin	Elizabeth Hudson	Nov. 8, 1810	98
Coker, Larkin	Ann Bray	Nov. 15, 1810	98
Cook, John	Polly Alexander	Feb. 25, 1810	116
Clark, Larkin	Lucy Welch	Dec. 25, 1810	118
Cawhorn, James	Jane Millican	Jul. 9, 1810	141
Collins, Willis	Phebe Martin	Dec. 2, 1810	188
Collidy, William	Tabitha Downer	Sep. 30, 1810	196
Chisholm, Andrew C.	Ann W. King	Jun. 8, 1811	197
Childs, John	Elizabeth Thornton	Oct. 17, 1811	251

HISTORICAL COLLECTIONS 275

Groom	Bride	Date	Page
Cunningham, Franklin	Nancy Dainel	Dec. 26, 1811	307
Casey, Stephen	Sally Anthony	Oct. 31, 1811	307
Carter, George	Martha Higginbotham	Jul. 15, 1812	355
Dye, Brown	Polly Martin	Apr. 23, 1809	1
Deadwiler, Martin	Rebecca Wilhite	Aug. 7, 1809	2
Denton, James	Silvey Pollard	Feb. 20, 1810	26
Davis, Benjamin	Patsy Wanslow	May 10, 1810	76
Dodds, James	Sarah Thomason	Sep. 6, 1810	110
Dollar, Ambrose	Sally Skelton	Mar. 28, 1811	188
Davis, Richard	Phebe Franklin	Feb. 7, 1811	196
Dobbs, John	Jane Haines	Sep. 14, 1810	197
Dye, William	Elizabeth Bullard	Aug. 22, 1811	251
Dunlap, Joseph	Mary Whitman	Dec. 18, 1811	307
Denny, Edward	Barbary Staples	Jun. 30, 1812	355
Easter, Booker B.	Catharine Yurman	May 21, 1809	2
Evans, Henry	Martha Whitney	Dec. 16, 1811	196
Foster, John S.	Martha Jones	Nov. 26, 1809	2
Fitts, John	Jinny Depriest	Nov. 2, 1809	22
Flaherty, Thomas	Milly Grace	Feb. 15, 1810	26
Freeman, Fleming	Martha Bibb	Apr. 16, 1812	335
Garner, William	Franky Pulliam	Jan. 27, 1808	1
Grimes, Thomas M.	Anney Power	Jun. 15, 1809	1
Gaar, William	Lucy Rucker	May 20, 1810	76
Gaines, Richard S.	Anna Alexander	Mar. 10, 1811	111
Gandy, Uriah	Polly Means	Mar. 20, 1811	196
Garner, John	Nancy Head	Feb. 14, 1811	196
Gaar, John	Polly Blair	Jan. 23, 1812	261
Gray, William	Peggy Bevers	Dec. 24, 1811	266
Glover, Richard	Elizabeth Glover	Sep. 21, 1811	307
Hudson, Buokes (?)	Elizabeth Burton	Sep. 15, 1809	1
Higginbotham, Wm. G.	Polly Eveston	Sept. 26, 1808	1
Ham, Reuben	Jane Jordan	Jan. 6, 1809	2
Hicks, William	Polly Phelps	Nov. 23, 1809	2
Hardy, Jethro	Polly Dennard	Feb. 10, 1810	13
Holloway, John	Martha Bryan	Jun. 5, 1808	22
Hales, Wiley	Jane Buchannon	Mar. 15, 1810	66
Henderson, George	Penina Wooldridge	Aug. 2, 1810	76
Hubbard, John	Betsy Cook	Nov. 17, 1810	110
Hendrick, Sylvan	Nancy Bailey	Dec. 4, 1810	111
Head, James	Patsy Richardson	Dec. 25, 1810	141
Human, Jesse	Sally Wood	Jul. 19, 1810	178
Higginbotham, Bartley C.	} Tabitha Oliver	Jan. 10, 1811	196
Hulsey, John	Polly Johnston	Feb. 2, 1809	196
Harper, Roderick	Susanna Selfridge	Feb. 10, 1806	251
Hightower, William	Mary Higginbotham	Oct. 3, 1811	251

Groom	Bride	Date	Page
Hoopwell, Thomas	Harriett Clements	Dec. 20, 1811	266
Hudson, Charles	Lucy McGehee	Oct. 30, 1811	266
Head, William	Sally Hall	Dec. 4, 1811	296
Higginbotham, Benj. C.	Polly Lollis	Jan. 2, 1812	325
Hilley, William	Patsy McGuire	May 30, 1812	325
Hamilton, James	Nancy Rucker	Jul. 30, 1812	325
Johnston, William	Sarah Grizzle	Nov. 17, 1808	2
Jenkins, Joshua	Milly Ellet	Apr. 19, 1810	75
Jordan, James	Beda White	Nov. 26, 1807	77
Jordan, James	Tabitha Murrah	Mar. 16, 1809	136
Jones, Standley	Ezza Alexander	Jan. 3, 1811	196
Kelly, William	Sarah Allen	Jan. 4, 1810	136
Key, James	Rebecca Grizzle	Oct. 17, 1811	296
Luce, Freeborn	Elizabeth Irons	Sep. 1, 1809	1
Moore, Lobard	Wineny Sanders	Aug. 17, 1809	1
Moss, Abraham	Betsy Smith	Oct. 5, 1809	26
Morgan, William	Lucy Karr	Nov. 9, 1809	66
Magesryth, Gardner	Susanna McGuire	Mar. 5, 1810	76
Mann, Asa	Betsy White	Jan. 24, 1810	76
McCane, William D.	Nancy Childs	Feb. 23, 1810	79
Middleton, Robert	Betsy C. Williamson	Nov. 11, 1810	110
Mann, Henry	Sally Haley	Jun. 26, 1809	116
McMullin, Charles	Nancy Breadin	Jan. 26, 1809	137
McMullen, Jeremiah	Sarah Harper	Feb. 8, 1811	196
McMullin, Lewis	Frances Stowers	Jun. 25, 1808	251
Moon, John	Tabitha Staples	Aug. 15, 1811	251
Morris, James	Lucy Parham	Sep. 8, 1811	251
McMullen, William	Eliz. Maxwell	Sep. 3, 1812	372
Nix, Jeremiah	Fanny Webb	Oct. 25, 1810	178
Nix, John	Sally Nix	Jan. 15, 1811	178
Nix, Joseph	Sally Colman	Mar. 10, 1811	188
Nelums, Nathaniel	Robema Carpenter	Mar. 3, 1809	196
Nunnelee, James F.	Jincy Naish	Sep. 28, 1810	251
Oliver, Major John	Susan Watkins	Feb. 19, 1811	116
Porterfield, James	Tabitha Bond	Sep. 6, 1808	1
Pulliam, Joseph	Betsy Bonds	Feb. 18, 1808	1
Pulliam, Matthew	Hannah Eavenson	Jan. 19, 1809	2
Pledger, Samuel	Hetty Shepherd	Sep. 28, 1809	2
Posey, Humphrey	Milly Key	Jan. 3, 1811	110
Plunket, Reuben	Patsy Taylor	Jul. 6, 1812	355
Rucker, Barton	Betsy Brown	Nov. .. 1809	2
Rucker, Azmond	Nancy Harper	Feb. 4, 1810	26
Richardson, William	Betsy Harrison	Oct. 29, 1809	58
Rucker, Barden	Frances Alexander	Aug. 23, 1810	77
Roebuck, Robert, Jr.	Franky White	May 27, 1810	99
Rice, Robert	Anny Pace	Nov. 16, 1809	178

HISTORICAL COLLECTIONS

Groom	Bride	Date	Page
Rice, William	Sally Brown	Jan. 30, 1812	339
Roberts, James W.	Polly Ledbetter	Jun. 28, 1812	355
Smith, Joseph	Nancy Morrow	Aug. 24, 1809	2
Smith, John	Zele Hill	Feb. 2, 1809	2
Spencer, John	Catherine Burton	Jan. 13, 1810	22
Story, William	Polly Dean	Aug. 18, 1808	26
Standifer, Andrew	Elizabeth James	Apr. 12, 1809	26
Spears, Mercer	Elizabeth Dodds	Apr. 19, 1810	75
Skelton, Jonathan	Elizabeth Cox	Jul. 17, 1810	78
Steedley, William	Patsy Ballinger	Sep. 13, 1810	99
Sterlings, William	Patsy Webb	May 16, 1811	188
Scales, Joel	Fanny Cash	Jan. 3, 1811	196
Spencer, William	Dama Gross	Feb. 28, 1811	196
Shoemaker, Jeremiah	Nancy Deadwiler	Aug. 31, 1809	2
Spencer, Octavius	Patsy Ann Gray	Nov. 26, 1810	197
Suttles, Micajah	Sarah Ford	Jun. 17, 1811	197
Stamps, Britton	Polly Sanders	Dec. 19, 1810	251
Satterwhite, James	Milly Wiche	Jul. 26, 1810	251
Sims, Edward	Sally Banks	Jul. 11, 1811	251
Shoemaker, Talton	Belenderon Booth	Dec. 22, 1811	307
Tait, Zimri	Susanna Tait	Oct. 28, 1809	1
Tait, James M.	Jane Watkins	Jul. 10, 1810	77
Thornton, Reuben, Jr.	Anna Crisler	Aug. 23, 1810	77
Tiner, Thomas B.	Polly Crump	Mar. 5, 1811	111
Thurman, John	Theney Irons	Dec. 11, 1810	196
Teasley, Joshua	Polly Christler	Mar. 4, 1812	315
Underwood, Ezekiel	Eliz. Wheeler	May 1, 1812	355
Woodley, John	Tempy Bullard	Mar. 5, 1808	1
Wootan, James	Rachel Rutherford	Oct. 5, 1809	1
Walker, John Wm.	Matlida Pope	Jan. 30, 1810	26
Walker, George C.	Milly Childers	Dec. 1, 1809	53
Wheeler, Henry	Polly Underwood	Mar. 18, 1810	75
White, John	Elizabeth Jones	Jan. 5, 1809	76
Wanslow, Thomas	Jemima Means	Apr. 15, 1810	137
Wade, John B.	Milly Hilley	Jan. 22, 1811	196
White, James E.	Janey Brown	Jul. 10, 1811	196
Williamson, Basil	Mary Skelton	Jul. 28, 1811	251
Worrell, Ramsom	Elender Harper	Nov. 3, 1811	251
Whitman, William	Sarah Colson	May 28, 1812	325
White, Stephen	Rebecca Pulliam	Dec. 6, 1808	339

GEORGIA D. A. R.

MARRIAGES 1812-1816
WILL BOOK "K" MIXED RECORDS

Groom	Bride	Date	Page
Alexander, Peter	Betsy A. Banks	Dec. 24, 1812	10
Allgood, Samuel	Fanny Naish	Nov. 10, 1814	163
Allgood, James Y.	Prudence Turman	Jul. 12, 1815	164
Aycock, Milton	Susan E. Aycock	Oct. 25, 1815	294
Alexander, Allen	Sarah M. Thompson	Feb. 5, 1815	309
Bell, Mayfield	Nancy Arnold	Nov. 1, 1812	10
Berry, Elijah	Sarah Rich	Feb. 8, 1811	32
Braswell, William B.	Polly Pollard	Oct. 26, 1812	32
Bird, John	Martha B. Tyner	Feb. 7, 1813	33
Brown, Jacob	Mary S. Higginbotham	July 15, 1813	161
Burton, John Jr.	Elizabeth G. Pate	Nov. 25, 1813	162
Butler, Daniel	Martha Naish	Sep. 29, 1814	164
Boughtright, Daniel	Eliz. Carpenter	Dec. 15, 1813	178
Blake, James	Susannah F. Horn	Oct. 28, 1813	187
Butler, Haley	Nancy J. Ward	Dec. 7, 1815	215
Burden, Henry	Sarah Burden	Aug. 20, 1815	308
Bird, Billions	Charity Tiner	Feb. 5, 1815	309
Butler, George	Polly Deprest	Apr. 13, 1815	309
Byrd, Edward	Marhala Pate	May 5, 1816	311
Burden, James	Elizabeth Bailey	Aug. 21, 1816	311
Craft, David	Elizabeth Elliott	Dec. 3, 1812	10
Childs, John	Elizabeth Rucker	Dec. 20, 1812	10
Cape, Brinkley	Jinny Braswell	Nov. 7, 1812	32
Clark, James	Mary Alston	Apr. 8, 1813	161
Colbert, William	Martha Clark	Jan. 24, 1813	161
Caldwell, Matthew T.	Eliza M. Jones	Dec. 22, 1814	162
Crittenden, Elijah	Eliz. Greenwood	Sep. 11, 1814	164
Chambers, John	Eliz. Shepherd	Dec. 29, 1814	164
Colly, Edward	Martha White	Sep. 7, 1813	179
Casey, Ephraim	Rebecca Anthony	Dec. 21, 1815	210
Carter, Robert	Patsy S. Wall	Oct. 15, 1815	308
Childers, Osborn	Malinda Burton	Jun. 28, 1815	309
Cook, John	Gilly Colbert	Jan. 16, 1816	310
Cabaniss, Henry	Sally Booker	Feb. 4, 1816	310
Cunningham, Menter	Polly Cunningham	Oct. 18, 1815	312
Dye, David	Rebecca Wilkins	Oct. 19, 1812	10
Davis, Thomas W.	Polly H. Banks	Dec. 24, 1812	10
Dickerson, John	Elizabeth Thornton	Dec. 29, 1812	32
Durratt, Marshall	Nancy K. Lindsay	Jan. 21, 1811	161
Dudley, William	Clemontyne Butler	May 20, 1813	162
Denny, Thomas	Polly Hanna	Sep. 1, 1814	163
Denney, Robert	Milita Staples	Feb. 2, 1815	309

HISTORICAL COLLECTIONS 279

Groom	Bride	Date	Page
Elliott, John	Elizabeth Agee	Oct. 30, 1814	163
Earp, Westly	Mornin Alexander	Sep. 8, 1814	193
Fields, Samuel	Milly Hill	Jul. 29, 1813	161
Fortson, John	Sarah Moore	Mar. 17, 1814	162
Fortson, James	Elizabeth Lewis	Dec. 16, 1814	163
Franklin, Job	Hannah Wheeler	Oct. 19, 1815	199
Gunter, John	Rebecca Bell	Dec. 31, 1812	32
Gunter, James	Rebecca Anderson	Dec. 13, 1813	162
Gully, John	Mary Ann H. Decker	Jul. 29, 1813	162
Gaines, John	Elizabeth Hearndon	Dec. 25, 1814	163
Ginn, Sherwood	Susannah Thomason	Jan. 12, 1815	164
Gober, John	Eliz. Bramblett	Dec. 15, 1813	179
Gully, William	Franky P. Taylor	Oct. 26, 1815	243
Gaines, Levingston	Sarah Johnson	Oct. 25, 1815	265
Grider, Jacob	Frances Wilkins	Jan. 12, 1815	309
Glover, John	Eliz. Y. Alston	Sep. 6, 1815	310
Higginbotham, Peter	Jinney Howard	Feb. 4, 1813	32
Harbin, John	Sophia Hendry	Nov. 17, 1814	161
Heard, George W.	Sarah Carter	Apr. 20, 1813	162
Harris, Richmond	Rachel Tait	Sep. 18, 1813	162
Higginbotham, Wm.	Susannah Bonds	Dec. 29, 1814	163
Hines, Restore	Jane Childs	Apr. 22, 1813	163
Hearndon, James	Sarah Thornton	Mar. 30, 1814	163
Higginbotham, Larkin	Polly Howard	Jan. 12, 1815	164
Hunt, Henry	Nancy Craft	Jul. 20, 1815	212
Hudson, George	Ann Samuel	Jan. 9, 1816	279
Hilley, Richard	Elizabeth Dillard	Apr. 20, 1813	308
Hill, Lewis	Nancy Anthony	Mar. 2, 1815	309
Hendrick, John	Rebecca Adams	Jul. 13, 1815	310
Heard, Charles M.	Sarah Whitman	Feb. 1, 1816	310
Hale, Henry	Levity Royal	Mar. 5, 1816	310
Henrey, Benjamin	Nancy W. Beck	Aug. 11, 1816	311
Hickman, Walker	Rebecca Harris	Sep. 27, 1816	312
Irons, McKinney	Syntha Brewer	Oct. 21, 1813	312
Jennings, John	Elizabeth Childs	Mar. 26, 1814	162
Jones, Wiley W.	Charlotte Jones	Dec. 1, 1814	164
Johnston, Solomon	Ann Campbell	Dec. 28, 1815	234
Jarratt, Archelus	Francis C. M. Brewer	Nov. 2, 1815	243
Jones, Lewis	Patcy Jones	Mar. 2, 1815	309
Johnston, Thomas	Peggy C. Gaines	Jan. 18, 1816	311
Kidd, Webb	Rebecca Allen	Dec. 1, 1814	164
King, Jacob W.	Mary A. Hackney	Sep. 5, 1815	309
King, William	Sarah Coleman	Sep. 8, 1815	310
Lovingood, Harmon	Martha Bell	Dec. 22, 1814	162
McGehee, Hugh	Sarah S. White	Sep. 29, 1814	164
McGuire, William D.	Jane Wimmes	Dec. 1, 1813	178

GEORGIA D. A. R.

Groom	Bride	Date	Page
McCoy, William	Nancy Shepard	Mar. 18, 1816	310
Mills, James	Nancy McMullan	Sep. 24, 1812	2
Moore, Joel	Sally Brady	Nov. 5, 1812	8
Mercer, John	Sally Kee	Sep. 1, 1812	33
Mitchum, John	Surreny Childs	Feb. 13, 1814	163
Moore, Henry	Polly L. Lewis	Jan. 9, 1815	164
Mills, William	Nancy Brown	Dec. 12, 1815	203
Mason, William	Fannay Penn	Nov. 14, 1814	210
Matthews, Philip	Elizabeth Clark	Feb. 8, 1815	309
Mullin, William	Susannah Brewer	Sep. 3, 1815	309
Milligan, James	Mary Smithwick	Aug. 10, 1815	310
Morgan, Isham	Mary Rich	1816	310
Northern, John	Molly Bedingfield	Mar. 13, 1813	33
Naish, Abraham	Polly Butler	Oct. 13, 1814	164
Oliver, Thomas W.	Frances Roebuck	Dec. 21, 1815	199
Owens, George	Margrett Childs	Feb. 23, 1816	311
Oliver, John	Leucy Penn	Apr. 7, 1816	311
Phipps, Lewis	Patsey Faulkner	Dec. 22, 1812	32
Phillips, Williamson	Betsey Coleman	Mar. 20, 1814	163
Powell, Francis	Nancy Dooly	Dec. 12, 1813	167
Pledger, Thomas	Nancy Ford	Mar. 2, 1815	309
Pace, Bazel	Claricy Shepard	Sep. 28, 1815	310
Payton, William	Polly McCormac	Feb. 11, 1816	311
Rich, James	Polly Gaines	Feb. 25, 1813	33
Ridgway, Thomas	Eliz. Irvin Morgan	May 14, 1812	162
Royal, John, Jr.	Martha H. Brewer	Dec. 1, 1814	163
Rose, Amos	Catharine Brown	Dec. 4, 1814	164
Rodgers, George	Carline Evans	May 20, 1815	265
Riddle, Anderson	Sarah Y. Tate	Feb. 21, 1815	309
Rumsey, Benjamin	Nancy Tomkins	Aug. 11, 1816	311
Roberts, Jesse O.	Susannah Coker	Oct. 13, 1816	312
Stone, William	Carah Colbert	Oct. 27, 1812	32
Simmons, Dudley	Elizabeth Spears	Sep. 1, 1813	161
Spencer, Griffeth	Elizabeth Owens	Sep. 50, 1813	162
Sullivan, John	Mima Booker	Apr. 15, 1814	163
Stowers, Benjamin	Ann Roebuck	Oct. 14, 1813	172
Stowers, Thomas	Jincy Gaines	Feb. 3, 1814	193
Snow, Joel	Gilley Patterson	Nov. 23, 1815	212
Scales, George	Polly Pledger	Oct. 5, 1815	294
Stowers, Lewis	Harriott Roebuck	Oct. 12, 1815	308
Stinson, Samuel	Nancy Gulley	Sep. 24, 1815	310
Smith, James	Deborah Adams	Jan. 18, 1816	310
Smithwick, Edmond	Piety Willis	May 2, 1816	310
Smith, Green W.	Margrett A. Cook	Feb. 22, 1816	311
Skinner, George M.	Polly Henry	Feb. 28, 1816	311
Tate, James	Maria S. Verdell	Jan. 14, 1813	33

HISTORICAL COLLECTIONS 281

Groom	Bride	Date	Page
Taylor, Hugh	Mahetable C. Sayre	Nov. 30, 1813	162
Thurmand, John	Theany Irions	Jul. 20, 1814	164
Thompson, William	Sarah Ragland	Mar. 3, 1814	191
Tate, Enos C.	Nancy M. Calister	Nov. 22, 1815	203
Thomason, Arnold	Eliz. Shackleford	Apr. 23, 1816	311
Thompson, Drury	Jane Thompson	Jan. 24, 1816	311
Tait, David	Frances Tait	Nov. 21, 1816	312
Upshaw, Leroy	Prudence T. Richardson	May 14, 1814	163
White, Nicholas	Sally Pollard	Oct. 25, 1812	2
White, David	Polly Hearndon	Feb. 14, 1813	33
Wansley, John	Sally Greenway	Mar. 14, 1813	33
Wallis, Jesse C.	Sally Stone	Sep. 14, 1813	161
White, John	Margaret Harbin	Dec. 15, 1814	164
Woods, Joseph	Polly Campbell	Jan. 3, 1815	164
White, Eppy	Catharine Hearndon	May 11, 1815	308
Wall, Burgess	Martha Carter	Oct. 6, 1815	309
Walker, James	Margaret Poelston	Mar. 16, 1816	311

MARRIAGES 1809-1824.

WILL BOOK "L" MIXED RECORDS

Alexander, Edmond	Catharine Alexander	Dec. 5, 1816	21
Allgood, William	Jincy Wright	Jan. 2, 1817	69
Adams, James B.	Polly Haley	Apr. 10, 1817	111
Alexander, Mordecai	Judey M. Shackleford	Aug. 7, 1817	193
Andrew, Burley	Caty Stinchcomb	Jan. 15, 1818	193
Andrew Benjamin	Lucy Tate	Dec. 18, 1817	217
Alexander, William	Jemmima Moore	Dec. 18, 1818	219
Anderson, James	Bathashe Hightower	Dec. 10, 1818	231
Anderson, James	Elizabeth Mobley	Dec. 24, 1818	230
Adams, William	Sarah Head	Jan. 11, 1819	296
Allen, John W.	Elizabeth McMullen	Aug. 6, 1818	304
Adams, Richard	Milley Murry	Dec. 30, 1819	350
Allen, Samuel	Pheba Rhodland	Nov. 25, 1819	435
Allmon, John	Mary V. Dillard	Jan. 20, 1820	435
Alexander, Willis	Sarah C. Banks	Mar. 15, 1820	475
Alston, William H.	Elizabeth Rucker	Jan. 25, 1820	476
Adams, John	Elizabeth Pledger	Feb. 7, 1821	477
Allmond, Isaac	Elizabeth Fortson	Dec. 20, 1821	477
Allen, Reuben	Patsy Rhodelander	Jul. 17, 1821	478
Anderson, Thomas G.	Elizabeth Smith	Jan. 1, 1823	479
Allgood, John	Jane Allgood	Jan. 17, 1822	481
Adams, John	Nancy Davis	Feb. 27, 1823	484

Groom	Bride	Date	Page
Aiken, William E.	Sarah K. Mann	Jan. 8, 1824	486
Alexander, William G.	Juliann Patterson	Mar. 16, 1824	487
Allgood, Asa	Sarah Wilkins	May 20, 1824	487
Allen, Joseph	Charlott Hendry	Mar. 11, 1824	488
Arnett, John Adams	Mary Chandler	Mar. 18, 1824	489
Allgood, John	Mary Allgood	Sep. 13, 1824	489
Breeding, Ancel	Frances Davis	Sep. 4, 1815	4
Bryant, Mason	Catharine Raine	Dec. 5, 1816	50
Brown, Daniel	Betsey Folley	Dec. 5, 1816	52
Brawner, Joel	Betsy King	Dec. 9, 1816	52
Bryant, Moses	Nancy Ginn	Jan. 19, 1817	95
Berreman, John	Sucky Bragg	Apr. 6, 1817	111
Bell, William	Elizabeth Thornton	Feb. 6, 1817	112
Barron, John	Polly Wright	Sep. 7, 1817	193
Burton, Alanson	Jane Curry	Jan. 15, 1818	193
Beard, John P.	Eliz. O. Pledger	Feb. 5, 1818	193
Brewer, Horatio G.	Susannah Davis	Nov. 27, 1817	216
Burton, Richard	Mary Snellings	Dec. 24, 1818	219
Banks, Ralph, Jr.	Elizabeth Maxwell	Dec. 22, 1818	261
Brawner, John	Nancy Allman	Aug. 6, 1818	262
Bell, James	Susan Key	Jan. 22, 1819	297
Brown, Aron	Elizabeth Cook	Mar. 21, 1819	297
Butler, David	Sarah S. King	Jun. 22, 1819	297
Brawner, Henry P.	Cherry Barnes	Dec. __ 1815	297
Brawner, James M.	Elizabeth Allman	Dec. 14, 1819	349
Banks, Willis	Mary W. Oliver	Oct. 3, 1819	384
Brown, James L.	Dicey Skelton	Aug. 22, 1819	399
Bolton, William	Sarah Nunnelee	Dec. 7, 1819	423
Banks, Thomas A.	Mary J. Chipman	Jan. 3, 1821	469
Beck, William A.	Ann Welch	May 30, 1820	475
Banks, James A.	Milly Oliver	May 25, 1820	475
Burton, Leroy	Harriett Burton	Jun. 4, 1820	475
Bowen, William U.	Ann A. Banks	Apr. 26, 1820	476
Barron, Barnabas	Polly Dooly	Feb. 17, 1820	476
Burton, Bins	Mrs. Eliz. Brewer	Feb. 10, 1820	475
Bradford, Nathaniel	Frances Carter	Jan. 4, 1821	476
Brown, Demsey	Martha Raines	Jan. 11, 1820	476
Brown, Robert	Mary Henderson	Apr. 26, 1821	476
Bond, John	Catharine Bond	Jan. 24, 1821	477
Black, Matthew J.	Mary Deadwiler	May 10, 1821	477
Banks, John H.	Sarah B. Clark	Jul. 4, 1821	478
Ball, Henry M.	Susan Tate	Aug. 2, 1821	478
Brown, Asa	Mariah W. Oliver	Nov. 1, 1821	478
Banks, Willis	Mary Gray	Sep. 3, 1822	479
Bruce, Walter	Polly David	Sep. 24, 1822	480
Brawner, Tilmon	Sarah B. Higginbotham	Aug. 13, 1822	480

HISTORICAL COLLECTIONS 283

Groom	Bride	Date	Page
Barr, Robert S.	Nancy Perrin	Jan. 20, 1822	481
Booth, Joel	Patsy Elder	Jan. 20, 1822	481
Bolton, Isaac N.	Rachel Gibbs	Mar. 2, 1823	482
Bell, Joseph	Mary Key	Jul. 13, 1823	482
Brantley, Joseph M.	Nancy J. Dooly	Mar. 18, 1823	482
Brewer, Edmund H.	Lucy F. Carter	May 7, 1823	483
Brown, Adam	Nancy Harbin	May 25, 1823	483
Butler, James	Elizabeth Hansard	Dec. 16, 1823	483
Butler, Patrick, Jr.	Jane Hansard	Jan. 16, 1823	484
Brown, Benjamin	Mrs. Prudence Richardson	Apr. 3, 1823	485
Bryant, William	Lucy D. Christler	Oct. 21, 1823	485
Bowers, Job	Eliz. Ballenger	Dec. 23, 1824	486
Brawner, Simeon	Mrs. Susannah Webb	Nov. 10, 1824	486
Beck, John, Jr.	Willie M. Bowman	Apr. 21, 1824	487
Cloud, Samuel G.	Elizabeth A. Cox	Jan. 9, 1816	32
Callaway, Jepthah	Mary McGehee	Feb. 27, 1817	85
Cook, Samuel	Anne Williams	Jan. 18, 1817	103
Cox, Jacob	Sally Wilkins	Feb. 20, 1817	111
Thomas P. Carter	Lucy C. Hudson	Dec. 22, 1818	231
Cook, Thomas S.	Nancy Patterson	Dec. 22, 1818	261
Colson, James	Frances Johnston	Aug. 11, 1818	285
Cash, Reuben	Elizabeth Buffington	Dec. 10, 1818	296
Cook, Fenton	Emaly Schofield	Jan. 10, 1819	296
Childers, Holman	Martha Colbert	Feb. 24, 1819	297
Crump, Robert	Milly Cason	Nov. 5, 1818	306
Clark, Edward	Rhody Davis	Dec. 9, 1819	327
Craft, Anderson	Lucy Alexander	Feb. 4, 1819	343
Chambers, William S.	Sarah Shepard	Nov. 18, 1819	396
Cason, Edmond	Sophia M. Turner	May 4, 1820	423
Craft, Washington	Polly Daniel	Dec. 26, 1820	446
Childers, John S.	Permelia Burton	Jan. 4, 1821	474
Campbell, William	Sally Dillard	Oct. 25, 1820	474
Carter, John	Sarah Ausley	Sep. 20, 1820	474
Coker, Asa	Mrs. Polly Ann Milligan	Oct. 12, 1820	475
Childs, John	Sarah Alexander	Feb. 15, 1820	476
Cheek, William	Sintha Coker	Sep. 13, 1821	476
Clark, James C.	Margaret Clark	Mar. 29, 1821	476
Chisenhall, Debany	Nancy Cunningham	Apr. 3, 1821	476
Christian, Elijah J.	Rebecca Coleman	Jan. 16, 1821	476
Craft, John	Elizabeth Daniel	Jan. 28, 1821	477
Childers, Jesse C.	Peggy Ferguson	Nov. 21, 1822	479
Corry, John S.	Elizabeth J. Carter	Nov. 26, 1822	479
Craft, Samuel	Lear H. Dunn	May 23, 1822	479
Chambers, Joseph S.	Frances A. Stinchcomb	Aug. 29, 1822	480

GEORGIA D. A. R.

Groom	Bride	Date	Page
Craft, John	Agatha Crump	Aug. 1, 1822	480
Collins, Samuel	Mary Cook	Oct. 17, 1822	480
Crump, Pleasant D.	Elizabeth Vauter	Mar. 9, 1822	481
Clark, William B.	Judith C. Rucker	Jan. 22, 1822	481
Cook, Franklin	Sarah Anderson	Sep. 21, 1823	483
Christian, Elijah W.	Mary Christian	Dec. 19, 1823	484
Cade, Bedford	Mrs. Agnes Wilkins	Nov. 5, 1823	484
Cunningham, John A.	Sarah Daniel	Apr. 13, 1823	485
Coker, John	Nancy Ballenger	Feb. 19, 1824	486
Cook, Lewis	Nancy Cook	Jan. 16, 1824	487
Cook, Theodocius	Nancy Wood	Jan. 15, 1824	487
Coleman, James	Polly Elder	Mar. 31, 1824	487
Christler, Benjamin	Sarah McGehee	Dec. 11, 1824	488
Christler, Westley	Anna Teasley	Oct. 28, 1824	488
Cash, Moses	Nancy Hunt	Jul. 6, 1824	489
David, Jacob W.	Peggy Allman	Jan. 2, 1817	14
Dooly, Bennett	Suckey Rice	Dec. 5, 1816	40
Doss, Hamlet	Alphia F. O. Crump	Jan. 3, 1817	46
Daniel, James	Peggy Means	Dec. 23, 1817	190
Dupuy, William L.	Frances T. Moore	Oct. 29, 1818	217
Depriest, James A.	Judith Booth	Jan. 7, 1819	296
Dobbs, David	Elizabeth McMullen	Apr. 28, 1819	297
David, Maraset	Elizabeth David	May 2, 1819	320
Dollar, Henry	Polly Self	Sep. 1, 1819	327
Dutton, Henry	Elizabeth Couch	Aug. 22, 1819	328
David, James	Nancy Henry	Dec. 9, 1819	349
Dudley, Ignatius	Sally Holton	Dec. 26, 1819	379
Downer, Joseph	Elcy Waters	Aug. 29, 1819	399
Dennard, John	Mary Ann Allman	Jul. 21, 1819	400
Dye, Burrell	Elizabeth Bell	Nov. 25, 1819	410
Davis, Pleasant	Polly Wheeler	Sep. 7, 1820	474
Dodds, James	Winny Burden	Oct. 12, 1820	474
Davis, William C.	Mary Burton	May 4, 1820	475
Deane, George	Mary Ann Anthony	Mar. 30, 1820	476
Dennard, Isaac	Edne Harris	Jan. 3, 1821	476
Daniel, David	Frances Means	1822	479
Dudley, James	Betsy Coleman	Dec. 26, 1822	479
Decker, Young A.	Nancy Chapman	Sep. 8, 1822	480
Dodds, Thomas	Mary Roberts	May 7, 1822	481
Dailey, Samuel C.	Milly T. Oliver	Feb. 14, 1822	481
David, Isaac	Patsy Sartin	Jul. 3, 1823	482
Davis, James	Louisa E. Hudson	Jul. 31, 1823	482
Downer, John	Elizabeth Butler	Jul. 6, 1823	482
Drake, Meredith	Della Wolen	Aug. 14, 1823	483
Downer, William W.	Elener Bell	Dec. 7, 1823	484
Duncan, Henry	Mary Vines	Dec. 23, 1823	485

HISTORICAL COLLECTIONS

Groom	Bride	Date	Page
Davis, Absolom T.	Martha Underwood	Oct. 27, 1824	488
Dobbs, Jesse	Mary Prothro	Aug. 31, 1824	489
Dooley, Allen D.	Letty M. Brantley	Apr. 22, 1824	490
Edwards, Isaac O.	Mary Clark	Oct. 24, 1816	79
Elliott, Thomas C.	Sally Key	Dec. 28, 1819	400
Edwards, Isaac O.	Frances Wyche	Nov. 7, 1824	488
Ford, Elisha	Eliz. Deadwyler	Jun. 11, 1818	193
Fortson, Easton	Tabitha Haley	Dec. 26, 1819	378
Fortson, Samuel H.	Vilate Higginbotham	Dec. 8, 1819	406
Fortson, William	Eliza Lane	Aug. 10, 1820	474
Fittes, William H. T.	Mary M. Christian	May 16, 1820	475
Freeman, Henry	Pamelia Cook	Jan. 11, 1820	476
Fannen, Lauchlen	Susannah Downer	Jan. 27, 1820	476
Fortson, Thomas	Mira Kennebrew	Feb. 9, 1821	476
Flemming, Benjamin	Frances Hudson	Sep. 18, 1821	477
Ferguson, William	Fanny Karr	Jul. 9, 1821	478
Fortson, William T.	Sarah H. Shackleford	Nov. 22, 1821	478
Foster, James M.	Nancy White	May 12, 1822	480
Faulk, Thomas	Louranie Largent	Jan. 11, 1822	481
Franklin, Richard	Polly Cunningham	Dec. 25, 1823	485
Felts, Walker	Ann P. Christian	Jan. 8, 1824	486
Fortson, Tavnah	Catharine D. Tate	Dec. 2, 1824	488
Farrar, Thomas J.	Martha Royster	Nov. 2, 1824	488
Glover, William	Milley Alexander	Jan. 4, 1816	40
Gartman, Daniel	Susannah Pledger	Sep. 26, 1816	85
Gully, Volintine	Elizabeth P. King	Jan. 8, 1818	193
Grinway, Elisha	Sally Hale	Jun. 8, 1818	193
Goode, James J.	Martha Clark	Dec. 8, 1818	217
Grizzle, John P.	Jane Key	Oct. 20, 1820	436
Gibson, Samuel	Dosha Franklin	Aug. 9, 1820	475
Gaines, Ralph	Elizabeth M. Turner	Jan. 3, 1822	478
Ginn, Wiley	Sintha Henry	Jan. 24, 1823	480
Gaines, James H.	Ann B. Henderson	May 2, 1822	481
Gaines, George	Polly Craft	Jan. 7, 1823	482
Ginn, Elisha	Charity Runnels	Sep. 9, 1823	483
Goss, Horatio J.	Ann Bradley	Sep. 18, 1823	484
Greenway, John W.	Lucy Hulme	Dec. 9, 1824	487
Grice, Demsey	Caty Williams	Jun. 23, 1824	489
Ginn, Isaac	Martha Burden	Jun. 17, 1824	489
Ginn, Jesse	Sarah Brown	Aug. 8, 1824	489
Hunt, William	Joicy Stowers	Dec. 4, 1815	14
Head, Benjamin	Rebecca Terrell	Apr. 22, 1817	86
Harris, John L.	Catharine W. King	May 7, 1817	89
Hausley, Newdeygate	Sarah Davis	Feb. 2, 1817	100
Higginbotham, Geo. G.	Sarah Fortson	Feb. 20, 1817	106

GEORGIA D. A. R.

Groom	Bride	Date	Page
Henry, William	Sucey Skinner	Mar. 20, 1817	106
Henderson, Simeon	Biddy Heard	Mar. 6, 1817	112
Horton, John	Winny Teasley	Aug. 21, 1817	133
Harcrow, Samuel	Alphia Ginn	Sep. 21, 1817	135
Huddleston, William	Sarah C. Rice	Nov. 13, 1817	154
Horton, Thomas	Betsy Teasley	Oct. 30, 1817	175
Harper, William W.	Lucy Allen	Nov. 4, 1817	175
Harbin, William	Elizabeth Kennedy	Dec. 18, 1817	190
Hudson, David	Matilda Oliver	Sep. 9, 1817	190
Haynes, Waller G.	Polly W. Harper	Dec. 29, 1818	231
Harper, Caselton B.	Polly Adams	Jan. 7, 1819	261
Hanley, Jarratt	Polly Coker	Dec. 23, 1818	291
Hubbard, John	Ann F. Nunnelee	Dec. 17, 1818	296
Holtzclaw, Silas	Rosannah Stone	Feb. 4, 1819	296
Hicks, Johnston	Martha G. Booth	Jan. 31, 1819	296
Holdbrook, Flemmon	Aggy Clark	Nov. 6, 1817	297
Henry, John	Polly Skinner	Jan. 25, 1818	306
Harris, John	Mary J. Shackleford	Dec. 6, 1820	469
Ham, Gideon	Elizabeth Terrell	Apr. 18, 1820	474
Hearndon, Edward	Nancy Brown	Aug. 17, 1820	474
Hardeman, Charles	Mrs. Betty Cook	Oct. 3, 1820	474
Hilley, Francis	Mary R. Oliver	Feb. 24, 1820	476
Harman, George W.	Susan Carpenter	Mar. 4, 1821	476
Howell, Samuel	Sally Brown	Mar. 22, 1821	476
Head, James B.	Elizabeth Allen	Jan. 7, 1821	477
Hammond, Herbert	Elizabeth Rich	May 7, 1821	477
Henry, William P.	Sarah L. Beck	Jun. 7, 1821	478
Hubbard, Vinson	Sarah Dye	Jul. 12, 1821	478
Harrison, John B.	Elizabeth Burton	Jan. 5, 1823	479
Hunt, George	Elizabeth Adams	Oct. 3, 1822	480
Hamilton, Robert	Louisey McGehee	Jan. 24, 1822	480
Holeyness, McKinney	Susannah W. Nunnelee	Jan. 22, 1823	482
Harris, Jonathan	Rachel W. Fortson	Oct. 17, 1823	483
Hunt, Sion	Priscilla Thornton	Jul. 31, 1823	484
Harper, Bedford	Gilly Y. Banks	Mar. 6, 1823	485
Hunt, James	Mary W. Haynes	Dec. 18, 1823	485
Hudson, David	Lucinda Jones	Feb. 8, 1824	486
Hicks, Wyatt	Melinda Phelps	Feb. 8, 1824	486
Hudson, John H.	Martha Snellings	Dec. 19, 1824	487
Hudson, William	Mary Ann Oliver	Jun. 13, 1824	488
Highsmith, Thomas	Elizabeth Parks	Aug. 12, 1824	489
Johnston, James	Jane Gains	Dec. 12, 1816	79
Jones, Heiram	Settey Jones	Mar. 19, 1818	193
Jones, Thomas	Hitty Pathro	Oct. 29, 1818	262
Johns, John D.	Nancy Booth	Dec. 24, 1818	285
Jones, John	Nancy Hambleton	Dec. 29, 1818	291

HISTORICAL COLLECTIONS 287

Groom	Bride	Date	Page
Jordon, Matthew	Elizabeth Magee	Oct. 31, 1820	435
Jones, Davis	Rhody Jones	Dec. 31, 1820	463
Jones, Micajah	Genoa Tate	Jul. 18, 1820	475
Johnston, John	Nancy Powell	Jan. 20, 1820	476
Jones, Garland	Winny Shackleford	Dec. 7, 1820	476
Jorden, Isaac	Elizabeth Bullis	Mar. 27, 1821	477
Jones, Simeon	Rebecca Banks	Sep. 6, 1821	478
Jack, James	Ann Gray	Oct. 27, 1822	479
Johnston, James	Ann F. Oglesby	Aug. 15, 1822	480
Jones, Joseph H.	Lucy Banks	Feb. 26, 1822	480
Jones, Standley	Frances Rucker	Jul. 24, 1823	483
Johnston, Daniel M.	Nancy Highsmith	Aug. 14, 1823	483
Johnston, Lindsay	Sarah Oglesby	Aug. 24, 1823	484
Jones, Edmond	Keziah Jones	Nov. 10, 1824	486
King, James	Minty Phelps	Aug. 27, 1818	219
Klugh, Pascoll D.	Martha M. Tate	Jun. 8, 1821	478
King, John	Matilada Bond	Dec. 12, 1822	479
King, William Jr.	Sukey King	Oct. 3, 1822	480
Kennedy, William J. C.	Elizabeth Cason	Jan. 24, 1822	481
Kemp, David V.	Nancy Butler	Dec. 25, 1823	484
Kerlin, David	Icy Kennebrew	Mar. 23, 1824	486
Lunsford, James	Polly White	Sept. 18, 1817	169
Lunsford, George	Winney White	Jan. 16, 1818	193
Lipford, H. F. M. M.	Frances A. Tate	May 20, 1819	297
Landers, John	Lotty Meret	Mar. 30, 1817	297
Lawrimore, Andrew	Margaret Kerlin	Dec. 22, 1820	473
Lewis, James H.	Elizabeth H. Kidd	Dec. 3, 1820	474
Landers, James O.	Frances Head	July 5, 1821	478
Lunsford, James	Honor Eaves	Mar. 17, 1822	480
Lunsford, William	Amela Teasley	Aug. 28, 1823	483
Logan, John	Matilda Craft	Jan. 2, 1823	485
Loftis, William	Catharine King	Feb. 10, 1824	487
Lofton, James	Lucinda A. Howard	Dec. 22, 1824	488
McMullin, Thomas	Sally Gaines	Jan. 12, 1815	4
McGarrity, Gardner	Sarah Hilley	Feb. 4, 1816	82
McCune, James A.	Ruth Ferrell	Mar. 20, 1817	116
McGehee, William	Eliza Watkins	May 22, 1817	133
McCurry, Lauchlen	Polly Penn	Jan. 21, 1819	296
McConnic, John	Rosannah Prewit	Jan. 17, 1819	297
McDonald, Alex	Martha P. Hudson	Mar. 22, 1821	477
McMullen, Daniel	Sally Wilson	Sept. 16, 1822	480
McMullen, Fielding	Polly Dollar	Mar. 3, 1822	482
McMullen, Sinclair	Crissa Richardson	Jan. 11, 1824	486
McCurley, Moses	Susannah Stowers	Feb. 5, 1824	487
McGarrity, John	Ann Burnett	Oct. 14, 1824	489
McGuire, John S.	Susannah A. Clark	Aug. 26, 1824	490

GEORGIA D. A. R.

Groom	Bride	Date	Page
Moon, Jacob	Anny Staples	Nov. 28, 1816	46
Mann, John	Polly Harper	Dec. 26, 1816	52
Mann, Abner L.	Diana Crittendon	Oct. 14, 1816	69
Morris, John W.	Anny Allgood	Feb. 6, 1817	85
Middleton, John	Elizabeth P. Tait	Jun. 26, 1817	133
Milton, William	Caty Baskins	Dec. 3, 1817	134
Mann, William H.	Dicey Bentley	Sep. 27, 1817	169
Meanes, Samuel	Sarah Elliott	Sep. 15, 1817	193
Merrell, Joshua	Betsy B. Williamson	Dec. 30, 1818	287
Morgan, William C.	Lucindey Oglesby	Mar. 30, 1819	297
Mason, Allen	Bathena Brannan	Nov. 24, 1819	349
Miller, Jedediah	Eliz. C. Edwards	Jun. 17, 1819	353
Maxwell, Simeon	Elizabeth Fortson	Dec. 9, 1819	353
Moore, Elijah	Sarah White	Dec. 10, 1819	379
Moon, Stephen	Fanny Phelps	Jan. 20, 1820	475
Mann, William H.	Fanny Hearndon	Jan. 6, 1820	476
Maxwell, William	Susannah Owens	Mar. 20, 1821	476
Mann, John R.	Rebecca Bentley	Feb. 17, 1821	477
Moon, James B.	Mary Davis	Aug. 2, 1821	477
Maxwell, Reuben	Elizabeth Thornton	Dec. 13, 1821	478
Means, Alexander	Judith Cridenton	Oct. 22, 1822	479
Mann, James	Esther Lewis	Apr. 7, 1822	481
Manning, Robert H.	Louisiana Thompson	Jan. 30, 1822	482
Moss, Beverly	Lucy Lewis	Dec. 18, 1823	483
Moon, Jesse	Mary Phelps	Oct. 28, 1823	484
Moss, Martin	Nancy Fannen	Nov. 20, 1823	484
Moss, William	Dosha Underwood	Feb. 20, 1823	484
Morgan, Thomas	Lucy Colbert	Feb. 5, 1824	486
Molden, Thomas	Nancy Christler	Feb. 20, 1824	486
Martin, Jesse	Elizabeth McMullen	Feb. 26, 1824	487
Mann, Stephen A.	Malinda Oliver	Jul. 8, 1824	489
Mewborn, Thomas	Frances Burden	Oct. 26, 1824	489
Nunnely, William	Mariah O. Tittle	Apr. 24, 1817	89
Nunnelee, John	Martha Thompson	Jan. 9, 1817	103
Nash, George B.	Nancy Butler	Aug. 28, 1817	193
Nunnelee, Howell	Melinda Morgan	Feb. 4, 1818	193
Nelmes, John	Mary Underwood	Jul. 23, 1818	306
Nunelee, Simeon	Martha Terrell	May 24, 1819	384
New, Samuel	Nancy Dudley	Oct. 5, 1820	474
Nix, William S.	Polly Smith	Mar. 2, 1820	476
Norman, Elijah B.	Polly S. Higginbotham	Apr. 3, 1821	476
Nelmes, Jesse	Alis Duncan	Jan. 10, 1822	482
Nelmes, Joshua B.	Nancy Wheeler	Aug. 19, 1823	483
Napier, John W. S.	Mary J. Jones	Aug. 3, 1824	488
Nelson, William	Grace A. Adams	Jul. 6, 1824	489

HISTORICAL COLLECTIONS

Groom	Bride	Date	Page
Ozburn, Pleasant	Letty Wood	Jan. 16, 1820	475
Oglesby, Robert C.	Zeriah G. Wilhite	Dec. 25, 1823	485
Patterson, Henry	Elizabeth Cook	Jun. 7, 1818	193
Pealor, Benjamin	Elitha Ginn	Mar. 18, 1819	297
Pealor, Abner	Elvey Allgood	Apr. 10, 1819	297
Parker, John D.	Nancy Merret	Oct. 23, 1819	314
Presley, Charles	Mildred Kerlin	Dec. 21, 1819	343
Pealer, Abner	Betsy Akens	Dec. 30, 1819	350
Prewet, John	Letha Craft	Dec. 23, 1819	400
Pledger, Johnston	Nancy Oglesby	Jul. 6, 1820	475
Pledger, Westly	Sarah Oglesby	Jan. 18, 1821	476
Penn, Thomas H.	Polly Burden	Jan. 18, 1821	477
Patterson, Thomas	Nancy Hendry	May 31, 1821	478
Pledger, Joseph P.	Frances P. Chambers	Jan. 3, 1822	482
Pledger, Isaac M.	Polly Ginn	Oct. 21, 1822	482
Page, Watson D.	Margarett Denna	Jan. 1, 1824	485
Prothro, Joshua	Lucy Dobbs	Jan. 4, 1823	485
Pulliam, William	Permelia Turman	Jan. 29, 1824	487
Perrin, Bannister	Nancy Carter	Dec. 2, 1824	487
Patterson, Robert H.	Martha Moore	Dec. 5, 1824	488
Patterson, James	Mary Jones	Aug. 17, 1824	489
Price, Matthew	Sally Skinner	May 12, 1824	490
Richards, Reuben	Rachel Bond	Nov. 12, 1809	2
Rembert, Andrew	Margaret M. Sayre	Feb. 12, 1819	297
Redwine, Lewis	Mary Merret	Jan. 14, 1817	297
Reay, Peter	Sarah Dooly	Jul. 1, 1817	304
Rice, Jesse	Webby Dooly	Sep. 3, 1818	304
Rose, Pleasant	Sarah Hubbard	Oct. 17, 1819	405
Ramsey, David B.	Polly Brown	Sep. 19, 1820	476
Runnals, Meredith	Milly Powel	Apr. 26, 1821	476
Roan, John	Jane Davis	Dec. 19, 1821	476
Roberts, Jesse	Tibitha Ruff	May 9, 1821	477
Ruff, Shadrack	Patsy Penn	Nov. 17, 1822	479
Roberts, Joseph	Polly Folk	Jan. 1, 1822	481
Runnels, Berry	Cresy Powel	Mar. 15, 1822	481
Rice, Richard	Eliza White	Jan. 1, 1823	482
Rodgers, John	Jane Dennard	Mar. 20, 1823	485
Reed, William P.	Harriett Allen	Jul. 22, 1824	486
Rone, John	Frances Tate	Apr. 15, 1824	486
Rose, Thomas G.	Sarah Christian	Mar. 11, 1824	486
Runnels, William	Sarah Bobo	Jun. 6, 1824	489
Shepard, James	Sarah Hilley	Apr. 24, 1810	2
Standeford, Bailey	Betsy Hales	Apr. 23, 1810	2
Smith, John M.	Nancy L. Suttles	Nov. 27, 1810	2
Smith, David	Selah David	May 15, 1817	86
Shorter, Eli S.	Sophia H. Watkins	Jun. 18, 1817	133

Groom	Bride	Date	Page
Simmons, John	Mary B. Harrison	May 25, 1817	190
Shelman, John	Unity Phillips	Aug. 3, 1818	193
Saxton, John M.	Elizabeth Burton	Dec. 31, 1817	217
Sheat, Burges	Milsy Ooker	Nov. 19, 1818	219
Shell, George	Sarah L. Hearne	Dec. 19, 1815	297
Skinner, Morris	Sally Hendrick	Aug. 12, 1819	349
Stricklin, Joseph	Sarah Davis	Jul. 14, 1819	386
Sanders, Thomas	Isabel Totman	Sep. 16, 1819	397
Smithey, Isaac	Polly Terrel	Nov. 25, 1819	406
Shephard, Richard	Judea J. Mann	Dec. 27, 1820	457
Smith, Thomas A.	Elizabeth Hullum	Nov. 28, 1820	473
Sheperd, Nathan	Betsy Bently	Nov. 30, 1820	474
Saggs, Henry M.	Polly Gregg	May 9, 1820	475
Smith, Welsey	Averilla Royal	Apr. 18, 1820	475
Self, Sinclair	Nancy James	Feb. 24, 1820	476
Smith, Charles	Martha T. Glenn	Jan. 20, 1820	476
Smith, Henry	Rachel Pemelton	Mar. 1, 1821	476
Smith, Archibald	Levina McMullen	Jan. 24, 1822	481
Statham, John Jr.	Nancy Hicks	Jan. 5, 1823	482
Schelds, Thomas E.	Matilda Bailey	Mar. 27, 1823	483
Stephens, Thomas	Patsy Lesuer	Mar. 11, 1823	485
Skelton, Jabez	Julia Davis	Feb. 14, 1823	485
Smith, William A.	Rebecca Anderson	Feb. 1, 1824	487
Sadler, James R.	Pressilla Jones	Jan. 8, 1824	487
Stephens, Henry H.	Martha Oglesby	Oct. 7, 1824	487
Sartin, James	Bethana Burnett	Nov. 18, 1824	488
Smith, Joseph	Mary Ann Harris	Dec. 30, 1824	488
Steelman, William H.	Eliz. T. Underwood	Jul. 8, 1824	488
Sanders, Benjamin	Nancy White	Jul. 15, 1824	489
Smith, Samuel	Mary Dobbs,	Oct. 17, 1824	489
Snow, Eli	Elizabeth Gully	Jan. 22, 1824	490
Thompson, Joel	Betsy Smith	Nov. 3, 1816	21
Tate, Zimri	Martha Owens	May 14, 1817	89
Thornton, Evans	Morening Adams	Oct. 23, 1817	171
Teasley, Levi	Elizabeth Horton	Nov. 27, 1817	190
Turner, John	Betsey Branham	Dec. 10, 1818	306
Tate, William	Sarah Upshaw	Nov. 4, 1819	314
Turner, Thomas	Anna Gregg	Dec. 23, 1819	378
Tate, James	Mary S. Brown	Jul. 27, 1819	396
Thornton, Benjamin	Nancy Pane	Sep. 16, 1819	397
Thornton, Jeremiah	Frances Colbert	Oct. 28, 1819	397
Thomason, John	Martha Gaines	Nov. 4, 1817	405
Tyner, Tollison	Jane Totman	Aug. 29, 1820	423
Thornton, Thomas A.	Polly Willis	Oct. 5, 1820	474
Toles, Suddeth	Nancy A. Nolan	Aug. 3, 1820	474
Thomas, Evan	Polly Moore	Jan. 11, 1821	477

HISTORICAL COLLECTIONS 291

Groom	Bride	Date	Page
Taylor, John	Rebecca Snelling	Jan. 7, 1821	477
Teasley, James S.	Mary A. Hansard	Oct. 17, 1822	479
Turman, Abner T.	Martha Jones	Dec. 9, 1822	479
Taylor, Jesse	Pheriby Decker	Nov. 14, 1822	479
Teasley, Benager	Lucy Haley	Oct. 31, 1822	482
Tate, Edmond B.	Mahala Fortson	Oct. 16, 1823	484
Thornton, Thomas A.	Sarah Fortson	Oct. 23, 1823	484
Thornton, John	Frances Adams	Oct. 23, 1823	484
Tucker, Robert	Martha Staples	Dec. 16, 1824	488
Threlkeld, Oliver	Mariah Cook	Nov. 18, 1824	488
Upshaw, John	Tabitha Lawlis	Apr. 2, 1818	193
Underwood, Jarratt	Nellie Moss	Jan. 1, 1818	327
Upshaw, Richard	Rebecca Elder	Feb. 27, 1820	475
Upshaw, George	Elizabeth Tate	Jan. 4, 1820	476
Upshaw, Huston	Rhoda Oglesby	Aug. 3, 1823	484
Unis, Samuel	Sarah Jorden	Jul. 5, 1824	486
Virdell, John A.	Sally C. Williamson	Jan. 21, 1819	297
Vaughn, Murphy	Sarah Ann Tate	Dec. 21, 1823	484
Wilson, Thomas	Polly Mattox	Mar. 14, 1816	40
Wallis, Burrell	Rhoda Dickenson	Dec. 12, 1816	46
White, John M.	Elizabeth Harper	Dec. 26, 1816	52
Webb, Wiley	Betsy Morris	Nov. 9, 1816	79
White, Asa	Agnes Moore	Dec. 26, 1816	79
Woods, John	Tabitha Ridgway	Mar. 27, 1817	116
Wood, Samuel	Lucy Cook	Mar. 29, 1818	193
Welborn, Burkett	Nancy Pace	Sep. 16, 1818	261
Wilhite, John B.	Elizabeth P. Wilhite	Aug. 17, 1820	474
Wilson, John	Fanny Sartin	Feb. 20, 1820	475
Webb, Milton P.	Letitia Deadwyler	Nov. 16, 1820	476
White, James	Lucy Cash	Oct. 25, 1821	478
Willis, Thomas F.	Milly Clark	Nov. 7, 1822	479
Wheeler, Thomas B.	Judith Bates	Jul. 4, 1822	480
Williams, John	Keziah Cook	Jan. 3, 1822	481
Wooldridge, Thomas	Nancy Banks	Feb. 13, 1822	481
West, William	Elizabeth P. Wood	Jul. 30, 1823	483
Ward, John B.	Rebecca Coulson	Jul. 1, 1823	483
Wheeler, Leroy	Sarah Wheeler	Oct. 8, 1818	304
Wilhite, Joseph W.	Nancy F. Wilhite	Dec. 19, 1820	463
White, Martin	Ann Burden	Feb. 27, 1823	485
Ward, Walter H.	Jane Gray	Jan. 23, 1823	485
Warren, Jeremiah S.	Elizabeth Thornton	Oct. 14, 1823	485
Webb, Abner	Nancy Deadwyler	Nov. 9, 1824	486
Young, John	Ann Cook	May 1, 1823	483

MARRIAGES 1825-1829
WILL BOOK "N" OLD No.

Groom	Bride	Date	Page
Almond, Simeon	Mary Fortson	Nov. 21, 1826	409
Adams, Lawrence M.	Nancy H. Hunt	Nov. 14, 1826	409
Arnold, William	Nancy Woodly	Sep. 3, 1826	410
Adams, Abner	Betsey A. Fortson	Jul. 20, 1826	410
Arnold, John	Mary W. Hudson	Dec. 15, 1825	410
Allen, Thomas J.	Elizabeth White	Jan. 26, 1826	411
Allgood, John	Nancy Burden	Dec. 27, 1825	411
Alexander, Elam	Lucy Terry	Dec. 8, 1825	411
Allen, Edmond B.	Sarah Ashworth	Jan. 12, 1826	411
Alston, James J. Y.	Mary A. R. Chambers	Apr. 12, 1827	413
Ashworth, Noah	Nancy O. Lockhart	Aug. 6, 1827	413
Anthony, William A.	Milly Hightower	Nov. 15, 1827	413
Adams, George	Jemima Anderson	Apr. 8, 1828	415
Akin, Johnson	Charity A. Banks	Oct. 28, 1828	416
Banks, Henry	Judith Oliver	Feb. 8, 1825	169
Bond, Daniel	Claricey Bond	Feb. 19, 1825	227
Bond, Willis	Leah Carpenter	Mar. 13, 1825	408
Bryant, William	Sarah Teasley	Dec. 31, 1820	408
Butler, Richmond	Martha Webb	Oct. 13, 1826	409
Bell, Thomas, Jr.	Polly Dye	Jul. 7, 1826	410
Butler, Peter P.	Milly L. Bell	Apr. 13, 1826	410
Barnes, Henry	Polly Stodghill	Mar. 5, 1826	410
Burden, Archibald	Lydia Fortenberry	Jan. 1, 1826	411
Bailey, Hezekiah	Sally Gaines	Jan. 12, 1826	411
Blair, Middleton	Peggy Wallis	Oct. 19, 1826	412
Brewer, William F.	Martha Fortson	Jun. 10, 1827	412
Brown, James	Sarah Alexander	Nov. 15, 1827	413
Bailey, Henry S.	Lucy Patterson	Nov. 22, 1827	413
Booth, Victor E.	Elizabeth Parham	Dec. 20, 1827	414
Black, John W.	Betsy Ham	Mar. 4, 1828	414
Burch, Benjamin	Mary Ann Cook	Mar. 20, 1828	414
Banks, John	Sarah Watkins	Feb. 14, 1828	415
Barnes, John	Martha C. Stodghill	Sep. 6, 1827	415
Bentley, Hiram	Levicy Bentley	Mar. 31, 1828	415
Bray, Masten H.	Elizabeth Faulkner	Apr. 17, 1828	415
Bell, Johnathan	Sarah Bell	Aug. 17, 1828	415
Burton, Nicholas	Eliza F. Nunnelee	Apr. 20, 1828	416
Benedict, Eli	Selah Smith	Dec. 18, 1828	416
Cunningham, Joseph	Polly Robertson	Mar. 13, 1825	201
Campbell, Daniel	Ann C. E. P. Wright	Mar. 31, 1825	408
Carpenter, Joshua S.	Mary W. Bond	Apr. 3, 1825	408
Canning, John	Elizabeth Moore	Oct. 9, 1825	408
Coker, Newell	Catharine Cunningham	Oct. 27, 1825	409

HISTORICAL COLLECTIONS 293

Groom	Bride	Date	Page
Childers, William B.	Nancy L. Hudson	Aug. 6, 1826	409
Carlisle, James W.	Mazy Pace	Mar. 26, 1826	410
Christian, Chas. W.	Mary Maxwell	Jan. 18, 1827	412
Christian, John	Marium Groose	Nov. 26, 1826	412
Cook, Issachar	Nancy Wood	Jan. 28, 1827	412
Cook, Beverly C.	Martha Tate	May 3, 1827	412
Childers, Seaborn	Permelia Rich	Jun. 28, 1827	413
Campbell, Obediah	Elizabeth Edwards	Jan. 24, 1828	414
Clark, Zachariah H.	Elizabeth Mattox	Jan. 10, 1828	414
Chandler, Mordecai	Elizabeth Banks	Feb. 26, 1828	414
Clark, James	Permelia T. Wilbern	Aug. 25, 1828	415
Cook, William T. O.	Nancy T. Ridgway	Sep. 16, 1828	415
Craft, John, Jr.	Ann Gaines	Oct. 23, 1828	416
Dooly, Thomas	Mary Brooks	Jul. 26, 1825	408
Deadwyler, Joseph P.	Martha P. Webb	Nov. 8, 1825	409
Dobbs, Asa	Frances McMullin	Oct. 18, 1826	409
Dickerson, Robt. P.	Martha Henderson	Jul. 20, 1826	410
David, Samuel	Harriett Threlkeld	May 25, 1826	410
Dean, Alvin	Eliza F. White	Jan. 3, 1826	411
Davis, Vatchel	Malinda O. Kelly	Jan. 23, 1827	412
Davis, James	Frances Terrell	Jan. 18, 1827	412
Dooly, William W.	Mary Brantley	Jul. 5, 1827	413
Dobbs, Silus	Nancy Mires	Oct. 4, 1827	413
Davis, Joseph	Susannah Wall	Nov. 4, 1828	416
Edmonson, James	Rebecca Jones	Mar. 15, 1826	409
Etchieson, Allen	Sarah M. Ragan	Jan. 20, 1826	411
Edmonson, Samuel	Eliza Perryman	Jun. 1, 1827	412
Everson, Willis	Frances Higginbotham	Dec. 9, 1827	414
Edwards, William H.	Elizabeth Burton	Dec. 23, 1828	416
Forrester, Jesse	Mary White	Sep. 26, 1826	409
Foster, William	Juda Parrott	Jan. 31, 1826	411
Fortson, Tavnah W.	Elizabeth D. Tate	Sep. 13, 1827	413
Franklin, Wiley	Elizabeth Dutton	Jan. 22, 1828	414
Ginn, Joshua	Nancy Statham	Nov. 3, 1825	408
Gunter, Jesse	Susan Butler	Nov. 10, 1825	409
Garey, Van D.	Eliz Dooley	Feb. 9, 1826	411
Grant, Gregory	Lucinda H. Davis	Jan. 25, 1827	412
Gaar, William	Keziah Davis	Oct. 25, 1827	413
Griffin, William W.	Elenor W. Smith	Dec. 18, 1827	414
Golding, Wm. Barnett	Eveline Adams	Oct. 9, 1828	415
Glenn, Simeon G.	Jane Ann Carden	Sep. 25, 1828	416
Harmon, Frederick	Rhody Carpenter	Apr. 4, 1825	4
Herring, William A.	Mary S. White	Jan. 18, 1825	104
Hutchenson, Moses	Nancy J. Brantley	Jul. 14, 1828	285
Hunt, John S.	Mary Gaines	Jul. 14, 1825	285
Hubbard, Woodson	Mary Dye	Jan. 20, 1825	408

Groom	Bride	Date	Page
Hardeman, Joel	Eliz. B. Upshaw	Dec. 5, 1825	408
Hendrick, Levi	Cloey Coker	Jun. 3, 1825	408
Hulme, William	Nancy Ann Oliver	Oct. 8, 1826	409
Handy, Joseph J. L.	Rebecca Martin	Sep. 28, 1826	409
Hendrick, Milum	Julia Ann Eaves	Aug. 17, 1826	410
Hammond, Alfred	Louisa Hudson	Jan. 24, 1826	411
Harris, Tryon	Sarah Alexander	Oct. 29, 1825	411
Hall, John	Mariah Turman	Apr. 12, 1827	412
Hendrick, James J.	Cissale Kelly	Jul. 5, 1827	413
Hendrick, James	Rebecca Maxwell	Aug. 2, 1827	413
Harcrow, Hugh	Sarah Powell	Jul. 11, 1827	413
Hickman, Thomas J.	Mary McCurry	Aug. 23, 1827	413
Higginbotham, John G.	Sally Thornton	Oct. 25, 1827	413
Hudson, Richard D.	Mary W. Burton	Jan. 13, 1828	414
Hill, Abram	Bitha Coker	Jan. 22, 1828	414
Horton, Walker	Melinda Colbert	Feb. 28, 1828	415
Heard, Thomas J.	Nancy P. Middleton	Apr. 1, 1828	415
Hilley, Thomas	Clary G. Higginbotham	May 13, 1828	415
Hearne, Thomas	Frances E. Williams	Jun. 3, 1828	415
Henderson, Simeon	Sarah D. Lewis	Jul. 20, 1828	415
Hall, Simeon	Lucy Stinchcomb	Jul. 29, 1828	415
Hinton, John L.	Elizabeth Hulme	Sep. 10, 1828	415
Hall, Thomas	Nancy Laremore	Oct. 14, 1828	416
Hudson, Lewellen W.	Eliza D. Jarratt	Oct. 22, 1828	416
Jarratt, James D.	Sarah Heard	Jan. 18, 1825	29
Jones, Jordan	Lucy Nix	Jan. 27, 1825	227
Johnston, James	Ann Prothro	Aug. 26, 1825	408
Jackson, William	Ann F. McGehee	Dec. 13, 1825	408
Jones, Samuel G.	Eliz. A. Edwards	Jan. 21, 1826	409
Johnston, Thomas	Mildred A. Roebuck	May 4, 1826	410
Jones, Dewy H.	Sophia Akin	Mar. 22, 1827	412
Jones, James W.	Delina Foster	Oct. 30, 1828	416
Koochagey, Samuel	Martha Carter	Feb. 10, 1825	29
Kirby, Willis	Barbary Jentry	Jul. 19, 1827	413
Lewis, Jeptha	Frances R. Harris	Oct. 13, 1825	408
Lunsford, Rolen	Patsey Roberts	Jan. 5, 1826	411
Legrand, John W.	Lucinda Christian	Aug. 8, 1827	413
Mattox, Nathan	Lucy Key	Feb. 19, 1826	410
Mannen, William	Sarah Deadwyler	Apr. 21, 1825	169
Martin, James S.	Rebecca Wright	Apr. 11, 1825	407
McCurry, John	Nancy P. Goss	Aug. 31, 1825	408
Moon, William H.	Susan Moon	Oct. 20, 1825	408
Mannen, Seaborn	Lucy Newborn	Sep. 28, 1826	409
Maxwell, Benson	Eliz. B. Johnston	Jul. 25, 1826	410
McCoy, Thomas	Lucy Brawner	Feb. 21, 1826	410
Mannen, William	Mary Ford	Dec. 4, 1827	413

HISTORICAL COLLECTIONS 295

Groom	Bride	Date	Page
Merrewether, Chas. S.	Mildred Banks	Dec. 1, 1827	414
Morgan, Kindred	Sarah T. Mann	Dec. 20, 1827	414
Moore, John N.	Martha Vaughn	Mar. 6, 1828	414
Martin, Henry	Permelia Nash	Apr. 6, 1828	415
McCalister, Richard	Phebe Powell	Jul. 14, 1828	415
Martin, James B.	Lucy Powell	Jun. 19, 1828	415
McGuire, Thomas M.	Elizabeth Skelton	Mar. 27, 1828	415
Nelmes, James M.	Susan Moss	Nov. 18, 1825	411
Nuckols, Nathaniel	Susannah Thornton	Nov. 13, 1826	409
Nellums, Wiley	Polly Gay	May 12, 1826	409
Nash, Henry E.	Mary Jones	Jan. 5, 1826	411
Oliver, Jaxson	Polly Maxwell	Feb. 14, 1826	410
Oliver, Thomas W.	Eliz. Ann. Oliver	Jun. 6, 1826	410
Oglesby, James	Sarah Booth	Mar. 6, 1826	412
Oliver, Shelton	Martha B. Williams	Sep. 9, 1828	415
Prater, James	Elizabeth Rowze	May 3, 1825	270
Prichett, John	Mary Farmer	Nov. 13, 1818	408
Pace, Dreadzil	Charlotty Sandridge	Oct. 4, 1825	408
Page, John	Emelia Akin	Oct. 26, 1826	409
Perrin, John	Lucinda Nash	Oct. 19, 1826	409
Patterson, William	Sarah Clark	Aug. 20, 1826	409
Prather, William M.	Nancy Rowsey	Nov. 17, 1825	411
Perryman, William J.	Lucinda Head	Sep. 30, 1823	411
Palmore, Thomas N.	Catharine Denna	Feb. 14, 1827	412
Prewet, Joshua.	Elizabeth Means	Dec. 21, 1826	412
Prothro, William	Mittey Powell	Nov. 29, 1827	413
Pealer, Joseph	Sarah Allgood	Nov. 29, 1827	414
Penn, Edmond T.	Katharine McCurry	Sep. 4, 1828	415
Rodgers, Isham G.	Sally R. Goss	Aug. 31, 1825	408
Ridgway, Samuel	Charlotte Brawner	Sep. 20, 1825	408
Rucker, Lemuel	Prisilla Teasley	Aug. 11, 1825	408
Rowsey, William	Martha Burden	Dec. 27, 1825	411
Rhodelander, Peter	Sally Howell	Oct. 28, 1825	411
Rosser, Jeptha	Sarah N. Harris	Oct. 6, 1825	411
Rice, Aaron	Letty Ballenger	Feb. 6, 1827	412
Rowsey, John	Martha S. Warren	Jan. 3, 1828	414
Raines, John W.	Lucinda Hicks	Dec. 18, 1828	416
Roebuck, John W.	Martha D. Brown	Dec. 30, 1828	416
Smith, Nathaniel	Selah Merrett	Mar. 6, 1825	4
Sparkes, Ellis	Elizabeth Harbin	Dec. 20, 1825	410
Smith, Zachariah	Mary Granshaw	Dec. 24, 1825	411
Shackleford, Joseph H.	Ann Thornton	Dec. 22, 1825	411
Stephens, Henry H.	Sarah Faulkner	Jan. 18, 1827	412
Shifflet, James	Judith Henderson	Dec. 14, 1826	412
Smith, Jesse	Patsy Bowers	Feb. 4, 1827	412
Saxon, Drury T.	Elizabeth Coleman	Jan. 3, 1827	412

Groom	Bride	Date	Page
Spalding, Albert M.	Lucinda Burton	May 3, 1827	412
Self, Samuel E.	Milly Ashworth	Mar. 13, 1827	413
Sewell, Joseph	Polley C. Stinchcomb	Nov. 1, 1827	413
Shelton, John	Mariah Sullivan	Jan. 8, 1828	414
Shiflett, Picket	Sarah Ann Henderson	Jan. 23, 1828	414
Shackleford, Henry	Martha Lewis	May 29, 1828	415
Scales, William	Ann R. Higginbotham	Dec. 16, 1828	416
Tucker, Ethal, Jr.	Nancy Davis	May 17, 1825	270
Thompson, Jesse	Permelia McGuire	Jan. 13, 1820	408
Tyner, Richard, Jr.	Elizabeth Harman	May 31, 1821	408
Thornton, Daniel	Lucy C. Bradley	Oct. 3, 1826	409
Tinsley, Thomas C.	Martha M. Harris	Apr. 7, 1826	410
Thornton, William	Nancy J. Shackleford	Jul. 20, 1826	410
Thornton, Elzey B.	Nancy Harper	Apr. 13, 1826	410
Thompson, Jeffrey	Tabitha Clark	Jan. 25, 1826	410
Taylor, Willis W.	Catharine Hall	Nov. 12, 1825	411
Tucker, Stephen H.	Mary Akin	Jan. 16, 1827	412
Tucker, John M.	Lucinda Tucker	Jan. 13, 1827	412
Tate, Jacob M.	Anna A. Keys	Jun. 7, 1827	413
Teasley, Thomas J.	Martha W. Teasley	Dec. 20, 1827	414
Turman, Samuel	Polley Fortson	Dec. 20, 1827	414
Tinsley, William D.	Sarah B. Edwards	Jan. 3, 1828	414
Teasley, Beverly A.	Eliz. Eavenson	Feb. 15, 1828	414
Tucker, Robert C.	Jane Akin	Aug. 12, 1828	416
Wilson, James	Fanny Prickett	Sep. 23, 1819	408
White, John M.	Milley Satterwhite	Dec. 19, 1826	409
Webb, Fortunatus	Lenna Almond	Nov. 22, 1826	409
Watson, John	Nancy Roberts	May 18, 1826	409
Williams, Thomas J.	Hannah Cook	Jul. 27, 1826	410
Wilkins, Clement	Mary Moon	Jul. 20, 1826	410
Webb, Walton P.	Susannah Deadwyler	Nov. 10, 1827	413
Wilson, George	Susan Cook	Jan. 13, 1828	414
Wimbish, Alex. F.	Eliz. P. Higginbotham	Dec. 18, 1828	416

MARRIAGES 1829-31

WILL BOOK "N" MIXED RECORDS

Groom	Bride	Date	Page
Almand, John	Mrs. Ann Johnson	Nov. 8, 1829	220
Adams, Nicholas N.	Drusilla Hunt	Dec. 2, 1829	220
Allen, William	Jincy Fannin	Dec. 9, 1829	220
Adams, Hiram G.	Mary A. Williams	Dec. 3, 1829	221
Andrew, Charles	Martha Christian	Jan. 5, 1830	221
Alexander, George	Elizabeth Cash	Sep. 9, 1830	222
Allmand, William M.	Mary Thornton	Jan. 6, 1831	351

HISTORICAL COLLECTIONS

Groom	Bride	Date	Page
Brown, Wiley B.	Sarah Clark	Dec. 13, 1827	218
Bobo, Sampson	Elizabeth Bobo	Sep. 4, 1828	218
Brock, James L.	Nancy Johnson	Dec. 23, 1828	218
Bell, David	Eliz. Snellings	Jan. 6, 1829	218
Booth, William S.	Lucy Parham	Feb. 12, 1829	218
Bobo, Lewis	Mrs. Letty Dooly	Jul. 7, 1829	219
Brown, Elbert	Eliz. Herndon	Jul. 28, 1829	219
Bell, James, Jr.	Martha Ousley	Sep. 13, 1829	219
Bullard, Thomas B.	Eliz. P. Gunter	Jul. 1, 1829	219
Barr, George I.	Rachel W. Willis	Dec. 15, 1829	219
Booth, Joseph G.	Jincey Hicks	Dec. 15, 1829	220
Bond, John M.	Lucy Harris	Sep. 15, 1829	220
Brown, Julian K.	Mrs. Catherine Alexander	Dec. 6, 1829	221
Burch, James J.	Mary Eades	Mar. 4, 1830	221
Bently, Jesse	Babba Moon	Feb. 16, 1830	221
Brown, John	Martha Eaves	Apr. 1, 1830	222
Burden, Micajah	Sarah Pulliam	Sep. 14, 1830	222
Boler, Bennett	Nancy Harris	Nov. 20, 1830	222
Bailey, Wesley S.	Harriett E. Morrison	Feb. 1, 1831	351
Blackwell, James M.	Irenia Coker	Dec. 26, 1831	352
Blackwell, Banks	Mrs. Elizabeth Clark	Jun. 28, 1831	352
Cleveland, James M.	Penina Haley	Dec. 20, 1827	218
Christian, Elijah L.	Elizabeth Edwards	Oct. 28, 1828	218
Crawford, Thomas	Martha A. Banks	Jul. 7, 1829	219
Callaway, Lawrence	Sarah Eaves	Jan. 7, 1829	219
Christian, Thomas J.	Mary J. Christian	Jun. 10, 1829	220
Childes, Elijah	Sarah Thornton	Jan. 14, 1830	221
Couch, Elijah W.	Nancy Allen	Jun. 8, 1830	222
Cook, Joseph	Adeline Threlkeld	Aug. 2, 1830	222
Cade, Drury B.	Julia A. Edwards	May 4, 1830	222
Clayton, George R.	Ann R. Harris	Oct. 7, 1830	222
Clark, William D.	Jane E. Hearne	Sep. 6, 1830	222
Crawford, Oliver	Barbary Cook	Jun. 24, 1830	222
Crawford, Burton E.	Lucy T. Gaines	Dec. 1, 1830	351
Cox, William B.	Rhoda Allen	Nov. 9, 1830	351
Collins, John W.	Pheba L. Hudson	Jun. 7, 1831	352
Downs, James	Dorcas Denna	Mar. 22, 1827	218
Dudley, James T.	Martha Bond	Jan. 14, 1829	218
Davis, Thomas F.	Matilda Brown	Aug. 20, 1829	219
Davis, Isaac N.	Mrs. Elz. Ann Oliver	Oct. 15, 1829	220
Davis, Jesse M.	Sophia M. Burton	Jan. 12, 1830	221
Dooly, Mitchell N.	Katharine Brantley	Nov. 11, 1830	222
Dobbs, Elijah	Cyrenea A. Smith	Dec. 12, 1830	222
Dobbs, Josiah	Elizabeth Prothro	Nov. 18, 1830	353
Eaves, William	Peggy A. Maxwell	Apr. 9, 1829	220

GEORGIA D. A. R.

Groom	Bride	Date	Page
Eavenson, Thomas	Sarah Thornton	Dec. 9, 1830	222
Fortson, Easton	Susan Ham	Feb. 10, 1831	351
Ginn, William	Nancy Dodds	Nov. 24, 1828	218
Gray, Reece	Martha Jane Pratt	Sep. 10, 1829	219
Gaines, Francis	Didama Haley	Dec. 17, 1829	220
Gaulding, John N.	Jane Kinnebrew	Sep. 16, 1829	220
Griffin, Robert T.	Mary Patterson	Nov. 2, 1830	222
Gay, James	Eliza Hendrick	Apr. 2, 1830	222
Gaar, William	Sarah Craft	Dec. 30, 1830	351
Gaar, George	Mary Rucker	Mar. 10, 1814	352
Goss, Benjamin	Sarah C. Roebuck	Jun. 3, 1830	352
Henry, Daniel N.	Caroline Edmondson	Mar. 20, 1827	218
Henry, Alexander	Keziah Mason	Jan. 7, 1829	218
Housley, John	Mrs. Francis Cook	Feb. 24, 1829	218
Hall, William	Orpha Nelms	Feb. 20, 1829	219
Hulme, John T.	Frances E. Rowzee	May 14, 1827	219
Hawthorne, William S.	Martha W. Davis	Dec. 3, 1829	220
Holmes, James	Nancy Adams	Oct. 18, 1829	220
Houston, Alex P.	Mrs. Martha P. Deadwyler	Dec. 8, 1829	220
Hubbard, Vinson	Mrs. Susan Gunter	Dec. 28, 1830	351
Harmon, John S.	Nancy A. Ford	Apr. 28, 1831	352
Jarratt, James D.	Jane H. Jack	Jul. 7, 1829	219
Jones, Willis B.	Manda B. Rucker	Jul. 24, 1829	219
Johnson, Larkin	Mrs. Milly Rucker	Jul. 19, 1827	219
Johnson, Bedford	Harriett Brawner	Dec. 9, 1829	220
Jones, Lewis R.	Elizabeth K. Dye	Sep. 29, 1829	220
James, William	Elizabeth Henderson	Jan. 11, 1829	221
Jordon, Stephen W.	Elizabeth Burden	Mar. 4, 1830	221
Johnson, Larkin	Mrs. Jane Martin	Mar. 11, 1830	221
Johnson, Neal	Katharine McCurry	Jan. 21, 1831	352
Kelly, Barnabas	Margaret M. Scales	Dec. 30, 1828	218
Kinnebrew, Edwin	Elizabeth Horton	Sep. 15, 1829	219
Kelly, Thomas O.	Eliz. L. Sandridge	Dec. 8, 1829	220
Lewis, Jeremiah	Rhoda Hansard	Dec. 30, 1829	220
Lee, Robert W.	Finetty Kinnebrew	Sep. 22, 1830	222
McAllester, Alex	Sarah Brown	Jan. 14, 1830	221
McStowers, Jeremiah	Mary Neal	May 7, 1829	219
McGuire, Frederick S.	Martha Goolsby	Jul. 7, 1831	352
McKerley, George	Nancy McMullin	May 12, 1831	353
Masters, Levi	Mary McCurry	Jan. 13, 1829	218
Mitchell, Isaac G.	Mary Dudley	Jan. 15, 1829	218
Morris, Garrett	Mary Keys	Dec. 30, 1829	220
Malden, Flemming	Eliza Hickman	Feb. 18, 1830	221
Maley, Johnston	Mrs. Eliz. L. Roebuck	Jan. 9, 1831	351
Maxwell, William T.	Sarah Horton	Sep. 28, 1830	352

HISTORICAL COLLECTIONS 299

Groom	Bride	Date	Page
Maxwell, Thomas J.	Ann B. Adams	May 31, 1831	352
Nix, James	Sophia Rich	Jan. 2, 1830	221
Nelms, Nathaniel H.	Ann Cash	Dec. 23, 1830	222
Oliver, Florence M.	Hannah K. Banks	Sep. 15, 1829	220
Oglesby, William	Plyne Wiley	May 21, 1830	221
Parham, Isham	Polly Booth	Nov. 15, 1828	218
Parham, Harrison	Polly Colvard	Dec. 27, 1829	220
Patterson, Wiley	Emeline E. Edwards	May 11, 1830	221
Perce, Jacob	Mary Downs	Mar. 27, 1830	221
Powell, Tinsley	Eliza Shiftlett	Mar. 17, 1831	352
Prichett, Nicholas	Polly Shiftlett	Mar. 18, 1830	353
Rich, Richmond	Frances W. Dye	Sep. 23, 1829	220
Richardson, James V.	Milly Bobo	Feb. 11, 1830	221
Rush, Lewis B.	Hannah Bobo	Jan. 20, 1831	352
Rowell, Joshua F.	Elizabeth Tucker	Sep. 23, 1831	352
Smith, Fielding	Lucy Davis	Nov. 11, 1824	218
Steel, Robert	Sarah Rice	Jan. 3, 1828	218
Speed, Terrell	Sarah D. Raymond	Feb. 22, 1829	219
Smith, Lindsay	Rhody Bell	Sep. 6, 1829	219
Sandridge, James W.	Mary Pulliam	Feb. 23, 1830	221
Shackleford, Allen	Eliz. Maxwell	Oct. 14, 1830	222
Smith, Drury	Susannah Harbins	Dec. 7, 1830	284
Shepherd, Thomas J.	Mary A. Henderson	Dec. 31, 1830	351
Shockley, James A.	Sarah E. Henderson	Mar. 26, 1831	352
Smith, Redick	Martha H. Glynn	Feb. 24, 1831	352
Shackleford, John H.	Sarah Hansard	Apr. 12, 1831	352
Teasley, John A.	Betsy C. Haley	Dec. 18, 1828	218
Tatum, Jesse	Sarah Rowsau	Apr. 9, 1829	219
Thornton, William D.	Sarah W. Cleveland	Jan. 7, 1829	221
Thomason, John	Mary Jenkins	Dec. 22, 1830	222
Taylor, Tavner	Sarow Craft	Jan. 12, 1831	351
Upshaw, Middleton C.	Eliz. H. Rucker	Feb. 2, 1830	221
Upshaw, Leroy	Mrs. Catharine Ellington	Nov. 18, 1830	222
Vines, Joseph	Mary McGarity	Mar. 22, 1829	219
Vineyard, Joseph	Susannah Christian	Mar. 28, 1830	221
Walters, Abraham	Margaret Salmons	Dec. 13, 1827	218
Webb, Urbin A.	Mrs. Sarah Lauremore	Jan. 21, 1829	218
White, Nathaniel H.	Mrs. Martha Pace	Jan. 28, 1829	219
Wheeler, Isaac	Sally Underwood	Aug. 6, 1829	219
Williams, Nathan	Polly Ballenger	Mar. 21, 1829	219
Ware, Francis	Lucy Hines	Dec. 26, 1829	220
Webb, Elijah W.	Ann B. Deadwyler	Dec. 24, 1829	220
Ward, Jeptha H.	Mary Terry	Jan. 15, 1829	221
Wiley, William S.	Katharine Morris	Mar. 7, 1830	221
Wall, Bud C.	Martha W. Nunnelee	Aug. 19, 1830	222
White, Martin	Martha N. Burton	Dec. 6, 1830	351
Williford, Reuben S.	Mary Bowers	Dec. 21, 1830	352

MARRIAGES
RECORD BOOK 1830-38

Groom	Bride	Date	Page
Almond, John W.	Mildred Gibbs	Sep. 7, 1831	199
Almond, James	Amanda N. M. Fortson	Oct. 20, 1831	199
Alexander, Fleming A.	Ann Jones	Oct. 7, 1831	199
Abney, Wiley	Elender Hailey	Apr. 19, 1832	201
Asher, Thomas J.	Moriah L. Housley	Dec. 11, 1832	201
Almond, Micajah	Eliza Cleveland	Oct. 3, 1833	408
Adams, William H.	Nancy Cheek	Oct. 3, 1833	408
Arnold, Wilton J.	Edna Ann Bell	Jan. 14, 1834	408
Adams, John M.	Agnes M. Hulme	Oct. 7, 1834	499
Alexander, Robert B.	Sarah L. Ward	Nov. 6, 1834	499
Ashworth, John S.	Julia Ann E. Gaar	Jan. 15, 1835	500
Black, Thomas	Hannah Rucker	Sep. 25, 1832	326
Bourne, Henry	Mrs. Mary Heard	Feb. 20, 1833	326
Brawner, James	Jemima W. Smith	Mar. 26, 1833	326
Brown, Thomas H.	Sarah D. Edwards	Mar. 28, 1833	326
Bryson, James	Eliza Banks	Jun. 28, 1833	326
Burton, Thomas	Ann Brown	Jul. 18, 1833	326
Bond, Henry W.	Sarah Caroline Floyd	Aug. 29, 1833	326
Bobo, Benjamin	Mary Bray	Sep. 15, 1831	199
Bell, Asmond	Sarah Ann Arnold	Sep. 6, 1831	199
Brown, Edward	Eliz. Hearndon	Dec. 28, 1831	199
Burnet, Pleasant	Martha Henry	Oct. 13, 1831	200
Banks, William R.	Eliz. Bowman	Apr. 3, 1832	200
Bentley, John E.	Adaline A. Arnold	Sept. 16, 1832	201
Bailey, James B.	Susan M. Foster	Dec. 13, 1832	201
Bonds, Isham R.	Nancy L. Harris	Nov. 12, 1832	201
Banks, Lemuel	Louisa A. Tate	Dec. 24, 1833	408
Burden, Nelson	Nancy Ginn	Dec. 19, 1833	408
Brown, William H.	Eliza Maxwell	Sep. 12, 1833	408
Butler, George S.	Katharine Booth	Feb. 17, 1830	498
Bailey, John M.	Harriett Dunn	Dec. 18, 1834	499
Butler, William J.	Frances J. Brewer	Sep. 30, 1834	499
Butler, Wiley W.	Malinda Jones	Dec. 19, 1834	499
Bell, Lucious J. M.	Sarah Ann Cheek	Jul. 3, 1834	500
Barnes, Barnabas	Milly McMullen	Aug. 7, 1834	500
Bowen, Samuel	Nancy Freeman	Mar. 17, 1835	500
Cheek, William F.	Elizabeth Cape	Sep. 25, 1831	199
Crawford, James L.	Mourning G. Gaines	Nov. 29, 1831	199
Carter, Lesley G.	Mary Gaulden	Dec. 25, 1831	199
Cleveland, John W.	Matilda Alexander	Dec. 28, 1831	199
Crawford, William H.	Sarah Ann Dooly	Aug. 20, 1832	200
Crawford, Richard C.	Elizabeth A. White	Sep. 27, 1832	201
Carlton, Henry A.	Elizabeth Rice	Oct. 25, 1832	201

HISTORICAL COLLECTIONS 301

Groom	Bride	Date	Page
Christian, Lindsey	Prudence S. Webb	Nov. 8, 1832	201
Clark, James	Flora McCurry	Dec. 6, 1832	201
Crawford, Leroy R.	Elizabeth A. Dooly	Dec. 13, 1832	201
Cox, Arus	Leah Boatright	Jan. 24, 1833	326
Cleveland, Peter	Merial K. Rowzee	Mar. 28, 1833	326
Coker, John	Martha Hathcock	Apr. 28, 1833	499
Clark, Bolen B.	Sophia Snellings	Feb. 21, 1833	499
Christian, Elijah L.	Mary J. Fitts	Apr. 9, 1832	498
Christian, John M.	Amelia A. Key	May 30, 1833	499
Cleveland, Daniel	Harriett McGarrity	Oct. 9, 1834	499
Christian, Drury	Sarah Stinchcomb	Mar. 5, 1834	499
Cristler, Abel	Ann Maxwell	Mar. 4, 1834	500
Cosby, Henry H.	Lucinda Clark	Jun. 10, 1834	500
Durrett, Richard J. D.	Martha E. Rucker	Jan. 8, 1833	327
Daniel, John	Averilla Fanning	Apr. 14, 1833	327
Dennard, Mitchell	Nancy Hanson	May 19, 1833	327
Edwards, John F.	Margarett S. Clark	Aug. 22, 1833	327
Evans, Zachariah	Mrs. Lucy Manning	Oct. 30, 1833	408
Flemming, Moses C.	Permelia Flanningham	Nov. 15, 1831	199
Fortson, Richard	Nancy Ham	Nov. 8, 1832	199
Frazier, James W.	Eliz. L. White	Mar. 27, 1833	327
Farmer, Josiah	Elizabeth White	Apr. 26, 1833	327
Flemming, Moses T.	Theodicia James	Jun. 20, 1833	327
Flemming, David C.	Averilla Cunningham	Aug. 27, 1833	327
Fowler, Robert	Sarah McGarity	Dec. 31, 1833	408
Faulkner, William	Mrs. Sarah Moon	Dec. 2, 1833	498
Griswell, John	Jenny King	Oct. 12, 1831	199
Gaines, Strawther	Merial Ann Ward	Nov. 27, 1834	499
Gray, Absolom	Rhoda Rowsey	Oct. 21, 1834	499
Gaulding, Richard	Mary Mattox	Dec. 16, 1834	499
Glasco, William	Elizabeth Turner	Sep. 2, 1834	499
Hall, Henry	Mrs. Eliz. Arnold	Oct. 2, 1831	199
Hill, Josiah W.	Sarah McGehee	Sep. 22, 1831	199
Harper, John Sr.	Polly Mitchell	Sep. 7, 1831	199
Hammond, Furney	Teresa Deadwyler	Oct. 6, 1831	199
Harper, Elijah	Martha Evenson	Oct. 29, 1833	199
Hendrick, Barnett	Mary Nelmes	Jan. 22, 1832	200
Harper, John A. H.	Susan Oliver	Sep. 25, 1832	201
Hunt, Hullum	Harriett C. Ward	Mar. 8, 1832	201
Hudson, John R.	Martha E. Banks	Jan. 17, 1833	327
Hammond, Amos W.	Eliza C. Hudson	Jan. 22, 1833	327
Hansard, James A.	Phebe Hardy	Aug. 23, 1833	327
Hunter, Alex. D.	Agnes Ann Harris	Aug. 14, 1833	327
Hall, Fenton	Lucinda D. Shepard	Sep. 26, 1833	408
Haynes, Charles W.	Flora McCurry	Dec. 15, 1833	408
Hunt, Willis	Priscilla T. Teasley	Nov. 7, 1833	408

Groom	Bride	Date	Page
Harris, James S.	Sarah Means	Dec. 3, 1833	408
Harcrow, David	Joicee Powell	Jul. 20, 1834	499
Herndon, Benjamin	Mahulda Almond	Nov. 27, 1834	499
Ham, Willis R.	Elizabeth Dickey	Feb. 25, 1834	499
Higginbotham, John S.	Sally Lowrimore	Mar. 30, 1834	500
Jones, William	Lucy Ann Brown	Sep. 27, 1831	199
Johnson, James	Milley Butler	Dec. 22, 1831	199
Johnson, William A.	Jane Tate	Dec. 29, 1831	200
Johnson, Nathan	Sarah Gaines	Feb. 9, 1832	200
Jinkins, James	Furlishe Warren	Jan. 26, 1832	200
Jones, Arthur, Jr.	Mary Dye	Nov. 6, 1833	498
Jones, James	Sarah T. Dye	Nov. 6, 1833	498
Jones, William S.	Sarah A. Brewer	Oct. 30, 1834	499
King, Francis W.	Sarah T. Smith	Jan. 8, 1832	200
Kirlen, Samuel	Mrs. Mary Fortson	May 15, 1832	200
Keys, John D.	Martha R. Teasley	Aug. 28, 1832	201
Kirbee, Lewis	Frances E. King	Nov. 20, 1832	201
Kilgore, William M.	Ann Alexander	Jul. 7, 1833	327
Lovingood, John	Priscilla Watson	Feb. 21, 1833	327
McDonald, Donald	Mary M. Johnson	Dec. 8, 1831	200
McCurry, Lauchlin	Eliza Brown	Feb. 14, 1832	200
McCurry, Daniel E.	Elizabeth Ashworth	Jun. 26, 1832	200
McGehee, Jesse	Susannah King	May 3, 1832	200
Moore, Jere. E.	Juley Ann Colson	Feb. 14, 1832	200
Marbury, Thomas W.	Mary Ann Booth	Jun. 20, 1832	200
Mann, Asa	Milly T. Oliver	Sep. 6, 1832	201
Moore, William J.	Elizabeth Booth	Sep. 20, 1832	201
Moore, John S.	Sophia Colson	Dec. 18, 1832	201
Myers, William	Sarah Highsmith	Feb. 21, 1833	327
Mann, Robert B.	Lucy Higginbotham	Jul. 27, 1833	408
Mantooth, Robert	Elizabeth Butler	Oct. 22, 1833	408
Medford, Demsey	Rebecca Dodds	Sep. 18, 1833	408
Mattox, John W.	Mrs. Caroline Whitlow	Dec. 31, 1833	408
Mattox, Henry P.	Sophia Nunnelee	Oct. 1, 1833	498
Moseley, Joseph	Sarah Cook	Dec. 24, 1833	499
Matthews, William	Jane Cook	Dec. 23, 1834	499
Moss, Christopher C.	Ann Nelms	Jul. 22, 1834	500
Maxwell, Martin	Julia Ann Upshaw	Jan. 29, 1835	500
Nelms, William T.	Elizabeth Banks	Aug. 2, 1832	200
Nelms, William B.	Eliz. Patterson	Dec. 20, 1832	327
Nelms, William R.	Ann J. Lewis	Jun. 9, 1833	327
Nash, Hudson J.	Mrs. Maria Nunnelee	Dec. 22, 1831	498
Osley, David	Elizabeth Nix	Oct. 2, 1831	199
Oliver, Winston	Elizabeth Brawner	Oct. 18, 1832	201
Oliver, James O.	Charity A. Chambers	Dec. 24, 1833	408
Oliver, Florence M.	Sarah A. H. Glenn	Mar. 13, 1834	500

HISTORICAL COLLECTIONS 303

Groom	Bride	Date	Page
Penn, James B.	Nancy Burton	Nov. 14, 1831	199
Prather, Josiah	Jane Ann Wall	Jan. 29, 1832	200
Prewet, Willis	Hester Lewis	Oct. 25, 1832	201
Perryman, Albert G.	Sarah Allgood	Dec. 24, 1833	409
Peeler, Allen	Eliz. Ann Coker	Mar. 28, 1833	499
Parham, George W.	Alcey W. Webb	Sep. 22, 1834	500
Penn, Benjamin J.	Harriett Penn	Dec. 3, 1834	500
Roberts, John	Sarah Faulk	Jan. 19, 1832	200
Reynolds, James H.	Penina J. Wheeler	Nov. 18, 1832	201
Richardson, James	Mary E. Clark	Feb. 7, 1833	327
Richardson, Willia	Drucilla E. Gaines	Feb. 28, 1833	327
Ragain, John	Nancy M. Brawner	Nov. 7, 1833	408
Rains, Josiah	Sarah Denna	Apr. 5, 1832	498
Ridgway, John T.	Sarah L. Colvard	Nov. 27, 1834	500
Steedey, James P.	Amanda M. Kelly	Aug. 18, 1831	199
Smith, William W.	Sarah J. Penn	May 26, 1831	200
Saxon, Drury T.	Elizabeth Bennett	Dec. 25, 1831	200
Salmons, Wiley	Elizabeth Chrisley	Oct. 27, 1831	200
Shiftlett, John	Polly Anderson	Mar. 4, 1832	200
Shearer, Alex.	Claricy Marbury	May 31, 1832	201
Shackleford, Starling M.	Frances Higginbotham	Jul. 16, 1833	327
Scott, Samuel N.	Martha M. Dillard	Dec. 27, 1832	409
Smith, Thomas A.	Winney Penn	Sep. 15, 1833	409
Smith, Samuel W.	Catharine Swindle	Dec. 26, 1833	409
Shackleford, Asa C.	Mary Christian	Jan. 21, 1834	409
Stovall, Thomas	Lucinda W. Key	Dec. 17, 1833	499
Smith, John Jr.	Sarah Watson	Jul. 15, 1834	499
Stribling, Simpson	Sarah Bates	Mar. 6, 1834	500
Semore, John W.	Nancy Christian	Jan. 20, 1835	500
Terrell, William B.	Eliza White	Mar. 20, 1834	500
Thornton, Reuben	Emilia Cleveland	Jul. 28, 1831	199
Tailor, William T.	Martha Means	Dec. 14, 1831	200
Thornton, Memory	Polley Higginbotham	Feb. 9, 1832	200
Tabor, Britton C.	Lidey Horton	Apr. 9, 1832	200
Teasley, Isham	Mary Maxwell	Dec. 6, 1833	327
Thornton, Eppy	Mary C. Higginbotham	Dec. 6, 1833	327
Thornton, Dozier, Jr.	Jane M. Fortson	Sep. 25, 1834	499
Tibbis, Joseph C.	Matilda Fowler	May 4, 1834	499
Terrell William B.	Eliza White	Mar. 20, 1834	500
Vasser, William O.	Mary W. Edwards	Dec. 30, 1833	498
Williamson, Stephen	Polly Reynolds	Mar. 4, 1831	199
Walker, Benjamin	Lucy Kirlen	Dec. 18, 1831	199
Wilson, Stephen	Feanetty Threlkeld	Feb. 28, 1832	200
Wanslow, Wiley J.	Martha L. Cleveland	Dec. 20, 1832	201
Wanslow, Flemming	Beckey Patterson	Dec. 13, 1832	201

GEORGIA D. A. R.

Groom	Bride	Date	Page
White, Wm. Bowling	Mildred Rucker	Jan. 8, 1833	327
Williamson, Walker	Betsey Farmer	May 2, 1833	327
Wiley, Hugh A.	Moddy W. Sullivan	Feb. 22, 1833	327
Webb, John B.	Nancy Christian	Jul. 30, 1833	409
Ward, Nisbet L.	Tabitha Hailey	Dec. 19, 1833	409
Ward, William W.	Nancy T. Greenway	Jan. 9, 1834	409
Walsh, Robert	Nancy E. Davis	Apr. 10, 1933	498
White, David O.	Catharine E. Rucker	May 6, 1834	500
White,, William Jr.	Rachel Eavenson	Sep. 11, 1834	500
Young, Thomas	Elizabeth Akin	Sep. 4, 1834	500

GENERAL INDEX

ABENATHEE, John, 207.
ACHESON, Nathan, 160.
ADAMS, Abner, 255; Alex, 60; Anne, 26; Calvin M., 252; David, 56, 59, 60, 142, 143, 151, 164, 181, 185, 187, 198, 201, 204; Geo., 250; Henry, 71, 79, 82, 89; James, 23, 39, 56, 60, 86, 93, 142, 143, 146, 179, 187, 198, 201, 239, 252; Jas. B., 46; John, 23, 26, 93; Josias P., 192, 194; Lawrence, 252; Nancy, 26, 60; Nicholas, 252; Richard C., 35; Ritter, 46; Robt., 253; Sally, 60; Samuel, 23, 93, 235; Solomon, 253; Thos., 252; William, 23, 26, 35, 93, 182, 224, 231, 240, 252; William H., 257.
ADERHOLD, Conrod, 216.
ADDERSON, Thomas, 243.
ADKINS, Lucy, 6; Thomas, 169.
AKEN—AKIN, Absolom, 246; Eliz., 47, 137; Fleming, 60, 145, 147; Jacob, 216; John, 216; Johnson, 47, 251; Joseph, 56, 59, 60, 144, 163; Martha C., 47; Mary, 170, 200; Nancy, 150; Sally, 56, 59, 60, 144; Samuel, 71, 146; Sarah M., 47; T., 60; Thos., 43, 47, 56, 59, 60, 97, 136, 137, 144, 169, 170, 200, 216; Warren, 47; William, 59; William E., 47.
ALBERT, Joseph, 6.
ALCORN, Elijah, 215, 224, 225.
ALEXANDER, Adly, 200; Ann, 128; Edmond, 14, 32, 79, 97; Edward, 256; Elam, 139, 251; Elias, 149; Elijah, 14; Eliz., 186; Ezza, 70; Fleming A., 48, 128; Geo., 14, 60, 70, 71, 79, 88, 100, 149; Geo. C., 254; Isaac, 139, 254; J., 200; James, 14, 79; Jas. B., 41, 48, 88; John, 14, 71, 79, 86; John B., 170; Judith, 32; Katharine, 256; Lucy, 70, 79; Mary, 70, 71, 79, 139, 254; Mordecai, 32, 112; Mourning, 70, 79; Nancy, 14, 70, 71, 79, 97, 148, 200; Peter, 14, 32, 45, 51, 70, 71, 79, 114, 115, 120, 124, 125, 128, 133, 135, 136, 140, 148, 233; Polly, 70; Tabitha, 86; Thos. J., 52; William, 14, 70, 71, 79, 88, 148, 156, 165, 200, 231, 240, 255; Willis, 115, 251.
ALFORD, James, 151, 170, 176; Luraner, 170.
ALICE, Chas., 154; Francis, 154.

ALIVEN, Elijah, 193; Josiah, 193.
ALLBRITTON, John, 162, 166, 202, 214, 220.
ALLEN, Aggie, 31, 187; Agnes, 48, 261; Almira A. C., 40; Asa, 15, 71, 74, 79; B., 232; Benj., 61, 119, 169, 173, 177, 193, 196; Betsy, 186, 193; Beverly, 21, 26, 27, 28, 32, 37, 38, 40, 41, 47, 86, 87, 99, 101, 107, 111, 115, 116, 124, 134, 135, 136, 137, 138, 169, 170; Caroline, 112; David, 225; Edmond, 254; Eliz., 169; Ephraim, 240; James, 31, 48, 225, 260; John, 48, 261; Joseph, 31, 48, 187, 261, 264; Joseph, J., 48; Josiah, 201; Martha, 112; Nathaniel, 10, 70, 144, 145, 166; 169, 170, 172, 186, 216; Nathaniel R., 257; Pamelia, 169, 170; Patsy, 42; Permelia, 112; Polly, 38, 42; R., 219; Reuben, 154, 158, 160, 163, 164, 169, 184, 199, 216, 223, 255; Rhoda, 48; Richardson, 112; Robt., 184; Rowland, 199; Sarah, 40; Singleton W., 27, 40, 41, 50, 108, 136; Thos., 40, 44, 112, 239, 248, 251; Wm., 14, 26, 40, 48, 69, 77, 87, 95, 97, 119, 147, 149, 150, 164, 169, 170, 200, 207, 223, 228, 229, 231.
ALLGOOD, James, 237; John, 68, 174, 246, 249; Mary, 249; Peter, 124, 249; Spencer, 190, 250; Wm., 94, 250.
ALLISON, John, 261.
ALMAN — ALMAND — ALMOND, Ann, 259; Catharine, 48; Isaac, 118, 134, 139, 258; James, 142, 151, 165, 179; John, 151, 244, 258; John W., 48; Jones R., 48, 258; Lucy A., 48; Lucyann F., 257; Mahulda K., 257; Micajah T., 259; Sarah, 250, 258; Simeon, 45, 118, 258; Usry, 249, 257.
ALSTON, Charity, 18, 34, 107, 200; Christeen L., 18; Christian, 34; Christian L., 107; Eliz., 21; Gilley, 21, 251; J., 227; James, 18, 21, 34, 66, 72, 145, 175, 190, 192, 193, 207, 211, 219, 226; John, 21, 28, 34; Martha, 21; Mary, 18; Nathaniel 18, 21, 192, 207; Philip H., 18, 34, 107; S., 169; Solomon, 18; Wm., 18, 58, 159, 174, 186, 200; Wm. H., 18, 21, 34, 107; Wm. J., 21.

GENERAL INDEX

ANDERSON, Ann, 249; Geo., 71; Henry, 259; James, 258; John, 24; Peter, 66; Thos., 255.
ANDREW, Benj., 92, 246, 265; Burley, 43, 263; Caty, 51; Chas., 38, 246; John, 65, 74, 84, 206, 211, 223; Joseph, 256; Lucy G., 7; Mary O., 7; Matilda H., 7; Thos., 65, 71, 74, 84, 147.
ANDREWS, B., 131; Eliz., 6, 23; Elbert, 102; Garnett, 140; John, 6, 145; Lewcy, 52; Lucy, 38; Nathaniel, 6, 145; Polly, 6; Robins, 6, 145.
ANGLIN, James, 228, 239.
ANSLEY, Eliz., 24.
ANTHONY, Barbara, 33, 106; Matthew J. W., 33, 106; Micajah, 106, 228, 235; Rebecca, 33, 34, 106.
APPLEBY, William, 4, 8, 58, 60, 143, 145, 202.
APPLING, John, 184.
ARMSTEAD, Dr., 109; Dr. Ajax, 122.
ARMSTRONG, James, 200; John, 170.
ARNETT, Mary, 127.
ARNOLD, Davis, 258; Jas., 18, 42, 50, 52, 79, 124, 135, 200, 239; Jas. Wm., 50, 124; Jenney, 18; John, 18, 251; Jonathan, 156, 175, 187, 189; Lemuel, 18; Lemuel N., 126, 136; Lucy, 18; Nancy, 18, 200; Polly, 18; Susanna, 18, 200; Susanna T., 50; Susan T., 124; Wm., 18, 61, 79, 136, 155, 158, 165, 170, 197, 200, 212, 251.
ASH, Thos. L., 170; John, 85, 243; Wm., 158.
ASHWORTH, Benj., 176, 232, 243; Elisha, 252; Joab, 243; John, 139, 232, 233, 243, 253; Noah, 253.
ATTAWAY, John W., 48; Joseph, 98.
AULSTON, James, 148.
AVREN, John, 6.
AYCOCK, Fielding, 258; James, 76, 160, 179; Jas. E., 141; Jewdo, 76; Milton, 76, 148; Patsy, 156; Patty, 2; Richard, 76, 148, 156, 210; Richard L., 52, 141, 258; Tabitha, 76, 148; Terrell, 76, 148; Wm., 2, 4, 56, 65, 76, 146, 147, 156, 220.
BAILEY, Amelia, 73; Eliz., 44, 73, 95, 239; Ezekiah, 47, 79; Ezekiel, 19; Fanny, 19; Henry, 255, 262; Hezekiah, 171, 173, 175, 239; Jas., 176, 239; Julin, 239; Mose, 114; Rebecca, 19, 79, 171; Samuel, 188, 239; Samuel N., 19, 29, 79, 97; Wesley S., 47; Westly, 133; Wm., 27, 29, 35, 39, 49, 102, 103, 113, 135.
BAGWELL, John, 46.

BAIRD, Benj., 103; William, 91.
BAKER, Absolom, 57, 152, 169, 180, 187, 200; Alphus, 91; Amos, 82, 109; Benj., 170, 187, 199, 213, 217, 222; Christopher, 187; Comfort, 170; Elias, 213; J., 219; Jas., 149, 170, 200; Jane, 170; Jean, 200; Jennett, 187; Jesse, 170, 187, 219, 220; John, 151, 171, 180, 184, 187, 200, 202, 204, 214, 217, 218; John A., 169, 170, 180, 187, 200; Madison, 52, 257; Mary, 152, 187, 200; Rachel, 217; Samuel, 161, 164, 179; Susannah, 170, 187.
BALDWIN, Edward, 151; Francis, 157, 167.
BALL, Edward H. 109.
BALLARD, Gardner, 42; Jesse, 245.
BALLENGER, David, 234, 245; John, 167, 236, 245, 261; Robt., 176; Wm., 230, 264.
BANKS, Ann, 114, 115, 251; Anny, 27; Betsy, 27; Charity, 21; Eliza, 114, 115, 124; Elmira, 21; Hannah, 21; Henry, 35, 99, 107, 125, 251; James, 14, 18, 27, 28, 41, 47, 49, 66, 86, 99, 115, 119, 125, 135, 147, 148, 194, 221, 224, 225; Jas. A., 21, 34, 107, 115, 120, 129, 138, 259; John, 35, 243, 248; John H., 27, 115; Josias R., 115; Lemuel, 35, 99, 107, 125, 255; Marion, 35, 99, 256; Martha, 115, 124; Mary, 115; Milly T., 34, 107, 138; Nancy, 27; Polly H., 27; Rachel, 35, 99; R., 23, 27, 34, 85, 100, 108, 116, 119, 167, 176, 225, 227, 256; Ralph, 27, 29, 35, 99, 107, 125, 194, 215, 216, 223; Richard, 34, 125, 251; Sally C., 27; Thos.,115; Thos. A., 27, 28, 35 39, 47, 49, 99, 102, 125, 256; Wm., 27, 29, 56, 114, 115, 194, 238, 239, 240, 244, 251; Wm. C., 34, 107, 120, 129, 138, 259; Wm. R.., 27, 115, 251; Willis, 34, 99,
BARDEN, Charlott, 171; Gilbert, 9,149. 171, 216; J. G., 9; Mary, 60; Will, 187.
BARGER, John, 80; Peggy, 80.
BARKER, Robert 24.
BARNES, Cordal, 65, 80, 88, 100; Henry, 88, 100; John, 42, 88, 100; John L., 129; Polly, 129; Priscilla, 65, 80, 88, 100.
BARNETT, Benj. J., 114, 152; Caroline, 188, 201; David, 36, 114; Isaac, 8; Jo., 152; Joel, 36; John, 160, 164, 167, 188, 201, 212, 218; Leonard, 114, 121; Lucy, 40, 152; Mial, 151; Nancy, 38; Nathan, 152; Nathaniel, 36, 107, 138, 175; Nelson, 11, 146; Nyal, 154; Patsy, 152; Peter, 11, 175; Sucky, 40; Thos. M., 11; Wm., 11, 36, 62, 142, 146, 151, 152, 154, 155, 159, 171, 173,

GENERAL INDEX 307

188, 193, 201, 202, 204, 216, 221, 222, 224, 225, 227, 230.
BARNWELL, Robert, 22.
BARR, Geo. I., 46, 120, 257; Robt. S., 249.
BARREN, Thomas, 165.
BARRETT—BARROTT, Isaac J., 73, 241; J. W., 44.
BARRON, Briton B., 248; David, 80; Sarah, 24; William, 80.
BARTON, Thomas, 97, 211.
BARWILL, Robert, 193.
BASINGER, John N., 257.
BASKIN, Robert, 228, 233, 245.
BASS, Jared, 167; Mrs. 117; Sally, 14.
BATES, George 245.
BATEY, Francis, 217, 220, 221.
BATTLE, Holleman, 211; Little B., 205.
BEAMAN, Lewis R., 40.
BEARD, John, 233; Robt, 244; Samuel, 244.
BEARDEN, Sally, 81.
BEASLEY, Ephraim, 69, 210, 223.
BECK, Beck & Bowman, 93; James, 97; Jesse, 110; John, 31, 52, 92, 93, 158, 222, 235; Lucy, 31; Sally, 53; Sary, 251; Reuben C., 81, 115; Wm., 97; Wm. A., 31, 51, 53, 124, 125, 135, 136.
BECKLEY, Joseph, 212.
BECXCY, Thomas, 10.
BEDDINGFIELD, Chas., 192.
BEEDON, Ephraim, 243.
BEEMAN, John D., 98.
BELL, Abraham, 32, 147, 206; Andrew, 13; Ann, 125, 137; Azmond B., 125; Capt, 248; Brockman, 133, 134; David, 19, 116, 125, 249; Eleanor, 26, 102; Eliz., 26, 45, 88, 152, 201, 249; Emily, 45; J., 220; Jas., 6, 8, 17, 18, 24, 30, 36, 45, 60, 65, 71, 81, 88, 103, 120, 125, 128, 145, 152, 159, 162, 163, 169, 172, 173, 174, 175, 176, 178, 180, 182, 183, 188, 194, 201, 222, 249; John, 254; Jonathan, 19; Joseph, 18, 19, 26, 45, 71, 81, 88, 90, 95, 100, 102, 118, 125, 152, 162, 175, 176, 180, 183, 188, 194, 195, 196, 201, 249; Lucious, 125; Lucious J. B., 137; Lucious K. M., 129; Martha, 88; Mary, 26, 45, 108, 125; Mayfield, 43, 79, 87, 125, 134, 135, 136, 137; Milly L., 102, 110, 118; Nancy, 19, 79, 135; Olive, 18, 19, 45, 163, 169, 201; Patsy, 19; Polly, 109; Rhoda, 254; Thomas, 18, 26, 32, 45, 88, 108, 109, 116, 125, 126, 133, 159; Wm., 18, 88, 125; Wm. G., 45.
BELLAMY, John, 114; Mary, 40.
BENNETT, Cooper, 98, 106; Eliz., 13; Frances, 106; Joel, 241; Moses, 241; Wm., 218.
BENSON, Chas., 10.
BENTLEY, Hiram, 257; Jesse, 259; John E., 258; Samuel, 225, 247, 259.
BERRY, Dabney, 17; Elijah, 115.
BERRYMAN, C., 234; Chas., 232.
BEVERLY, Anthony, 167, 239.
BEVERS, Alsa, 243; Wm., 31, 243.
BEVIL—BEVILLE, Dicy, 19; Edward, 79; Jas., 79; John, 71, 89; Nancy, 89; Patsy, 79; Peter, 89; Thos., 89, 248; Wm., 89.
BIBB, Benajah, 91; John D., 96, 188; Jos. W., 35, 188; Mrs. 64; Payton, 149; Sally, 188; Sally B., 188; Sally S., 2, 202; Thos., 190; Wm., 2, 188, 202, 203, 214; Wm. W., 13, 188.
BIGGS, William, 62.
BINFORD, John K., 142.
BIRD, Billings B., 113; Charity, 39, 113; Elijah, 113; John, 113; Martha, 39, 113; Martha B., 113; Mary, 113; Nancy, 113; Sarah, 113.
BIRDIN, Nelson, 263.
BLACK, John, 187; John W., 110, 257; Lemuel, 106, 179, 189, 199; Mary A., 33, 34, 106; Matthew J., 133; Mathew W., 33; Polly, 45; Robt., 200, 224; Thos., 187; Wm., 182, 187.
BLACKBURN, S., 171; Samuel, 155, 162, 173.
BLACKWELL, Banks, 26, 48, 72, 138, 231, 232, 239; Capt., 255; Doster, 188; Dunston, 26, 44, 50, 72, 90, 95, 100, 108, 115, 119, 239, 240; Eliz., 48; Geo., 205; Hambleton, 172; Hardie, 120, 139; Joseph, 26, 36, 44, 48, 49, 72, 85, 95, 122, 149, 188, 227, 239; Matthew, 69; Michael, 229; Park, 26, 72, 256; R., 72, 231; Ralph, 26, 236, 239; Sally, 27; Sally C., 188, 256; Sally N., 239; Sarah, 245.
BLAIR, John, 199; Middleton, 264.
BLAKE, Happy, 6, 201; John, 6, 75, 85, 220, 222, 224, 230; Joseph, 6; Lucy, 6, 144, 201; Martha, 20, 75, 85; Nancy, 6; Olive, 6; Patsy, 6; Walton, 57; Wm., 6, 57, 144, 170, 188, 189, 201, 206.
BLANGET, Jeremiah, 259.
BLANKENSHIP, Wm., 145, 226; Womack, 155, 171, 173, 208.
BLARE, Polly, 48.
BOATRIGHT—BOATWRIGHT, Daniel, 253; Eliz., 39, 113; James, 27; Wm., 113.
BOBO, Benj., 15, 37, 92, 148, 241; Burrell, 228, 235; Hannah, 15, 148; Lewis, 171, 180, 241, 253; Mary, 15,

148, 187; Sarah, 37; Susannah, 37; Wm., 18.
BOLTON, Isaac N., 42; Rachel, 42.
BOND—BONDS, Cleacy, 24; Eliz.; 21, 24, 35, 90, 151, 152, 171; Ephraoditus, 262; Esom, 97; Gabriel, 97; Henry W., 51, 261; John, 222; Joseph, 35, 164, 213; Martin, 258; Nathan, 21, 35, 90, 92, 150, 151, 152, 168, 171, 192, 213, 239, 252; Polly, 24; Richard, 21, 90, 164; Richard C., 35; Wm., 35, 51, 53, 96, 97, 246, 264; Willis, 252.
BOOKER, Alex., 263; James, 139; Richardson, 146; Richerson, 15; Wm., 3.
BOOTH, David S., 26, 72, 80, 90, 91, 92, 114; D. S., 72; Eliz., 81; Eliz. J., 81; G., 232; Gabriel, 30, 43, 80, 81, 89, 100, 259; Geo., 26, 77, 80, 81, 89; Geo. J., 258; Henry, 26, 257; Joel, 80, 81, 89, 100, 245; John, 65, 72, 80, 81, 90, 114, 235, 258; Jos. G., 258; Martha, 72; Mary, 258; Mary A., 26; Nancy, 26, 81, 244, 258, 263; Nathaniel, 26, 80, 81, 89, 224, 244; Prudence, 90, 244, 262; Prudence U., 114; Prudence W., 72; Robt., 26, 43, 81, 258, 263; Robt. D. S., 81; Sally, 26; Sarah, 48, 81; Sudith, 26; Thos. W., 72; T. W., 90; Victor E., 259; Wm., 80, 81, 89; Wm. N., 258.
BORDER, Michael, 171; Paschal, 222.
BOSLER, Henry, 152.
BOUCHER, Dr. J. C., 90.
BOUGHTRIGHT, William, 240.
BOURNE, Dr. H., 90; Henry, 52, 102, 115, 122, 127, 251; Mary, 127.
BOWEN, Christopher, 78, 114, 141; Christopher O., 18; Frances D., 257; Horatio C., 45, 250; John, 168, 180; Wm. M., 47; Wm. W., 115.
BOWER—BOWERS, Charity, 208; Edy, 56, 261; Joel, 260, 261, 264; Wm., 48, 53, 227, 228, 239, 264.
BOWMAN, Willis W., 254; Zachariah, 93.
BOWREN, Henry, 28.
BOYD, John, 158, 171.
BRADBERRY, Stephen, 222; Wm., 227.
BRADBURY, Joseph, 26.
BRADDY, James, 148, 150; Mary, 148.
BRADEN, Hannah, 243; John, 243; Rachel, 243; William, 241.
BRADFORD, William, 151, 161.
BRADLEY, Ann, 244; Anna, 35; Drury, 14, 28, 173, 196, 237; Eliz., 14, 89; Jeptha M., 35, 115; Joshua, 157; Lucy, 35; Lucy C., 108; Robt. C., 35,

100, 107, 115, 244, 253; Wm., 14, 89, 148, 186.
BRADY, Eli, 150; Jas., 150, 179; Sally, 150.
BRAGG, Jo., 234; John W., 23; Maston H., 259; Mary, 23, 76, 250.
BRAMBLET, Eliz., 261; Henry, 228, 239; John, 92, 239; Lott, 239; Margrett, 239; Reuben, 239; Rn., 229; Robt., 229.
BRANAN, William, 38.
BRANTLET, Henry, 245; Lott, 245.
BRANTLEY, Jos. M., 36, 116; Nancy J., 36, 116.
BRANTLY, Black, 133; Catharine, 133; William, 133.
BRASEL, Frederick, 159; John, 182.
BRAWNER, Asa, 250; Basil, 161, 223; Henry, 81; Henry P., 40, 45, 88; James, 29, 48, 49, 130, 263; Jas. M., 263; Jesse, 5, 216; Joel, 246; John, 81, 165, 194, 202, 227; John W., 250; Joseph, 29, 104, 250; Middleton, 257; Simeon, 139; Simuel, 249; Susannah, 139; Wm., 211, 223; Wm. M. 250.
BRAY, Avy, 48, 260; Bannister, 250, 251; Benj., 260; David, 48, 245, 261; Delinda, 48; Eliz., 48; John, 48, 74, 135, 169, 216, 245, 260; Lewis, 259; Nancy, 48; Patience, 48, 260; Rhoda, 48; Zoe, 48.
BRAZDAL, John, 56; Mary, 56.
BRAZEL, Eliz., 187; Frederick, 187; John, 65.
BREEDEN, Richard, 240.
BREWER, E., 17, 73, 85; Edmond, 60, 66, 71, 77, 143, 156, 188; Edmond H., 250; Elijah, 187, 198; Elisha, 24, 56, 60, 61, 125, 143, 179, 188, 189, 199; Eliz., 265; Fanny C. M., 21; Frances C. M., 89; Frances K., 125, 133; Horatio, 250; Horatio G., 60, 61, 108, 116, 124, 125, 133; Hundley, 27; Hundley J., 249; Jas., 27, 60, 66, 71; John, 12, 27, 56, 60, 116, 124, 125, 143, 188; John H., 18, 19, 21, 89; John W., 27; Leroy, 27; Martha, 124; Martha G., 125; Martha J., 133; Mary A., 125; Mary M., 133; S., 18; Sackville, 19; Sarah, 60; Sarah A. R., 125, 133; Susan, 124, 125, 133, 250; Susannah, 108, 116; Wm., 77, 179, 198; Wm. B., 19, 60; Wm. F., 27, 116, 118, 124, 125, 261.
BRITT, Daniel, 148.
BROACH, Jonas, 67; Littleberry, 84; Sarah, 84.
BROOK, James, 63, 174, 194, 221, 226; Jones, 152.

GENERAL INDEX 309

BROWN, Aaron, 249; Abraham, 63, 71, 80, 81, 89, 146, 229, 245, 264; Abram, 50; Absolom, 63; Adam, 264; Amy, 147, 172, 188; Andrew, 213, 243, 261, 264; Ann, 80; Asa A., 250; B., 125; Bedford, 171; Benj., 45, 81, 97, 100, 105, 125, 136, 164, 169, 171, 199, 205, 225, 236, 239, 256; Betsy, 63; Catharine, 71, 80; Caty, 63, 146, 147; Daniel, 241; David, 154; David B., 101; Dozier T., 255; Edward, 81, 83, 89, 236, 246, 257; Elbert, 256; Francis, 151; Geo., 151; Henry, 6, 245; Jacob, 81; Jas., 44, 63, 81, 152, 200, 210, 221, 243, 256; Jas. E., 261; Jas. N., 29, 81, 87, 94, 239, 250; Jesse, 105, 234, 263; Jincey, 201; John, 38, 71, 86, 121, 147, 149, 157, 172, 175, 188, 229, 261; Julia, 200; Keziah, 101; Lewis, 263; Lucy, 38, 48, 81; Mary, 157; Mary S., 81; Meroday, 157; Middleton W., 260; Nancy, 171; Patrick, 188; Peggy, 63, 71; Peter, 63, 165, 171, 188, 191, 216; Polly, 37, 49, 63, 243; Reuben, 23, 48, 114, 131, 236, 246; Robt., 63, 71, 80, 86, 89, 146, 147, 218; Roland, 61, 226, 243; Rolen, 163, 253; Rot., 176; Sally, 80, 147; Sarah, 152, 188, 201; Thos., 60, 151, 152, 154, 168; Thos. H., 258; Wm., 14, 19, 20, 32, 97, 149, 152, 159, 172, 173, 176, 179, 187, 188, 193, 201, 202, 207, 208, 217, 226, 233, 234; Wm. A., 264; Wm. H., 260; Wiley B., 260.
BRUMFIELD, Ann C., 260, 263.
BRYAN, Augustine, 159; Sarah, 253; Thomas, 217.
BRYANT, Thomas, 219.
BRYSON, Eliza, 124; James, 124.
BUCKLES, E., 79.
BUCHANAN, John, 164, 168.
BUCKHAM, William, 172.
BUCKHANNON, Ebenezer, 201, 212.
BUFFINGTON, Ann, 100, 255; Joseph, 100, 255; William, 254.
BUGG, Jacob, 154, 170, 173; Nancy, 170, 173.
BUKLEY, Joseph, 205.
BULLARD, Allen, 35; Ann, 35, 249; Anna, 26; Tapley, 35, 133, 134, 135; 136; Thos., 35, 137, 180, 194; Thos. B., 125, 134, 136; Wm. G., 133.
BULLIS, John, 133.
BURCH, Benj., 35, 258; Cheadle, 35; Eliz., 6, 34, 35, 100, 174, 258; John, 35; Moza, 35; Thos., 35; Wm. S., 8, 34, 100, 179, 187, 201, 205, 223.
BURDELL, Robt., 5; Thomas, 5.
BURDEN, Archer, 24; Archibald, 51, 218, 237; Clary, 15; E., 81; Edmond, 81, 89, 95, 237; Hannah, 81, 237, 252, 264; Henry, 89; Jas., 224, 237; John N., 89, 95, 111; Wm., 50, 84, 224, 237, 261, 264.
BURGAMY, Nathaniel, 237.
BURGESS, Bethany, 16; Betsy, 16; Jas., 16; Nancy, 16; Sanders, 16; Thos., 16.
BURGS, Mary, 116; Thomas, 116.
BURK—BURKE, Fleming, 219; Priscilla, 98; Robt., 23, 29, 98, 160, 164, 171, 231, 233; Thos., 56, 151, 172, 177, 201.
BURKS, Robert, 239.
BURNETT, Jeremiah, 245, 264; John, 260; Pleasant, 260; Reason, 261.
BURNS, William, 246.
BURROUGH, John, 63.
BURTON, A., 79; Abraham, 19, 34, 41, 71, 72, 73, 80, 89, 90, 125, 137, 150; Ann, 22, 187; Archer, 56, 90, 143, 147, 149, 187, 201; Archibald, 198; Ba., 90; Barsheba, 80; Bathsheba, 90, 100; Benj., 201, 205, 223; Blackbourn, 148, 150; Blackman, 31, 34, 41, 43, 66, 90, 100, 125; Eliza, 21; Eliz., 79, 80, 150; Eliz. H., 90, 100; Eliz. N., 72; Geo., 140; Germain, 34, 66, 90, 125, 148, 150, 248; Harriett, 21, 41; Henry, 34, 148, 187; Jacob, 152, 172; Jane, 125; Jenny, 19; John, 71, 72, 79, 80, 82, 89, 90, 96; Joseph, 249; Leroy, 34, 41, 100, 108, 125; Mary, 8, 79, 90, 100, 108, 140, 249; Nancy, 15, 41, 108, 152; Nelson B, 248; Nicholas, 41, 125, 248; Paten S., 248; R., 198; Rhoda, 8; Rhody, 80, 90; Richard, 79, 80, 90, 97, 100, 108, 125, 140, 249; Richard A., 108; Robt., 21, 41, 64, 145; Robt. C., 144, 197; Siphia M., 41; Tabitha, 21, 108; Thos., 15, 19, 21, 34, 41, 59, 61, 64, 71, 72, 79, 85, 89, 90, 100, 142, 145, 155, 159, 187, 207, 227, 230, 231, 248, 262, 264; Thos. H., 64; Thos. J., 261; Thos. W., 90; Wm., 34, 150; Wm. C., 137.
BURWELL, William A., 78.
BUTLER, Daniel, 43, 112; David, 27; David C., 249; Eliz., 188, 201; Hannah, 113; Jabez, 75; Haley, 24, 53, 262; Jas., 152, 165, 188, 218; John, 45, 116, 250; John H., 126; Js., 79; Martha, 45, 116; Mary, 172, 201; Milly L., 118; Nancy, 35; Nathan, 43, 198; Patrick, 112, 148, 152, 177, 188, 189, 201, 250; Patsy, 45; Peter D., 250; Peter P., 45, 113, 118, 263; Sally, 152; Zachariah, 165, 169, 172, 188, 201.

BUTT, Moses, 125; Wililam, 175.
CABBENESS, Henry, 139, 252, 258; LaFayette, 138; Napoleon B., 139.
CADE, Drury, 61; Robt., 223; Wm., 60, 222.
CAIN, Cornelius, 208, 209; Rosannah, 221; Ruth, 221; Wm., 178, 205.
CALDWELL, Catharine, 202; Harry, 163, 164, 166, 202.
CALHOUN, E. N., 99, 107; John, 173, 176; Wm., 198.
CALL, Richard, 153.
CALAHAN, A. E., 94.
CALVART—CALVERT, John, 4, 60, 173, 207; Jos., 58, 143, 146.
CAMERON, James, 58, 142; Thos., 58, 142.
CAMPBELL, Caleb, 14, 147; Daniel, 250; Wm. B., 48, 257.
CAMRON, James, 154; John, 220; Thos., 202.
CANE, John, 177.
CANNADA, Eliz., 249.
CANNING, John, 49, 136, 257, 263; Wm., 49; Wm. E., 49.
CANTERBURY, Jederson, 14.
CAPE, Meriam, 249.
CAPELL, Britton, 22, 43; Jabez B., 43; Louisa, 43; Sary, 43.
CARDEN, Chas., 46, 234; Moses, 46, 254; Robt., 242; Sarah, 46.
CARDIN, Nancy, 136; Robt., 136.
CAREW, Jean, 216.
CAREY, Joseph, 161.
CARGILL, Chas., 173; Mary, 173.
CARGILE—CARGYLE, John, 154, 203.
CARITHERS, William, 210.
CARLTON, Henry S., 261; Isham W., 261; John M., 261; Stephen, 229, 264.
CARNES, Peter, 209.
CARPENTER, Capt., 252; James, 50; Joshua, 75, 227, 234; Joshua S., 253.
CARR, David, 232, 245; Geo., 152; John, 232, 234, 245; Judith, 152; Samuel, 232, 239.
CARRELL, Edward, 67, 71, 73, 74, 79; Jas., 24, 96; Jessy, 239; John, 206, 225, 227, 228, 229, Lizzie, 24; Mary, 154; Nancy, 74; Peter, 154.
CARROLL, John, 29, 36, 98; Mary, 28, 36.
CARSON, Jean, 193; John, 192, 208.
CARTER, Betsy, 73; Chas., 66, 72, 74, 81, 149, 237, 238, 240, 244; Chas. N. B., 41, 116, 255; Chas. N. P., 133; Eliz., 41, 64, 116, 172, 249, 255; Francis S., 186, 192; Geo., 81, 109, 117, 140, 246, 261; James, 16, 58, 66, 72, 81, 91, 153, 169, 172, 202, 215, 219, 232, 239; John, 27; John J., 36, 255; John M., 168; John W., 49, 91, 107, 116, 258; J. W., 209; Leslie G., 127; Lewis, 16; Lucy, 41, 172, 255; Micajah, 44; Nathias, 249; Nelly, 16; Polly, 16; Ro. M., 36, 38; Robt. M., 46, 246 255; Sarah, 242; Sterling, 139; Thos., 66, 72, 75, 81, 91, 143, 153, 157, 162, 166, 168, 169, 172, 183, 191, 194, 202, 204, 220, 237, 242; Thos. L., 153; Thos. P., 72, 81, 91, 100, 255; Thos. S., 66, 72, 81, 91, 94, 97, 107, 146, 261; Wm., 172, 175; Willis, 147.
CARY, Eliz., 51; John, 51.
CASEY, Abraham P., 209; Daniel, 169.
CASH, Howard, 67, 73; 83, 93, 100, 148, 215, 228, 229, 233, 240, 241; Jas., 241; Jesse, 46, 229, 240; John, 241, 255; Moses, 234; Nancy, 241.
CASHWELL, Peter, 3.
CASON, Betsy, 28; John, 28, 32, 36, 133, 243.
CATSTINS, John M., 96.
CASTLE, William, 62.
CAUTIH, John, 242; Polly, 242.
CEALOR, David, 62.
CECIL, Leonard, 176.
CERTAIN, Eliz., 190, 202; James, 191, 199; John, 74, 190; Josiah, 159, 190, 202.
CHAMBERS, Edward M., 34, 260; James, 203; James E., 257, 260; John, 246; Lettice, 153, 203; Robt., 5, 153, 168, 186, 187, 203; Sarah, 18, 34; Thos., 18, 34; Wm. S., 246.
CHAMBLESS, James E., 244.
CHANDLER, Joseph, 17, 183; M., 119; Mordecai, 251; Washington, 247.
CHAPMAN, David, 254; Frederick, 254.
CHAPPELL, Thos. B., 244.
CHATMAN, Stephen, 103.
CHARLTON, John K., 95.
CHAVES, Charlotte, 59; Gilbert, 59, 144; Harry, 59; Philip, 59, 144.
CHEEK, Burgess, 245; John, 264; Wm., 245; Wm. C., 48.
CHILDERS, Holman, 101; Jas., 68; Jesse C., 254; John, 41, 101, 235; Malinda, 41; Martha A., 41; Patsy, 27; Robt., 230; Thos., 91, 237; Wm., 249.
CHILDRES, Sally, 18, 27; Wiley, 19, 234, 236.
CHILDREYS, James, 145.
CHILDRUS, Robert, 242.
CHILDS, Ann W., 66, 72, 88, 107, 148; Eliz., 51; Jane, 66, 72, 148; John,

GENERAL INDEX 311

51, 66, 72, 147, 182, 230, 243, 250; Lewis G., 250; Nathan, 66, 72, 81, 147, 155; Richard, 72; Susan, 130; Susannah S., 51; Wm., 130; Wm. R., 51.
CHIPMAN, Joseph, 32, 241.
CHISENHALL, Delany, 36, 248.
CHISHOLM, Andrew, 257; Andrew J., 257; Ann, 257; Eliz. L., 22; Patrick J., 257; Sarah, 204; Sarah A., 257; Wm., 58, 82, 91, 149, 190, 229; Wm. Sr., 73.
CHOLSTON, Chas. T., 250.
CHRISTIAN, Chas. W., 229, 230, 244; C. W., 26, 38, 43, 51; Drewry, 258; Elijah D., 246; Elijah L., 258; Elijah W., 246; Geo. W., 262, 264; Ira, 244; Isaac, 87; James, 14, 35, 38, 69, 91, 121, 137, 147, 148, 149, 186, 202, 226, 227, 228, 229, 231, 237, 246; Jas. G., 246; Jesse, 237; Jesse G., 262, 264; John, 45; John M., 250; J. P., 228; Lindsay, 261; Lucy, 14; P., 77, 87; Pressley, 81, 137, 150, 237; Presley G., 104; R., 229; R. B., 230; Reuben, 26, 227, 235; Robt. B., 33, 45, 222; Robt. R., 35; Rufus, 236, 244; R. W., 118; Samuel, 250; Thos. J., 264; Turner, 192, 219, 221, 223, 260; Washington, 259; Wm., 231; Wm. P., 237, 246, 265.
CHRISLAR, Benj., 252.
CHRISTLER—CHRYSTLER, Eliz., 126; Henry, 64; Joseph, 14, 64, 83, 108; Jos. L., 91; Julius, 108, 126, 188, 239; Wesler, 113.
CHRISTLY, Henry, 145; Jos., 145, 148; Julius, 145.
CHRISTMAS, Robert, 161.
CHRISTOPHER, William, 166.
CRITTINGTON, Henry, 237; Henry P., 237; Prior, 237; Robt., 237; Wm., 237.
CLARK, Abigail P., 72, 73, 82; Agatha, 168; Bolling, 173; C., 168, 217; Charity A., 34; Christopher, 7, 27, 57, 91, 101, 116, 146, 153, 174, 179, 180, 186, 190, 223, 249; Christopher H., 27, 116, 249; D., 168; David, 7, 25, 27, 60, 146, 153, 206; E., 217; Edward, 50, 66, 171, 205, 212, 245; Elijah, 215; Francis, 66, 72, 239; Geo., 101; Geo., W., 27, 116, 138, 139; Jas., 33, 34, 83, 116, 134, 138, 149, 234, 236, 240, 264; Jas. O., 35, 101, 249; John, 154; John H., 138, Johnston, 5; Joshua, 7, 23, 27, 79, 92, 146, 149; J. & W., 93; Judith, 153; Larken, 81, 85, 147, 251, 260, 264; Lewis, 66, 186, 195; Lucinda M., 48, 138; Margaret, 27, 91; Martha, 173; Martha A., 138; Mary, 27, 34, 101, 116, 134, 138, 140; Mary A. E., 138; Micajah, 7, 146; Rebecca, 91, 101, 249; Robt., 138; Samuel, 27, 101, 223, 248; Sarah, 5; Susannah, 26, 91; Susannah A., 101; Tabitha, 98, 104, 112; Thos. B., 48, 138; Thos. J., 27, 101, 116, 134, 257; Wm., 91; Wm. D., 27, 101, 116, 134, 138, 139, 251; Williamson, 48, 232, 239, 264; Zachariah, 18, 72, 82, 91, 101, 138, 149, 172, 182, 248; Zachariah H., 101, 138.
CLARKSON, John, 156, 170, 184, 219, 220.
CLATON, Rebecca, 15.
CLAY, John, 78, 88, 142.
CLAYTON, P., 173.
CLEGHORN, Geo., 68; Jas., 154; John, 154; Wm., 17, 181.
CLEMM, Adam, 172; Jemima, 172.
CLEMONT, Simon, 239.
CLEVELAND, Benj., 215; Daniel, 2; Early, 251; Eliz., 2; Ibrey, 137; Jacob, 2; Jacob M., 51, 117, 251; Jacob N., 126; Jas. M., 117; Jeremiah, 2, 142; John, 37, 68, 94, 108, 117, 126, 137; Milly, 142; Permelia, 51; Rhoda, 137; Rhody, 12, 117, 126; Reuben, 2, 37, 79, 117; Rice, 142, 219; Sarah W., 117; Temperance, 22; Wiat, 83.
CLIFT, Henry, 75; Sally, 75.
CLOUD, Ezekiel, 153, 203; Jeremiah, 153; Noah, 226; Samuel G., 102; Sarah, 153.
CLOWD, Samuel G., 21.
CLOWNEY, Robt. G., 129.
COATS, N., 215.
COBBS, John, 172; Mary, 172.
COCKBURN, George, 162, 165.
COCKRAN, William, 114, 190.
COCKS, George, 264.
COFFEE, James, 191, 192; John, 207.
COHORN, William, 220.
COIL, James, 4; John, 144, 227.
COKER, Abraham, 237; Alsea, 263; Anne, 48; Isaac, 4, 56, 152, 173, 190, 227; Jacob, 84, 233; John, 245, 259; Larkin, 48, 135; Malachi, 237; Malicha, 190; Nancy, 173.
COLAT, John, 81.
COLBERT, Anne, 203; Fanny, 203; James, 217, 220, 222; John, 27, 157, 203; Lucy, 27; Malinda, 27, 101, 126; Martha, 203; Nicodemus, 198, 203, 208; Patsy, 203; Philpot, 203; Rhoda, 27, 101; Richard, 27, 83, 91, 101, 126, 149, 157; Susanna, 154, 157, 175, 248; Thos., 66, 101, 126, 146, 148,

GENERAL INDEX

167, 167, 170, 203, 205, 209; Thos. J., 27, 101; Tukedmark, 167; Turman W., 159; Wm., 91, 101.
COLEMAN, Anna W., 15; Jas., 69, 74, 154, 174, 182, 190, 196, 197, 204, 248; Jesse, 246; John, 143, 154, 163, 170, 173, 182, 197, 198, 216, 223; Michael, 203, 205; Mitchell, 196; Polly, 5, 154; Thomas, 74.
COLLERS, Matthew, 57, 142.
COLLETT, John, 229, 235.
COLLIER, Thomas, 164.
COLLIN—COLLINS, Henry, 197; John, 216, 231; Richard, 147; Samuel, 251; Zachariah, 154, 204.
COLLEY—COLLY, Edward, 114; John, 147; Mary W., 12; Maynard, 147; Sally, 40; Sarah, 11, 12; Zachariah, 11, 147; Zacharias, 12, 114.
COLSON, A., 11, 31, 213; Abraham, 10, 74, 154, 170 173, 174, 204; Jacob, 174; Jas., 31; Nancy, 10, 74, 170, 173; Rebecca, 31; William, 212.
COLVARD, John S., 258.
CONNOLLY, Thomas, 211.
CONWAY, Edwin, 173; Marget, 204; Peter, 173, 181; Philip, 204.
CONYERS, John, 61, 145, 180, 203, 221; Mrs., 61; William, 61.
COOK, Abraham, 262, 265; Alcy, 6; Aley, 189; Allen, 35, 203; Benj., 6, 12, 20, 22, 61, 75, 100, 101, 108, 121, 145, 147, 154, 162, 168, 179, 180, 187, 188, 189, 198, 201, 203, 213, 218; Betty, 22, 35; Beverly C., 12, 47, 108, 117, 122, 139, 140, 249; Daniel, 249; David, 254; Deborah, 154; Delilah, 35; Dudley, 22; Edoshus, 153; Effie, 6, 145; Elijah M., 36, Elisha, 22; Eliz., 36, 203; Emila, 89; F., 219, 220, 221, 222; Fenton, 89, 246; Frances, 91, 101, 129; Francis, 16, 22, 152, 154, 157, 160, 162, 165, 173, 182, 183, 189, 212, 217, 218, 219, 220, 222; Frank, 216; Geo., 11, 40, 47, 76, 81, 86, 103, 144, 145, 146, 179, 186, 189; Geo. H., 12; Gilly, 27; G. W., 203; Henry, 143, 197; Isaac, 230; Jas., 16, 143, 153, 154, 160, 162, 164, 168; Jas. W., 143, 203; Jesse M., 36, 249; John, 22, 24, 36, 94, 101, 108, 175, 178, 187, 189, 207, 222, 249; Joseph, 26, 82, 1, 173; Joshua, 22, 36, 108, 249; Josiah, 22, 189, 203; Lewis, 250; Mary, 12, 36, 108, 147, 188, 249; Mary A., 36; Patsy, 203; Polly, 6; Rebeckey, 6; Reuben, 188, 207, 214; Richard, 36; Sally, 203; Samuel, 249; Sarah, 36, 152, 179, 249; Smith, 24, 36, 125, 134, 249; Theodocus, 199; Theodosius, 249;

Thos., 4, 8, 12, 22, 56, 91, 101, 146, 176, 203, 214, 215, 219, 220, 221, 222, 224, 226, 227, 228, 229, 230, 231, 249; Wiley, 35; Wm., 6, 35; Wm. T., 91, 101, 102, 145, 173, 189, 197, 242, 246; Wm. T. O., 35, 129, 262.
COOKE, James, 56; Jas. W., 56; Reuben, 56.
COOPER, Jonathan, 20, 76, 79; Thos., 259.
CORBETT, Rachel, 38.
CORETHERS, Robert, 162.
CORITHERS, Robert, 222.
COSBY, Barbara M., 7; Chas., 6, 10, 146, 187, 203; Chas. S., 7, 205; Cynthia, 154; David, 7, 172, 177, 183, 185; Eliz., 6; Eliz. S., 7; Fortunatus, 7, 178; H. H., 49; Jas., 7, 57, 61; Jas. O., 146, 147, 190, 203; John, 11; Lucy H., 7; R., 180, 190; Richmond, 7, 146; Richmond T., 72, 147; Robt., 6, 7, 10, 146, 154, 162, 172, 173, 187, 189, 190, 202, 212, 223; R. T., 146, 226; Sydnor, 154, 215; Thos., 61.
COTHERS, William, 157.
COTTLE, Delila, 19; Lurina, 19.
COUCH, Nancy, 48; Sarah, 254.
COUDEN, Robert, 199, 208.
COURSEY, Daniel, 22, 34.
COULTER, Chas., 152, 165, 174, 189, 202, 203, 206; Eliz., 189; Francis, 154, 189, 204; Mary, 189; Rebecca, 153, 189; Richard, 57, 153, 165, 171, 173, 174, 189, 203; Robt., 174, 189; Sarah, 154.
COULSTON, Mariam, 252; Nancy, 254.
COWAN, William, 177.
COWDEN—COWDON, Robt., 59, 144, 149, 153, 160, 193, 224.
COWDERY, John, 209.
COX, Jacob, 123; Jesse, 163; Sally, 44; Zachariah, 60.
CRAB, Asa, 65.
CRAFFORD, Oliver, 167.
CRAFT, Archable, 256; Anderson, 45; John, 12, 22, 27, 47, 82; 239, 239, 254, 255; Samuel, 255; Washington, 255; Wm., 25, 254.
CRANE, Joel, 208.
CRAWFORD, Ann, 11, 36; Arthur, 58; Benj., 48; Burton, 22, 48; Burton E., 102, 135; David, 224; Earls, 22; Henrietta, 22; Jas., 48; Jas. L., 45, 125; Joel, 11; John, 22, 48, 82, 102, 135; Leroy, 22, 48; Leroy K., 102; Leroy R., 135; Lucy, 22, 45, 48, 125, 135, 136, 254; Lucy A., 48; Matilda, 48; Milly, 45, 48; Milly L., 45, 125, 136; Nancy B., 48; Oliver, 45, 48, 125, 254; Richard G., 134;

GENERAL INDEX 313

Richmond, 48; Richmond G., 45, 125; Wm., 37, 41, 45, 46, 48, 102, 110, 125, 134, 136; Wm. H., 22, 48, 102, 135.
CREAGH, John G., 213; Rebecca, 14, 190; Thos., 178; Thos. B., 18, 69, 87, 161, 190, 194, 199, 211, 213, 219, 220.
CRENSHAW, Maybourn, 56, 143, 194.
CREWS, Thomas, 66, 72.
CRIDENDON—CRITTENTON—CRIDDINGTON, Abigail, 39; Elijah, 246, 262; Henry, 174, 205, 206; Juda, 246; R. L., 42, 117; Wm., 189, 203, 205.
CRISLER, Julius, 221.
CRISWELL, David, 152, 161, 168, 173, 184, 190, 202.
CROCKET, Robt., 56, 64, 143, 190, 203; Samuel, 56, 64, 143, 190, 203.
CROOK, Robert, 73.
CROSBY, John, 154, 161, 164, 165, 178, 179, 189, 216.
CROSS, William, 225.
CROSSLEY, John, 152.
CROW, Hannah, 172; James, 145, 157, 161, 172, 203, 221; Samuel, 86, 242.
CROWDER, Frederick, 145; Fodrick, 225; John, 176.
CRUMP, Aggy, 27; Agnes, 39; Chas., 27, 91, 102, 241; Lemuel, 27; Louise, 189; Pleasant D., 27, 102, 253; R. D., 106; Richard L., 102; Robt., 113, 196; Wm., 27, 114.
CRUTCHFIELD, George, 153.
CULBERSON, James, 113.
CULBRETH, A., 263.
CUMMINGS, Parson, 64.
CULPEPPER, John, 195.
CUNNINGHAM, Abraham, 248; Alex., 6; Andrew, 174; Ann, 152; David, 6, 61; Eliz., 174, 191, 204; F., 47; Franklin, 240; J., 157, 162, 222, 231; Jas., 191; John, 24, 41, 73, 92, 152, 156, 157, 162, 184, 222, 226, 227, 241, 255; Joseph, 255; Martha, 61; Minter, 248; Nancy, 16; Patsy, 6; Polly, 6; Sarah, 6, 145; Thos., 6; Wm., 6, 36, 61, 82, 145, 151, 165, 206, 248.
CURDY, David M., 149.
CURTIS, Reuben, 60.
DAILEY, Hezekiah, 173; John, 22, 168, 183; Samuel C., 100, 247.
DALY, Rachel, 7.
DANIEL, A., 174, 226; Allen, 102, 155, 160, 162, 169, 174, 186, 226, 227, 228, 230, 231; Aln., 229; Amy, 154; David, 136; Eliz., 190; Jas. S., 46; John, 73, 74, 225, 230; Nancy, 154, 155, 174; Peggy, 30; Wm., 154, 155, 160, 161, 162, 174, 186, 190, 203, 206.
DARDEN—DARDIN, Buckner, 207; Eliz., 28, 111; Geo., 56, 144, 174, 186, 192, 207, 216, 225; John, 155, 204, 205, 211, 219; Martha, 174.
DARRACOTT, Rebeckah, 257.
DAUGHERTY, John, 174.
DOUGHTY, Joseph, 155.
DAVID, Humphrey, 245; Isaac, 151, 181, 247; Jacob W., 244, 263; Samuel, 131, 262.
DAVIS, A., 218, 220; Abraham, 230; Absolom, 15, 16, 18, 22, 57, 61, 73, 78, 92, 147, 150, 204, 217, 250; Absolom T., 22; Ann, 155; Ann M., 7; Augustine, 16; Augustine J., 127; Benj., 7, 144, 155, 167, 193, 216, 217, 228; Chislen, 16; Edward, 117, 147; Eliz., 7; Frederick, 16; G., 217; Gideon, 16, 61, 145; Hickman, 238; Isaac N., 49, 133, 134, 135, 257; J., 174; Jas., 45, 255; Jesse M., 42; John, 7, 117, 144, 155, 162, 254; Jos., 44, 145, 220; Jos. T., 16, 78, 217; Jos. W., 50; L., 221; Larkin, 183; Lewis, 16, 57, 142, 155; Mary, 7; Margaret, 204; Meredith, 239; Milly, 145, 225; Moses, 165, 218, 261; Nancy, 16, 22, 28, 238, 250; Patsy, 53; Patsy W., 22; Patty, 11; Ransom, 42; Rebecca, 204; Richard,16; Rody, 155; Sally, 73, 147, 183; Sally S., 147; Samuel, 127; Sarah, 37, 78, 150, 155, 239; Sarah F., 15; Suckey, 155; Susannah, 255; Terry, 22; Thos., 21, 109, 117, 140, 147, 185; Thos. F., 22, 42, 117, 126, 130, 136, 139, 250; Thos. L., 245; Thos. W., 15, 42, 78, 115, 148; W. C., 91; Wiley, 16, 155, 174, 176, 217; Wm., 13, 15, 16, 28, 57, 87, 92, 115, 117, 143, 147, 150, 190, 193, 194, 245; Wm. C., 100, 108, 125, 140, 204, 248; Wm. H., 155.
DAWSON, Thomas, 172.
DEADWILER—DEADWYLER, Alice, 45; Arrenna, 45; Asa, 45, 134, 258; Eales, 191; Eve, 19; Henry R., 258; John, 45; John G., 134; Joseph, 19, 35, 45, 82, 100, 107, 114, 115, 117, 123, 126, 133, 134, 135, 136, 141, 191, 198, 244, 258; Margaret A., 45, 126, 133, 135, 141, 258; Martha, 141; Martha P., 133, 141; Martin, 19, 44, 45, 82, 92, 106, 109, 114, 117, 123, 126, 134, 137, 140, 142, 233, 234, 235, 244, 263; Nancy, 19.
DEAN, Alvia, 109; John, 254; Shadrick, 149; Wm., 156, 157.

GENERAL INDEX

DECKER, Edey, 174, 190; John, 174, 185, 190, 224.
DENNA, Edward A., 105; Robt., 105.
DENNARD, John, 27, 250; Phebe, 27.
DENNIS, Stephen, 250.
DENNY, Barbara, 38; David, 259; Edward, 224; Edward A., 259; Geo. W., 259, 263; Melita, 38; Robt., 245, 259.
DEPRIEST, Amey, 204; Jean, 191; Jas. A., 247, 265; John, 151, 152, 155, 167, 168, 174, 187, 190, 191, 210, 222; Randolph, 184, 204, 212.
DEWHIT, Samuel, 62.
DESKINS, Sarah, 178; William, 178.
DEVEREUX, Samuel, 161.
DICKENSON—DICKINSON, John, 78, 196, 204, 211; Jos., 204; Josiah W., 78, 87; Robt. N., 78, 87.
DICKERSON, David, 49; Dolly, 49; Eliz., 142; John, 49, 252; Josiah W., 142; Nancy, 49; Patsy, 49; Polly, 49; Rhody, 49; Robt., 49; Robt. N., 142; Robt. W., 255; Zachariah, 49, 135.
DICKEY, John, 111, 261, 265.
DICKSON, Arthur B., 155; Blackman, 248; David, 149; Jas., 228; Samuel, 248.
DILLARD, Isaac, 250; Jas., 250; Neheniah V., 250; Sarah, 23.
DINGLER, John, 191, 200.
DIVINE, Jinney, 35.
DIXON, Charlotte, 34; Elenner A., 34; Eleven, 204; John L., 34, 174; Lemuel, 34; Mary, 57, 59; Outlerbridge, 174, 204; Roann B., 34; Robt., 34; Wm., 57, 59.
DIXSON, Mary, 145; Wm., 145..
DOBB, David, 252.
DOBBINS, Joseph, 23.
DOBBS, Capt., 253; David, 30, 31, 51, 113, 135, 136; Elijah, 102; Jane, 127; Jesse, 38, 129, 135, 136; John, 29, 30, 31, 38, 73, 92, 120, 127, 190, 242; Josiah, 73, 92, 149, 242, 254; Lewcey, 242; Lot, 242; Louisania, 254; Luzany, 73, 92; Peter, 242; Silas, 15, 242, 254.
DOCTH, Joseph, 197.
DODD, Eliz., 243; William, 243.
DODDS, Jas., 235; Thos., 264; Wm., 252, 254.
DOLINGS, Joseph, 174.
DOLLAR, Ambrose, 68, 229, 233, 235, 242; Henry, 92, 102; Jas., 91, 242; Mary, 102.
DONALD, H. M., 170.
DONOVAN, A., 109.

DOOLEY—DOOLY, Allen, 141; Allen D., 253; Eliz., 36, 141; Frances, 36; Geo., 155; Nancy, 243; Wm., 116, 141, 243; Wm. W., 133, 141.
DOSS, Geo., 192; Jean, 165; Joel, 6, 85, 206, 235, 241; John, 156, 204.
DOUGLAS, John, 165.
DOWNER, Elenor, 110; Jos., 188; Wm. W., 110, 133.
DOWNS, James, 259.
DRAKE, Turner, 228.
DRIVER, Betsy, 239; Bird, 239; John, 51; Simeon, 51; William, 243.
DUDLEE—DUDLIE, William, 164, 221.
DUDLEY, Ignatius, 259; Jas., 57, 143, 190, 221; Jas. L., 245, 263; Jarrott, 245; John, 57, 143, 149, 190; John B., 245; John T., 245; Mary, 174; Nicholas, 239; Sarah, 189; Wm., 68, 146, 174, 175, 181, 189, 211.
DUGGER, A., 93.
DUGLASS, Thomas, 205.
DUKE, Abraham, 177.
DULA—DOOLY, Thos., 227, 232; Wm., 227, 232.
DUMERE, C., 98.
DUNAHOO, Cornelius, 68.
DUNCAN, Aaron, 264; Henry, 48, 155, 168, 213, 245, 264; Joanna, 155; John, 28, 221, 260, 264; Mark, 156; Mary, 156; Matthew, 17; Moses, 232, 264; Nathaniel, 245, 259; Pearson, 199, 220, 230, 259, 264; Sally, 17; William, 232.
DUNLAP, Joseph, 32, 99; Robt, 19; Wm., 19, 67, 73, 74, 82, 90, 92, 109, 110.
DUNN, Capt., 254; Francis, 133; John, 33, 162; Joseph, 254.
DUNNAL, Soloman, 145.
DUNNYHOO, Cornelius, 242.
DURRETT, Marshall, 75; Nancy, 75.
DUSKIN, Hannah, 92.
DUTTON, Jas., 239; Thos., 241, 253; William, 252.
DYE, Beckham, 146, 148; Beckman, 81, 82; Brown, 108, 109, 117, 126, 249; Burrell, or Burwell, 90, 109, 116, 117; David, 109, 116, 117, 123; Eliz., 35, 88, 90, 109, 116, 117; Francis, 109; Geo. J., 109; Geo. W., 108, 116, 133; Jane, 109, 116, 117, 126, 134, 249; John A., 116, 126, 133; Martin, 18; Martin B., 108, 116, 133; Mary, 108, 109, 126, 249; Polly, 109, 126; Rebecca, 44; Sarah, 109, 126; Susan A., 108, 116; Susan A. F., 133; Susan F. A., 116; Thompson, 17, 134, 249; Thompson B., 109, 126; William, 109, 116, 117.

GENERAL INDEX 315

DYER, Jacob, 200.
EADES, John, 175; Ramey, 258; Sarah D. 258.
EAGIN, John, 259.
EAKIN, Samuel, 224, 226.
EARLY, Joab, 78; Joshua, 62.
EASTEN, Chas., 190; John, 191.
EASTER, Campain, 147; Champion, 2, 64, 239; Booker B., 2, 59, 156, 231; Dolly, 2; Eliz., 2; Jas., 2, 57, 66, 72, 143, 156, 182, 187; John, 163; John C., 21, 22; Lewis, 2; Lieut., 85; Lotty, 2, 156; Marjary, 2; Mary, 22, 205; Mary A., 2; Moneyca, 59; R., 13, 166; Richard, 2, 17, 22, 37, 66, 69, 72, 143, 144, 156, 186, 198, 205, 207, 211, 212, 213, 229; Richard J., 22; Robt., 58; Sarah, 2, 143, 156; Sophia, 2, 156; Tabby C., 156; Tere, 2, 156; Wm., 16, 64, 147, 156; Wm. F., 22; Wm. T., 2, 143, 156.
EASTIN, Reuben, 16.
EASTON, Chas., 57, 143; John, 57, 143; Reuben, 57, 143; Sally, 57, 143; William, 59.
EAVES, Alford, 261; Jas., 261; Polly, 75; Rhoday, 260; Wm., 263.
EAVENSON, Eli, 149, 171, 173, 177, 187, 201, 204, 214, 224, 225; Willis, 255.
EAVENSTON, Eli, 239; Geo., 239; Susannah, 239.
EAVERHURT, Jacob, 160.
EBERHART—ABERHART, David, 12, 20, 149, 156, 157; Frances P., 104; Geo. 12, 20, 63, 75, 149, 156, 226; Jacob, 20, 156; James, 20.
EDES, Mary, 152.
EDMONDSON, Samuel, 119.
EDWARDS, Augustine, 38, 39, 43, 210; Emaline, 117; Emily E., 118; Felix G., 117, 118, 129, 134; Gilbert, 117; Jas., 102, 109, 117, 128, 129, 134, 248; Jesse, 149, 265; John, 92, 234, 244, 259; Lamar G., 129; Laura G., 117, 118, 134; Peter, 186; Robt. L., 122, 131, 250; Sarah, 117; Sarah B., 102, 109, 117, 118, 129; Sarah M., 117, 118, 134; Sarah P., 248; Susannah, 156, 175; Wm., 156, 157, 175, 215.
ELBERT, Samuel, 166.
ELDER, Penelope, 24; William, 245.
ELLICOTT, Robert, 62.
ELLINGTON, Ann 16; Catharine 16; Eliz., 146; Garland, 66; Jane, 66; Nancy, 10; Rice, 66; Robt., 66; Stephen, 3, 5, 64, 66, 146, 147, 166, 185, 198, 213, 247.
ELLIOTT, Alex., 145; Andrew, 3, 5, 180, 183; Arthur, 227; Eliz., 53; Geo., 153; Jas., 82, 109, 156, 158; Sarah, 156; Sharlot, 82, 110; Thos. C., 91; Wm., 156, 160, 161, 181, 215, 221; Wm. P., 203.
ELLIS, Chas., 166, 205; Robt., 175, 184; Zillar, 238.
ELLISON, John, 200.
ELSWORTH, M. M. A., 108.
ELLS, John, 168.
EMBRY, Mary, 20.
EMORY, Nancy, 117.
ENGLAND, Anderson, 12.
ENLO, John, 253.
EPPERSON, S., 218; Samuel, 219.
EUBANKS, Richard, 189.
EVANS, Elam, 248; Eliam, 149; Eliz., 34, 248; Geo., 194, 205; Harden, 188; Matilda, 34; Stephen, 66.
EVENS, George, 156; Major, 154, 215.
EVINGSON, Sarah, 53.
EVINS, Andrew, 153; Hardin, 206.
EWING, Chas., 64, 147; David, 60, 228; Jas., 64, 77, 88, 147; Matthew, 185; Thos., 185, 188; Wm. A. D., 64, 179, 188.
FAGUSON, Norman, 243.
FAIN, Chas., 184, 252; Epperson, 254; Jas., 184; John, 254; John H., 254; Judy, 184; Robert, 254.
FALK, Thomas, 245.
FALKNER, John, 244.
FANNIN—FANNING, Aberialer, 205; Avery, 205; Benj., 8, 41, 42, 169, 170, 200, 201, 203, 205, 239; Chas., 233; John, 42; John H., 82, 169; Laughlin, 239; Middleton, 205; Susanna, 156; Wm., 82.
FARER, Parent, 164.
FARGUS, John, 220.
FARR, Jonathan, 222.
FARROW, Britton, 156; John, 156; Micajah, 156; Needham, 156; Perin, 156; Perren, 212; Sally, 156; Willie, 156.
FAUBES, Henry, 255.
FAULKENBERRY, Jacob, 239.
FAULKNER, Jas., 16, 75, 82, 85, 92, 96; Jas. H., 16; Jas. J., 258; Jas. M., 256; John, 16, 28, 82, 85, 92, 96, 193; Nancy, 75; Patsy, 16, 75; Peter, 16, 28; Sally, 92; Sarah, 28; Wm., 28, 92, 191, 193, 233, 234, 258; Zachariah, 75.
FERGUS, Jo., 216; John, 218, 219, 220, 221; Wm., 216, 221, 222, 231.
FERGUSON, Daniel, 253; John, 182, 254.
FERRELL, James, 143, 191; John, 30, 57, 142, 143, 215; Margaret, 30;

GENERAL INDEX

Martin, 57, 143, 191; Micajah, 241; Wylie, 30, 84, 241.
FERINGTON, Aron, 238.
FIELDING, Mary, 117.
FIELDS, Jeremiah, 228.
FILPS, Francis, 214.
FILSON, John, 146.
FINCHER, Mary, 61; Moses, 61, 145.
FINLEY, James, 214.
FINNEY, Abadiah, 175.
FINNY, Laughlin, 145.
FITCHGARRALD, John, 145.
FITS, Eliz., 259; James O., 259; Jincy, 259; John, 259; John T., 259; Keziah D., 259; Mary, 259; Mary J., 259; Rhoda A., 259; Tandy W., 259; Wm. G., 259; Wm. H., 246.
FITSGERRALD, Geo., 226.
FITZGARRALD, Geo., 146.
FITZJARRELD, Geo., 242.
FLANIGAN, Wm., 162, 175.
FLEMING, Henry, 36, 248; John, 62, 216, 219, 239; Margaret, 36, 248; Martha, 9; Moses, 23, 102, 110, 118, 149, 211, 219, 224, 239; Robt., 36, 215, 221; Rosanna, 36; Sarah, 110, 118.
FLINT, John, 191; Wm., 191.
FLOOD, Chas., 171; James, 171, 190.
FLOYD, Barbara, 33; James, 67; Richard, 153; Robt., 231; Shadrick, 74; Wm. K., 223.
FOOTE, Newton, 171.
FORBES, A., 219; Arthur, 221.
FORBIS, Patrick, 176.
FORD, Barbary, 82; Barrett, 82; Benj., 81, 89; Daniel, 12, 146; Dorcas, 12; Elisha, 133, 264; E., 81; Eliza, 89; Eliz., 12, 45; Isaac, 212; Jesse, 12, 92, 233; John, 12, 83, 92, 146, 239; Joseph, 246; Mary, 12, 146, 256; Sarah, 239.
FORGUSON, Katharine, 29; Norman, 29.
FORK, Henry, 263.
FORTSON, Alemeda H., 134, 140, 258; Amanda M., 110; B., 97; Benj., G., 110; Benj., 36, 58, 102, 110, 134, 172, 239, 256; Benj., H., 128, 136; Benj. W., 257; Eastin, 102, 110, 130; Easton, 46, 134, 257; Edward K., 128; Edwin K., 136; Eliza, 46; Eliz., 46, 52, 102, 110, 140, 256; Eliz. D., 122; Eliz. E., 110; Geo. G., 134; Haley, 134; Harriett, 118; James, 110; Jane M., 118, 134, 140, 258; Jesse, 36, 73, 82, 87, 102, 110, 118, 134, 139, 140, 150; Jesse M., 118, 139; John, 102, 110; Katherine D., 122; Laura P. E., 122; Permelia E.
L., 139; Permelia L. E., 127; Rachel, 191; Rachel A., 128, 136; Richard 36, 38, 41, 79, 94, 105, 107, 110, 112, 114, 118, 138, 139, 247; Rich'd E., 128, 136; Sarah, 4; Tabby, 46; Tavner, 251; Tavner W., 102, 122, 127, 257; T. W., 122, 131; Thos., 36, 45, 46, 102, 110, 118, 126, 128, 136, 143, 153, 175, 191, 197, 224, 225, 226, 247, 250; Thos. D., 140, 258; Thos. J., 134; Wm., 36, 46, 103, 149, 172, 191, 247.
FOSTER, Geo., 184; Samuel, 175, 179, 205; Warsham, 243; Wm., 250.
FOWLER, Arthur, 238; James, 253; Jeremiah, 223; Rachel, 253.
FRANKLIN, David, 117, 216, 241; Edmond, 241; Henry, 241; Job, 132; John, 230; Mary, 241; Milly E., 241; Philemon, 241; Polley, 241; Sampson, 241; Sarah, 241.
FREELAND, Lewis, 147.
FREEMAN, James, 22, 83, 156, 158, 175, 206, 214, 217; Jenny, 5; Joel, 19, 231.
FRY, Michael, 218.
FUGES, Wm., 63.
FULGHUM, Matthew, 57, 142, 175; Stephen, 57, 142, 175; J., 218.
FUQUA, Joseph, 157, 173.
FURGUS—FERGUS, John, 58, 151, 153, 161, 165, 167, 173, 175, 191, 192, 205.
GAAR, Abraham, 57, 63; Adam, 28, 57, 61, 63, 82, 83, 95, 102, 144, 200, 239; Benj., 57; Catharine, 176; Fanny, 57, 59, 61; Frances, 57; Geo., 36, 57, 59, 61, 73; Joel, 59, 61, 239; Lewis, 14, 57, 176, 209, 212, 239; Michael, 57, 59, 61, 144; Mikel, 239; Nancy, 57, 59, 61, 102; Sally, 59; Wm., 36, 57, 59, 61, 73.
GADDIS, John, 204.
GAINES, Anna, 49; Anne T., 23; Francis, 41, 46, 110, 241, 254; Henry, 12, 146, 225; Hierome, 23, 27, 29, 93, 233; Hiram, 148, 206, 212; James, 23; James H., 23; Jeney, 23; Judith B., 110, 140; Judy, 41; Judy B., 41; Leavenston P. 29; Livingston P., 37, 41, 110, 140; L. P., 94, 234; Margaret O., 23; Mary E., 41, 110, 140; Ralph, 37, 106; Rich'd S., 41, 241; Robert, 60; Robt., T., 70; R. T., 41; Sally, 29, 37, 70, 110; Sarah, 103, 140; Taliaferro, 70, 71, 241; Wm., 206, 212, 227, 239; Wm. S., 23.
GANDY, Patsy, 30.
GANES, Henry S., 254; Levingston W. 254; Sarah, 254; Wm., 255.

GENERAL INDEX 317

GARDNER, Elijah, 254; Nancy, 38, 120, 254.
GARNER, Mary, 61, 144; Stephen, 59, 61, 64, 144, 182.
GARRETT, Archalas, 147; Catharine, 16; John, 16, 206; Julian, 16; Margaret, 16; Martha, 16; Maria, 16.
GARVIN—GARVEN, Daniel, 67, 73, 109, 110, 146; Jane 67, 146; John E., 73, 109, 110; Nancy, 67; Robt., 67, 73, 110; Wm. D., 73, 109.
GARVIS, Jay, 68; Sally, 68.
GATES, James, 118, 140; John, 229; Josiah, 175.
GATEWOOD, Betsy, 12, 16; Betty, 3, 14, 16, 143; Catharine, 12, 238; Caty' 147; Chas. C., 16; Eliz., 23; Flemming, 67; Henry, 13, 16, 145, 189, 192, 204, 223, 226; James, 146, 197; John, 3, 14, 16, 67, 143, 189, 191; Larkin, 12, 147, 158, 160, 197, 205; Nancy, 16; Richard, 3, 16, 67, 143, 156, 189, 191; Sally, 15, 16, 67.
GAULDING, Alex., 127, 135, 136; Eliz., 127; Lucy, 127; Mary Ann, 127; Nancy, 127, 135, 136; Richard, 127; Wm., 127, 137; Wm. B., 127.
GAY, Ann, 93, 102, 243; James, 259.
GENTRY, Wiatt, 245.
GEORGE, David, 192; Jas., 191; Wm., 191.
GERDAN, William, 208.
GERIDINE, John, 108.
GIBBS, Eliz., 36, 41; Francis, 41, 42; Fortson, 39, 42, 118; Milly, 41, 42; Nancy, 42; Rachel, 42; Thos. F., 42, 129; Wm., 39, 41, 118, 247.
GIBSON, Thomas, 144.
GILBERT, William G., 171.
GILES, Jas., 160, 171; John, 3, 57, 61, 143, 145, 182, 184, 206, 212; John M., 206.
GILL, Eliz., 253; John, 56, 182, 201, 216, 220; Robt., 253.
GILLESPIE, Geo., J., 251; James, 208.
GILLEYLEN, Agness, 157, 175; Jacob, 144, 154, 157, 168, 175, 200, 212; Nancy, 144.
GILLY, Frances, 13.
GILMER, John T., 20; Thos., 216, 220.
GILMORE, Thos. M., 11.
GINN, Jesse, 84, 145, 193, 218, 221, 233, 239, 245, 261, 265; Luke W., 264; Sarah, 260; Silvana, 102; Thos., 252; Transylvania, 252; Wiley, 259; Wm., 252.
GINNINGS, James, 174.
GITLEY, Francis, 59.

GLASS, James, 217.
GLENN, Clement, 23; Edwin, 201, 207; Eliz., 23; Jas., 19, 23, 65, 93, 110; Jane, 46; Joseph, 23, 40, 87, 114, 123, 201, 206, 211; Jos. L., 206; Martha T., 23; Mitchell, 110, 250; Radford, 110; Simeon, 23, 73, 83, 93, 110; Simeon G., 44; Wm., 23, 79, 83, 110.
GLOVER, Anna, 157; Benj., 148, 159; Ellender, 175, 191; Jas., 150; John, 157, 175, 176, 191, 219; Wm., 157, 206, 207.
GODDEN, Samuel, 19.
GOIN, Elisha, 154.
GOING, Thomas, 67.
GOLDEN, Alexander, 250; Matthew, 239.
GOOD, John, 174; John M., 249.
GOODE, Abraham, 90; Edward, 4, 158, 177, 221, 222; Nicholas, 26, 90, 102, 110, 118; Robt., 17; Wm., 17, 61, 154, 174.
GOODS, Edwd., 172.
GOODWIN, William, 180.
GOODWYN, Thomas, 192.
GOOLSEY, Reuben, 23, 135.
GORDEN—GORDAN—GORDON, Alex, 168; Catharine, 175; Chas., 97; Ephraim, 81; Gilbert, 243; John, 29, 37, 47; John L., 18; Neal McD., 29; Wm., 172, 175.
GORE, Lydia, 242.
GORMAN, J., 156, 158, 167, 184; Jean, 175; Jenny, 156; John, 156, 175.
GOSS, Ann, 45, 100; Benj., 23, 157, 206, 208; Betsy, 24; Chas., 23, 153, 197, 203, 206, 207; Eliz., 23, 157, 206; Horatio J., 23, 92, 100, 115, 183; Isham, 23; Jesse, 23; John, 191; John C., 23; Martha, 23; Mary, 23; Matilda, 23; Micha H., 23; Sarah C., 53; Sopha, 23.
deGRAFFENREIDT, Trehamer, 177.
GRAG, Susannah, 251.
GRAGG, Henry, 221; Joannah, 148; Thos., 148.
GRAHAM, David, 226; Nancy, 206; Wm., 165, 206.
GRAIG, Ann, 148; Keziah, 148; Polly, 148; Thos., 148.
GRANSHAW, Maben, 183.
GRANT, Michael, 189.
GRAVES, Humphrey, 157, 173; Thos., 140, 157.
GRAY, Elijah, 37; H., 226; Hezekiah, 23, 57, 87, 193, 199, 223, 226; Jas., 37, 83, 123, 157, 161; Jane, 37; John, 37, 42, 44, 123; Jonathan, 3, 37; Joseph, 37, 236; Mary, 157; Plea-

sant, 78; Sarah, 37; Susannah, 37, 83; Susannah M., 23; Thos., 8; Wm., 36, 37.
GREEN, Burton, 4, 56; Castoe, 247; Robt. H., 44.
GREENSTREET, James, 160, 179, 192; Jean, 192.
GREENWOOD, Beverly, 16, 202, 206, 225, 238; Fleming, 191, 216; Geo., 206, 238; Jas., 16; John, 68, 159, 191, 204, 211, 216; Lucy, 12, 205; Martha, 14; Nancy, 14; Polly, 12; Wm., 12, 84.
GREGG, Ann, 83, 93, 100; Anna, 230; Jonathan, 67; Joanas, 241; Keziah, 83, 93, 100, 230; Polly, 83, 93, 100, 230; Thos., 6, 22, 67, 73, 83, 93, 100, 157, 203, 206, 224, 230, 241.
GRESHAM, J., 152, 155.
GRIFFITH—GRIFFETH, Ann, 206; Jas., 226; John, 59, 61, 83, 93, 145, 206, 207; Martha, 61; Patsy, 62, 145; Peter, 49; Robt., 61, 62, 83, 145, 206; Thos., 144; Wm. L., 83.
GRIFFEN, Margaret, 258; Marshall W., 258; Wm. W., 258.
GRIFFIN, Joseph, 72, 247; Margaret, 247; Winny, 37.
GRIFFIN & MONTAGUE, 92.
GRIMES, Anne, 6; Betsy, 3; Carter, 3; Eliz., 5; Mildred, 3; Mildredge, 143; Patsy, 64; Sarah, 5; Thos., 64; Thos. M., 3, 73, 147, 150; Wm., 3, 62, 64, 73, 139, 140, 143, 145, 147, 150, 158.
GRISSOP, James, 255.
GROSS, Joshua, 225.
GROVE—GROVES, Edward, 204; Jas. A., 21; John J., 48, 49, 118, 122, 127, 131, 134, 139; Joseph, 197; Lemuel, 148; Robt., 228; Samuel, 69, 146, 147, 228; Sarah, 21; Stephen, 173, 202, 221.
GULLY, Eliz., 261; George, 261.
GULLEY, Richard, 241.
GUNN, Elisha, 239.
GUNNELS, John, 10; Joseph, 172; Wm., 157.
GUNNOLDS, Joseph, 157; Marget, 157.
GUNNS, William, 172.
GUNTER, Chas., 32, 72, 82, 226; Jas., 26, 27; Jesse, 45, 118, 127, 134, 136; John, 88, 134; Rebecca, 26, 88; Susan, 45, 118, 127, 134.
GUTHREE, Betsy, 7; Betty, 7; John, 7; Leroy, 7; Molly, 7; Robt., 7; Thos., 7; Wm., 7.
GUTHRIE, Gabriel, 228; Lee, 220; Robt., 220, 222.

GUTTERY, Betsy, 145, 157; Betty, 192; Robt., 157, 184, 192, 199.
GUY, Mary, 206; Wm., 158, 202, 206, 224.
HAGINS, Richard, 245.
HAILEY, Reuben, 241; Thos., 254; Wm., 157, 175, 241, 254.
HAINES, Moses, 57; Stephen, 57, 215.
HAINEY, Bridger, 114; Patsy, 40, 114.
HAIRCROW, Ezekiel, 252; Hugh, 252.
HAIRSTON, Eliz., 141; Robt., 141; Samuel, 78, 88, 141.
HAIRON, Hugh, 172.
HALCOM, Zachariah, 62.
HALE, Jehu, 78, 87, 141; Joseph, 78; Mary, 141; Polly, 78.
HALEY, James, 46, 102, 103; John, 46; Mary, 46, 159; Polly, 39; R., 231; Reuben, 46, 231, 233; Thos., 46; Wm., 46, 134, 149, 159, 169, 185, 230.
HALK, John, 104; Piety, 104.
HALL, Alcy, 72; Blake, 72; Eliz., 50, 136; Henry, 50, 97, 121; Hughy S., 141, 260; Joannah, 138; J., 181; John, 52, 72, 111, 130, 138, 215, 220, 247, 264; Katharine, 256; Leverta, 97; Levita, 121; Lucy M., 51; Mariah, 130; Nathaniel, 225; Robt., 169, 239, 256; Sally, 66; Sarah, 6; Samuel, 247; Seals, 111, 138, 250; Simeon, 111; Tarlton, 68, 94; Tolliver, 66; Thos., 72, 247, 250, 265; Wm., 48, 72, 74, 83, 193, 196, 211, 215, 216, 217, 218, 234, 239.
HALLEY, William, 165.
HAM, Ambrose, 224, 238; Abros, 223; Bartlet, 20, 74; Betsey, 28, 43, 110; Clary, 28; Eliz., 262; Eliz. A., 118; Ezekiel, 16; Gideon, 28, 102, 110; Jas., 28, 102; Jinny, 245; John, 3, 14, 16, 28, 67, 74, 102, 110, 119, 148, 238, 262; Lucinda, 28; Nancy, 16, 28, 111, 119, 262; Reuben, 139, 245, 254; Samuel, 28, 110; Sophia, 28, 102, 110; Stephen 28, 102, 110, 111, 119; Sucky, 28, 110; Theophilus, 262; Wesley, 139; Wm., 28, 29, 110; Willis R., 28, 111, 261.
HAMBLETON, Francis, 57; Isaiah, 216; Luke, 218.
HAMILTON, Bedford, 23; Elisha, 248; Jas., 21, 23, 25, 75, 86; Jane A., 23; Nancy, 23.
HAMMOND, A., 103, 111; Alfred, 103, 133; Ann, 40; D. W., 117; Furney, 259; Job, 59, 103, 111, 235; Lucy, 103, 111; Wm., 103.
HANAY, Thomas, 206.

HANCOCK, P., 195, 196; Thos., 171, 185, 195, 210.
HANDLEY, Drury B. P., 245; Geo., 176, 184; Jarrett, 245.
HANDLIN, Stephen, 175.
HANEY, Thomas, 57.
HANNA—HANNAH, Jas., 67, 153, 156, 216, 218, 223, 226, 244; John, 192.
HANSARD, Brown, 7; Chaney, 7; Gessey, 7; Jane, 42, 239; Janet, 255; Jennett, 7; John, 7, 42, 239; Richard, 170; Susannah, 93, 239; Thos. S., 7, 21, 85, 93, 96, 236, 264; Wm., 7, 143, 144, 153, 169, 239.
HANSFORD, William, 231.
HARBIN, John, 28, 229, 264; Mary, 193; Nancy, 28; Sally, 28, 245; Sarah, 260; Susannah, 28; Thos., 28, 165, 181, 193, 229; Wm., 28, 169, 215, 217, 219, 222, 229, 245.
HARBOUR, Catharine, 158, 177; Esaias, 157, 158, 177, 184, 217; Noah, 158; Talmon, 158, 177; Thos., 157.
HARCROW, Hugh, 243.
HARDEN—HARDIN, Henry, 6, 35; John, 173; Mary, 261; Rhoda, 261; Sarah, 35.
HARDIMAN, Eliz. B., 262; Joel, 262.
HARDMAN, Joel, 52; Middleton C., 52.
HARDY, Jetha, 250; Mary, 249.
HARMAR, Christ., 158, 177; Rebeckah, 177.
HARMON, John, 246, 262; John S., 264.
HARPER, Ann, 28, 177; Averelle, 147; Bedford, 23, 28, 52, 111, 177, 251; Charter, 68, 149, 185; Drucilla, 28, 111, 177; Edmond, 28, 32, 177, 197; Edward, 68, 111, 242; Elender, 28, 177; Eliz., 177; Frederick, 25; Henry, 70, 209, 223, 243; Henry A., 234; Jas., 177; John, 255; John P., 8, 9, 60, 144, 146, 163, 177, 188, 207, 215, 216, 218, 223, 224; J. P., 222; Lucy, 177; Mary, 177; Nancy, 12, 177; Polly, 12, 136; Polly R., 84; Rhoderick, 243; Richard, 41; Sally, 9, 145, 146; Sarah, 9, 177, 242; Thos., 243; Webb, 12; Wm. G., 253; Wm. M., 255; Wm. W., 84, 94; Williamson, 177.
HARR, David, 153.
HARRINGTON, William, 172.
HARRIS, Agnes A., 52; Christopher, 211, 223; Darvin, 68, 198, 224; E. G., 108; Ezekiel, 254; Henry L., 105; Jas., W., 46, 257; Jeptha, 32, 40, 44, 51; Jeptha V., 98, 107, 124, 132, 141, 142, 238; Jesse, 121; Joannah, 230; John, 158, 176, 254, 255; Jonathan, 110; J. V., 66, 87, 140; Mary, 158, 176; Rachel, 52; Rebecca, 256; Robt., 146; Sally, 28; Sarah, 40; Sherwood, 193, 197; S. W., 20, 140; Tryon, 27, 86, 234; Thos., 123.
HARRISON, Barbara C., 33, 34, 106; Chas. 174, 212; Clement K., 33; Henrietta, 34; Matthew R. T., 33, 34, 106.
HART, Frederick, 221.
HARTHORN, James, 194.
HARTSFIELD, Peletiah, 104; Wm., 104.
HARVEY—HARVIE—HARVY, Blasingame,11; Eliz. S., 7; Lucy C., 7; Richard, 6, 153; Wm., 3, 143.
HATCHCOCK, Denton, 68; Harbert, 328; John, 68; Oziah, 238; Wm., 238, 242.
HATHCOCK, Hosey, 137; John, 17, 24; Oziah, 259.
HATCHER, Jas., 69; Priscilla, 15, 207; Robt., 159; W., 187; Wm., 5, 15, 59, 61, 67, 69, 74, 86, 145, 152, 159, 163, 166, 167, 168, 184, 192, 195, 198, 207, 230.
HAWK, Thomas, 103.
HAWSEY, John, 158; Sarah, 158.
HAWTHORN, Eli, 238; Jas., 219; John, 58, 203, 219; Jos., 238; Robt., 192, 202, 203.
HAWTON, John, 205.
HAY, G., 193; William, 193.
HAYES, Jesse, 112.
HAYLEY, Frances G., 29; Jas., 29; William, 231.
HAYNES, Chas. W., 46; Jas., 46, 62; Jas. W., 261; Jane, 46; John M., 264; M., 229; Mary, 62; Moses, 8, 22, 31, 46, 58, 59, 62, 64, 68, 69, 73, 75, 83, 86, 119, 127, 136, 144, 145, 148, 156, 158, 160, 167, 172, 177, 190, 209, 223, 224, 231, 232, 242, 254; Moses G., 254; Moses M., 261; Nancy, 46; Robt., 62; Robt. P., 25; Sarah, 46, 62, 127, 160; Stephen, 46, 59, 62, 144, 242; Thos., 46, 62, 127, 136, 139, 227, 229, 235, 260; Thos. J., 46; Waller, 148; Walter, 62; Wm., 46, 62, 224, 242; Wm. D., 264.
HAYNIE, Anthony, 201, 207; Bridger, 67, 142, 147, 148, 152, 182, 214, 222, 226; Chas., 67, 147, 148; Jemima, 150; Richard, 67, 150; Wm., 67.
HEAD, Benj., 4, 29, 58, 64, 67, 143, 148, 156, 176, 192, 200, 254; Daniel, 192; Eliz., 48, 176; Eliz. J., 4, 144; Jas., 4, 70, 105, 144, 145, 150, 153, 176, 184, 207; Jas. B., 245; John S.,

145; Martha, 4, 38; Peggy, 158; Ritter, 176; Sarah, 262; Simon, 4; Tavnah, 30, 74; Thos., 66, 155, 209; Wm., 74, 83, 142, 143, 154, 158, 170, 176, 191, 192, 193, 207, 241, 249; Wm. C., 262.

HEARD, A., 215; Armstrong, 192, 218; Barnard, 95, 154, 207; Barnard C., 34, 41, 93, 103, 111, 119, 127, 139; Eliz., 93, 103, 207, 251; Geo., W., 90, 102, 112, 257; H., 207; Jenny, 192; Jesse, 207; John, 154, 192, 207; John A., 43, 83, 93, 101, 119, 131, 137, 138, 140; John S., 31; Mary, 119, 127, 139; Sarah H., 93, 103; Stephen, 83, 93, 103, 153, 170, 175, 200, 203, 205, 208, 212, 215, 225, 229; Stephen T., 119; Thos. J., 50, 93, 103, 111, 119, 131, 137.

HEARN—HEARNE, Frances E., 119, 124, 140; Thos., 114, 119, 121, 124, 127, 130, 140.

HEATLEY, James, 151.

HEMPHILL, Andw., 160; Mary, 10; Thos., 161; Wm., 222, 225.

HENDERSON, Amelia, 49, 135; Beverly A., 107, 115, 124; Cinthy, 135; Jas., 239, 255; Jas. B., 41, 99, 107, 115, 119, 251; Jas. N., 49, 130, 135; John, 57, 99, 107, 111, 115, 119, 124, 142, 206, 216, 251; John J., 115, 124, 135; Jos., 57, 82, 142, 239; Jos. W., 107, 115, 124; Martha, 16; Mary A., 99, 107, 115, 124; Nancy, 49; Polly, 41; Richard S., 255; Robt. 216; Sarah E., 49; Sarah W., 99, 107, 111; Simeon, 21, 44, 49, 52, 103, 135, 230, 239, 255; Syntha, 49; Thos. B., 49, 135; Wm., 239; Wm. J., 49, 135.

HENDON, Thos., 243; Wm., 144.

HENDRICK—HENDRICKS, Anna, 74; Abijah, 74, 83, 93, 129, 238, 246; Benj., 202; Brantley, 245, 264; Camnel, 74, 83; Eli, 245, 259; Elias, 74, 187, 206, 207, 229, 238; Elijah, 83, 84, 93; Eliz., 159; Enoch, 83; Frances, 207, 257; Hillery, 159, 230, 233; Isaac, 232; Jas., 83, 245, 264; Jesse, 207, 215, 232, 245, 264; Milam, 245, 263; Nelson, 84, 129; Nimrod, 230; Pattern, 26; Polly S., 129; Rebecca, 26; Russell, 259; Sarah, 238; Siah, 227; Wesley, 259; Whited, 70; Whitehead, 245, 259; Wm., 74, 247.

HENDRY, Alex., 263; Chas., 261; Nancy, 48.

HENLEY, Darby, 118; John, 4, 178.

HENRY, Alex., 233, 260; Benson, 153, 172; Daniel N., 261; Jas. M., 260,

263; Patrick, 176; Sarah, 263; Sarah A., 260; Sarahann, 263.

HERD, Armstrong, 191; John, 191.

HERNDON, Benj., 12, 147; Edward, 12, 83, 147, 239, 255; Geo., 243; Israel, 243; John, 176, 178; Susannah, 12, 147.

HERRIN, Edwd., 187.

HERRING, Jas., 91; James & Co., 96; John, 46, 258; John A., 40; Mary S., 46; Wm. A., 46, 108, 141.

HERRINGTON, John, 159.

HERVEY, Daniel, 186.

HESTERS, Robt., 49, 257.

HICKMAN, Martha, 119, 140, 142, 253; Thos., 253; Thos. S., 120; Waker, 253; Walker, 247; Wm., 253.

HICKS, Anderson, 119; Bishop, 119; David, 13, 246; Frederick, 246; Holeberry, 13; James, 42, 119; Johnson, 50, 90, 265; Josiah, 42; Josiah R., 119; Nancy, 26; Patsy, 90; Samuel, 246; Wm., 263; Wm. B., 42, 119; Willis B., 127.

HIDE, Jesse, 215.

HIDSPETH, Sally, 11.

HIGGASON, Larkin, 183.

HIGGINBOTHAM, A., 64, 103; Anna, 238; Anne, 3; Anny, 20; Aron, 64, 65; Benj., 3, 12, 20, 32 '4, 76, 94, 103, 142, 146, 147, 224, 226, 232, 238; Benj. G., 20, 84, 149; B. G., 97; Caleb, 3, 20, 196; Clary, 65; Dolly, 12; Dorothy, 176; Eliz., 3, 15, 20; Frances, 158; Francis, 3, 12, 74, 142, 147, 149, 158, 214, 227, 238; Gabriel, 191; Geo. G., 97; Jacob, 20, 61, 92, 176, 221, 239, 252; James, 239; Jane, 146; Jeane, 258; John, 149, 239; John S., 38, 64, 65, 67, 74, 84, 103, 105, 146, 232, 239, 263; Joseph, 3, 142, 144, 158, 238; J. S., 227; Larkin, 20, 74, 84, 94, 103, 147; Mary, 12, 20, 74; Peter, 20, 74, 94, 103; Riley, 252; S., 220, 221, 222, 223, 224, 225, 226; Samuel, 7, 64, 67, 103, 144, 146, 153, 177, 180, 201, 217, 224; Sarah, 20, 238; W., 154; Wm., 3, 94, 160, 164, 165, 166, 167, 176, 177, 215, 216, 217, 218, 219, 221, 222, 223, 224, 225, 238.

HIGGINS, Richard, 84.

HIGH, John, 62.

HIGHSMITH, James, 15, 161, 199, 204, 243; John, 37, 51, 253; Milley, 37, 253; Nancy, 37; Thos., 37; Thos. B., 253.

HIGHTOWER, Epaphroditus, 196; John, 159, 195; Sarah, 159; Sterling, 180; Wm., 60, 143, 147, 150, 187, 198, 215, 217, 221, 222, 223, 226, 227, 231.

GENERAL INDEX 321

HILL, Abraham, 62; Ann, 157, 167; Ealum, 253, 259; Eliz., 141; Francis, 78, 88, 141; Jacob, 160, 161, 215, 243; John, 157, 167, 177; Moses, 158, 161, 177; Sarah, 10.
HILLERY, Thos., 151.
HILLRY, Milly, 239; Sarah, 239; Thos., 165, 216, 239, 252.
HILLYER, Shaler, 25, 91, 141.
HILLYRE, Shaler, 13.
HINES, Lucy, 40; Margaret C., 135, 141; Polly, 135; Robt., 26, 109.
HINTON, Jas. L. 111; Jas. S., 254; John L., 255; Peter, 111, 241, 254, 255; Robt., 133, 254; Thos., 256.
HOBBY, Wm. J., 57, 143, 154, 180, 204, 209; Winsley, 213.
HOBSON, Nicholas, 177; Sally, 177.
HODGE, Alex., 8, 145, 157, 188, 191; Catrina, 8; Cynthia, 4; Eliz., 4; Elliott, 3, 207; Francis, 3, 191; James, 4; John, 4, 8, 143, 145, 216; John A., 3; John H., 8; Mary, 4; Nancy, 4; Wm., 3, 8, 60, 143, 172, 182, 191, 196, 207.
HOLBROOK, Fleming, 264; Jesse, 166, 176; Susannah, 176.
HOLLOOM, John, 19.
HOLLIDAY, Jerimah, 62; John, 62; Robt., 62, 65; Tabitha, 67, 143, 148, 191.
HOLLINSHED, Samuel, 185.
HOLLMAN, Geo., 179.
HOLLY, James, 24.
HOLLYDAY, Tabitha, 14.
HOLMES, Ezekiel, 242; Gideon, 62, 160, 161, 177, 242; James, 257; Joshua, 242; Mary, 177; Richard, 177, 242; Shadrack, 242.
HOLT, David, 88; Dr., 64; Wm., 13, 25, 147, 148.
HOOKER, Thos., 187, 226, 242; Wm., 242.
HOPKINS, Elijah, 10; Josiah, 178; Sam'l, 10.
HOOPER, Moses, 62; Thos. 228.
HORTON, Eliz., 39, 245, 260; James, 49, 84, 264; James J., 261; Jeremiah, 113; Jeremiah T., 261; John, 39, 113; Joshua P., 261; Rebecca, 49; Thos., 39, 81, 113, 147, 264; Walker, 126, 245; Wm., 111, 113, 264; Winny, 39.
HOUSE, Brinkley, 67, 148.
HOUSLEY, Frances, 129; Wm., 257.
HOUSTON, Alex. P., 117, 126, 133, 135, 136, 259; Benajah, 36, 42, 46, 49, 109, 117, 136, 140, 141; J., 215; Moses W., 125.

HOWARD, Archer, 8; Benj., 8, 144; Eliz., 207; Francis, 6; James, 8; John, 8, 110, 186; Joseph, 8, 242; Julius, 74, 159, 170, 180, 186, 198, 207; Lucy, 16, 28, 111, 251; Mark, 8; Nehemiah, 160, 167, 242; Nemiah, 8, 144; Sarah, 12; Susannah, 159, 207; Wm., 13.
HOWELL, Abel, 82, 190, 193; Ann, 193; Anna, 82; John, 159; Joseph, 62; Thomas, 193.
HOWINGTON, Wm., 215, 216, 223.
HOWINTON, Wm., 171, 177, 196.
HUBBRAD, Benj., 8, 65, 159; Caty, 159; John, 8, 100, 145, 159, 187, 199, 226; Joseph, 8; Polly, 126; Richard, 8, 9, 11, 15, 16, 17, 24, 26, 71, 74, 145, 148, 159, 187, 190; Sally, 159; Susan, 118, 127, 134; Vincent, 249; Vinson, 116, 117, 127, 136.
HUDDLESTON, Joseph, 175, 176, 201; Patsey, 176, 206; Robt., 159, 175, 176, 186, 206; Sally, 6, 201; Sarah, 176.
HUDSON, Anne, 62; Benj., 26; Bethsheba, 8; Booker, 21, 41; Chas., 31, 144, 146, 166, 168, 169, 177, 193, 250; Christopher, 8, 145, 158; Cuthbert-Cuthberd-Cutbird, 8, 57, 144, 145, 153, 156, 158, 196; Cudt., 59; Daniel, 76; David, 10, 25, 27, 35, 59, 62, 67, 71, 73, 74, 91, 94, 101, 116, 119, 131, 134, 144, 166, 177, 186, 213, 249, 261; David B., 50, 248; David N., 184, 261; Eliz., 8, 158, 251; Eliza, 138; Eliza C., 101, 108, 121, 129; Eliz. A., 134, 261; Frances, 101; Gilliam, 74, 80; Gilliom, 8; Gyllum, 100; Joacim, 8, 145; Joakim, 199; Joakin, 15; John, 103, 119; John H., 112, 248; John R., 124; Joshua, 8; Louisa, 101, 108; Lucy, 50, 91, 250; Martha, 112, 177, 193; Mary, 113, 134, 140; Mary D., 71, 74, 79; Mary L., 261; Molly, 28, 36, 101, 256; N., 16, 146, 223, 224, 227, 228; Nancy, 59, 62, 67, 144; Nathaniel, 8, 9, 11, 36, 59, 62, 67, 74, 82, 94, 101, 103, 108, 119, 121, 129, 138, 144, 146, 158, 184, 185, 207, 223, 224, 225, 227, 228, 231, 232, 256; R. D., 108, 113; Richard D., 140, 250; Susannah, 8; Thos., 8, 79, 90; Virginia, 71, 73, 74, 79; W., 22, 185; Wm., 17, 119, 134, 146, 158, 177, 193, 249.
HUES, James, 31.
HUDSPETH, Sally, 15.
HUFF, Jas., 92; Martha, 43; Mathis 234.
HUGHES, Caty, 31.
HULLUM, Duke W., 25, 32.

GENERAL INDEX

HULMN, John, 30.
HUMBER, John, 241.
HULME, Agnes M., 127; Agnius, 136; Eliz., 70; Henry B., 127, 136; John, 70, 241; John R., 119; John T., 119, 127, 255; Joseph, 255; Jos. R., 127, 140; Margaret, 119, 127, 136, 140; Susanna, 127, 136; Thos. M., 127, 136; Wm., 111, 119, 127, 140, 239; Wm. A., 127, 136.
HUMAN, Alex., 4, 26, 143, 158, 177; Anny, 4; Bazzle-Bazell-Bazdel, 4, 143, 156, 177, 184, 205; Isabel, 4, 177; Rutha, 4; Susanna, 4.
HUNT, Dr. E., 105; Elijah, 28; Fitz. M., 192; Geo., 45, 254; Henry, 49, 180, 192, 194, 254; Hullum, 49; Jas., 28, 30, 49, 137, 161, 233, 243, 252; Jemima, 49; Joel, 125, 255; John S., 255; Joshua, 27; J. R., 229; Mary, 49; Moses, 49, 113, 254; Nancy, 183, 262; Nancy M., 28, 192; Nathaniel, 239; R., 12, 151, 152, 158, 167, 172, 185, 186, 191, 201, 217, 218, 220, 221, 222, 223, 224, 225, 226, 227, 228, 229, 230, 231; Richard O., 49; Richardson, 7, 20, 22, 28, 31, 76, 144, 151, 159, 160, 166, 171, 173, 177, 183, 188, 192, 194, 202, 204, 215, 216, 218, 219, 224, 238, 240, 244; Sion, 49, 120, 137; Tamer, 39, 113; Virginia S., 45; Wm., 49; Wm. H., 28; Willis, 49, 137.
HUNTER, Chas., 105; David, 193; Dr., 157; Samuel, 158, 180, 215, 217.
HUTARSEN, Moses, 253.
HUTCHENS, Zach., 228.
HUTCHERSON, Moses, 116; Nancy J., 116.
HUTCHINGS, Chas., 156, 158; Zachariah, 243.
HUTCHINSON, Joel, 52.
HUTSON, James, 212.
HYSMITH, John, 28.
INGRAHAM, J., 93.
INSHEEP, Geo., 46, 247.
IRBY, Charles, 56.
IRIONS, Cynthis, 27; McKinney, 27, 43, 235.
ISHAMS, Edward, 222.
ISOM, Charles, 175.
JACK, Abner McG., 111; Archabald E., 111; Harriett, 94, 103, 111; Harriet K., 111; Jas., 94, 103; John, 154; Margaret E., 111; Patrick, 27, 94, 103, 111; Patrick C., 111; Samuel, 176, 180; Spencer A., 111; W. H., 94, 103; Wm., 103.
JACK & McGEHEE, 97.
JACKSON, Absolom 171, 173, 176, 178; Robt., 152.

JAMERSON, William, 145.
JAMES, Aaron, 213; Angus, 243; David R., 257; Eliz., 49; Enoch, 227, 238, 243; Jos., 201; Samuel, 18, 243; Thos., 227, 243; Wm., 255.
JAMISON—JAMESON, Wm., 61, 91, 101, 103.
JARRATT, A., 211, 226, 227, 228, 229, 230; Archilus, 211; Jas. D., 42, 44, 247; Martha B., 42; Thos. K., 42.
JARRELL, Arch., 188; Archabald, 242; Elijah, 7; Gibson, 7; Samuel F., 242; Simeon, 7; Wm. F., 242.
JARRETT, A., 74; Archelaus, 20, 29, 40, 42, 65, 71, 74, 84, 87, 89, 192; Archibald, 187; Eliza D., 42; Frances C. M., 89.
JARVIS, William, 147.
JENKINS, E. B., 96; Eliz., 53; Milly, 53.
JENNINGS, Molly, 94; Polly, 12; Robt., 193; Wm., 68, 94, 208.
JETER, Anderson, 42; B., 16, 147, 228; Barnett, 18, 42, 78, 83, 91, 119, 127, 148, 230, 251; Catharine, 127; Caty, 42; Dudley, 42, 127; Jas., 127; Mary E., 127; Nancy, 119; Robt., 42, 119, 127; Samuel, 127; Wm., 127.
JINKENS, Samuel, 241.
JINKS, Polly, 9.
JOHNS, Mary, 172.
JOHNSON, Alex., 9, 253; Andrew, 58, 160, 164, 196; Angus, 9, 75, 146, 187, 234, 243, 252; Archibald, 9, 146, 187, 214, 243; Catharine, 9; Caty, 243; Daniel, 253; Donald, 9; Edmond, 161, 178, 198; Elisha, 178, 179; Eliz., 9; Isaac W. 110; Jas., 244, 250; John, 9, 146, 148, 161, 185, 202, 227, 253; John H., 50, 58, 152, 160, 183, 186, 202, 251; Julius, 257; Lindsey-Lindsay, 253, 258, 263; Littleton, 29, 66, 72, 81, 147, 148; Malcom, 9, 243; Mary, 9, 14, 117; Milly, 53; Nancy, 9, 160; Nathan, 198; Neil, 9, 253; Peter, 9; Philip, 52, 79, 251; Rachel, 243; Sarah, 160; Susan, 251; Thos., 14, 146, 225; Thos., A., 265; Wm., 208.
JOHNSTON, Anquish, 214; Elisha, 69; Eliz. B., 29, 103; Equincy, 77; Geo., 160, 164; J., 22, 228; Jas., 77, 86; Jane, 52; J. M., 61; John, 23, 29, 94, 103, 241, 243; John H., 178, 179; Larkin, 29, 103; Lauchlin, 75; Lindsay, 77, 86; Littleton, 231, 232, 233; Margaret C., 93; Marshall, 77; Martha, 86; Mary, 29, 77, 86, 94, 254; Philip, 84, 94; Polly, 35; Sally, 39; Susannah, 84; Thos., 29, 48, 52,

GENERAL INDEX 323

86, 89, 93, 103; Wm., 29, 37, 52, 77, 86, 94, 103; Yancy, 86.
JONES & JUSKUP, 91.
JONES, Abraham, 159; Abram, 180; A. C., 196; Allen, 68, 204; Amanda, 42; Ann, 42, 43, 120, 128, 140; Aron, 174, 178, 190; Arthur, 16, 50, 68, 73, 74, 80, 84, 85, 91, 94, 101, 103, 104, 128, 201; Asa, 234; B., 173; Capt., 85; Cartna, 178; Charlot, 17, 23; Charlota, 42; Cyrus, 9; Cynthia, 50; Davis, 50, 72, 74, 82, 84, 91, 94, 101, 103; D. H., 47; Drewey N., 261; Edmond, 50, 128, 250; Elijah, 43, 119, 120, 128, 140; Eliz., 160; Eliz. K., 126; Elwylie, 264; Emily, 42; Fanny, 9, 250; Frances, 42, 43, 51, 119, 120, 128, 130; Garland, 43, 128; Geo., 68, 74, 84, 147; Gilly, 201, 207; Harriett, 50; Hiram, 50, 128; Hulday, 17, 23, 42, 92; Isaac, 153, 160, 180; Jas., 42, 43, 62, 68, 79, 84, 115, 120, 128, 133, 138, 147, 196, 206, 207, 241, 244; Jane, 17, 23, 42, 92; Janes, 179; Jemima, 260, 263; Jesse, 6, 9, 68, 74, 94, 104, 128, 152, 162, 169, 176, 178, 188, 199, 249; John, 6, 7, 19, 43, 68, 76, 120, 128, 140, 144, 159, 160, 162, 165, 207, 230; Jordan, 42, 52, 124; Jos. H., 253; Keziah, 128; Lewis, 9, 71, 145; Lewis J., 50; Lewis R., 126; Malinda, 50; Marshall, 43, 120, 128, 251; Martha, 42, 43, 120, 128, 140; Mary, 28, 50, 213; Mary E., 138; Mary M., 53; Mehetebal, 38; Micajah, 244; Nancy, 68, 74, 111; Nathan, 50, 68, 72, 74, 84, 91, 94, 101, 103, 169, 175, 178; Obediah, 7, 10; Patsy, 50; Polly, 68; Rebecca, 253; Reuben, 226; Rhody, 50; Richard, 158; Rn., 232; Robt., 227; Samuel, 250; Sarah, 42, 43, 128, 140, 178; Seaborn, 121; Simeon, 128, 138, 253; Solomon, 17, 24, 97, 121; Sophia, 47; Stanby, 68; Standley, 42, 71, 74, 79, 84, 115, 119, 120, 128, 133, 140, 147; Thos., 6, 9, 17, 23, 43, 68, 71, 74, 91, 119, 120, 128, 140, 144, 196, 201, 207, 211, 257; Thos. W., 42; Wiley W., 17, 24, 42, 120; Wm., 43, 48, 68, 74, 84, 115, 119, 120, 128, 140, 190, 213, 251; Willis B., 130.
JORDAN, Eliz. C., 261; Jas., 25, 229, 234, 261; Jas. B. H., 261; Jas. N., 261; John, 25; Joshua R., 261; Levy H., 261; Littlebury, 261; Matthew, 245; Rachel, 245; Stephen W., 141, 264; Wm., 246.
JORDEN, Absolom, 9, 145; Geo. W., 9; Jas., 238; Joshua, 9, 144; Marget, 9; Mary, 9, 144; Redden, 238; Sarah, 9; Thos., 9.
JORDON, Abner, 228; John, 230; Obedience, 261.
JOSEPH, William, 179.
JOURDAIN, Fountain, 254; Isaac, 254; John, 254;
JOURDAN—JOURDIN, Absolom, 218; John, 160, 162, 176; Over River, 178; Reuben, 177.
JURDEN, Fountain, 241; Jas., 241; John 241; Margaret, 241.
JURDIN—JURDON, Nancy, 37; River, 176, 178.
KAAR, Samuel, 140, 220.
KAIN, Christian, 178; John, 178; Richard, 178, 207, 221, 224; Rosanna, 178, 207; Ruth, 178, 207; Wm., 207.
KANNADY, William M., 238.
KARR, Samuel S., 260.
KEE, Benj., 32.
KEELING, Eliz., 46; L., 119; Leonard, 46; Leonard W., 254; L. Matteson, 46; Marcy, 46; Polly, 46; Susannah, 46; Thos., J., 253.
KEES—KEYS, Cornelius, 242; Jacob, 149; Winny, 193, 208.
KELLETT, Solo., 202; Wm., 202.
KELLY, Barnabas, 260, 264; Barney, 264; John, 261; Sarah, 48; Wm., 254, 264.
KEMP, David V., 249.
KENDRICK, Siah, 229.
KENNEDY, Campbell, 75; Chas., 155, 175, 181, 208; Eliz., 133, 160; Jas. M., 133; John, 224; John A. H., 133; John C., 234; John S., 31; R., 227; Ro., 228, 229, 230, 231, 232; Robt., 28, 69, 75, 81, 86, 145, 146, 160, 220, 228, 229, 232, 234; Sophronia J., 133; Wm. J. C., 133.
KENNY, James, 112.
KERLEY, Samuel, 250.
KERLEN—KERLIN, Daniel, 141; David, 40, 128, 134, 136; Eliz., 95, 104, 244, 249; Jacob, 94, 95, 104, 128, 134, 141, 258; Jas., 94, 95, 104, 128, 134, 136, 141; Lucy, 95, 104; Mildred, 94; Peter, 94; Samuel, 126, 128, 136, 244; Wm., 29, 81, 94, 104, 141, 250.
KERR, Charity, 208; Samuel, 208.
KERSEY, Stephen, 160.
KETTLER, John, 239.
KEY, Chiles T., 23; Geo., 52; Mourning C., 7; Terrell, 18; Thos. J., 249; Wm. B., 18, 153, 159, 249.
KEY—KEES, John, 170, 193, 208; John D., 251; Thos., 41, 165, 209.

KIDD, Eliz., 193, 207, 208; Frances, 74; Francis, 68; Jas., 9, 168, 171, 187, 193, 199, 201, 207, 208; Jas. H., 146, 208; J. H., 146; John, 12, 94, 147; John W., 68, 74, 84; Martain, 12, 68, 74, 84, 94, 147, 242; Webb, 2, 12, 68, 74, 84, 94, 142, 147, 184, 208; Wm., 12, 74, 84, 94, 147, 213.
KILGORE, William, 202.
KINCADE, Hugh, 142.
KING, Ambrose B., 246; Anne, 50; Benj.; 154; Catharine, 243; Elisha, 75, 84; Eliz., 178; Ezekiel, 196; Francis W., 258; Hugh, 180; Jacob W., 247; Jas., 42, 244, 263; John, 56, 154, 158, 161, 174, 243, 246; Joseph, 58, 196; Lembird, 183; Samuel, 171, 173; Thos., 133, 177, 178, 181, 241, 255; Wm., 29, 50, 75, 84, 238, 247, 257, 262; Zenriah, 133; Zuriah, 255.
KINKADE, Hugh, 57.
KINNEBREW, Edwin, 250; Henry, 80, 88.
KISER, Sarah, 35.
KLUGH, Martha, 105; Martha M., 122; Paschal D., 122, 136.
KNIGHT, Cullen C., 117.
KNOTT, Thomas, 120.
LAGRAND, William, 245.
LAMAR, Basil, 160, 162, 179, 180, 185, 186, 208; Mary, 160, 179; Peter, 119, 127; Z., 160; Col. Z., 33.
LAMBETH, John, 159.
LANCASTER, Eliz., 15.
LAND, Isaac, 62, 172, 177.
LANDERS, Jas. O., 39, 256; Tyree, 65, 234; Wm., 39.
LANE, John, 46; John A., 46, 47, 128, 250; Thos., 46, 128; Wm., 22.
LANGDON, John, Jr., 66.
LANIER, Sampson, 174.
LARGENT, Jesse, 245.
LANKESTER, William, 5.
LAWLESS, John, 238.
LAWLIS, Betsy, 77; Catharine, 127; Eliz., 97; Jas., 127; John, 77, 97; Tabitha, 77, 97.
LAWREMORE, Alex., 238; Andrew, 134, 141; Anna, 238; Jas., 238; Nicholas, 238; Sally, 238; Samuel, 238; Sarah, 238.
LAWSON, Ann, 145; David, 145; Henry, 64, 145, 146; Jas., 145, 149; Jonas, 64, 146; Robt., 64.
LEACH, William, 157.
LEAR, Jonathan, 58.
LEATREM, John, 10.
LEDBETTER, Drury, 4.
LEEPER—LEPER, Allen, 63, 207; Jas., 60, 194, 203, 219.

LEGETT, John, 160.
LEGRAND, Jesse, 245; John N., 138, 245, 259.
LEITH, John, 196.
LENORE, William W., 9.
LESUER, Drury, 149; Drewry M., 95, 104; John O., 95, 104; Mede, 244; Samuel, 45, 104, 244.
LEWIS, Ellender, 37; Hester, 133; Jeptha, 37, 251; Jeremiah, 33; John, 37, 133; John W., 133; Mary M., 133; Phillip, 37, 167, 179; Sarah, 37, 179; Thos., 37; Thos. W., 133.
LINDSAY, Jacob, 76; Nancy C., 20; R., 222, 227, 228, 229; Reuben, 20, 75, 222, 227; Rm., 3; Rn., 211; Wm. A., 40.
LINES, Joseph, 260.
LIONS, John, 239.
LITTALS, James, 15.
LITTLE, Isaac, 161; Isabell, 160; Jas., 15, 160, 203, 217, 220; J. H., 199; John, 200; Reuben, 229; Wm., 161.
LIVELY, Charles, 241.
LOCKHART—LOCKHARD, John, 207, 241, 254.
LOFTON, Eli, 100; Jas., 49, 115, 118, 120, 121, 130, 257.
LONG, Evans, 154; Jas., 17, 75; Joseph, 17, 75, 179, 212, 216, 218, 219; Nicholas, 158, 193, 221; Nimrod, 215; Rebeccah, 193; Samuel, 17, 196; Sarah, 17, 22, 179.
LOVELADY, Jane, 160, 208; Thos., 157, 161, 196, 204, 208, 209, 216, 218, 219, 222.
LOVELL, Gabrile, 241; John, 160, 161; Wm., 153.
LOVEMAN, Robert, 156.
LOVENGOOD, Harmon, 242; Polly, 242.
LOVINGOOD, Ann, 62, 145; Harmon, 62, 64, 81, 88, 125, 145, 212; Patsy, 81; Samuel, 62, 253.
LOURIMORE, Rob., 67; Samuel, 234.
LOWREMORE, Andrew, 128; Sarah, 43, 50.
LOWREYMORE, Sarah, 262.
LOWRIMORE, Anne, 50; Sally, 50; Samuel, 261.
LOWRYMORE, Robert, 226.
LOWREY-LOWRY-LOWERY, Caty, 42; Edmond, 23, 170, 200, 208; Jas., 183, 185, 208; John, 183, 208, 218; Mary, 208; Mashack, 183, 208; Wm., 179, 208, 214, 217.
LUCKIE, Hez., 164; Jane, 179; John, 179, 181; Wm. F., 179.
LUMPKIN, Ann, 160; Geo., 62, 160, 167, 179, 193; John, 179; Jos. H., 117.

GENERAL INDEX

LUNSFORD, Addie, 50; Geo., 50, 235; Jas., 50, 128, 137, 139, 142; Katy, 50; Patsy, 50; Peggy, 50; Polly R., 50; Rachel M., 50; Rolle, 50; Rollin, 262; Rowland, 264; Wm., 39, 50, 111, 113, 138, 140, 208, 252.
LYMON, Elihu, 209.
LYON, Edmond, 213; Edward, 68, 85, 95, 96, 104, 177; Eliz., 95, 104; Henry, 95, 104; John, 95, 263; Mary C., 104; Nancy, 95, 104; Nathan, 95; Nathaniel, 104; Thos., 251.
McALPIN, Ann, 145; Mary, 241; Patsy, 145; Robt., 209; Solomon, 56, 145, 158.
McCALL, T., 174; Thos., 185.
McCANN, John, 218.
McCARTY, Daniel, 208.
McCELLEY, Hugh, 195.
McCLEARY-McCLARY, John, 188, 206, 224; Reuben, 188; Robt., 58, 142.
McCLESKEY-McCLUSKEY, David, 161, 174, 179, 208, 214, 217; Isabella, 187, 208; J., 221; Jas., 58, 142, 151, 164, 174, 187, 194, 208, 216, 218, 219, 220; Mary, 161, 179, 208.
McCOMBS, John, 201.
McCOMMACK, John, 245.
McCOMMON, James, 3.
McCORMICK, John, 231.
McCONNELL, Alex., 178; Jas., 161; John, 161, 165, 174, 184, 220; Joshua, 204, 221, 223; Jos., 220; Manuel, 57; Newell, 224.
McCOY, Nancy, 246; Reuben, 238; Wm., 77, 227, 238, 246.
McCREDY, Robt., 216; Silas, 216.
McCREIGHT, Robert, 17.
McCUNE, Alex., 148; Jas., 68, 148; Jas. A., 30; Jane, 241; Jean, 241; John M., 30; Margaret, 148; Mary, 241; Peggy, 68, 148; Polly B., 148; Samuel, 64; Thos., 148, 241; Thos. B., 68, 84, 233; Washington, 148; Wm., 64, 68, 84, 148, 153, 158, 174, 215, 241; Wm. S., 84.
McCURDY, D., 60; David, 8, 58, 60, 144; Geo., 128; Jas., 4, 18, 60, 144, 176; John, 8, 58, 60, 69, 144, 146, 147, 173, 202, 231.
McCURLEY, Moses, 252.
McCURRY, Anguish, 228; Angus, 29, 47, 75, 104, 243, 253; Benj. C., 120, 129, 139; Daniel, 243; Dan'l. N. 120, 129, 139; Edmond S., 139; Flora, 29, 243; Flora M., 120, 139; Gardner M., 139; John, 47, 75, 243, 253; Kathrine, 252; L., 147; Lauchlin, 39, 75, 95, 111, 113, 120, 129, 139, 252; Lyon H., 139; Martha B., 129, 139; Nancy, 75, 95; Neal McDougal, 29; Patsy B., 120.
McCUTCHEON, Wm., 3, 182.
McDONALD, Alex, 233; Allan, 179; Angus, 37, 254; Chas., 212; Daniel, 37; Donald, 75, 158, 180, 214, 243, 254; Eliz., 161; Flora, 37; H., 197, 200, 203, 227, 228, 229; Helen, 161, 179, 180, 208; Hugh, 37, 92, 144, 147, 152, 159, 161, 179, 180, 183, 194, 208, 209, 214, 219, 222, 223, 224, 225, 227, 228, 233; James, 159, 161, 171, 180, 217; John, 29, 37, 75, 95, 154, 160, 242, 243, 253; John Lauchlin, 37; Margaret, 29, 37, 253; Mary, 29; Nancy, 29, 37; Patrick, 161, 172, 175, 202; Roderick, 37, 75, 243; Ronnald, 243; Sarah, 180.
McDOUGALL, Alex, 208; Eliz., 208; Neal, 29.
McDOWELL, Dan'l., 107, 138; David, 93, 98; John, 164, 216; Robt., 172, 177, 199.
McEVER, McEAVER, Andrew, 63, 155, 168, 174, 224, 226; John, 189.
McEAVERT, Andrew, 167.
McELHANEN, McALHENAN, John, 179, 181.
McELROY, Avington-Evington, 179, 180; Chas., 104; Edward, 84; Henry, 75, 84, 104; James, 75, 84, 104; John, 84, 193; Pellatia, 84, 104; Polly, 84; Sarah, 179, 180.
McENY, John, 59.
McFARLIN, Robt., 216.
McFERRON, Wm., 259.
McGAHEE, Samuel, 184.
McGARITY, Archabald, 264; Delilah, 260; Gardner, 126; John, 264; Kindred, 260; Sarah, 260; Willson, 254.
McGARRITA, Gardner, 242.
McGARRY, E., 217, 226; Elward, 161, 174, 178, 180, 215, 226; Jeanett, 180.
McGEE, Allen, 50; Ansel, 50; Jane B., 50; Jesse, 50; John, 50; Jonathan, 50; Mary H., 50; Nancy, 50; Rachel, 50; Sarah, 50; Wm., 261.
McGEHEE, Abner, 21, 89, 97; Abraham, 233; Hugh, 43; Samuel, 7, 43, 63, 82, 149, Thos. G., 250.
McGHEE, Nancy, 11; Richard, 11.
McGOWAN-McGOWEN, Elijah, 95; Hannah, 209; J., 7; James, 188; John, 95, 165, 200, 209.
McGOWING, John, 241.
McGOWN, John, 215.
McGRATH, Robt. & Co., 37; Robt., 37, 38.
McGUIRE, Allegany, 65, 146, 218, 219, 221, 241; Anderson, 130, 241, 255;

GENERAL INDEX

Eliz., 130; Frances, 36, 39; Thompson, 113, 158, 218, 219, 222; Thos. M., 253; Wm., 243, 244.
McHENRY, Nancy, 98; Thos., 98.
McKEE, John, 209; Mary, 209.
McKEEN, Wm., 161.
McKENZIE, John, 157, 171, 216; Wm., 56, 158.
McKIE, Wm., 226.
McKLEROY, Jacob, 13.
McLAUCHLIN, D. E., 102; Duncan C., 121.
McLEAN, Lewis, 213.
McLEOD, M., 105; Murdock, 121.
McLESTER, Horatio, 257.
McMARTIN, Duncan, 86, 95, 104, 242.
McMILLIAN, Jon., 5.
McMORRIS, Alex., 79.
McMULLEN, McMULLAN, McMULLIN, Archabald, 67; Daniel, 30, 129, 252; Eliza, 30; Eliz., 30, 129; Fielding, 30; Frances, 129; James, 30; Jeremiah, 30; John, 14, 30, 224, 242; Joice, 129; Jones, 18, 101; Levina, 30; Lewis, 30, 128; Nail, 30; Neal, 242; Patrick, 30, 129, 229, 233, 235, 243; Sally, 41; Sinclair, 30, 128; Thos., 30, 129; Willis, 254.
McNEEL, John, 3.
McNEIL, James, 181; John, 180.
McRIGHT, Matthew, 221.
MABRY, Thos. W., 255, 258.
MACGEE, John, 253.
MACGEHEE, Jesse, 253; Jonathan, 253.
MACHEL, John, 196.
MACKEY, John, 58.
MACKIE, John, 9, 10, 144, 149, 200; Rosannah, 9; Samuel, 9, 10, 144, 161; Thos., 9, 144, 161; Wm., 9, 149.
MACNEILL, John, 182.
MADDOX, Betsy, 7; Daniel, 7.
MAGARY, Robt., 160.
MAGEE, Ansell, 243; Lewis, 240; Wm., 240.
MAINS, Robt., 206.
MALEY, John, 128, 136; Johnson, 53, 128, 136; Sidney, 128, 136.
MALLARY, John, 25.
MANN, Asa, 29, 33, 53, 95; Asa V., 47; Ester, 37; Henry, 25, 29, 46, 95; James, 29, 37, 95, 209, 222; James W., 246; Jeremiah, 29, 95; Jesse, 29, 225; Joel, 29, 97; John, 29, 85, 94; John B., 262; John R., 265; Judith, 29, 95, 256; Nancy, 53; Robt. B., 260; Sally, 46; Stephen A., 43; Thos., 256; Wm., 246; Wm. H., 246.
MANNEN, Wm., 44.
MANNING, James, 202.

MARBURY, Horatio, 173, 176, 180, 181, 209.
MARKS, James, 4, 142; Nicholas, 29, 87.
MARSH, Minor, 186.
MARSHALL, Eliz., 6.
MARTAIN, Robt., 59.
MARTEN, Robt., 215.
MARTIN, Archabald, 162; Barkley, 162; Beverly, 93, 98, 251; David, 152, 176, 183; Eliza, 162; Eliz., 162; Geo., 152, 162, 201; Henry, 249; Hugh, 78, 88; James, 194; John, 162, 207, 209, 238; Lewis, 104; Lucy, 141; Luther Henry, 52; Murdock, 161; Nathaniel, 249; Peggy, 141; Peter, 162, 218; Rebecca, 249; Robt., 143, 154, 162, 168, 194, 218.
MASON, Andy, 260; Ann, 129; Eliz., 260; Evelina, 260; Jane A., 260; John, 129, 223; Joseph P., 247; Joshua, 260; Kitty, 260; Lucinda, 260; Polly, 260; Wm. J., 260.
MATHIS, Wm., 178.
MATKIN, MADKIN, Daniel, 155, 165; James, 155, 209.
MATLOCK, J., 215; James, 162.
MATTHEWS, Geo., 190, 192, 208; John, 155, 180; Nancy, 165.
MAUPIN, Jesse, 249.
MAXWELL, Audley, 168, 180; James, 218, 221; Jesey, 252; Joel, 80, 240; John, 92, 153, 222, 227, 252; Martin, 252; Reuben, 256; Simon, 247; Thos., 199, 218, 219, 221, 222, 223, 230, 240, 252; Wm., 252; Wm. T., 260, 264.
MAYES, Thos., 185, 196.
MEADOWS, Isaac, 163, 167; Mary, 163.
MEANES, Hugh, 241; Wm., 241.
MEANS, Alex, 262; Betsy, 30; Elij., 30, 181, 254; Fanny, 30; Jacob, 30, 254; James, 177, 218; John Seal, 30; Nancy, 30; Patsy Morgan, 30; Robt., 178, 181; Rossy Colbert, 30; Sally, 30; Samuel, 30; Wm., 30, 178, 181, 225, 228, 254.
MECUNE, Wm., 180.
MEDLOCK, James, 175.
MEGARITY, Abner, 242; Kindred, 240, 245.
MEGREDY, Robt., 4; Silas, 4.
MENEFEE, Geo., 180, 183.
MENNEFEE, Nathaniel, 13.
MEREDITH, Francis S., 8; James, 4, 75, 142, 165; Molly, 4; Nancy, 4; Patty, 4; Sally, 4; Sarah, 4, 142.
MERET, Towan, 240.
MERIWETHER, Milly T., 120.
MERRELL, Joshua, 94; Joshua & Co., 92.

MERRETT, MERRITT, Benj., 157, 163; John, 141, 245, 261, 264; Mary, 163; Tom, 232; Torren, 245, 264.
METZLER, Sophia E., 120.
NEWBOURN, Archibald, 89, 95, 111; Thos., 252.
MICOU, Wm., 17.
MIDDLETON, Betsy, 100, 104; Betcy C., 85, 95; Eliz., 15, 162; James L., 90, 95, 100, 104, 108, 115; John, 95, 104; Nancy P., 90, 95, 100, 104, 108; R., 63; Ro., 18; Robt., 84, 95, 100, 104, 108, 115, 142, 146, 147, 155, 159, 162, 176, 177, 180, 181, 194, 215, 218, 219, 223, 228, 231, 250; Samuel, 95.
MILES, Thos., 263.
MILLER, Carter, 190; Eliz., 134; Eliz. C., 128; James, 188; Jedidah, 248; Jedidah H., 134; Jedidah S., 128; Joel, 219, 222; John, 58; Mary Ann, 147; Peter, 154; Miller & Hanks, 91; Miller & Hawks, 93.
MILLICAN, Andrew, 174, 181, 224; John, 67, 148, 181, 202.
MILLIGAN, A., 67.
MILLIRONS, Christopher, 183.
MILLOR, John, 143.
MILLS, James, 30, 75; Moses, 252; Nancy, 30; Wm., 48.
MITCHELL, Eliz., 242; Emily, 136; Isaac, 68, 242; Jane, 170; John, 242; Patrick, 62, 68, 160, 161, 212, 242; Wm., 62, 242.
MOBLEY, Allen, 201; Frances, 82, 259; Francis, 249; Isaac, 82, 249, 258; John, 154, 182; Martin D., 258; Stephen, 201; Wm., 6, 188, 201, 248.
MOLDING, Thos., 251.
MONACK, John, 58, 144; Mary, 58, 144.
MONDAY, Chas., 110.
MONTAGUE, Susan G., 259.
MONTGOMERY, John, 149, 200.
MOODY, John, 62.
MOON, A., 75, 85; Anna, 38; Archelaus, 20, 76, 79, 85, 96; B., 75, 85; Boller, 20; Eliz., 19, 125, 249; Gabrilla, 30, 260; J., 207; Jacob, 20, 85, 105; James B., 30, 259; Jesse 20, 76, 249; John, 20, 85, 244, 263; John B., 260; John P., 30; Pleasant, 20, 30, 230, 259, 260; Polly, 19; Robt., 20, 62, 64, 76, 149, 158, 228; Sally, 76; Sarah, 19, 20, 30, 76, 85, 125, 245, 263; Stephen, 76, 244; Tabitha, 88, 105; Wm., 20, 75, 85, 207; Wm. H., 19, 20, 30, 72, 76, 84, 85, 125, 207, 249, 265.
MOONEY, Christopher, 189, 218.
MOONY, Wm. H., 45.

MOOR, John, 242; Nancy, 242.
MOORE, Davis, 209; Elijah, 33; Francis, 59; Jamima, 37; Jesse, 231; John, 179, 194, 209; John N., 259; Joseph, 167, 194; Robt., 66, 72; Sarah, 33, 66, 72; Thos., 263; Wm., 4, 40, 114, 145, 163, 197, 203, 244.
MORE, Lizzie, 96; Mary, 37; Martha, 37; Wm., 142; Wm. J., 259.
MORGAN, Andrew, 256; Eliz., 30, 31; Isham, 27, 30, 31, 85, 96, 104, 143, 168, 235; Isom, 225; John, 30; Samuel, 193, 218, Sarah, 30; Silus, 30; Stephen, 30, 31, 87; Thos., 30; Wm. C., 30.
MORRIS, Burrell, 220; Burwell, 219; Isaac, 58, 143, 194, 222; James, 58, 143, 194, 199; John, 155, 168, 174, 178, 180, 211; Milly, 53; Sally, 58, 143, 194; Sherod, 58, 80, 224, 226, 258.
MORRISON, Clary, 64, 65; Ezra, 64; Frances, 64, 65; Francis, 64, 65; James, 3, 17, 24, 32, 71, 72, 73, 82, 85, 91, 94, 95, 96, 101, 103, 104, 111, 112, 120, 149, 182, 198; John, 68; Joseph H., 65, 179, 190; N., 9; Peter, 240; Polly D., 64, 65; Thos., 111, 112, 120; Vilet, 190; W., 95; Washington, 44, 47, 64.
MORSE, John J., 162, Sam'l., 162.
MOSELY—MOSELEY, Benj., 10, 146, 194; Eliz., 22; Elijah, 19; Geo., 180; Henry, 10, 160, 162, 163, 173, 180, 185, 194, 201; Lewis, 10, 86, 194, 226; Mary, 10, 162; Polly, 180, 194; Robt., 160, 162, 163, 180, 185, 212; Sarah, 163, 180; Wm., 104.
MOSES, Joseph, 193.
MOSS, Abraham, 83; Beverly, 128, 137; Ephraim, 12, 82, 224, 236, 240; Jos., 205; Lucresy B., 137; Wm., 22, 51, 58, 143, 164, 170, 174, 183, 194, 196, 203, 218, 220.
MOULDER, Daniel, 214.
MOUNGER, Henry, 165.
MOUSON, Jean, 166.
MUCKLEROY, Andrew, 146; Edward, 19; Henary, 193; Wm., 193.
MULLINS, Susannah, 27.
MUNDY, Israel D., 146.
MURDOCK, Patrick, 218, 219.
MURPHY, James, 19; Sarah, 35.
MURRAH, John, 206, 240; Nancy, 240; Tabitha, 240.
MURRY, Nancy, 252.
MUSE, James W., 149.
MYERS, Daniel, 31; Donel, 31; Eurazemes, 31; Jacob, 217; Patsy, 31; Rachel, 31; Wm., 31.

NAIL, Benj., 30, 140, 142, 226, 242; J., 217; Julian, 39, 163, 222, 240; Mary, 163.
NAILER, James, 157.
NAISH, Frances, 248, 249 Jeremiah, 76, 245.
NAPIER, Cloe, 17; Dorothy, 17, 68, 96; Mary C. D., 96; Rene, 17, 68, 85, 96; Tabby, 2; Theo., 17; Thos., 2, 56, 60, 76, 143, 146, 148, 176, 194, 201; Walker, 143, 194.
NASH, Henry, 146; Henry C., 50; James, 26, 235; Polly, 50; Thos., 50.
NEAL, Benj., 30, 119, 209; Chriswell, 254; Eliz., 209; John, 161; Jos., 69, 227; Julian, 209; Linsey, 120, 253; Robt., 185, 194.
NEIL, Daniel, 221.
NELLEMS, Wm., 85.
NELLUM, Jesse, 259, 263.
NELMS—NELMES, Ann, 240, Anna, 12; Anna Dillard, 15; D., 219; David, 209, 218; James, 255; Jesse, 263; John, 185, 215, 219; Jonathan, 245; Joshua B., 252; Jurden, 240; Nathaniel, 85, 96; Penelepy, 240; Polley, 85, 240; Unity, 209; Wiley, 264; Wm., 96, 240, 245, 251, 26), 263.
NELSON, Daniel, 217; Major, 165; Martha, 181, 194; Matthew, 181; S., 220; Samuel, 59, 180, 181, 194, 199, 220; Wm. A., 52.
NEWBERRY, Nancy, 256.
NEWBOURN—NEWBORN, Archibald, 81, 229, 230, 232, 240.
NEWMAN, Archibald, 227; John, 58, 143, 180, 198.
NEWTON, Josiah, 13.
NICHOLSON, Right, 216.
NICKOLS, John, 80, 102.
NICKS, Joseph, 265.
NIX Edward 244; Eliz., 27; Geo., 120; James, 116, 120, 126; John, 126, 229, 251; Jos., 120, 126, 228, 229, 230, 240; Lucy, 120, 126, 240, 245; Samuel, 245; Sarah, 126; Thos., 229, 232.
NOBLE, Alex, 78.
NOLAN, Wm., 235.
NORMAN, Argal, 9i; John, 226.
NORRIS, Anny, 12; Diana, 12; Eliz., 12; Evins, 12; James, 12, 14, 68, 76, 146, 208, 240; Jane, 181; John, 5; Robt. Y., 68; Roy, 208; Royal Young, 12; Samuel, 12; Sarah, 12, 68, 76; Wm., 181.
NORTHEN, John, 263.
NORTHINGTON, Eliz., 8.
NORWOOD, Eliz., 39; Permelia, 39.
NUNNELEE, Eliz., 163; James, 15; Jas. F., 12, 15, 31, 41, 43, 148, 154, 160, 163, 228, 229, 230, 234, 250; John 43; Keziah, 163; Susannah, 8; W., 202, 228, 229, 230, 231; Wallis, 148; Walter, 15, 146, 155, 193, 230; Watt, 63; Watters, 184, 197; Wm., 15, 25; Wm. W., 148, 163.
ODAM, David, 19; Jacob, 146, 147, 148, 149, 160.
OFFUTT, E., 190; Wm. J., 209.
OGLESBY, Adkins, 258; Drewry, 263; Drury, 32; Geo., 16, 77, 92; Geriah G., 106; James, 258; Leroy, 234; Lindsay—Lindsey, 121, 244; Martha, 14; Nancy, 32; Robt. C., 106, 264; Thos., 14, 89, 204, 263; Wm., 45, 77, 263.
OLIVE, James, 39, 138.
OLIVER, Anthony, 59; Barbara, 10, 196; Berrien, 249; Caleb, 43, 58, 143, 197, 213, 251; Dionysius, 135, 149, 159, 163, 164, 181, 182, 185, 195, 196, 197, 205, 210; Dyonecious, 238; Elinor, 181, 195, 210; Eliz., 182; Fanny, 195; Francis, 181; Jackson, 117, 134, 140, 265; James, 30, 37, 87, 120, 149, 163, 182, 195, 199, 210, 244, 258; Jane, 262; John, 31, 96, 98, 106, 111, 149, 163, 168, 181, 182, 190, 195, 197, 205, 210, 259; Lucy, 7; McCarty, 17, 27, 73, 88, 117, 195, 196, 210; Malinda, 94; Matilda, 76; Maria, 76; Martha B., 124, 140; Mary, 7; Mary Ann, 76, 94, 163, 181, 182, 195, 196, 210; Milly, 34; Nancy, 43, 213, 251; Peter, 17, 73, 163, 182, 195, 196, 210, 249; Polly, 182; Richard, 37; Samuel (Dr.), 101; S. C., 116; Shelton, 124, 263; Simeon, 34, 107, 115, 120, 129, 235, 259, 263; Susan, 96; Susannah, 7, 31; Thos., 24, 32, 76, 91, 98, 102, 129, 135, 149, 159, 163, 164, 178, 196, 199, 205, 210, 211, 224, 237, 238, 247, 258; Wm., 15, 59, 68, 76, 94, 148, 159, 163, 171, 182, 185, 195, 200, 201, 220, 221, 222, 225; Winston, 49.
ORMOND, Giles M., 141; James, 141; Peggy, 141.
ORR, Daniel, 61, 64, 144, 182, 203; Robt., 149.
OWENS, Barashaba, 251; Clement, 192, 199, 211; Elijah, 8, 144, 160, 167, 179, 192, 211, 226; Elisha, 8; James, 251; John, 154, 251; Nancy, 8; Patsy, 18; Ralph, 8, 192, 199, 211; Thos., 12.
OZLEY, Jesse, 42, 50.
PACE, Agnes, 164, 182; B., 176, 204, 229; Barnabas, 11, 50, 51, 63, 70, 74, 135, 146, 156, 164, 178, 182, 185, 222; Bazil, 51; Dreadzil—Dredzil, 51, 135,

263; James, 228; Leroy, 199, 204, 223; Mary, 11, 50; Noel, 51; Paris, 51; Thos., 15, 50.
PAGE, Berry, 23; James B., 259 John, 138; John S., 260; Laval, 264; Level, 234; Levil, 238; Wadson D., 264; Wm., 70, 79, 138, 229, 243, 245.
PAIN, B., 178.
PALMER, John, 217.
PALMARE, Catharine, 262.
PANNILL, J., 179.
PARHAM, Cannon, 13; Dickson, 13, 26; Francis, 13; Geo. W., 258; Harrison, 265; Isham, 80, 147, 258, 263; Isom, 13, John, 13, 147, 258; Lucy, 13; Mary, 13; Mildred, 13; Sarah, 244; Southern, 244; Thos., 13.
PARK, Abriam, 148; Chas., 148; John, 148; Mary, 254; Theophilus, 148.
PARKER, Benj., 245; Dan'l, 170, 204, 226; John, 204; Jos., 139, 235, 264; Jos. H., 261; Wm. H., 264.
PARKS, Abraham, 15, 231, 243; Chas., 15, 215; John, 15; Marshall, 15; Mary, 15, 242; Theopeles, 15.
PARNALL, John, 208.
PARNELL, Cyrus, 10; Daniel, 10; Eliz., 10; James, 10; Jesse, 10; John, 10, 146; Samuel, 10; Sarah, 10, 146.
PARROTT, Ledford, 207, 217; Wm. S., 37.
PATEN, Margarette, 238; Mary, 238.
PATTEN, Catherine, 20; James, 63, 145, 204; Margaret, 20; Polly, 20; Samuel, 10, 12, 20, 75, 76, 145; Wm., 20.
PATTERSON, Alex, 17, 201, 241; Anna, 39; Eliza, 112; Eliz., 36; Elza, 137; Elzy, 104; Emily E., 118; Geo., 17; James, 17, 241; Jesse, 31, 92; John, 17, 31, 85, 155, 160, 163, 171, 221, 224, 240, 241; Jonathan, 186; Joseph, 17, 241; Margaret, 17; Nimrod, 31; Rebecca, 31, 245; Robt., 17; Samuel, 17, 140; Thos., 17, 171; Wiley, 129, 134, 255; Wm., 31, 42, 85,. 112, 137, 149, 164, 183; Wm. B., 17.
PATTON, James, 211, 215; Samuel, 221, 228, 230; Thos., 181; Wm., 180.
PAXTON, John, 68; Lemuel, 148; Samuel, 32, 76, 148, 225, 228.
PAYNE, Jonathan, 229.
PAYTON, Geo., 259, 263; John, 260, 263; Moses, 263; Wm., 164, 221, 260, 263.
PEALER, Abner, 233, 241.
PEARCE, Jacob, 260.
PEARPOINT, Charity, 4; Larkin, 4, 144.
PEARSON, Enoch, 65; James, 176.

PECK, Abel, 260; Eliz., 260; Solomon, 260; Stephen, 260; Winny, 260.
PEDEGREW, Matthew, 62.
PEEK, John C., 164.
PEELER, Abner, 246; Benj., 246; Cader, 260, 264.
PEEN, Abner J., 129; A. J., 129; Benj., 111, 120, 129, 149, 238, 246; Eliz., 43; Eliz. R., 238; Fanny, 43, 238; Frances, 260; Francis, 20; John, 43, 189, 235, 260, 265; Lewcy, 238; Lucinda, 260; Mary, 43, 259; Philip, 182, 238, 245; Sally, 238; Sarah, 43; Sinda, 43; Thos., 65, 81, 158, 172, 219, 238; Wm., 238, 246, 262; Wilson, 20; Winny, 43.
PENNINGTON, Abel, 152.
PERCEL, Ignatius, 83.
PERKINS, Joshua, 210; Wm., 225.
PERRIN, John, 249.
PERRY, James, 202; Thos., 61, 155, 168, 190.
PERRYMAN, Albert G., 257; Anthony A., 257; Wm. J., 251.
PETTIGREW, Geo., 164, 196, 203.
PEW, Isaac, 210.
PHAIR, Jonathan, 212.
PHARR, Francis, 13; Jonathan, 13.
PHELPS, Anna, 15; James, 258, 263; Johnson, 262; Thos., 105, 259, 263; Wm., 12, 16, 189.
PHILIPS, Geo., 141; Dr. Geo., 76; Henry K., 139; James, 139; Martha, 10; Wiley, 260; Wm., 139, 186.
PHILPOT, Warren, 215.
PHINIZY, F., 222; Ferdinand, 212.
PHIPS, Caleb, 180; John R., 97; Lewis, 14, 85, 92, 96, 97, 227; Patsy, 92; Richard, 97; Tabitha, 24.
PICKENS, Eliz., 17; John, 176.
PICKINGS, Wm., 70, 172.
PICKINS, Joshua, 204.
PINNEL, Thos., 154.
PINION, Ann, 182; Thos., 182.
PITCHFORD, Nathan, 62; Wm., 216.
PLEDGER, Isaac M., 246, 262; James, 236; John S., 247, 262; Joseph P., 246; Lemuel, 246; Mary S., 262; Murrell, 80; Sally, 238; Simeon L., 51, 264; Thos., 50, 51, 238, 246, 261, 265; Wesley, 50, 51, 262, 265; Wm., 51.
POLESTONE., Jesse, 262.
POLLARD, John, 57, 164, 182, 217, 220; Major, 211; Mary, 182; Polly, 164; Richard, 164.
PONDER, Abner, 223, 240; Betsy, 240; Jesse, 229, 240; Reuben, 229, 240.
POPE, Henry, 56; Judith, 196, 210; Leroy, 13, 147, 148, 159, 186, 196,

GENERAL INDEX

200, 202, 210, 222, 226; W., 154; Pope & Walker, 209.
POPPLACELL, Isaac, 191.
POPWELL, Isaac, 188.
PORTER, B., 209; Benj., 164, 166.
PORTERFIELD, D., 220; David, 201, 218.
POSEY, Thos., 104, 161, 234.
POST, John, 182; Wm., 226.
POTTER, Solo., 185.
POWELL, Francis, 210, 224, 243, 253; Honoria, 85; Honourrias, 240; Killis, 243; Lauston, 243; Lurany, 243; Mary, 30; Sarah, 24; Wm. R., 39, 85, 243, 255.
POWER, David, 75, 85; James, 20; Sally Green, 20; Susannah, 20; Wm., 75.
POWERS, Eliz., 182, 196; Francis, 182, 196.
PRATER, Wm. M., 102.
PRATHER, Wm., 255.
PRESBURY, Geo. G., 184.
PRESLY, Chas., 94, 104; Mildred, 94.
PRESSEL, James, 22; Susannah, 22.
PRESSLES, Elijah, 40.
PREUIT, Jacob G., 254; John, 254.
PREWET, John, 136, 218; Wm., 136.
PREWETT, Jacob, 175, 177.
PREWIT, John, 129; Joshua, 254; Wm., 25, 129, 241; Willis, 129; Zilpha, 129.
PRICE, Eliz., 210; Thos., 209, 210, 224.
PRIER, Archelas, 147; Archibald, 148; Harden, 147.
PRINCE, Hudson, 89.
PRINGLE, Wm., 93.
PRIOR, Archibald, 142.
PRITCHETT, Delpha, 253; Geo., 242; Nicholas, 242, 253; Thos., 252.
PROTHRO, Eliz., 38; Evan, 31, 38; Geo., 129; Harriott, 38; James, 31, 253; Joshua, 38, 253; Lydia, 38; Mary, 38; Massee, 38; Nathaniel, 31, 38, 120, 253; Solomon, 38; Wm., 31, 38, 129, 253; Zilpha, 38, 120, 129, 253; Zilphy, 135.
PRUETT, John, 196; Samuel, 196.
PRUITT, David, 246; Susannah, 246; Wm., 246.
PRYOR, Eliz., 5.
PUCKET, James, 138, 246; John, 138; Rebecca, 138.
✢PULLEN, Samuel, 63.
PULLIAM, Elinor, 182; Hannah C., 35; J. N., 112; John, 262; Jos., 147, 164, 182, 240, 265; Robt., 61, 144, 176, 182, 205, 215, 252; Wm., 129, 130, 137, 145, 155, 168, 193.
PULLING, Major, 160.

PURCELL, John, 171.
PURKINS, Eliz., 238, Wm., 238.
PURYEAR, Mary, 8.
PUTNAM, Sarah, 8.
QUINN, Matthew, 26, 245; Wm., 119.
QUIRY, Chas., 178; Wm., 178.
RADFORD, John M., 47.
RAGAN, Evan, 85; John, 257; Wm., 263.
RAGANS, Chas., 22; James, 22; Nancy, 22.
RAGLAND, Benj., 3, 13, 182, 184; Col., 185; E., 112; Eliz., 195; En., 112; Evan, 59, 61, 88, 98, 104, 145, 151, 157, 164, 166, 168, 171, 173, 179, 181, 188, 196, 197, 202, 204, 205, 210, 211, 213, 247; Frances, 68; Franky, 13, 68, 146; Henry G., 190; Hudson, 85, 112, 206, 212; James, 85; Jas. O., 88, 98, 112; John A., 225; John R., 13, 60, 68, 146, 182, 190, 197, 206, 212, 213; Milly, 5; Pamela, 13; Patsy,7, 13, 68; Thompson, 85, 96, 98, 104, 112, 149.
RAIFORD, John M., 45, 115.
RAIN, Rich'd, 142.
RAINES, Dabney, 259; John W., 259; Josiah F., 259.
RAINS, Dabney, 245.
RAMSEY, B., 251.
RANDALL, Nany, 204; Saloannah, 204.
RANDOLPH, Joseph, 17; N., 31.
RANEY, Entreken, 142; Matilda, 142.
RAWSON, C. W., 112.
RAY, James H., 253; John, 131; P., 112; Wm. C., 261, 264.
RAYMOND, Sarah D., 99, 100, 101, 121.
REACH, Wm., 27.
READY, Eliz., 164; James, 164, 215.
REATHERFORD, Claiborn, 230.
REAVES, Nelly, 7.
REDWINE, Jacob, 260; Wm., 230.
REECE, Alford B., 258.
REED, Alex, 203; Collin, 155, 164, 210; James, 17; Piety, 48; Sarah, 261; Wm. P., 264.
REESE, David A., 29, 90, 96.
REEVES, Alex., 160.
REID, B., 98.
REILY, James, 217.
REMBERT, Mr., 33; Samuel H., 248.
RENOLDS, Mark, 146.
REYNOLDS, Martha, 210; Patty, 182; Wm., 182; 207, 210.
RHOADES, James, 225.
RHODES, Hannah, 253; James, 149; John W., 253; Moses R., 253; Zachariah, 91.

GENERAL INDEX

RICE, Aaron, 260, 264; Asa, 53; Chas., 53; Christian, 13; Eliza, 53; Francis, 53; James, 62; Leonard, 28, 160, 164, 187, 221, 229, 245, 264; Milly, 53; Richard, 53, 256; Robt., 229, 231, 243; Sarah, 164; Walton, 261; Wm., 80, 233, 235, 264.
RICH, Eliz., 24; Frances W., 126; James, 24, 96, 112, 257; Jesse, 24, 104, 112; John, 24, 85, 96, 104, 112, 115, 201, 248, 249; Mary, 24, 85, 115, 138, 139; Pamela, 24; Richmond, 24, 115, 126, 138, 139, 248; Sarah, 24; Sophia, 24, 112, 115; Wm., 24, 43, 85, 96, 97, 104, 112, 115, 121, 122, 126, 130, 131, 138, 140.
RICHARDS, A., 234; James, 169; Letha, 261; Mary, 261; Piety, 261; Rachel, 105, 121, 246, 261, 265; Reuben, 96, 105, 121, 246, 261; Wm., 261.
RICHARDSON, A., 226; Amos, 38, 73, 135, 177, 184 189, 204, 229, 231, 242, 253; Ann, 242; Dr., 41; Eliz., 33, 34; James R., 31; John W., 34; Livonia J., 52; Nancy, 42; Prudence, 9, 38, 197; Rebecca, 34, 106; Richard, 25, 38, 42, 105, 161, 235; Robt., 106; Robt. W., 34; Safrony A., 51; Susannah, 40, 51, 52; W., 182, 220; Walker, 9, 11, 22, 38, 105, 112, 155, 164, 179, 184, 185, 191, 193, 197, 198, 200, 213; Wm., 106, 175; Wm. N., 25, 31, 34, 38, 39, 116, 121, 122, 123; Dr. Wm. N., 96, 105; Richardson & Hunt, 96.
RICKERSON, Mary A., 196; Marmaduke, 196.
RICKETSON, Marmaduke, 184.
RIDDLE, Anderson, 105, 136; Archibald, 192; Sally, 144, 210; Sarah,4; Sarah Y., 122.
RIDGEDALL, David, 238.
RIDGDELL, Betsy, 15.
RIDGEWAY—RIDGWAY, Bazel,244; Burrel, 263; Drury, 26, 104; Eliz., 30; James, 244, 258; James E., 259; John T., 258; Lemuel T., 259; Lucy, 146; Robt., C., 258; Thos., 65, 146, 224.
RILEY, Ann, 196; Eliz., 226; James, 196, 225, 241, 255.
ROAN, Frances, 112; John, 112, 121, 126, 130, 139, 248; Stephen, 148.
RONE, Thos., F., 117, 126, 130, 136, 139.
ROBBARDS, John, 245.
ROBERSON, Samuel, 254.
ROBERT, Moses J., 260; Presley B., 260.

ROBERTS, Armstrong, 128, 137, 139; Jas., 62; Jesse, 246; John, 193, 233, 263; John W., 128, 137, 139; Joseph, 62, 259, 263; Josiah, 50; Martha, 139, 142; Nace, 137; Patsy, 137; Zilly, 15.
ROBERTSON, Gen. Jas., 18; John, 217; Wm., 240.
ROBBINS, Isabella, 76; Plenny, 76; Wm. O., 76, 149.
ROBINSON, David, 183.
ROCK, Oliver, 9, 224.
RODGERS, Isham G., 250; John C., 97; John W., 249.
RODLANDER, Wm. B., 255.
ROE, Susannah, 243.
ROEBUCK, Eliz., 29; Eliz. L., 121; Eppy, 53; Eppy W., 121; Fanny, 24; Frances, 53; Geo. 24, 95, 240; Harriott, 24; Polly, 24; Robt., 24, 33, 44, 121, 130, 241; Wm., 24, 44, 53, 121, 231, 256.
ROGERS, Benj., 60, 164, 229; Caroline M., 41; Elisha, 238; Geo. 41, 180; Isham G., 23; Jas., 60, 164, 188, 196, 198; Jo., 216; John, 58, 60, 152, 164, 165, 180, 183, 196, 218; Martha, 183; Mary, 60, 68, 76, 164; Michael, 151; Milly, 15; Nancy, 22, 58, 60, 183, 196; Peleg, 188; Rhoda, 6; Simeon, 83; Simeon G., 23, 73; Susannah M., 73; Thos., 60, 164, 165, 180, 183, 196, 199; Unity, 165; Wm., 68, 76, 173, 182, 191.
ROGGERS, Jas., 144; Nancy, 144; Thos., 144.
ROLAND, Mastin, 260.
ROSE, Amos, 24, 235; Benj., 24; Drury, 96; Grantham, 24; H., 220; Henry, 56, 183; Jemima, 183; Sally, 24; Sarah, 251; Thos., 24, 96; Wm., 16, 24, 174; Winny, 24.
ROSEL, Jona., 168.
ROSS, Daniel, 234; Drury, 216; Jesse, 215, 219; John, 58, 143, 164, 198, 210; Marget, 164, 210; Richard, 146; Robt., 157, 210.
ROSSELL, Jonathan, 214.
ROSSER, Jeptha, 117, 251, 265; Wm., 117.
ROSSITER, Nathaniel, 183.
ROWE, William, 68, 149.
ROWELL, Jesse, 186, 222.
ROWS, Amos, 48; Eliza, 48; Francis, 48; Grantham, 48; Lucy A., 48; Milton B., 48; Thos., 48; Washington, 48.
ROWSEY, Clary, 238; Edmond, 24, 96, 238, 247; Forester, 249; Foster, 24, 92, 97; Jas., 24, 77, 85, 94,

96, 233, 234; John, 24, 67, 77, 83, 96, 98, 211, 238; Mary, 14, 24, 96; Rhoda, 53; Stephen, 24, 96, 210; Tabitha, 97; Wm., 264.
ROWZIE, Winslow, 149.
ROWZY, John, 166.
ROYAL, Abraham, 97; Averilla, 97; Eliz, 97, 255; Jas., 97, 121; John, 121, 124, 146, 217; Levita, 121; Martha, 124; Martha H., 27; Wm., 97.
ROYSTER, Robert, 249.
ROYSTON, Robert, 210.
RUCKER, Amanda B., 47; Ann, 28; Azmon, 76, 85, 149, 240; Barden, 45, 51, 71, 79, 125, 126, 130; Catharine, 165; Fielding, 184; Geo., 152, 165, 232; Jas., 29, 47, 112, 130, 251; Jeremiah, 51; John, 76, 86, 221, 223, 240, 251, 255; Joseph, 27, 49, 121, 129, 130, 138, 221, 222, 223, 224; Lemuel, 51, 130; Margaret, 51; Mary, 51; Milly, 47, 251; Nancy, 76; Peter, 51; Tavener, 37, 51, 94, 102, 112, 130; Wm., 37, 51, 112, 130, 253; Willis, 51, 79, 91; Zachariah, 121, 130, 251.
RUFF, Allen, 245; Shadrick, 263; Stephen, 245.
RUMSEY, Benj. 263; Fanny, 242; Henry, 242; John, 242; Nancy, 259; Polly, 242; Richard, 252; Thos., 242; Wm., 242.
RUNNALS, William, 252.
RUNNELS, William, 138.
RUNNOLDS, Samuel, 224, 225.
RUSH, Moses, 161.
RUSSELL, John, 20, 61, 62, 145; Mary, 210; Thos., 155, 166; Thos., C., 183, 184, 194, 202, 210, 211, 222.
RYAL, John, 216.
RYAN, Berry, 68, 94.
RYLAND, Robert, 159.
RYELYE, James, 165.
RYLEY, Jas., 62, 144; Mary, 39.
RYONS, Philip, 11.
SADLER, Jas. R., 252; John F., 255; Wm. B., 254.
SAFFOLD, Bird, 91.
SALE—SAIL, Anthony, 58, 144; Cornelius, 56, 58, 68, 86, 144, 188; Dudley, 28, 68; Jas., 86; Joseph, 68, 86; Lewis, 205.
SALMON—SALMONS, Geo., 184; Jeremiah, 253; Lewis, 233, 236; Mary, 15, 148.
SAMMONS, Lewis, 242.
SANDERS, Benj., 155; Calvin P., 253; Elias, 229; Ephraim, 173;

Henry, 230; Jesse, 173; Lewis M., 253; Richard, 206; Wm., 13, 146.
SANDEDGE—SANDIDGE, Clabourn, 166, 183, 185, 240, 252; John, 183, 215, 216; Thos., J., 252.
SANDRADGE, Claibourne, 67.
SANDRIDGE, James M., 262.
SANFORD, Robert, 9.
SAMSON, William, 161.
SARR, Charles, 219.
SARTAIN, James, 206; John, 48, 234.
SATTERWHITE, Anna, 32; Chas., 32; Eliz., 32, 121, 130, 258; Francis, 8, 20, 32, 58, 84, 97, 121, 130, 144, 146, 215, 217; Franky, 72; Frans., 151, 153; Jas., 32,.66, 72, 121, 130; John, 32, 64; Milly, 27; Nancy, 238; Reubin, 32; Stephen, 182.
SAUNDERS, Richard, 67, 215.
SAWYER, Robert, 243.
SAXON, Drury T., 15, 34; Hugh, 15, 150, 211; Jensy, 15; John M., 15; Lewis W., 15, 43, 150; Mary, 15, 211; Timothy, 202, 223.
SAXTON, Eliz. M., 248.
SAYER, Robert S., 92.
SAYLER, Christ., 157.
SAYLORS, Eliz., 184; Michael, 201.
SAYRE, B. W., 121, 122.
SCALES, Ann, 62, 63, 144; Anna, 28; Benj., 62, 63, 83, 145; Elijah, 62, 63, 83, 145; Eliz., 62; Geo., 233, 243, 246, 262, 265; Joel, 38, 253; John, 97, 153, 197, 198, 223, 242, 243; Nathan, 69; Nathaniel, 62, 63, 83, 145; Thos., 38, 58, 62, 63, 69, 83, 144, 145, 158, 180, 223, 235, 242, 243, 253; Wm., 147, 253.
SCHOFIELD, Eliza, 81, 89; Emily, 81, 89; Robt., 81, 89.
SCOTT, Betsy, 165, 211; Eliz., 211; Jas., 69, 154, 196; Nancy, 165; Thos., 25, 165, 216; Thos. B., 3, 4, 62, 142, 143, 151, 152, 153, 165, 181, 182, 188, 210, 218, 221; Wm., 156.
SCRINE, Peter, 62.
SEAL—SEALS—SEALE, Eliz., 32, 250; Ivey, 23, 93; John, 32, 101, 135, 198.
SEAMORE—SEEMORE, John W., 258; Zachariah, 245, 259.
SELF, Frances, 253; Franky, 38; Mary, 38; Nancy, 38; Samuel, 38, 223, 233; Samuel, E., 38; Samuel L., 253; Sarah, 38; Sinclair, 38.
SELFRIDGE—SULFRIDGE, Agnes, 184; Nancy, 243; Robt., 184, 243.
SELMAN, Thomas, 196.
SELPEDY, Robert, 62.
SERMONS, Wesley, 96.
SERTAIN, John, 148, 187.

GENERAL INDEX 333

SEWELL, Henry, 213; Jas., 226; Joseph, 50, 51, 264; Nicholas, 217; Polly C., 51; Samuel, 155, 197, 213; Wm., 217.
SHACKLEFORD, Asa, 139; Asa C., 112, 256; Betsy, 32; E., 112; Edmond, 13, 32, 47, 97, 112, 152, 161, 165, 186, 197, 234, 235; Fanny, 32; Henry, 32, 43, 95, 97, 112, 121, 139, 161, 186, 197, 256; Howard B., 28; Jas., 29, 139, 231, 233, 241, 256; Jefferson, 32; Jenney, 32; John, 32, 139, 197, 216, 219; Judith, 32, 112; M., 220; Madison, 139; Martha, 29, 112, 139; Mordecai, 216; Nancy, 32; Philip, 32, 112, 232; Polly, 32; R. E., 112; Reuben, 32; Sally W., 112; Stephen, 139; Thos. J., 112; T. J., 112; Wm., 167.
SHAMMELL, Zachariah, 145.
SHANNON, Owen, 210; Quinton, 222, 223.
SHARP, John, 13, 197; Lucrecy, 65; Lucy, 145; Patsy, 13; Wm., 63, 65, 145, 150, 197, 203, 209.
SHAPPARD, Anna, 15; Geo. D., 15; John, 15; Peter, 15; Robt., 15; Samuel, 15.
SHARYER, Joseph, 243; Wm., 243.
SHAW, Daniel, 186, 198, 205, 217; Molly, 198; Zachariah, 211.
SHEARMAN, Robert, 165.
SHEARMOND, Tabitha, 197.
SHEEMAN, Ann, 192.
SHELLNUT, Anderson, 234.
SHELTON, William, 223.
SHEPHERD, Jas., 157, 169, 170; Nathan, 246; Richard H., 246; Samuel, 246.
SHEPPARD, Anna, 148, 238; John, 148; Mary A., 124; Nancy, 238; Peter, 148, 238; Robt., 148, 215, 238; Samuel, 238; Thos. J., 124.
SHEPPERD, Robt., 222; Samuel, 224.
SHERMAN—SHARMAN, Ann, 58, 143; John, 107; John A., 111, 115; Sarah W., 107.
SHEWMAKER, Jeremiah, 82; Lindsey, 154; Nancy, 82.
SHIELDS, James, 62, 63, 146, 214, 224, 226, 227; John, 149, 165; Samuel, 144.
SHIFLET—SHIFFLET, James, 253; Joseph, 255, Katharine, 30; Pickett, 241, 253; Powell, 75, 243.
SHIVES, Wm., 212.
SHOCKLEY, James, 8; James A., 130, 135; Thos., 8, 160.
SHOEMAKER, Bellender A., 80; Eliz., 211; John B., 262; Lindsay, 211; Talton, 264; Tarlton, 80.
SHORTER, Polly, 17; Sophia, 40.
SHREWSBURY, Joel, 78.
SIGMON, John, 56, 167, 218.
SILMAN, Thos., 217, 225.
SIMMONS, Ann, 22, 52; E. A., 33; Eliz. A., 34; Hollman, 22; Hollman F., 51, 52; James, 22; James B., 51; Jane Ann, 51; John, 22, 51, 52, 83; Moses W., 52, Polly B., 34.
SIMPKINS, Chas., 179.
SIMPSON, Mary, 233, 235.
SIMS, Edward, 28, 77, 232; Martain, 59; Martin, 186, 207, 210.
SINGLETON, Wm., 225.
SITTIN, Wm., 252.
SKAGGS, Henry M., 52, 101; Polly, 101; Tabitha, 254.
SKELTON, Jabez, 253; Jacob, 190; John, 92, 158, 177, 197, 243, 252; Lucretia, 37; Martin, 254; Reecy, 242; Richmond, 253; Robt., 158, 171, 180, 228, 229; Wm., 190, 193, 197; Zachariah, 242.
SKINNER, A., 228; Archer, 25, 152, 183, 208, 226, 247; Clary, 25, 183, 245; Geo., 245; Geo. Martin, 25; James, 25; Morris, 25, 105, 247.
SLACK, Jacob, 226.
SLAYTON, Benj., 62.
SLED, Joshua, 168.
SMETHER, Gabriel, 255.
SMITH, Alex, 10; Archibald, 254; Archer, 193, 242; Asa, 260; Averilla, 97, 100; Benj., 41, 130, 165, 240, 258; Betsy, 31; Betty, 4; Catharine, 52; Chas. L., 93; David, 240; Delila Winnie, 10; Drury, 260; Eady, 10; Ebenezer, 191; Elijah, 259; Eliz., 165, 172; Francis M., 256; Fulden, 246; Gabriel, 190; Gideon, 63, 146; Henry, 63, 146; Isham, 259; J., 217; Jasper, 4, 142, 217; Jemima, 165, 240; Jesse, 240, 264; John, 57, 86, 142, 161, 165, 184, 193, 200, 218, 222, 238, 240, 260; John M., 257; Jos., 236, 256; Larkin, 260; Levy, 248; Levy D., 146; Mark, 4; Martha T., 93; Mary, 165, 216; Mial, 33, 114, 133, 141; Micajah M., 259; Miles, 44, 106, 123; Nathaniel, 4, 146, 157, 206, 246, 264; Nelly W., 40; Patsey, 242; Peter, 230; Priscilla, 165; Prudence, 38; Ralph, 149, 242; Rebeckah, 4, 142; Richard, 241; Robt., 189, 223, 225, 232, 255, 259, 263; Rt., 231, 232; Sally, 4; Sarah, 10; Sara Margaret, 10; Singleton W., 40, 260, 264; Stephen, 10, 146; Thos., 4, 46, 76, 146, 247, 257; Thos. J., 262; V., 129, 131; Valentine, 105, 130, 136, 139, 146, 159, 199, 215; Voluntine, 46, 257; Wells, 251;

Wm., 10, 62, 105, 147, 165, 172, 184, 188, 217; Wm. W., 260, 261, 263; Wells, 97; Z., 66; Zachariah, 40, 41, 49, 66, 72, 240, 258.
SMITHWICK, Edmond, 38; Mary, 233.
SMYTH, Thos., 173, 183, 184.
SNEED, Elijah, 97; Israel, 123; Polly, 44; Sarah, 97.
SNELLINGS, Eliz., 32, 113; Geo., 11, 32, 85, 97, 105, 112; Hannah, 32; James, 112; John, 24, 32, 45, 112, 250; Martha, 32; Mary W., 32; Rebecca, 32, 97, 105, 112, 248; Samuel, 32, 45, 90, 97, 105, 249.
SNOE, Eli, 255.
SNOWDEN, Chas., 187.
SORRELS, Chas., 19; Wm., 19.
SOWELL, Chas., 226, 229.
SPAULDING, Albert M., 117.
SPEAR, Wm., 205.
SPEARER, W. Waldough, 118.
SPEARS, Eliz., 36; Joshua, 246; Salian, 246; Samuel, 57, 190; Shadrick, 246.
SPEED, Terrell, 257; Wade, 248.
SPEERS, John, 217; Samuel, 143, 222, 224.
SPERES, Eliz., 11.
SPIER, Benj., 151; Wm., 151.
SPIVEY, James, 176.
SPURLOCK, James, 215, 217; John, 184.
STANDERFER, Anderson, 243.
STANDEFORD, Bailey, 97; Benj., 243; Tilman, 246.
STAPLES, David, 38, 75, 105, 148; Fanny, 38, 105; Frances, 259; John, 13, 14, 38, 58, 105, 149, 151, 160, 164, 172, 177, 197, 214, 223, 224, 238; Patsy, 38, 105; Thos., 38, 105, 263.
STARNES, Esther S., 166.
STARR, Christopher, 204, 211; Mary, 211.
STATHAM, A. D., 121; Aug. D., 127; Augustine D., 122; Augustus D., 251; Barnett, 119; Chas., 38, 42, 119, 127; James, 38; Jesse, 38, 221; John, 38, 121, 154, 246; Love, 2; Lucy B., 122; Memory, 121; Nathaniel, 38, 121; Pleasant, 38, 224; Richard W., 127; Robt., 38; Wm., 38, 42, 246; Wm. R., 119, 127.
STATOM, John, 251.
STEAGALL, Eliz., 184; Richard, 184.
STEEDLEY—STEEDLY, James P., 259; Wm., 235.
STEEL, Henry, 197; Margaret, 190, 211; Robt., 246, 261.
STEPHENS, Alex., 165; Fereby, 246; Henry, 250; Henry H., 42; John, 238;
Jos., 228; Nancy, 182, 184; Stephen, 181; Wm., 69, 230.
STEWARD, Alex., 216.
STEWART, Alex., 219; Cyrus, 46, 118; Wm., 227.
STICKALL, Richard, 177.
STILL, H., 220.
STINCHCOMB, A., 50, 98, 222, 223, 224, 226, 227, 228, 229, 230, 231, 316; Absolom, 14, 51, 63, 67, 91, 148, 155, 165, 182, 189, 199, 218, 236, 262; Alex., 161; Aron, 226; Levi, 29, 51, 246, 258; Mary, 51; Nathaniel, 51, 246; Philip, 51, 98.
STO, Warren, 219.
STOOKS, Joseph, 172.
STODGEHILL—STODGILL, Durrat, 36, 82; Joel, 58, 143, 172, 183, 197; Martitia, 58, 143, 197; Willis, 247.
STOGDON, John 2.
STOKES, Archibald, 25, 86; Archd., 91, 103; Armstead, 25; Jane, 5; Martha, 5; Richard H., 25; Sarah, 5; Thos., 25, 86; Wm., 5, 25, 60, 144, 208; Wm. M., 5, 144; Young, 25; Stokes & Sayre, 91, 96.
STONE, John, 228; Karenhappeck, 27; Marbil, 197; Uriah, 197; Wm., 32, 101, 130, 257.
STOREY—STORY, Edward, 149; Lucy, 245; Thos., 226, 227.
STOVALL, Eliz. D., 38; Geo., 14, 69, 77, 86, 94, 147, 148, 228; John, 105; Thos., 258.
STOW, Warren, 208.
STOWERS, Anna, 24; Eliz., 30; Jeremiah, 252; Lewis, 180, 229, 233, 243, 253.
STREETMAN, Garrett, 165; Mary, 165.
STRIBLING, Thos., 127.
STRICKLAND, Eliz., 13, 69, 146; Barnaby, 226; Barnes, 217; H., 13; Hardy, 69; Isaac, 13, 146; Jacob, 13, 69, 146; Jos., 255; Rachel, 9; Solomon, 198.
STRONG, Peggy, 5; Samuel, 177; Wm., 5, 144, 155, 164, 208.
STROUD, Isham, 58, 143, 178, 194, 220.
STUART, Cyrus, 121, 130; James M., 184.
STUBBLEFIELD, Catharine, 80, 86; Seth, 165; Theodrick, 192; Wm., 184, 215.
STUBBS, Ann, 52; Eliz., 153; Harrison Y., 153; James 41; John, 32; Mary, 153; Peter, 32, 58, 146, 153, 219, 240; Thos., 41; Thos. B., 41.
SULLIVAN, Wm. H., 253.
SULLIVANT, Patsy, 240.
SUMNER, Nazareth, 238.

SUTTEN, Geo., 63, 65; James, 63, 65, 221, 223; Joel, 63, 65; Sally, 63, 65; Wm., 63, 65.
SUTTLE, John, 75; Margaret, 183; Wm., 83, 183.
SUTTLES, Isaac, 75, 92, 151, 152, 154, 165, 180; Stephen, 227, 228.
SUTTON, Abner, 123; Alcy, 142; Alsay, 58; Eliz., 44; Jeams, 158; Reuben, 158; Wm., 58, 142.
SWEPSON, John, 174.
TABAR, Benj. K., 262, 264.
TABOR, Brittain C., 264; P. A., 102.
TAILER, Eliz., 255; Garrett, 255; John, 255.
TAIT, America, 10; Betsy, 25; Betty, 97; Caleb, 232; Charity, 10, 69; Charity Ann, 34, 107; Chas., 10, 13, 34, 69, 86, 213, 225; Daniel, 25, 131; David, 25, 39; Eanos, 211; Edmond B., 256; Edward B., 110; Elisha, 25, 131; Eliz., 213; Enos, 25, 39, 40, 52, 97, 122; Hudson, 169, 170; James, 10, 11, 25, 39, 43, 52, 56, 69, 86, 108, 117, 122, 131, 151, 152, 154, 155, 158, 159, 163, 166, 168, 170, 171, 173, 175, 183, 184, 185, 186, 188, 200, 202, 204, 211, 213, 215, 216; Jas. M., 10; Jesse C., 82; John, 14, 25, 86, 97, 105, 131; Louisa, 10; Lucy, 25, 86, 97; Lucy B., 122; Martha, 147; Nancy, 18; Patsy, 10; Rebecca, 10, 168, 184, 185, 211; Robt., 145; Robt. L., 7, 10, 60, 71, 77, 149, 207, 211; Susannah, 25; Thos., 11, 59, 69, 82, 97, 105, 113, 121, 122, 225; Thos. L., 232; Wm., 6, 14, 25, 39, 69, 71, 86, 97, 113, 131, 247; Wm. H., 10, 34, 59, 69, 154, 169, 177, 184, 222, 226; Zimri, 11, 25, 40, 43, 52, 56, 105, 108, 113, 117, 122, 130, 131, 159, 169, 193, 213, 235; Zinny, 185.
TALBERT, Samuel, 199.
TALBOT, John, 160, 185; Sam'l., 187; Thos., 185.
TALBOTT, Matthew, 185; Phebe, 185.
TALIAFERRO, Benj., 2, 16, 20, 156; Judge, 59; Lewis B., 17; Martha, 40.
TALLEY, Littleberry H., 163.
TATE, Asbury, 52; Barbara, 185; Beatrice J. A., 105, 113, 121, 122, 127, 136, 139; Caleb, 73, 74, 75, 84, 86, 97, 104; Catharine, 105; Chas., 145, 146, 147; Elisheba, 167, 185; Eliz., 52, 248; Eliz. D., 122, 138; Enos., 52, 68, 71, 82, 131, 136, 138, 140, 250; Enos C., 52; Enos M., 248; Frances, 39; Henrietta, 22; Horatio, 108, 117, 122, 139; Isaac M., 48, 52, 122, 140, 248; J. A., 122; Jacob M., 112, 122, 130, 131, 138; James, 139, 143, 144, 145, 147; James M., 41, 43, 52, 69, 113, 122, 136, 137; Jane, 40, 52; Jesey C., 248; John, 250; John D., 105; John W., 105, 113, 122, 136; Jos. P., 105; Katharine D., 122; Lawrence P., 136; Lucy B., 136; Madison, 52; Martha, 11; Martha J., 122, 138; Martha M., 122; Milton, 52; Permelia, 105, 113, 122, 136; Sarah, 105, 250; Sarah A., 105; Susan, 52; Thos., 136, 147, 248; Thos. J., 105, 122, 248; Uriah M., 122; Uriah R., 138; Waddy, 87; Wm., 14, 71, 167, 168, 169, 185, 186; Wm. A., 107; Wm. H., 145; Wm. J., 105; Wm. M., 122; Zilphy 136; Zimri, 134, 138, 139, 140; Zimri A., 136; Zimri M., 122, 138; Zimri W., 39, 121, 122, 127, 136, 248; Tate & Verdell, 93.
TATUM, Jese, 250; Sally, 22.
TAYLOR, Benj., 185, 240; Burden Rice, 25; Chas., 145, 210; Edmond, 60, 215; Elisha, 242; Eliz., 47, 130; Grant, 193; James, 47; Jesse, 254; John, 43, 47, 105, 222; John C., 249; Moses, 191; Nathan, 43; Nathias, 196, 225, 249; Patsy, 25, 43; Philisha, 47; Rebecca, 43, 112, 249; Robt. H., 158; Roland, 185; Susannah, 185; Wm., 58, 172, 241, 250, 254; Wm. A., 43; Wm. T., 257; Winny, 43.
TEASLEY, Alfred H., 52; Amelia, 39; Ann, 111, 140; Anna, 39; Ausborn G., 52; Benager S., 254; Benajah, 46, 49, 52; Beverly A., 252; Betsy, 46; Drusilla, 21, 40; Fanny, 167; Isham, 23, 39, 52, 93, 113, 252; Isom, 240; James, 21, 240, 252; Job, 46, 58; John, 46, 185, 212, 252; John A., 49, 50, 52; Joshua, 50; Levi, 39, 105, 111, 113, 252; Lucy, 46; Sarah, 39, 252; Silas, 167; Silus, 243, 253; Thos., 111, 113; Thos. J., 39, 49, 111, 140; Wm., 39, 50, 96, 105, 111, 113, 145, 184, 193, 196, 221, 229, 240.
TELFAIR, Edward, 157.
TEMPLE, Rosannah, 10.
TEMPLETON, John, 183, 196; Rosannah, 183.
TERONET, Daniel, 168; Salley, 168.
TERRELL, Amanda E., 118, 127, 134, 139; Booker S., 131; Brittian, 118, 127; Eliz. A., 131; Francis F., 118, 127, 134, 139; Geo., 165; J., 227; James, 131; James T., 43, 118; Jeremiah, 9, 25, 218, 220, 241; Joel, 121; John, 25, 155, 216; John W., 43, 118; Joseph, 43, 118, 250; Jos. R., 43, 118; Levisa, 255; Louisa, 25; Margaret, 43; Mary, 241; Mary E., 131, 133; Micajah, 17; Nancy W.,

GENERAL INDEX

131, 133; Philip, 122; Philip P., 131, 137; Polly, 25; Rachel, 25; Rosanna, 25; Robt. W., 255; Sarah, 122, 131, 133; Sarah Ann, 131, 133; Susanna, 25; Timothy, 122, 131, 133, 137, 250; Wm., 25, 118, 241; Wm., O., 43, 118, 134, 139.
TERRILL, Joseph, 166; Jowel, 250.
TERRY, Joseph, 44; Thos., 255.
THACKER, Ector, 225; Hannah, 10, 145; Jonl., 13; Voluntine, 10, 145; Wm., 10, 145.
THEARMOND, Tabither, 189.
THOMAS, E. L., 23; Geo., 108; Joel, 58, 143, 217; Leroy, 100; Wm., 58, 143, 198.
THOMASON, Geo., 145.
THOMASSON, John, 19, 47, 217; Wm., 19.
THOMPSON, Alex., 17, 18, 77, 153; Allen, 212; Alsomain, 147; Andrew, 242; Ann, 62, 63; Asa, 25, 77, 97, 107, 137, 190, 198; Beat., 93; Betsy, 60; Drewry (Drury), 10, 77, 145, 163, 166, 185, 198; Eliz., 18; Eliz. W., 59, 144, 211; Esther, 18; Farley, 5, 25, 143, 156, 198, 211; Gaines, 35, 51, 92, 138, 149, 232, 233, 235, 246; Geo., 233; Isham, 5, 59, 60, 63, 86, 144, 147, 166, 168, 185, 195, 211; James, 17, 18, 77; Jency E., 86; Jesse, 10, 58, 142, 145, 185, 242, 252; John, 5, 17, 59, 151, 164, 195, 198, 212; John F., 5, 143, 166, 211; Lamentation, 212; L. B., 211; Lewis, 211; Lewis B., 5, 143; Mary, 5, 166, 198; Nathan, 230, 242; Oliver, 58, 142, 166; Patsy, 86, 147; Peter, 5, 156; Polly, 40; Ro., 13; Robert, 2, 5, 10, 15, 17, 58, 142, 156, 166, 181, 184, 211; Ruth, 17; Sally, 5, 86, 166; Samuel, 242; Samuel M., 3; Sarah, 17, 25, 138, 166, 185, 198, 212; Solomon, 242; Tabby, 5, 9, 147; W., 232; Wells, 3, 9, 25, 97, 198, 210; Wiley, 22, 38, 42, 60, 63, 64, 66, 86, 146, 147; Wm., 2, 5, 11, 17, 25, 57, 58, 66, 68, 72, 97, 143, 146, 147, 156, 163, 166, 169, 181, 184, 185, 188, 192, 198, 211, 212, 213, 215, 216, 221, 223; Willis, 77; W. G., 232.
THORNHILL, John, 204; Leonard, 185; Mary, 185.
THORNTON, Anne, 21; Benj., 131, 252; Daniel, 21, 40, 94, 107, 125, 225, 252; Dillard, 51; Dozer, 240, 255; Dozier, 200; Elsey B., 252; Eliz., 21, 53, 40, 98, 251; Eppy, 53; Hudson A., 28, 39; Jeremiah, 83, 240; John, 131, 252; John M., 53; Jonathan, 255; Lucy O., 107; Lucy K., 53, 105; Mark, 29, 58, 144, 194, 209, 212, 231, 240; Mary, 212; Memorable, 53; Middleton, 43; Molly, 212; Priscilla, 21; Reuben, 21, 51, 86, 98, 113, 163, 252; Thos., 21, 29, 53, 98, 104, 170, 200, 203, 212, 217, 252; Thos., A., 247; Wiley, 231; Wm., 21; Wm. D., 137.
THRELKELD—THRELKILL, Banebridge, 262; Delila, 40, 106, 122, 131, 262; John, 105; John W., 250; Marcus D., 122; Marcus D. F., 131; Marian F., 261; Oliver, 40, 106, 121, 122, 131; Thos., 106, 262, 263; Thos. D., 262; Tuly, 262; Wm. 88; Wm. H., 105, 129, 249; Willis, 48, 106, 250, 264.
THURMAN, John, 198; Philip, 208.
THURMAND, James, 194; Polly, 201.
THURSTON, Benj., 66.
TIBIS, Thomas, 252.
TIDWELL, Peter, 176.
TILER—TILLER, Reuben, 47, 254.
TINAR, Cabel, 252; Tolison, 252; Wm., 252.
TINER, Richard, 58.
TINSLEY, Sarah B., 109, 117, 118; W. D., 101; Wm. D., 45, 108, 109, 117, 127, 129, 249.
TIPPIN, Dennis, 88, 96.
TOLLETT, John, 166, 167, 171, 176, 183, 185, 199; Margaret, 166, 185.
TOMASON, George, 240.
TOMS, William, 172.
TONEY, Sherwood, 228.
TOTMAN, Rebecca, 253.
TORRENCE, Hester, 8.
TOWNLEY, Henry, 198.
TOWNS, Ankey, 13; Betsy, 13; Oaty, 13; Diury, 13, 32, 147, 198; Elisha, 13, 60, 147, 206; Nancy, 13; Patsy, 32.
TRAMMELL, William, 259.
TRANTHAM, A., 223; Absolom, 157.
TRENTHAM, Ab., 220; Absolom, 167; Ann, 167.
TRIMBLE, Oaty, 37; John, 167, 184; Katharin, 167, 184; Moses, 166, 167, 184.
TUCKER, Bartlett, 43; Daniel, 13, 32, 76, 225, 231; Dicy, 19; Eppes, 32; Ethil, 32; Frances, 32; Gabriel, 18, 32, 226, 229; Godfrey, 43, 122, 250; H. D., 52; Jane, 47; Jesse, 43; John M., 259; Martha, 134; Martha W., 131; Mary, 47; R. C., 47; Reuben, 18, 32; Robt., 32, 43, 76, 79, 90, 245; Robt. W., 264; Sarah, 134; Sarah H., 131; S. H., 47; Shem, 32, 234; Stephen H., 131, 133; Susannah, 32; Wm., 259.

GENERAL INDEX 337

TUGGLE, Henry, 173.
TUREMAN, Eliz., 167; Geo., 167; Martin, 167.
TURK—TURKE, John, 190, 216.
TURMAN, Abner, 17; Benj., 149; Catharine, 17; Oaty, 69; Eliz., 15; G., 220; Garrett, 15, 178, 198, 210, 220, 221, 225, 226; Geo., 15, 17, 67, 69, 71, 103, 113, 123, 130, 138, 180, 198, 212; Isaac, 15; Jacob, 15, 71; Jas., 17; John, 15, 17, 168; Mariah, 113, 130; Martha, 154; Martin, 77, 168, 183, 198, 207, 212; Mary, 198, 249; Matilda, 77; Nancy, 15; Prudence, 17, 77; Robt., 15, 17, 67, 69, 74, 86; Robt. G., 74, 249; Samuel, 38, 113, 123, 130, 247; Seaborn, 246; Seaborn J., 113; Thos., 15, 17, 69, 198, 210, 212; Thos. J., 113, 130, 263; Viletty, 262; Violet, 138;Violetty, 113; Wm., 220.
TURNBULL, Joseph, 205.
TURNER, Anna, 101; Eliz., 106, 148; Eliz. M., 77, 86, 150; John, 74; Martin, 77, 86, 106, 150, 241; Sally, 23, 77, 86, 148, 150, 235; Sarah, 106; Thos., 77, 86, 101, 106, 148, 150, 168, 255.
TUTTLE, Betty, 166, 211; Isaac, 5, 211; J., 219; Jas., 56, 142, 151, 165, 167, 178, 179, 185, 196, 198, 211; Jesse, 211; Nicholas, 166, 167; Nicholas H., 211; W. H., 221.
TWEEDLE, Jas., 242; John, 160, 162, 165, 167, 171, 199, 211; Sarah, 167, 199.
TYLER, Anne, 86; Henry, 86; Reuben L., 86.
TYNER, Harris, 39, 50, 113, 232, 244; Joshua, 39; Nancy, 39, 113; Noah, 39; Richard, 39, 62, 113, 231, 243; Samuel, 39.
TYSON, Abm., 171.
UNDERWOOD, Ann, 147, 240, 252; Ezekiel, 132, 240; Joseph, 39, 215, 219, 241, 254; Joshua, 147, 221, 222, 240; Reuben, 39, 113, 123, 140; Wm., 25; Wm. F., 17; Wm. H., 33, 39, 241; Winneford, 123; Winney, 113; Winnifred, 39, 140; Wyneford, 255.
UNIS, Samuel, 244.
UPSHAW, Adkins, 63, 145; Amy, 12; Ann, 238; Catharine, 238; Eliz., 14, 52; Eliz. B., 33; Geo., 29, 52, 130, 131, 136, 262; Geo. L., 52, 130, 136, 262; Haston, 264; Jas., 29, 52, 81, 102, 110, 118, 131, 136, 261, 262; John, 12, 16, 20, 24, 33, 35, 52, 98, 147, 197, 238, 262; John A., 52, 130, 136, 262; Leroy, 20, 38, 41, 52, 105, 206, 214, 238, 265; Louisa, 261; Louisa E., 52, 130, 136; Middleton, 262; Middleton C., 33, 52; Prudence, 38; Rebecca, 33, 35, 98, 265; Richard, 14; Sarah, 238; Wm., 89, 244.
URQUHART, John A., 248.
VACRAY, Jos., 252.
VANHOOK, Aron, 185, 202.
VANN, Martha, 163.
VARNER, JAMES, 238.
VASSER, John, 263, Wm. O., 259.
VAUGHN, Alex., 263; Isaac D., 258.
VAUGHTERS, Lindsey, 253; Russell, 253.
VAWTER, Eliz., 106; Jas., 98, 106; Johannah, 44, 98, 106; John, 73, 98, 106, 114, 131; Lindsey, 44, 106; Nancy, 106; Richard, 44, 98, 106; Russell, 44, 98, 106; Wm., 44, 106.
VERDEL, John A., 247, 256.
VICK, Elijah, 33; Elisha, 30, 33.
VICKERY, Aron, 132, 235; Jas., 132, 253; Mary, 132.
VINES, Isaac, 246; Isaiah, 98; Jas., 246; John, 246; Jos., 264; Parnal, 246; Sarah, 98, 246.
VINEYARD, David, 69, 153, 199; Geo., 69; Isham, 153; Ishmael, 63, 69, 146; Jas., 69, 224, 231; Jane, 69; John, 69, 223; Jonathan, 199; Jos., 69; Philip, 166, 167, 199.
VINING, Thomas, 208.
VINSON, Eliab, 223; Liab, 172; Jesse, 167, 177, 179.
VIRDAL, John A., 147.
VODEN, B., 215; Braddock, 59, 142, 162.
WADE, Anna, 241; David, 37; John 261; Joshua, 241.
WADDLE, Moses, 93.
WADSON, Abner, 259.
WAILES, Edward L., 225.
WALAS, Thomas, 260.
WALES, Levin, 63.
WALKER, Andrew, 184; Ann, 133; Archelaus, 177, 184, 212, 222; Eliz., 168; Geo., 162; Henry G., 5, 13, 69, 146, 186, 198, 213, 215; H. G., 11, 203, 223, 228; H. Graves, 170; J., 153; Jas., 12, 26, 162, 168, 198, 203; Jas., S., 6, 186; Jere., 61; Jeremiah, 5, 37, 74, 143, 146, 153, 156, 158, 167, 168, 170, 174, 186, 195, 206; John, 146; John W., 6, 13; M., 37, 154, 184, 198, 212; Melanda, 5; Memorable, 5, 13, 37, 146, 205; Milly, 5, 153, 159, 174; Narcissa, 5; Sally, 133; Sally B., 13; Sanders, 6, 143; Thos., 90.

GENERAL INDEX

WALL, Bud C., 250; Cade, 250; Jesse C., 43; Lucy, 43; Wiley, 44, 50, 122.
WALLACE, Edward, 212.
WALLER, John, 170, 200.
WALLIS, Jesse, 37; J. F., 108; Michael J., 98, 106; Rhody, 252; Thos., 246.
WALRAVEN, John, 172.
WALTHALL, Edward, 11, 14, 87, 168, 169, 211, 213; G., 86, 220; Garard, Gerrard, 11, 14, 58, 69, 77, 87, 147, 178, 199, 213, 219; Nancy, 168, 213; Singleton, 14, 26, 70, 77, 87, 147, 150; Sophia, 9; Susanna, 26, 87; Tom, 77; Wm., 9, 14, 70, 77, 87, 147, 150.
WALTON, Benton, 96; Geo., 152; Harris, 122; John, 169, 178, 212; John J., 199; Mary, 186; Matthew, 186; Nancy, 199, 212; Wm., 179, 186.
WANSLEY, Jamima, 30; John, 255; Larkin, 256; Reuben, 255.
WANSLOW, John, 53; Larkin, 53; Nathan, 53; Reuben, 53; Thos., 53.
WARD, Abner, 30, 44, 94, 123, 132, 137; Ann, 44; Finley, 44; Jane, 44, 123; John B., 44; Martha, 123, 256; Martha W., 123, 132; Mary A., 44; Matthias, 187, 204, 242; Richard, 24, 44, 137; Sally, 24, 123, 137; Sarah, 44, 132; Thos., F., 44; Walter H., 44, 123; Wm., 44, 67, 123, 143, 148, 181, 192, 229, 256; Wm. B., 44; Wm. H., 106, 132, 137.
WARE, Edward, 63, 69, 149, 196, 201, 211; Henry, 160; Hudson T., 10; Jas., 69, 149, 160, 183, 213, 221, 223; Jane, 25; Robt., 208.
WARNER, Eliz., 123, 134, 141; Nathan, 123, 141; Nathan B., 134; Nathan R., 123, 141.
WARREN, Eliz., 53; Jeremiah, 29, 94, 241; Jeremiah S., 47, 123, 131; Voluntine, 229.
WATKINS, Edward, 88; Elenor, 10; Henry M., 248; H. M., 103; Isam, 198; Jacob, 221; Jas., 13, 25, 40, 137, 166, 185, 213; Jane, 10; John, 31, 103, 131, 140, 166, 235, 236; Jos., 146; Jos. P., 25; Prudence T., 31; Robt. 31, 40, 98, 106, 111, 140, 166, 181, 182; Samuel, 13, 25, 31, 58, 66, 77, 97, 131, 142, 147, 156, 198; Susannah, 168; Thos. 181; Thomason, 20; Wm., 149, 168, 170, 215; Z. T., 40.
WATKINS & SPEED, 115.
WATSON, John, 152, 168, 180, 194; Moses, 263; Thos., 232, 252.
WATTS, Edward, 168; Geo., 212; Thos., 220.
WEAR, William, 176.
WEBB, Abner, 44, 87, 99, 106, 114, 123, 133, 250; Alcean M., 258; Alice A. M., 123, 132; Allison M., 44; Andrew J., 33, 123, 139; Anna, 23; Archer, 244; Austin, 40, 80, 114, 157, 199, 234; Barbara, 90; Bridger, 87, 99, 106, 114, 123, 258; Burrell, 90, 114; Claborn-Claiborn-Claibourn, 40, 44, 87, 99, 106, 114, 123, 132, 152, 157, 163, 199, 207, 211, 244, 258; Elijah, 87, 99, 106, 114, 123; Elijah W., 258; Evelina, 87, 99; Fortunatus, 258; Francis, 208; Jas., 234; John, 40, 90, 114, 199, 233; John B., 263; John C., 33, 87, 99, 114, 123, 139; John D., 263; Letitia, 44; Letty, 45, 123, 132, 258; Margaret, 87, 99, 106, 114, 123, 244, 259; Martha, 87, 99, 106, 114; Milly, 40; Milton P., 40, 44, 87, 99, 106, 114, 123; Nancy, 45; Peggy, 199; Pleasant, 40, 114; Pope, 40; Susannah, 33, 139; Thos., 152; Urbin A., 262; Walton P., 258; Wm., 40, 87, 99, 114, 168, 180; Wm. C., 33, 106, 139.
WEBSTER, Jonathan, 153; Moses, 223; Peter, 15.
WELBORN, Curtis, 195.
WELLS, Jeremiah, 3; Joannah, 225; Peggy, 4; Wm., 244.
WEST, Andrew, 39; Barbara, 65; Eliz. W., 39; Henry, 39.
WESTBROOK, Anphelady, 8; Elen, 15; John, 79, 200; Stephen, 57, 155, 158, 216.
WESTON, Job, 32, 35, 49, 128, 137, 140, 247, 257.
WESTMORELAND, Z. F., 46.
WEVER, John, 56.
WHALEY, William, 199, 221, 224.
WHEELER, Benj., 132; Chas., 17, 39, 75, 76, 229; Colby, 132; Geo., 123, 131, 147, 241; Jas., 22; Leroy, 123, 132; Mary, 22, 83; Sarah, 47, 123; Thos., 47, 123, 132, 229, 241, 256; Thos., B., 123, 132; Wm., 22.
WHIPPLE, Jesse, 21, 93; Welcome, 149.
WHITE, Anderson, 244; Andrew J., 53; Asa, 53, 70, 73, 83, 87, 150; Barbary, 14; Benj., B., 257; Benj., H., 137; Col., 157; Daniel, 70, 77, 83, 87, 150, 219, 240; David, 47, 99, 137, 220, 251; Eliza, 53; Eliz., 7, 33, 80, 137, 213; Eliz. E., 53; Epaphodetus, 150; Eppy, 53, 77, 81, 246, 261;

GENERAL INDEX 339

Geo. W., 137; Henry, 36, 38, 213, 240; Jas. E., 36, 47, 71, 255; Jas. F., 47, 53; Jeany, 244; Jeremiah, 53; Jesse, 7, 47, 132, 191, 254; John, 2, 7, 12, 47, 52, 77, 87, 150, 152, 155, 167, 168, 176, 198, 213, 236; John H., 250; John M., 32, 53, 137, 256, 264; John W., 253; Joshua, 238; Luke, 147, 212, 220, 226, 227, 230; Lydia, 47, 132; Martha E., 53; Martin, 75, 77, 87, 150, 246, 262, 263; Mary, 14, 47, 251; Mildred, 150; Milly, 53, 168; Molly, 7; Moses, 64, 65, 146; Nicholas, 14, 147, 244; Oliver, 210; Palatere, 14; Patsy, 53; Pleasant, 65, 146; Polly, 53; Rebecca, 14; Reuben, 2, 33, 53, 99, 152, 185, 197, 251; Reuben H., 53; Rn., 228, 231; Sabrina L. A., 53; Sally, 244; Samuel, 174; Sarah, 53; Shelton, 27, 46, 76, 78, 137, 175, 176; Silas, 71, 80; Solomon, 14, 147; Stephen, 35; Sucka, 14; Tabitha, 253; Thos., 4, 12, 144, 161, 175, 176, 213, 240; Thos. J., 250; Thos., S., 49, 256; W. B., 130; Wm., 28, 33, 37, 45, 49, 53, 86, 93, 98, 108, 109, 112, 117, 121, 130, 132, 135, 137, 139, 140, 240, 242, 254; Wilson, 123.
WHITFIELD, Geo., 205; Matilda J., 124; Wm., 107, 115, 124.
WHITMAN, Eliz., 18, 78, 99; John, 18; Polly, 18; Sally, 18; Wm., 18, 71, 78, 99, 115, 116, 117, 124, 250, 263.
WHITNEY, Bridget, 212; John M., 188, 202, 208, 212, 221.
WHYTE, John, 209, 213; O., 163, 202; Reuben, 209, 213.
WIDEMAN, Henry, 163, 168; Mary, 168.
WILBORN, Burket, 51; Nancy, 51.
WILBOURN, Polly, 35; Thos., 35; Wm., 208.
WILEY, Geo., 263; Hugh A., 50; Wm. S., 259.
WILHIGHT, Philemon R., 263; Philip A., 258; Thos. O., 258.
WILLHIGHT, John, 62; Philemon R., 132; Young, 132.
WILHITE, Eliz. P., 92, 138; Geriah G. 106, 137; John, 64, 208; John B., 92, 138, 247, 263; John R., 137, 244; Joseph G., 247, 258; Jos. Y., 92, 94, 138, 259, 263; Lewis, 247, 259; Meshack T., 106, 137; Nancy F., 92, 137, 138; Philip, 16, 92, 106, 117, 138, 142; Philip A., 106, 109, 117, 126, 137; Thos. O., 137.
WILHOIT, Adam, 63; Geo., 63; Michael, 63.

WILKINS, Ann, 185, 199; O., 218; Clary, 199; Clement, 4, 44, 53, 123, 144, 165, 190, 199; Eliz., 169; Francis, 87; John, 44, 79, 87, 123, 163, 185, 192, 199, 250; Nancy, 44, 53, 123; Thos., 44, 78, 87, 148, 150, 169, 178; Wm., 9.
WILKINSON, Dabney D.; 32; John 99, 106.
WILLEFORD, Chas., 227; John, 199; Nathan, 226; Samuel, 69.
WILLIAM, John, 93.
WILLIAMS, Barbara, 33, 34, 106, 119, 124, 127; Barbara E., 139, 140; Eliz., 142; Frances, 119, 124, 127; Frances E., 114, 124, 139, 140, 249; Frances M., 139, 140; Harmon, 135; Henrietta J., 33, 98; Ja., 4; Jas., 26; John, 5, 143, 186, 220, 247, 249; Joseph, 5, 70, 77, 87, 99, 143, 150; Martha B., 33, 124, 139, 140; Mary A., 135; Matthew, 73; Matthew J. 5, 33, 34, 56, 66, 70, 72, 73, 87, 99, 106, 114, 124, 139, 140, 143, 148, 150, 159, 179, 186, 189, 198, 199, 248; N., 218; Nehemiah, 185, 199, 215, 217, 219; Philip, 59, 60, 144; Polly J., 150; Rachel, 59, 60, 144; Sarah, 47, 135; Thos., 212; Thos. W., 33, 34, 91, 99, 106; Wm., 132, 135, 186.
WILLIAMSON, Betsy B., 27; 95; Betsy O., 26, 72, 240; Dunston, 27; John, 198, 242; Matthias, 189; Sally O., 27, 97; Stephen, 233; Thos., 117; W., 152; Walker, 254.
WILLIFORD, Chas., 20; Maxfield H., 255; Nathan, 19; Reuben S., 260; Stephen, 186, 199; Thos., 223.
WILLIS, Benj., 257; Eliz. C., 257; Jas. M., 257; John, 22, 107, 138, 257; Louisa A., 257; Milly, 36, 107, 138, 257, 258; Richard, 258; Thos. F., 53; Wm., 257.
WILLY, Thomas, 3.
WILMOTH—WILMOUTH, Eliz., 212; Ezekiel, 186; Nancy, 186; Stephen, 212; Thos., 186, 201, 212; Wm., 186, 212, 242.
WILSON, Benj., 11, 70, 228; Jason, 165, 170, 201, 212; John, 11, 22, 70, 86, 146, 176, 199, 230, 232; John & Co., 199; Joseph, 11, 169, 212; Littleberry, 202, 205, 212; Mary, 11, 146; Stephen, 131; Whitfield, 205; Wm., 11.
WILLSON, John S., 107.
WIMBISH, Alex., 213; Frances S., 213; Samuel, 168, 205.
WINGFIELD, John, 185, 194; Mary, 185.

WINKFIELD, John, 263; John Y., 247.
WINGOM, Philip, 166.
WINN, Benj., 246, 264; Edw. G., 11; Gustavus A., 261; Jane, 66; John, 66; Wm., 10, 217.
WITCHER, Benj., 75, 76.
WITT, Chas., 240.
WODLEY, John, 249; Temporine, 248.
WOLDRIDGE, Edward 11, 15; Gibson, 11, 15, 16, 78; Rachel, 11; Sarah, 11, 15, 144, 148; Thos., 146, 147, 148, 213; Wm., 11, 78, 144, 162, 213.
WOMACK, Abraham, 170.
WOOD, Agrippe, 63; Bennett, 63; Francis, 244; Geo., 164, 214; Jas., 20, 25, 26, 63, 70, 75, 79, 85, 150, 218; Jas. L., 247; John, 63; Pennel, 63; Sarah, 150, 244; Susannah, 63.
WOODALL, Joseph, 240.
WOODLY, Andrew, 19; Temperance, 35.
WOODLY & BELL, 91, 95.
WOODS, Andrew, 70, 78, 88, 148; Ann, 70, 77, 78, 88, 148; Bailey, 78, 141; Bailey M., 33, 35, 88, 98, 141; Bennett, 244; Citizen S., 141; Eliz., 79, 85, 96, 141, 150; Eliz. H., 141; Francis, 148; Geo., 63, 141, 179; Hugh, 18, 78; J., 78, 88, 98; John, 65, 70, 78, 79, 88, 96, 141, 150; Joseph, 62; Josiah, 18, 78, 141; Lucy, 141; M., 6, 22, 61, 86, 151, 152, 153, 155, 162, 165, 168, 171, 176, 185, 202, 217, 218, 219, 220, 221, 222; Mary, 141; Middleton, 9, 18, 21, 60, 63, 65, 78, 87, 98, 114, 124, 132, 141, 142, 143, 145, 146, 147, 148, 163, 169, 186, 187, 188, 197, 202, 212, 215; Middleton G., 141, 215; Peter M., 141; Reuben, 141; Richard, 160, 188; Robt., 26, 70, 75, 77, 78, 87, 88, 98, 141, 148; Robt. T., 87, 88, 141; Sally, 18; Samuel, 10, 148, 172, 206; Samuel H., 141; Sarah, 79, 85, 96; Wm., 18, 19, 25, 28, 32, 35, 73, 78, 84, 87, 88, 95, 98, 104, 107, 112, 124, 131, 141, 142, 169, 210, 229, 236; Wm. H. C., 124, 132, 141.
WOODSON, William, 62.
WOODWARD, Mary, 8; Robt., 184; Thos., 149, 193, 242.
WOODY, Pleasant, 49; Wm., 49; Wm. C., 116.
WOOLDRIDGE, Chirial, 16; Gibson, 148; Lucy B., 16; Thos., 11, 15, 16, 65, 76, 78, 252; Thos. D., 115.
WOOTAN, James, 234.
WOOTEN, Thos., 186, 198, 203; Tobitho, 198.
WOOTON, Hannah, 259.
WORD, Richard, 255; Sarah, 255; Wm., 255.
WORRILL—WORRELL, Edmund F., 257; Ransom, 48, 100, 111, 263.
WORSHAM, R., 168, 215.
WRAY, John, 169; Philip, 3.
WRIGHT, Chas., 250; Elisha, 33; Eliz. V., 33; Estley H., 33; Gabriel, 33, 252; Henry, 33; Isaac, 254; Mary, 33; Warren, 250.
WYCHE, Agatha, 7, 23, 36; Alfred, 117; Frances, 34; Geo., 23, 36, 44, 53, 79, 201, 217; Joshua C., 36, 137, 250; Judith, 7; Peter, 19, 65, 149, 168, 201, 203, 214, 217; Susannah, 117; Thos., 168; Wm. H., 250.
WYLLY, Richard, 176.
WYNNE—WYNN, Geo., 77, 88, 107; John, 72, 88, 107.
WYTER, D., 154.
de YAMPERT, John, 172.
YOES, Katharine, 255.
YOUNG, Eliz., 40; Lemuel, 213; Nancy, 53; Reuben, 261; Samuel, 61, 143, 190; Thos., 257.
ZIMMERMAN, William, 31.

MARRIAGES, PAGES 271-304

Arranged Alphabetically and Chronologically as to Men's Names as Found in Will Books

FEMALE INDEX

ADAMS, Ann B., 299; Deborah, 280; Eliz., 286; Eveline, 293; Frances, 291; Grace A., 288; Morening, 290; Nancy, 298; Polly, 286; Rebecca, 279.
AGEE, Eliz., 279.
AKENS, Betsy, 289.
AKIN, Eliz., 304; Emelia, 295, Jane, 296; Mary, 296; Sophia, 294.
ALEXANDER, Ann, 302; Anna, 275; Catharine, 281; Mrs. Catherine, 297; Ezza, 276; Frances, 276; Lucy, 283; Matilda, 300; Milley, 285; Milly, 273; Mornin, 278; Polly, 274; Sarah, 283, 292, 294.
ALLEN, Eliz., 286; Harriett, 289; Lucy, 286; Nancy, 297; Rebecca, 279; Rhoda, 297; Sarah, 276.
ALLGOOD, Anny, 288; Elvey, 289; Jane, 281; Mary, 282, Sarah, 295, 303.
ALLMAN, Eliz., 282; Mary A., 284; Nancy, 282; Peggy, 284.
ALMOND, Lenna, 296; Mahulda, 302.
ALSTON, ELIZ. Y., 279; Mary, 278.
ANDERSON, Jemima, 292; Polly, 303; Rebecca, 279, 290; Sarah, 284.
ANTHONY, Mary A., 284; Nancy, 279; Rebecca, 278; Sally, 275.
ARNOLD, Adaline A., 300; Mrs. Eliz., 301; Nancy, 278; Sarah A., 300.
ASHWORTH, Eliz., 302; Margaret, 273; Milly, 296; Sarah, 292.
AUSLEY, Sarah, 283.
AYCOCK, Susan E., 278.
BAILEY, Eliz., 278; Matilda, 290; Nancy, 275.
BALLENGER, Eliz., 283; Letty, 295; Nancy, 284; Patsy, 277; Polly, 299.
BANKS, Ann A., 282; Betsy A., 278; Charity A., 292; Eliza, 300; Eliz., 293, 302; Gilly Y., 286; Hannah K., 299; Lucy, 287; Martha A., 297; Martha E., 301; Mildred, 295; Nancy, 291; Polly H., 278; Rebecca, 287; Sally, 277; Sarah C., 281.
BARNES, Cherry, 282.

BARNETT, Patsey, 272.
BASKINS, Caty, 288.
BASSILE, Patience, 273.
BATES, Anny, 274; Judith, 291; Sarah, 303.
BECK, Nancy W., 279; Sarah L., 286.
BEDINGFIELD, Molly, 280.
BELL, Anna, 271; Edna A., 300; Elener, 284; Eliz., 272, 284; Martha, 279; Milly L., 292, Rebecca, 279; Rhody, 299; Sarah, 292.
BENNETT, Eliz., 303.
BENTLY, Betsy, 290; Dicy, 288; Levicy, 292; Rebecca, 288; Sally, 272.
BEVERS, Peggy, 275.
BIBB, Martha, 275; Sally S., 271.
BLAIR, Polly, 275.
BOATRIGHT, Leah, 301.
BOBO, Eliz., 297; Hannah, 299; Milly, 299; Sarah, 289.
BOND, Catharine, 282; Claricey, 292; Martha, 297; Mary W., 292; Matilda, 287; Permelia, 271; Rachel, 289; Tabitha, 276.
BONDS, Betsy, 276; Susannah, 279.
BOOKER, Sally, 278; Mima, 280.
BOOTH, Belenderon, 277; Eliz., 302; Judith, 284; Katharine, 300; Martha G., 286; Mary A., 302; Nancy, 286; Polly, 299; Sarah, 273, 295.
BOWMAN, Eliz., 300; Willie M., 283.
BOWERS, Mary, 299; Patsy, 295.
BRADEN, Eliz., 271.
BRADLEY, Ann, 285; Lucy C., 296.
BRADY, Sally, 280.
BRAGG, Sucky, 282.
BRAMBLETT, Eliz., 279.
BRANHAM, Betsey, 290.
BRANNAN, Bathena, 288.
BRANTLEY, Katharine, 297; Letty M., 285; Mary, 293; Nancy J., 293.
BRASWELL, Jinny, 278.
BRAWNER, Charlotte, 295; Eliz., 302; Harriett, 298; Lucy, 294; Nancy M., 303.

BRAY, Ann, 274; Mary, 300; Sally, 272.
BREADIN, Nancy, 276.
BREWER, Mrs. Eliz., 282; Frances C. M., 279; Frances J., 300; Martha H., 280; Polly, 273; Sarah A., 302; Susannah, 280; Syntha, 279.
BROOKS, Mary, 293.
BROWN, Ann, 300; Betsy, 276; Catharine, 280; Caty, 273; Eliza, 302; Janey, 277; Lucy A., 302; Martha D., 295; Mary S., 290; Matilda, 297; Nancy, 280, 286; Polly, 274, 289; Sally, 271, 277, 286; Sarah, 285, 298.
BRYAN, Martha, 275.
BUCHANNON, Jane, 275.
BUFFINGTON, Eliz., 283.
BULLARD, Eliz., 275; Tempy, 277.
BULLIS, Eliz., 287.
BURDEN, Ann, 291; Eliz., 298; Frances, 288; Martha, 285, 295; Nancy, 292; Polly, 289; Sarah, 278; Winny, 284.
BURNETT, Ann, 287; Bethana, 290.
BURTON, Catherine, 277; Catty, 271; Eliz., 275, 286, 290, 293; Harriett, 282; Lucinda, 296; Malinda, 278; Martha, 299; Mary, 284; Mary W., 294; Nancy, 303; Permelia, 283; Sophia M., 297.
BUTLER, Clemontyne, 278; Eliz., 284, 302; Martha, 272; Milley, 302; Nancy, 287, 288; Polly, 280; Sally, 272; Susan, 293.
CALISTER, Nancy M., 281.
CAMPBELL, Ann, 279; Nancy, 274; Polly, 281.
CAPE, Eliz., 300.
CARDEN, Jane A., 293.
CARPENTER, Eliz., 278; Leah, 292; Rhody, 293; Robema, 276; Susan, 286.
CARTER, Eliz. J., 283; Frances, 282; Lucy F., 283; Martha, 281, 294; Nancy, 289; Sarah, 274, 279.
CASH, Ann, 299; Eliz., 296; Fanny, 277; Lucy, 291.
CASON, Eliz., 287; Milly, 283.
CHAMBERS, Charity A., 302; Frances P., 289; Mary A. R., 292.
CHANDLER, Mary, 282.
CHAPMAN, Nancy, 284.
CHEEK, Nancy, 300; Sarah A., 300.
CHILDERS, Milly, 277.
CHILDS, Eliz., 279; Jane, 273, 279; Margaret, 280; Nancy, 276; Surreny, 280; Susanna, 274.
CHIPMAN, Mary J., 282.
CHRISTIAN, Ann P., 285; Lucinda, 294; Martha, 296; Mary, 284, 303; Mary J., 297; Mary M., 285; Nancy, 303, 304; Sarah, 289; Susannah, 299.
CHRISLEY, Eliz., 303.
CHRISTLER, Lucy D., 283; Nancy, 288; Polly, 277.
CLARK, Aggy, 286; Eliz., 280; Mrs. Eliz., 297; Judah, 271; Lucinda, 301; Margaret, 283; Margaret S., 301; Martha, 278, 285; Mary, 285; Mary E., 303; Milly, 291; Sarah, 272, 295, 297; Sarah B., 282; Susannah, 287; Tabitha, 296.
CLEMENTS, Harriett, 276.
CLEVELAND, Eliza, 300; Emilia, 303; Martha L., 303; Sarah W., 299.
COKER, Bitha, 294; Cloey, 294; Eliz., 271; Eliz. A., 303; Irenia, 297; Milsy, 290; Polly, 286; Sintha, 283; Susannah, 280.
COLBERT, Carah, 280; Frances, 290; Gilly, 278; Lucy, 288; Martha, 283; Melinda, 294.
COLE, Mahala, 271; Sally, 273.
COLEMAN, Betsy, 280, 284; Eliz., 295; Rebecca, 283; Sarah, 279.
COLMAN, Sally, 276.
COLSON, Juley A., 302; Sarah, 277; Sophia, 302.
COLVARD, Polly, 299; Sarah L., 303.
COOK, Ann, 291; Barbary, 297; Betsy, 275; Mrs. Betty, 286; Eliz., 282, 289; Mrs. Francis, 298; Hannah, 296; Jane, 302; Keziah, 291; Lucy, 291; Margaret A., 280; Mariah, 291; Mary, 284; Mary A., 292; Nancy, 272, 284; Pamelia, 285; Sarah, 302; Susan, 296.
COUCH, Eliz., 284.
COULSON, Rebecca, 291.
COX, Eliz., 277; Eliz. A., 283.
CRAFT, Letha, 289; Matilda, 287; Nancy, 279; Polly, 285; Sarah, 298; Sarow, 299.
CRAWFORD, Jane, 272.
CRIDENTON, Judith, 288.
CRISLER, Anna, 277.
CRITTENDEN, Nancy, 274.
CRITTENDON, Diana, 288.
CRUMP, Agatha, 284; Alphia F. C., 284; Polly, 277.
CUNNINGHAM, Averilla, 301; Catharine, 292; Eliz., 271; Nancy, 283; Polly, 278, 285.
CURRY, Jane, 282.
DANIEL, Eliz., 283; Nancy, 275; Polly, 283; Sarah, 284.
DAVID, Eliz., 273, 284; Milly, 273; Polly, 282; Selah, 289.
DAVIS, Frances, 282; Jane, 289; Julia, 290; Keziah, 293; Lucinda H., 293; Lucy, 299; Martha W., 298;

MARRIAGES—FEMALE INDEX 343

Mary, 288; Nancy, 281, 296; Nancy E., 304; Rhody, 283; Sarah, 273, 285, 290; Susannah, 282.
DEADWILER—DEADWYLER, Anna, 274; Anna B., 299; Eliz., 285; Letitia, 291; Mrs. Martha P., 298; Mary, 282; Nancy, 277, 291; Sarah, 294; Susannah, 296; Teresa, 301.
DEAN, Polly, 277.
DECKER, Mary A. H., 279; Pheriby, 291.
DENNA, Catharine, 295; Dorcas, 297; Margaret, 289; Sarah, 303.
DENNARD, Jane, 289; Polly, 273, 275.
DEPRIEST, Jinny, 275; Polly, 278.
DICKENSON, Rhoda, 291.
DICKEY, Eliz., 302.
DICKSON, Sally, 272.
DILLARD, Eliz., 279; Martha M., 303; Mary V., 281; Sally, 283.
DOBBS, Lucy, 289; Mary, 290.
DODDS, Eliz., 277; Nancy, 298; Rebecca, 302.
DOLLAR, Polly, 287.
DOOLEY—DOOLY, Eliz., 293; Eliz. A., 301; Mrs. Letty, 297; Nancy, 280; Nancy J., 283; Polly, 282; Sarah, 289; Sarah A., 300; Webby, 289.
DOWNER, Susannah, 285; Tabitha, 274.
DOWNS, Mary, 299.
DUDLEY, Mary, 298; Nancy, 288.
DUNAHOO, Susanna, 271.
DUNCAN, Alis, 288.
DUNN, Harriett, 300; Lear H., 283.
DUTTON, Eliz., 283; Patsy, 273.
DYE, Eliz. K., 298; Frances W., 299; Mary, 293, 302; Polly, 292; Sarah, 286; Sarah T., 302.
EADES, Mary, 297.
EASTER, Eliz. L., 274.
EASTRIDGE, Mary, 272.
EAVENSON, Eliz., 296; Hannah, 276; Rachel, 304.
EAVES, Honor, 287; Julia A., 294; Martha, 297; Sarah, 297.
EDMONDSON, Caroline, 298.
EDWARDS, Eliz., 293, 297; Eliz. A., 294; Eliz. C., 288; Emeline E., 299; Julia A., 297; Mary W., 303; Sarah B., 296; Sarah D., 300; Susan, 273.
ELDER, Patsy, 282; Polly, 284; Rebecca, 291.
ELLET, Milly, 276.
ELLINGTON, Mrs. Catharine, 299; Jane, 272.
ELLIOTT, Eliz., 278; Sarah, 288.
ENGLAND, Jane, 274.
EVANS, Carline, 280; Sally, 273.
EVENSON, Martha, 301.
EVESTON, Polly, 275.
EWING, Rebecca, 272.
FALKNER, Rhoda, 274.
FANNEN, Nancy, 288.
FANNIN, Jincy, 296.
FANNING, Averilla, 301.
FARMER, Betsy, 304; Mary, 295.
FAULK, Sarah, 303.
FAULKNER, Anna, 274; Eliz., 292; Patsey, 280; Sarah, 295.
FERGUSON, Peggy, 283.
FERRELL, Ruth, 287.
FIGGS, Betsy, 273.
FINCHER, Mary, 271.
FITTS, Kissia, 271; Mary J., 301.
FLANNINGHAM, Permelia, 301.
FLOYD, Sarah C., 300.
FOLK, Polly, 289.
FOLLEY, Betsey, 282.
FORD, Mary, 294; Nancy, 280; Nancy A., 298; Sarah, 277.
FORGUS, Rachel, 272.
FORTENBERRY, Lydia, 292.
FORTSON, Amanda N. M., 300; Betsey A., 292; Eliz., 281, 288; Jane M., 303; Mahala, 291; Martha, 292; Mary, 292; Mrs. Mary, 302; Polley, 296; Rachel W., 286; Sarah, 285, 291.
FOSTER, Delina, 294; Susan M., 300.
FOWLER, Matilda, 303.
FRANKLIN, Dosha, 285; Phebe, 275.
FREEMAN, Nancy, 300.
GAAR, Julia A. E., 300.
GAINES—GAINS, Ann, 293; Drucilla E., 303; Jane, 286; Jincy, 280; Lucy T., 297; Martha, 290; Mary, 293; Mourning G., 300; Peggy C., 279; Polly, 280; Sally, 287, 292; Sarah, 302; Susannah, 273.
GARRETT, Catherine, 272.
GARVIN, Jane, 271.
GAULDEN, Mary, 300.
GAY, Polly, 295.
GIBBS, Mildred, 300; Rachel, 283.
GINN, Alphia, 286; Elitha, 289; Nancy, 282, 300; Polly, 289.
GLENN, Martha T., 290; Sarah A. H., 302.
GLOVER, Eliz., 275.
GLYNN, Martha H., 299.
GOOLSBY, Martha, 298.
GOSS, Nancy P., 294; Sally R., 295.
GRACE, Milly, 275.
GRAGG, Joannah, 272.
GRANGER, Mahala, 272.
GRANSHAW, Mary, 295.
GRAY, Ann, 287; Jane, 291; Mary, 282; Patsy A., 277.
GREENWAY, Nancy T., 304; Sally, 281.

GREENWOOD, Eliz., 278.
GREGG, Anna, 290; Polly, 290.
GRIFFITH, Ann, 271.
GRIZZLE, Rebecca, 276; Sarah, 276.
GROOSE, Marium, 293.
GROSS, Dama, 277.
GULLEY, Nancy, 280.
GULLY, Eliz., 290.
GUNTER, Barshaba, 273; Eliz. P., 297; Mrs. Susan, 298.
HACKNEY, Mary A., 279.
HAILEY, Elender, 300; Tabitha, 304.
HAINES, Jane, 275.
HALE, Sally, 285.
HALES, Betsy, 289.
HALEY, Betsy C., 299; Didama, 298; Henrietta, 274; Lucy, 291; Penina, 297; Polly, 281; Sally, 276; Tabitha, 285.
HALL, Catharine, 296; Lucy, 274; Sally, 276.
HAM, Betsy, 292; Nancy, 301; Susan, 298.
HAMBLETON, Nancy, 286.
HAMMOND, Lucy, 273.
HANNA, Polly, 278.
HANSARD, Eliz., 283; Jane, 283; Mary A., 291; Rhoda, 298; Sarah, 299.
HANSON, Nancy, 301.
HARBIN, Anna, 273; Eliz., 295; Margaret, 281; Nancy, 283; Susannah, 299.
HARDY, Phebe, 301.
HARMAN, Eliz., 296.
HARPER, Avariller, 273; Charlotte B., 271; Elender, 277; Eliz., 291; Nancy, 276, 296; Polly, 288; Polly W., 286; Sarah, 276.
HARRIS, Agnes A., 301; Ann R., 297; Edne, 284; Frances R., 294; Lucy, 297; Martha M., 296; Mary A., 290; Nancy, 297; Nancy L., 300; Rebecca, 279; Sarah N., 295.
HARRISON, Betsy, 276; Mary B., 290.
HATCHER, Nancy, 273.
HATHCOCK, Martha, 301.
HAYNES, Mary W., 286.
HAYS, Tabitha, 272.
HEAD, Frances, 287; Jinsey, 272; Lucinda, 295; Nancy, 275; Sarah, 281.
HEARD, Biddy, 286; Mrs. Mary, 300; Sarah, 294.
HEARNDON, Catharine, 281; Eliz., 279, 300; Fanny, 288; Polly, 281.
HEARN, Jane E., 297; Sarah L., 290.
HENDON, Ruth, 272.
HENDERSON, Ann B., 285; Eliz., 298; Judith, 295; Martha, 293; Mary, 282; Mary A., 299; Sarah A., 296; Sarah E., 299.
HENDRICK, Betsy, 272; Eliza, 298; Sally, 290.
HENDRY, Charlott, 282; Nancy, 289; Sophia, 279.
HERNDON, Eliz., 297; Polly, 274.
HENRY, Martha, 300; Nancy, 284; Polly, 280; Sintha, 285.
HICKMAN, Eliza, 298.
HICKS, Eliz., 273; Jincey, 297; Lucinda, 295; Nancy, 290.
HIGGINBOTHAM, Ann R., 296; Clary G., 294; Clarysa, 274; Eliz. P., 296; Frances, 293, 303; Lucy, 302; Martha, 275; Mary, 275; Mary C., 303; Mary S., 278; Polley, 303; Polly S., 288; Sarah B., 282; Vilate, 285.
HIGHSMITH, Nancy, 287; Sarah, 302.
HIGHTOWER, Bathashe, 281; Milly, 292.
HILL, Milly, 279; Zele, 277.
HILLEY, Milly, 277; Sarah, 287, 289.
HINES, Lucy, 299.
HOLBROOK, Peggy, 271.
HOLTON, Sally, 284.
HORN, Susannah F., 278.
HORTON, Eliz., 290, 298; Lidey, 303; Sarah, 298.
HOUSLEY, Mariah L., 300.
HOWARD, Jinney, 279; Lucinda A., 287; Polly, 279.
HOWELL, Sally, 295.
HUBBARD, Sarah, 289.
HUDSON, Eliza C., 301; Eliz., 274; Frances, 285; Louisa, 294; Louisa E., 284; Lucy C., 283; Martha P., 287; Mary W., 292; Nancy, 271; Nancy L., 293; Pheba L., 297.
HULLUM, Eliz., 290.
HULME, Agnes M., 300; Eliz., 294; Lucy, 285.
HUNT, Drusilla, 296; Nancy, 284; Nancy H., 292.
INGRAHAM, Polly, 273.
IRIONS, Theany, 281.
IRONS, Catharine, 271; Eliz., 276; Theney, 277.
JACK, Jane H., 298.
JAMES, Eliz., 277; Nancy, 290; Theodicia, 301.
JARRATT, Eliza D., 294.
JENKINS, Mary, 299.
JENNINGS, Betsy, 272.
JENTRY, Barbary, 294.
JOHNSON, Mrs. Ann, 296; Mary M., 302; Nancy, 297; Sarah, 279.
JOHNSTON, Eliz. B., 294; Frances, 272, 283; Polly, 275.

MARRIAGES—FEMALE INDEX 345

JONES, Ann, 300 Charlotte, 279; Eliz., 277; Eliza M., 278; Keziah, 287; Lucinda, 286; Malinda, 300; Martha, 275, 291; Mary, 289, 295; Mary J., 288; Milly, 274; Patcy, 279; Patsey, 272; Polly, 272; Presilla, 290; Rebecca, 293; Rhody, 287; Settey, 286.
JORDAN, Betsy, 272; Jane, 275.
JORDEN, Sarah, 291.
KARR, Fanny, 285; Lucy, 276.
KEE, Sally, 280.
KELLY, Amanda M., 303; Cissale, 294; Malinda O., 293.
KENNEBREW, Icy, 287; Mira, 285.
KENNEDY, Eliz., 286.
KERLIN, Margaret, 287; Mildred, 289.
KEY, Amelia A., 301; Jane, 285; Lucinda W., 303; Lucy, 294; Mary, 283; Milly, 276; Sally, 285; Susan, 282.
KEYS, Anna A., 296; Mary, 298.
KIDD, Eliz. H., 287; Frances, 273.
KING, Ann W., 274; Betsy, 282; Catharine, 287; Catharine W., 285; Eliz. P., 285; Jenny, 301; Sarah S., 282; Sukey, 287; Susanna, 302.
KINNEBREW, Jane, 298; Sarah, 298.
KIRLEN, Lucy, 303.
LAIN, Charlotte, 273.
LANE, Eliza, 285.
LAREMORE, Nancy, 294.
LARGENT, Louranie, 285.
LAUREMORE, Mrs. Sarah, 299.
LAWLIS, Tabitha, 291.
LEDBETTER, Polly, 277.
LESUER, Patsy, 290.
LEWIS, Ann J., 302; Eliz., 279; Esther, 288; Hester, 303; Lucy, 288; Martha, 296; Polly L., 280; Sarah D., 294.
LINDSAY, Nancy K., 278.
LOCKHART, Mary, 271; Nancy C., 292.
LOLLIS, Polly, 276.
LOWRIMORE, Sally, 302.
LOWRY, Delilah, 271.
LUNCEFORD, Polly, 273.
McCLARY, Mary E., 272.
McCARMAC, Polly, 280.
McCUNE, Peggy, 272.
McCURRY, Catharine, 272; Flora, 301; Katharine, 295, 298; Mary, 294, 298.
McGARITY, Mary, 299; Sarah, 301.
McGARRITY, Harriett, 301.
McGEHEE, Ann F., 294; Eliz., 274; Louisey, 286; Lucy, 276; Mary, 283; Sarah, 284, 301.
McGUIRE, Cynthey, 273; Patsy, 276; Permelia, 296; Susanna, 276.
McKINNEY, Sally, 273.
McLEROY, Frances, 273.
McMULLAN, Nancy, 280.

McMULLEN, Dosha, 274; Eliz., 281, 284, 288; Levina, 290; Milly, 300.
McMULLIN, Frances, 293; Nancy, 298.
MAGEE, Eliz., 287.
MANN, Judea J., 290; Sarah K., 282; Sarah T., 295.
MANNING, Mrs. Lucy, 301.
MARBURY, Claricy, 303.
MARTIN, Mrs. Jane, 298; Phebe, 274; Polly, 275; Rebecca, 294.
MASON, Keziah, 298.
MATTOX, Eliz., 293, 301; Polly, 291.
MAXWELL, Ann, 301; Eliza, 300; Eliz., 276, 282, 299; Mary, 293, 303; Peggy A., 297; Polly, 295; Rebecca, 294.
MEANS, Eliz., 295; Frances, 284; Jemima, 277; Martha, 303; Peggy, 284; Polly, 275; Sarah, 302.
MERET—MERRET, Lotty, 287; Mary, 289; Nancy, 289; Selah, 295.
MICOU, Margaret, 274.
MIDDLETON, Martha N., 273; Nancy P., 294; Polly, 273.
MILLICAN, Jane, 274.
MILLIGAN, Polly A., 283.
MIRES, Nancy, 293.
MITCHELL, Eliz., 272; Polly, 301.
MOBLEY, Eliz., 281.
MOON, Baba, 297; Mary, 296; Mrs. Sarah, 301; Susan, 294.
MOORE, Agnes, 291; Eliz., 292; Frances T., 284; Jemima, 281; Martha, 289; Polly, 290; Sarah, 279; Susanna, 272.
MORGAN, Eliz. I., 280; Melinda, 288.
MORRIS, Betsy, 291; Katharine, 299.
MORRISON, Harriet E., 297.
MORROW, Nancy, 277.
MOSS, Nellie, 291; Susan, 295.
MURRAH, Tabitha, 276.
MURRY, Milley, 281.
NAISH, Fanny, 278; Jincy, 276; Martha, 278.
NASH, Lucinda, 295; Permelia, 295.
NEAL, Mary, 298.
NELMES, Mary, 301.
NELMS, Ann, 302; Orpha, 298.
NEWBORN, Lucy, 294.
NIX, Eliz., 302; Lucy, 294; Sally, 276.
NOLAN, Nancy A., 290.
NUNNELEE, Ann F., 286; Charlotte C., 274; Eliza F., 292; Mrs. Maria, 302; Martha W., 299; Sarah, 282; Sophia, 302; Susanna W., 286.
OGLESBY, Ann F., 287; Lucindey, 288; Martha, 290; Nancy, 289; Rhoda, 291; Sarah, 287, 289.
OLIVER, Eliz. A., 295; Mrs. Eliz. A., 297; Judith, 292; Malinda, 288; Mariah W., 282; Mary, 274; Mary A., 286;

MARRIAGES—FEMALE INDEX

Mary R., 286; Mary W., 282; Milly, 282; Milly T., 284, 302; Matilda, 286; Nancy A., 294; Sarah, 271; Susan, 301; Tabitha, 275.
OUSLEY, Martha, 297.
OWENS, Eliz., 280; Martha, 290; Susannah, 288.
PACE, Anny, 276; Mrs. Martha, 299; Mazy, 293; Nancy, 291.
PANE, Nancy, 290.
PARHAM, Eliz., 292; Lucy, 276, 297; Milly, 271.
PARKS, Eliz., 286.
PARROTT, Juda, 293.
PATE, Eliz. G., 278; Marhala, 278.
PATHRO, Hitty, 286.
PATTERSON, Beckey, 303; Eliz., 302; Gilley, 280; Juliann, 282; Lucy, 292; Mary, 298; Nancy, 283.
PEMELTON, Rachel, 290.
PENN, Fannay, 280; Harriett, 303; Leucy, 280; Patsy, 289; Polly, 287; Sarah J., 303; Winney, 303.
PERRIN, Nancy, 283.
PERRYMAN, Eliza, 293.
PHELPS, Fanny, 288; Mary, 288; Melinda, 286; Minty, 287; Polly, 275.
PHILLIPS, Unity, 290.
PLEDGER, Eliz., 281; Eliz. O., 282; Polly, 280; Susannah, 285.
POELSTON, Margaret, 281.
POLLARD, Polly, 278; Sally, 281; Silvey, 275.
POPE, Matilda, 277; Ruth, 273.
POWEL, Cresy, 289; Milly, 289.
POWELL, Joicee, 302; Lucy, 295; Mittey, 295; Nancy, 287; Phebe, 295; Sarah, 294.
POWER, Anney, 275.
PRATT, Martha J., 298.
PREWIT, Rosannah, 287.
PRICKETT, Fanny, 296.
PROTHRO, Ann, 294; Eliz., 297; Mary, 285.
PULLIAM, Franky, 275; Mary, 299; Rebecca, 277; Sarah, 297.
RAGAN, Sarah M., 293.
RAGLAND, Frances, 272; Sarah, 281.
RAGLIN, Tabitha, 274.
RAINE, Catharine, 282.
RAINES, Martha, 282.
RAYMOND, Sarah D., 299.
REILY, Amely, 274.
REYNOLDS, Polly, 303.
RHODELANDER, Patsy, 281.
RHODPHEBA, 281.
RICE, Eliz., 300; Sarah, 299; Sarah C., 286; Suckey, 284.

RICH, Eliz., 286; Mary, 280; Permelia, 293; Sarah, 278; Sophia, 299.
RICHARDSON, Crissa, 287; Patsy, 275; Mrs. Prudence, 283; Prudence T., 281.
RIDGWAY, Nancy T., 293; Polly, 273; Sally, 274; Tabitha, 291.
ROBERTS, Mary, 284; Nancy, 296.
ROBERTSON, Eliz., 272; Polly, 292.
ROEBUCK, Ann, 280; Mrs. Eliz. L., 298; Frances, 280; Harriott, 280. Mildred A., 294; Sarah C., 298.
ROGERS, Polly, 271.
ROSE, Betsy, 271.
ROWSAU, Sarah, 299.
ROWSEY, Clary, 274; Nancy, 295; Rhoda, 301.
ROWZEE, Eliz., 295; Frances E., 298; Merial K., 301.
ROYAL, Averilla, 290; Levity, 279.
ROYSTER, Martha, 285.
RUCKER, Catharine, 304; Eliz., 278, 281; Eliz. H., 299; Frances, 287; Hannah, 300; Jane, 272; Judith C., 284; Lucy, 275; Manda B., 298; Martha E., 301; Mary, 298; Mildred, 304; Mrs. Milly, 298; Nancy, 276.
RUFF, Nancy, 271; Polly, 272; Tabitha, 289.
RUNNELS, Charity, 285.
RUTHERFORD, Rachel, 277.
SALMONS, Margaret, 299.
SAMUEL, Ann, 279.
SANDERS, Polly, 277; Wineny, 276.
SANDRIDGE, Charlotty, 295; Eliz. L., 298.
SARTIN, Fanny, 291; Patsy, 284.
SATTERWHITE, Milley, 296.
SAUNDERS, Eliz. D., 274.
SAXTON, Jinsy, 271.
SAYRE, Mahetable C., 281; Margaret M., 289.
SCALES, Margaret M., 298; Susanna, 271.
SCHOFIELD, Emaly, 283.
SELF, Polly, 284.
SELFRIDGE, Susanna, 275.
SHACKLEFORD, Eliz., 281; Judey M., 281; Mary J., 286; Nancy J., 296; Sarah H., 285; Winny, 287.
SHEPHARD, Clarecy, 280; Lucinda, 301; Nancy, 280; Sarah, 283.
SHEPHERD, Eliz., 278; Hetty, 276.
SHIFTLETT, Eliza, 299; Polly, 299.
SKELTON, Dicey, 282; Eliz., 295; Mary, 277; Sally, 275.
SKINNER, Piety, 273; Polly, 286; Sally, 289; Sucey, 286.

SMITH, Betsy, 276, 290; Cyrena A., 297; Elenar W., 293; Eliz., 281; Jemima W., 300; Polly, 288; Sarah T., 302; Selah, 292.
SMITHWICK, Mary, 280.
SNELLINGS, Eliz., 297; Hannah, 271; Martha, 286; Mary, 282; Rebecca, 291; Sophia, 301.
SPEARS, Eliz., 280.
SPENCER, Sally, 273.
STATHAM, Nancy, 293; Polly, 274.
STAPLES, Anny, 288; Barbary, 275; Lucy, 274; Martha, 291; Milita, 278; Tabitha, 276.
STEPHENS, Betsy, 271.
STINCHCOMB, Betsy, 271; Caty, 281; Frances A., 283; Lucy, 294; Polley C., 296; Sarah, 301.
STODGHILL, Martha C., 292; Polly, 293.
STONE, Rosannah, 286; Sally, 281.
STOWERS, Frances, 276; Joicy, 285; Susannah, 287.
SULLIVAN, Mariah, 296; Moddy W., 304.
SUTTLES, Nancy L., 289.
SWET, Anna, 274.
SWINDLE, Catharine, 303.
TAIT, Charity, 274; Eliz. P., 288; Frances, 281; Mary J., 273; Rachel, 279; Susanna, 277.
TATE, Catharine D., 285; Eliz., 291; Eliz. D., 293; Frances, 289; Frances A., 287; Genoa, 287; Jane, 302; Louisa A., 300; Lucy, 281; Martha, 293; Martha M., 287; Sarah A., 291; Sarah Y., 280; Susan, 282.
TAYLOR, Franky P., 279; Patsy, 276.
TEASLEY, Amelia, 287; Anna, 284; Betsy, 286; Martha R., 302; Martha W., 296; Nancy, 274; Priscilla, 295; Priscilla T., 301; Sarah, 292; Winny, 286.
TERRELL, Eliz., 286; Frances, 293; Martha, 288; Polly, 290; Rebecca, 285; Sarah, 274.
TERRY, Lucy, 292; Mary, 299.
THOMASON, Sarah, 275; Susannah, 279.
THOMPSON, Charlotte, 273; Eliza. E., 278; Jane, 281; Louisiana, 288; Martha, 288; Sarah M., 278.
THORNTON, Ann, 295; Eliz., 274, 278, 282, 288, 291; Mary, 296; Polly, 272; Priscilla, 286; Sally, 294; Sarah, 279, 297, 298; Susannah, 295.
THRELKELD, Adeline, 297; Feanetty, 303; Harriett, 293.

TIDWELL, Sally, 274.
TINER, Charity, 278.
TITTLE, Mariah O., 288.
TOMKINS, Nancy, 280.
TOTMAN, Isabel, 290; Jane, 290.
TOWNS, Nancy, 272.
TUCKER, Eliz., 299; Lucinda, 296.
TURMAN, Mariah, 294; Permelia, 289; Prudence, 278.
TURNER, Eliz., 301; Eliz. M., 285; Sophia M., 283.
TYNER, Martha B., 278.
UPSHAW, Catharine, 273; Eliz. B., 294; Julia A., 302; Sarah, 290.
UNDERWOOD, Dosha, 288; Eliz. T., 290; Martha, 285; Mary, 288; Polly, 272, 277; Sally, 299.
VAUGHN, Martha, 272, 295.
VAUTER, Eliz., 284.
VERDELL, Maria S., 280.
VINES, Mary, 284.
WALL, Jane A., 303; Patsy S., 278; Susannah, 293.
WALKER, Martha, 271.
WALLIS, Peggy, 292.
WALTERS, Dosha, 272.
WANSLOW, Patsy, 275.
WARD, Harrett C., 301; Merial A., 301; Nancy J., 278; Sarah L., 300.
WARREN, Furlishe, 302; Martha S., 295.
WATERS, Elcy, 284.
WATKINS, Eliza, 287; Eliza H., 273; Jane, 277; Martha, 273; Sarah, 292; Sarah H., 272; Sophia H., 289; Susan, 276.
WATSON, Priscilla, 302; Sarah, 303.
WEBB, Alcey W., 303; Fanny, 276; Martha, 292; Martha P., 293; Patsy, 277; Prudence S., 301; Mrs. Susannah, 283.
WELCH, Ann, 282; Lucy, 274.
WHEELER, Eliz., 277; Hannah, 279; Nancy, 288; Penina J., 303; Polly, 284; Sarah, 291.
WHITE, Beda, 276; Betsy, 276; Eliza, 289, 303; Eliza F., 293; Eliz., 292, 301; Eliz. A., 300; Eliz. L., 301; Franky, 276; Martha, 278; Mary, 293; Mary S., 293; Milly, 271; Nancy, 285, 290; Patsy, 273; Polly, 287; Sally, 274; Sarah, 288; Sarah S., 279; Winney, 287.
WHITLOW, Mrs. Caroline, 302.
WHITMAN, Mary, 275; Sarah, 279.
WHITNEY, Martha, 275.
WICHE, Milly, 277.
WILBERN, Permelia T., 293.
WILEY, Plyne, 299.

WILHITE, Eliz. P., 291; Nancy F., 291; Rebecca, 275; Zeriah G., 289.
WILKINS, Mrs. Agnes, 284; Frances, 279; Rebecca, 278; Sally, 283; Sarah, 282.
WILLIAMS, Anne, 283; Caty, 285; Frances E., 294; Martha B., 295; Mary A., 296.
WILLIAMSON, Betsy B., 288; Betsy C., 276; Sally C., 291.
WILLIS, Piety, 280; Polly, 290; Rachel, 297.
WILSON, Sally, 287.
WIMMES, Jane, 279.
WOLEN, Della, 284.
WOOD, Eliz. P., 291; Letty, 289; Nancy, 284, 293; Sally, 272, 275.
WOODLY, Nancy, 292.
WOOLDRIDGE, Penina, 275.
WRIGHT, Ann C. E. P., 292; Jincy, 281; Polly, 282; Rebecca, 294.
WYCHE, Frances, 285.
YURMAN, Catharine, 275.